Mastering AutoCAD

Level up your AutoCAD skills with advanced methods and tools, including AutoCAD Web and Trace

Shaun Bryant

Mastering AutoCAD

Copyright © 2025 Packt Publishing

All rights reserved. No part of this book may be reproduced, stored in a retrieval system, or transmitted in any form or by any means, without the prior written permission of the publisher, except in the case of brief quotations embedded in critical articles or reviews.

Every effort has been made in the preparation of this book to ensure the accuracy of the information presented. However, the information contained in this book is sold without warranty, either express or implied. Neither the author, nor Packt Publishing or its dealers and distributors will be held liable for any damages caused or alleged to have been caused directly or indirectly by this book.

Packt Publishing has endeavored to provide trademark information about all of the companies and products mentioned in this book by the appropriate use of capitals. However, Packt Publishing cannot guarantee the accuracy of this information.

Publishing Product Manager: Tejashwini R
Book Project Manager: Sonam Pandey
Senior Editor: Ayushi Bulani
Technical Editor: Simran Ali
Copy Editor: Safis Editing
Indexer: Rekha Nair
Production Designer: Prashant Ghare
DevRel Marketing Coordinator: Nivedita Pandey

First published: February 2025

Production reference: 3100425

Published by Packt Publishing Ltd.
Grosvenor House
11 St Paul's Square
Birmingham
B3 1RB, UK

ISBN 978-1-83763-969-4

www.packtpub.com

To my wife, Michelle, for enduring the numerous late nights of writing and editing and for being my ever-patient partner on our journey together. Your creativity and love always amaze me as we move forward in life. You are my safe harbor, especially in recent times.

To my children, stepchildren, and grandchildren. Some of you are fully grown now. Keep that childlike curiosity to ensure that you are always learning and pass that knowledge on to your children and my grandchildren.

To my sister and her family. You have been a rock in difficult times, ensuring I remain grounded during recent challenging circumstances. Thank you for your love and kindness at all times.

To Mum and Dad. You're not here to see this book finally get published, but I do hope that, wherever you are, you can see the hard work and dedication put in to finally achieve my life goal of writing a book about AutoCAD, the Autodesk application that has been the foundation of my whole career. Inheriting your tenacious spirit and attention to detail has made me the person I am now. Thank you for everything. You will both always be loved.

- Shaun "CADjedi" Bryant

Foreword

It is my privilege to introduce "Mastering AutoCAD," written by Shaun Bryant. As the Senior Director of Community at Autodesk, I've had the chance to work with some truly passionate and skilled professionals, and Shaun is a standout in our community.

Shaun started his journey with AutoCAD back in 1988 and has been dedicated to mastering and sharing his expertise ever since. His credentials are impressive: Autodesk Certified Instructor since 2000, AUGI Board Director from 2010 to 2016, and an Autodesk Expert Elite since 2017. He's also been a LinkedIn Learning instructor since 2015, reaching countless learners around the world.

As the Group Leader for the AutoCAD User Group, which boasts over 12,000 members, Shaun has demonstrated exceptional leadership and community-building skills. His contributions as an experienced AU Speaker since 2006 have solidified his reputation as a trusted voice and mentor in the field.

I've witnessed firsthand the amazing impact that leaders like Shaun have on our community. His dedication and contributions truly capture the essence of what the Autodesk Community is all about. Enjoy the journey with "Mastering AutoCAD" and happy learning!

Jessica Langston

Senior Director, Autodesk Community

The views and opinions expressed in this book are those of the author and do not necessarily reflect the views or position of Autodesk, Inc. Autodesk is not affiliated with this book and did not endorse, sponsor, or compensate the author for this book. Autodesk does not take responsibility for the content or any outcomes resulting from use of the information presented in this book.

I have known Shaun Bryant for over 30 years. We met through our shared experiences at Autodesk University and enjoyed exchanging tips and tricks about CAD and its ever-evolving technology. Shaun is an Autodesk Certified Instructor in AutoCAD and Revit, boasting over 34 years of experience. As a leading expert in AutoCAD, Shaun is among the most sought-after consultants, trainers, CAD managers, and users globally. As the owner and author of the acclaimed CAD blog "Not Just CAD" and a LinkedIn Learning author, he offers a wealth of online instructional materials to help users excel in their fields. Shaun is recognized worldwide as a top instructor and speaker at Autodesk University. He recently served as an Autodesk Speaker Mentor, showcasing his exceptional ability to help others advance in their careers.

In this book, Shaun demonstrates some of the more advanced functionality of AutoCAD to enhance efficiency and productivity, helping you to get started quickly with AutoCAD processes and workflows. Shaun uses this book to demonstrate how to easily create a diverse range of drawings with examples that incorporate best practices and techniques utilizing the latest AutoCAD technology.

Jeanne Aarhus

President of Aarhus Associates, LLC

Author *of AutoCAD 2025 Best Practices, Tips, and Techniques*, *MicroStation for AutoCAD Users*, *AutoCAD for MicroStation Users* and several other training manuals.

Contributors

About the author

Shaun "CADjedi" Bryant is a seasoned CAD expert and technologist in the AECO industry. With 36+ years of experience with AutoCAD, Shaun is also an **Autodesk Certified Instructor** (**ACI**), **Autodesk Certified Professional** (**ACP**), and a member of the Autodesk Expert Elite program. He is also a seasoned **Autodesk University** (**AU**) speaker, starting his AU speaking career in 2006. As an active AU speaker mentor, he also assists first-time AU speakers in developing their AU classes for a global audience.

Shaun lives in East Yorkshire, UK, and works from his home-based, self-built office studio, affectionately known as *The Workshop*.

I want to thank everyone at this point in my career, including the amazing Autodesk Community team – Vikram Dutt, Jessica Langston, April Robinson, Chris Coumbe, Jonathan Hand, Amanda De Pancrazio, Amanda Pruyn, and all other Community team members and Expert Elites who remain too numerous to mention. Thank you.

I also want to thank the past and present Autodesk Expert Elite program team. I would not be an Expert Elite without them – Mark Gunn, Katinka Sante, Kate Merriman, and Maureen Higgins. The Autodesk Expert Elite program would not exist without you.

About the reviewer

Nisreen Khlefat is an experienced interior designer and educator dedicated to fostering creativity and functional design. At Milwaukee Area Technical College, she supports students in mastering AutoCAD and SketchUp, helping them build strong foundations in design software. In addition to teaching, Nisreen manages NK Interior Design, where she works with clients to create personalized, inviting spaces. With a balance of technical expertise and creative vision, Nisreen is passionate about enhancing interiors and guiding aspiring designers toward success.

Table of Contents

Preface — xv

Part 1: The AutoCAD Interface – Enhanced

1
Customizing the AutoCAD Interface — 3

Technical requirements	4
Introducing the default AutoCAD interface settings	4
Understanding the AutoCAD ribbon settings	6
Using sticky panels	12
Using the QAT effectively	15
Customizing the QAT	16
Other QAT settings	18
Introducing the CUI command	21
Summary	26
Exercise	27

2
Developing Your Own AutoCAD Workspace — 29

Technical requirements	30
Exercise files	30
Using workspaces effectively	30
Choosing the right default workspace	30
Creating your own AutoCAD workspace	32
Saving AutoCAD interface changes to a custom workspace	33
Removing a redundant workspace from the AutoCAD CUI	37
Summary	41

3

Using the AutoCAD Interface to Work Smarter — 43

Exercise files	44	The AutoCAD navigation bar	66
Working with file tabs	44	Navigation Wheels	67
Working with the Model and Layout tabs	47	Real-time Pan	68
		Zoom	69
Utilizing the drafting settings on the status bar	53	Orbit (flyout)	70
		3Dconnexion	70
The AutoCAD ViewCube	63	ShowMotion	71
		Summary	73

4

Using Advanced Drafting Settings — 75

Exercise files	76	Working with ISODRAFT settings to create isometric views	83
Selecting objects using selection cycling	76	Changing units via the status bar	85
Utilizing 3D object snaps when 3D modeling	80	Working with annotation scale to improve drawing legibility	87
		Summary	92

Part 2: Advanced Drafting Techniques and Annotation

5

Developing Advanced Geometry Using Object Snaps — 95

Technical requirements	96	Locking the cursor orthogonally with ORTHOMODE	100
Exercise files	96		
Measuring angles accurately with Polar Tracking (POLAR)	96	Using Object Snap Tracking (AUTOSNAP) to draw efficiently with multiple Osnaps	102

Drawing accurately and effectively with Object Snaps (OSNAP) and snap overrides	106	Working with Snap Overrides	112
		Summary	119
Finding the Geometric Center	108		

6

Measuring and Modifying Geometry and Objects — 121

Exercise files	122	Adding and subtracting areas using the Area tool	129
Using Noun/verb selection for quick and easy object selection	122	Measuring precise angles with the Angle tool	134
Calculating lengths and angles with Quick Measure and Distance	125	Refining drawings using the Modify panel	137
		Summary	143

7

Developing Annotative Annotation Styles — 145

Exercise file	146	Setting up specific leader styles	165
Creating text styles to manage text sizes and fonts	146	Working with accurate table styles	172
		Summary	182
Managing dimension annotation with dimension styles	152		

8

Working with Annotative Scaling — 183

Exercise files	184	Adding and deleting object annotation scales	204
Setting up viewports and varying viewport scales	184	Summary	209
Working with annotation scales in the Model tab	197		

Part 3: Content Re-Use Including Dynamic Blocks

9

Developing Block Libraries — 213

Exercise file	213	Adding the block library to the Blocks palette	231
Bringing blocks and dynamic blocks into drawings	214	Creating a new block library tool palette	236
Adding a regular door block	215	Summary	244
Adding a dynamic Door block	219		
Using the Clipboard to create a new block library drawing	227		

10

Working with Block Attributes — 245

Exercise file	246	Using Block Attribute Manager (BATTMAN)	260
Defining attributes within a block	246	Summary	264
Editing attributes in a block using Enhanced Attribute Editor	257		

11

Creating a Dynamic Block with Parameters and Actions — 265

Exercise file	266	Testing the new dynamic block in the drawing	286
Creating the regular door block	266	Summary	291
Adding a vertical flip to the door	271		
Adding a horizontal flip to the door	279		

12

Creating a Dynamic Block with Visibility States — 293

Exercise file	294	Adding visibility states in a dynamic block	306
Creating the washbasin block drawing	294	Setting up the first visibility state	307
Adding the front block	294	Adding two more visibility states	313
Adding the top and side blocks	298	Using the new dynamic block with visibility states	316
Adding the necessary blocks for each view	303	Summary	320

Part 4: Communicating and Collaborating

13

Sharing Your AutoCAD Drawings — 323

Exercise file and requirements	324	Using the Shared Views palette	335
Using the Share Drawing tool	324	Working with shared views in the Autodesk Viewer	340
Working with shared drawings in AutoCAD Web	327	Summary	346

14

Comparing Drawings and External Reference Files — 347

Exercise files	347	Working with reference file comparisons generated with Xref Compare	364
Comparing drawings with DWG Compare	348		
Working with drawing comparisons generated with DWG Compare	353	Summary	367
Comparing drawings with Xref Compare	357		

15

Working with AutoCAD Web — 369

Exercise file	370	Opening and working with drawings in the AutoCAD mobile application	384
Saving DWG files to the cloud from the AutoCAD desktop	370	Using drawings updated in AutoCAD Web or the AutoCAD mobile application	392
Using the Drawing History tool	372		
Opening and working with drawings in the AutoCAD web application	376	Summary	395

16

Collaborating using Traces in AutoCAD — 397

Exercise files	398	Using traces in AutoCAD Web	412
Using traces with AutoCAD desktop	398	Reviewing traces in the AutoCAD desktop app	417
Using traces in the AutoCAD mobile application	406	Summary	423

Index — 425

Other Books You May Enjoy — 432

Preface

AutoCAD is over forty years old and has had many versions. The full version of AutoCAD provides 2D drafting capabilities and 3D modelling tools that can be professionally lit and rendered, providing photo-realistic visualizations that can be incorporated in professional presentations. Precise 2D drawings can be created that include accurate drafting annotation, including dimensions, leaders, and data tables.

This book encourages the reader to master AutoCAD, introducing techniques and workflows that allow the reader to become even more competent with the AutoCAD application, empowering them to use the knowledge gained in this book to improve and enhance their existing AutoCAD skill set.

Who this book is for

This book is for existing users of AutoCAD who have already used AutoCAD professionally in their careers. Ideally, readers should already have a basic level of knowledge of AutoCAD to understand the concepts, workflows, and processes mentioned in this book. Typical readers would include intermediate level CAD technicians, CAD managers, and those who use AutoCAD on a regular daily basis.

What this book covers

Chapter 1, Customizing the AutoCAD Interface, looks at the AutoCAD interface and how it can be customized quickly and easily. With this customizability, you can make quick and easy changes to your AutoCAD interface to enhance productivity.

Chapter 2, Developing Your Own AutoCAD Workspace, will help you learn how to use workspaces in AutoCAD effectively and make the necessary interface changes to create a custom workspace. You will also learn how to remove a workspace that isn't needed.

Chapter 3, Using the AutoCAD Interface to Work Smarter, shows how AutoCAD provides many functions and features that allow you to work smarter, not harder. These include file tabs, the Model and Layout tabs, drafting settings on the status bar, the AutoCAD ViewCube, and the AutoCAD navigation bar. This chapter teaches you how to use these tools effectively, enhancing your AutoCAD productivity

Chapter 4, Using Advanced Drafting Settings, talks about AutoCAD and its extensive range of drafting settings located on the AutoCAD status bar. This chapter will take you through some of the lesser-used, advanced drafting settings so that you can work more effectively and productively by working smarter, not harder.

Chapter 5, Developing Advanced Geometry Using Object Snaps, elaborates that AutoCAD is a precise design application, and accuracy must be maintained in your drawing files. This chapter will show you how to use specific drafting settings and object snaps (often referred to as Osnaps) that will allow you to draft and model precisely and accurately

Chapter 6, Measuring and Modifying Geometry and Objects, To achieve a high level of accuracy, AutoCAD users spend a lot of time modifying geometry and objects in drawings, often needing to measure lengths, areas, and angles. AutoCAD provides a comprehensive set of drafting and modeling tools to modify and measure the geometry quickly and accurately in your DWG files

Chapter 7, Developing Annotative Annotation Styles, This chapter you will learn the methodologies needed to use annotative annotation in your DWG files, including creating text styles to manage text sizes and fonts, managing dimension annotation with dimension styles, setting up specific leader styles, and working with accurate table styles

Chapter 8, Working with Annotative Scaling, This chapter takes you through how to utilize annotation styles with annotative scaling by setting up viewports and varying viewport scales, working with annotation scales in the Model tab, and adding and deleting object annotation scales. This allows annotation to be displayed appropriately to communicate design intent effectively and accurately

Chapter 9, Developing Block Libraries, By the end of this chapter, you will be able to work with regular and dynamic blocks in drawings and create your own block libraries using various methods, including the Clipboard. You will also learn how to use the Blocks palette and utilize tool palettes with your blocks

Chapter 10, Working with Block Attributes, Drawings become occupied with more and more blocks over time. Attributes allow you to identify your blocks and provide valuable information to anyone using your drawings. The methodologies you will need are in this chapter, such as defining attributes within a block, editing attributes in a block using Enhanced Attribute Editor, and using Block Attribute Manager (*BATTMAN*)

Chapter 11, Chapter Creating a Dynamic Block with Parameters and Actions, Dynamic blocks need both a parameter and an associated action, so if you were working with a block representing a door, you may need to add a parameter and action to control the swing direction of the door in the door opening in the drawing. This chapter covers the methodologies for working with those parameters and actions in your drawings.

Chapter 12, Creating a Dynamic Block with Visibility States, Visibility states allow you to create a dynamic block with numerous views in the same block. This chapter shows you how to create a washbasin block with three different views: top, front, and side

Chapter 13, Sharing Your AutoCAD Drawings, Sharing drawings and drawing views allows you to share aspects of your design in real-time, using the power of the internet and the cloud. This saves valuable drawing management and collaboration time by providing a much more dynamic drawing revision path.

Chapter 14, *Comparing Drawings and External Reference Files*, Comparing drawings and Xrefs is much easier and less time-consuming than it used to be. AutoCAD can compare drawing files and Xref drawing files. This technology also allows you to make a drawing file of the comparison and incorporate the compared objects into the relevant drawing

Chapter 15, *Working with AutoCAD Web*, The AutoCAD subscription comes with the AutoCAD Web offering, which incorporates the AutoCAD web and mobile applications. Both applications allow DWG file collaboration in the cloud, and the AutoCAD mobile application adds full mobility to your DWG files

Chapter 16, *Collaborating using Traces in AutoCAD*, As of AutoCAD 2023, the Trace function is also available in the AutoCAD desktop application and is much enhanced in the AutoCAD 2026 version. This availability provides full trace functionality across all three AutoCAD applications: desktop, web, and mobile.

To get the most out of this book

You will need a full version of AutoCAD 2026 installed on your computer (not AutoCAD LT 2026). All exercises and examples have been tested using AutoCAD 2026 on Windows OS. However, they should work with AutoCAD for Mac 2026 as well, and any differences between the Windows OS version of AutoCAD 2026 and AutoCAD for Mac 2026 are noted where applicable.

Software/hardware covered in the book	Operating system requirements
AutoCAD 2026	Windows OS
AutoCAD for Mac 2026	macOS
AutoCAD Web	Google Chrome, Microsoft Edge Chromium
AutoCAD mobile application	iOS for iPhone or iPad, Android OS

If you are using this book's physical or digital version, we advise you to download the exercises files mentioned in each chapter to a known location, such as your hard drive, network drive, or a cloud-based drive, for easy access.

After reading this book, the reader should utilize their extended AutoCAD knowledge to become more effective in their daily AutoCAD processes and workflows. It is also suggested that the reader consider looking into Autodesk Certification in AutoCAD to gain a recognized Autodesk Certification.

Download the exercise (DWG) files

You can download the exercise (DWG) files for this book from GitHub at `https://github.com/PacktPublishing/Mastering-AutoCAD`. If there's an update to the exercises, it will be updated in the GitHub repository.

We also have other code bundles from our rich catalog of books and videos available at `https://github.com/PacktPublishing/`. Check them out!

Conventions used

There are a number of text conventions used throughout this book.

`Filenames in text`: Indicates the filenames of exercise files that should be used to work through the workflows and processes demonstrated in each chapter. Here is an example: "Having a DWG file open ensures you get access to all of the AutoCAD interface, so make sure to have the `Workspaces.dwg` file open and current in AutoCAD."

Bold: Indicates a new term, an important word, or words that you see onscreen. For instance, words in menus or dialog boxes appear in **bold**. Here is an example: "You can also access the **New** command via the **Application** menu (top-left corner) and the **Start** screen in AutoCAD."

> Tips and tricks #25
>
> When you select a viewport, it is not only the grips that are displayed. If you select the triangle dropdown in the center of the selected viewport, you will be able to see all available viewport scales. If you select a different scale from the existing viewport scale, the viewport will be resized and rescaled, as shown in *Figure 8.5*. This also works in AutoCAD for Mac.

Get in touch

Feedback from our readers is always welcome.

General feedback: If you have questions about any aspect of this book, email us at `customercare@packtpub.com` and mention the book title in the subject of your message.

Errata: Although we have taken every care to ensure the accuracy of our content, mistakes do happen. If you have found a mistake in this book, we would be grateful if you would report this to us. Please visit `www.packtpub.com/support/errata` and fill in the form.

Piracy: If you come across any illegal copies of our works in any form on the internet, we would be grateful if you would provide us with the location address or website name. Please contact us at `copyright@packtpub.com` with a link to the material.

If you are interested in becoming an author: If there is a topic that you have expertise in and you are interested in either writing or contributing to a book, please visit `authors.packtpub.com`.

Share Your Thoughts

Once you've read *Mastering AutoCAD*, we'd love to hear your thoughts! Scan the QR code below to go straight to the Amazon review page for this book and share your feedback.

https://packt.link/r/1-837-63969-8

Your review is important to us and the tech community and will help us make sure we're delivering excellent quality content.

Free Benefits with Your Book

This book comes with free benefits to support your learning. Activate them now for instant access (see the "*How to Unlock*" section for instructions).

Here's a quick overview of what you can instantly unlock with your purchase:

PDF and ePub Copies | Next-Gen Web-Based Reader

- Access a DRM-free PDF copy of this book to read anywhere, on any device.
- Use a DRM-free ePub version with your favorite e-reader.

- **Multi-device progress sync**: Pick up where you left off, on any device.
- **Highlighting and notetaking**: Capture ideas and turn reading into lasting knowledge.
- **Bookmarking**: Save and revisit key sections whenever you need them.
- **Dark mode**: Reduce eye strain by switching to dark or sepia themes

How to Unlock

Scan the QR code (or go to `packtpub.com/unlock`). Search for this book by name, confirm the edition, and then follow the steps on the page.

Note: Keep your invoice handy. Purchases made directly from Packt don't require one

Part 1: The AutoCAD Interface – Enhanced

The AutoCAD interface is fundamental to the effective use of AutoCAD in either 2D or 3D environments. Regardless of whether you are drafting a 2D floor plan or modeling a 3D automotive part, the interface is incredibly important. This part of the book teaches you how to customize the user interface and work with user-defined workspaces to make it work more effectively for you. You will also learn how to work smarter, not harder, when using the AutoCAD interface and how to use advanced AutoCAD drafting settings to your advantage.

This part has the following chapters:

- *Chapter 1, Customizing the AutoCAD Interface*
- *Chapter 2, Developing Your Own AutoCAD Workspace*
- *Chapter 3, Using the AutoCAD Interface to Work Smarter*
- *Chapter 4, Using Advanced Drafting Settings*

1
Customizing the AutoCAD Interface

AutoCAD is the world's most well-known **Computer-Aided Design** (**CAD**) application. Globally used by architects, engineers, and designers, AutoCAD has been around for over 40 years. It has been the go-to CAD application for millions in that time, and the DWG file format is universally recognized.

This chapter looks at the AutoCAD interface and how it can be customized quickly and easily. With this customizability, you can make quick and easy changes to your AutoCAD interface to enhance productivity. You will also be able to work with different interface setups for different production environments.

By the end of the chapter, you will be able to work with your ribbon settings in AutoCAD, work effectively with the **Quick Access Toolbar** (**QAT**), and be more knowledgeable about the AutoCAD **CUI command**.

This chapter covers some of the best practices associated with the AutoCAD user interface. We also look at the following topics in depth:

- Introducing the default AutoCAD interface settings
- The AutoCAD ribbon settings
- Using sticky panels
- Using the QAT effectively
- The AutoCAD CUI command

Free Benefits with Your Book

Your purchase includes a free PDF copy of this book along with other exclusive benefits. Check the *Free Benefits with Your Book* section in the Preface to unlock them instantly and maximize your learning experience.

Technical requirements

Using AutoCAD will require you to have a licensed version of AutoCAD installed either on your desktop computer or your laptop. You will also require the following:

- A subscription (license) for AutoCAD. This will need to be the *full* version of AutoCAD, not AutoCAD LT. Ideally, this will be the latest version of AutoCAD: AutoCAD 2026. You can use earlier versions, but it is suggested that you go no further back than AutoCAD 2022.

- In order to use AutoCAD with a subscription, you will need an Autodesk account. If you do not have one, you can set one up at `https://accounts.autodesk.com/`.

- This book covers AutoCAD 2026, running on the Microsoft Windows **Operating System (OS)**. All figures and graphics are from AutoCAD 2024 and the Windows 11 OS. However, this book contains instructions for both Windows and Mac users. While comprehensive instructions have been provided for Windows users, special instructions relating to deviations in the Mac interface have also been provided within callout boxes.

- All the graphics and drawings for this book can be found here: `https://github.com/PacktPublishing/Mastering-AutoCAD`.

Okay, let's get into the chapter now!

Introducing the default AutoCAD interface settings

Before we jump into the rest of the chapter and learn about how to tweak AutoCAD's UI for our benefit, let us familiarize ourselves with the default AutoCAD interface settings. These are known as workspaces. As an AutoCAD user, you will have more than likely already been using these workspaces without knowing it.

The following default workspaces are available in AutoCAD:

- **Drafting & Annotation**: The Drafting & Annotation workspace is used primarily for 2D drafting in AutoCAD. This is the most-used AutoCAD workspace.

- **3D Basics**: The 3D Basics workspace is exactly what it says: a basic 3D interface that is used for 3D modeling. It is, however, a limited, cut-down 3D interface with only basic functionality.

- **3D Modeling**: The 3D Modeling workspace is a comprehensive 3D workspace that includes all the 3D ribbon tabs, panels, and commands. It would normally be the 3D workspace that you would use for everyday 3D modeling.

    I have introduced you to these default workspaces now so that you can check where to find them and ascertain which workspace you are currently using. To check which workspace is being used, you can click on the fly-out arrow to the right of the gearwheel icon on the status bar, as shown in *Figure 1.1*.

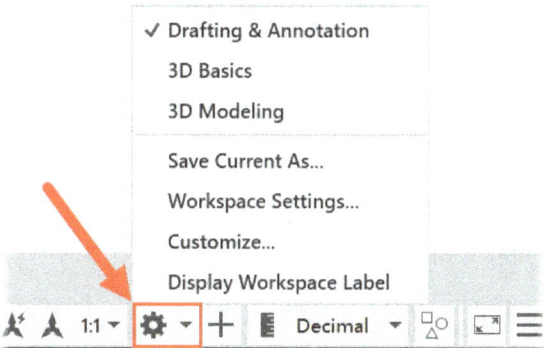

Figure 1.1: The gearwheel icon on the status bar

When clicking on the fly-out arrow, the **Workspace** menu appears. The preceding figure shows that the **Drafting & Annotation** workspace is the current one (as indicated by the checkmark next to it).

Make sure to check which workspace you are using, and for the purposes of this chapter, make sure to set the **Drafting & Annotation** workspace as current. We will go into workspaces in more depth in *Chapter 2*.

> **AutoCAD for Mac**
>
> Some of you might be using AutoCAD for Mac on an Apple computer that uses the macOS OS. The AutoCAD for Mac interface is decidedly different from the AutoCAD interface you would see when running it on Windows OS. Workspaces in AutoCAD for Mac work differently. You will find the **Drafting** and **Modeling** workspaces in AutoCAD for Mac at the top of the icon menu on the left-hand side of the screen, as shown in *Figure 1.2*.

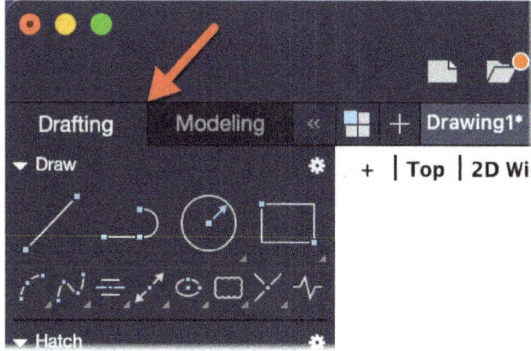

Figure 1.2: The Drafting and Modeling tabs in the AutoCAD for Mac interface

Customizing the AutoCAD Interface

Now that you have an understanding of the AutoCAD interface, the next section introduces the AutoCAD ribbon and its settings.

Understanding the AutoCAD ribbon settings

The AutoCAD ribbon is a fundamental part of your AutoCAD interface. It provides you with ribbon tabs, each of which is occupied by ribbon panels, which incorporate most of the commands you need to operate AutoCAD effectively.

AutoCAD has four ribbon settings. These can sometimes inadvertently be activated, making you think you have broken AutoCAD somehow. You haven't, trust me. It takes a lot to break AutoCAD nowadays!

The ribbon settings are activated by clicking on a small button on the top of the ribbon. If you blink, you might miss it, and many AutoCAD users do. It is one of those buttons that gets clicked on, and then you're not sure how to get things back to what they looked like before.

If you check the top of your AutoCAD ribbon, you will see a small white rectangular button with an arrow on it. *Figure 1.3* shows you where you will find it.

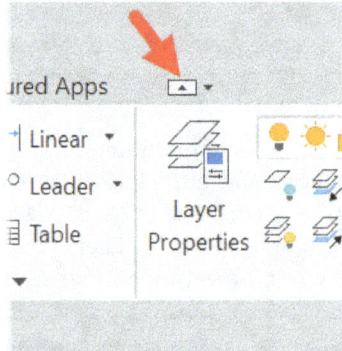

Figure 1.3: The ribbon settings button

Based on its size, you can understand why it gets missed easily, right? If you click on the button (not the fly-out arrow to the right of it), you will see the appearance of your ribbon change. Don't panic. All you have done is change the appearance of the ribbon.

Each of the four settings displays the ribbon differently, giving you varying methods of utilizing the ribbon during your day-to-day AutoCAD work.

I'll briefly explain how each setting works. The ribbon settings change based on whether you have clicked the ribbon settings button at the top of the ribbon and how many times you have clicked it consecutively:

- **The default ribbon (no click required):** This ribbon setting is set by default when you first start using AutoCAD. As you can see in *Figure 1.4*, it provides a view of all the ribbon tabs, panels, and icons.

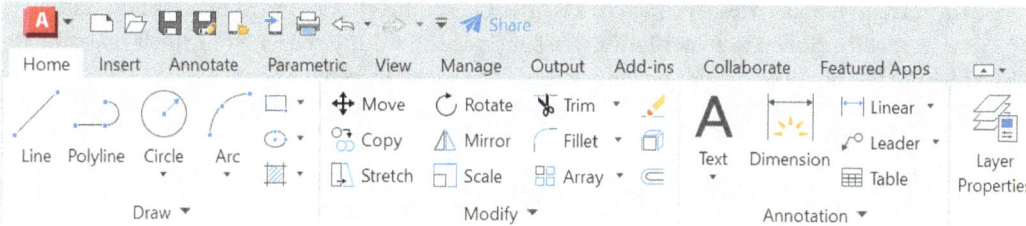

Figure 1.4: The default ribbon display

- **Minimize to Panel Buttons (first click):** After the first click of the ribbon settings button, you will set the ribbon to **Panel Buttons**. The ribbon tabs are still available, but each panel on its respective tab will now only display as a button, as shown in *Figure 1.5*.

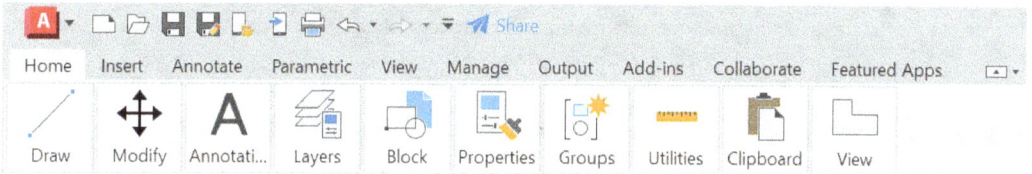

Figure 1.5: The ribbon display using Minimize to Panel Buttons

Upon clicking on any panel button, the selected ribbon panel will display, as shown in *Figure 1.6*.

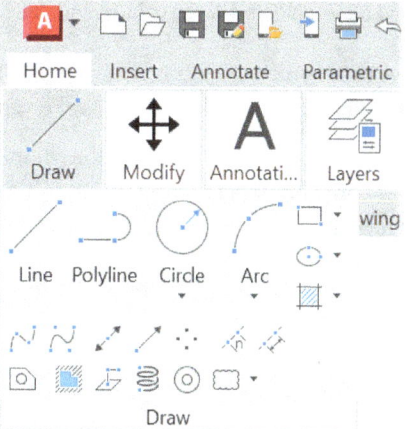

Figure 1.6: The Draw panel selected while using Minimize to Panel Buttons

The preceding figure shows the **Home** tab as current, and the **Draw** panel after the **Draw** panel button has been clicked.

As you can see, this ribbon setting reduces the footprint of the ribbon, providing more screen space for your AutoCAD drafting and modeling, by only displaying the panel selected by the panel button. If you move the cursor away from the selected panel, it will revert back to the panel buttons view.

- **Minimize to Panel Titles (second click)**: After the second click of the ribbon settings button, you will set the ribbon to **Panel Titles**. The panels are now displayed with only their titles, thus reducing the ribbon footprint on your screen even more as seen in *Figure 1.7*.

Figure 1.7: The ribbon display using Minimize to Panel Titles

Upon clicking on any panel title, the selected ribbon panel will display, as shown in *Figure 1.8*.

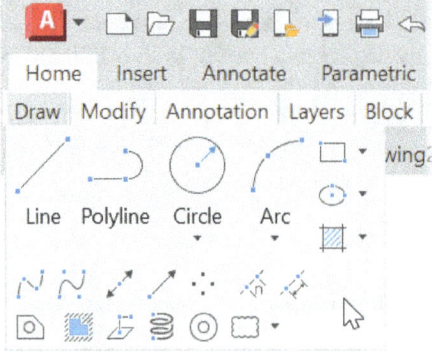

Figure 1.8: The Draw panel selected when using Minimize to Panel Titles

The preceding figure shows the **Home** tab as current with the **Draw** panel title selected. As before, when you move the cursor away from the panel, it will revert back to the panel titles view.

- **Minimize to Tabs (third click)**: After the third click of the ribbon settings button, you will set the ribbon to Tabs. There are now no panel buttons or titles displayed, only the ribbon tabs. This is the most minimal view of the ribbon in AutoCAD as you can see in *Figure 1.9*.

Figure 1.9: The ribbon display using Minimize to Tabs

Understanding the AutoCAD ribbon settings   9

To access the ribbon panels when using the **Minimize to Tabs** setting, you will need to select the ribbon tab first, then select the required command icon on its respective panel, as shown in *Figure 1.10*.

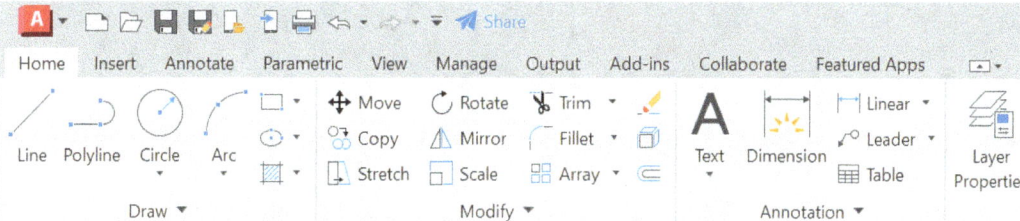

Figure 1.10: The Home tab selected when using Minimize to Tabs

As you can see in the preceding figure, all the panels in the selected tab are displayed. In this case, the **Home** tab on the ribbon has been selected, displaying the **Draw** panel, the **Modify** panel, and all panels that display under the **Home** tab on the ribbon

> **Note**
>
> *Figure 1.10* has been truncated slightly to fit better on the page. Hence, only the **Draw** and **Modify** panels are displayed in full.

- **Back to default (fourth click)**: A fourth click on the ribbon settings button will bring you back to the default ribbon setting, as shown in *Figure 1.11*.

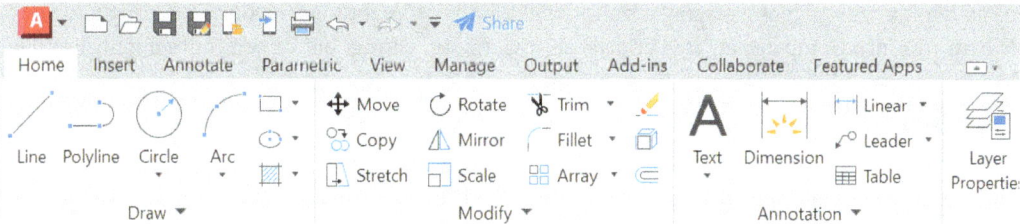

Figure 1.11: Back to the default ribbon setting on the fourth click

So, as you can see, it is easy to click on the ribbon settings button and make these changes in error. If you have never used the ribbon settings button before, it can cause a certain amount of trepidation as you wonder what you have done to your AutoCAD interface. However, by using the sequence of clicks I have described in this section on the ribbon settings button, you can now get back to the default ribbon setting if required.

You can now also see how the ribbon settings can be changed to suit your specific requirements. This allows you to utilize more screen space in AutoCAD by reducing the ribbon footprint. This is especially useful when your screen space is restricted. A typical example would be running AutoCAD on a laptop with a smaller screen.

Until this point, I have not mentioned the small fly-out arrow to the right of the ribbon settings button, as shown in *Figure 1.12*.

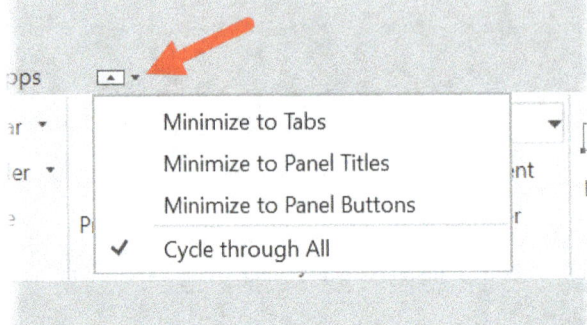

Figure 1.12: The fly-out menu on the ribbon settings button

Upon clicking on the fly-out arrow, you will see the small fly-out menu as shown in the preceding figure. This allows you to select a specific ribbon setting rather than clicking through them on the ribbon settings button, as mentioned earlier.

Once a specific ribbon setting has been selected, it will remain set. You will need to set the menu back to **Cycle through All** to use the ribbon settings button to cycle through each ribbon setting.

The ribbon settings in AutoCAD are a great way of gaining that little bit more screen real estate when working on smaller displays. As we move toward workstation replacement laptops, this will help. Yes, you can hook up to a gigantic display monitor when in the office, but when you're traveling and you only have a 15-inch laptop display at your disposal, that ribbon settings button will prove mighty useful!

> **Tips and tricks #1**
>
> You will notice a fly-out arrow on the title bars of some of the ribbon panels. If you click on the fly-out arrow on the panel, the hidden command icons from that panel are displayed. Click on the small pin icon and those hidden command icons will remain pinned open and will display until the pin icon is clicked again. The hidden icons will then revert into the ribbon. *Figure 1.13* shows you where you will find the pin icon using the **Draw** panel on the **Home** tab of the ribbon.

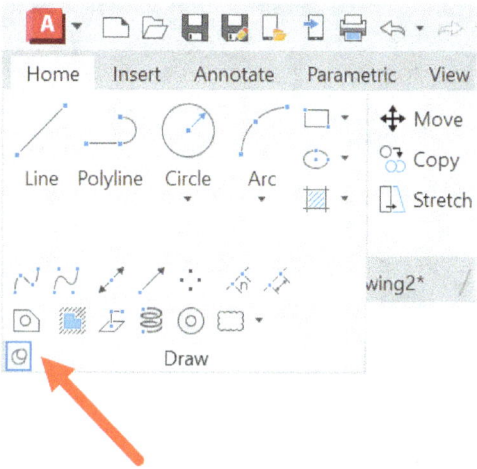

Figure 1.13: The pin icon that allows the hidden command icons to be pinned open (shown pinned)

Now that you know how you can fix the AutoCAD ribbon settings to suit your workflow without feeling like you have broken AutoCAD, let us move on to learning how we can improve the UI even further using sticky panels.

> **AutoCAD for Mac**
>
> AutoCAD for Mac does not have a ribbon interface like AutoCAD for Windows does, so there is no way of changing the ribbon appearance. AutoCAD for Mac uses an icon menu to the left of the AutoCAD for Mac screen. You can edit the icon settings for each icon panel by clicking on the gearwheel icon. *Figure 1.14* shows the Draw panel and its default icon settings. In AutoCAD for Mac, you still click and hold for the fly-out icon menus, much like in AutoCAD for Windows, to get access to more instances of a command, such as the Arc fly-out menu.

12　Customizing the AutoCAD Interface

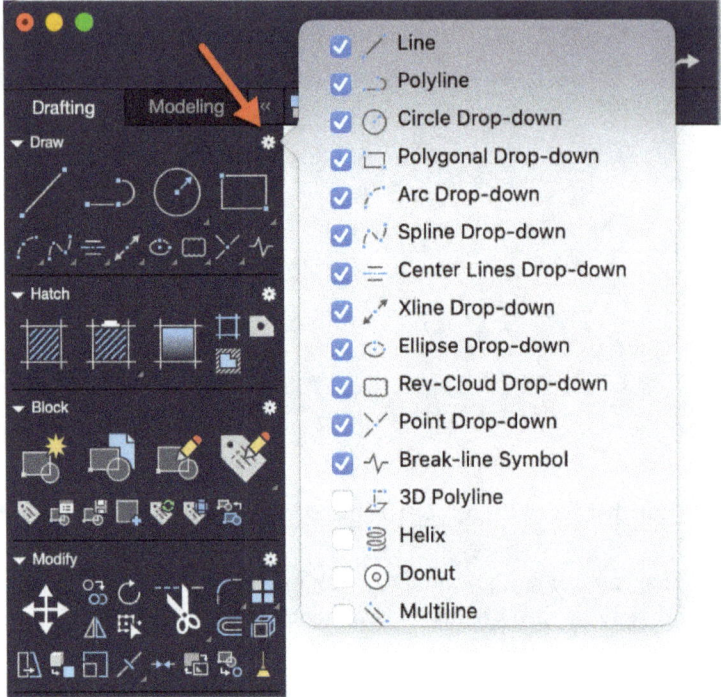

Figure 1.14: The icon settings in the Draw panel in AutoCAD for Mac

You now have a good understanding of the AutoCAD ribbon and its settings and functionality. In the next section, you will learn how to use sticky panels (from the ribbon) to your advantage.

Using sticky panels

In this chapter, the assumption has so far been made that ribbon panels stay in the ribbon. That's not the case. Ribbon panels can be moved into the AutoCAD drawing area and can float in the same way as dialog boxes and palettes can.

The following figure shows the **Draw** panel (from the **Home** tab) floating in the AutoCAD drawing area. This section covers how to get a sticky panel there, as well as how to get it back into the ribbon.

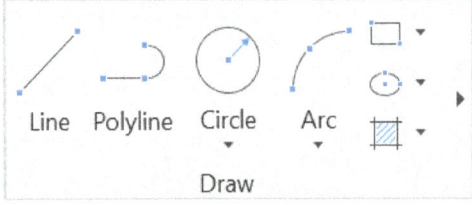

Figure 1.15: The floating Draw panel in the AutoCAD drawing area

To keep things simple, stay in the **Home** tab on the ribbon.

Move the cursor over the title bar of the **Draw** panel. Click and drag the **Draw** panel. You will see the **Draw** panel start to move and you can simply drop it into the AutoCAD drawing area by releasing the mouse button. Yes, it really is that easy!

This is known as a **sticky** panel. The description derives from the Post-It sticky notes you might use in the office. You are sticking the ribbon panel where you need it to be so that you can see it and use it more effectively.

The benefit of this is that the sticky panels are then not constrained by the ribbon. You can now go to other ribbon tabs to use other AutoCAD commands but still have quick and easy access to the commands on the sticky panels.

A typical scenario might be that you need the **Draw** panel so that you can create geometry, but you might be in the **Annotate** tab working on the annotation in the drawing. *Figure 1.16* highlights that scenario.

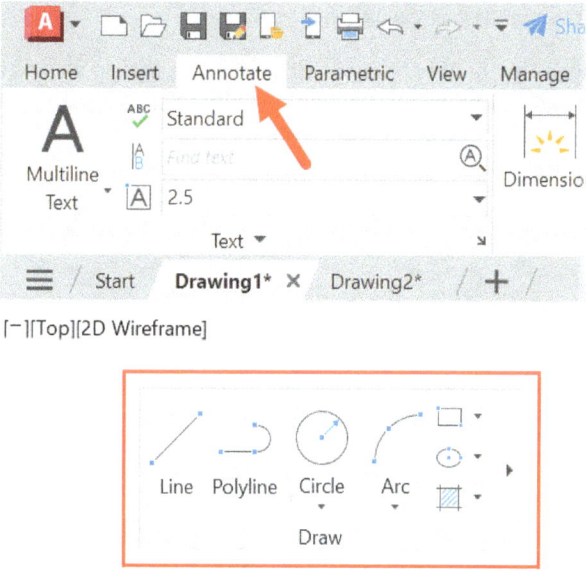

Figure 1.16: The Draw panel is the sticky panel, while the Annotate ribbon tab is current

Getting the sticky panel back into the ribbon is not as difficult as you might think. Click and drag are not required, and AutoCAD even remembers which ribbon tab you took the sticky panel from.

To get the sticky panel back into the ribbon, you need to hover over the sticky panel in place. You will see the panel highlight and sidebars appear on both the left and right sides of the panel. *Figure 1.17* shows the sidebars, as indicated by the arrows.

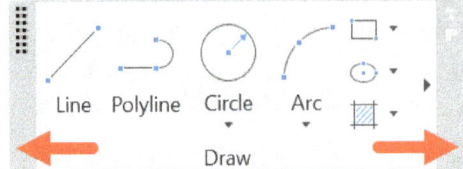

Figure 1.17: The sticky panel with sidebars indicated

On the left sidebar, you will see a graded or dotted area. You can click and drag this to relocate the sticky panel.

On the right sidebar, there are two small icons. The lower of these two icons will allow you to rotate the sticky panel from horizontal to vertical and vice versa.

You need the top-right icon. If you hover the cursor over it, the tooltip will read **Return Panels to Ribbon**. You can see this shown in *Figure 1.18*.

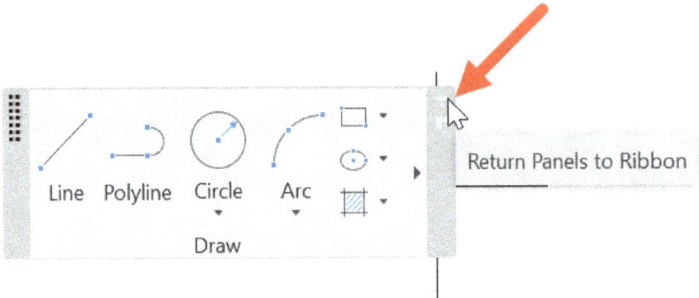

Figure 1.18: The sticky panel with Return Panels to Ribbon indicated

Upon clicking on this icon, the sticky panel will be returned to the ribbon. Regardless of which ribbon tab is current, AutoCAD will put the panel back on the appropriate ribbon tab.

If you are in the **Annotate** tab and you return your sticky **Draw** panel to the ribbon, not only will AutoCAD make sure it is placed on the appropriate ribbon tab, but it will even make sure it is back in the correct location on that ribbon tab!

This is done using the AutoCAD CUI settings, which we will touch on later in this chapter.

> **Tips and tricks #2**
>
> AutoCAD now has a feature known as floating drawing windows. This means that any drawing file tab can be dragged and dropped into any display location. This is often used when AutoCAD is used across a dual (or sometimes triple) monitor hardware setup. Sticky panels will remain in place even when the floating drawing is moved to another location. *Figure 1.19* gives you an idea of what this might look like.

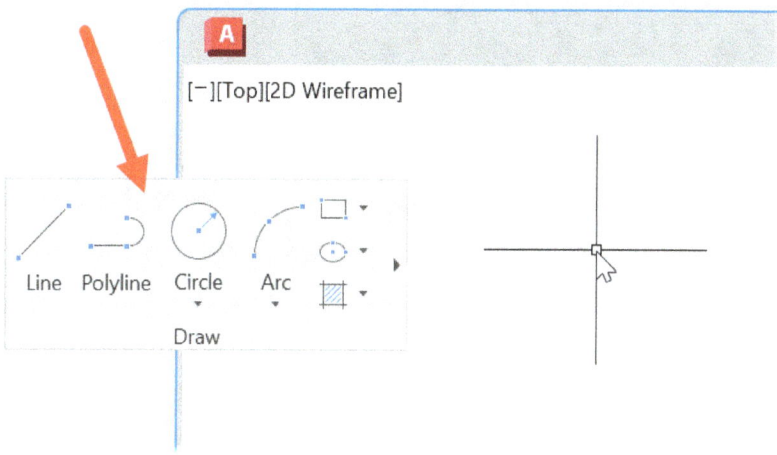

Figure 1.19: The Draw sticky panel is still in place with the floating drawing window behind it

Sticky panels are a great way of customizing your AutoCAD interface to suit the way you work. They can be located anywhere, especially when you need specific ribbon panels to always be available.

Now that you understand how to utilize sticky panels and put them back into their place, let us divert our attention to learning about the items in the QAT.

Using the QAT effectively

The AutoCAD QAT is located in the top-left of your AutoCAD 2024 application window. You may have used it already when working with AutoCAD. *Figure 1.20* shows you the default non-customized QAT.

Figure 1.20: The QAT (non-customized)

In this section, we will learn about some useful workflows with the QAT that will help you become just that bit more efficient and productive.

Customizing the QAT

There is a very small but powerful icon on the QAT. For those of us who are over a certain age, it will remind us of the era of **Compact Discs** (**CDs**). These were used primarily for music and replaced vinyl albums. They were also used for software installations. AutoCAD used to be installed from CD media too. Music CDs were played on a CD player. The **Customize Quick Access Toolbar** icon on the QAT looks remarkably like the eject button on those old CD players. *Figure 1.21* highlights the **Customize Quick Access Toolbar** button.

Figure 1.21: The Customize Quick Access Toolbar button

Upon clicking the icon, a drop-down menu will appear, as shown in *Figure 1.22*.

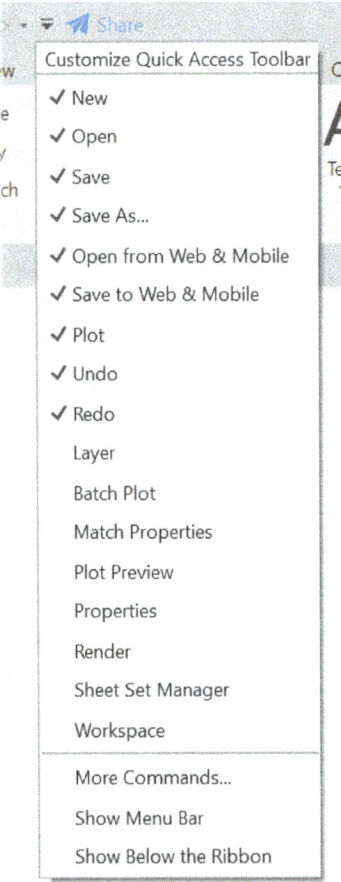

Figure 1.22: The Customize Quick Access Toolbar dropdown with default settings

You will notice that several of the settings have checkmarks next to them. This indicates that these functions are already displayed on the QAT. The functions without checkmarks can be selected to display on the QAT to improve your day-to-day AutoCAD work. This is the customization that we will focus on.

If the **Layer** option is selected from the drop-down menu, you will see that the **Layer** drop-down menu is added to the QAT, as shown in *Figure 1.23*.

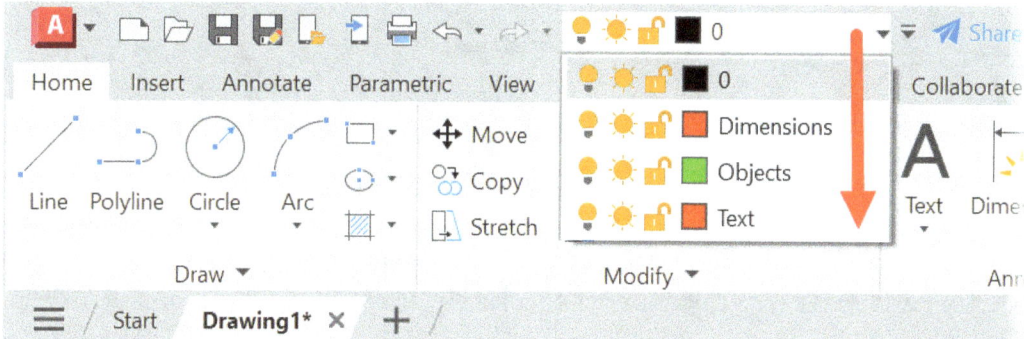

Figure 1.23: The QAT with the Layer drop-down menu added and in use

The major benefit of this customization is that you now have access to all the AutoCAD layer controls all of the time. Regardless of which ribbon tab you use, you can control your layer properties at any time, thus not needing to keep returning to the **Home** tab on the ribbon to change any specific layer properties. *Figure 1.23* also shows the QAT with the **Layer** drop-down menu added while it is in use. You can now see how easy it is to access your AutoCAD layers.

If you want to turn off the **Layer** dropdown on the QAT, you will need to repeat the customization process by clicking on the **Customize Quick Access Toolbar** icon. Then click on **Layer** on the drop-down menu and the checkmark will be removed. The **Layer** dropdown will also be removed.

Another useful drop-down menu to add to the QAT is the **Workspace** function. As mentioned previously, this is another function you can tick in the **Customize Quick Access Toolbar** dropdown. *Figure 1.24* shows the **Workspace** function added to the QAT and in use.

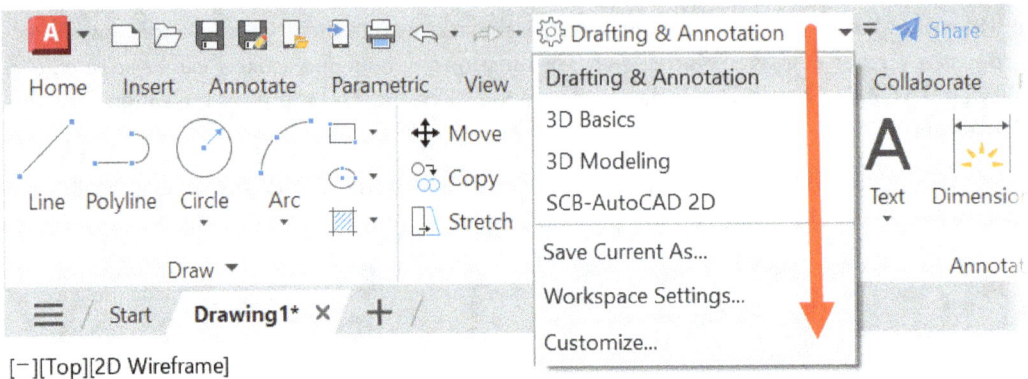

Figure 1.24: The QAT with the Workspace function added and in use

As you can see, adding functionality to the QAT gives you a customized AutoCAD user interface that will enhance your workflows and provide you with that little bit of extra efficiency every day when using AutoCAD.

Other QAT settings

On the **Customize Quick Access Toolbar** dropdown for the QAT, you will also see other settings that can be used to customize your AutoCAD interface a little further.

The **Show Menu Bar** option will display a classic AutoCAD menu bar at the top of the AutoCAD application window, as shown in *Figure 1.25*.

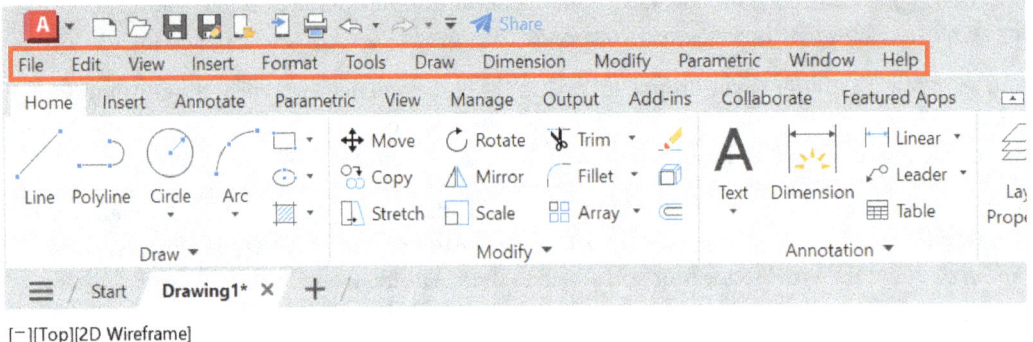

Figure 1.25: The AutoCAD menu bar in position after being set in the QAT

Using the QAT effectively | 19

This classic menu bar provides the older, more traditional AutoCAD drop-down menus from previous versions of AutoCAD. In *Figure 1.26*, the **Draw** function is selected, with the **Modeling** sub-option displayed.

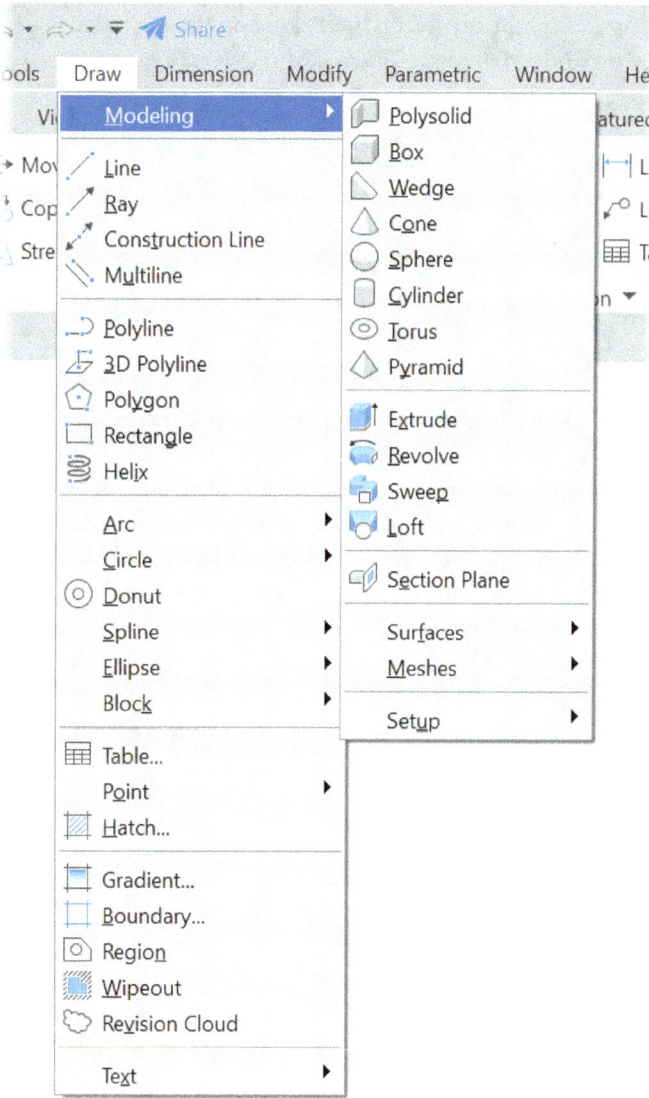

Figure 1.26: The Draw dropdown from the menu bar, with the Modeling sub-option selected

You can utilize this option from the QAT to create a more classic AutoCAD interface, which more seasoned AutoCAD users might opt for, in conjunction with the ribbon settings button mentioned earlier in the chapter.

The **Show Menu Bar** option can be turned off by clicking on the QAT **Customize Quick Access Toolbar** icon and selecting **Hide Menu Bar**. This is shown in *Figure 1.27*.

Figure 1.27: The Hide Menu Bar option on the Customize Quick Access Toolbar dropdown

Another excellent setting on the **Customize Quick Access Toolbar** dropdown is the ability to move the QAT above or below the AutoCAD ribbon. This, again, is selected from the **Customize Quick Access Toolbar** dropdown. The default position of the QAT is above the ribbon, but if you select **Show Below the Ribbon**, you will position the QAT as shown in *Figure 1.28*.

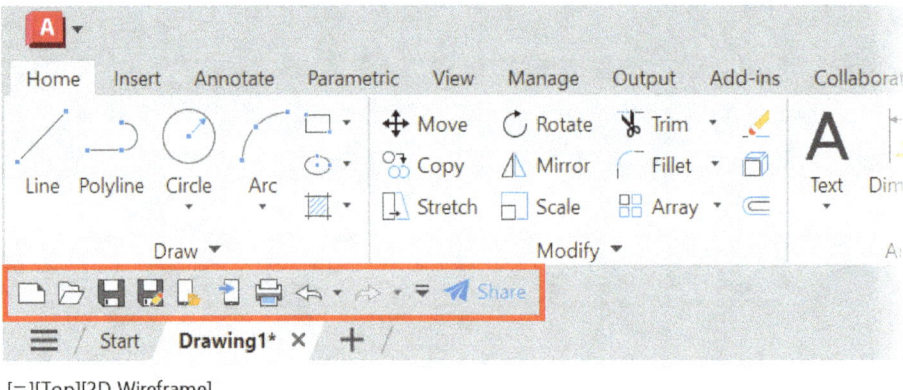

Figure 1.28: The QAT positioned below the AutoCAD ribbon

If you go back to the QAT Customize dropdown, you can click on **Show Above the Ribbon** and the QAT will return to its default location above the ribbon.

While changing the position of the QAT or adding functionality to it may seem like a small, insignificant change to the AutoCAD interface, it's amazing how many users use those tools to tweak and adjust their AutoCAD interface to suit their daily use. As they say, it's the small things. And when combined with saving these settings to your own customized AutoCAD workspace, it all starts to make sense. When we look into workspaces in more detail later in the book, you will start to see their advantages and how they can allow you to have a fully customized AutoCAD workspace just for you.

> **AutoCAD for Mac**
>
> AutoCAD for Mac does not have a QAT. It has a simplified toolbar across the top of the AutoCAD for Mac application window, as shown in *Figure 1.29*. This can be customized by right-clicking on the toolbar and selecting **Customize Toolbar**.

Figure 1.29: The toolbar in AutoCAD for Mac

Introducing the CUI command

Up until now, we have used the AutoCAD interface to customize the AutoCAD interface. There is also an AutoCAD command that allows you to adjust the AutoCAD interface. That command is the **Customize User Interface** (*CUI*) command.

The quickest way to start using the CUI command is to type CUI and press *Enter*. You can type this directly, and it will appear near the cursor (crosshair), or you can type it on the command line at the bottom of the AutoCAD screen.

This will bring up the **Customize User Interface** dialog box. *Figure 1.30* shows the **Customize User Interface** dialog box with the three default AutoCAD workspaces: **Drafting & Annotation Default**, **3D Modeling**, and **3D Basics**. These are found in the **Customize** tab in the dialog box.

Customizing the AutoCAD Interface

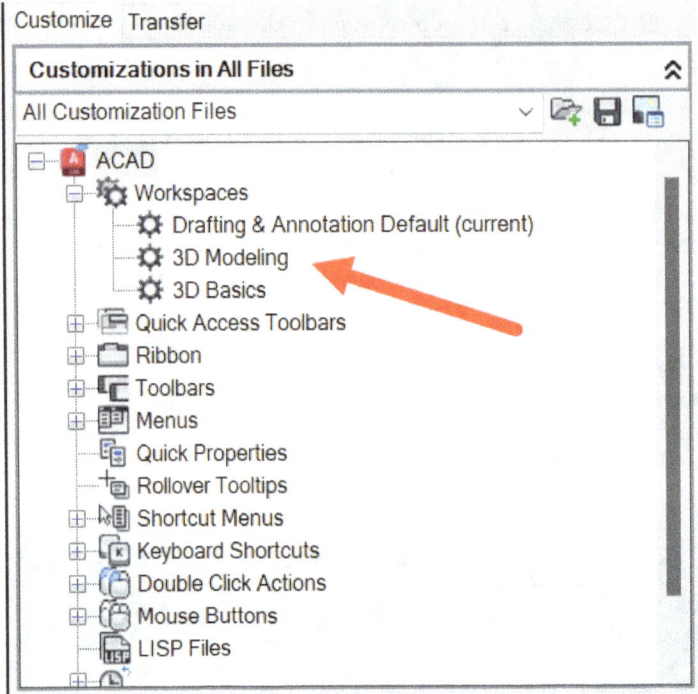

Figure 1.30: The Customize User Interface dialog box with the default AutoCAD workspaces indicated in the Customize tab

If you make the dialog box bigger by dragging a corner or side of the dialog box, you can start to investigate how to customize your AutoCAD user interface.

> **Tips and tricks #3**
>
> Before committing to any changes in the **Customize User Interface** dialog box, it is always beneficial to duplicate the workspace you want to work with. This is to avoid any errors you might make that would affect one of your default workspaces beyond the point of no return! Simply right-click over the specific workspace in the dialog box and select **Duplicate** from the shortcut menu. It will save you from a whole world of pain later when you realize that you have changed a default workspace beyond all recognition!

If you select a workspace in the top-left pane of the dialog box (noting *Tips and tricks #3*), you can then select that workspace and start to see its structure and how it is made up of its component parts, ribbon tabs, panels, and commands.

In *Figure 1.31*, you can see that **Drafting & Annotation** is selected, with the ribbon/panel contents expanded. You can see all of the individual panels listed.

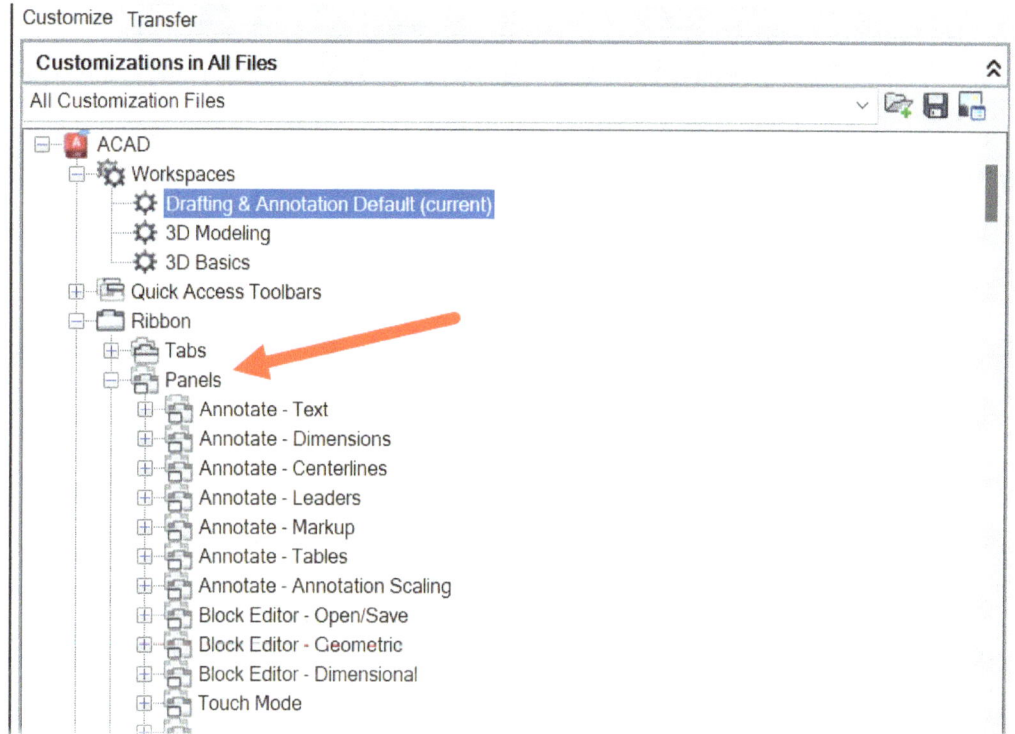

Figure 1.31: The Ribbon | Panels contents expanded in the CUI dialog box

Using the slider bar, you can slide down the list to find the **Home 2D: Draw** ribbon panel. If you expand this content and expand **Row 1**, you can see the **Line**, **Polyline**, **Circle**, and **Arc** commands there.

Expand the **Circle** command. You will then see all the different command options you would otherwise see when you click on the **Circle** fly-out arrow in the ribbon when drafting in AutoCAD. This is highlighted in *Figure 1.32*.

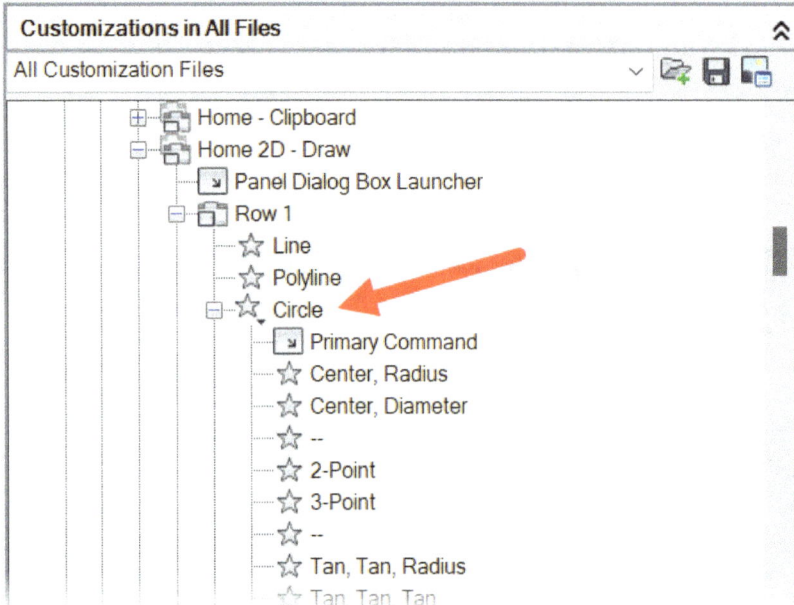

Figure 1.32: The different Circle command options displayed in the Customize User Interface dialog box

If the **Center, Radius** option is selected in the dialog box, all the settings for that command option will be displayed in the right-hand pane of the dialog box, allowing for command customization.

The right-hand pane also displays a panel preview so that you can check its display on the ribbon. The macro coding for that command is also shown. Look at *Figure 1.33* to see how this looks in the dialog box.

Introducing the CUI command 25

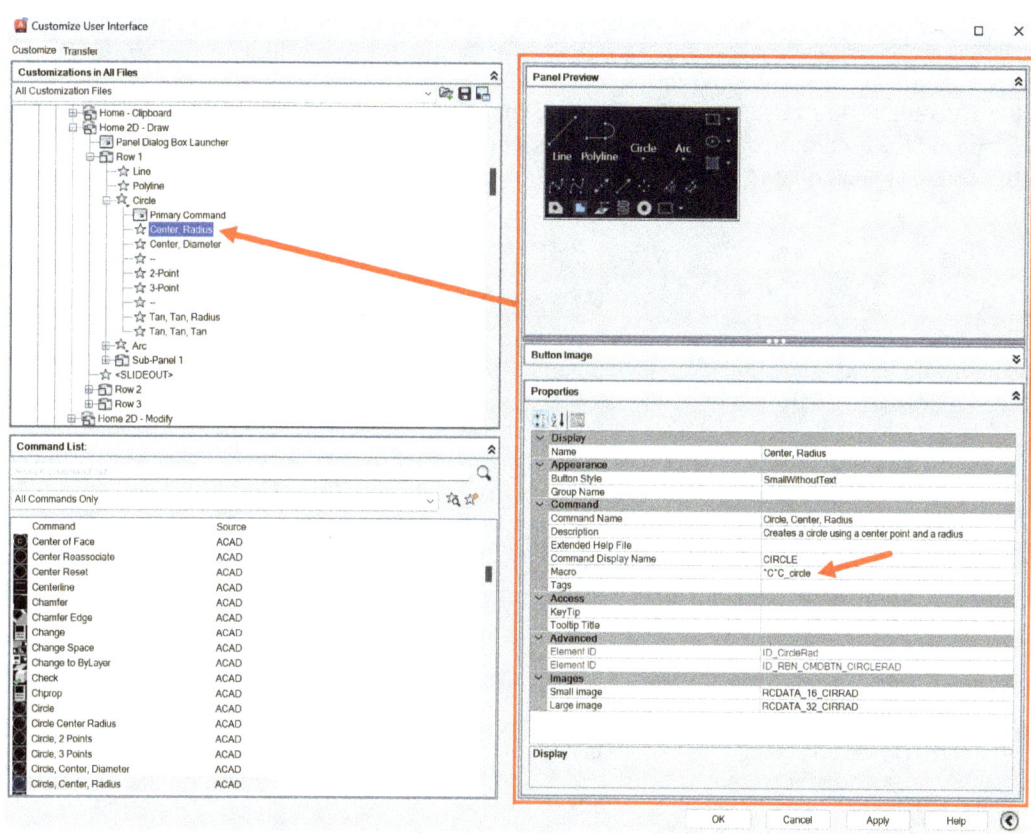

Figure 1.33: The Customize User Interface dialog box with the Circle | Center, Radius command selected

The CUI command can edit or duplicate existing workspaces down to the command macro level. This means that programming in (full) AutoCAD can be applied to create new commands that might occupy new panels and tabs on the AutoCAD ribbon.

There are numerous methods to use the CUI command to dive deeper into customizing the AutoCAD interface. They are not covered in this book, but the internet is full of many resources and communities (including the Autodesk Community) where you can investigate this and discuss it with your fellow peers. Autodesk provides some great internet locations for you to talk to your fellow AutoCAD users. You will need to use your Autodesk Account to sign into any of the Autodesk communities below: -

- Autodesk Forums, located here: `https://forums.autodesk.com`
- **Autodesk Knowledge Network (AKN)**, located here: `https://knowledge.autodesk.com`
- Autodesk Community Tips: AutoCAD Products: located in the AutoCAD forum
- Autodesk Community Voices blog: located in the preceding Autodesk Forums link

> **AutoCAD for Mac**
>
> The CUI command is also applicable in AutoCAD for Mac, but the interface and dialog boxes are different. *Figure 1.34* shows the Customize dialog in AutoCAD for Mac after the CUI command has been started. You will need to click on the tabs at the top of the dialog to access the necessary areas of the CUI command.

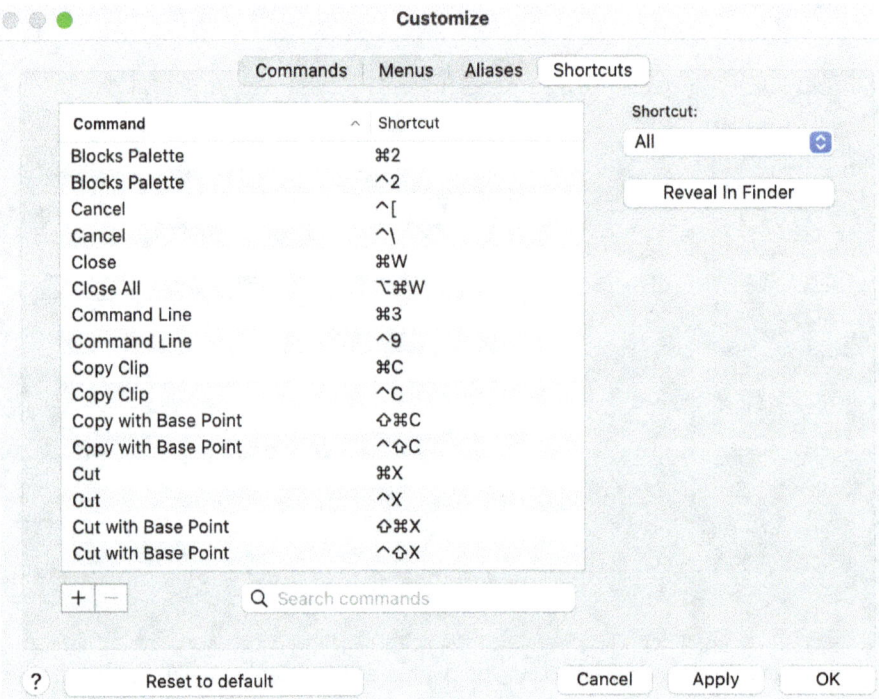

Figure 1.34: The Customize dialog box in AutoCAD for Mac

In the previous section, you learned how to customize the AutoCAD user interface, using the **CUI** command and the **Customize User Interface** dialog box. The next section summarizes what you have learned in this chapter.

Summary

In this chapter, you learned about changing and managing AutoCAD ribbon settings and set up sticky panels. We also looked at how to use the QAT effectively and how to work with AutoCAD **CUI** command and the **Customize User Interface** dialog box.

All of these workflows and concepts are important to allow you, as an AutoCAD user, to enhance and customize the AutoCAD interface to suit your preferences and ideal working environment. In the next chapter, we will talk about how to develop and customize your own workspace in AutoCAD.

Exercise

Open a blank drawing in AutoCAD and follow along to explore the user interface customization options shown across all the sections in this chapter. This applies to AutoCAD for Windows and AutoCAD for Mac.

From *Chapter 2* onward, I will be sharing exercise files so you can follow along and learn hands-on with AutoCAD.

Get This Book's PDF Version and Exclusive Extras

Scan the QR code (or go to packtpub.com/unlock). Search for this book by name, confirm the edition, and then follow the steps on the page.

Note: Keep your invoice handy. Purchases made directly from Packt don't require one.

2
Developing Your Own AutoCAD Workspace

AutoCAD 2026 comes with preset default workspaces for specific working environments. These are used primarily for 2D drafting and 3D modeling. Individual workspaces can be set up for use in specific production environments, thus making for a productive interface for each environment.

AutoCAD workspaces have already been introduced in *Chapter 1*. By the end of this chapter, you will be able to use workspaces in AutoCAD effectively and make the necessary interface changes to create a custom workspace. You can also remove a workspace that isn't needed using the AutoCAD **Customize User Interface** (*CUI*) command.

Developing your own workspace personalizes the AutoCAD interface and allows you to utilize your screen and monitor space. A typical example is that you might only use a laptop screen when using AutoCAD, compared to a dual screen monitor setup for a desktop PC. You would then need to optimize your screen space to use AutoCAD effectively. Workspaces allow you to work in both screen configurations if required.

In the *Introducing the default AutoCAD interface settings* section in *Chapter 1*, we learned about the default workspaces available in AutoCAD. Make sure to check which workspace you are using, and for the purposes of this chapter, set the **Drafting & Annotation** workspace as current.

This chapter will take you through the AutoCAD workspace settings and teach you the following:

- Using workspaces effectively
- Saving AutoCAD interface changes to a custom workspace
- Removing a redundant workspace from the AutoCAD CUI

Technical requirements

For this and later chapters within this book, you would need to enable **Dynamic Input** and **command prompt** in AutoCAD. For instructions on how to do this, visit https://www.autodesk.com/support/technical/article/caas/sfdcarticles/sfdcarticles/How-to-enable-or-disable-dynamic-input-in-AutoCAD.html.

The AutoCAD command line or *command prompt* is always on the AutoCAD screen by default. You can hide it by typing COMMANDLINEHIDE and pressing *Enter*. You can bring it back by typing COMMANDLINE and pressing *Enter* or using *Ctrl + 9*.

Dynamic Input (*DYNMODE*) is also on by default. However, the **Dynamic Input** icon is not displayed on the status bar. Click on the **Customization** icon at the right-hand end of the status bar (*three horizontal lines*), and on the menu click on **Dynamic Input**, ensuring there is a check mark next to it. It will then display on the status bar. You can then turn **DYNMODE** off and on and access its settings by right-clicking on the **Dynamic Input** icon.

Exercise files

This chapter used a simple DWG file to ensure you had full access to all workspace-related features in AutoCAD. The filename of the DWG file is Workspaces.dwg.

Using workspaces effectively

Workspaces are incredibly useful. They allow you to work in specific *spaces* that are related to the AutoCAD environment you are working in. For example, the **Drafting & Annotation** workspace is the default AutoCAD workspace, used primarily for 2D drafting, whereas the **3D Basics** and **3D Modeling** workspaces are used for 3D modeling in AutoCAD.

Each workspace displays a certain set of ribbon tabs, panels, and icons, ensuring that AutoCAD's necessary tools and features can be utilized effectively, based on what task AutoCAD is being used for at the appropriate time. But how do we choose the right workspace for our project?

Choosing the right default workspace

At the beginning of this chapter, I asked you to ensure that your default workspace is set to **Drafting & Annotation**. This is because we are going to complete an exercise to determine which AutoCAD workspace would work for your particular project, such as 2D drafting or 3D modeling. You will learn how to change your default workspace or customize your workspace to suit the project environment.

Before we start, I would like you to open this chapter's exercise file called Workspaces.dwg, which you should have already downloaded from the link provided within the *Preface*.

Using workspaces effectively   31

Locate the exercise file and open it in AutoCAD. It will look like *Figure 2.1*

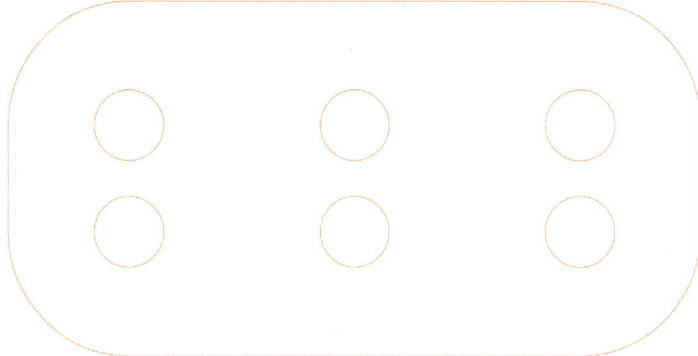

Figure 2.1: The Workspaces.dwg file when first opened

The `Workspaces.dwg` file looks like a flat 2D drawing of a polyline with six regularly spaced circles. It isn't. It is a 3D solid with six regularly spaced holes, but due to the default settings you are working with, in this case, the **Drafting & Annotation** workspace, AutoCAD is set up for 2D drafting.

Therefore, the question is how do you set a workspace that is more suited to 3D modeling? This is where you need to change your AutoCAD workspace to fit your needs.

Return to the gearwheel icon on the status bar. Click on it, and you will see the **Workspace** menu. Select the **3D Modeling** workspace. A tick will appear next to it on the menu, and you will see the AutoCAD ribbon change to display tools that are more suited to a 3D modeling environment. *Figure 2.2* shows you the **Workspace** menu with the **3D Modeling** workspace set as current.

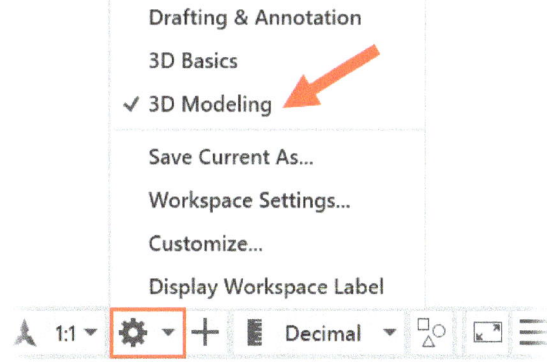

Figure 2.2: The Workspace menu with 3D Modeling set as the current workspace

The AutoCAD ribbon now displays all the necessary tools you may need to work on the 3D solid in the Workspaces.dwg file. *Figure 2.3* shows an excerpt of some of the 3D modeling tools available on the ribbon now that the workspace has been changed.

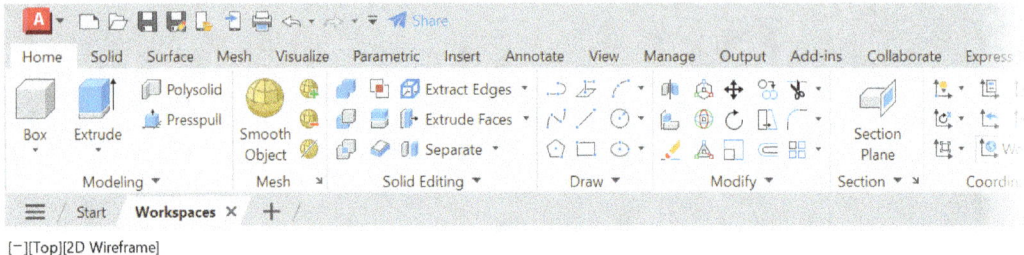

Figure 2.3: The ribbon with the 3D Modeling workspace active

With the **3D Modeling** workspace active and comparing the **Home** tab on the ribbon to the **Home** tab when using the **Drafting & Annotation** workspace, you can see that they are dramatically different. The **Home** tab now includes panels such as **Modeling**, **Mesh**, and **Solid Editing**, which are used regularly when 3D modeling.

You don't have to use the preset workspaces in AutoCAD. You can save a workspace with its own name for your own purposes. This is often preferred if you make any changes to the ribbon, as it preserves the settings of the default workspaces.

Creating your own AutoCAD workspace

Whenever a separate named workspace is required, you need to click on the gearwheel icon on the status bar again. On the **Workspace** menu, select **Save Current As…**, as shown in *Figure 2.4*.

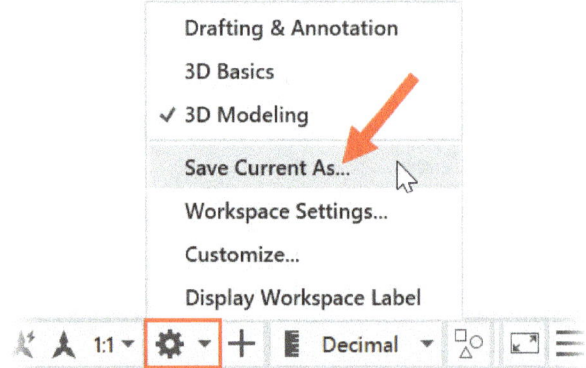

Figure 2.4: The Workspace menu with Save Current As… displayed

The **Save Workspace** dialog box will display as shown in *Figure 2.5*. Type in the name you want your workspace to be named as. You can see the new workspace has been named **3D Modeling-CURRENT**. Click on **Save**, and you now have a new workspace with that name available in the **Workspace** menu.

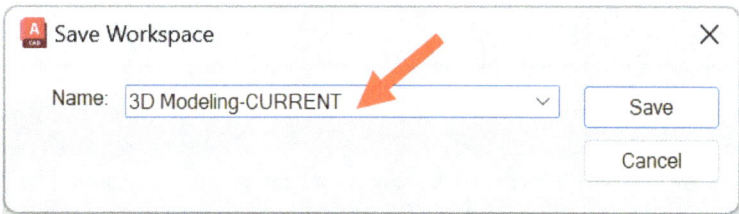

Figure 2.5: The Save Workspace dialog box with the new workspace name displayed

When clicking on the gearwheel icon again, *Figure 2.6* shows how the newly saved workspace is displayed on the **Workspace** menu and is now the current workspace.

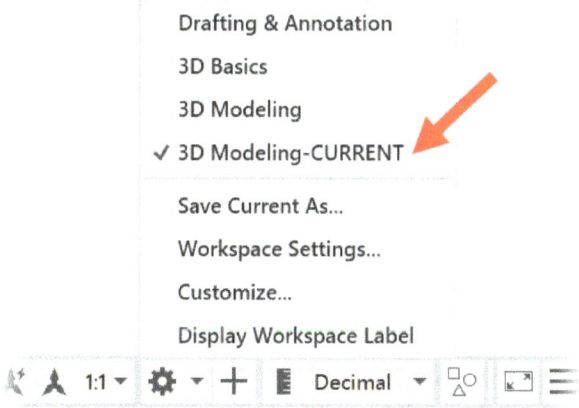

Figure 2.6: The Workspace menu with the new workspace name displayed and set as current

Workspaces are a fantastic way to personalize your working environment in AutoCAD, and as we work further through this chapter, you will discover ways to make the AutoCAD interface your own, thus enhancing your daily productivity. Let's learn how to customize the **3D Modeling** workspace to complete our exercise.

Saving AutoCAD interface changes to a custom workspace

In the previous section, you were shown how to change your workspace so that you could use it in a specific environment. You went from a 2D drafting workspace (**Drafting & Annotation**) to a 3D modeling workspace (**3D Modeling**).

Staying in the **3D Modeling** workspace with the `Workspaces.dwg` file still open in AutoCAD, you will now make changes to the AutoCAD interface and save those changes in a saved custom workspace.

The changes to the interface are going to involve utilizing the ribbon panels. Ribbon panels can easily be moved from the ribbon and placed in the drawing area in AutoCAD. They are known as sticky panels and are similar to Post-It notes – discussed in *Chapter 1*.

Take a look at the **Home** tab on the ribbon. You will see various panels available when using the **3D Modeling** workspace. For this exercise, you will move the **Modeling** and **Mesh** panels into the AutoCAD drawing area. This will create *sticky* panels that can be moved around like Post-It notes in the AutoCAD drawing area, independently of their original positions on the AutoCAD ribbon.

Click and drag on the title bar of the **Modeling** ribbon panel. You will see the panel move away from the ribbon as you move the mouse. Position the **Modeling** panel in a suitable location in the drawing area and release the mouse button. The panel is now placed in the drawing area.

Repeat this workflow for the **Mesh** ribbon panel, placing it underneath the **Modeling** panel. *Figure 2.7* shows how the panels should appear in the drawing area.

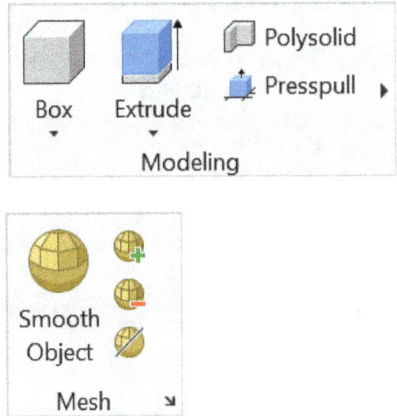

Figure 2.7: The Modeling and Mesh sticky panels

> **AutoCAD for Mac**
>
> As mentioned previously, the interface is different on AutoCAD for Mac. There is no way of moving panels in AutoCAD for Mac as the **Drafting** and **Modeling** workspaces in AutoCAD for Mac are fixed at the top of the icon menu on the left-hand side of the screen and cannot be changed.

You have now altered the AutoCAD interface to suit your needs. The two panels have been moved to a suitable location, ready for use when 3D modeling.

To maintain the location of the two *sticky panels*, you now need to save a custom workspace. The reason for this is that if you revert back to one of the default AutoCAD workspaces, the *sticky panels* will be returned to their original positions in the ribbon due to the **Customize User Interface** (**CUI**) settings in each preset workspace.

Saving a new custom workspace ensures that the CUI settings are set to keep your *sticky panels* where you placed them.

To save the custom workspace, you need to use the workflow covered earlier in the chapter. Click on the gearwheel icon and select **Save Current As…**, as shown in *Figure 2.8*.

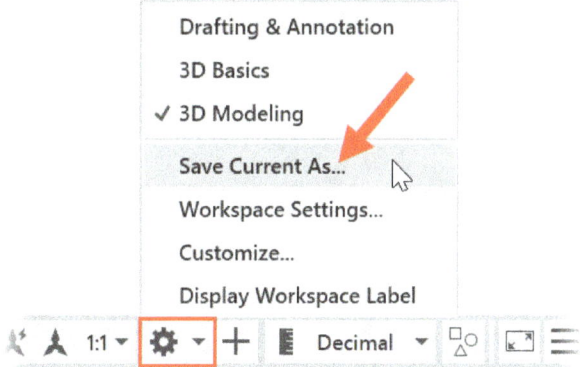

Figure 2.8: Selecting Save Current As… to save a custom workspace

The **Save Workspace** dialog box will appear. Name your custom workspace 3D Modeling-CUSTOM and click on **Save**. *Figure 2.9* shows you the dialog box.

Figure 2.9: The Save Workspace dialog box with the custom workspace name

This is now a saved workspace and is now also the current workspace. This workspace includes the position of the sticky panels in the AutoCAD CUI settings.

If you click the gearwheel icon again, you will see your custom workspace listed on the **Workspace** menu, as shown in *Figure 2.10*.

You can also see the previously saved **3D Modeling-CURRENT** workspace. The check mark next to the **3D Modeling-CUSTOM** workspace indicates the current workspace.

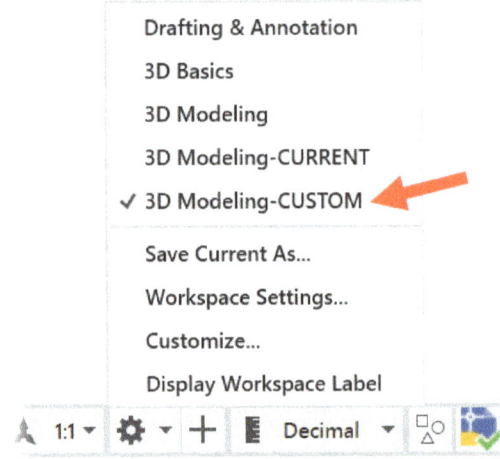

Figure 2.10: The Workspace menu displaying the new custom workspace

Your custom workspace includes your sticky panels. If you select the default **3D Modeling** workspace from the **Workspace** menu, you will see your sticky panels disappear from the drawing area to be repositioned in their respective positions on the **Home** tab on the ribbon.

> Tips and tricks #4
>
> You can use sticky panels in AutoCAD in any workspace. As mentioned in this chapter and the *Using sticky panels* section in *Chapter 1*, they can be returned to the ribbon at any time using the **Return Panels to Ribbon** function. Sticky panels are a great timesaver when using a dual monitor setup for your workstation. You can set up all the necessary panels you use daily in one area of the screen and save this interface configuration as your own personalized AutoCAD workspace. Should the time come when you need to reset to default settings, you simply select the appropriate default AutoCAD workspace as the current workspace, and all the *sticky panels* will be returned to the relevant locations on the ribbon. *Figure 2.11* shows how your customized interface would look when using the **3D Modeling-CUSTOM** workspace set up in this chapter.

Select your **3D Modeling-CUSTOM** workspace from the **Workspace** menu, and you will see the sticky panels reappear in their locations in the drawing area, as shown previously in *Figure 2.7*.

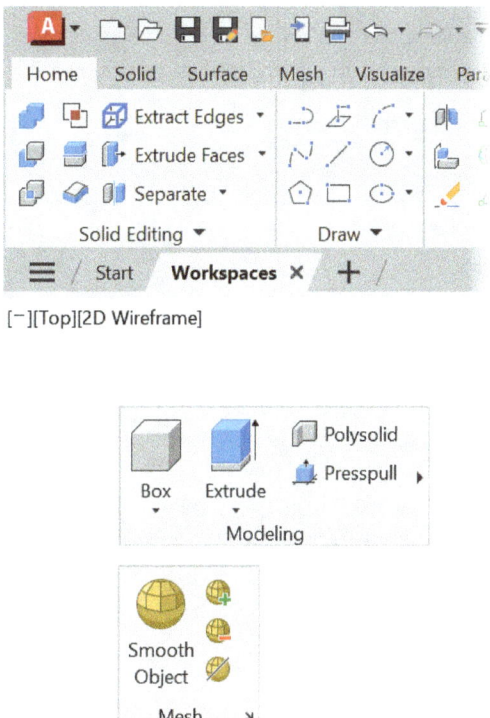

Figure 2.11: The sticky panels in the drawing area when using the 3D Modeling-CUSTOM workspace

Sometimes, after creating new workspaces, and customizing existing ones, there may be a need to remove redundant workspaces from the AutoCAD interface. In the next part of the chapter, we will look at how to do this, using the CUI tool.

Removing a redundant workspace from the AutoCAD CUI

Workspaces are incredibly useful and versatile, but there will come a time when you need to remove redundant workspaces from the AutoCAD CUI. You may want to rationalize how many workspaces are displayed in the **Workspace** menu, or you may just want to return back to the preset workspaces AutoCAD provides.

You will need to run the AutoCAD CUI command to remove unwanted workspaces. We learned about this command in the *Introducing the AutoCAD CUI command* section in *Chapter 1*.

Having a DWG file open ensures you get access to all of the AutoCAD interface, so make sure to have the Workspaces.dwg file open and current in AutoCAD.

Using **Dynamic Input** or the **command line**, type in CUI and press *Enter*.

The **Customize User Interface** dialog box will appear on the screen, and you will see your workspaces listed in the top-left pane of the dialog box. *Figure 2.12* shows you how the workspaces are displayed.

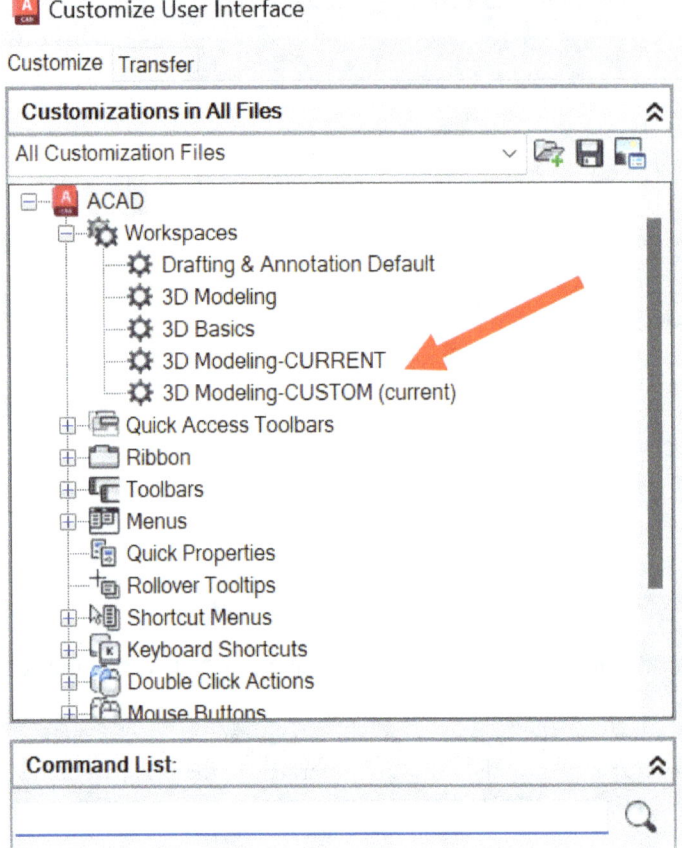

Figure 2.12: A partial view of the Customize User Interface dialog box, with the workspaces arrowed

You can see that your current workspace (**3D Modeling-CUSTOM**) is listed. In this case, the **3D Modeling-CURRENT** workspace needs to be removed as the name of the workspace could be misleading to other users.

Click on the **3D Modeling-CURRENT** workspace in the list to select it. The name of the workspace will be highlighted in blue, as shown in *Figure 2.13*. Then, right-click on the selected workspace. *Figure 2.13* also shows you the right-click shortcut menu that is displayed.

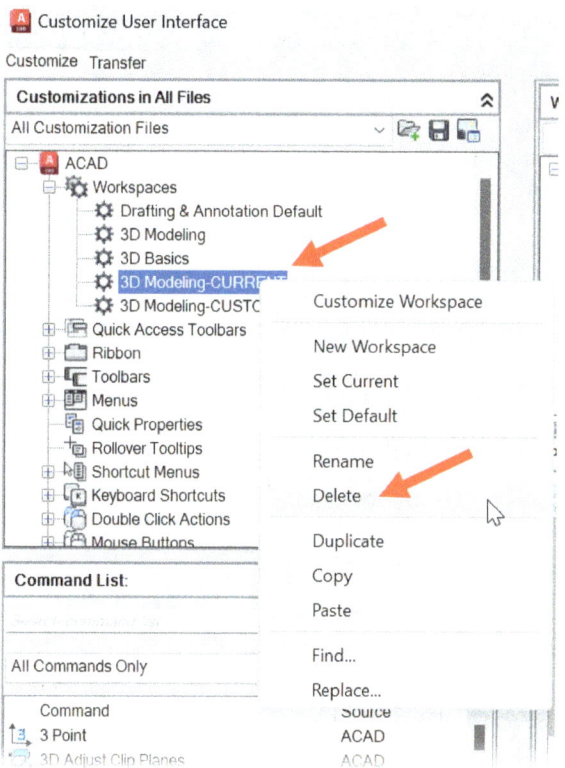

Figure 2.13: 3D Modeling-CURRENT shown highlighted, with the right-click shortcut menu displayed

Click on **Delete** on the shortcut menu and you will be asked whether you really want to delete the *element* (the AutoCAD CUI calls all CUI items elements). *Figure 2.14* shows the prompt that is displayed.

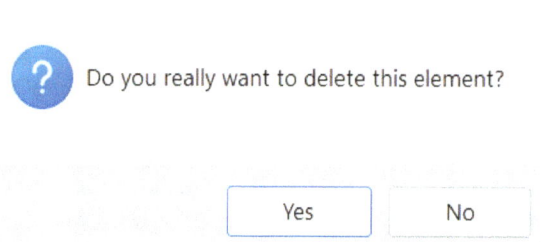

Figure 2.14: The prompt displayed after selecting Delete on the shortcut menu

Click on **Yes**, and the **3D Modeling-CURRENT** workspace will be removed from the CUI workspace list.

To close out the **Customize User Interface** dialog box, click **Apply** (to apply the changes), then click **OK**, and the dialog box will close.

You can click **OK** to apply the changes and close the dialog box, but it is a good practice to click on **Apply** just to be sure all changes have been applied before closing the dialog box.

You have now successfully removed an unwanted workspace from the AutoCAD CUI and applied the necessary changes.

If you click on the gearwheel icon on the status bar, you will see that the **3D Modeling-CURRENT** workspace is not listed on the **Workspace** menu. You can see this in *Figure 2.15*.

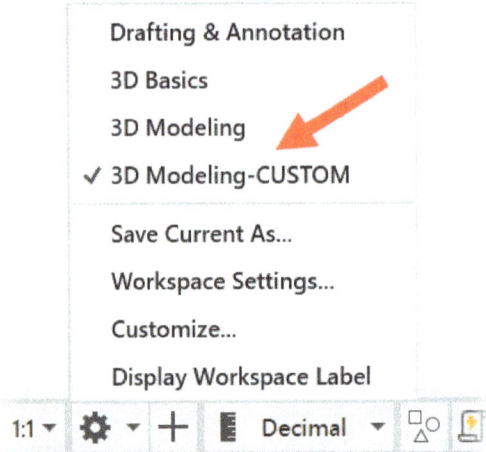

Figure 2.15: The Workspace menu without the 3D Modeling-CURRENT workspace

You can also see that your current workspace is the **3D Modeling-CUSTOM** workspace. This is the workspace that includes the *sticky panels* set up earlier in the chapter.

> **AutoCAD for Mac**
>
> As mentioned in *Chapter 1*, the CUI command is also applicable in AutoCAD for Mac, but the interface and dialog boxes are different. *Figure 2.16* shows you the CUI dialog in AutoCAD for Mac after the `CUI` command has been started. You will need to click on the tabs at the top of the dialog to access the necessary areas of the CUI command. It is also important to note that there are no *workspaces* or *sticky panels* available in AutoCAD for Mac.

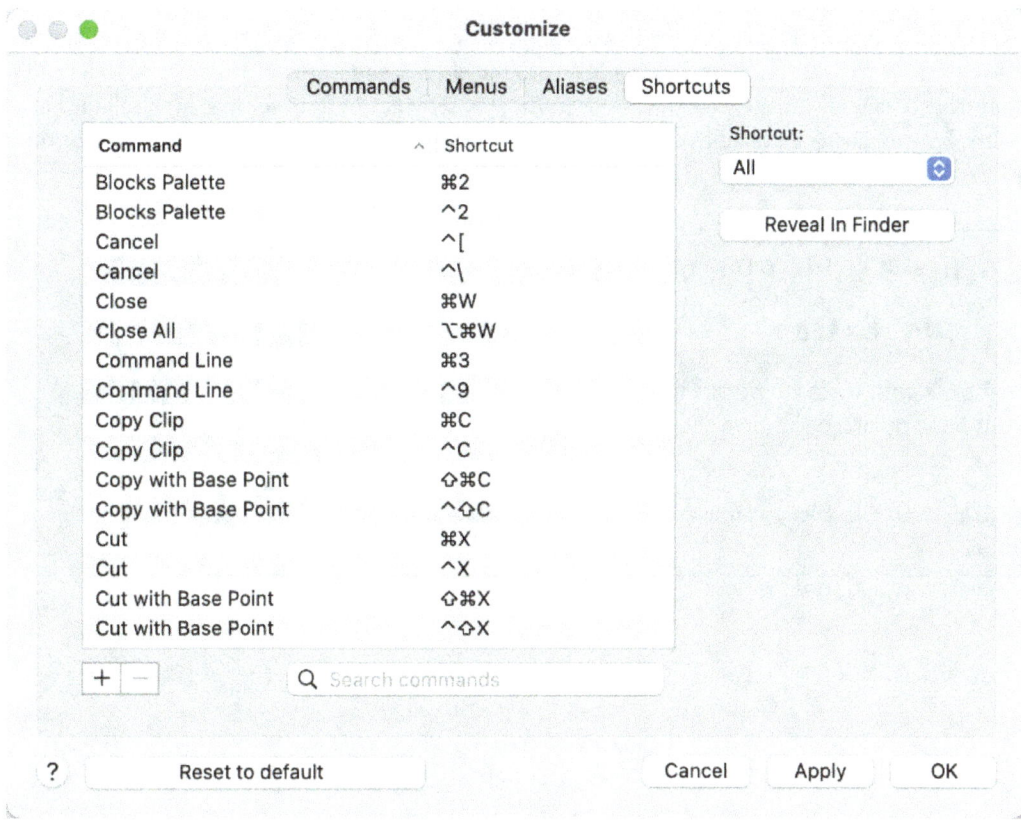

Figure 2.16: The Customize dialog box in AutoCAD for Mac

You have now learned how to remove a redundant workspace from the AutoCAD CUI, making sure that only currently used workspaces are maintained. Your workspaces define your interface, and it is important to keep the CUI organized.

Summary

Workspaces are fundamental, allowing you, the AutoCAD user, to enhance and customize the AutoCAD interface, ensuring you can access the appropriate tools for the environment in which you are working. In this chapter, you ensured you used a 3D-related workspace as the exercise contained a 3D solid. You learned how to save AutoCAD interface changes and remove redundant workspaces, which will help you in customizing your work environments within AutoCAD. You also learned how to utilize *sticky* ribbon panels to allow easy access to specific ribbon panels in the AutoCAD drawing area.

In the next chapter, we will discuss how to work smarter with the AutoCAD interface. You will learn how to effectively navigate multiple drawing files with the file tabs and learn how to use the **Model** and **Layout** tabs to your advantage. You will also learn how to set your drafting settings in the status bar, as well as how to navigate drawings quickly and easily with the **ViewCube** (*3D*) and the **Navigation Bar** (*2D*).

Get This Book's PDF Version and Exclusive Extras

Scan the QR code (or go to `packtpub.com/unlock`). Search for this book by name, confirm the edition, and then follow the steps on the page.

Note: Keep your invoice handy. Purchases made directly from Packt don't require one.

3
Using the AutoCAD Interface to Work Smarter

AutoCAD is now over 40 years old. In that time, the AutoCAD interface has adapted and evolved to become more efficient and intuitive. This chapter will take you through several methods to enhance how AutoCAD is used, allowing you to work smarter, not harder.

We will go through some of the AutoCAD interface tools that make your daily use of AutoCAD easier, thus enhancing your efficiency and productivity. In this chapter, you will learn about the following interface tools:

- Working with file tabs
- Working with the Model and Layout tabs
- Utilizing the drafting settings on the status bar
- The AutoCAD ViewCube
- The AutoCAD navigation bar

All the preceding tools provide specific methods with which to navigate the AutoCAD interface and also navigate your AutoCAD drawing. AutoCAD drawings can be complex, and the AutoCAD interface, when used effectively, can help you work smarter, not harder. Learning how to work smarter using the AutoCAD interface will not only allow you to become a more seasoned AutoCAD user but also enhance your efficiency and productivity on a day-to-day basis.

In *Chapter 2*, you worked with AutoCAD's workspaces. Please ensure your AutoCAD workspace is now set back to the default **Drafting & Annotation** workspace.

Exercise files

Later on in the chapter, in *The AutoCAD ViewCube* section, we will be utilizing an exercise file called `3D Solid.dwg`. Please ensure you have it downloaded and ready in AutoCAD.

Working with file tabs

AutoCAD can have more than one drawing (DWG) file open during an AutoCAD session. Each file is displayed as a file tab just below the ribbon at the top left of the AutoCAD application window. This is shown in *Figure 3.1*.

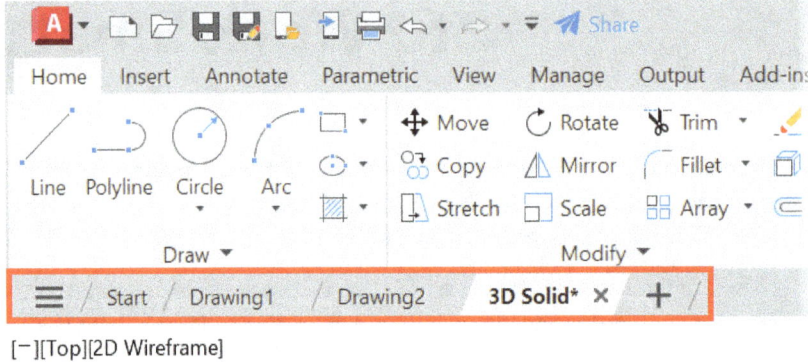

Figure 3.1: The File tabs underneath the AutoCAD ribbon

The AutoCAD **Start** tab is there by default, and three drawing files are displayed: **Drawing1**, **Drawing2**, and **3D Solid**. Each of these is a DWG file open in the current AutoCAD session. The `3D Solid.dwg` file is the exercise file for this chapter. If you open the file in AutoCAD, you will see the filename in the corresponding file tab.

File tabs can be dragged and dropped horizontally to change the order of the file tabs displayed. For example, if required, you could drag the **3D Solid** file tab in front of the other file tabs.

You can see three horizontal lines to the left of the file tabs area. This is often known as the *hamburger* icon (for obvious reasons). The hamburger icon gives you a drop-down menu, allowing you to work with the file tabs. This is shown in *Figure 3.2*.

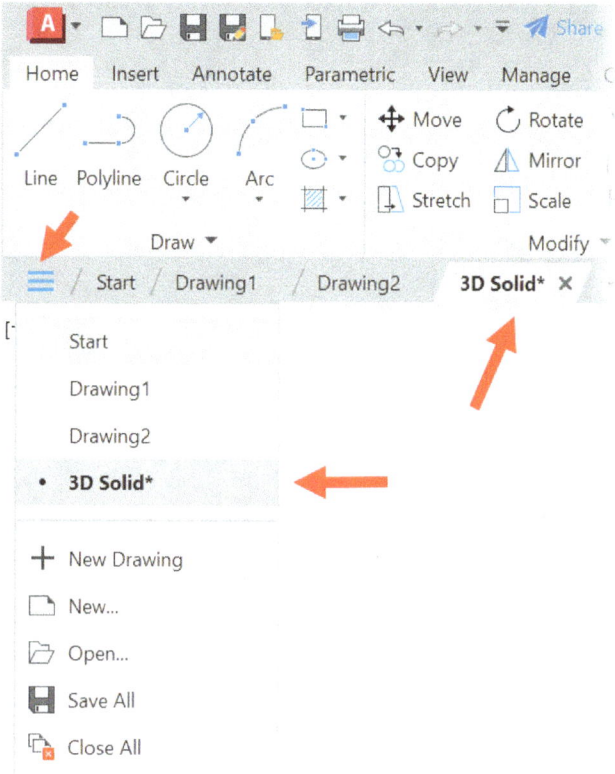

Figure 3.2: The drop-down menu displayed after the hamburger icon is clicked on

The current file tab is the **3D Solid** file tab, highlighted in bold on the file tab itself and in bold on the drop-down menu. The drop-down menu allows you to select any file listed to make it current, such as by clicking the corresponding file tab.

Figure 3.3 shows how if you hover over a filename in the drop-down list, you are also given options to go to the **Model** and **Layout** tabs for the file hovered over. This is a highly efficient way to navigate the files open in an AutoCAD session.

46 Using the AutoCAD Interface to Work Smarter

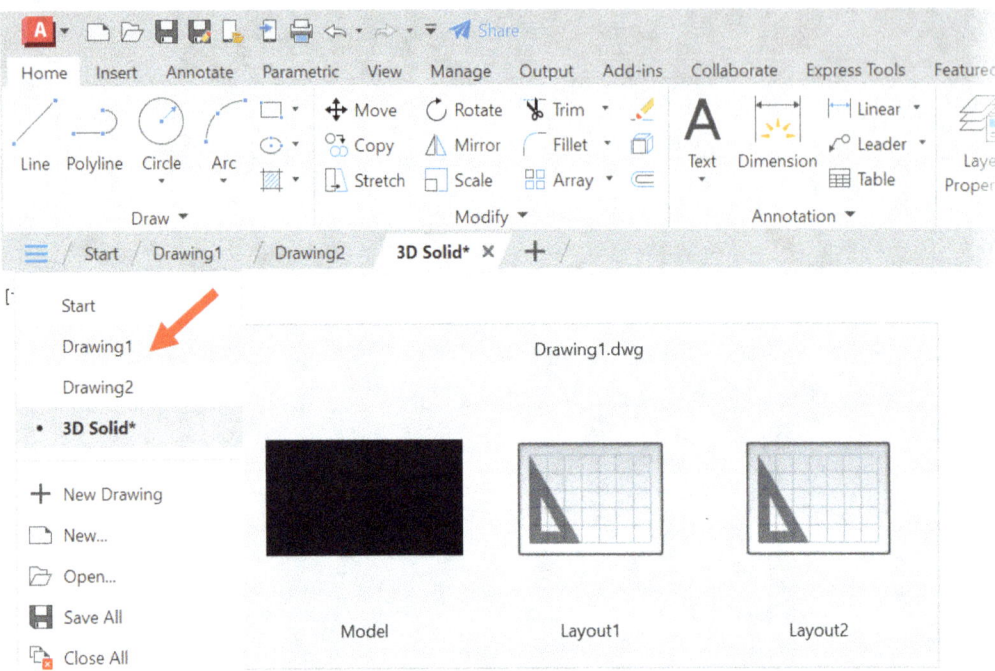

Figure 3.3: When hovering over Drawing1 in the drop-down menu, the Model and Layout tabs are displayed

A corresponding + symbol is next to the file tabs and on the drop-down menu. As you can see in *Figure 3.3*, in the drop-down menu, this will open a new blank drawing file. AutoCAD opens these blank drawing files sequentially, naming them **Drawing1.dwg**, **Drawing2.dwg**, and so on. Hence, the file tabs are displayed in *Figure 3.2* and *Figure 3.3*.

The drop-down menu also provides great flexibility when working with multiple AutoCAD files by offering quick access to the **New…**, **Open…**, **Save All**, and **Close All** commands.

> **Tips and tricks #5**
>
> Becoming a seasoned AutoCAD user is about more than just the knowledge contained in the drawing. It is often about the knowledge of AutoCAD itself. Navigating multiple drawings when working in AutoCAD can help you work smarter, not harder, and over time, saves you time. Try and build the file tabs into your daily AutoCAD workflows and processes to become more productive and efficient.

Both AutoCAD for Windows and AutoCAD for Mac use file tabs for currently open drawing files. They are a superb efficiency tool, allowing for an easy transition from one open drawing to another.

> **AutoCAD for Mac**
>
> In AutoCAD for Mac, there is a similar methodology for using file tabs. In *Figure 3.4*, you can see similar file tabs, with the current drawing tab, **3D Solid**, highlighted. The small icon with the blue corner (indicated by the arrow), is a tool that works in a similar way to the *hover* tool on the drop-down menu in the Windows version of AutoCAD. When clicked on, it provides an easy method to navigate the **Model** and **Layout** tabs of the current drawing.

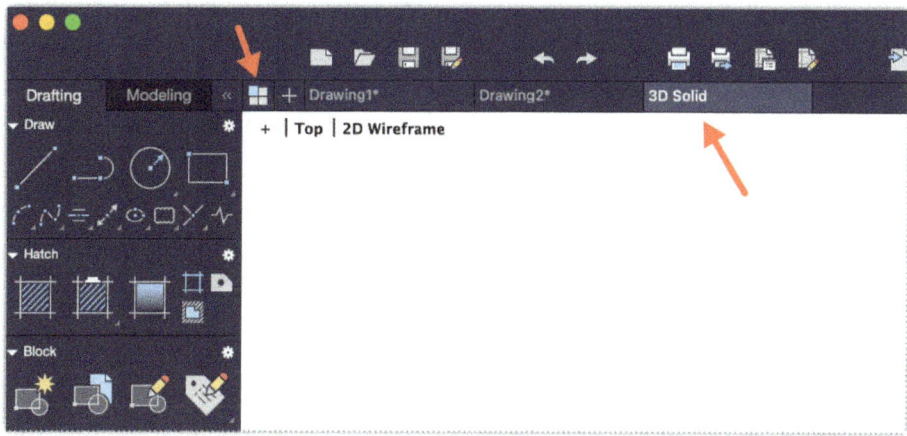

Figure 3.4 – The file tabs in AutoCAD for Mac

You are now proficient with the file tabs in the AutoCAD interface. This will allow you to work that little bit smarter when you have multiple files open in an AutoCAD session, giving you greater flexibility to move in and out of multiple drawing files. We will now move on to using the **Model** and **Layout** tabs with your DWG files.

Working with the Model and Layout tabs

AutoCAD works across two spaces: *model space* and *paper space*. Model space is represented by the **Model** tab, with paper space being represented by the **Layout** tabs. You can have multiple layout tabs, which display different scaled views of what is in model space.

The **Model** and **Layout** tabs are in the bottom-left corner of the AutoCAD application window (for both Windows and Mac versions). *Figure 3.5* shows the **Model** and **Layout** tabs in the Windows version of AutoCAD.

48   Using the AutoCAD Interface to Work Smarter

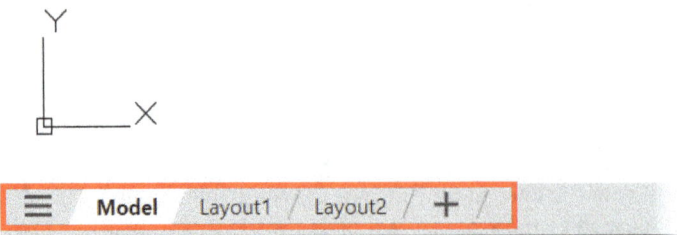

Figure 3.5: The Model and Layout tabs in AutoCAD

As with file tabs, there is a hamburger icon for the **Model** and **Layout** tabs too. When clicked on, this also provides a menu allowing quicker navigation of the **Model** and **Layout** tabs. *Figure 3.6* shows the menu with the current tab arrowed. In this case, the drawing is currently being worked on in *model space*, in the **Model** tab.

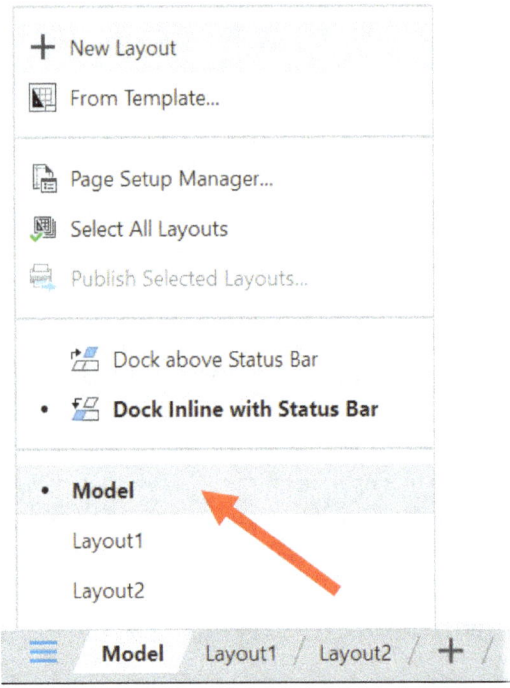

Figure 3.6: The Model and Layout tabs menu

There are some incredibly useful tools on the menu. Starting at the top of the menu, the + symbol allows a new layout to be created with one click. This can also be done with the + symbol next to the **Model** and **Layout** tabs.

Other tools include adding a new layout from an AutoCAD template file (DWT file) using the **From Template…** option.

The AutoCAD **Page Setup Manager…** is also accessible from the menu, allowing for fast access to existing page setups and creating new page setups to be used with both the **Model** and **Layout** tabs.

Generating document output is now quick and easy with the **Select All Layouts** option. With all the layouts selected, the **Publish Selected Layouts…** tool becomes available, allowing for the output of multiple layouts from the drawing. *Figure 3.7* shows the layouts selected in the menu.

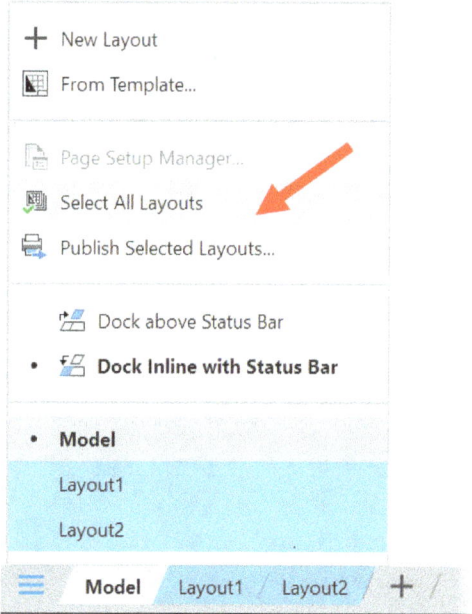

Figure 3.7: The menu with all layouts selected

All selected layouts are highlighted in blue for easy reference, with the **Publish Selected Layouts…** option now active and ready for use.

By default, the **Model** and **Layout** tabs are docked in line with the status bar on the right side of the application window. Using the menu, you can dock them above the status bar, allowing for more status bar settings to be displayed if required. This is a very subtle interface change, but it is incredibly useful if needed.

Figure 3.8 shows the **Model** and **Layout** tabs displayed above the status bar. The arrow indicates the gap below the tabs.

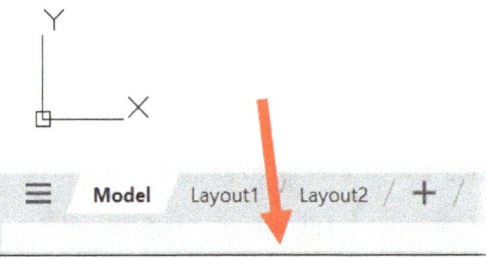

Figure 3.8: The Model and Layout tabs docked above the status bar

While these tools on the menu may seem simple, they are also highly effective methods of accessing the necessary tools when managing the **Model** and **Layout** tabs in a drawing.

Right-clicking on either the **Model** tab or **Layout** tabs provides shortcut menus specific to each tab type. This menu will also give you quick access to various **Model** and **Layout** tools, enabling faster workflows when working with AutoCAD. *Figure 3.9* shows the shortcut menu when you right-click on the **Model** tab.

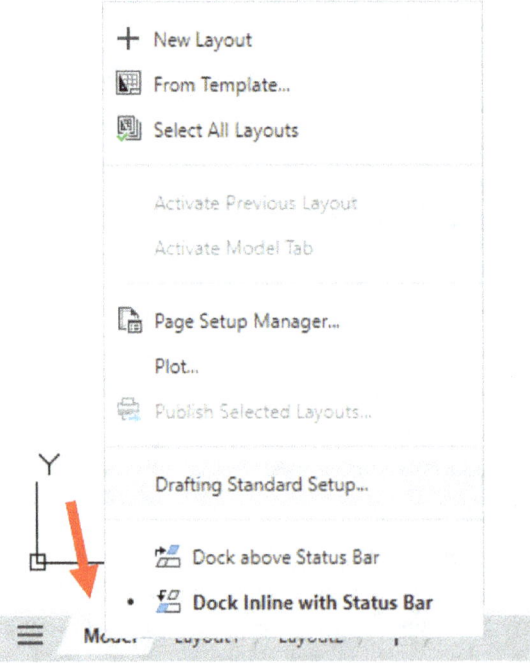

Figure 3.9: The Model tab right-click shortcut menu

As you can see, some of the content from the hamburger icon is replicated. The **Plot…** option is available, as is **Drafting Standard Setup….** Again, these are quick shortcuts to what is already available on the AutoCAD ribbon, thus providing quicker ways to get to commands in context. You normally set up the drafting standards when working in the **Model** tab. This is just that little bit quicker than trying to find it on the ribbon, and those few mouse clicks saved each time daily improve your efficiency.

A **Layout** tab has a similar shortcut menu displayed after right-clicking on it. Each of these shortcut menus is contextual, so different options are displayed. *Figure 3.10* shows the shortcut menu displayed.

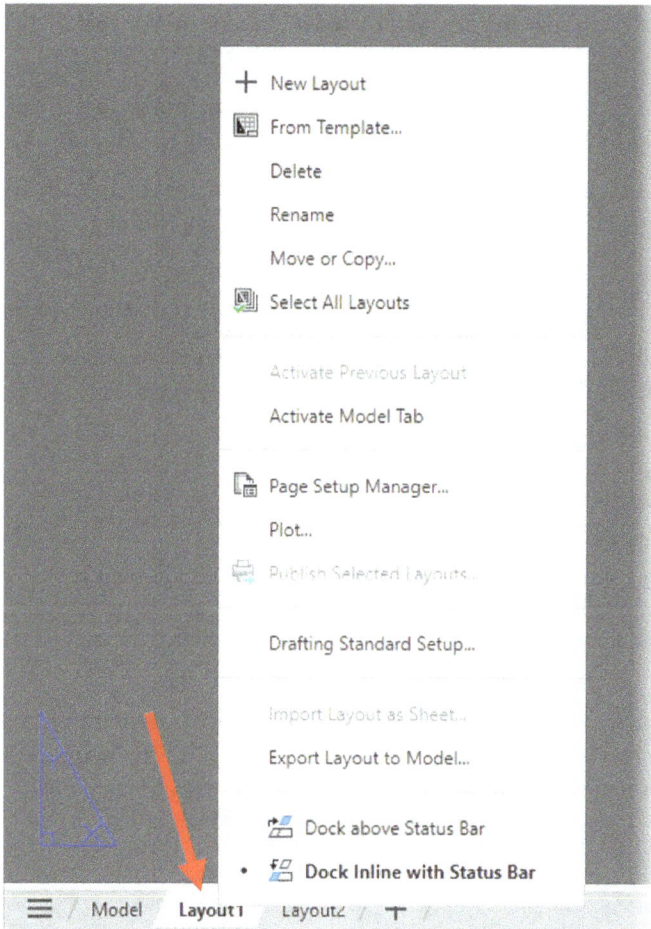

Figure 3.10: The Layout tab right-click shortcut menu

There are some different options on this shortcut menu as compared to the **Model** tab version. Again, all options are designed to give you a contextual interface, and reduce mouse clicks, to improve productivity.

Some of these **Layout** options with brief descriptions are listed as follows:

- **New Layout**: This generates a new blank **Layout** tab, like clicking on the + symbol next to the **Model** and **Layout** tabs.
- **From Template…**: This allows you to insert a layout into the existing drawing from a drawing template file (*DWT*).
- **Delete**: This does exactly what it says. It allows for the deletion of a **Layout** tab.
- **Rename**: **Layout** tabs can be renamed for easy identification and context. This option highlights the tab text, allowing for renaming, similar to Microsoft Excel worksheets.
- **Move or Copy…**: Layouts can be moved along the tab display or copied to be renamed/reused. This option opens a dialog box to expedite a move or a copy of a **Layout** tab.
- **Select All Layouts**: It is sometimes required to select all **Layout** tabs to publish them all (see **Publish Selected Layouts…** in *Figure 3.10*). You would use this option after all **Layout** tabs have been selected).
- **Activate Model Tab**: This is a simple switch toggle to allow you to make the **Model** tab active.
- **Export Layout to Model…**: There will be times when the **Layout** tab content may need to be taken into the **Model** tab. This option expedites this quickly with one click from the shortcut menu.

> **Tips and tricks #6**
>
> Being a seasoned AutoCAD user, you (more than likely) already have a daily methodology when working with the **Model** and **Layout** tabs. The preceding options provide a more context-related approach, utilizing the enhanced hamburger icon and right-clicking shortcut menus available in AutoCAD 2026. They save a few mouse clicks, and when used repetitively daily, they will save you time in the longer term. The only way to find out is to try them!

If you remember to perform all of your design work in the **Model** tab, and ensure that **Layout** tabs are used to present those designs only, you are on the right track. Try to maintain that in all of your drawing work to keep your AutoCAD drawings organised and professional.

> **AutoCAD for Mac**
>
> The workflow for **Model** and **Layout** tabs in AutoCAD for Mac is different. The right-click shortcut menus require preset page setups, defined in **Page Setup Manager**, accessible from the **File** drop-down menu. The shortcut menu is only available on the **Layout** tabs and is less extensive than the AutoCAD for Windows version. This much smaller menu is shown in *Figure 3.11*.

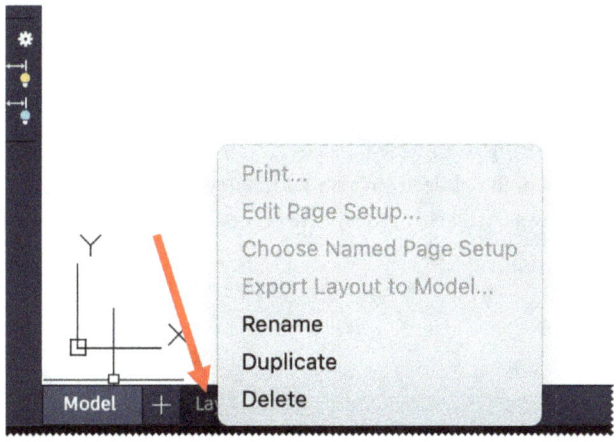

Figure 3.11: The AutoCAD for Mac right-click shortcut menu on the Layout tab

You now know how to work effectively with the **Model** and **Layout** tabs in AutoCAD. These tabs are fundamental when using model space and paper space with your DWG files. We will now move on to using the AutoCAD drafting settings on the status bar.

Utilizing the drafting settings on the status bar

Most of the AutoCAD drafting settings are located on the status bar. You will find this at the bottom right of your screen, as shown in *Figure 3.12*.

Figure 3.12: The AutoCAD status bar

If a drafting setting is currently in use (*on*), the status bar's corresponding icon is *blue*. If the drafting setting is not being used (*off*), the corresponding icon will be *gray* in color. You can see in *Figure 3.12* that some of the icons are blue, indicating that those drafting settings are on.

After the initial AutoCAD installation, specific drafting settings will be current on the status bar. This includes the following settings (with their system variable names displayed in *italics*):

- **Polar** (*POLAR*)
- **Object Snap Tracking** (*AUTOSNAP*)
- **Object Snaps** (*OSNAP*)

The preceding three preset drafting settings will be covered in this chapter, followed by the **Dynamic Input** (*DYNMODE*) setting, which, while always on with a new AutoCAD install, is not displayed on the status bar. *Figure 3.13* shows each setting from the preceding list on the status bar.

Figure 3.13: The default drafting settings on the AutoCAD status bar

The definitions of the drafting settings are as follows:

- **Polar:** This drafting setting defines the polar angle increments for drafting. The default value for the system variable *POLAR* is ninety (90) degree angle increments. AutoCAD has numerous preset values, and user-defined angle increments can be used.

    To work with the *POLAR* settings, right-click on the corresponding icon (denoted by *1* in *Figure 3.13*), and select **Tracking Settings…**. This will bring up the **Drafting Settings** dialog box, with the **Polar Tracking** tab open. This is shown in *Figure 3.14*, where you can see that all things POLAR can be set and adjusted when required.

Utilizing the drafting settings on the status bar   55

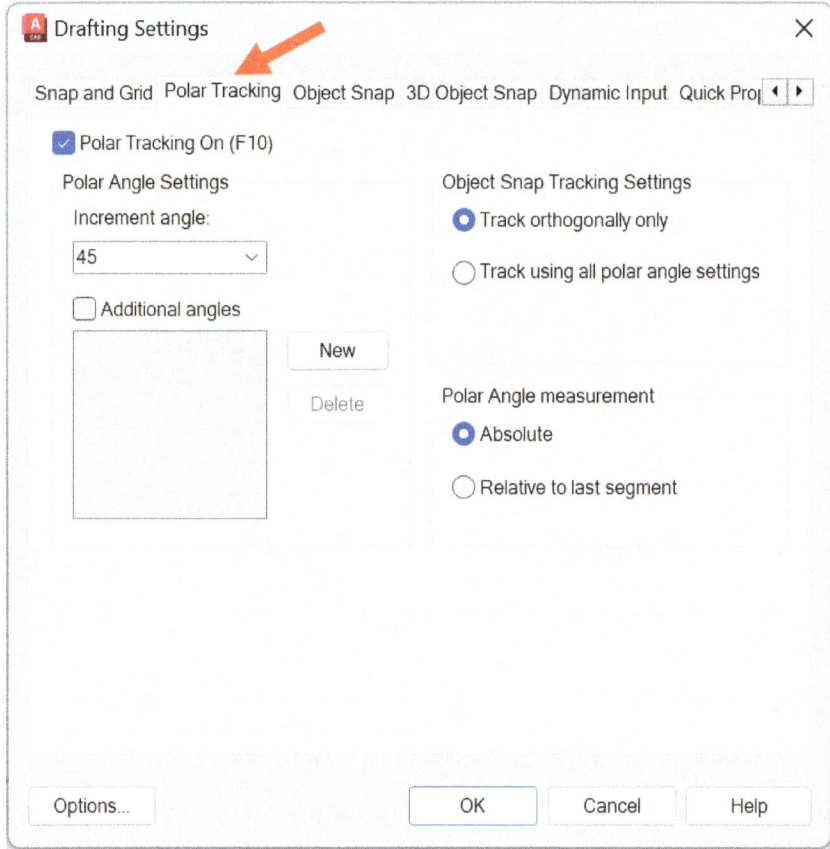

Figure 3.14: The Drafting Settings dialog box with the Polar Tracking tab open

There is also a flyout arrow to the right of the **Polar** icon on the status bar. Clicking on this will open the **Polar Tracking** flyout menu, where polar tracking angles can be quickly adjusted to preset increments. *Figure 3.15* shows this.

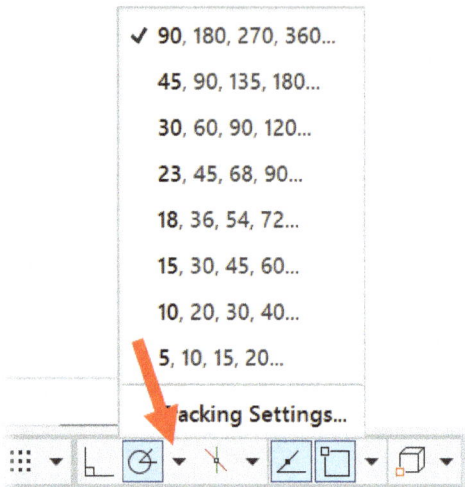

Figure 3.15: The Polar Tracking flyout menu

You can also access **Tracking Settings** from the flyout menu, as well as setting a preset angle increment.

- **Object Snap Tracking**: This drafting setting is purely an on/off switch to switch on the *AUTOSNAP* system variable. Used in conjunction with **Object Snaps** (*OSNAP*), this drafting setting allows for multiple object snap points when drafting.

You can right-click on this icon to select **Object Snap Tracking Settings**. It will open the **Drafting Settings** dialog box with the **Object Snap** tab open. To enable this setting in the dialog box, you must ensure the checkbox is checked, as shown in *Figure 3.16*.

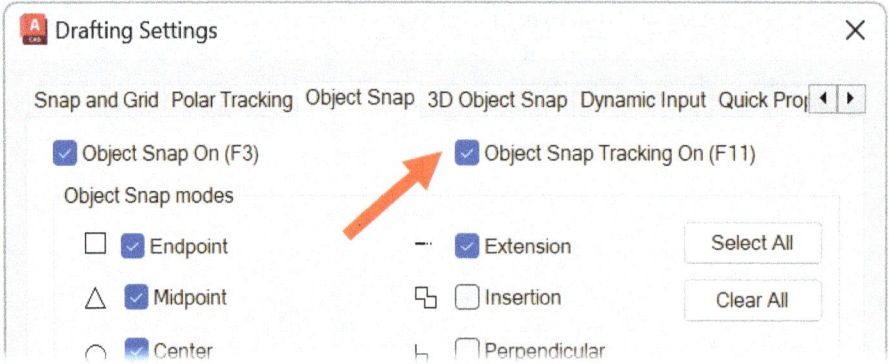

Figure 3.16: The Drafting Settings dialog box with Object Snap Tracking switched on

- **Object Snaps**: The use of object snaps (*OSNAP*) in AutoCAD is fundamental to accurate 2D drafting and 3D modeling. It is good CAD practice to ensure that you are always using object snaps for accuracy, but there might be an occasion when object snaps would need to be switched off, hence the icon being available on the status bar.

As with **Polar Tracking**, the icon for **Object Snaps** (*OSNAP*) is available, and you can see it in *Figure 3.13*. If you right-click on the icon, you can select **Object Snap Settings…** and this will display the **Drafting Settings** dialog box with the **Object Snap** tab open.

The dialog box is shown in *Figure 3.17*, with the **Object Snap** tab open.

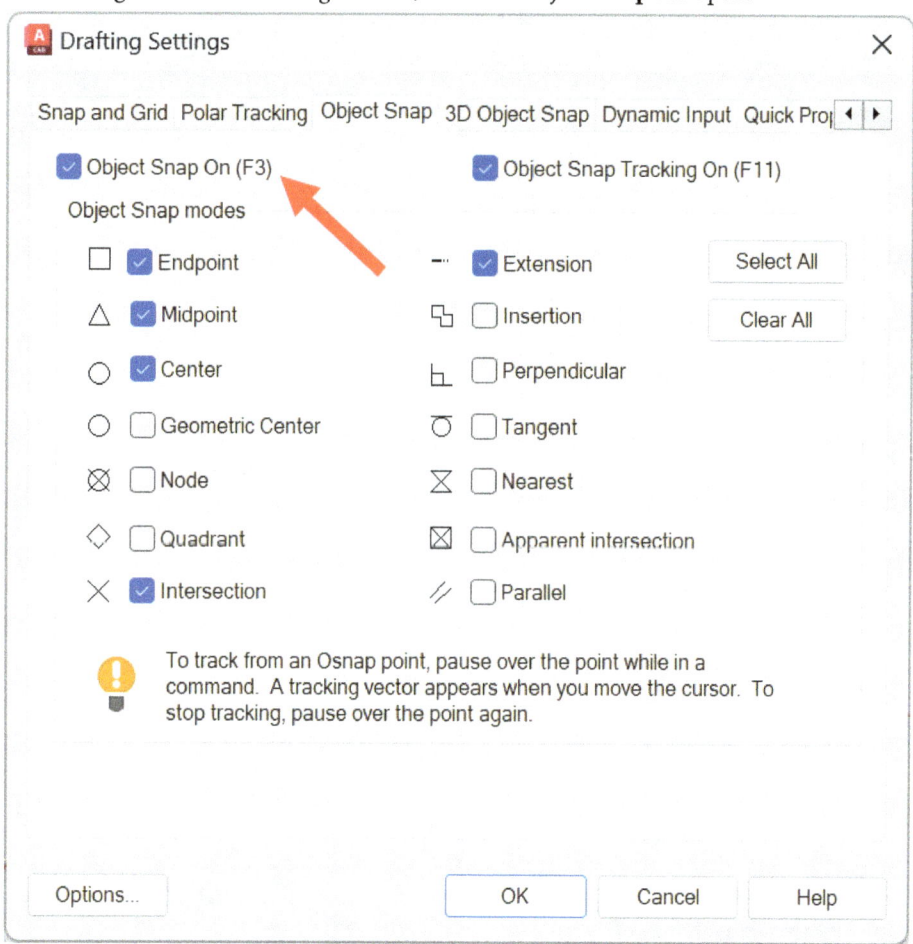

Figure 3.17: The Drafting Settings dialog box with the Object Snap tab open

58 Using the AutoCAD Interface to Work Smarter

Various object snap modes are checked in the dialog box, and those checked are known as the *running object snaps*. It is a good idea to check only some checkboxes. Otherwise, this will make for a frustrating drafting experience! The object snaps selected in *Figure 3.17* comprise a good start. Once the object snap modes are set, click **OK** to close the dialog box.

There is also a flyout menu for **Object Snap**, as there is for **Polar Tracking**. When the flyout arrow is clicked, the flyout menu shown in *Figure 3.18* displays, allowing you to change your running object snap selection quickly and easily. Those that are switched on have a check mark displayed next to them.

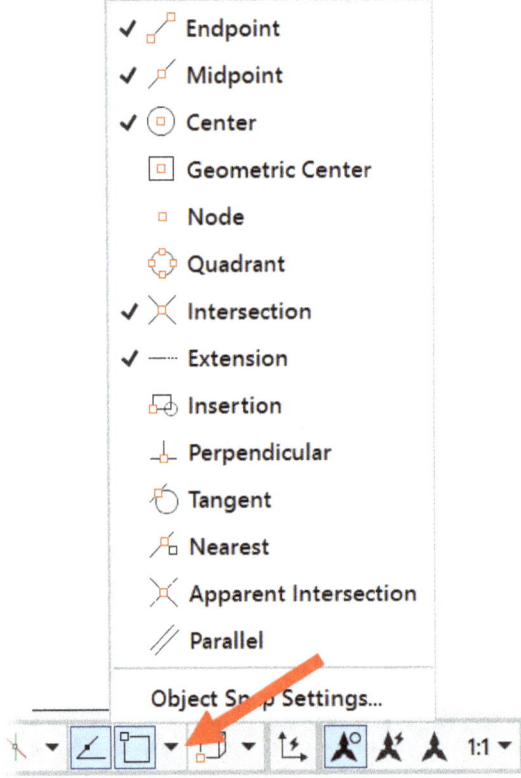

Figure 3.18: The Object Snap flyout menu

You can also select **Object Snap Settings…** on the flyout menu to display the **Drafting Settings** dialog box with the **Object Snap** tab open.

The object snaps mentioned so far are generally used for 2D drafting. When working in a 3D modeling environment, you can also utilize the 3D object snaps (*3DOSNAP*) in AutoCAD by clicking or right-clicking the **3D Object Snap** icon on the status bar, as shown in *Figure 3.19*.

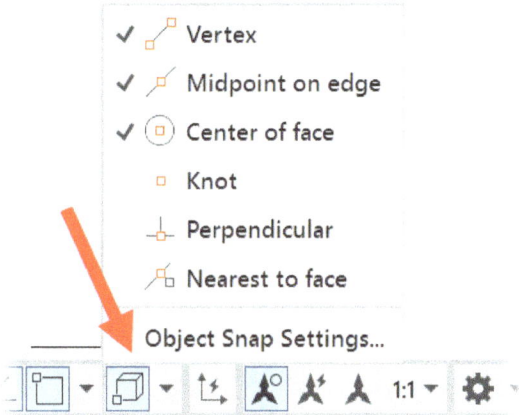

Figure 3.19: The 3D Object Snap flyout menu

> **Tips and tricks #7**
>
> This section has only touched the surface regarding the main drafting settings in AutoCAD. There are many drafting settings, and it is suggested that you open the exercise file for this chapter (`3D Solid.dwg`) and investigate the status bar in more depth at your own pace. Start with 2D drafting, using regular object snaps (*OSNAP*), for example, and then progress forward with 3D modeling with 3D object snaps (*3DOSNAP*).

One drafting setting is always on when you first install and run AutoCAD. That is **Dynamic Input**, known as *DYNMODE*. However, there is something you should know about this drafting setting. While it is on, the icon is *not* initially displayed on the status bar.

To get other drafting settings to display on the status bar, you must click on the hamburger icon in the lower-right corner (in AutoCAD for Mac, it is shown as a gearwheel icon in the same location). If you hover over the hamburger icon, it will display the **Customization** tooltip.

Figure 3.20 shows the menu when you click on the hamburger icon. As you can see, it is a long list!

AutoCAD for Mac

To customize the status bar in AutoCAD for Mac, you would need to click on the gearwheel icon at the bottom left of the AutoCAD for Mac application window. This displays a similar menu to the one in *Figure 3.20*. The list of drafting settings is shorter, and each has a checkbox next to it to switch settings on and off, unlike the Windows version of AutoCAD, where you click on the setting name to toggle it on or off and display a check mark. To close the menu in AutoCAD for Mac, you will need to click on the gearwheel icon again.

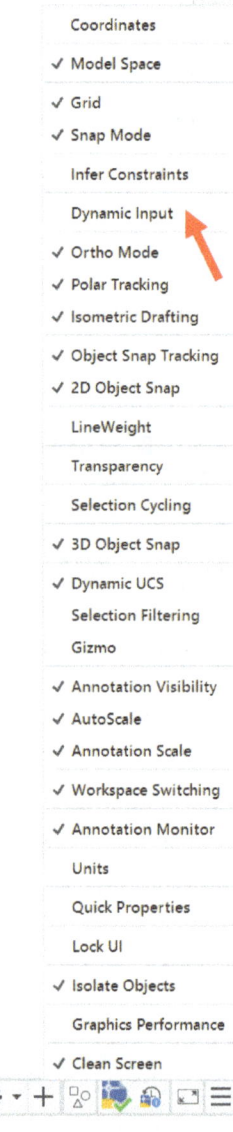

Figure 3.20: The status bar customization menu

Note in *Figure 3.20* that **Dynamic Input** is arrowed. The **Dynamic Input** drafting setting does not have a check mark next to it, indicating that it is not currently displayed on the status bar. Clicking **Dynamic Input** on the menu will switch it on, and a check mark will appear next to the setting name.

To close the menu, click on the hamburger icon again. This is the only way to close the menu, and you must do that to return to work in AutoCAD.

The **Dynamic Input** drafting setting is now displayed on the status bar. This is shown in *Figure 3.21*.

Figure 3.21: The Dynamic Input icon displayed on the status bar

Dynamic Input (*DYNMODE*) is incredibly useful. It allows you to input commands in information at the cursor (crosshair), instead of using the command line at the bottom of the screen. This gives you a more dynamic interface with which to use AutoCAD commands, hence the term **Dynamic Input**.

Like with all other drafting settings on the status bar, you can right-click on the icon and select **Dynamic Input Settings…** Clicking on this will open the **Drafting Settings** dialog box with the **Dynamic Input** tab open, allowing you to update any dynamic input settings you need to use to work effectively in AutoCAD. *Figure 3.22* shows you the **Dynamic Input** tab in the **Drafting Settings** dialog box.

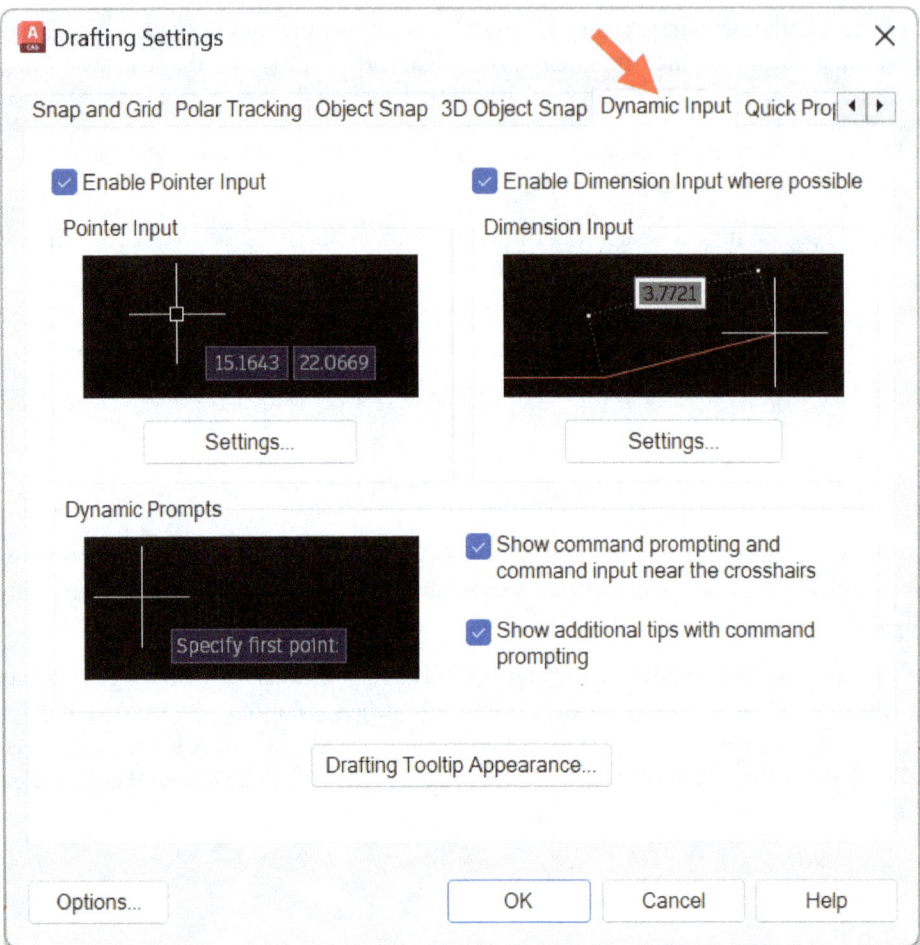

Figure 3.22: The Drafting Settings dialog box with the Dynamic Input tab open

All the drafting settings on the AutoCAD status bar are unique to you. You set them up to make your daily AutoCAD work easier. There is no defined setup. The settings are there if you need them, and you turn them off and on according to your needs and requirements. Use them to your advantage, so that you can use AutoCAD as quickly and efficiently as you can.

> **Tips and tricks #8**
>
> When 3D modeling in AutoCAD, you can utilize **3D Object Snap** (*3DOSNAP*) on the status bar. Make sure they are visible on the status bar by using the **Customize** (*hamburger*) icon, and then switch them on. You can set running 3D object snaps in the same way as regular object snaps on the status bar, thus enhancing your productivity when working in 3D.

All of the previous interface tools you have learned about can be used in both 2D and 3D environments. The next section takes us directly into 3D modeling and the incredibly useful AutoCAD ViewCube.

The AutoCAD ViewCube

In this chapter, 3D modeling has been mentioned numerous times. When working in 3D, there is a need to be able to view a 3D object or solid in various isometric views.

The **ViewCube** is a navigation tool that displays in the top-right corner of the drawing area in AutoCAD, regardless of whether you are working in the 2D model space or a 3D visual style. The **ViewCube** allows you to switch between standard and isometric views.

The **ViewCube** is what is called a persistent, clickable, and draggable interface that allows you to switch between standard views and isometric views of your model. *Figure 3.23* shows you the **ViewCube** in place at the top right of the AutoCAD drawing area.

Figure 3.23: The ViewCube in the AutoCAD drawing area

The **ViewCube** uses three types of view, as listed:

- **Edge**
- **Corner**
- **Face**

Clicking on any of these will re-align the AutoCAD view in the drawing area to correspond with the orientation of the **ViewCube**. Using the exercise file, 3D Solid.dwg, click on the *lower-left corner* of the **ViewCube** in its default position, as shown in *Figure 3.24*.

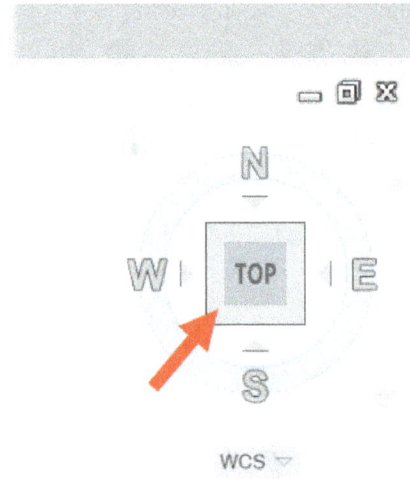

Figure 3.24: The lower-left corner of the ViewCube

As you hover over the corner, it will light up so that you can ensure you are clicking on the correct part of the **ViewCube**. After clicking, the drawing will look as it does in *Figure 3.25*. That corner of the **ViewCube** takes the display to a preset **SW Isometric** view, as indicated by the view control display. Using the edges, corners, and faces of the **ViewCube** allows you to effectively navigate in AutoCAD, especially when working with 3D models.

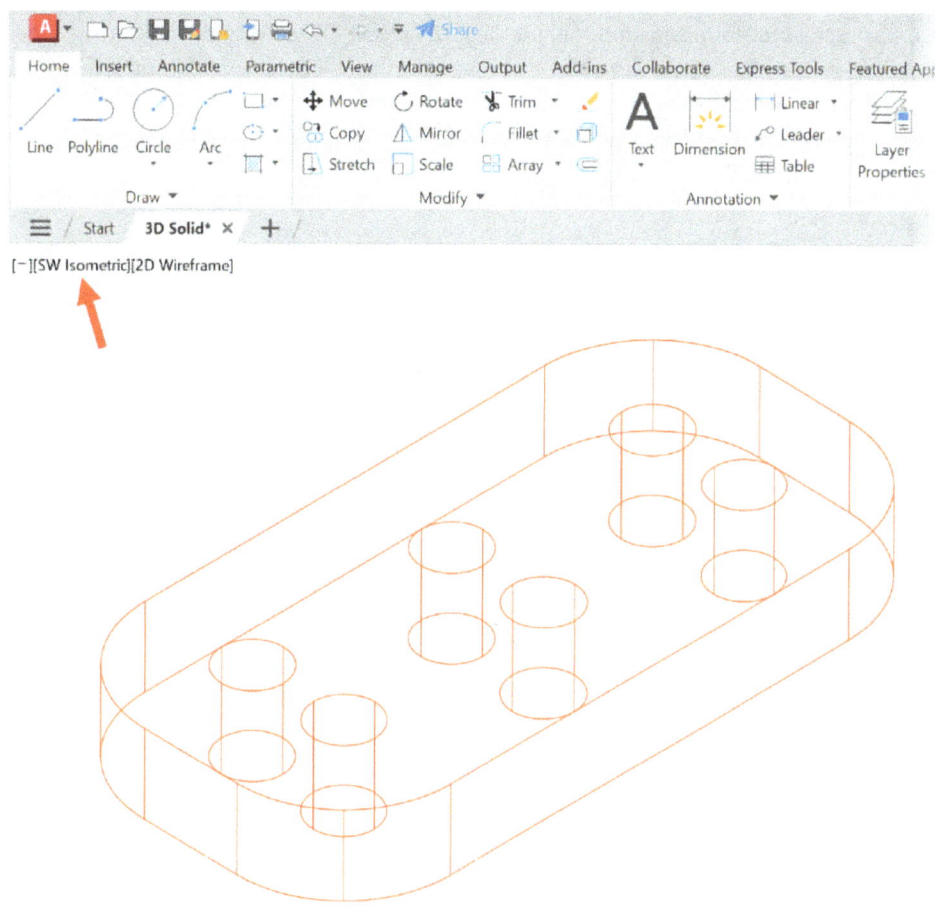

Figure 3.25: The drawing displayed in the SW Isometric view

Tips and tricks #9

When working with the ViewCube, you can use the compass display by clicking on the arrows to rotate any view you are using. You can also go back to the **Home** view by clicking on the *house* symbol. Right-click on the ViewCube and use **Set Current View as Home** on the shortcut menu to set the required home view. Also, test the other settings on the shortcut menu to investigate their effects on the visual display of the drawing. Use the AutoCAD system variables *DISPLAYVIEWCUBEIN2D* and *DISPLAYVIEWCUBEIN3D* to turn the display of the ViewCube on and off in either of the 2D or 3D workspaces.

The **ViewCube** is an excellent navigation tool for all of the preset 3D views and elevations you need when modelling in AutoCAD. You can also orbit manually using a combination of the *Shift key + holding down the mousewheel button*. As you move the mouse, you will orbit manually in the 3D model view. Use the ViewCube to select a preset view once you are done orbitting manaually.

> **AutoCAD for Mac**
> The ViewCube tools in AutoCAD for Mac are the same as in AutoCAD for Windows. Visually, they are the same and use the same right-click shortcut menu and system variables.

In this section, we looked at how useful the AutoCAD **ViewCube** is when navigating, especially in 3D models. We will now take a detailed look at how the **navigation bar** is just as useful, especially when working with 2D drawings.

The AutoCAD navigation bar

The AutoCAD **navigation bar** (sometimes known as the *navbar* for short) is another highly effective way of navigating your AutoCAD drawings.

Positioned by default on the right-hand side of the AutoCAD drawing area, the navigation bar provides several methods of navigation:

- **Navigation Wheels (flyout menu)**
- **Real-time Pan**
- **Zoom (flyout menu)**
- **Orbit (flyout menu)**
- **3Dconnexion (if connected)**
- **ShowMotion**

Figure 3.26 shows the **navigation bar** highlighted in the AutoCAD drawing area. It is highlighted because the cursor (crosshair) is close to it.

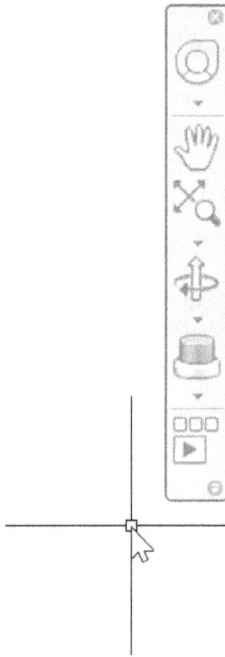

Figure 3.26: The AutoCAD navigation bar

Starting from top to bottom, the following briefly describes the icons on the navigation bar and explains their use when working in AutoCAD.

> **AutoCAD for Mac**
> Please note that there is no navigation bar functionality in AutoCAD for Mac.

Navigation Wheels

The navigation wheels (also known as steering wheels) on the **navigation bar** combine various navigational tools by way of a wheel displayed on the screen. Hovering over various parts of the wheels allows you to navigate the drawing accordingly. Typical navigational aids include *Zoom*, *Pan*, *Orbit*, and *Rewind*.

A flyout menu is also available on this icon to allow you to change the wheel configuration, as there are several wheels to choose from, ranging from a **2D wheel** to the **full navigation wheel** (default). *Figure 3.27* shows the default full navigation wheel. Also, notice the darker background in the drawing area, which has changed automatically due to this wheel being normally used in a 3D environment. These drawing area background colors can be changed in the AutoCAD **options** if required.

68 Using the AutoCAD Interface to Work Smarter

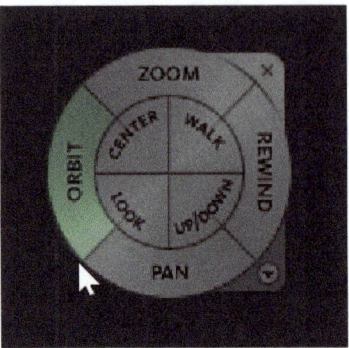

Figure 3.27: The full navigation wheel in AutoCAD

Let's look at the **Real-time Pan** tool next.

Real-time Pan

The **Pan** icon on the **navigation bar** starts the **Real-time Pan** tool. This tool provides you with uninterrupted panning around your AutoCAD drawing or model. You can right-click and use the shortcut menu when in *Real-time Pan* mode. This then allows you to utilize other **Zoom** and **Pan** tools. *Figure 3.28* shows the shortcut menu when activated.

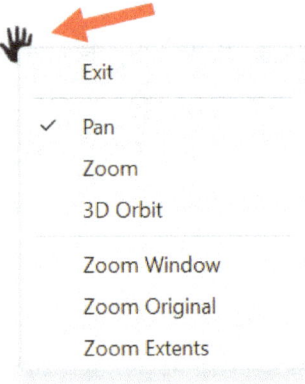

Figure 3.28: The Real-time Pan shortcut menu (flyout)

Using **Real-time Pan** is a great way to move around in a DWG file. In the next section, you will learn how to use **Zoom** to magnify the view in your DWG to see the design in more detail.

Zoom

Zooming in and out of your drawing is essential for you to see close-up details in your drawing, as well as being able to view the overall design. The **Zoom** icon on the **navigation bar** provides a flyout menu that gives access to the AutoCAD **Zoom** commands. *Figure 3.29* shows the **Zoom** flyout menu activated.

The flyout provides a menu listing all the AutoCAD **Zoom** commands, which are selected by clicking on them. The most recent **Zoom** command will then display on the **navigation bar** until the next **Zoom** command is chosen. The most current **Zoom** command is highlighted with a check mark on the flyout menu.

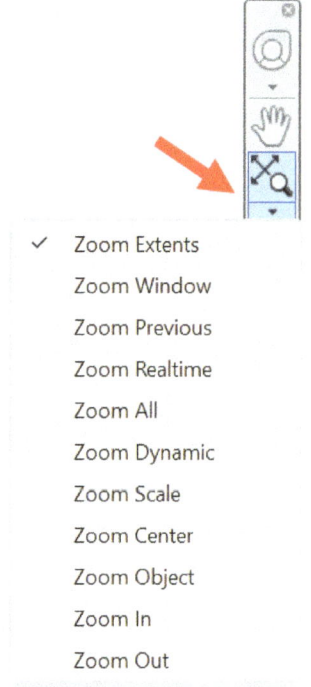

Figure 3.29: The Zoom flyout menu with Zoom Extents current

You now have the knowledge to use **Zoom** effectivley. In the next section, you will learn how to utilize the **Orbit** tool to navigate models quickly and easily.

Orbit (flyout)

Orbiting in a 3D drawing is essential for you to see important details in your drawing, as well as being able to showcase the overall design. The **Orbit** icon on the **navigation bar** provides a flyout menu that gives access to the AutoCAD **Orbit** commands. *Figure 3.30* shows the **Orbit** flyout menu activated.

The flyout provides a menu listing all the AutoCAD **Orbit** commands, which are selected by clicking on them. The most recent **Orbit** command will then display on the **navigation bar** until the next **Orbit** command is chosen. The most current **Orbit** command is highlighted with a check mark on the flyout menu.

Figure 3.30: The Orbit flyout menu with Orbit current(flyout)

You can use **Orbit** to navigate your model in your DWG file. Using a **3Dconnexion** device allows you to be much more precise as you orbit and zoom in your 3D designs.

3Dconnexion

The **3Dconnexion** icon is only available if you have a 3Dconnexion device, such as a **SpaceMouse** or **CadMouse**, configured for use with AutoCAD. These devices enhance the human interface with AutoCAD, with the SpaceMouse often being used in 3D modeling. *Figure 3.31* shows the **3Dconnexion** flyout menu activated.

You will find all the necessary information about 3Dconnexion devices on the website at `www.3dconnexion.com`, and you can also download any necessary AutoCAD drivers there.

The flyout provides a menu listing all the available 3Dconnexion modes (depending on the 3Dconnexion device), which are selected by clicking on them. The most recent 3Dconnexion mode will then display on the **navigation bar** until the next one is chosen. The most current mode is highlighted with a check mark on the flyout menu. You can also get access to **3Dconnexion Settings…** for your device on the flyout menu.

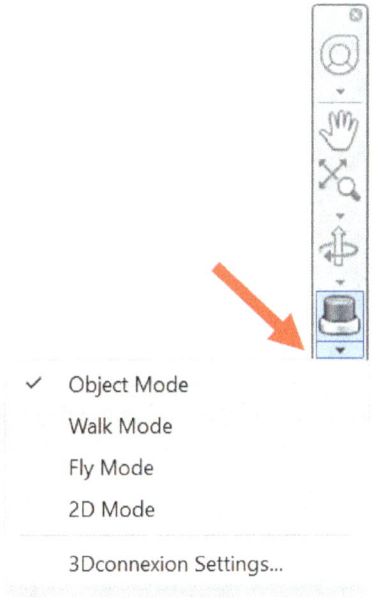

Figure 3.31: The 3Dconnexion flyout menu with Object Mode current

A **3Dconnexion** device is a great addition to AutoCAD. Combining that with **ShowMotion** in AutoCAD allows you to create seamless presentations of specific views of your design in AutoCAD.

ShowMotion

The **ShowMotion** tool provides an onscreen display for creating and playing back cinematic camera animations of various views in your drawing. These views can then be utilized for design review, presentation, and bookmark-style navigation. *Figure 3.32* shows the **ShowMotion** icon on the **navigation bar**.

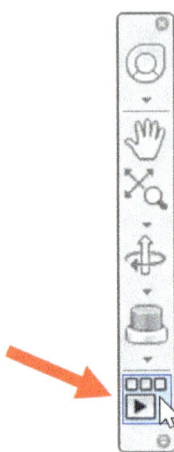

Figure 3.32: The ShowMotion icon on the navigation bar

ShowMotion has three main parts: control bar, shot sequence thumbnails, and shot thumbnails. Shots are named locations showing specific parts of the model, with related shots being able to be organized into a shot sequence. *Figure 3.33* shows **ShowMotion** in a 3D modeling environment, with two saved shots and the **ShowMotion** control bar displayed.

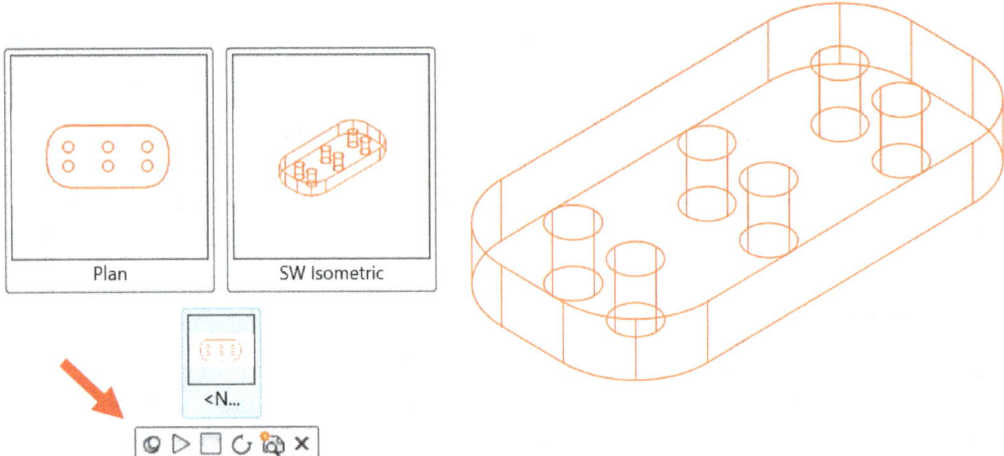

Figure 3.33: The ShowMotion control bar with two saved shots displayed

> **Tips and tricks #10**
> **ShowMotion** is a highly under-used and underrated AutoCAD tool that can enhance the visual and presentation qualities of any design. If any design needs a quick presentation to a stakeholder, **ShowMotion** should be your go-to tool of choice.

Consider using **ShowMotion** as your go-to tool for creating presentation material. It is integrated into AutoCAD and saves the need for third-party applications.

> **AutoCAD for Mac**
> Please note that there is no **ShowMotion** functionality in AutoCAD for Mac.

As you can see, the **navigation bar** is incredibly versatile – not just for navigating in 2D drawings and 3D models. It provides a comprehensive navigation toolbox that enhances productivity in your daily AutoCAD workflows and also provides a useful presentation tool in **ShowMotion**.

Summary

In this chapter, you have learned how to work with file tabs and floating drawing windows using them to manage your open drawing files.

You have also learned how to use the **Model** and **Layout** tabs and how to copy tabs and set up their required settings.

You have also learned how to utilize drafting settings on the status bar to draft and model effectively and productively.

You have learned how to work with the ViewCube when 3D modelling and use the ViewCube settings, and also how to use the navigation bar and work with the tools available.

Working smarter with the AutoCAD interface will make you more productive.

It is important that you not only understand the AutoCAD interface but also utilize it to its full advantage. The interface has seen many iterations over the years and is now at a point where it works incredibly well for you, allowing you to be much more efficient with your day-to-day work. In the next chapter, we will look at how advanced drafting settings will enhance your AutoCAD productivity.

4
Using Advanced Drafting Settings

AutoCAD has an extensive range of drafting settings, located on the AutoCAD status bar. This chapter will take you through some of the lesser-used, advanced drafting settings so that you can work more effectively and productively by working smarter, not harder.

We'll show you how to use specific drafting settings that will enhance your daily AutoCAD usage, providing you with additional skills that will allow you to use AutoCAD for more complex drafting tasks.

You will learn about the following drafting tools:

- Selecting objects using selection cycling
- Utilizing 3D object snaps when 3D modelling
- Working with ISODRAFT settings to create isometric views
- Changing units via the status bar
- Working with annotation scale to improve drawing legibility

Learning more advanced methods of drafting in AutoCAD helps you build your AutoCAD skill set which, in turn, will make it easier to be more efficient and productive when using AutoCAD on a daily basis.

In *Chapter 3*, we touched upon how to work with the drafting settings located on the AutoCAD status bar. In this chapter, we will be taking that knowledge up a notch to work with specific drafting settings within a drawing.

Exercise files

For this chapter, make sure you have downloaded the following exercise files:

- `DraftingSettings.dwg`
- `Office Project.dwg`

Both files will be used in different sections of the chapter, so make sure you have them open in AutoCAD, ready to use.

Selecting objects using selection cycling

There will always be occasions in an AutoCAD drawing where geometry or objects *overlap* or share the same line or edge. Making sure the correct geometry or object is selected is important, as it assists with accuracy and saves valuable time. That's where selection cycling (*SELECTIONCYCLING*) can be very useful.

Selection cycling is also a great method for *filtering* objects. There will always be times when you need to select overlapping objects for modification or deletion. In order to select the appropriate object, you can use selection cycling to select the correct object from a list of overlapping objects. As you work through this section, you will see how selection cycling does this and makes your daily AutoCAD work much easier.

Before working with selection cycling, you will need to make sure it is available on the AutoCAD status bar. Click on the customization (*hamburger*) icon, located in the far bottom-right corner of the AutoCAD screen. Select **Selection Cycling**. A tick mark will appear next to it. Click on the customization icon again to close the menu.

You can now see the selection cycling icon on the status bar. Ensure it is displaying blue, indicating it is switched on. *Figure 4.1* shows you the selection cycling icon switched on:

Figure 4.1: The AutoCAD status bar with selection cycling displayed and switched on

Using the exercise file for this chapter (DraftingSettings.dwg), make sure you are in the AutoCAD **Model** tab. You will see two rectangles, one blue and one red. They are displayed in the preset **Top** view on the **ViewCube**. They are both 3D solids viewed from above (top) and are adjacent to each other, as shown in *Figure 4.2*:

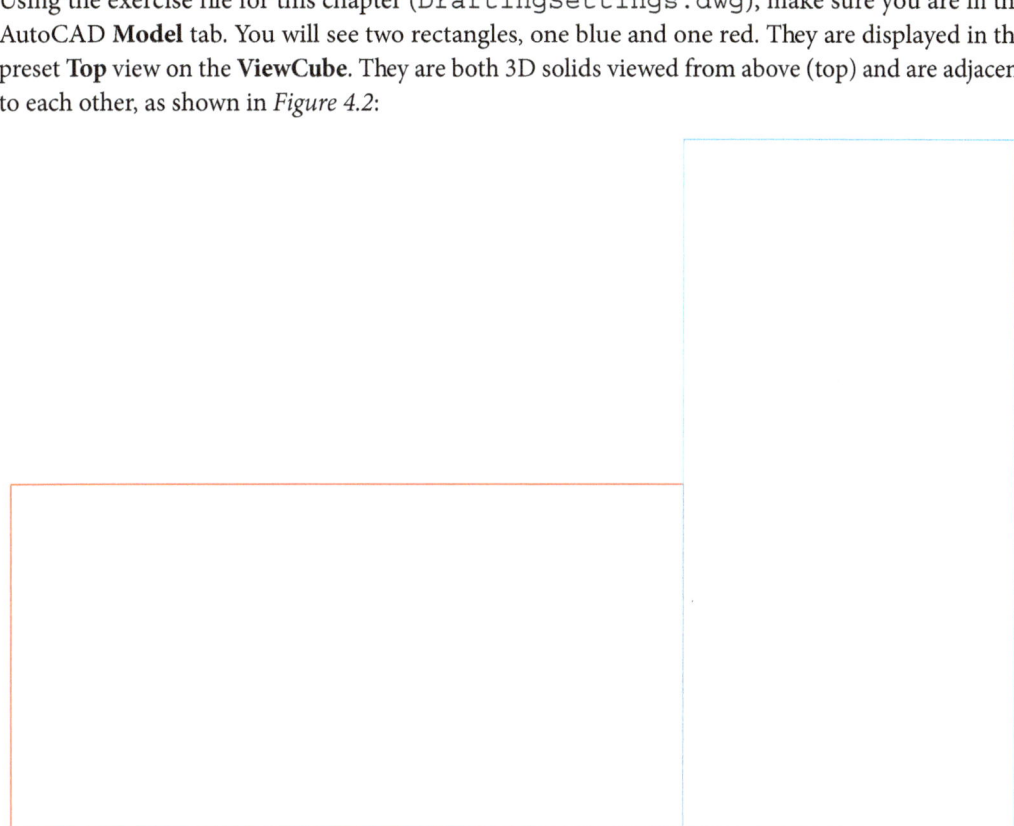

Figure 4.2: The two rectangles in the preset Top view in the Model tab

Figure 4.2 is a simple example of two adjoining rectangles. Even in a more complex drawing than this one, the geometry of objects is often adjacent or next to each other. Whether we are dealing with a simple or complex drawing, selection cycling provides an efficient method of selecting one single object among many.

Now, let's see how to select an object. With selection cycling on, hover over the line where the two adjoining rectangles meet. Click on the adjoining line. You will see the **Selection** prompt appear. You now have the option to select either object, as shown in *Figure 4.3*, by clicking on the objects in the list displayed:

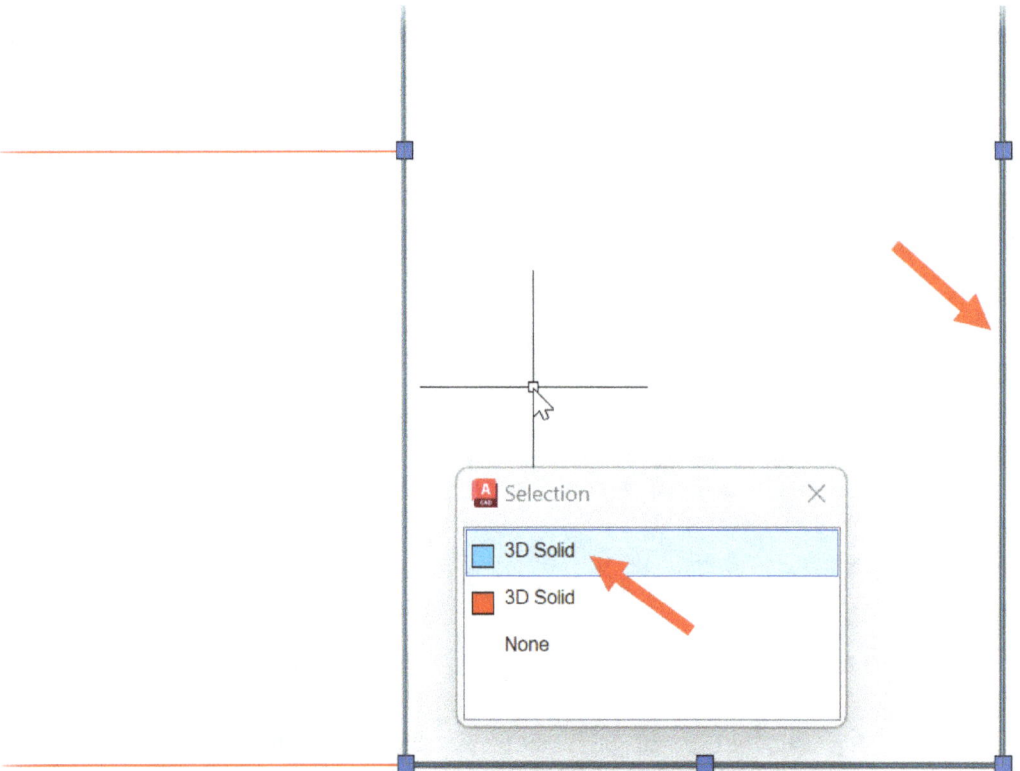

Figure 4.3: The selection cycling prompt with the blue rectangle (3D Solid) selected

In *Figure 4.3*, you can see that the object currently selected is the blue rectangle (a 3D solid in the **Top** view) with the AutoCAD grips displayed.

If you repeat this workflow and select the red 3D solid in the **Selection** list, you will see the red rectangle highlight and the grips on that object display:

Selecting objects using selection cycling 79

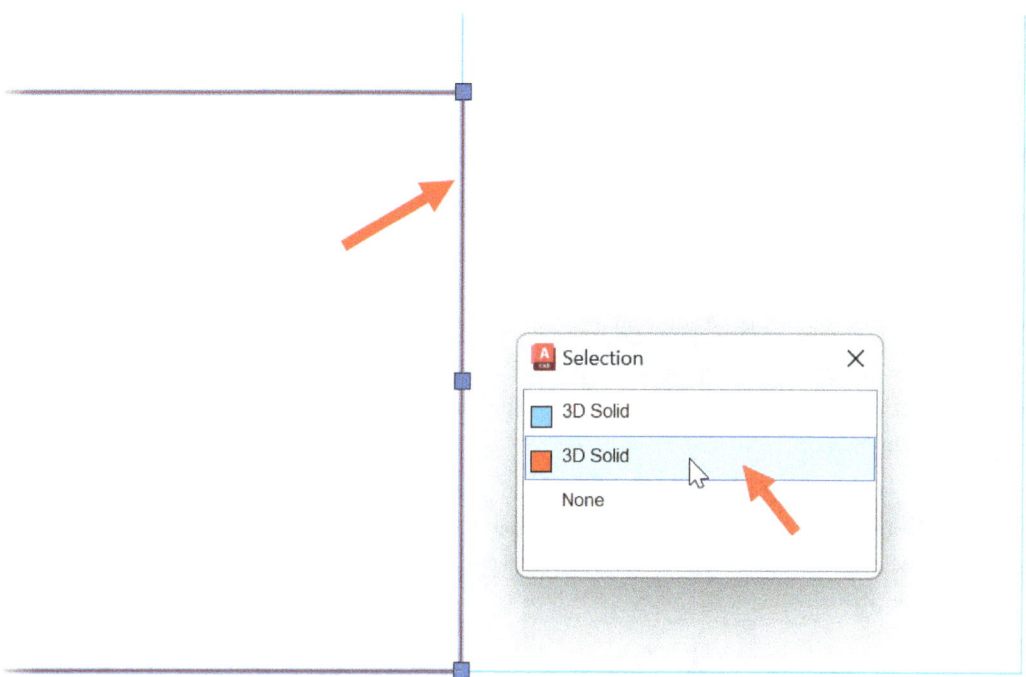

Figure 4.4: The selection cycling prompt with the red rectangle (3D Solid) selected

So, whichever 3D solid you select at the **Selection** prompt is then selected and highlighted in the drawing with its grips displayed. If you do not want either object selected, click on **None** within the **Selection** prompt.

> Tips and tricks #11
>
> **Selection cycling** is a great tool for simple object selection in any drawing, complex or otherwise, 2D or 3D. When 3D modeling, consider using the **Selection Filtering** drafting setting on the status bar. This will give you the selection options for **Vertex**, **Edge**, **Face**, **Solid History**, and **Drawing View Component**.

Selection tools are fundamental to your design workflow in AutoCAD. Try to use them and keep using them to build up that "muscle memory." That way, your workflows will improve, making you more effective and productive.

> AutoCAD for Mac
>
> There is no option for **Selection cycling** in AutoCAD for Mac. However, you can use **Selection Filtering** when 3D modeling.

Now that you know how to select objects within a drawing to change or delete them, let's learn how to model accurately in 3D, utilizing 3D object snaps.

Utilizing 3D object snaps when 3D modeling

When 3D modeling in AutoCAD, regular object snaps can sometimes snap you to the wrong point on the 3D model. For example, you might be in a plane (top) view of the model and select an **Endpoint** object snap to add geometry to the model. As you are looking down from the top of the model, that endpoint snap could be on the top face or the bottom face of the model, depending on the model's orientation.

3D Object Snap (*3DOSNAP*) is a drafting setting on the status bar that gives you a selection of object snaps that function only in a 3D environment, allowing you to be more accurate when working with 3D models in AutoCAD.

Before working with **3D Object Snap** (*3DOSNAP*), you will need to make sure it is available on the AutoCAD status bar. Click on the **Customization** (*hamburger*) icon (as mentioned in previous chapters) and select **3D Object Snap**. A tick mark will appear next to it. Click on the **Customization** icon again to close the menu.

You can now see the 3D object snap icon on the status bar. Ensure it is displaying blue, indicating it is switched on. *Figure 4.5* shows you the **3D Object Snap** icon switched on:

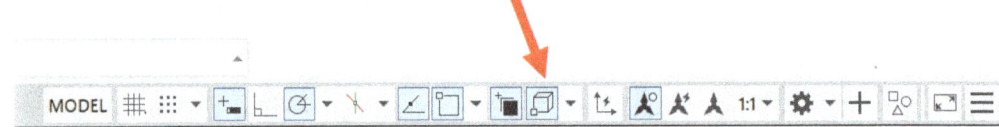

Figure 4.5: The AutoCAD status bar with 3D Object Snap displayed and switched on

3D Object Snap operates in the same way as the regular **Object Snap** drafting setting. You switch it on and select your running 3D object snaps from the flyout menu. If you click on the flyout arrow to the right of the **3D Object Snap** icon, you will see the 3D object snaps on the flyout menu. This is shown in *Figure 4.6*:

Utilizing 3D object snaps when 3D modeling | 81

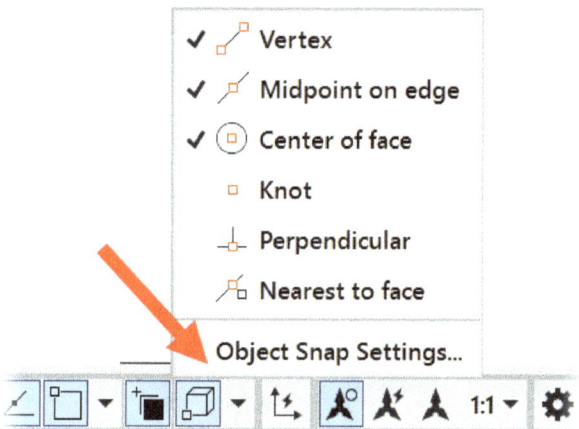

Figure 4.6: The 3D Object Snap flyout menu

You will notice in *Figure 4.6* that **Vertex**, **Midpoint on edge**, and **Center of face** have tick marks against them, which signify that these are currently the running 3D object snaps.

Now, let's go to the drawing area and select the lower left corner of the **ViewCube**. This will put the drawing into a preset **SW Isometric** 3D view. You can now see the rectangles looking as they should, as 3D solids. This is shown in *Figure 4.7*:

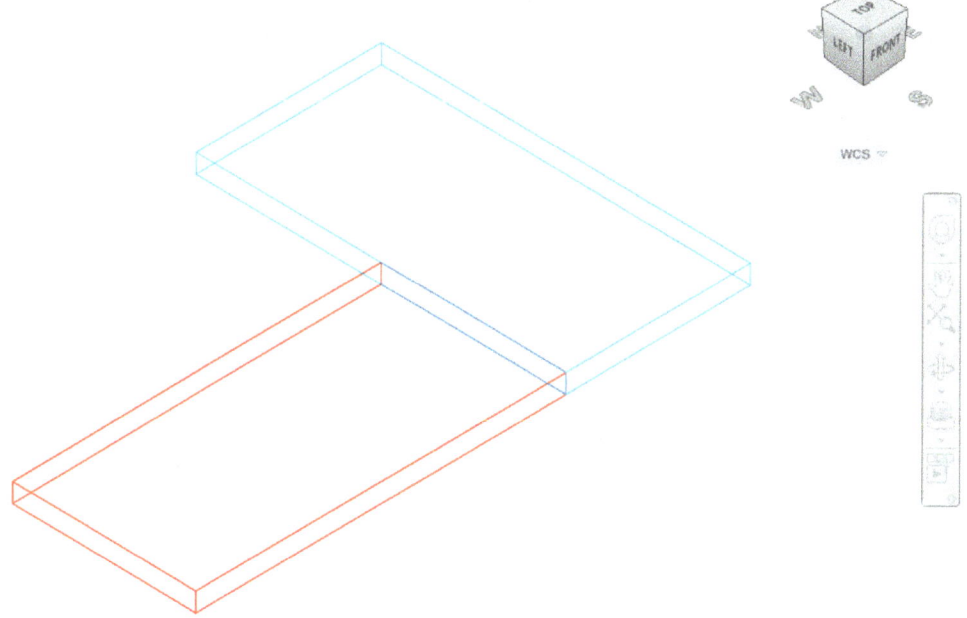

Figure 4.7: The rectangles (3D solids) in the SW Isometric preset view with the ViewCube displayed

You can utilize the 3D object snaps more effectively now that you are in a 3D view. In *Figure 4.8*, you can see a line being drawn from one 3D snap to the **3D Vertex** object snap, as displayed by the tooltip:

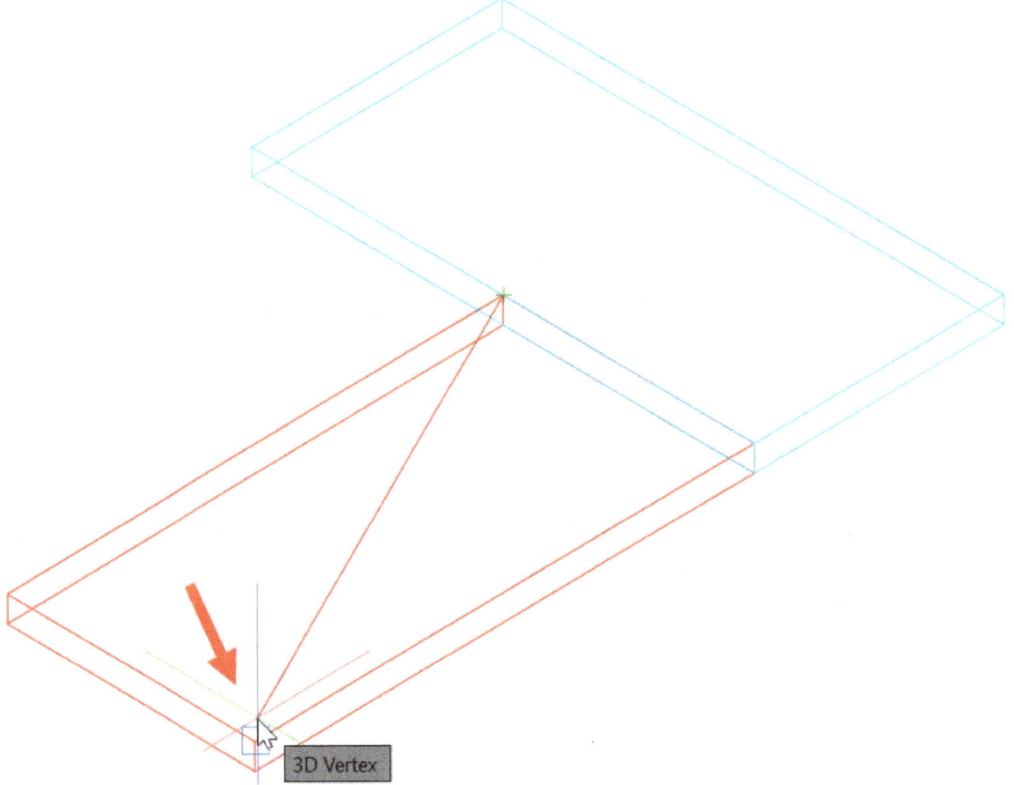

Figure 4.8: A line drawn from one 3D object snap to the 3D Vertex object snap

> **Tips and tricks #12**
>
> When working in 3D, you will find the **3D Object Snap** (*3DOSNAP*) drafting setting more accurate than your regular **Object Snaps** (*OSNAP*), as you can snap to 3D vertices and faces rather than having to keep changing your 3D view to find the appropriate object snap.

3D Object Snaps (*3DOSNAP*) are incredibly useful tools in a 3D environment. They accurately snap to geometric points on 3D objects when 2D object snaps (*OSNAP*) might snap to the incorrect point.

> **AutoCAD for Mac**
> The **3D Object Snap** (*3DOSNAP*) drafting setting is also available in AutoCAD for Mac. You can set it up in the same way as you would in AutoCAD for Windows, as described in this chapter.

3D Object Snaps are a great tool when working in a 3D modeling environment, and you now know how to use them effectively when creating 3D geometry in AutoCAD. Sometimes, a 2D interpretation of 3D is all that is required. That's where isometric drafting becomes useful and the *ISODRAFT* settings in AutoCAD allow you to create isometric views quickly and efficiently.

Working with ISODRAFT settings to create isometric views

Isometric drafting in AutoCAD is a useful tool that allows you to generate isometric views in a 2D drafting environment, thus communicating design intent more effectively. This is often done when there is no 3D model of the design created, and when a simple isometric view would be sufficient for understanding the overall design.

You can start with a blank drawing for this part of the chapter. Use a metric default template file such as `acadiso.dwt` (*full AutoCAD*) or `acltiso.dwt` (*AutoCAD LT*).

To gain access to one of the aforementioned templates, you will need to select **New** in AutoCAD. You can do that via the **Quick Access Toolbar** (**QAT**), covered in *Chapter 1*. You can also access the **New** command via the **Application** menu (top-left corner) and the **Start** screen in AutoCAD.

After clicking on the **New** icon, you will see the **Select Template** dialog box. You can then select the `acadiso.dwt` template file (*full AutoCAD*) or the `acltiso.dwt` template file (*AutoCAD LT*). Click on **Open**, and a new DWG file will be created using the selected template. You can then save the new DWG file with a filename of your choosing.

Also note here that templates with *ISO* in their filenames are preferred for metric units, and filenames without ISO in their name, such as `acad.dwt` and `aclt.dwt`, are the preferred templates when working in imperial units. This philosophy is not set in stone, however, as templates can be used in many different environments.

> **AutoCAD for Mac**
> Be aware that there is no **ISODRAFT** drafting setting in AutoCAD for Mac, so if you're a Mac user, you can jump to the next part of the chapter, *Changing units via the status bar*.

Sometimes, isometric drafting is all that is needed to create a suitable design. To do this, you will need to switch on **Isometric Drafting** (*ISODRAFT*) on the status bar. The icon should already be displayed on the status bar, but if it isn't, utilize the **Customization** (*hamburger*) icon in the same way as you have previously to display drafting settings. *Figure 4.9* shows **Isometric Drafting** switched on and displays the flyout menu available:

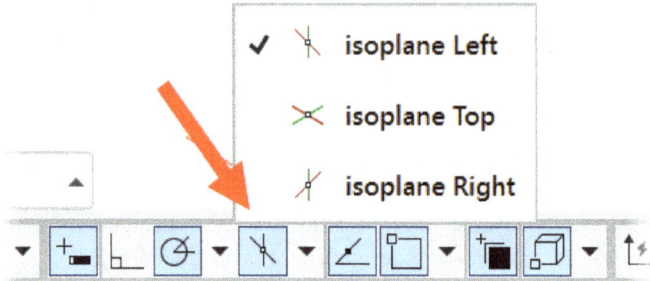

Figure 4.9: The Isometric Drafting (ISODRAFT) setting with the flyout menu displayed

The settings in *ISODRAFT* are self-explanatory. If you want to work on the left of the isometric view of the design, select **isoplane Left**. For working on the top of the view, use **isoplane Top**, and for working on the right, select **isoplane Right**.

The setting you choose then sets up the relevant polar tracking angles you will need to draft in an isometric view (normally 30 degrees and 60 degrees).

Figure 4.10 shows a simple 2D isometric view of what would be a 3D rectangular solid:

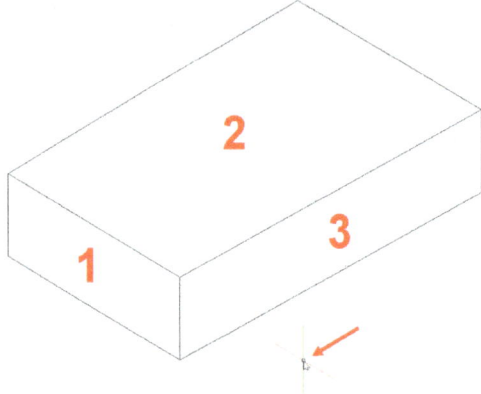

Figure 4.10: A simple rectangular 2D isometric view with the isoplane Left mode selected (note the cursor display)

The numbers indicate where the different *ISODRAFT* modes would be used to create the 2D isometric view:

- **1**: isoplane Left
- **2**: isoplane Top
- **3**: isoplane Right

Only the **Line** (*LINE*) command was used to create the view with a little bit of help from object snaps (*OSNAP*). The isometric view in *Figure 4.10* is purely made up of line segments drawn at the isometric angles *ISODRAFT* provides. After the first line segment has been drawn (which could be any of the lines shown), with *ISODRAFT* on, the remaining lines can easily be drawn at the appropriate angles using object snaps (*OSNAP*) to snap to the relevant endpoints of each line drawn in sequence.

You now know how to work with isometric drawing utilizing the *ISODRAFT* setting. All entities and geometry need relevant units, so next up is how to change your unit settings in AutoCAD via the status bar.

Changing units via the status bar

There will sometimes be occasions where your AutoCAD unit settings need to be changed. It might be that you need to convert units from one format to another (imperial to metric, for example), or you might just need to be able to work with a different unit set because a certain element in the drawing is imperial, and not metric, such as a mechanical gearwheel.

There are two methods by which you can update your unit settings in AutoCAD. Let's look at the first one using the **Drawing Units** dialog box.

To change your units (*UNITS*) in AutoCAD, you would need to type UNITS and press *Enter*. This would then display the **Drawing Units** dialog box, as shown in *Figure 4.11*. You can either type UNITS in the command line and press *Enter*, or, if **Dynamic Input** is on, you can type UNITS anywhere in the drawing area of the screen and press *Enter*:

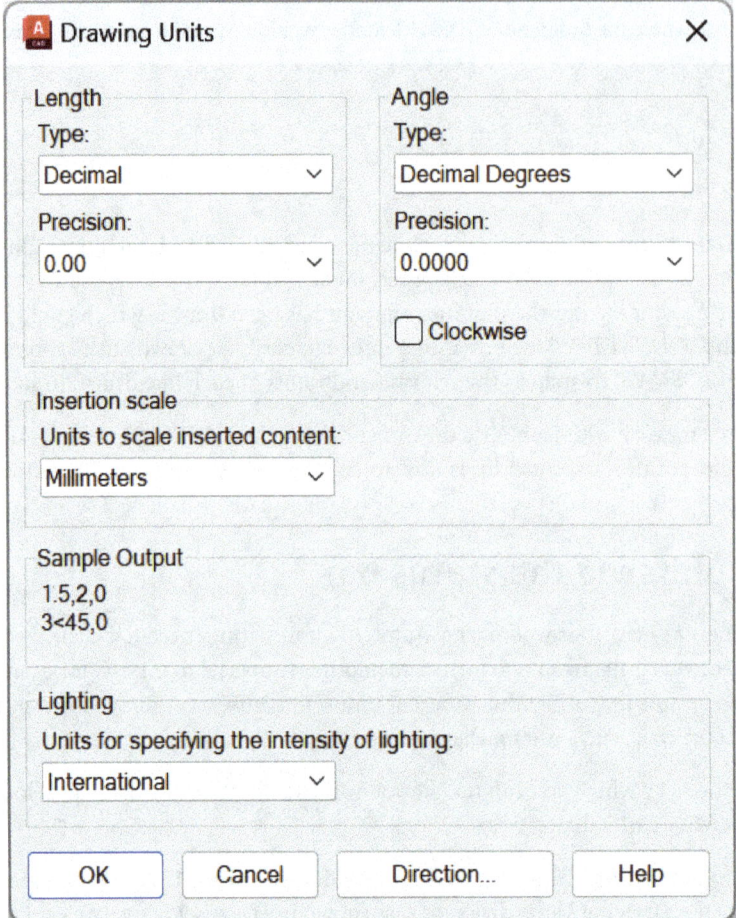

Figure 4.11: The Drawing Units dialog box

This is a somewhat long-winded way of updating your unit set in a drawing. There is a much quicker and easier way of doing this.

If you click on the **Customization** (*hamburger*) icon located in the bottom-right of the AutoCAD screen (at the end of the status bar) and then select **Units** from the flyout menu, a tick mark will appear next to **Units** in the list. It will also be added to the status bar as a drafting setting, as shown in *Figure 4.12*, which also shows the flyout menu displayed:

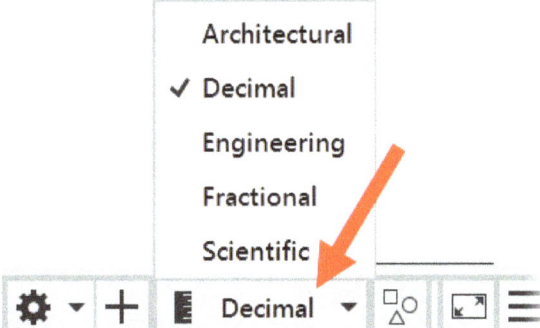

Figure 4.12: The Units drafting setting with the flyout menu displayed and Decimal units selected

Using this as a drafting setting on the status bar is a much quicker and easier method to change the units in your drawing, rather than having to keep going to the **Drawing Units** dialog box.

> **Tips and tricks #13**
>
> **Units** on the status bar, as a drafting setting, is for linear units only. You will still have to use the **Drawing Units** dialog box to alter any angular unit settings.

Units are only part of the design workflow in AutoCAD and allow you to draft effectively. You also need to communicate your design intent via annotation on your drawings. Next, we will look at using annotative scaling and annotation scales to enhance and improve your drawing legibility.

Working with annotation scale to improve drawing legibility

The **Annotation Scale** feature (*CANNOSCALE*) is used when using annotation scaling in your drawings. It is often used for drawing elements such as dimensions, text, and hatching to make for a neat, easy-to-read drawing when working at differing viewport scales in the layout tabs.

We will learn more about this by using another exercise file provided for this chapter, `Office Project.dwg`. Open the file so that you are in the **ISO A3-Landscape** layout tab. *Figure 4.13* shows you the layout tab and how it should be displayed on the AutoCAD screen:

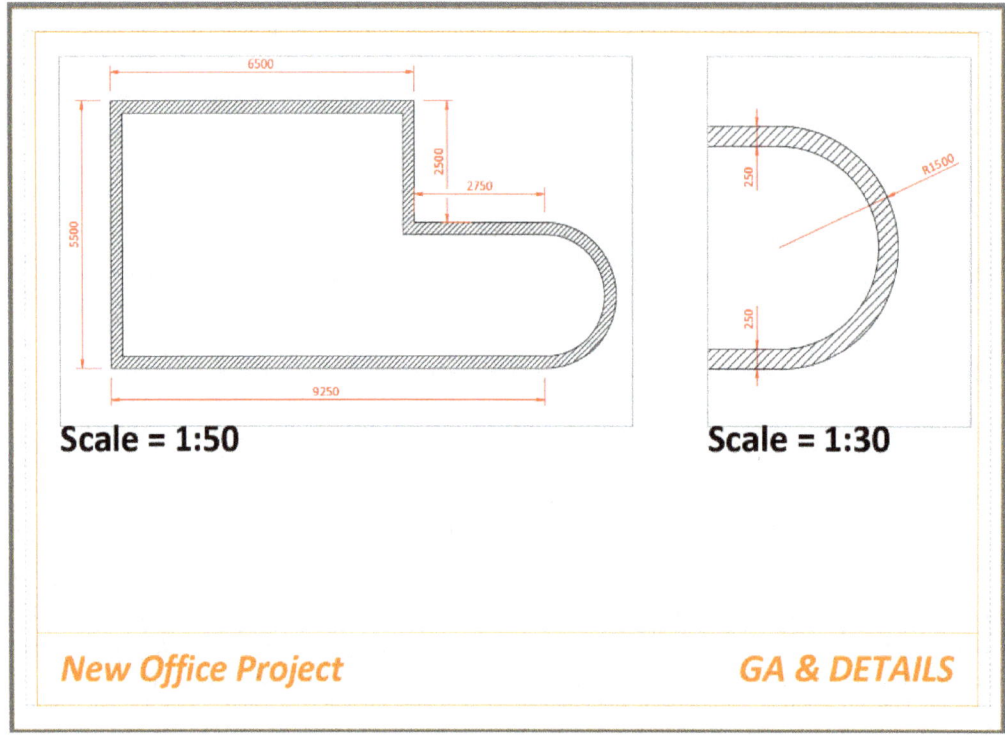

Figure 4.13: The Office Project.dwg file with the layout tab displayed

You will notice in the layout tab that there are two obvious viewports, one at a scale of **1:50** and one at a scale of **1:30**. You will also notice that all dimension annotation is consistently sized, even though the layout viewports are at different scales. This is where annotative scaling is incredibly useful.

In any layout tab, there are often viewports of differing scales, and the annotation scale of annotative objects (especially dimensions) can make for easy, consistent dimensioning.

If you return to the **Model** tab, you will see the dimension annotation in the drawing displayed at differing sizes. This is because the dimensions have different annotation scales, which can be seen in *Figure 4.14*:

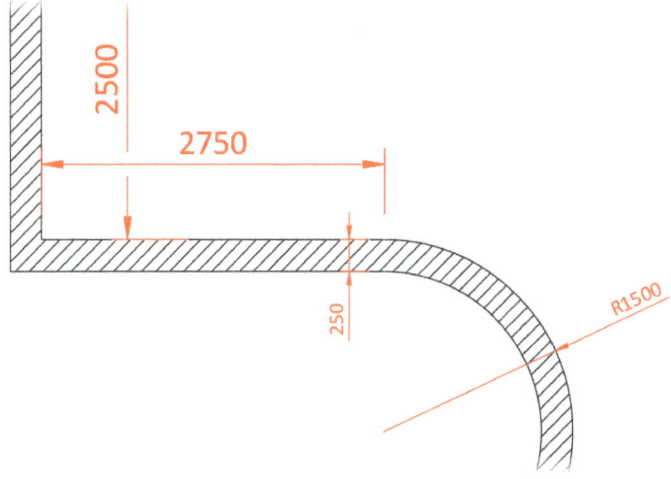

Figure 4.14: Dimensions with different annotation scales

In *Figure 4.14*, the larger dimensions (**2500** and **2750**) have an annotation scale of **1:50**, and the smaller dimensions (**250** and **R1500**) have an annotation scale of **1:30**. These then correlate to the scale of the layout viewports in which they are displayed, by way of annotative scaling, using an annotation scale applied to each dimension object.

The benefit of these annotative dimensions is that due to the annotation scales applied to the dimension objects, they display consistently in the layout viewports. You can also apply multiple annotation scales so that annotative objects display in more than one scaled layout viewport.

All that is required for this to work effectively is an annotative dimension style. In the `Office Project.dwg` file, an annotative dimension style called **Metric-mm** is used. This is shown in *Figure 4.15*. The figure shows the **Dimension** panel, which you will find in the **Annotate** tab on the AutoCAD ribbon:

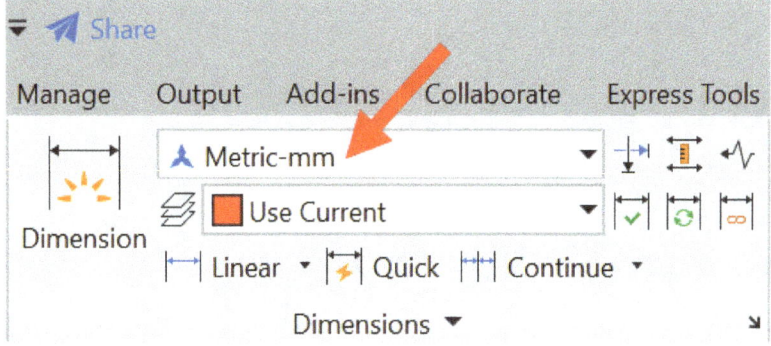

Figure 4.15: The current annotative dimension style shown in the Dimension panel

Using Advanced Drafting Settings

The annotative dimension style uses a small blue triangular symbol to indicate it is an annotative dimension style.

With an annotative dimension style, you set the annotation scale in the **Model** tab, using the flyout menu on the status bar, as shown in *Figure 4.16*:

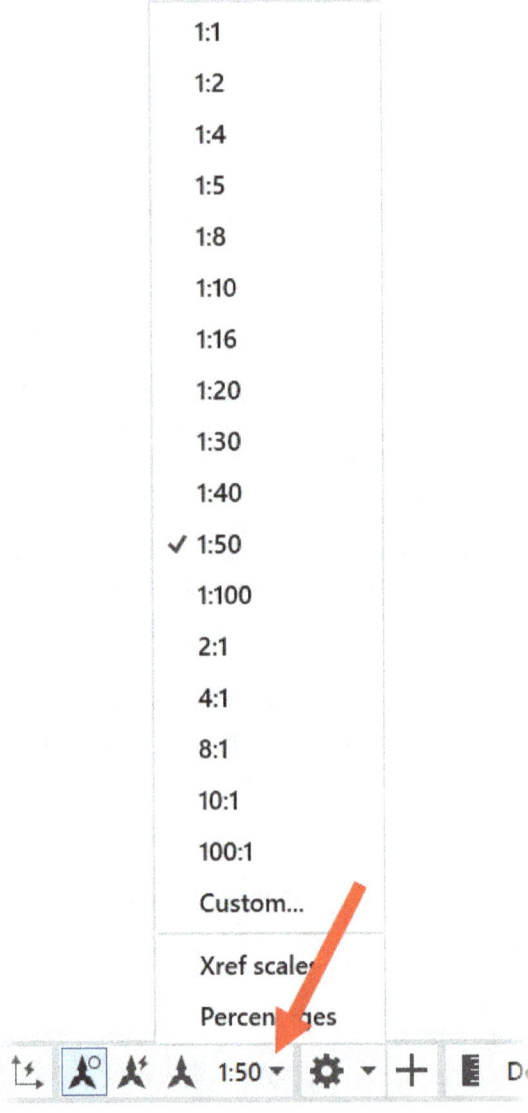

Figure 4.16: The annotation scale flyout menu with 1:50 as the current annotation scale

Dimensions are added to your design in a drawing to communicate design intent. Typical examples of this would be the length and width of a room, the size of a window or door opening, or the shaft length and thread length of a bolt. You would normally add dimensions to a drawing using object snaps (*OSNAP*) to snap accurately to the geometry representing real-world objects to communicate these values for construction and manufacture. By setting the annotation scale when working in the **Model** tab, you are letting AutoCAD know how to scale the dimension in the appropriate layout tab.

Any subsequent dimensions placed using the annotative dimension style will adopt a **1:50** annotation scale, thus making sure they are displayed in the **1:50** layout viewport. The same workflow would be adopted for the **1:30** layout viewport, where the annotation scale for the annotative dimensions would be set to **1:30**.

All objects in an AutoCAD DWG file have known properties, whether that be the **Layer**, **Xolor**, **Linetype**, or in this case, the **Annotative Scale**. You can check whether a dimension object is annotative or not by looking at its properties in the **Properties** palette. The properties of an annotative dimension should be displayed as shown in *Figure 4.17*:

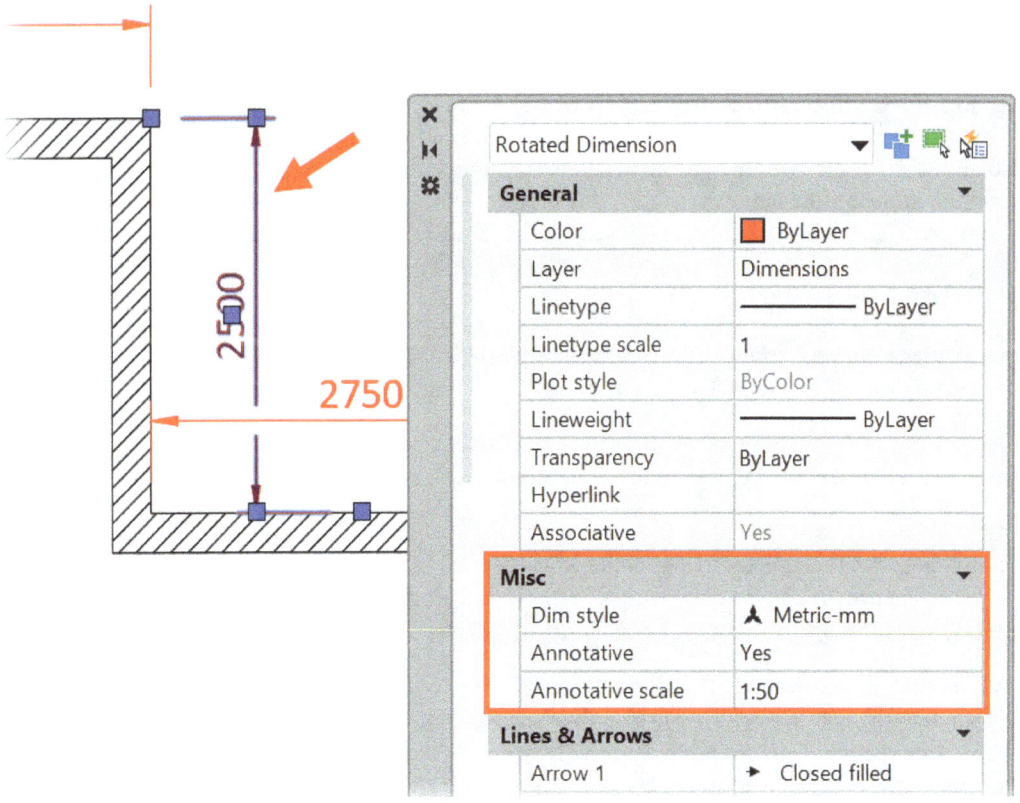

Figure 4.17: The properties of a selected annotative dimension object displayed in the Properties palette

The biggest benefit of annotative scaling when used with annotative dimensions is that you can stick with one annotative dimension style and one layer for all your dimension annotation, knowing that it will display consistently in all layout viewports of differing scales.

> **Tips and tricks #14**
>
> When using annotation scaling with annotative dimensions, you can also add multiple annotation scales to a single dimension object. For example, if you had a dimension that needed to be displayed in both a **1:50** layout viewport and a **1:30** layout viewport, you would add **1:50** and **1:30** annotation scales to the dimension object. This can be done via the **Properties** palette by clicking on the **Annotative scale** value (see *Figure 4.17*). After clicking on the value, a small button appears next to the displayed annotative scale value. Click on the button, and you will be able to add new annotation scale values using the dialog box that appears.

Annotation scaling is a fantastic time-saver. When using it with annotative dimensions, you only have to create one dimension style and one layer for your dimensions.

> **AutoCAD for Mac**
>
> Annotation scaling is also available in AutoCAD for Mac. You would set up your annotative dimension styles using a similar workflow. Place your annotative dimension objects as you do in AutoCAD for Windows, using the annotation scale flyout menu on the status bar when working in the **Model** tab.

Summary

In this chapter, we have learned how to select multiple overlaid objects and select the required object for updating or deletion, as well as how to model in 3D much more effectively using **3D Object Snap** (*3DOSNAP*).

We have also learned how to create accurate 2D isometric drawings, utilizing the isometric drafting (*ISODRAFT*) settings.

We have also gained valuable knowledge of the units (*UNITS*) function in AutoCAD, allowing for quick and effective changes to units in drawings, as well as learning how to set and/or change the annotation scale (*CANNOSCALE*) to work in line with annotative scales set in layout viewports in the drawing.

The advanced drafting settings in this chapter will allow you to work in a more effective way, enhancing your productivity. They also allow you to utilize various tools in AutoCAD to their full advantage. Now that you know how to use them, your daily AutoCAD use will become less onerous, and you will start to work smarter with AutoCAD, not harder.

In the next chapter, we will look at how you can develop advanced geometry in AutoCAD using object snaps.

Part 2: Advanced Drafting Techniques and Annotation

Drafting and annotation in AutoCAD go hand in hand. In order to effectively convey your design intent, you need to communicate your design using both effective drafting and geometry, as well as precise and accurate annotation that allows stakeholders and third parties to read and interpret your designs in your AutoCAD DWG files. This part of the book takes you through how to develop advanced geometry in your drawings using object snaps and how to modify and measure geometry and objects. You will also gain valuable knowledge of creating annotative styles and working with annotative scaling.

This part has the following chapters:

- *Chapter 5, Developing Advanced Geometry Using Object Snaps*
- *Chapter 6, Measuring and Modifying Geometry and Objects*
- *Chapter 7, Developing Annotative Annotation Styles*
- *Chapter 8, Working With Annotative Scaling*

5
Developing Advanced Geometry Using Object Snaps

AutoCAD is a precise design application and accuracy must be maintained in your drawing files. This chapter will show you how to use specific drafting settings and **object snaps** (often referred to as **Osnaps**) that will allow you to draft and model precisely and accurately and provide you with the necessary knowledge to utilize the drafting settings and Osnaps in your daily AutoCAD workflows. When drafting or modeling, **Object Snaps** (*OSNAP*) in AutoCAD allow you to snap to specific points on geometric objects. For example, you can snap to an *endpoint,* or the *midpoint* of a line drawn in AutoCAD.

To develop advanced geometry, such as for mechanical parts, geographical plans, or construction blueprints, you need a good knowledge of Osnaps in AutoCAD. This chapter will take you through a workflow that will help you develop these skills.

In this chapter, we'll cover the following topics:

- Measuring angles accurately with Polar Tracking (*POLAR*)
- Restricting the cursor orthogonally using *ORTHOMODE*
- Using Object Snap Tracking (*AUTOSNAP*) to draw efficiently with multiple Osnaps
- Drawing accurately and effectively with Object Snaps (*OSNAP*) and Snap Overrides

In *Chapter 4*, you looked at how advanced drafting settings could assist you in working more productively and efficiently with the AutoCAD interface. In this chapter, you'll be utilizing Osnaps in AutoCAD, which provide so much more than just endpoints, midpoints, and centers. You'll also be using drafting settings such as **Polar Tracking** and **Object Snap Tracking** so that advanced geometry can be created quickly and easily.

Technical requirements

To use AutoCAD, you'll need to have an AutoCAD license installed either on your desktop computer or your laptop. You'll also require the following:

- A subscription (license) to AutoCAD. This will need to be the *FULL* version of AutoCAD, not AutoCAD LT. Ideally, this will be the latest version of AutoCAD, which is *AutoCAD 2026* at the time of writing. You can use earlier versions, but it's suggested that you go no further back than *AutoCAD 2022*.
- To use AutoCAD with a subscription, you'll need an Autodesk account. If you don't have one, you can set one up at https://accounts.autodesk.com/.
- This book covers AutoCAD 2026, running on the Microsoft Windows **operating system** (**OS**). All images and graphics are from AutoCAD 2026 and the *Windows 11* OS.

  This book contains instructions for both Windows and Mac users. While comprehensive instructions have been provided for Windows users, special instructions relating to deviations in the Mac interface have also been provided within callout boxes.

Exercise files

You'll need to make sure you've downloaded the exercise file, `BearingCase.dwg`, to complete this chapter.

Measuring angles accurately with Polar Tracking (POLAR)

Before working with **Polar Tracking** (*POLAR*), you'll need to make sure it's available on the AutoCAD status bar. Follow these steps to do so:

1. Click on the **Customization** (*hamburger*) icon and select **Polar Tracking**. A check mark will appear next to it.
2. Click on the **Customization** icon again to close the menu.
3. You'll now see the **Polar Tracking** icon on the status bar. Ensure that it's blue, indicating it's been switched on.

Figure 5.1 shows the **Polar Tracking** icon once it's been switched on:

Figure 5.1: The AutoCAD status bar with Polar Tracking displayed and switched on

Why do you need **Polar Tracking**? It allows you to work with preset angle increments and add individual angle increments on an as-needed basis.

Now, let's explore some properties of this feature. You'll notice that the **Polar Tracking** icon on the status bar has a flyout menu arrow to the right of it. If you click on this arrow, the flyout menu will display the different preset angle increments that can be used. *Figure 5.2* shows this flyout menu:

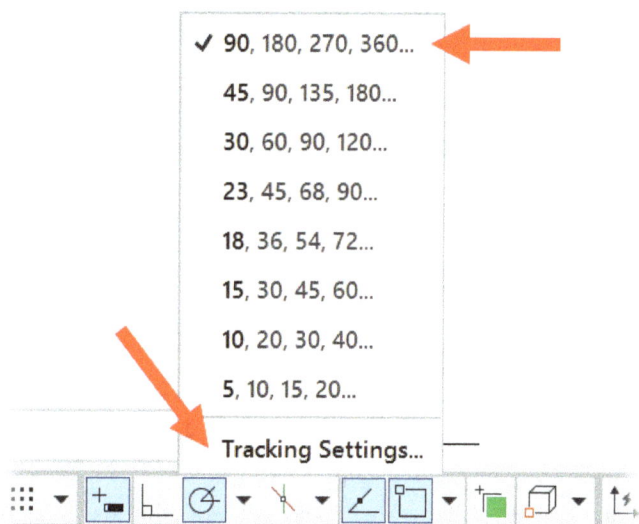

Figure 5.2: The Polar Tracking flyout menu, showing the default angle increment and the location of the flyout arrow

This flyout menu displays the preset angle increments that can be used. These include increments of 90 degrees (*default*), 45 degrees, and 30 degrees, all the way down to 5-degree increments. To view more properties, you can click on **Tracking Settings**. This will open the **Drafting Settings** dialog box with the **Polar Tracking** tab currently open. *Figure 5.3* shows this dialog box:

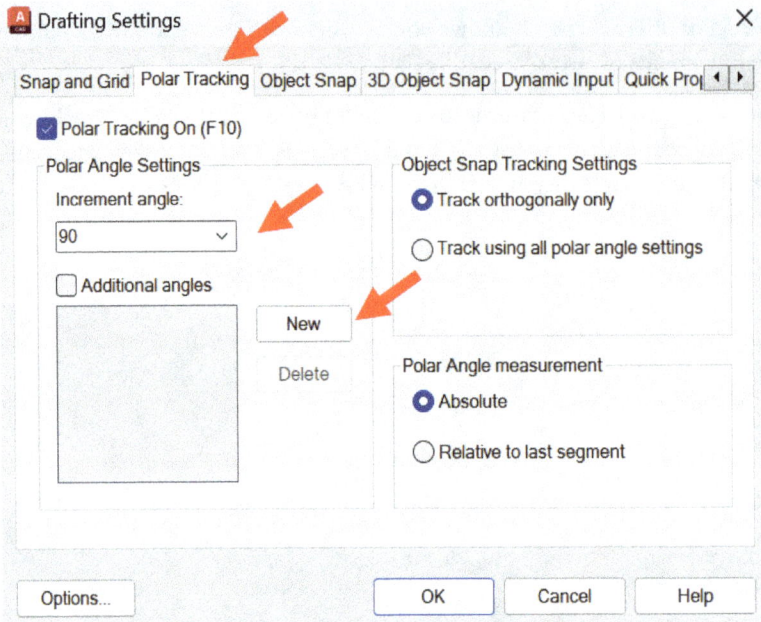

Figure 5.3: The Drafting Settings dialog box with the Polar Tracking tab currently open

In this dialog box, the **Polar Tracking On** checkbox is checked, indicating that **Polar Tracking** (*POLAR*) is currently on (the icon will also be highlighted *blue* on the status bar). The preset angle increments can also be updated in the dialog box, not just selected on the flyout on the status bar. You can do this by using the drop-down menu showing 90 degrees (highlighted by the arrow).

If the **Additional angles** checkbox is checked, you can add individual angle increments by clicking on the **New** button. To remove any unwanted individual angle increments, use the **Delete** button. Unchecking the **Additional angles** box will turn off any additional angles that were added previously.

Now, let's try out **Polar Tracking** with the `BearingCase.dwg` exercise file, which is a 2D drawing of a small bearing case that requires manufacturing. Using a clear area in the file, draw the symmetrical bearing plate outline shown in *Figure 5.4*. The completed bearing plate outline is included in the exercise file for reference:

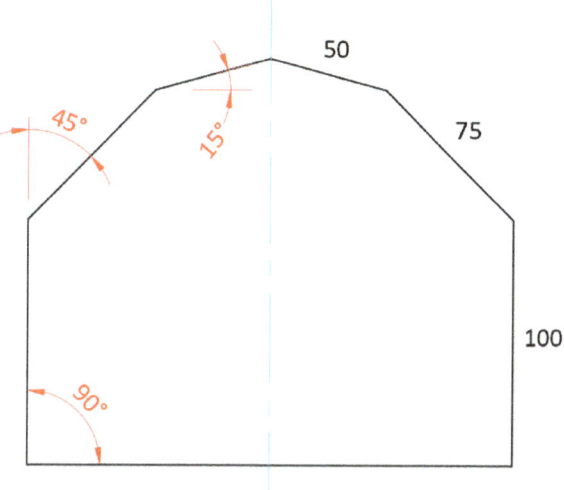

Figure 5.4: The new bearing plate with distances, angles, and centerlines shown for clarity

Draw the outline in the **Model** tab while using the **Polar Tracking** preset's angle increments. Use the 90-degree, 45-degree, and 15-degree angle increment settings. You can draw the outline as lines or as a polyline. Once you've done this, make sure you save your drawing. You can save it with the same filename or use a different filename if you want to differentiate it from the original exercise file.

Polar Tracking allows you to automate the angles at which you draw your AutoCAD geometry, thus saving you from having to input the angles manually. Not only does this enhance your productivity, but it also maintains accuracy and reduces errors.

> Tips and tricks #15
>
> When working with **Polar Tracking** (*POLAR*) in AutoCAD, the drafting settings on the status bar can be changed at any time, even mid-command. When drawing the outline shown in *Figure 5.4*, try to create the outline in one *pass*, changing the polar angle increments on the status bar when needed while using the **Line** (*LINE*) or **Polyline** (*PLINE*) command.

Polar Tracking is a great method to use to automate regularly used angles when drafting and modeling. Make sure it becomes part of your daily workflow when you're designing in AutoCAD.

> AutoCAD for Mac
>
> You'll find **Polar Tracking** (*POLAR*) on the status bar in AutoCAD for Mac. It can be used in the same way as in AutoCAD for Windows.

Now that we know how to get accurate angles with **Polar Tracking**, let's look at achieving orthogonal movements using AutoCAD's **ORTHOMODE**.

Locking the cursor orthogonally with ORTHOMODE

There will be times when you'll need to draw lines that are geometrically straight in both the horizontal and vertical directions. To do this, you can utilize the **Restrict cursor orthogonally** (*ORTHOMODE*) draft setting.

You can turn *ORTHOMODE* on and off by clicking the icon on the status bar, just like other drafting settings. *Figure 5.5* shows the status bar with *ORTHOMODE* on:

Figure 5.5: The AutoCAD status bar with ORTHOMODE on

ORTHOMODE restricts the AutoCAD cursor to only two directions: horizontally and vertically, using the current coordinate system. AutoCAD's default coordinate system is the World Coordinate System, where the *X*-axis (horizontal) and the *Y*-axis (vertical) intersect at the *0,0* coordinates. This is normally known as the **origin**.

In its default setting, **ORTHOMODE** makes sure that any geometry is drawn exactly horizontally and vertically. This is ideal when the geometry that needs to be drawn is perpendicular (at 90 degrees to each other).

Let's learn how to put **ORTHOMODE** into practice. Using the exercise file (`BearingCase.dwg`), create the simple metal plate outline shown in *Figure 5.6* in a clear space in the drawing. You can use the outline layer as the current drafting layer (already provided in the drawing file):

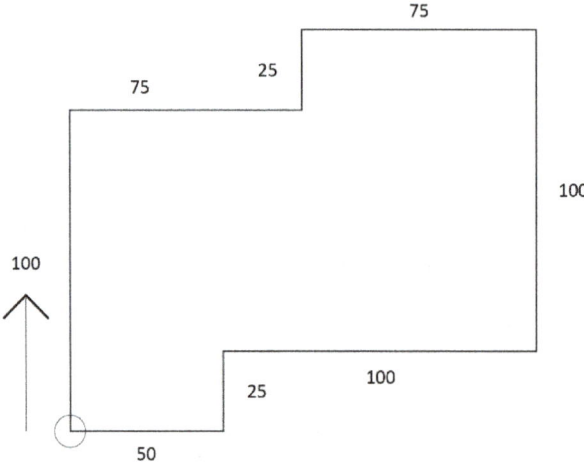

Figure 5.6: The new metal plate outline (dimension text and arrow shown for clarity)

The lengths of the sides of the plate are shown purely for clarity. Just like the new bearing plate shown in *Figure 5.4*, try to draw the plate outline in one go, using either the **Line** (*LINE*) or **Polyline** (*PLINE*) command.

Start at the bottom-left corner of the plate, indicated by the circle, and go in the direction of the arrow, typing in each distance and pressing *Enter* before moving in the direction of the next line segment. You can also use the **Close** right-click shortcut menu option to close the line (or polyline) to the point you started from.

As you draw the plate outline with **ORTHOMODE** on, you'll notice that as you move your mouse to draw the line segments, you can only move the cursor horizontally and vertically, thus negating the need to consider any angle increments. This saves a considerable amount of time when you're drawing regular geometry such as this.

There will be times when exact horizontal and vertical lines will be needed. A typical example would be gridlines on a floor plan, or as in this section, where perpendicular lines are needed for a plate outline. Using **ORTHOMODE** ensures that all the lines are at 90 degrees to each other, hence they're perpendicular.

> Tips and tricks #16
>
> When drawing lines using the **LINE** command, or polylines using the **PLINE** command, there's a neat little workaround you can use if you place a line or polyline segment incorrectly. Simply right-click to bring up the shortcut menu and click **Undo** via the shortcut menu. Note that this won't undo the entire command – it will simply undo the last line (or last polyline) segment that was placed, taking you back to the last point of the last segment. It's also a great way of getting back to a particular point in the line (or polyline) when used multiple times.

Consider using **Ortho Mode** (*ORTHO*) if you have to draft a lot of lines and geometry that are perpendicular (at 90 degrees) to each other. Due to the way that **Ortho Mode** (*ORTHO*) constrains you to the *X* and *Y* axes, it's a great tool for this.

> AutoCAD for Mac
>
> You'll find **Ortho Mode** (*ORTHO*) on the status bar in AutoCAD for Mac. It can be used in the same way as in AutoCAD for Windows, to restrict the cursor orthogonally.

Now that we've discovered the benefits of using **ORTHOMODE**, let's look at how we can work with multiple Osnaps using **Object Snap Tracking** (*AUTOSNAP*).

Using Object Snap Tracking (AUTOSNAP) to draw efficiently with multiple Osnaps

Numerous AutoCAD drafting settings make your daily routine simpler. **Object Snap Tracking** (*AUTOSNAP*) is one of those drafting settings; you'll find that once you've turned **AUTOSNAP** on and used it, you'll never turn it off again.

This drafting setting uses an in-built AutoCAD technology known as **AutoTrack** that tracks which Osnaps you select before combining them and forming a datum point, such as a center, midpoint, or intersection.

When combined with **Object Snaps** (*OSNAP*) and **Polar Tracking** (*POLAR*), **AUTOSNAP** allows you to work with multiple snap points on AutoCAD geometry, giving you the ability to create insertion points and intersection points without the need to generate unnecessary construction lines.

Figure 5.7 shows where you can find the **AUTOSNAP** icon on the status bar. The icon acts simply as an ON/OFF toggle. However, you need to ensure that your running **Object Snaps** (*OSNAP*) are defined and switched on; otherwise, **AUTOSNAP** will be null and void:

Figure 5.7: The status bar with Object Snap Tracking (AUTOSNAP) switched on (arrowed for clarity)

Working with the drawing you used in the previous section, `BearingCase.dwg`, let's learn how to utilize **Object Snap Tracking** (*AUTOSNAP*) so that you can place new geometry in the bearing case that was already in the drawing when you originally opened the DWG file, as shown in *Figure 5.8*.

Use **ZOOM** and **PAN** to centralize the bearing case in the AutoCAD drawing area to make it easier to work on the geometry:

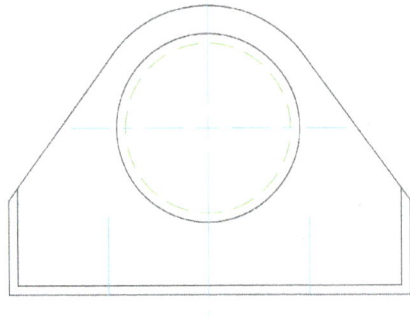

Figure 5.8 – The bearing case, as displayed in the BearingCase.dwg file

Make sure that you have the following drafting settings switched on:

- **Object Snaps** (*OSNAP*)
- **Polar Tracking** (*POLAR*)
- **Object Snap Tracking** (*AUTOSNAP*)

You'll need the following Osnaps switched on:

- **Endpoint**
- **Midpoint**
- **Intersection**
- **Center**

You'll also need to have applied the following polar angle increment: **90, 180, 270, 360….**

For this exercise, you'll be placing two circles inside the bearing case outline to represent two drilled holes. *Figure 5.9* shows how the drawing will look once the two circles have been placed:

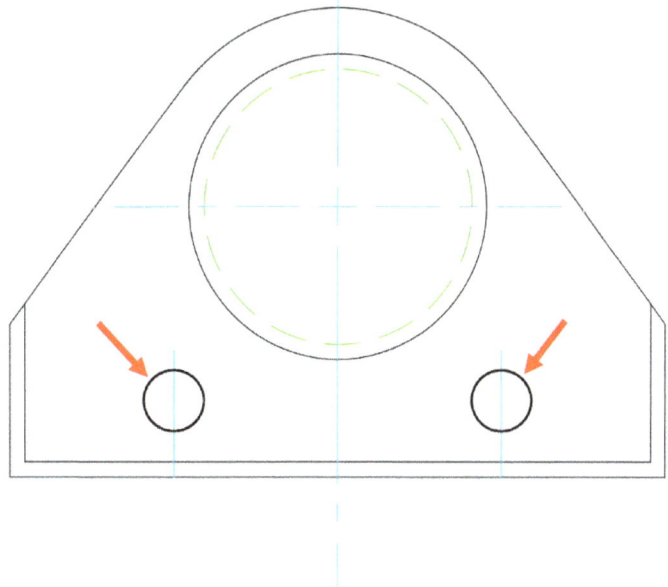

Figure 5.9: The bearing case with the new circles (arrowed and bold for clarity)

104   Developing Advanced Geometry Using Object Snaps

Let's begin this exercise:

1. Select the **Circle** flyout on the **Draw** panel on the **Home** tab on the ribbon to draw the new circles.
2. Then, select **Center, Radius**. AutoCAD will prompt you for the center of the circle to be drawn.

   It's at this point in the workflow that we'll be using **Object Snap Tracking** (*AUTOSNAP*).

3. Using the settings described previously, hover over the **Midpoint** Osnap of the left-hand outside edge of the bearing case in the drawing.

   However, *don't click* on it; simply hover over it for a few seconds. You'll see a small cross symbol appear *inside* the snap symbol. That's **Object Snap Tracking** memorizing the **Midpoint** Osnap.

4. Then, drag your mouse to the right. You'll see the green, dashed tracking line. *Figure 5.10* shows what this will look like onscreen:

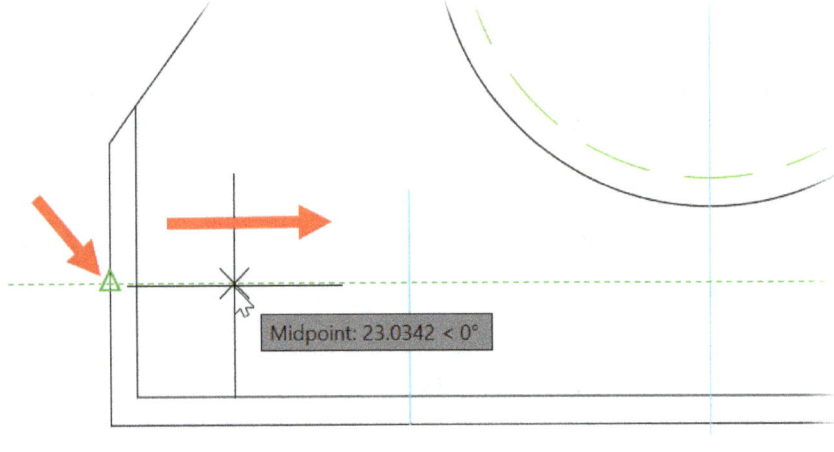

Figure 5.10: The Midpoint Osnap being used as an Object Snap Tracking point (arrowed for clarity)

As you drag your mouse over the blue, vertical centerline to the right of the **Midpoint** Osnap, you'll see an **Intersection** Osnap appear. This is **Object Snap Tracking** picking up the intersection at a 90-degree increment concerning the **Midpoint** Osnap you hovered over. *Figure 5.11* shows the **Intersection** Osnap:

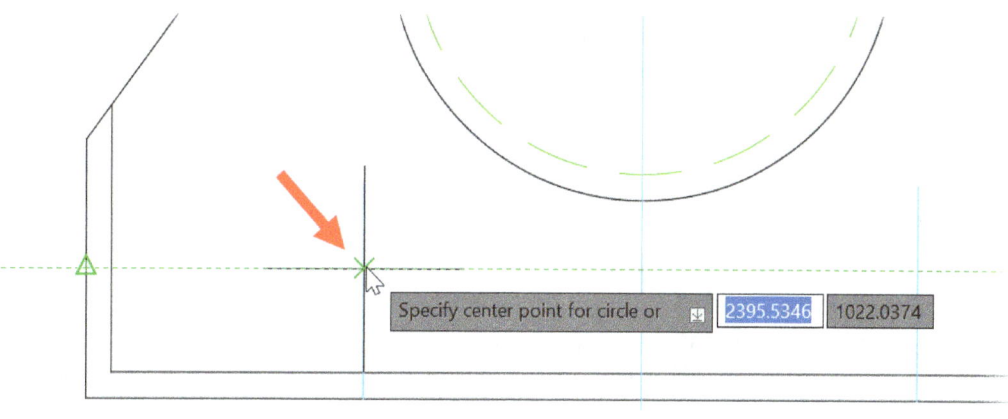

Figure 5.11: The Intersection Osnap aligned with the Midpoint Osnap (arrowed for clarity)

5. Click on the **Intersection** Osnap – that's where your circle center will now be placed. You'll be prompted for a circle radius. Type 10 for the radius value and press *Enter*. The circle will now be placed like so:

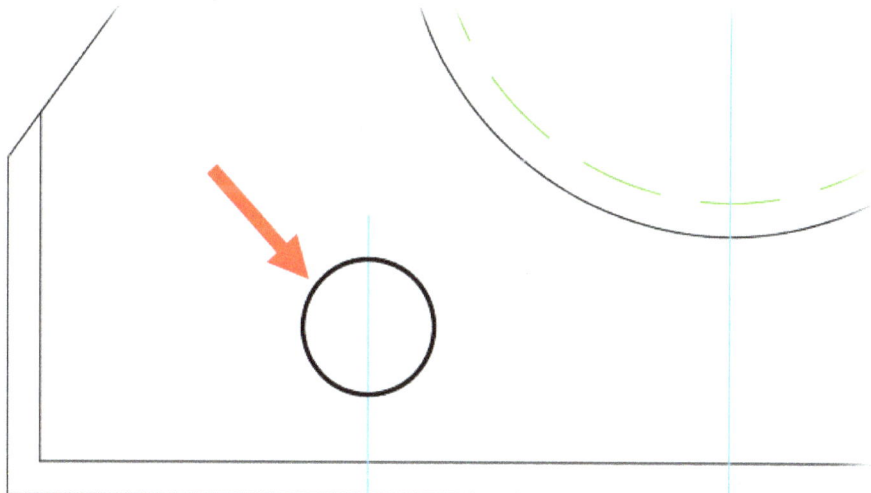

Figure 5.12: The circle placed after using Object Snap Tracking (AUTOSNAP)

6. Using the **Midpoint** Osnap on the right-hand outside edge of the bearing case, repeat this workflow, but drag to the left toward the right-hand, blue, vertical centerline (in the opposite direction to the previous example). This will give you the same result that was shown in *Figure 5.9* but on the other (right) side of the bearing case.

Just using this simple workflow, you can now see the advantages of **Object Snap Tracking** (*AUTOSNAP*). If this wasn't available in AutoCAD, you would have needed to draw sacrificial construction lines to place the **Intersection** Osnaps needed to place the new circles.

AUTOSNAP is a great efficiency tool, negating the need to draw numerous construction lines to obtain the necessary data and snap points. It also removes the need to draw unnecessary geometry that might have to be erased later.

> Tips and tricks #17
>
> **Object Snap Tracking** (*AUTOSNAP*) allows you to use up to seven tracking points in any one reference. This can be any sensible combination of Osnaps or temporary tracking points. When selecting tracking points, no mouse click is required. Simply hover over the point required until the relevant Osnap description appears, but *don't click*! As you hover, AutoCAD will recognize the point as a tracking point and add it to your possible seven points. We're all taught to move our mouse and click when necessary. When using *AUTOSNAP*, you don't need to click!

Make sure you use **Object Snap Tracking** (*AUTOSNAP*) combined with your running Osnaps. That way, you can ensure that you're taking full advantage of the functionality that **Object Snap Tracking** (*AUTOSNAP*) provides.

> AutoCAD for Mac
>
> You'll find **Object Snap Tracking** (*AUTOSNAP*) on the status bar in AutoCAD for Mac. It can be used in the same way as it can in AutoCAD for Windows when working with **Object Snaps** (*OSNAP*) and **Polar Tracking** (*POLAR*).

Object Snap Tracking (*AUTOSNAP*) is a great way to utilize Osnaps. In the next section, we'll learn how to utilize not only our **Object Snaps** (*OSNAP*) but also how to work with **Snap Overrides**.

Drawing accurately and effectively with Object Snaps (OSNAP) and snap overrides

Object Snaps (*OSNAP*) were mentioned in the *Utilizing 3D object snaps when 3D modeling* section in *Chapter 4*, and they're a fundamental function of AutoCAD, making sure that all drafting in 2D and modeling in 3D is performed with accuracy and precision.

You should now be used to the regularly used Osnaps such as **Endpoint**, **Midpoint**, and **Center**. Other typical Osnaps that are used include **Intersection** and **Extension**. If you're not familiar with these, you can use the AutoCAD Help function or take a look at the *Hitchhikers Guide to AutoCAD* (also part of the AutoCAD Help function – it can be found in AutoCAD's **Start** tab).

Drawing accurately and effectively with Object Snaps (OSNAP) and snap overrides

In this section, we'll look at some of the lesser-used Osnaps that can help you become more efficient and productive. We'll also continue to work with the `BearingCase.dwg` file that you used in the previous sections of this chapter.

All of your Osnaps can be accessed via the AutoCAD status bar, which is located at the bottom right of the AutoCAD application window. You can also type `OSNAP`, and press *Enter*. This will open the **Drafting Settings** dialog box of the **Object Snaps** tab.

Object Snaps (*OSNAP*) is an AutoCAD drafting setting and is normally displayed on the status bar by default. The icon is normally switched on (blue), with the **Endpoint** and **Center** Osnaps set as running Osnaps.

Running Osnaps are snaps that are switched on and always available when drafting. *Osnap overrides* are the snaps that haven't been switched on but can be used when you're overriding the running Osnaps. We'll learn more about **Snap Overrides** later in this section.

The **OSNAP** drafting setting is displayed on the status bar, as shown in *Figure 5.13*:

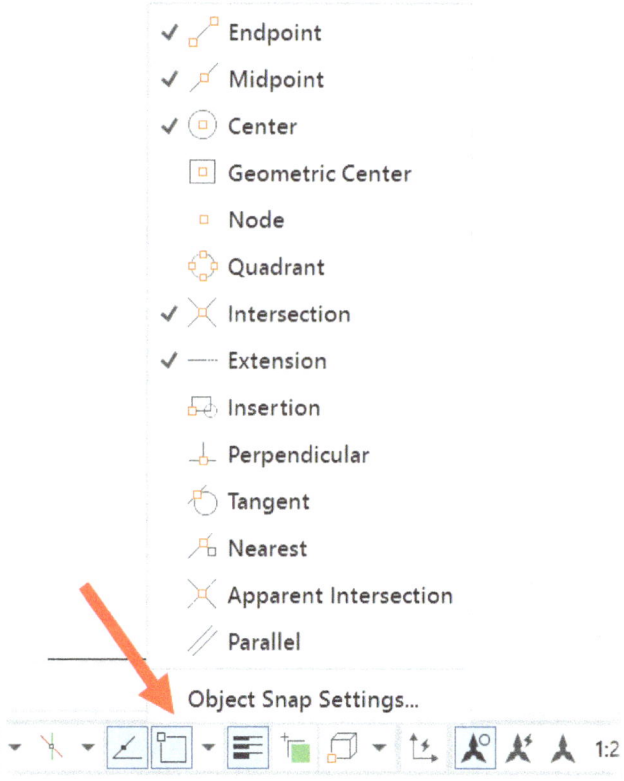

Figure 5.13: The flyout Object Snaps (OSNAP) menu on the status bar, displayed after clicking on the Osnap icon (arrowed)

The preceding figure also displays the flyout menu that's available when clicking on the flyout arrow to the right of the **OSNAP** icon on the status bar. This menu displays the currently running Osnaps, all shown with check marks. A check mark indicates that the Osnap is on. A non-checked Osnap is off.

> **Tips and tricks #18**
>
> You can also select **Object Snap Settings…** from the flyout menu. This will display the **Drafting Settings** dialog box, with the **Object Snap** tab currently open. In this tab, you can clear all existing running Osnaps and select *ALL* Osnaps as running Osnaps. However, doing this isn't recommended because you then have no geometry snaps to snap to, leading to drafting inaccuracies. You can also turn **Object Snaps** on and off from this dialog box, as well as **Object Snap Tracking**.

Object Snaps (*OSNAP*) are fundamental to accurate and precise drafting and modeling. Make sure you use them when you're creating your designs.

> **AutoCAD for Mac**
>
> You'll find **Object Snaps** (*OSNAP*) on the status bar in AutoCAD for Mac. It can be used in the same way as in AutoCAD for Windows, including selecting **Settings…** to display the **Drafting Settings** dialog box with the **Object Snap** tab displayed.

A good set of running Osnaps is **Endpoint**, **Midpoint**, **Center**, **Intersection**, and **Extension**. It's advisable not to select all of them as running Osnaps as this becomes unworkable; AutoCAD will try and snap to every Osnap available.

The set of running Osnaps shown checked in *Figure 5.13* should have you in good stead for most of your drafting and modeling tasks. However, there may be times when alternative Osnaps might need to be running. For example, a circle has various Osnaps. The most obvious is **Center**, but you might also use the **Quadrant** Osnap or the **Tangent** Osnap when working with circle geometry.

Finding the Geometric Center

One of the alternative Osnaps that can be incredibly useful is a newer snap known as **Geometric Center**. In the same way that the **Center** Osnap snaps to the center of an arc or a circle, **Geometric Center** snaps to the geometric center of a closed geometric shape, such as a closed polyline.

In this section, you'll convert the existing geometry of a bearing case into a closed polyline and find the **Geometric Center** Osnap. Then, you'll use the located **Geometric Center** to place a circle.

To do this, you'll need the exercise file, `BearingCase.dwg`, the external outline of which is made up of individual lines and an arc. Follow these steps to find the Geometric Center Osnap:

1. Type PE. You'll see **PE** (*EDIT*) in the **Dynamic Input** suggestion menu. Click on it; the **Select polyline or** prompt will appear.
2. Select the arc on the outline of the bearing case, as shown in *Figure 5.14*:

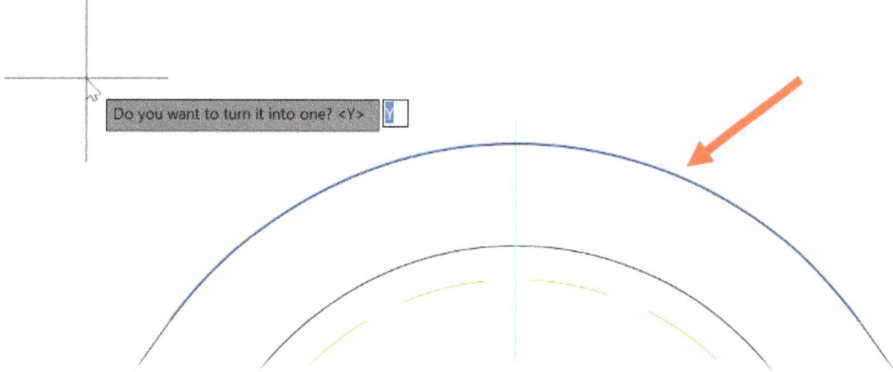

Figure 5.14: The selected arc with the relevant AutoCAD prompt displayed

You'll receive a prompt stating **Do you want to turn it into one? <Y>**.

3. Press *Enter* when the default **Y** option is highlighted. This confirms that you want the selected arc to be converted into a polyline segment. Typing **N** and pressing *Enter* will stop the arc from being converted into a polyline segment. The **Edit Polyline** (*PEDIT*) menu will appear, as shown in *Figure 5.15*:

Figure 5.15: The Edit Polyline menu with Join highlighted and arrowed

4. Select **Join** from the flyout menu and select all the remaining elements that form the bearing case outline. *Figure 5.16* shows all the selected elements, which AutoCAD highlights in blue.

   Note that at this point, you can re-select the arc you originally selected earlier. It won't affect the **Edit Polyline** (*PEDIT*) command's workflow:

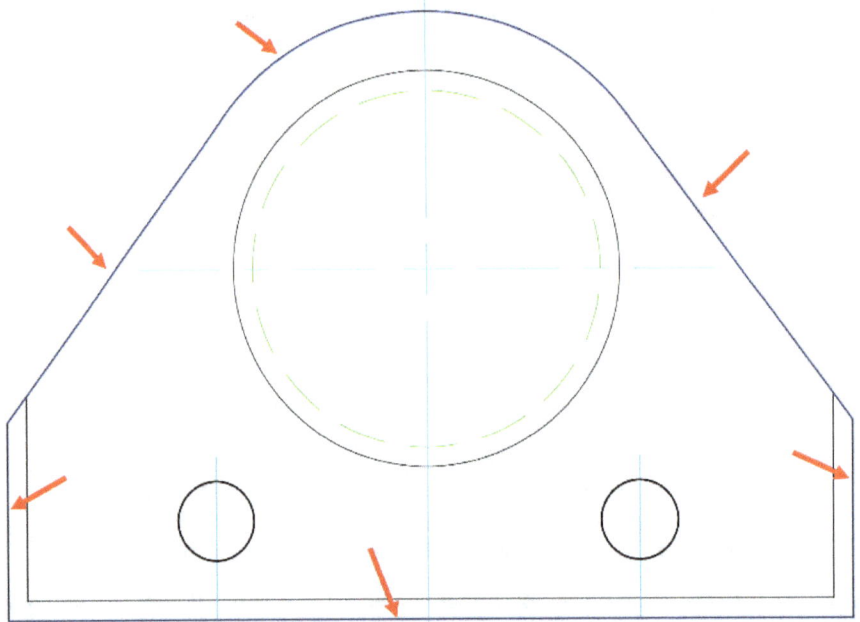

Figure 5.16: The selected elements (arrowed) to be joined into a polyline using the Edit Polyline (PEDIT) command

5. Press *Enter*. You'll be returned to the menu.
6. Press *Enter* again to close the **Edit Polyline** (*PEDIT*) command.

   The external boundary of the bearing case is now a closed polyline.

7. Click on it to select it. You'll see that it's now one closed object with blue AutoCAD grips, as shown in *Figure 5.17*:

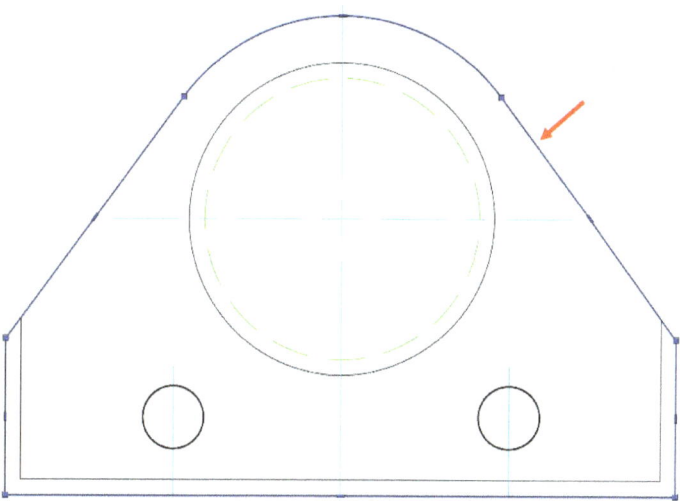

Figure 5.17: The selected polyline with grips displayed

8. Click on the **Object Snaps** flyout menu on the status bar, as shown in *Figure 5.13*.
9. From the menu, click **Geometric Center**. You'll see a check mark appear next to it. It's now a running Osnap.
10. Select the **Circle, Radius** command from the **Circle** flyout menu of the **Draw** panel on the **Home** tab on the ribbon. You'll be prompted for the center of the circle.
11. Hover your cursor/crosshair over any part of the newly created outside polyline. Ignoring the other Osnaps, you'll see a small asterisk-like symbol (*) toward the center of the bearing case, as shown (arrowed) in *Figure 5.18*.

This is the **Geometric Center** Osnap:

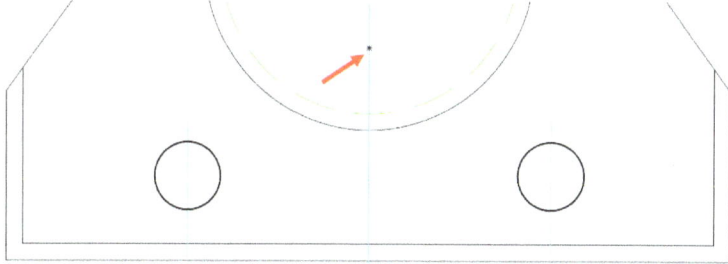

Figure 5.18: The Geometric Center Osnap (arrowed) of the bearing case outline polyline

112 Developing Advanced Geometry Using Object Snaps

12. Move the cursor/crosshair over the Osnap (it will be highlighted with a green circle) and click. This will now be the center of your circle.
13. Type 15 as the radius value and press *Enter*. You'll see your new circle appear, as shown in *Figure 5.19*:

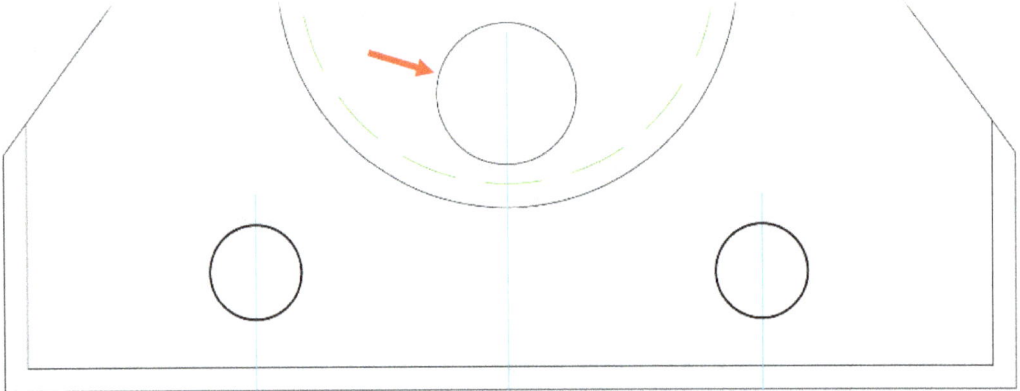

Figure 5.19: The new circle (arrowed) placed with the Geometric Center Osnap

In closed polylines, such as a rectangle or a square, we can use the **Midpoint** Osnaps of opposing sides to find the geometric center. However, this method may not work in irregular shapes, such as the bearing case outline. This is why using the geometric center is an extremely accurate method of finding the exact center of a shape that might not conform to the usual constraints.

Working with Snap Overrides

Sometimes, you don't want to set an Osnap as a running Osnap. This is where your Osnap overrides become useful. Known as **Osnap Overrides**, you can use it to override the running Osnaps to utilize just one specific Osnap for one-off usage.

Osnap Overrides allows you to use Osnaps that aren't currently set in the Osnaps drafting setting. You can always gain access to **Osnap Overrides** without a command running. You can do this by holding down the *Shift* key and right-clicking. This will bring up the **Osnap Overrides** menu at any time. Note that it's more useful if this is performed in a command workflow as you then have access to **Snap Overrides** within the command you're working in. *Figure 5.20* shows the **Osnap Overrides** menu when accessed with the *Shift* and right-click method:

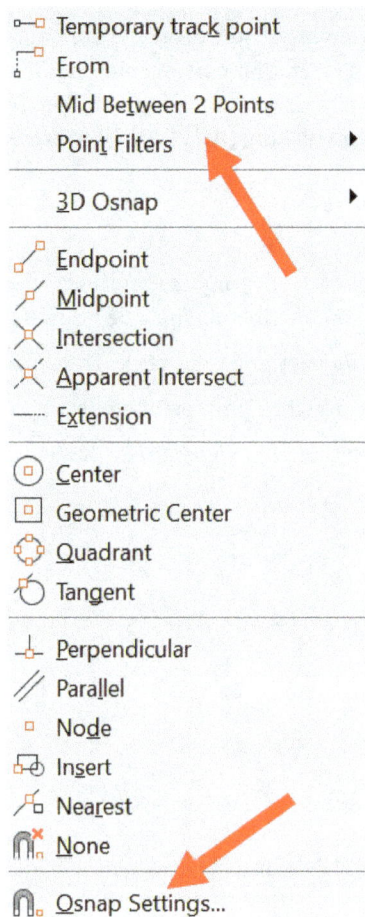

Figure 5.20: The Osnap Overrides menu displayed when using Shift and right-click

Note that in *Figure 5.20*, you can still gain access to the **Drafting Settings** dialog box by clicking on **Osnap Settings…** (arrowed). This will open the dialog box with the **Object Snap** tab currently displayed, in the same way as when using the **Object Snaps** flyout menu on the status bar.

Several alternative Osnaps are incredibly useful, especially when used in a command workflow. To explore Osnaps further, take a look at the Autodesk website: `https://help.autodesk.com/view/ACD/2023/ENU/?guid=GUID-8F5E5431-9EFB-414E-BC6D-2C65EFB2DAC3`.

We're going to look at one of the alternative Osnaps, called **Mid Between 2 Points** (*M2P*). This snap function is highlighted with an arrow in *Figure 5.20*.

This snap allows you to specify two points on any geometry (or coordinates) and find the midpoint between them. We'll be using this to create some new centerlines in the BearingCase.dwg file, so make sure you're using the **Centerlines** layer as the current layer. Also, ensure that you have **Polar Tracking** (*POLAR*), and **Object Snap Tracking** (*AUTOSNAP*) switched on. They should be displayed in blue on the status bar.

To create new centerlines, follow these steps:

1. Zoom to the lower left corner of the bearing case outline. Select the **Line** command from the **Draw** panel of the **Home** tab on the ribbon. You'll be prompted for the first point of the line.
2. At this point, hold down the *Shift* key and right-click. The **Osnap Overrides** menu will appear.
3. Click **Mid Between 2 Points**. You'll be prompted to select **First point of mid**.
4. Click on the **Endpoint** Osnap shown in *Figure 5.21*. This will be the first midpoint:

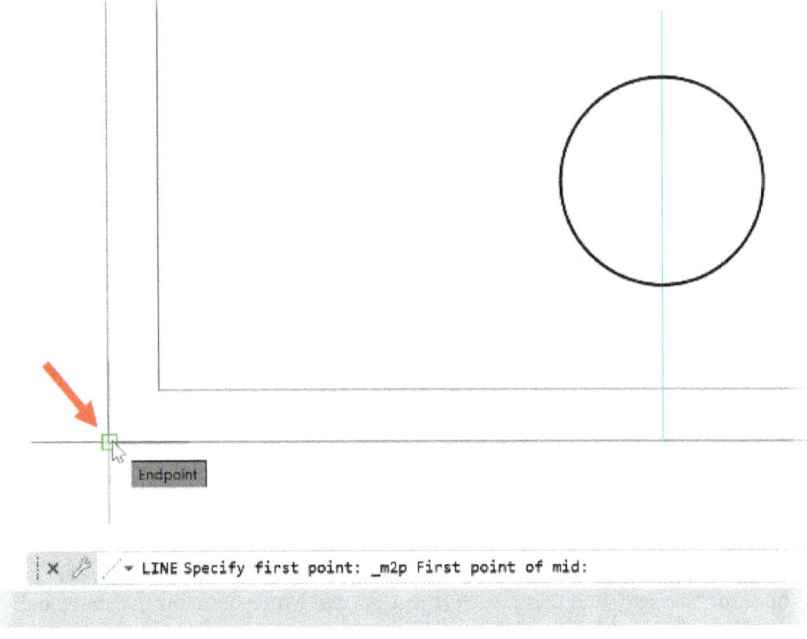

Figure 5.21: The first midpoint is the Endpoint Osnap shown (arrowed)

5. Then, click on the **Endpoint** Osnap shown in *Figure 5.22*. This will be the second midpoint:

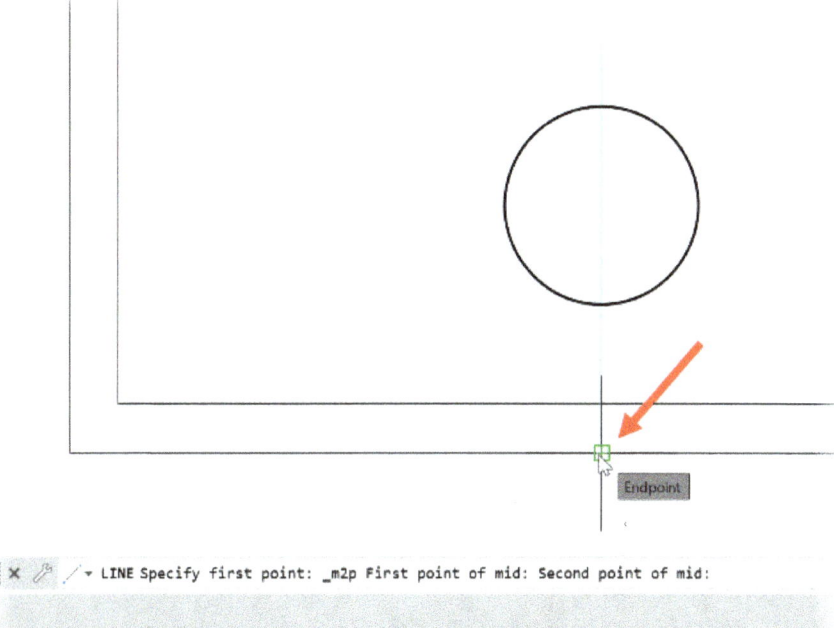

Figure 5.22: The second midpoint is the Endpoint Osnap shown (arrowed)

The first point of your new centerline will now be on the lower edge of the bearing case outline (point **1** in *Figure 5.23*), between the two midpoints that have been selected.

6. Drag your mouse and hover over the top endpoint of the existing centerline, shown as point **2** in *Figure 5.23*. This will activate **Object Snap Tracking** (*AUTOSNAP*) for that **Endpoint** Osnap:

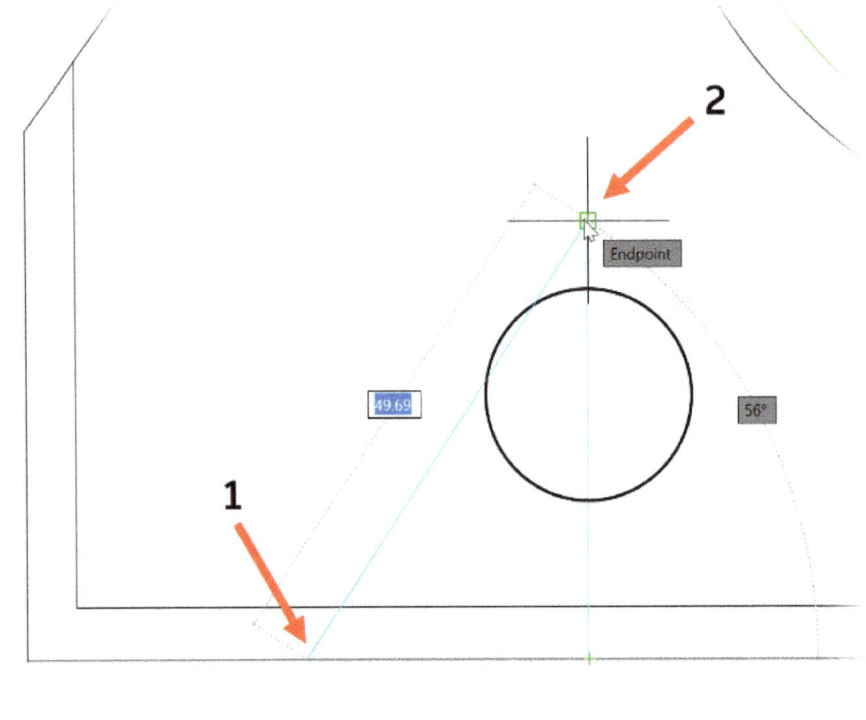

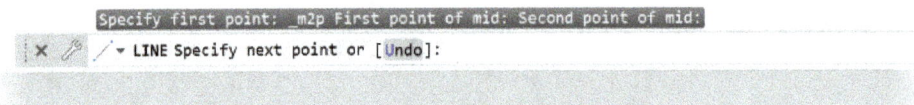

Figure 5.23: The M2P Osnap override has placed the first point of the line (1). Hovering over the Endpoint Osnap of the existing centerline (2) creates an Object Snap Tracking point

7. Remember not to click on it, and then drag your mouse to the left, as shown in *Figure 5.24*:

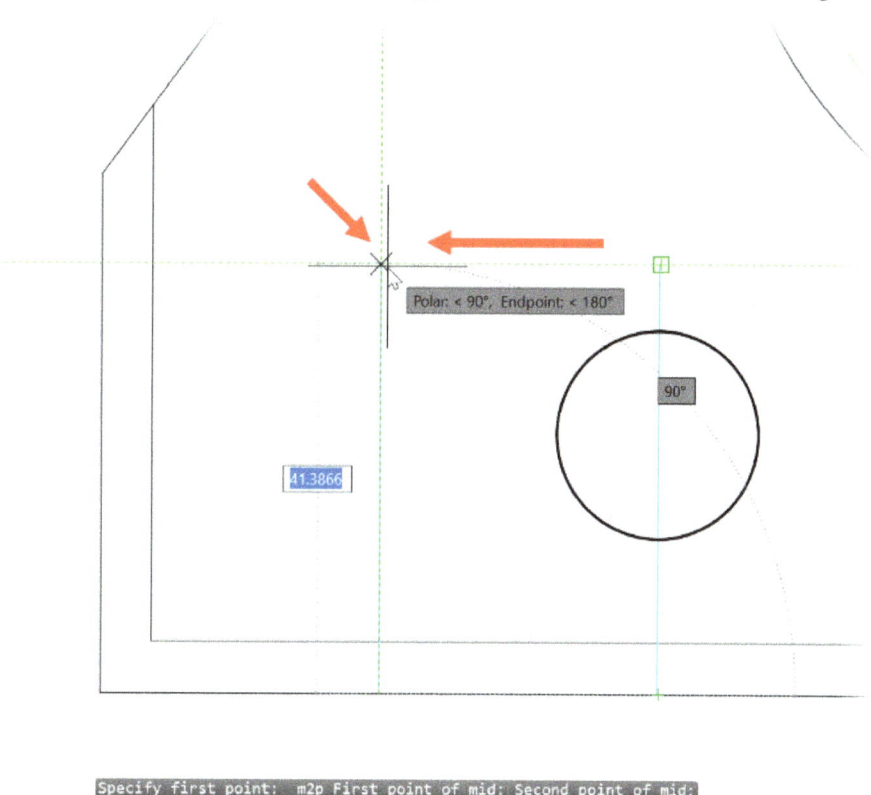

Figure 5.24: Moving to the left (arrowed) to create the Object Snap Tracking point for the second point (endpoint) of the new centerline

8. Click on the point indicated when the vertical and horizontal tracking lines intersect (shown as green dashed lines). This will be the endpoint of your centerline.
9. Press *Enter* to close the **Line** command.

At the end of this workflow, you'll have a new centerline that's the same length as the existing centerline, to the left of the existing centerline and circle, as shown in *Figure 5.25*.

If you wish, you can now repeat this workflow on the right-hand side of the bearing case to create another new centerline. This would be great practice to reinforce how to utilize the **Mid Between 2 Points** (*M2P*) Osnap function:

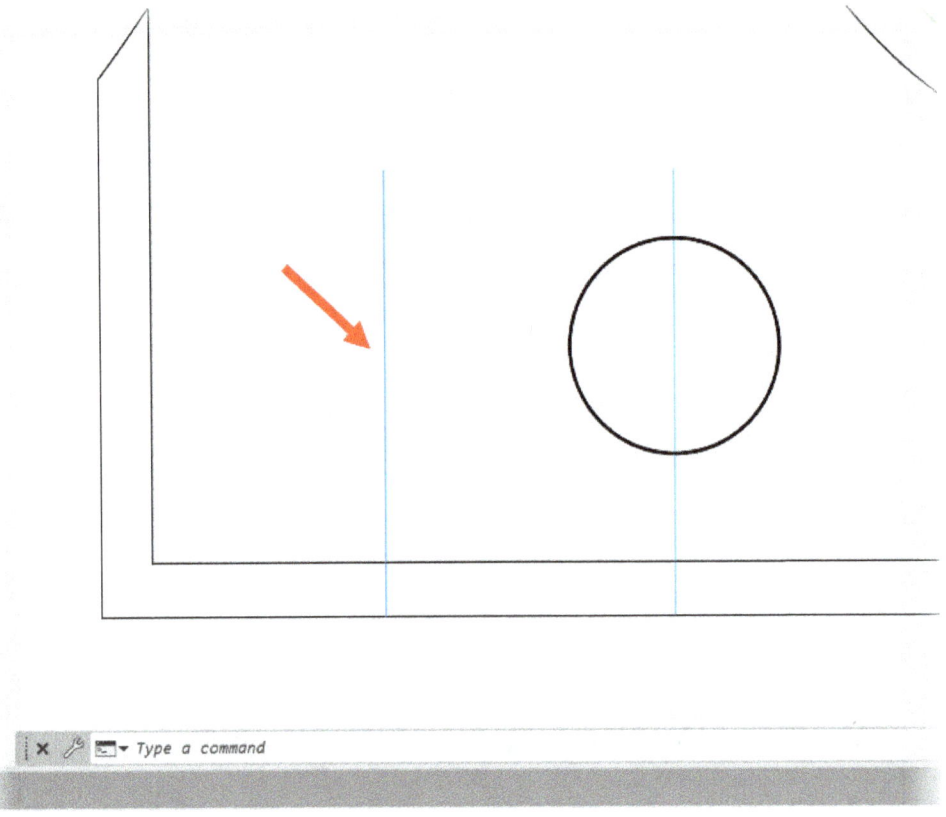

Figure 5.25: The new centerline, placed using the M2P Osnap function

> **Tips and tricks #19**
>
> You can also select **Osnap Overrides** from the right-click shortcut menu in the middle of a command. This is an alternative to the *Shift* and right-click method. Simply right-click mid-command and select **Osnap Overrides** from the shortcut menu. This will bring up the same menu you see when you use the *Shift* and right-click method. However, note that you can only bring this menu up *after* the first point (or base point) of the geometry has been placed. You'll always need to use *Shift* and right-click for the first point (or base point).

You're now conversant with not only Osnaps in AutoCAD but also how to utilize **Snap Overrides**. This will make for highly accurate and more efficient drafting and modeling.

Summary

In this chapter, we learned how to work with **Polar Tracking** (*POLAR*) and use it effectively when creating geometry and objects.

You also learned how to utilize orthographic projection and draft straight and perpendicular geometry with the **ORTHOMODE** setting.

Then, you learned about **Object Snap Tracking** (*AUTOSNAP*), an intuitive drafting tool that removes the need for sacrificial construction lines. When combined with both **Polar Tracking** (*POLAR*) and **Object Snaps** (*OSNAP*), it allows for highly accurate drafting and modeling.

After, you learned how to use the **Geometric Center** Osnap, one of the lesser-used Osnaps, and draft effectively with it.

Finally, you learned how to use a quick, on-the-fly method of snapping to existing geometry using **Osnap Overrides**.

The Osnaps and settings demonstrated in this chapter unraveled how important they are when drafting in AutoCAD. They're fundamental to the accuracy and precision of any geometry created to further your design.

Osnaps allow you to work with your drafting tools in AutoCAD to their full advantage. And some Osnaps can be incredibly useful. **Geometric Center** and **Mid Between 2 Points** (*M2P*) are just two of the lesser-known Osnaps that can make your daily AutoCAD work much easier to manage.

In the next chapter, we'll learn how to modify and measure geometry and existing objects in AutoCAD drawings by using commands such as **Quick Measure** and **Distance**.

Get This Book's PDF Version and Exclusive Extras

Scan the QR code (or go to packtpub.com/unlock). Search for this book by name, confirm the edition, and then follow the steps on the page.

Note: Keep your invoice handy. Purchases made directly from Packt don't require one.

6
Measuring and Modifying Geometry and Objects

Accuracy is paramount when you are working with AutoCAD. If you are developing the design of a gasket for a car engine, for instance, the gasket must fit exactly to ensure the safe and economical running of the engine.

To achieve such accuracy, AutoCAD users tend to spend a lot of time modifying geometry and objects in drawings, often needing to measure lengths, areas, and angles.

With AutoCAD, you have a comprehensive set of drafting and modeling tools at your disposal that allow you to modify and measure the geometry quickly and accurately in your design as well as your DWG files. This chapter shows you how to make these modifications and measurements using some of the lesser-known AutoCAD tools available. This will expand your AutoCAD knowledge and allow you to modify and measure smarter, not harder when working with AutoCAD daily.

You will learn about the following:

- Using Noun/verb selection for quick and easy object selection
- Calculating lengths with Quick Measure and Distance
- Adding and subtracting areas using the Area tool
- Measuring precise angles with the Angle tool
- Refining drawings using Modify tools

In *Chapter 5*, you looked at how you could develop advanced geometry using AutoCAD's object snaps. In this chapter, you will not only utilize these object snaps but will also use some interesting AutoCAD tools combined with those snaps to achieve pinpoint accuracy when calculating distances, areas, and angles.

Exercise files

You must ensure you have downloaded the exercise files, `Sawblade.dwg`, `Sawblade2.dwg`, and `Sawblade3.dwg` to follow the sections in this chapter.

Using Noun/verb selection for quick and easy object selection

Noun/verb selection is normally on by default in AutoCAD. It allows you to select AutoCAD objects *before* executing the appropriate command to manipulate the selected objects.

It is a particularly useful feature as it saves you from a longer and relatively more complex workflow. Without **Noun/verb selection**, you would be forced to choose a command first, then select objects at the **Select objects** prompt, and then press *Enter* to confirm object selection before using the command on the selected objects.

Even though this is a default setting, it's best to check that it's enabled. To get to it, simply right-click with no objects selected and no commands running, and then select **Options** on the shortcut menu. Alternatively, you can click on the AutoCAD icon (top left) to open **Application Menu** and find the **Options** button there.

You will find **Noun/verb selection** in the **Selection** tab of the **Options** dialog box. As shown in *Figure 6.1*, the **Noun/verb selection** checkbox appears at the top left.

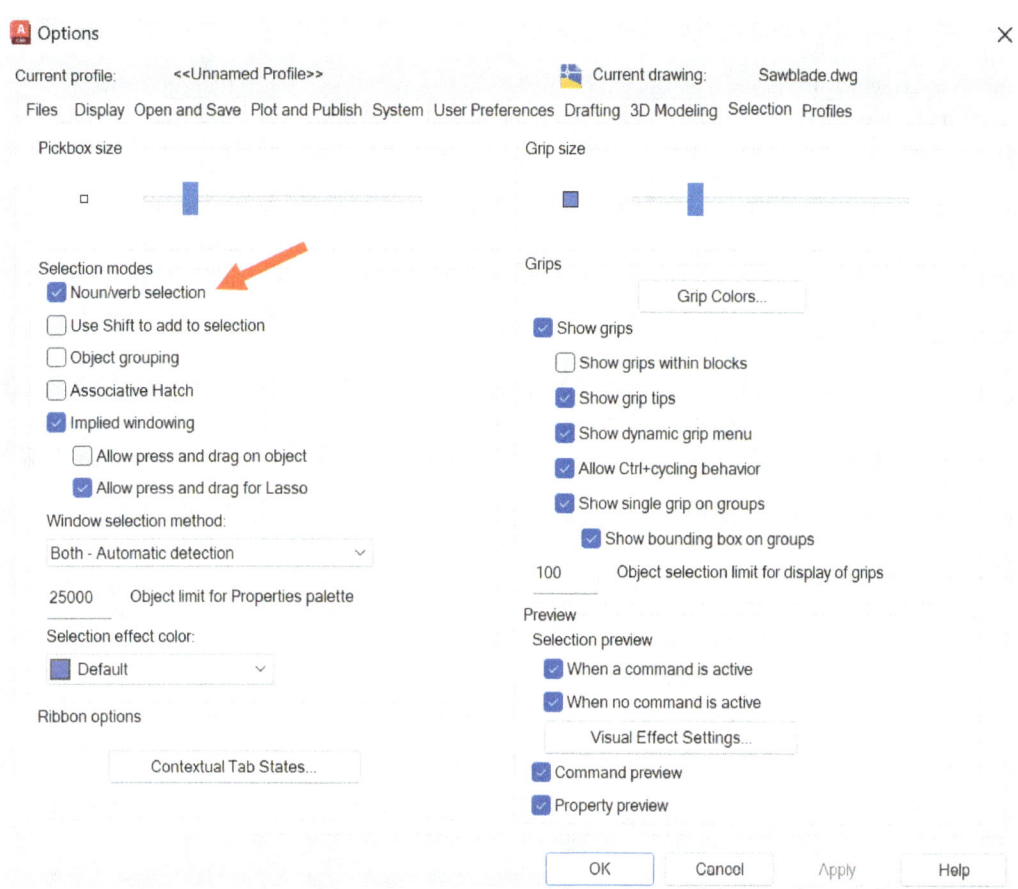

Figure 6.1: The Options dialog box with Noun/verb selection checked

You will notice that the **Noun/verb selection** checkbox is already checked, which means that **Noun/verb selection** is switched *on*. The **Noun/verb selection** checkbox works similarly to a human brain when picking up an object. Before picking up an object (*noun*), it will choose the object first and then pick it up (*verb*).

> **Tips and tricks #20**
>
> **Noun/verb selection** *should* be switched on by default in any AutoCAD installation. However, users do (sometimes) switch it off. A typical reason might be that more than one object needs to be selected. With **Noun/verb selection** off, the command (*verb*) can be selected first, followed by the **Select objects** prompt (*noun*), where multiple objects can easily be selected, followed by the *Enter* key to confirm selection during the command workflow. Depending on personal preference, this type of workflow might be adopted by the user. To get the most out of this chapter, it would be ideal if you keep it switched on. You can also type PICKFIRST and press *Enter* to change the variable value. To turn it on, **PICKFIRST** should be set to **1**. Setting it to **0** (zero) turns it off.

Noun/verb selection is incredibly useful. It makes for a much more fluid AutoCAD experience. Try using AutoCAD with it and without it, and you will see the difference it makes to your daily AutoCAD workflow.

> **AutoCAD for Mac**
>
> **Noun/verb selection** is not supported in AutoCAD for Mac. You will also find that the **Options** dialog box is called **Application Preferences**. You can find this by clicking on **AutoCAD 2024** (top left – if you use the 2024 version; it will be **AutoCAD 2023** for AutoCAD 2023, etc.). Select **Preferences…** and the **Application Preferences** dialog box will open. Mac users can utilize this dialog box to manage their AutoCAD settings. These settings include **Look & Feel**, where the user interface can be adapted to suit the Mac user, and **Units & Guides**, where the user can set specific source content units and target drawing units, similar to how they would be set in the Windows version of AutoCAD. The dialog box is shown in *Figure 6.2*.

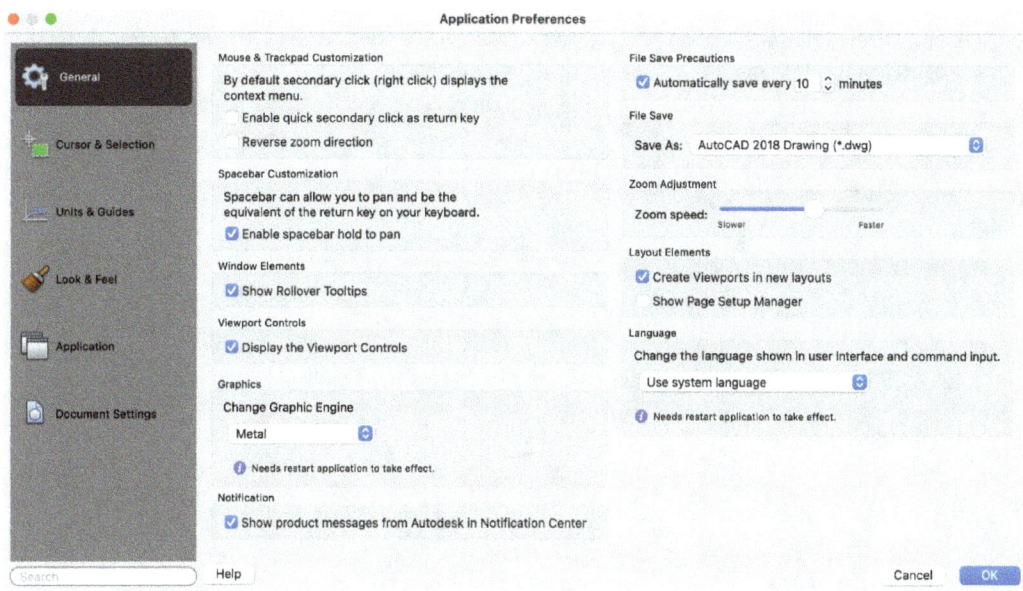

Figure 6.2: The Application Preferences dialog box in AutoCAD for Mac

Now that we have learned how to use the **Noun/verb selection** feature, let us look at other AutoCAD tools: **Quick Measure** and **Distance**.

Calculating lengths and angles with Quick Measure and Distance

AutoCAD is a drafting application that allows you to communicate your design intent. With that intent comes the need to measure distances accurately.

In versions of AutoCAD from AutoCAD 2021 onward, you can do this in two ways:

- **Quick Measure**: This tool measures all distances and angles as you move the cursor over the geometry in your drawings
- **Distance**: This tool measures individual distances (lengths) using object snaps for precision and accuracy

Using the `Sawblade.dwg` file, you will now use both tools to accurately measure distances (and, in the case of **Quick Measure**, angles as well). Follow these steps to see how:

1. Open the `Sawblade.dwg` file and zoom into the saw teeth at the top of the circular sawblade.

126 Measuring and Modifying Geometry and Objects

2. On the **Home** tab on the ribbon, click on the **Measure** flyout on the **Utilities** panel. You will see **Quick** (**Quick Measure**), as shown in *Figure 6.3*. Click on it.

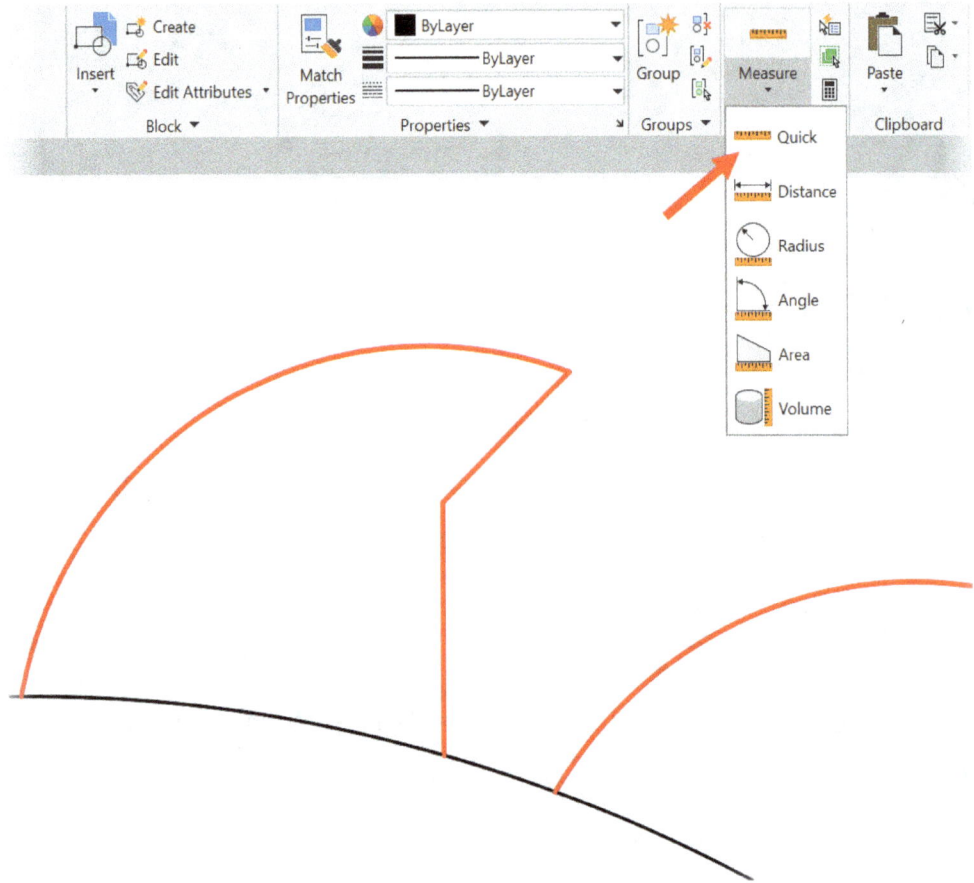

Figure 6.3: The Measure flyout with Quick Measure (arrowed)

3. Move the cursor around the sawblade in the drawing file. You will see numerous measurements shown, including angles, as shown in *Figure 6.4*.

   The geometry being measured is highlighted in a different color (purple) than the geometry color. Also, note that arc lengths are measured.

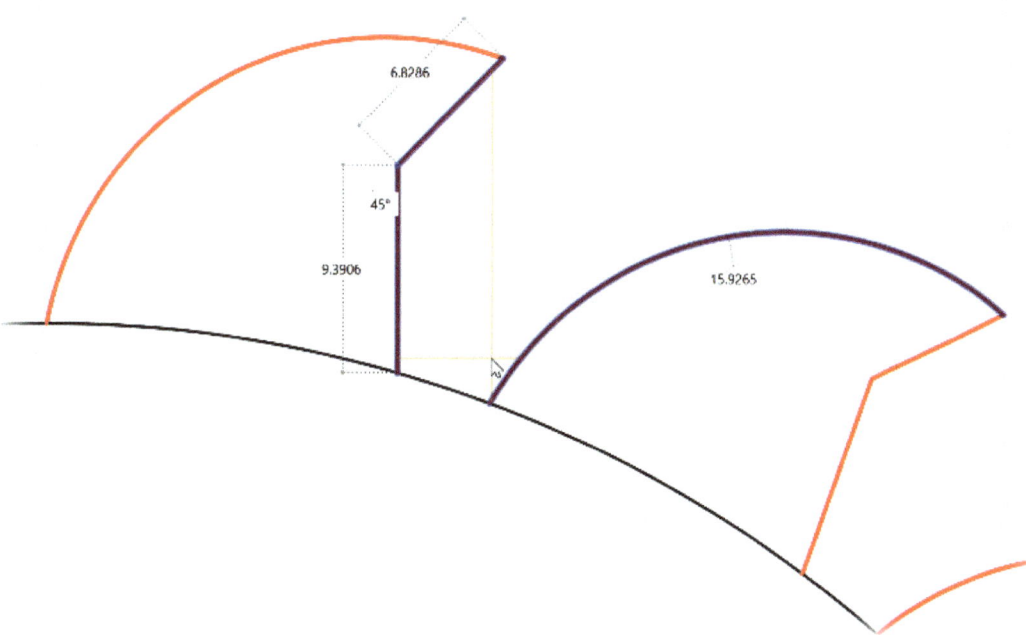

Figure 6.4: Measured geometry shown highlighted by Quick Measure

4. To close **Quick Measure**, hit *Esc* on the keyboard. You can also right-click and select **Enter** on the shortcut menu.
5. Check that your object snaps are *on* down on the status bar and, again, click on the **Measure** flyout. This time, select **Distance**.
6. You will be prompted to select a point to measure from. This is why you need object snaps to measure the distance accurately.
7. Select the lower point on the saw tooth (shown as **1** in *Figure 6.5*), and then select the point below it (shown as **2** in *Figure 6.5*).
8. The measured distance will then be displayed, along with the **Measure** menu, so you can continue measuring using any of the **Measure** tools, as shown in *Figure 6.5*.

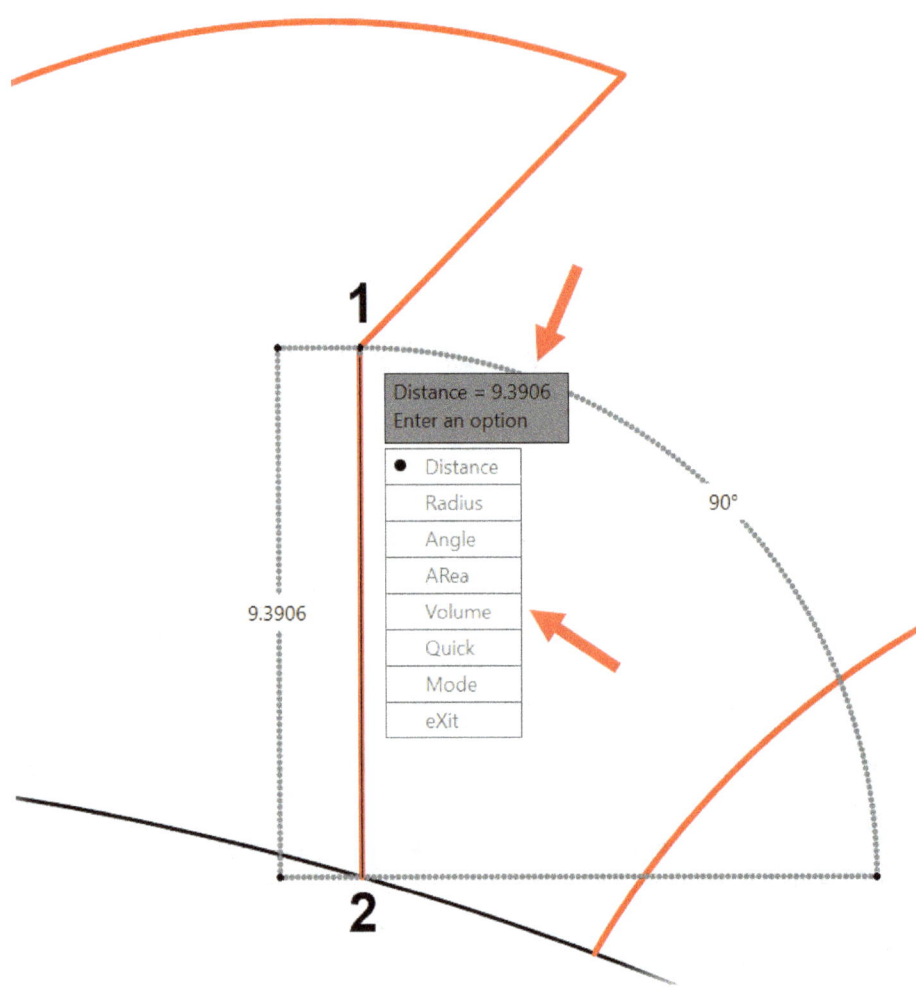

Figure 6.5: Using the Distance tool to measure between points

9. You can select **eXit** in the **Measure** menu to close the tool anytime or press *Esc* on the keyboard to cancel the **Measure** (*MEASUREGEOM*) command.

Quick Measure is a great way of checking existing distances and angles visually when you just need to look at and confirm them. The **Distance** tool allows for more detailed measurement of existing distances, utilizing accuracy tools such as **Object Snap**.

> **AutoCAD for Mac**
>
> The **Measure** (*MEASUREGEOM*) command is available in AutoCAD for Mac, but there is no default icon or flyout menu. Simply type MEASUREGEOM and press *return* to activate the **Measure** tools, and right-click to bring up the shortcut menu that will display the measuring tools available in the command, such as **Quick Measure** and **Distance**.

You now know how to measure distances and angles effectively in AutoCAD, utilizing **Quick Measure** and **Distance**. Let us now look at how we can add and subtract areas using the **Area** tool.

Adding and subtracting areas using the Area tool

Sometimes, areas will need to be calculated from your AutoCAD geometry. The **Area** tool in the **Measure** (*MEASUREGEOM*) command allows you to do this quickly, easily, and, more importantly, accurately.

The workflow of this tool is similar to that of **Quick Measure** and **Distance**. However, you can use the **Area** tool to perform simple area calculations by adding and subtracting areas of geometry, such as closed polylines.

In the following exercise, you will quickly and accurately add and subtract areas in order to calculate a final required area:

1. Open the Sawblade2.dwg file. Note that there is a closed polyline forming the outline of the saw teeth and a central circle representing the hole in the center of the saw plate.
2. As with **Quick Measure** and **Distance**, select the **Measure** flyout from the **Utilities** panel on the **Home** tab on the ribbon. Click on **Area**.
3. You will see the **Specify first corner point** prompt. This is for when you may need to select individual points around an area to define it. You can do this using object snaps, but you don't need to do this, as your areas are fully closed by a closed polyline (saw teeth) and a circle (the hole in the saw plate).
4. Right-click and select **Add area** on the shortcut menu. You will get the same corner point prompt. Simply ignore it and right-click again. Select **Object** on the shortcut menu. You will now see the **(ADD mode) Select objects:** prompt, as shown in *Figure 6.6*.

130   Measuring and Modifying Geometry and Objects

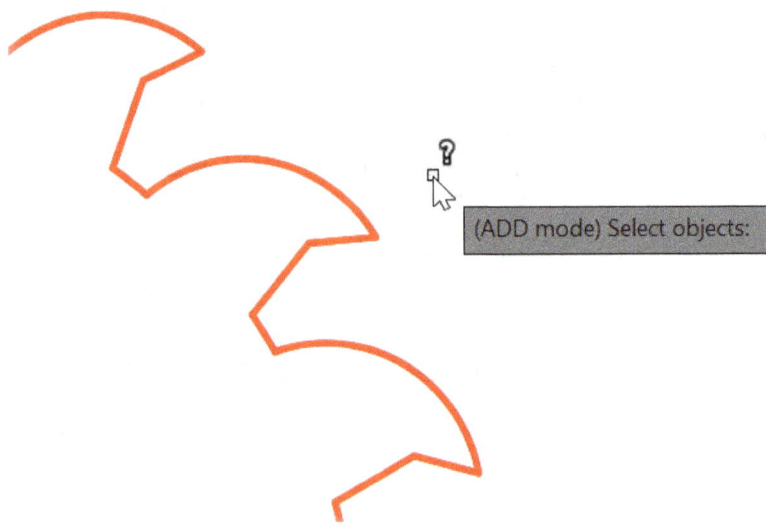

Figure 6.6: (ADD mode) Select objects, ready to select the saw teeth

5. Select the saw teeth. They are a closed polyline, so they will be selected as one object. They will highlight green, showing the area added, as shown in *Figure 6.7*. Press *Enter* to confirm the selection.

Figure 6.7: The saw teeth closed polyline selected as an added area

6. You will see the area displayed in a small gray box in the AutoCAD drawing area, listing **Area**, **Perimeter**, and **Total area**. There will also be the corner prompt again, expecting you to start tracing another area to add. This is shown in *Figure 6.8*.

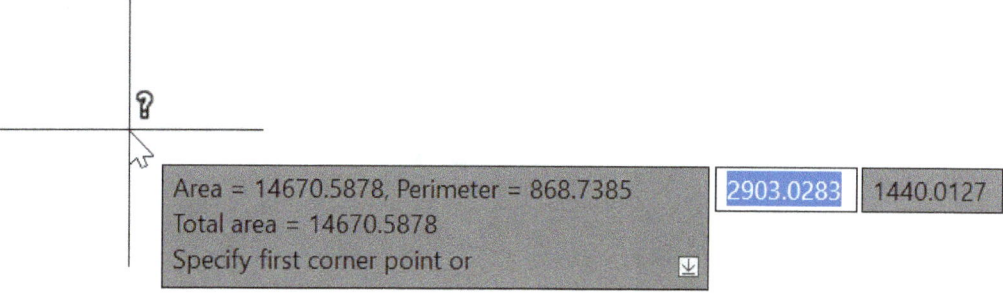

Figure 6.8: The calculated area of the saw teeth displayed, as well as the perimeter, and total area

7. Right-click again and select **Subtract area** on the shortcut menu.
8. Right-click again and select **Object**. You will now see the **(SUBTRACT mode) Select objects** prompt, similar to when you added the sawtooth area. This is shown in *Figure 6.9*.

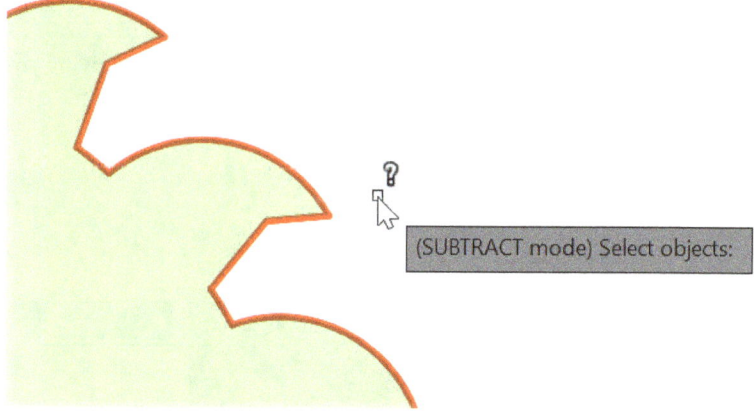

Figure 6.9: (SUBTRACT mode) Select objects, ready to select the circle

9. Select the circle representing the circular hole in the saw plate. It is now highlighted in brown, indicating it will be subtracted from the saw tooth area, as shown in *Figure 6.10*.

Figure 6.10: The circle is highlighted brown, indicating it will be subtracted

10. Press *Enter*. In the same gray box you saw when you added the saw tooth area, you will now see the area of the circle displayed (**1963.4954**), along with **Total area** (**12707.0923**). The total area is the area of the saw tooth polyline with the circle area subtracted, giving you the actual physical area of the sawblade. This is shown in *Figure 6.11*.

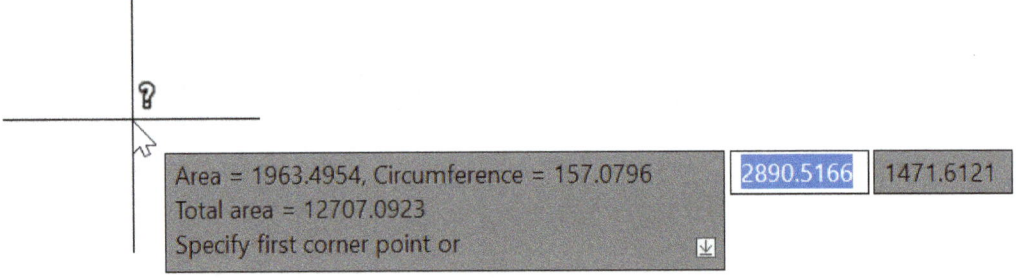

Figure 6.11: The area of the circle and the total area of the sawblade with the circle area subtracted

11. Press *Enter* to finish. You can now select **eXit** to close the **Measure** command.

> **Tips and tricks #21**
>
> Should you expand the AutoCAD command line, you will see *all* of the commands and data used when using the **Add** and **Subtract** functions of the **Area** tool, as shown in *Figure 6.12*. This text can be copied and pasted for other applications where required. Typical examples of where copy-pasting might be needed would be pasting into a project document, such as a specification, or into a spreadsheet being used to calculate quantities. Simply highlight any text and right-click. You can then select **Copy** from the shortcut menu.

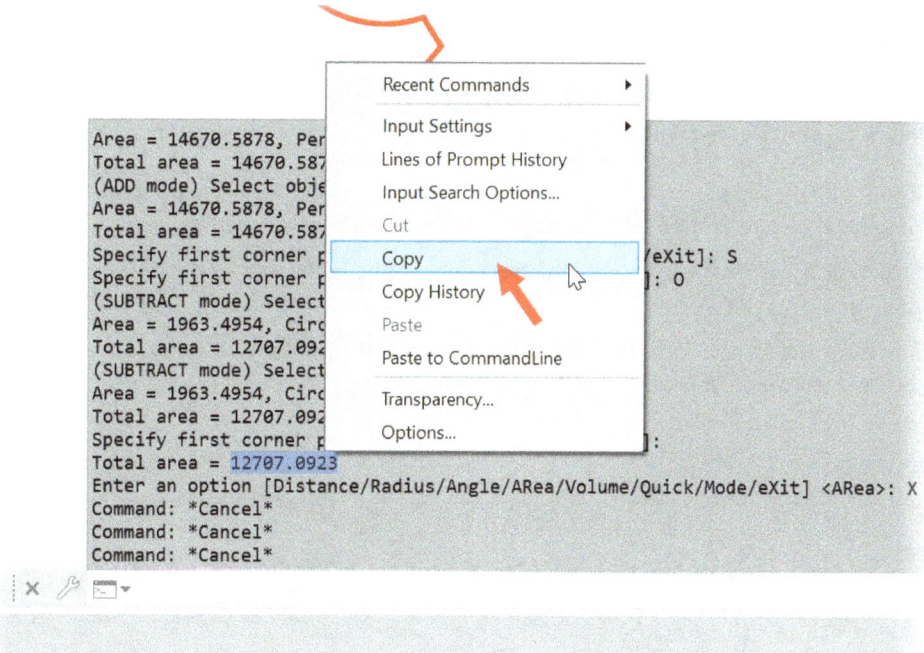

Figure 6.12: The AutoCAD command line with the area of the sawblade highlighted and ready to be copied

Should you want to change the settings for the command line, they can be opened using the spanner icon on the left-hand end of the command line.

> **AutoCAD for Mac**
>
> The **Measure** (*MEASUREGEOM*) command is available in AutoCAD for Mac, but there is no default icon or flyout menu. Simply type MEASUREGEOM and press *Enter* to activate the **Measure** tools, and right-click to bring up the shortcut menu that will display the measuring tools available in the command, where you will find the **Area** tool.

134 Measuring and Modifying Geometry and Objects

Now that you know how to calculate areas quickly and precisely, using the add and subtract tools, let us now look at how angles can be measured precisely in AutoCAD.

Measuring precise angles with the Angle tool

Angles are a fundamental part of geometry in your AutoCAD drawings. Measuring them precisely is essential but it is also essential that this can be done quickly and effectively.

For this section, you will continue to use the `Sawblade2.dwg` file. Ensure you do not have any commands or objects selected by pressing *Esc* on the keyboard twice. This cancels any commands and then clears any selection sets.

In the following exercise, you will learn how to measure precise angles in your AutoCAD drawing:

1. Zoom into the top of the sawblade so that you can see one of the sawblade's teeth closely. Note that there are numerous angles forming each tooth on the sawblade.

2. Select the **Measure** flyout on the **Utilities** panel on the **Home** tab on the ribbon, as you have done in the previous sections of this chapter. Select **Angle** this time.

3. You can select an arc, circle, line, or specify vertices at the prompt that appears. Select the large arc on a saw tooth. You will see the angle displayed (**99** °), as shown in *Figure 6.13*.

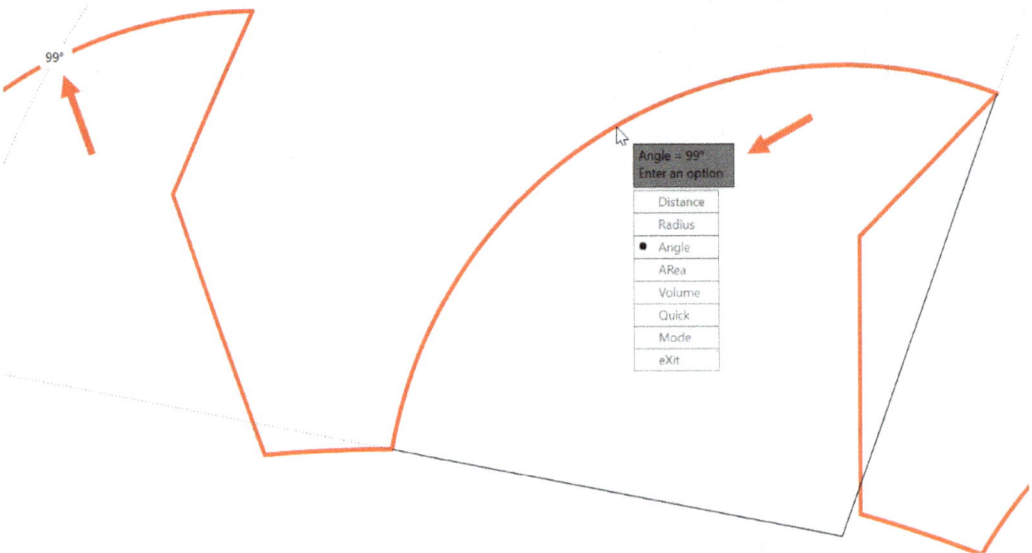

Figure 6.13: A measured angle with the Measure menu displayed

4. Select **Angle** again on the **Measure** menu.

5. Angles can also be measured by using two divergent lines. Select the two lines arrowed in *Figure 6.14*, and you will see the angle measurement displayed between them as **135°**.

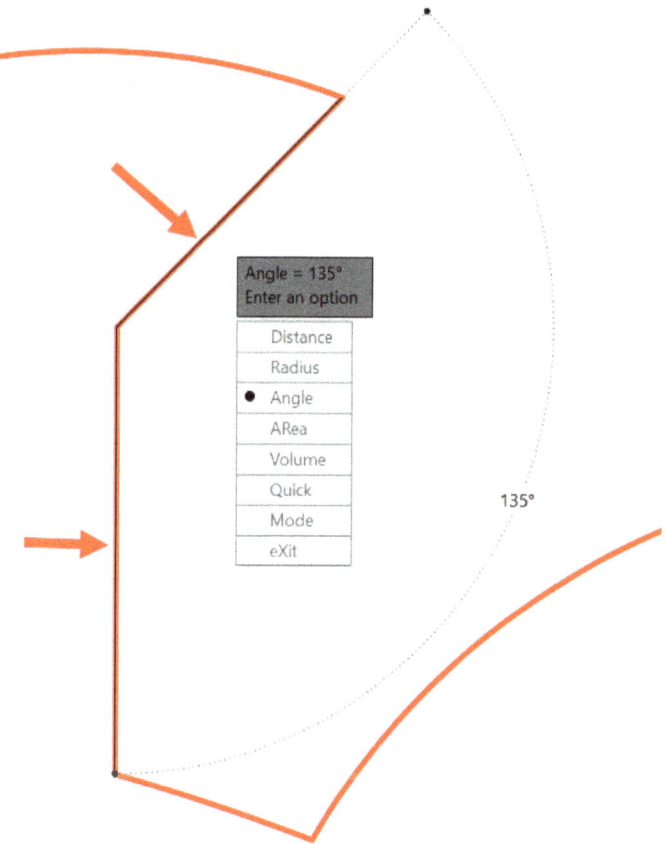

Figure 6.14: The displayed angle is measured using the two lines (arrowed)

6. You can also measure angles using vertices. Select **Angle** again from the **Measure** menu, and press *Enter* to confirm the **<Specify vertex>** prompt. Select the three points in the order shown in *Figure 6.15*. You will see that the measured angle is *108 degrees*. Make sure that the first point selected is the apex of the angle to be measured (**1**), followed by the other two vertices that make up the angle (**2** and **3**).

136   Measuring and Modifying Geometry and Objects

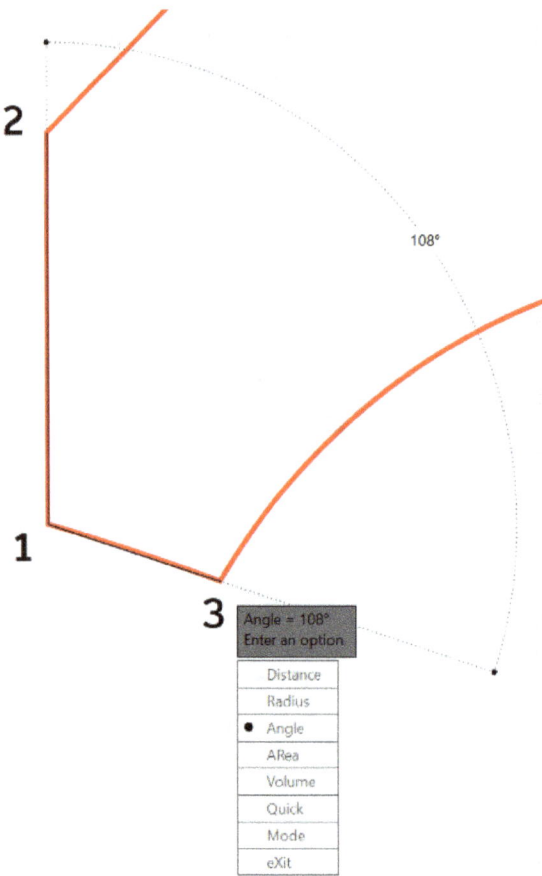

Figure 6.15: The displayed angle measured using three vertices (numbered)

7. To close the menu and the command, select **eXit** on the **Measure** menu.

Measuring angles is essential for accuracy in AutoCAD, and the **Angle** tool allows this to be done quickly and easily. In the case of the sawblade, the angles used for the saw teeth have to be measured precisely to allow the sawblade to be manufactured. The ability to measure exactly makes sure that any **Computer Aided Manufacturing** (**CAM**) has accurate angles to cut the saw teeth from the source materials.

AutoCAD for Mac

The **Measure** (*MEASUREGEOM*) command is available in AutoCAD for Mac, but there is no default icon or flyout menu. Simply type MEASUREGEOM and press *Enter* to activate the **Measure** tools, and right-click to bring up the shortcut menu that will display the measuring tools available in the command, where you will find the **Angle** tool.

You can now measure angles with precision in your drawings. Let's now look at how you can refine your drawings using the **Modify** panel.

Refining drawings using the Modify panel

Your AutoCAD drawings are constantly evolving. Revisions and design iterations must be made as the project you are working on gets refined toward construction or manufacture.

AutoCAD provides many tools that allow you to modify existing drawing geometry quickly, effectively, and, most importantly, accurately and precisely. One of these features is the **Modify** panel.

In the exercise that follows, you will use `Sawblade3.dwg` and learn how to utilize some of the AutoCAD **Modify** tools to change the saw teeth configuration on the sawblade:

1. Upon opening the drawing, you will see that the sawblade only has one tooth. You will use some of the **Modify** tools to add the required saw teeth and edit the sawtooth profile.
2. Make sure you are on the **Home** tab on the ribbon and that the **Modify** panel is displayed, as shown in *Figure 6.16*.

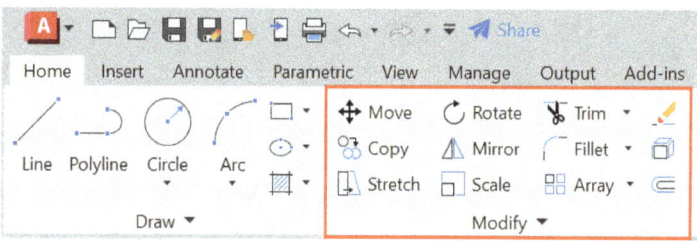

Figure 6.16: The Modify panel on the Home tab of the ribbon

3. Click on the **Array** flyout to display the various arrays that can be created in AutoCAD, as shown in *Figure 6.17*.

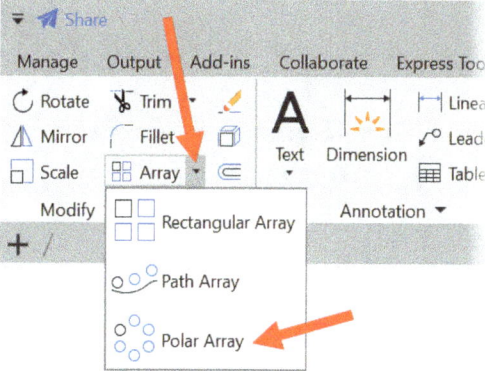

Figure 6.17: The Array flyout menu

4. Select **Polar Array** (*ARRAYPOLAR*). You will be prompted to make a selection in the **Select objects** menu. Select the red arc and lines that form the single saw tooth, and press *Enter* to confirm your selection.

5. You will then encounter the **Specify center point of array** prompt. Select the center of the circles that form the sawblade using the **Center** object snap. You can do this now, having learned to set object snaps in *Chapter 5*, in the *Finding the geometric center* section.

6. Upon clicking on the **Center** object snap, you will see the ribbon update to the contextual **Array Creation** tab, and the prompt change to **Select grip to edit array or**. You will also see that AutoCAD has automatically displayed *six* saw teeth, including the original, as shown in *Figure 6.18*.

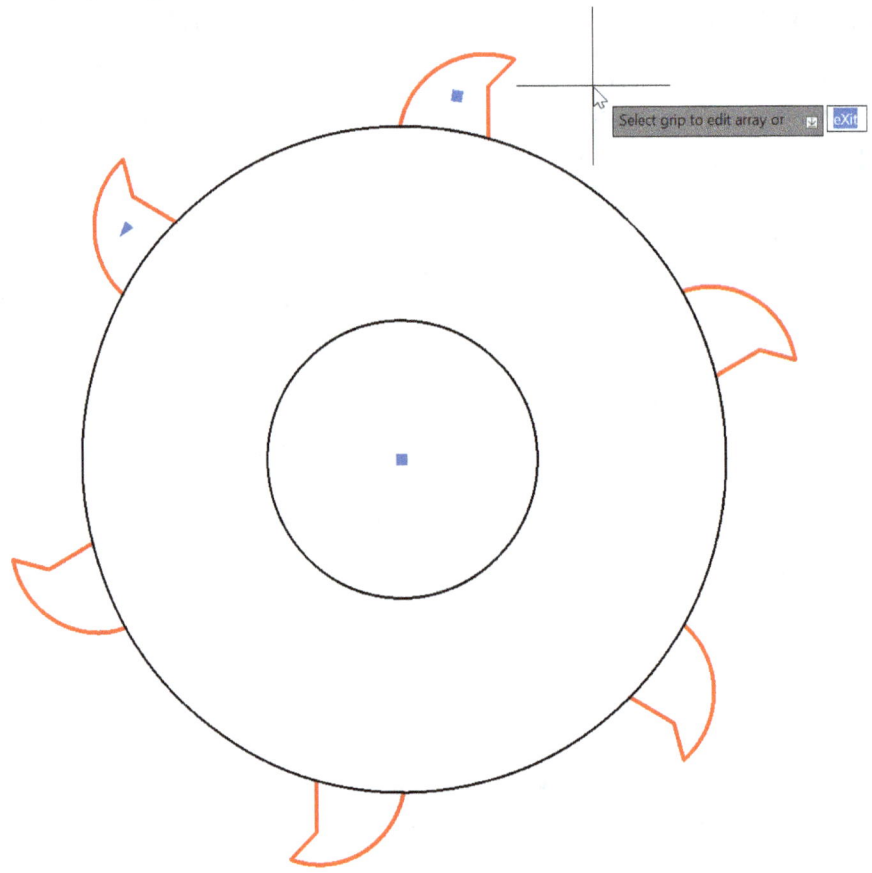

Figure 6.18: The default polar array with six saw teeth

7. The design specification is for *eighteen* saw teeth, so the polar array needs to be updated. This can be done in the **Items** panel on the contextual **Array Creation** tab.

Refining drawings using the Modify panel   139

8. Change the number of items to 18 in the **Items** field, as shown in *Figure 6.19*. Then, press *Enter*.

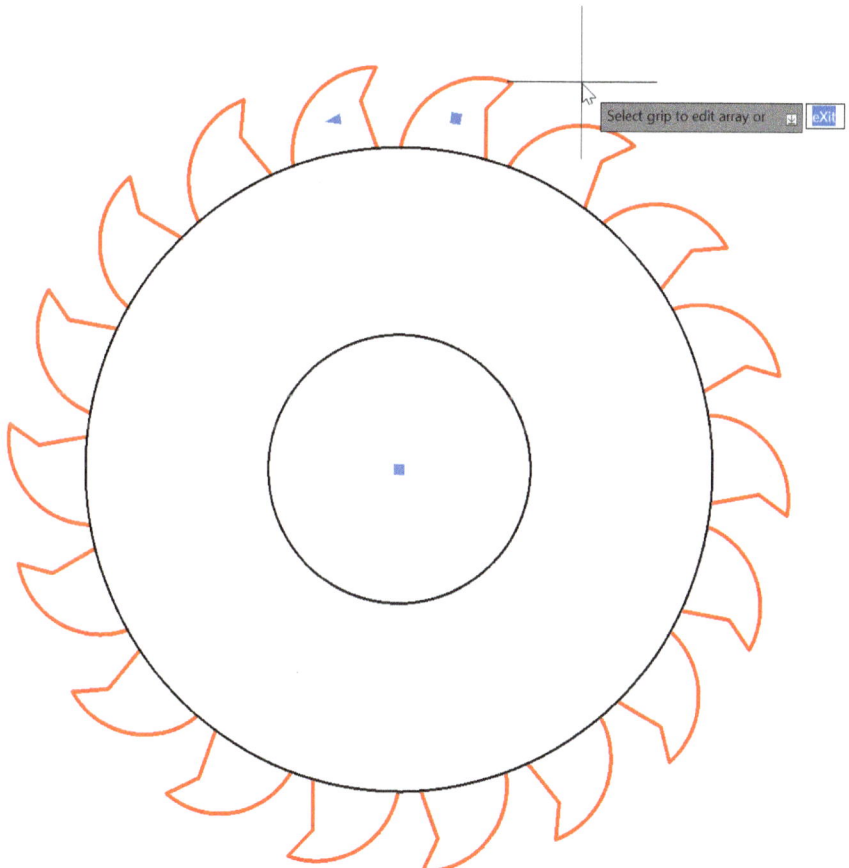

Figure 6.19: The Items field on the Items panel on the contextual Array Creation tab

9. You will see the number of saw teeth updated to *18* in the drawing, as displayed in *Figure 6.20*.

Figure 6.20: The sawblade with 18 saw teeth

140   Measuring and Modifying Geometry and Objects

10. To close the **Polar Array** command, press *Enter* to confirm the **eXit** prompt, or click on the **Close Array** icon (green check mark) on the ribbon.

11. You now have 18 saw teeth in an associative **Polar Array**. Clicking on one of the saw teeth will select the array, highlighting it, as shown in *Figure 6.21*. Also, note that the contextual **Array** tab on the ribbon is displayed.

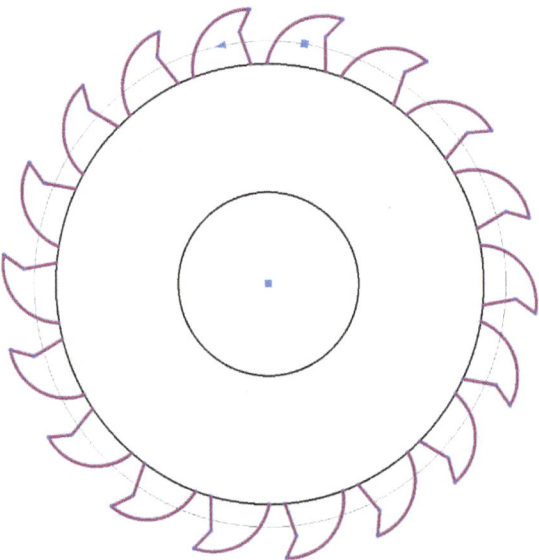

Figure 6.21: The associative Polar Array shown highlighted after selection

The saw tooth design on the sawblade needs to be revised, for easier manufacture. To do so, some AutoCAD users might use the **Explode** (*EXPLODE*) command to break the associative array back into its component objects and then re-array the saw teeth. This is a long-winded approach, open to error. The following workflow is not only quicker, but will also help to avoid any transferred errors:

1. Locate the **Edit Source** icon on the **Options** panel on the contextual **Array** tab on the ribbon, as shown in *Figure 6.22*. Click on the **Edit Source** icon. You will return to the **Home** tab on the ribbon.

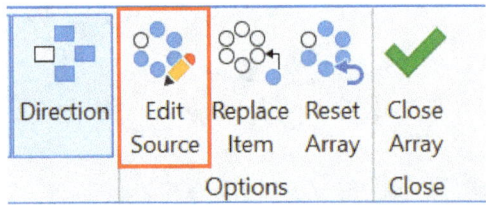

Figure 6.22: The Edit Source icon on the Options panel

2. Using the **Layer** drop-down menu on the **Layers** panel, ensure that you use the **Sawteeth** layer as the current drafting layer.
3. You will see a **Command** prompt. Select the original saw tooth used to create the array.
4. A small dialog box will appear, as shown in *Figure 6.23*. It is a confirmation that you want to edit the source objects of the array. Click on **OK**.

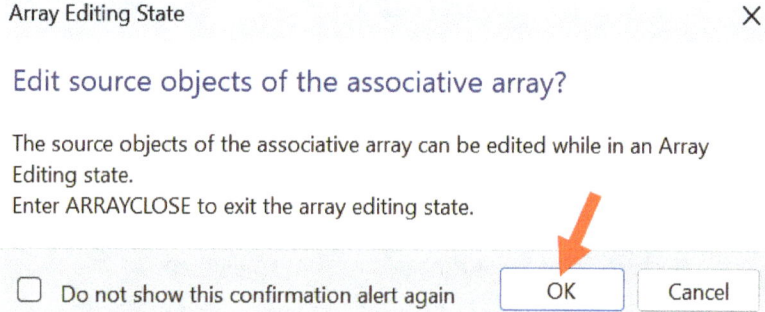

Figure 6.23: The Edit Source confirmation dialog box

5. Using the **Line** (*LINE*) command and the **Erase** (*ERASE*) command, edit the original saw tooth to a similar configuration, as shown in *Figure 6.24*.

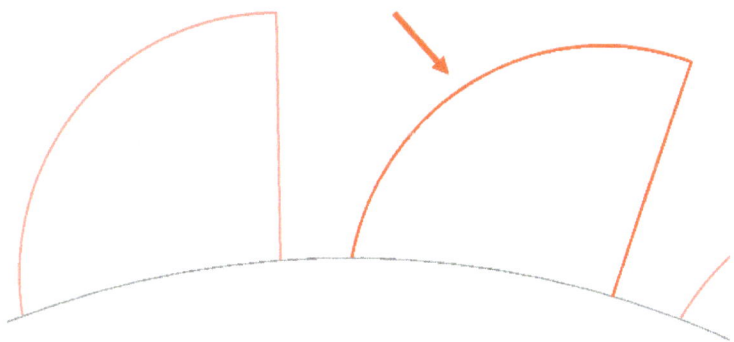

Figure 6.24: The reconfigured saw tooth

6. As you edit the original saw tooth, you will see the other saw teeth in the array update to suit. Once the editing is complete, click the **Save Changes** icon in the **Edit Array** panel, now displayed on the right-hand end of the **Home** tab on the ribbon. The **Save Changes** icon is shown in *Figure 6.25*.

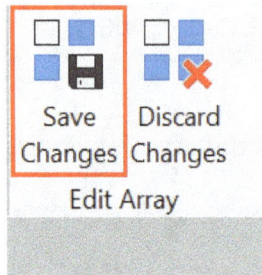

Figure 6.25: The Save Changes icon on the Edit Array panel

Upon saving the changes to the array, you will now see that all of the 18 saw teeth are set to the new saw tooth configuration.

Select the array, and you will see that it is still in place, fully associative, without needing to re-array to make the necessary changes. *Figure 6.26* shows the revised array, selected and highlighted.

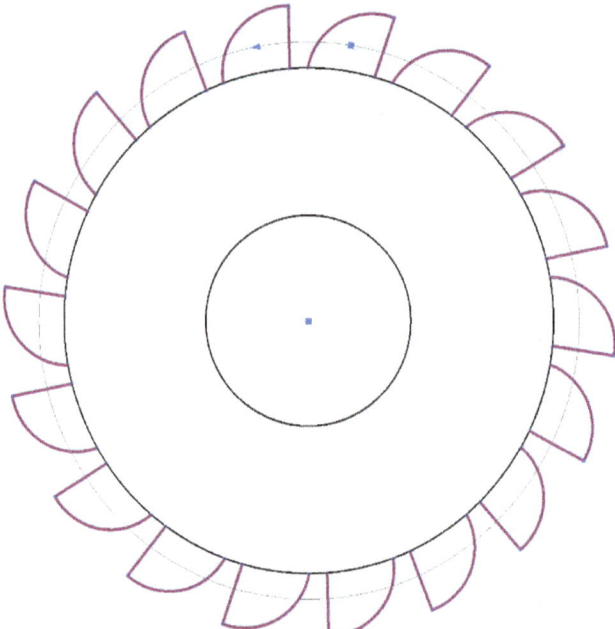

Figure 6.26: The reconfigured Polar Array, shown selected and highlighted

Lastly, press *Esc* on the keyboard to de-select the array. This avoids the array object being part of the selection set should you start another command.

The **Modify** panel contains many valuable tools that will allow you to revise and update your drawings quickly and accurately. Drawings are used in many disciplines and environments, and the **Modify** tools can be adapted and used in any workflow.

Summary

In this chapter, you have learned how to work with **Noun/verb selection** to ensure the quick selection of objects you wish to modify in your drawings. You have also learned how to measure geometry lengths quickly and efficiently using **Quick Measure** and **Distance**.

Calculating exact areas of geometry is now quick and easy, having learned how to use **Measure** (*MEASUREGEOM*), using the **Area** tool, with the **Add** and **Subtract** functions. You have also learned how to measure angles accurately, quickly, and effectively using the **Angle** tool in the **Measure** (*MEASUREGEOM*) command, utilizing circles, arcs, lines, and vertices.

Using the **Polar Array** (*ARRAYPOLAR*) command, you have learned how to modify an existing sawblade design, working with the **Edit Source** function to update the existing saw teeth configuration.

AutoCAD also carries a comprehensive editing toolset on the **Modify** panel on the ribbon. In this chapter, you have only touched the surface of those tools through the **Polar Array** tool, but with more practice on your own, you will find that most editing requirements in AutoCAD can be met with the **Modify** panel.

This chapter demonstrated how important the aforementioned tools are when modifying and editing drawings in AutoCAD. They are fundamental to the accuracy and precision of any edits to any geometry in your design. In the next chapter, we will look at how you can use annotative annotation to communicate your design intent effectively in your AutoCAD drawings.

Get This Book's PDF Version and Exclusive Extras

Scan the QR code (or go to `packtpub.com/unlock`). Search for this book by name, confirm the edition, and then follow the steps on the page.

Note: Keep your invoice handy. Purchases made directly from Packt don't require one.

7
Developing Annotative Annotation Styles

AutoCAD is used to draft, draw, and create your designs. With that comes a need to communicate your design intent. A builder, for example, needs to know how big the building is that needs to be built. The factory needs to know how big the item is that needs to be manufactured. This is where AutoCAD's highly versatile and comprehensive annotation tools come in handy.

Not only do these annotation tools allow you to add annotation text and dimensions to your drawings but they can also be made annotative, working with annotation scales that represent the annotation at the appropriate scales when using scaled viewports in your layout tabs.

Annotating effectively allows users to communicate their design intent accurately. Much time in AutoCAD is spent annotating designs, and annotation styles must be set appropriately.

This chapter covers the following methodologies you will need to learn to use annotative annotation in your DWG files:

- Creating text styles to manage text sizes and fonts
- Managing dimension annotation with dimension styles
- Setting up specific leader styles
- Working with accurate table styles

In previous chapters, you looked at how you could develop advanced geometry using AutoCAD's drafting tools. In this chapter, you will create annotation styles to assist you in communicating your design intent accurately and effectively.

Exercise file

You must ensure you have downloaded the `New Office Proposal.dwg` exercise file to follow the sections in this chapter.

Creating text styles to manage text sizes and fonts

Text is fundamental in an AutoCAD drawing. You need text to add labels to describe and annotate objects and areas in a design, as well as provide numerical values, such as the number of instances of objects (for example, doors), and use dimension text to add values to important dimensions. This section will look at how you can use text styles to manage text sizes and fonts and use annotative text scaling in your drawings.

You can have as many text styles as you like in an AutoCAD DWG file, but what is more important is the naming philosophy of those text styles. It is no use having text styles called *Shaun1*, *Shaun2*, and so on. The text styles need a naming philosophy that means something to everyone using the AutoCAD DWG file. Even if you're working alone, it's a good practice to name your styles such that they are identifiable in terms of their attributes. Having this system in place will be helpful in your AutoCAD projects in the long run.

Annotative text styles allow you to specify the paper space height of text annotation in the **Layout** tab, regardless of the scale of the viewport in which it is displayed. For example, if you use an annotative paper space height of `2.5` mm in a viewport of 1:100, the height of the actual text in the **Model** tab will be `250` mm. Providing an annotation scale of 1:100 is used when placing the annotative text in the **Model** tab, the annotative text will display correctly in the **Layout** tab viewport.

Using the file that accompanies this chapter, you will now learn how to define text styles. Open the exercise file, `New Office Proposal.dwg`. It will be in the **Model** tab when it opens, displaying a simple office floor plan without annotation. Your first step is to define text styles that are needed in the drawing. If you wish, you can develop more text styles once you have completed the exercise in this section. For now, let's jump into the file:

1. To create new text styles, you need to access the **Text Style** dialog box. You can do this in two ways. The first is from the **Home** tab/**Annotation** panel, as shown in *Figure 7.1*.

Creating text styles to manage text sizes and fonts   147

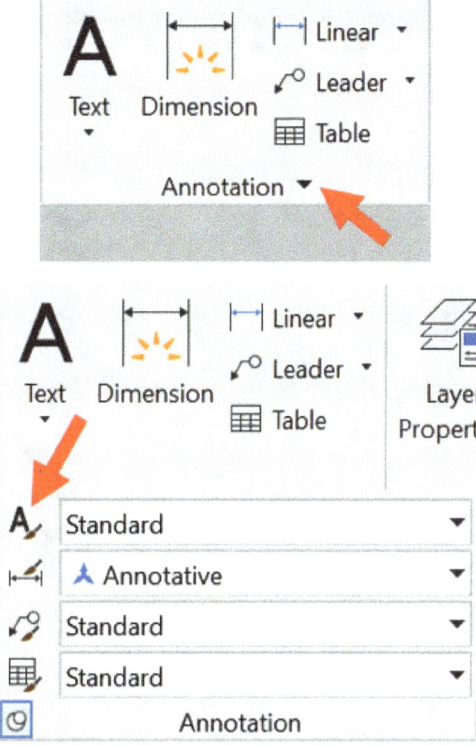

Figure 7.1: Expanding the Annotation panel on the Home tab and then clicking on the Text Style icon

You can also use the **Annotate** tab/**Text** panel, as shown in *Figure 7.2*. Each method differs slightly but you end up in the same dialog box.

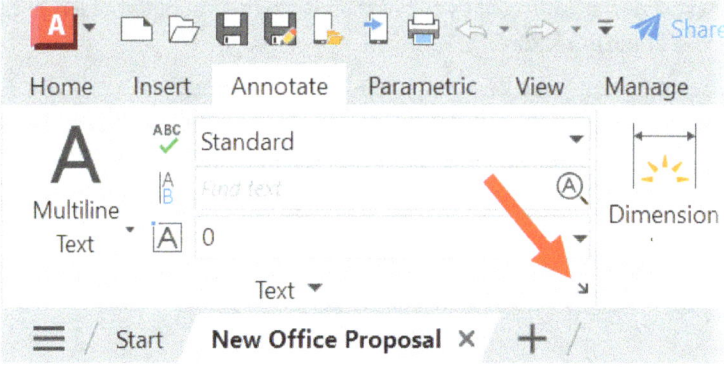

Figure 7.2: Clicking on the arrow icon on the Text panel title bar in the Annotate tab on the ribbon

148 Developing Annotative Annotation Styles

2. The **Text Style** dialog box is now open and ready for use, as shown in *Figure 7.3*.

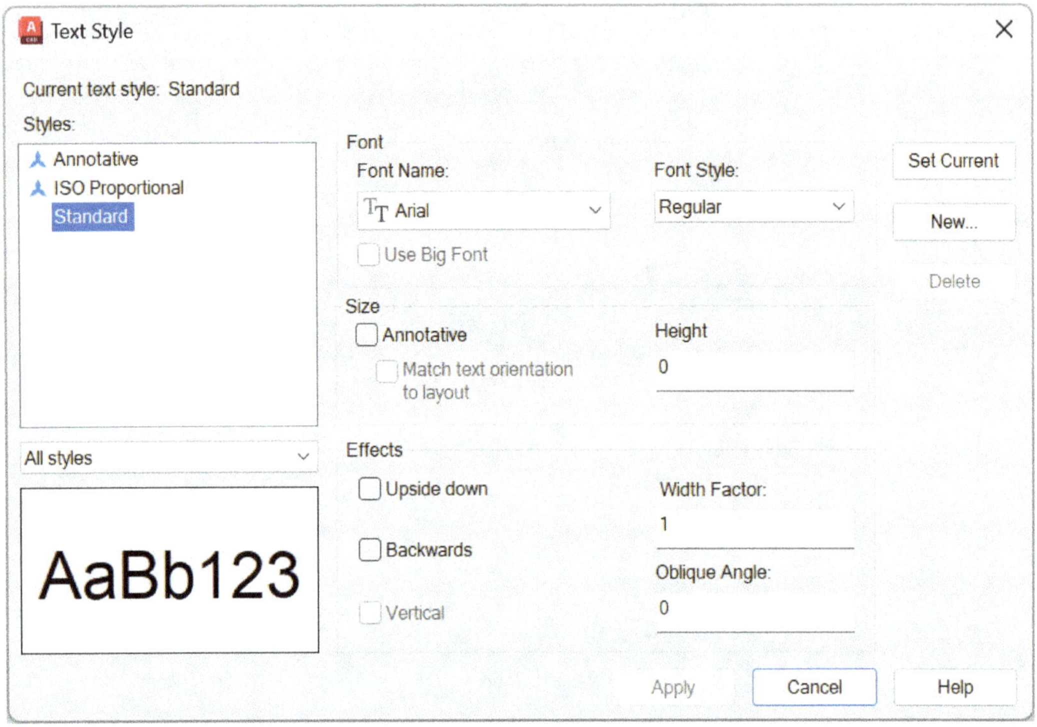

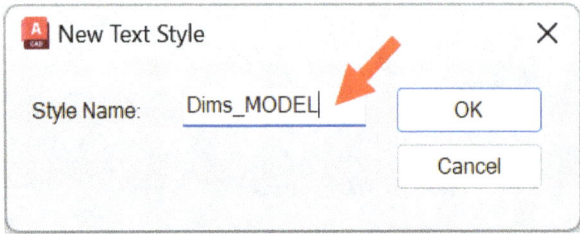

Figure 7.3: The Text Style dialog box

3. Note that some default text styles are already in this drawing file. Also note that there are *two* annotative text styles, as indicated by the *blue* annotative symbol to the left of each text style name in the list at the top left.

4. To create a new text style, click on **New...**. You will be prompted for a new text style name, as shown in *Figure 7.4*.

Figure 7.4: Creating a new text style

5. Type in the name `Dims_MODEL` and click on **OK**. You will be returned to the **Text Style** dialog box, with the **Dims_MODEL** text style showing in the list. Click on the style name in the list to prepare it for property editing. It will be highlighted in *blue*, as shown in *Figure 7.5*.

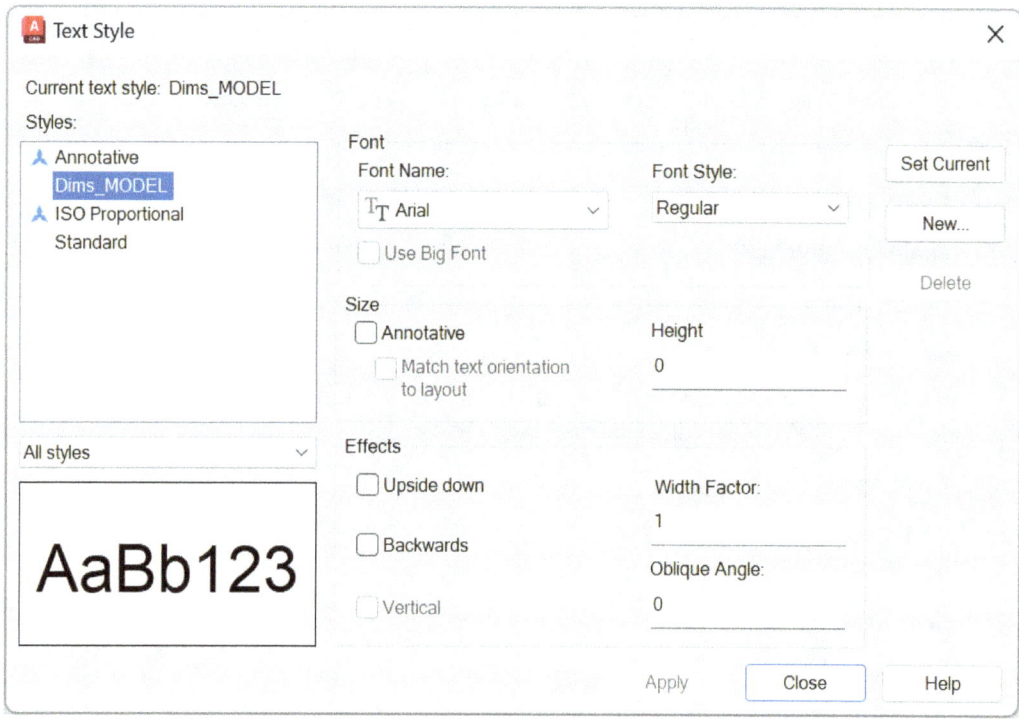

Figure 7.5: The Text Style dialog box with the Dims_MODEL text style highlighted

6. Using the settings in the dialog box, you can now change the properties of the **Dims_MODEL** text style, as follows:

   - **Font Name: Calibri**
   - **Font Style: Regular**
   - **Height**: 0

7. Make sure that the **Annotative** box is unchecked (this text style will be used for annotative dimensions, which will already be set to annotative in the dimension style later in the chapter).

8. No effects will be used in this text style, so leave them all as they are. You can, however, create another text style if you wish, to experiment with effects that can be used. These effects can be used to manipulate the text style so that it displays in different ways when used, such as displaying text backward or upside-down.
9. Once these properties have been set, click on **Apply**. You will remain in the dialog box.
10. Click on **New…** again. Call the new text style `Title_LAYOUT_10mm` and click **OK**.
11. Select the new text style in the dialog box, and set the following properties:

    - **Font Name**: Calibri
    - **Font Style**: Bold Italic
    - **Height**: `10mm`

    Again, no **Effects** options will be needed.

    This text style will *only* be used in the **Layout** tabs on title blocks, hence the naming philosophy and height for the style. It will *not* be used in the **Model** tab.

12. Click on **Apply**.
13. Using the workflow above, create one more text style called `Labels_MODEL_5mm`. Set the following properties:

    - **Font Name**: Calibri
    - **Font Style**: Regular
    - **Annotative**: Yes (check the box)
    - **Paper Text Height**: 5mm
    - **Effects**: None

14. Your **Text Style** dialog box will now look as shown in *Figure 7.6*.

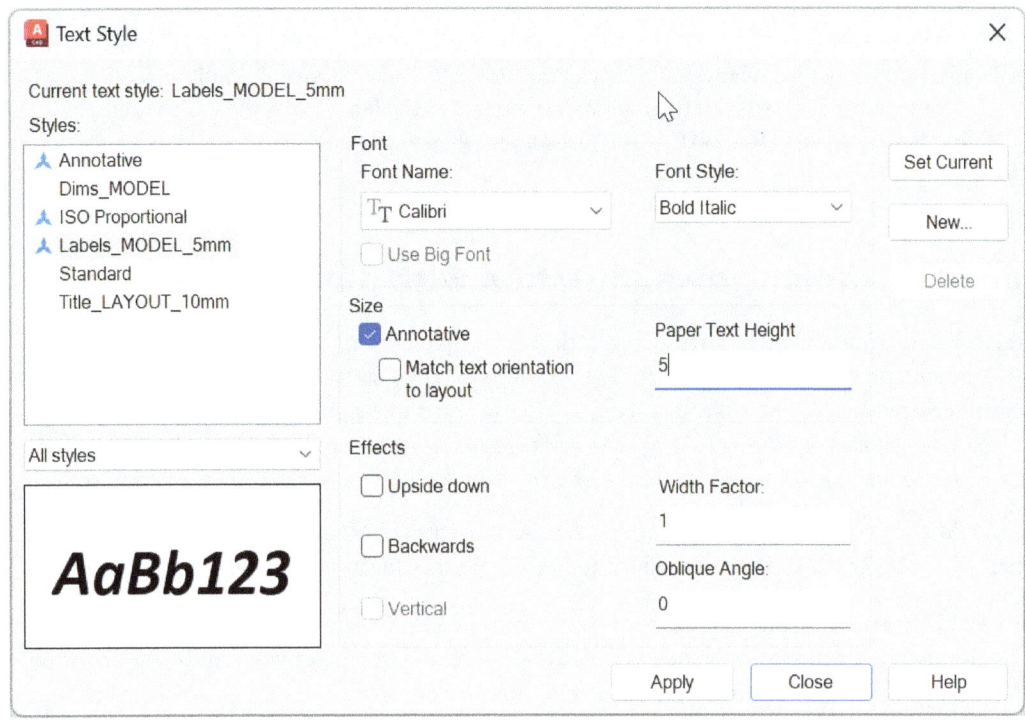

Figure 7.6: The Text Style dialog box with the Labels_MODEL_5mm style selected

15. Click on **Apply** and then **Close**. The dialog box will close.
16. At this point, make sure to save your drawing. You can save with the existing file name or use **Save As…** to create a new one. This will ensure that your text styles are saved.

You now know how to create, manage, and apply text styles in a drawing, utilizing text fonts and sizes. In the next section, you will learn how to work with dimension annotation using dimension styles.

> **Tips and tricks #22**
> When creating text styles, if you set the **Height** property to zero (0), AutoCAD will prompt you for the text height when using that text style to place text annotation in your AutoCAD drawings.

A fixed text height in a text style ensures that AutoCAD places text at that height every time text is placed using that style. For example, if you are working on a drawing using metric millimeters and a text height is set to 200, the text will always be placed at 200 millimeters in the drawing.

> **AutoCAD for Mac**
>
> When creating any type of annotation style in AutoCAD for Mac, you will find the icons for each type of annotation style in their appropriate panel in the left-hand toolbar. For example, the **Text Style** icon is in the **Text** panel. This also applies to dimensions styles, leader styles, and table styles.

Managing dimension annotation with dimension styles

In the previous section, you learned that creating and implementing text styles is fundamental to adding annotation to your drawings. Creating and implementing suitable dimension styles is also an essential requirement. You need the text styles in place to add dimension text to your dimensions, and this is all set up as part of a dimension style. In this section, you will learn how to use dimension styles to manage and maintain dimension annotation across multiple layout viewports of differing scales.

You should already have the `New Office Proposal.dwg` exercise file open from the previous section. You will now add an annotative dimension style to the drawing by undertaking the following steps:

1. As with text styles, there are several ways to open **Dimension Style Manager**. You can use the flyout on the **Annotation** panel on the **Home** tab on the ribbon, or you can use the arrow on the title bar of the **Dimensions** panel on the **Annotate** tab on the ribbon. Each of these methods will open the **Dimension Style Manager** dialog box. *Figure 7.7* shows the flyout.

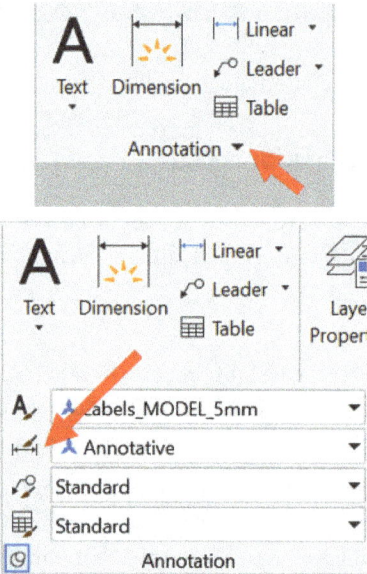

Figure 7.7: Expanding the Annotation panel on the Home tab and then clicking on the Dimension Style icon

Managing dimension annotation with dimension styles   153

Figure 7.8 shows the arrow on the title bar.

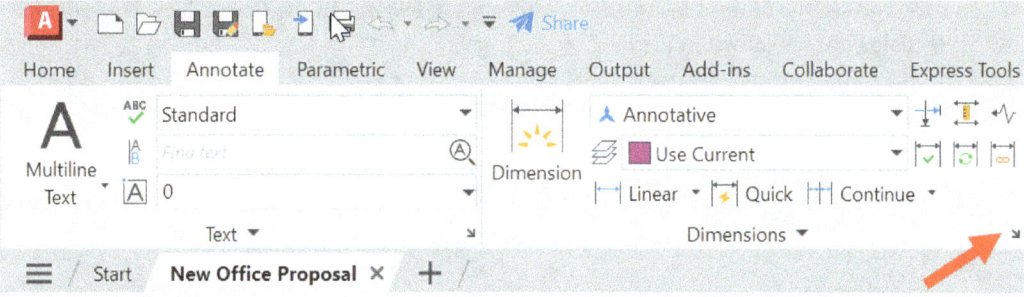

Figure 7.8: Clicking on the arrow icon on the Text panel title bar in the Annotate tab on the ribbon

2. Using either method, you will see the **Dimension Style Manager** dialog box appear, as shown in *Figure 7.9*.

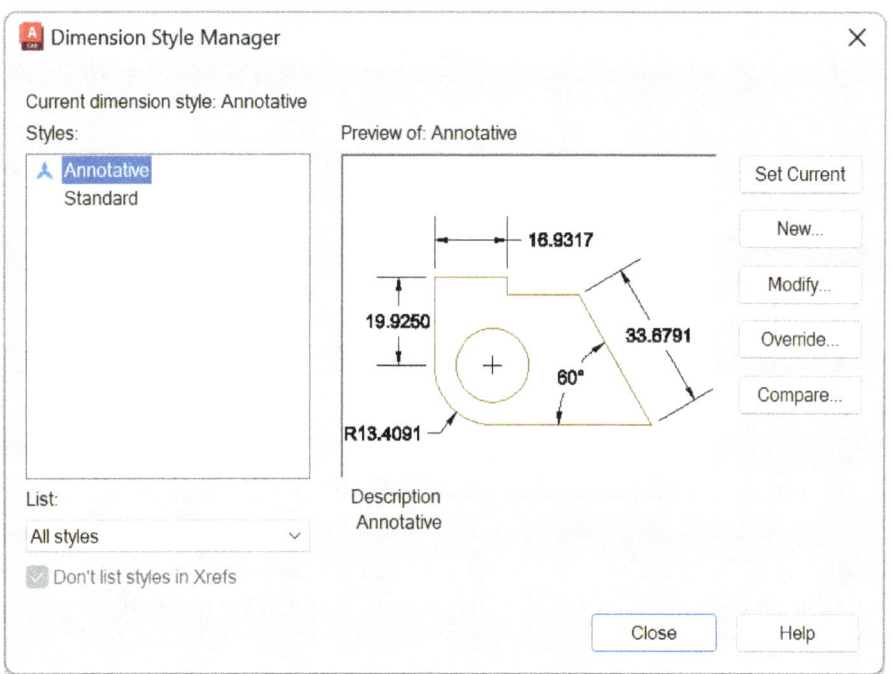

Figure 7.9 – The Dimension Style Manager dialog box

True to its name, **Dimension Style Manager** manages all your dimension styles in your DWG file. You will notice two default dimension styles: **Annotative** and **Standard**. In *Figure 7.9*, the **Annotative** style has a blue symbol next to it, indicating that it is, indeed, an annotative dimension style.

3. You will now create an annotative dimension style for use in your drawing file. Click on **New…**, and you will see the prompt for the new dimension style name in the **Create New Dimension Style** dialog box, as shown in *Figure 7.10*.

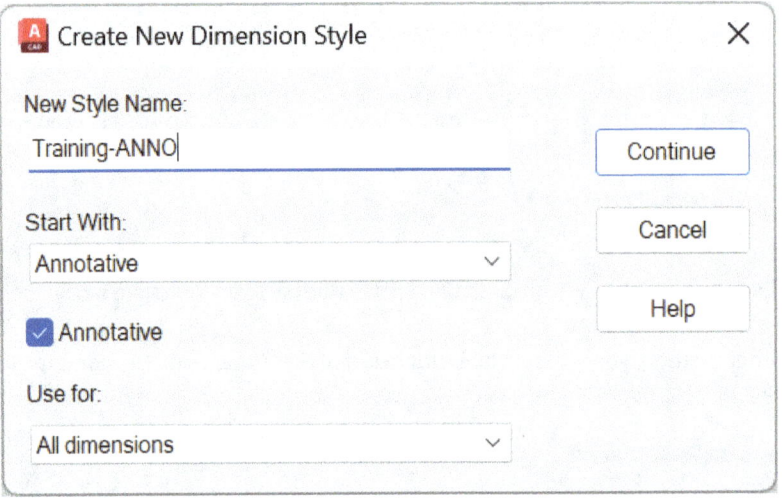

Figure 7.10: The Create New Dimension Style dialog box

4. Create a new style named `Training-ANNO`, and set **Start With** to the **Annotative** style in the dropdown.
5. Ensure that the **Annotative** box is checked, as shown in *Figure 7.10*. This will make sure that you are creating an annotative dimension style.
6. In the **Use for** dropdown, select **All dimensions**.
7. Click on **Continue**.
8. You will now see the **New Dimension Style** dialog box specific to the new dimension style that you created, along with its name, displayed in the title bar of the dialog box, as shown in *Figure 7.11*.
9. You can see tabs at the top of the dialog box, and you will be working across those tabs from left to right to customize the dimension style. Ensure the **Lines** tab is current and all settings in the tab in your dialog box are the same as in *Figure 7.11*.

Managing dimension annotation with dimension styles | 155

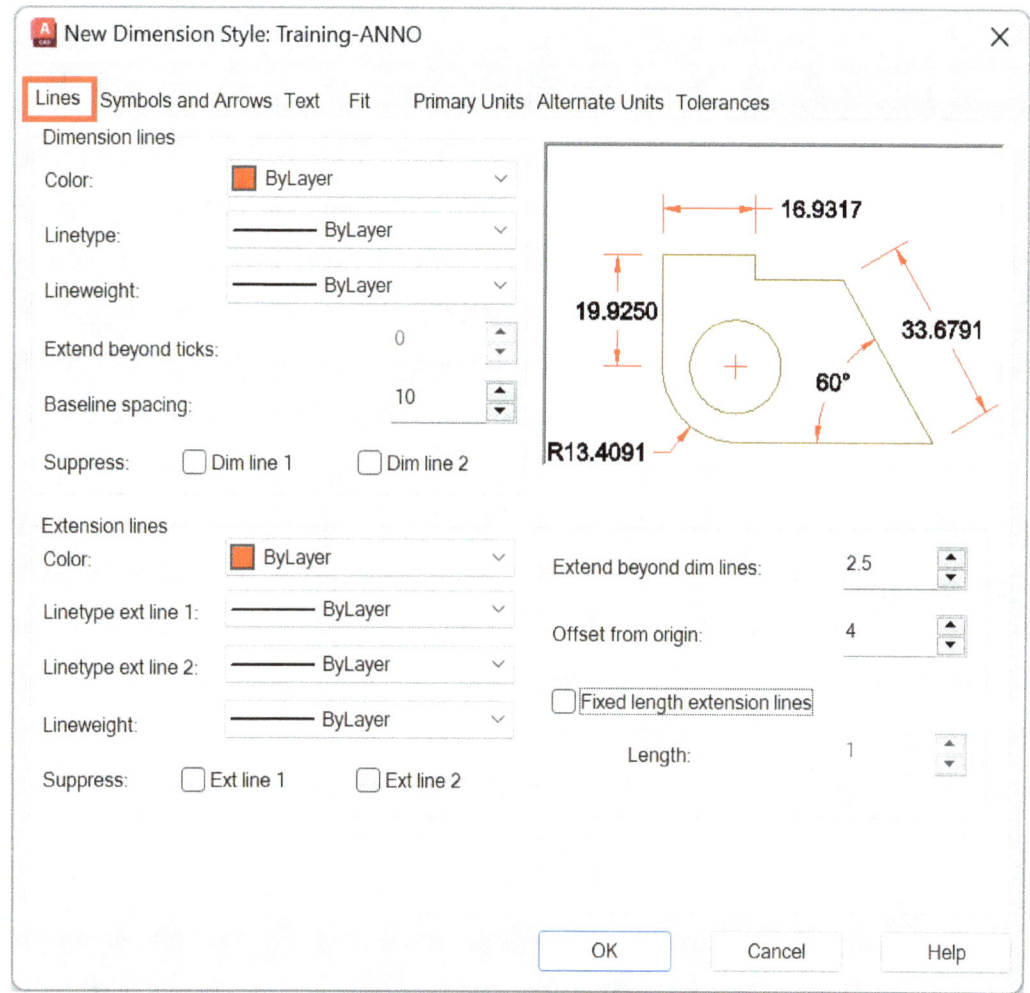

Figure 7.11: The New Dimension Style: Training-ANNO dialog box with the Lines tab

10. Once the **Lines** tab settings are all in place, select the **Symbols and Arrows** tab.
11. Make sure to set all the settings in the **Symbols and Arrows** tab to the same as shown in *Figure 7.12*.

Developing Annotative Annotation Styles

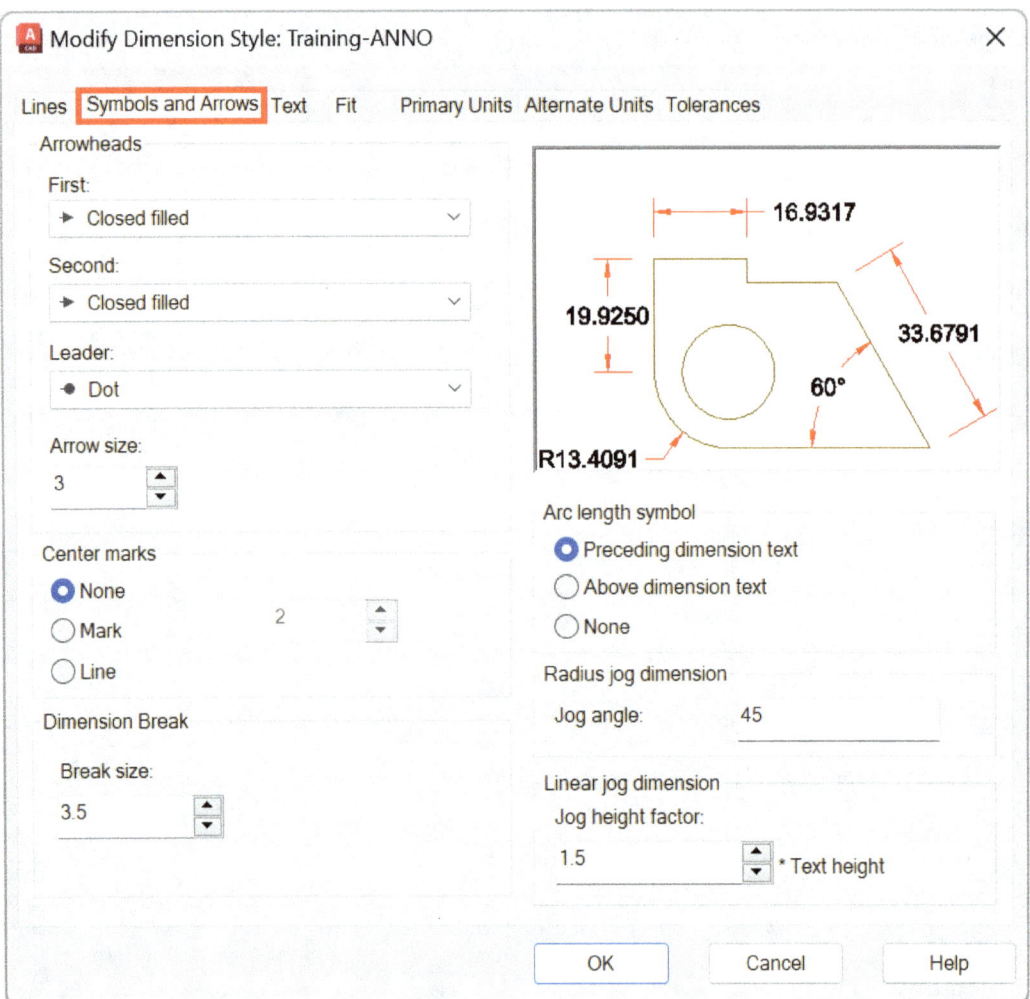

Figure 7.12: The Symbols and Arrows tab

12. Next, select the **Text** tab. Using the **Text style** drop-down menu, you can now select the **Dims_MODEL** text style you created earlier. Note that this text style is *not* annotative, as it is being used in a dimension style that *is* annotative.

    Ensure all the other settings shown in *Figure 7.13* are also set. There are many settings for text in a dimension style, and it is worth investigating these at another time, exploring what can be displayed by way of dimension annotation on a drawing.

Managing dimension annotation with dimension styles 157

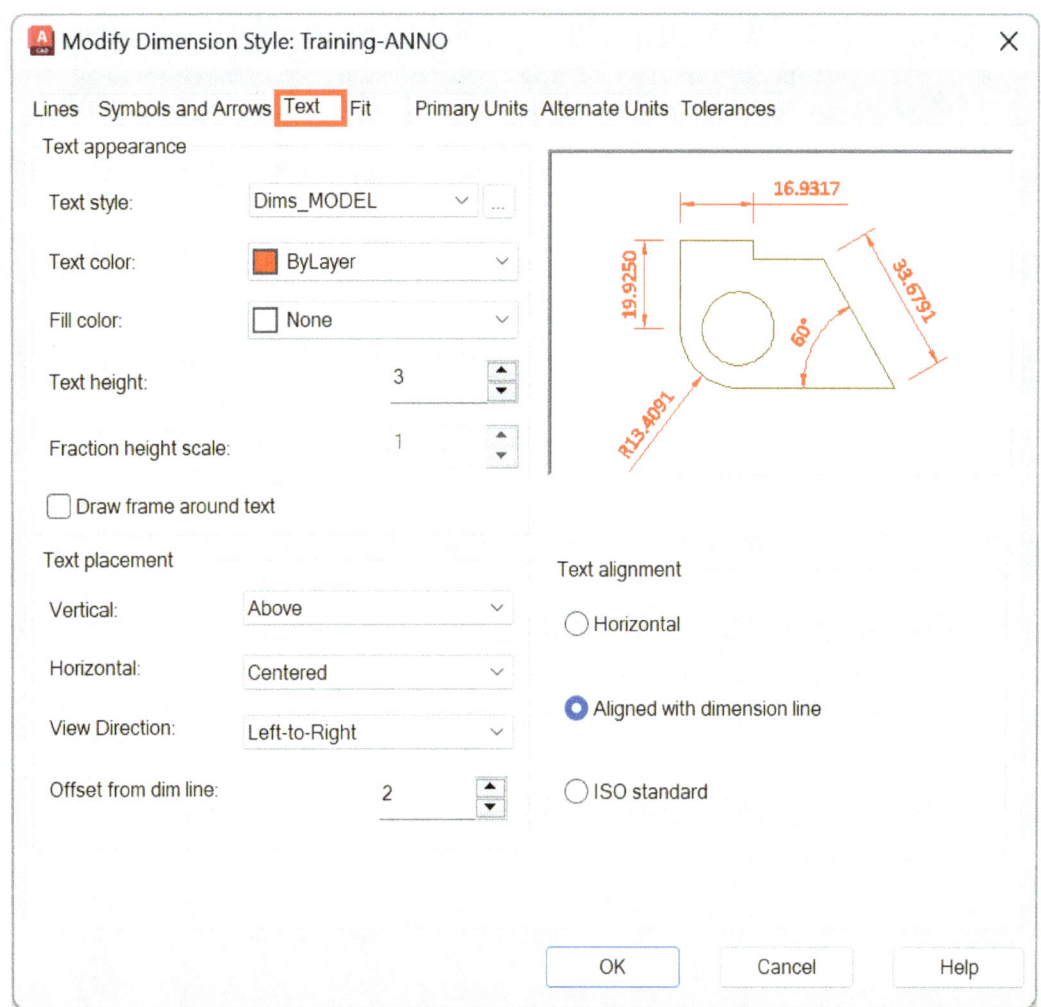

Figure 7.13: The Text tab

13. For now, moving along the tabs at the top of the dialog box, select the **Fit** tab.

158 Developing Annotative Annotation Styles

14. The dimension style you create is annotative, so the **Annotative** checkbox will already be checked. If it isn't, though, make sure it *is* ticked. You don't need to make any other changes to the **Fit** tab, as you will be using the default settings, so make sure your **Fit** tab looks the same as the one displayed in *Figure 7.14*.

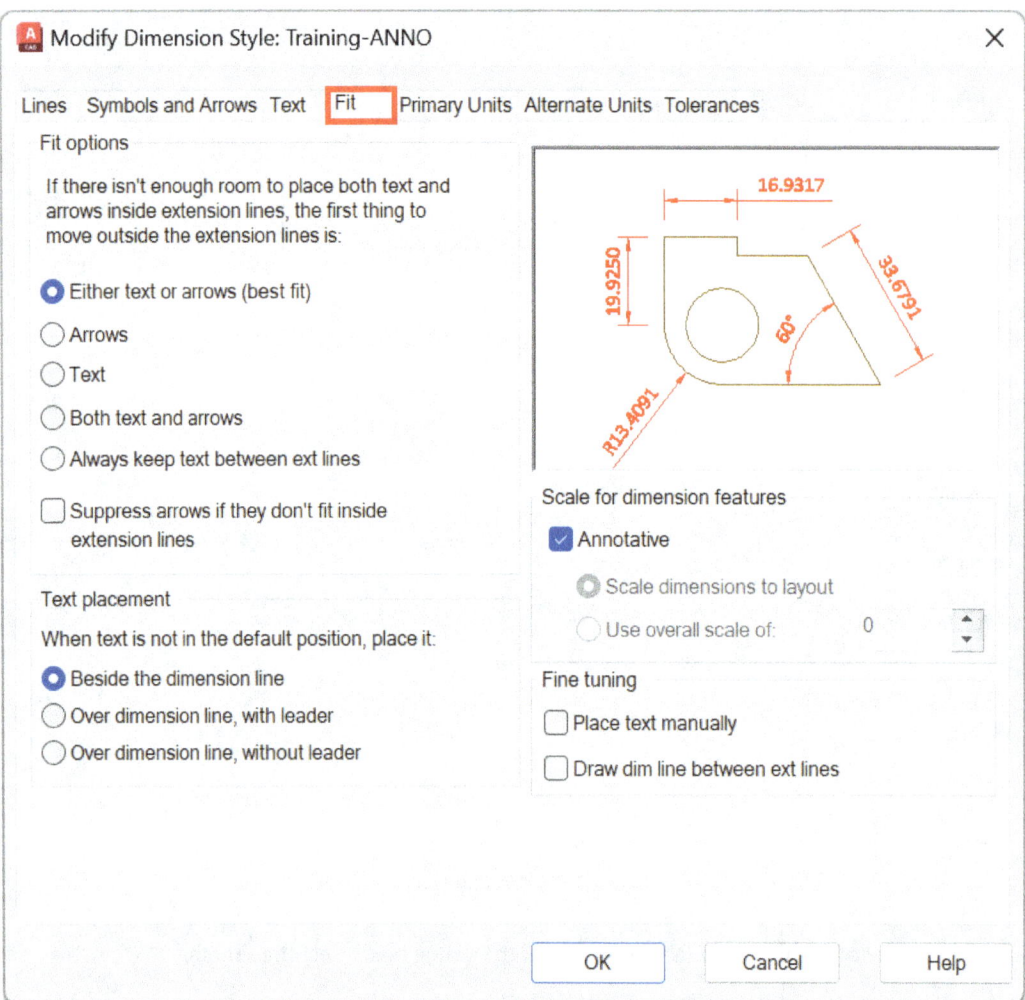

Figure 7.14: The Fit tab with the Annotative checkbox checked

15. Click on the **Primary Units** tab to the right of the **Fit** tab. This is where you can override any settings in the **Units** settings (set with the *UNITS* command) for annotation display purposes. For example, you might be working to units setting of *four* decimal places for accuracy when drafting in AutoCAD, but only need an accuracy of *one* decimal place when placing annotation to communicate design intent, so the **Precision** setting would be set to `1.0`, overriding the `1.0000` setting originally set with the **Units** (*UNITS*) command.

16. Make sure all your **Primary Units** settings are set, as shown in *Figure 7.15*.
17. Ensure that **Decimal separator** is set to **Period** (.). **Comma** (,) or **Space** ( ) might also be used, but bear in mind that this setting *is* displayed when placing dimension annotation and is one of the display settings that could be defined by the CAD standard you might be using.

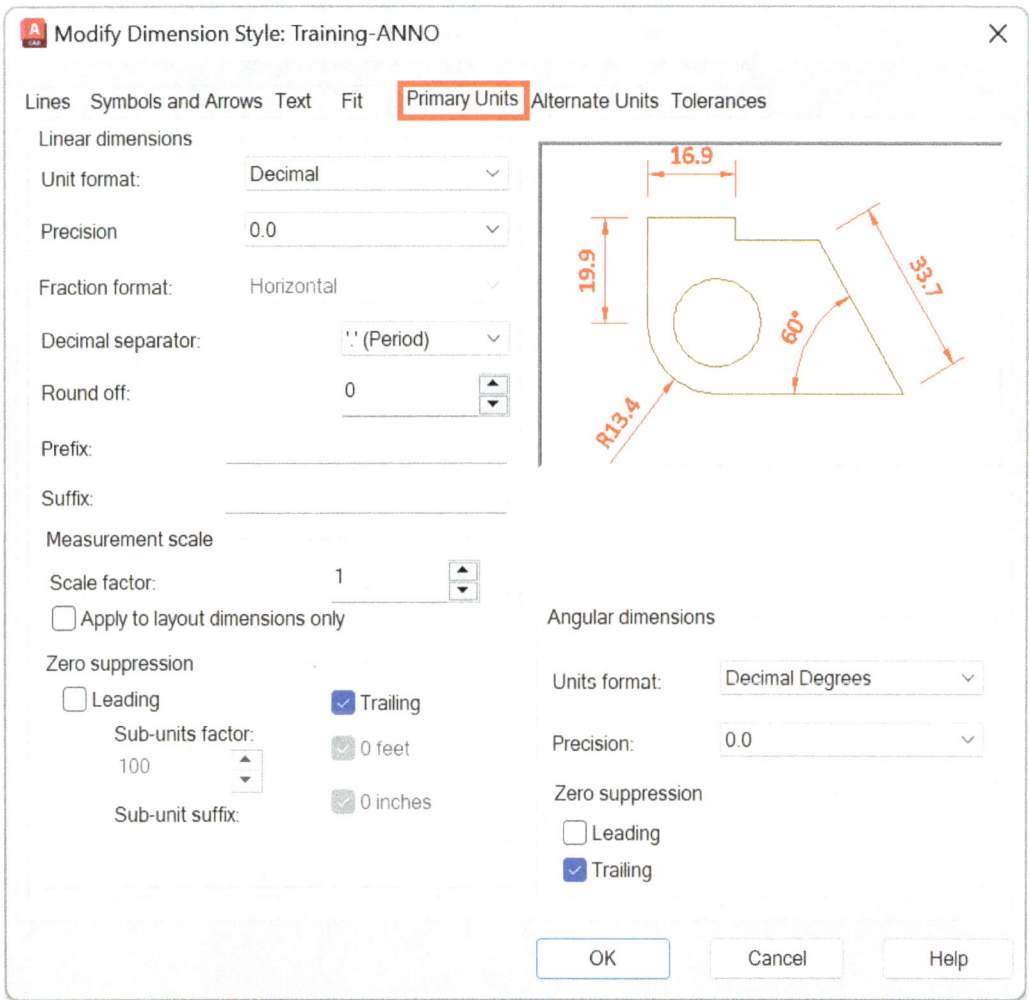

Figure 7.15: The Primary Units tab with the Decimal separator set to Period

160   Developing Annotative Annotation Styles

In this chapter, we will not set any options on the **Alternate Units** tab. You can investigate this at another time if you wish. Alternate units allow for the display of a different set of units when placing dimension annotation. For example, you may be using **METRIC** units for your **PRIMARY** dimension annotation, and you want to display **IMPERIAL** units as your **ALTERNATE** units. To display both in your dimension annotation, you would set your alternate units to the imperial settings you would need to display. *Figure 7.16* shows how the **Alternate Units** tab needs to be set for this chapter. Take note that the **Display alternate units** checkbox is *unchecked*.

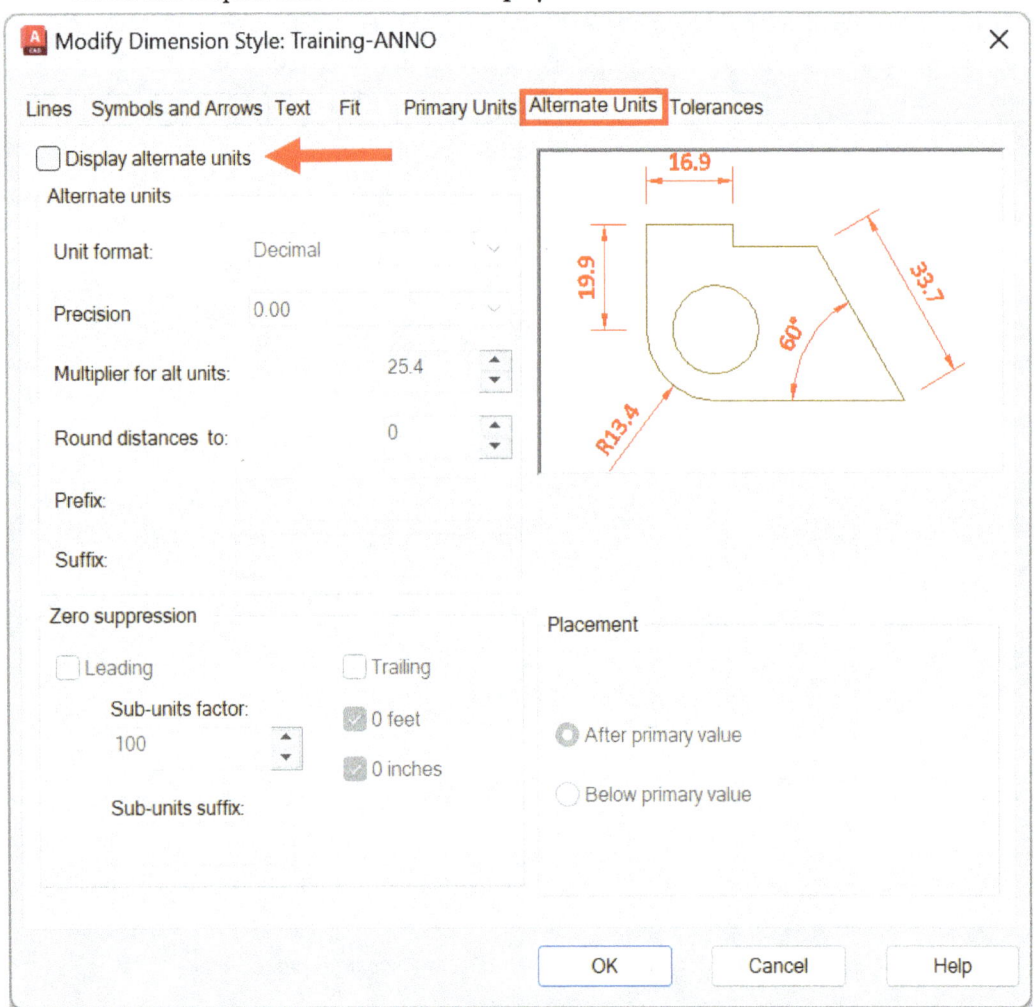

Figure 7.16: The Alternate Units tab with Display alternate units unchecked

Managing dimension annotation with dimension styles 161

18. There will be no **tolerances** needed in this dimension style. Tolerances tend to be used in machining and manufacturing to display lateral tolerances in a material when it is machined for manufacture. These tolerances apply to an aspect of a part, such as a point, line, axis, or surface. Tolerances are often used in mechanical and production drawings, where the drawn objects are cut, planed, or milled. These production processes require a tolerance as the tools and machinery used are (normally) cut into a material such as metal. These processes will never be absolute, so the appropriate tolerances are needed. In the case of the exercise file, you do not need any tolerance values.

19. Click on the **Tolerances** tab.

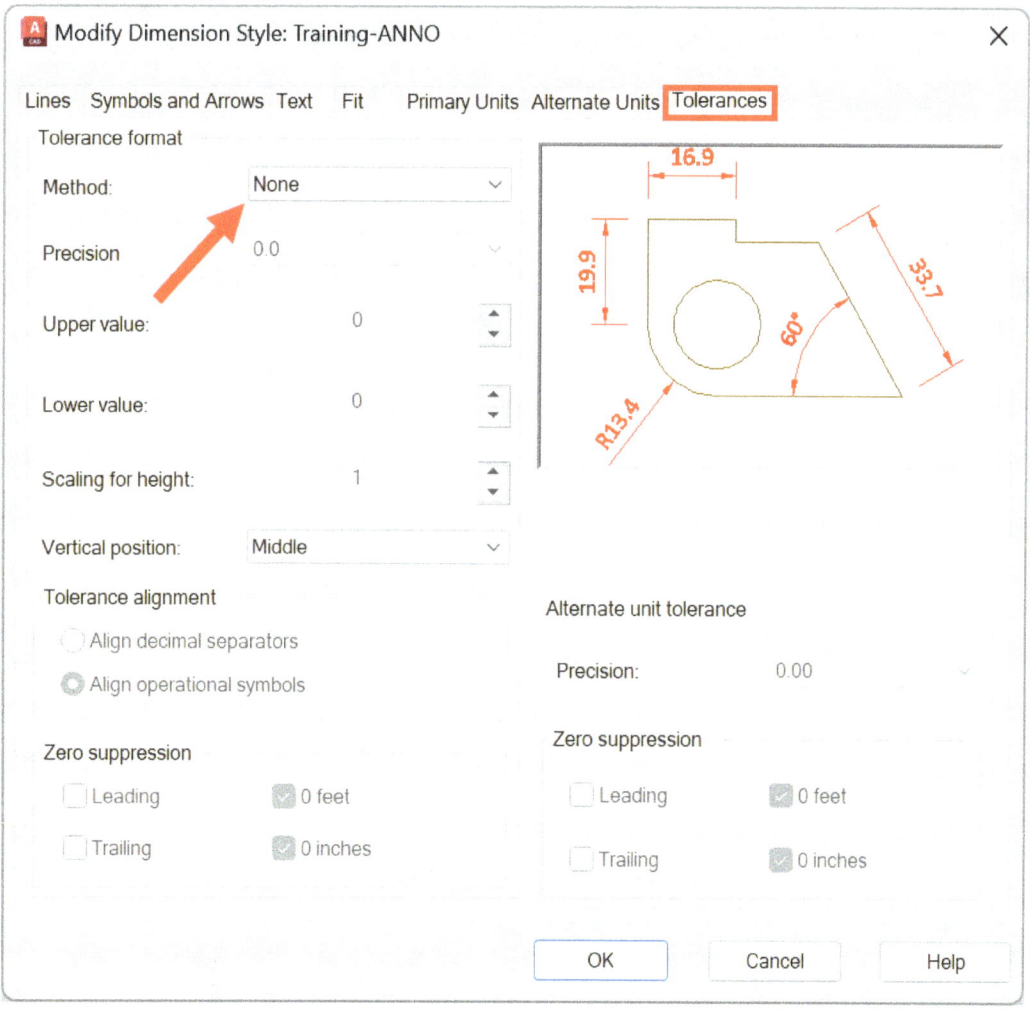

Figure 7.17: The Tolerances tab

20. Ensure the **Method** option under **Tolerance format** is set to **None**, as shown in *Figure 7.17*. Also, ensure that all other settings in the **Tolerances** tab are set as per *Figure 7.17*. You are then ensuring that no tolerances are used in your dimension style.

21. Click on **OK**. Your dimension style is now set up and displayed in **Dimension Style Manager**, as shown in *Figure 7.18*.

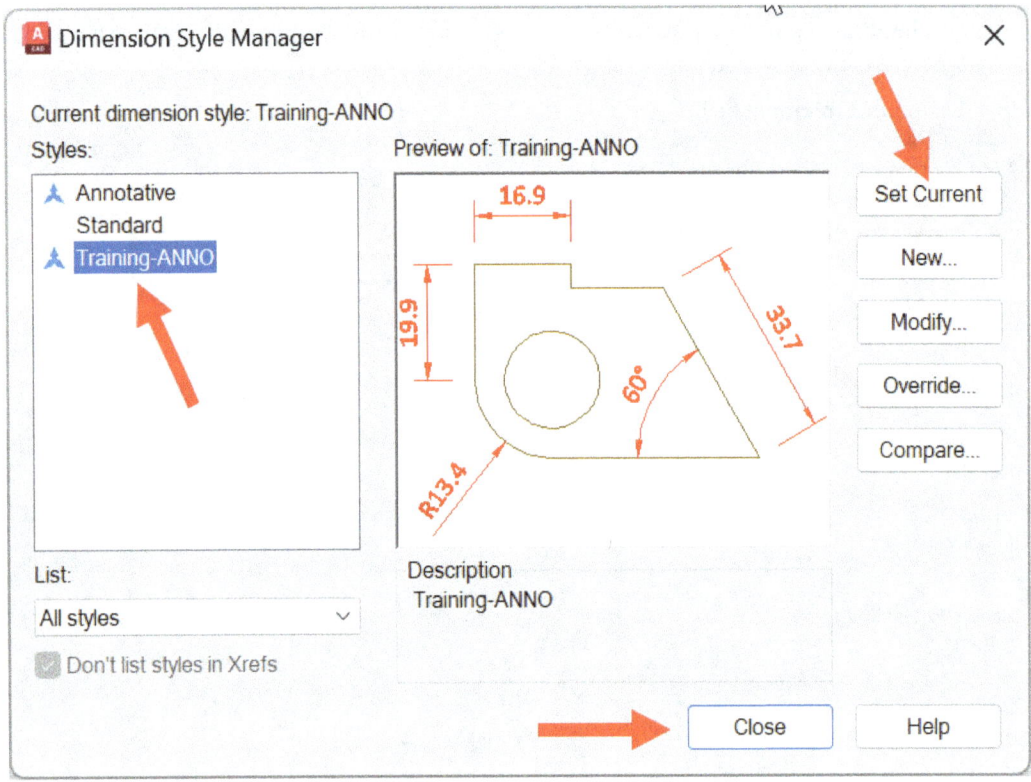

Figure 7.18: Dimension Style Manager with the Training-ANNO dimension style current

22. Select the new **Training-ANNO** annotative dimension style in the left pane so that it highlights in blue, as shown in *Figure 7.18*.

23. Click on **Set Current**, and then click on **Close**.

24. Your new annotative dimension style (**Training-ANNO**) is now the current dimension style in the `New Office Proposal.dwg` file.

25. Make sure to save the drawing so the dimension style is saved in the DWG file.

Tips and tricks #23

When working with dimension styles, there is often a need to remove unused dimension styles from the drawing file to maintain file size and for general housekeeping of your DWG files. To do so, you can right-click over non-used dimension styles in **Dimension Style Manager** and use **Delete** in the shortcut menu (see *Figure 7.19*). You can also remove non-used dimension styles with the **Purge** (*PURGE*) command.

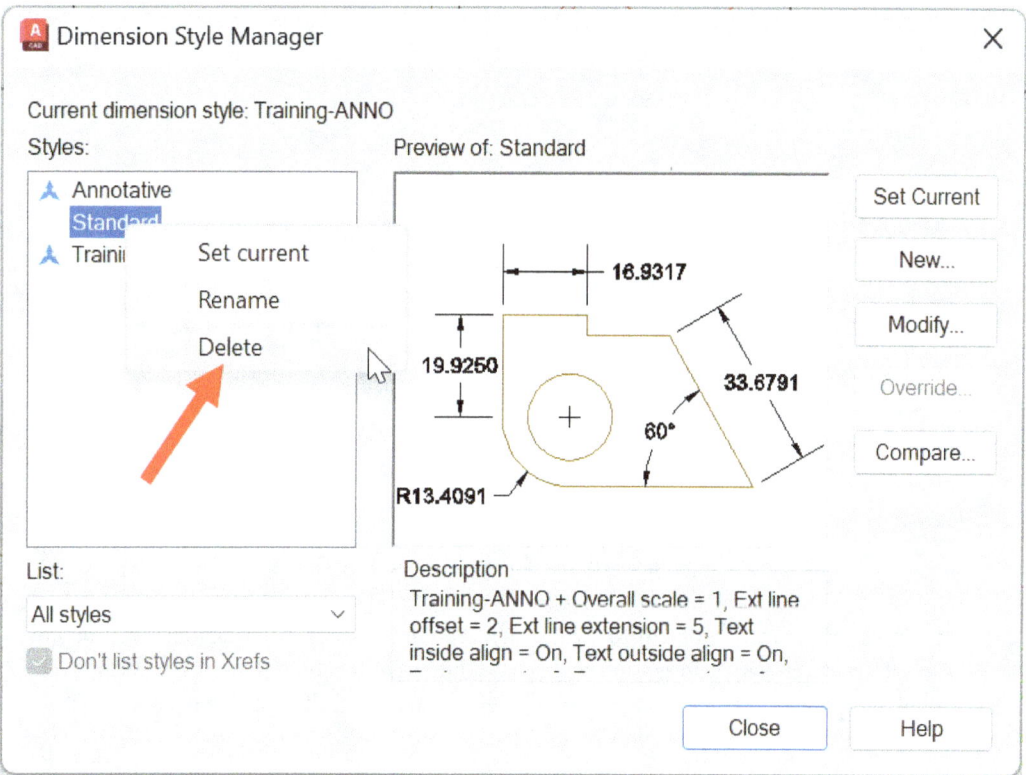

Figure 7.19: Deleting a dimension style using the shortcut menu in Dimension Style Manager

AutoCAD for Mac

When creating a dimension style in AutoCAD for Mac, you will find the **Dimension Style** icon in the **Dimension** panel in the left-hand toolbar. When working with dimension styles in Mac, the dialog boxes are similar but use the usual Mac interface, as shown in *Figure 7.20*.

164 Developing Annotative Annotation Styles

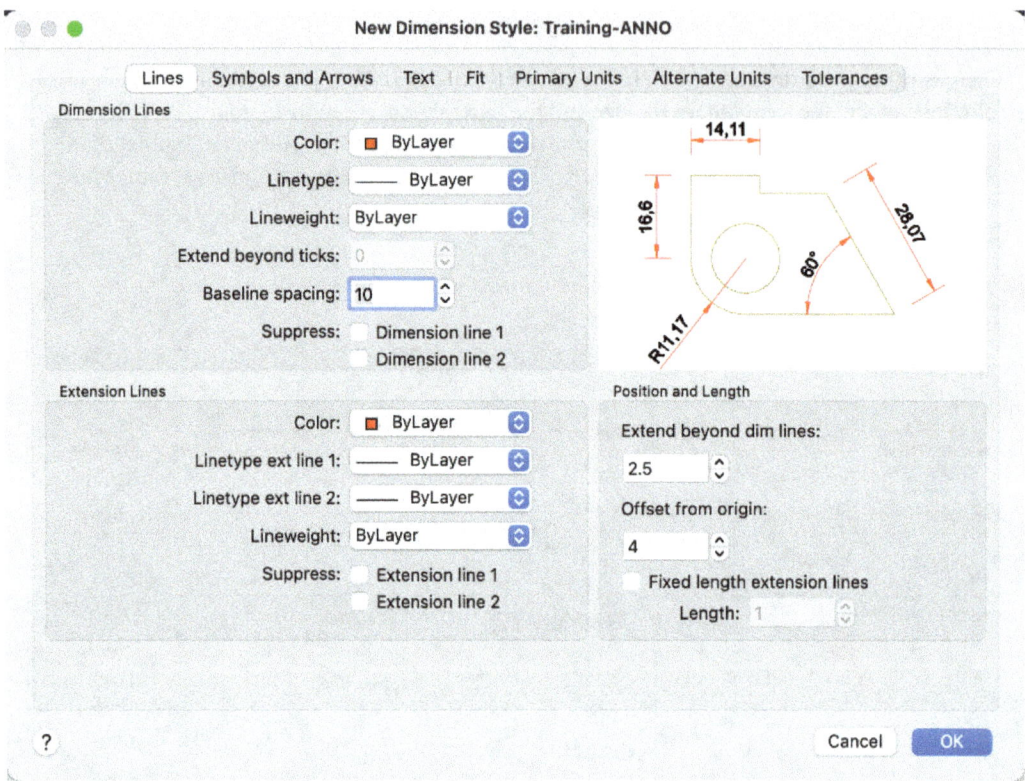

Figure 7.20: Creating a dimension style in AutoCAD for Mac

Dimension annotation is fundamental to your drawings. It communicates your design intent. You now know how to set up an annotative dimension style to add dimension annotation to your drawings. This applies to all drawings, no matter how large or small they are. They will all need dimension annotation to communicate the designs contained in them.

In this section, you learned how to create and implement a new annotative dimension style. Building on that knowledge, you will next set up styles for both **multileaders** (*MLEADER*) and **Quick Leaders** (*QLEADER*) in the upcoming section.

Setting up specific leader styles

In the **Training-ANNO** dimension style, which is now current in the `New Office Proposal.dwg` file, you had set **Dot** for **Leader** lines in the **Symbols and Arrows** tab, as shown in *Figure 7.21*.

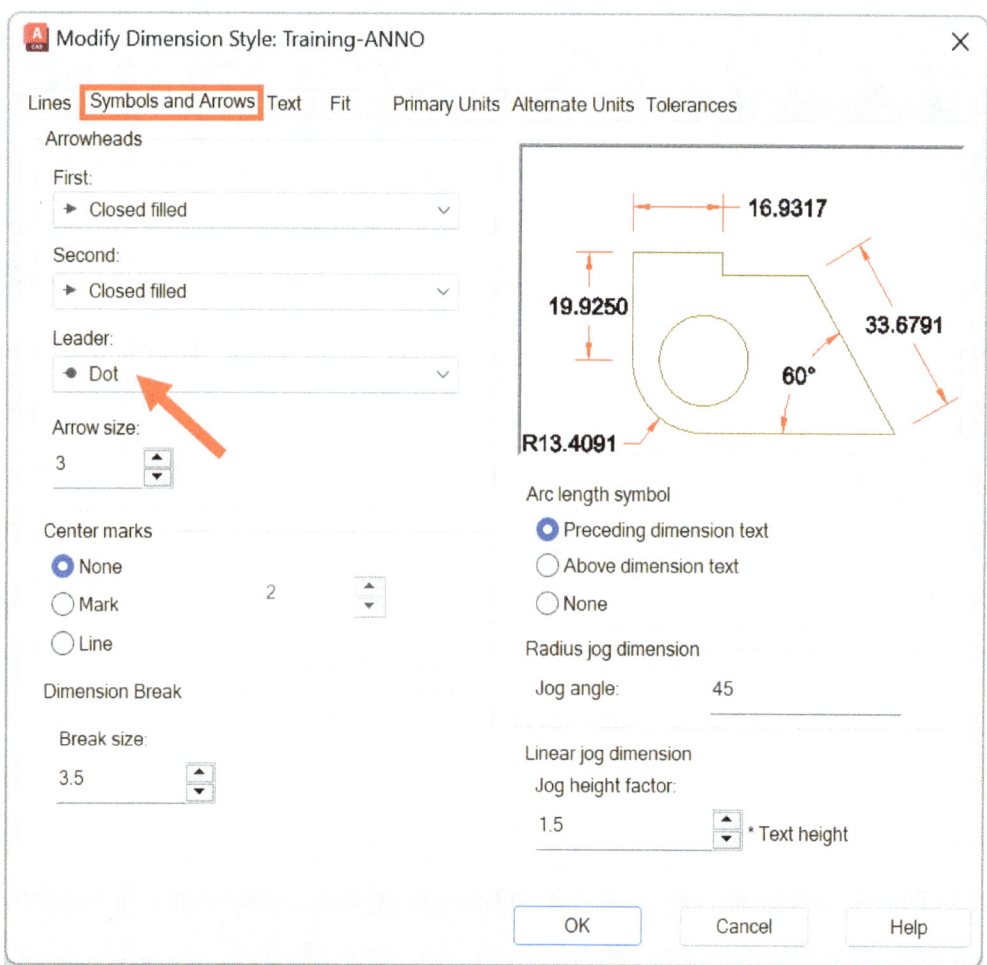

Figure 7.21: The Symbols and Arrows tab with the arrowhead set to Dot for the Quick Leader (QLEADER) command

This dimension style setting will apply to any leaders you may create using the older **Quick Leader** (*QLEADER*) command. You can find out about this leader annotation method in the AutoCAD Help files here:

```
https://help.autodesk.com/view/ACDLT/2019/ENU/?guid=GUID-5FEC133A-5EBD-4EFA-9E44-771E85480DAD
```

166 | Developing Annotative Annotation Styles

As the AutoCAD Help page states, it is recommended, in most cases, that you use the **Multileader** (*MLEADER*) command to create leader objects. There are several reasons for this:

- The *QLEADER* command does not have an icon as it is an older, legacy command. You must always type the command.
- Leaders created using *QLEADER* are not as easy to manipulate in drawings as leaders created using *MLEADER* are.
- You can set up multileader styles quickly and easily and make them annotative, using a similar workflow to your dimension styles. Being annotative in nature also makes multileaders function in a similar way to the dimensions in your drawings.
- Future versions of AutoCAD will see the development of the **Multileader** (*MLEADER*) command, as it is now the preferred method of adding leaders to drawings.

Now, let's go back to the exercise file, New Office Proposal.dwg, which should still be open. You will use this drawing to create a new, annotative, multileader style with the help of the following steps:

1. To create new multileader styles, you need to access the **Multileader Style** dialog box. You can do this in two ways. The first is from the **Home** tab/**Annotation** panel, as shown in *Figure 7.22*.

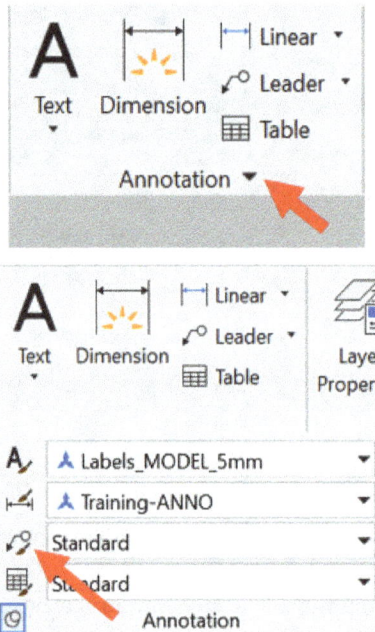

Figure 7.22: Expanding the Annotation panel on the Home tab and then clicking on the Multileader Style icon

You can also use the **Annotate** tab/**Leaders** panel, as shown in *Figure 7.23*. Each method differs slightly, but you end up in the same dialog box.

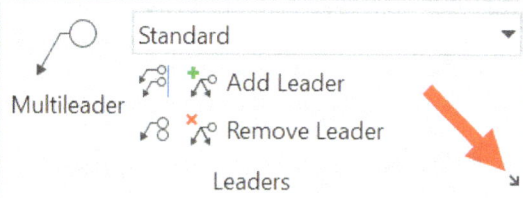

Figure 7.23: Clicking on the arrow icon on the Leaders panel title bar in the Annotate tab on the ribbon

2. Using either method, the **Multileader Style Manager** dialog box appears, with two default multileader styles: **Annotative** and **Standard**, as shown in *Figure 7.24*.

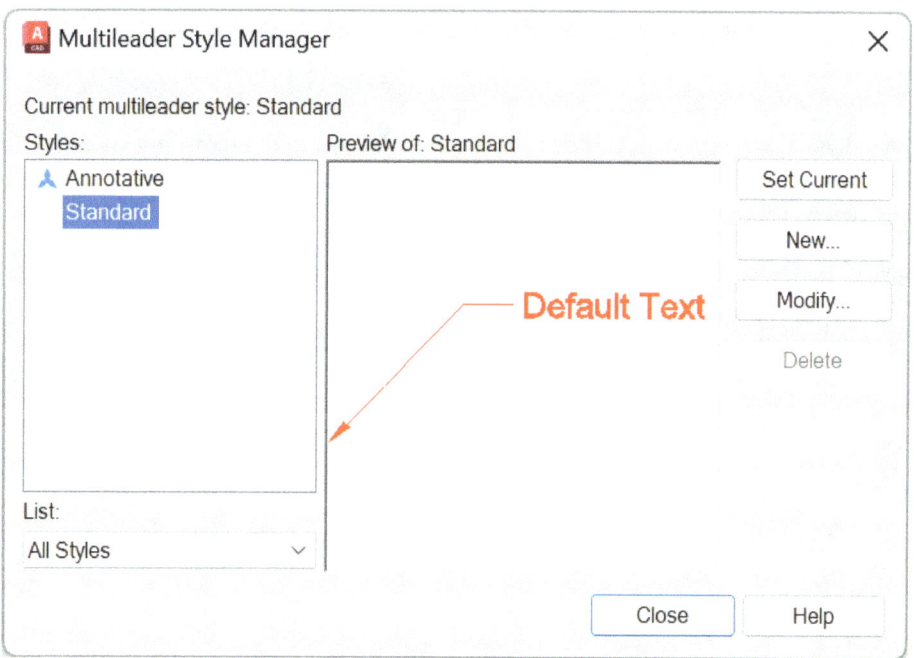

Figure 7.24: Multileader Style Manager

The workflow used to create an annotative multileader style is remarkably similar to that of creating an annotative dimension style. There are just fewer tabs in the dialog box to be considered.

3. Click on **New…** in **Multileader Style Manager**.

4. In the **Create New Multileader Style** dialog box that appears, set a new multileader style with the name Training-ANNO (like the dimension style), set the **Start with** dropdown to **Annotative**, and make sure you check the **Annotative** checkbox, as shown in *Figure 7.25*.

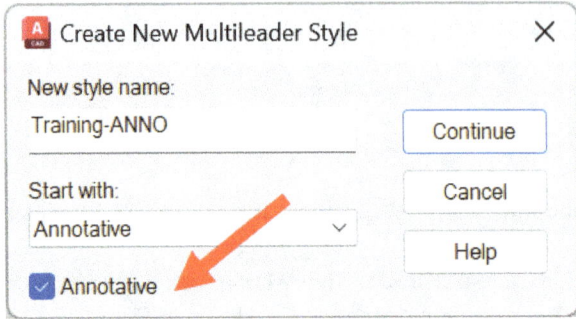

Figure 7.25: The Create New Multileader Style dialog box

5. Click on **Continue**.
6. You will now see a very familiar dialog box. It looks like the one you used for your annotative dimension style, but you are now developing an annotative multileader style. Ensure you have the **Leader Format** tab current and set it to the settings shown in *Figure 7.26*.

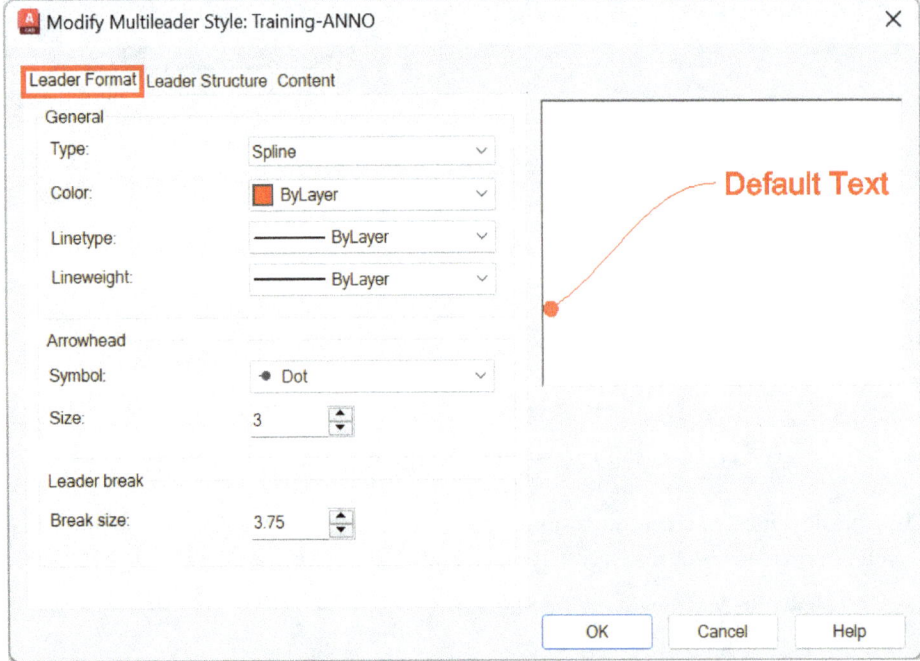

Figure 7.26: The Modify Multileader Style dialog box set to the Leader Format tab

7. Once the **Leader Format** settings are configured, click on the **Leader Structure** tab to make it current.
8. There are no settings that need to be changed in this tab. Just ensure that they are the same as shown in *Figure 7.27*, and that the **Annotative** checkbox is checked, making it an annotative multileader style.

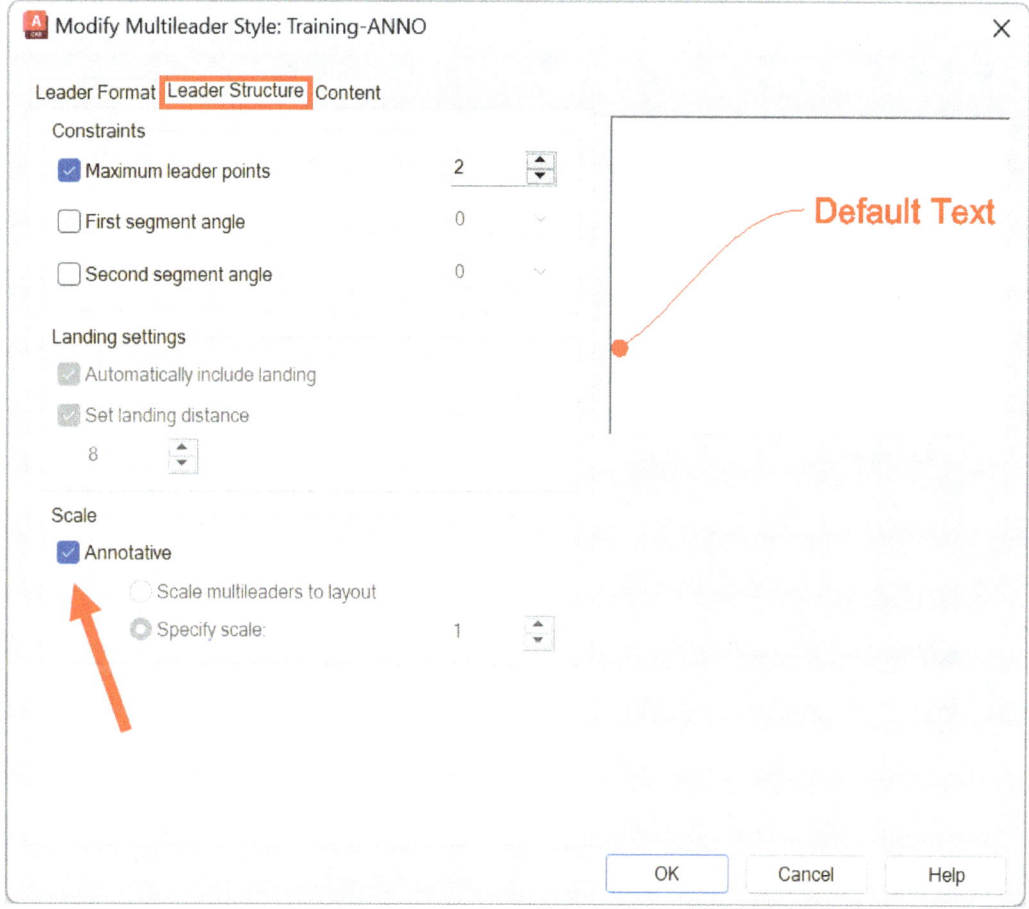

Figure 7.27: The Leader Structure tab as current, ensuring that the Annotative checkbox is checked (arrowed)

9. Now, click on the **Content** tab to make it current.
10. You will be creating a multileader that has **Mtext** content. Multileaders use multiline (*MTEXT*) content so that you can utilize the contextual **Text Editor** ribbon tab.

11. Ensure that you have set all the settings shown in *Figure 7.28* in the **Content** tab.

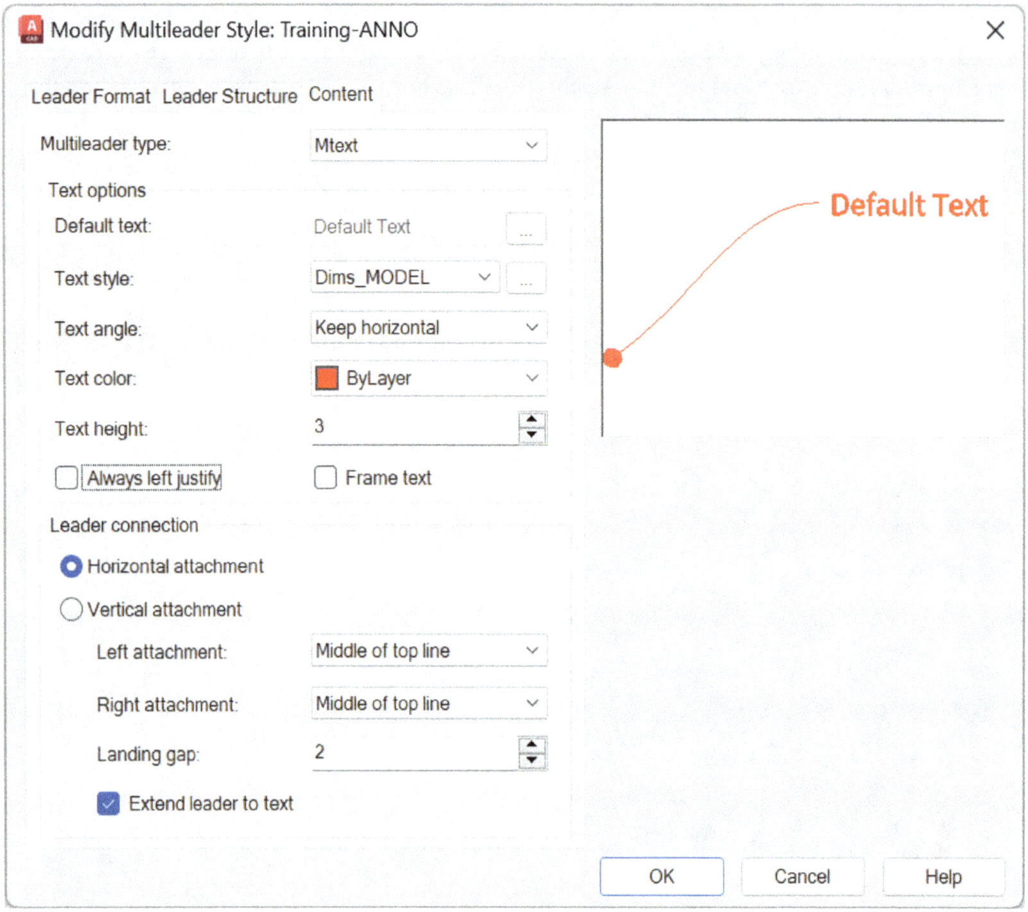

Figure 7.28: The settings in the Content tab

12. Now that your multileader style settings are complete, click on **OK**.
13. You will now be returned to **Multileader Style Manager**. Like with the **Dimension Style Manager** workflow in the previous section, select the **Training-ANNO** annotative multileader style in the list in the left-hand pane, and click on **Set Current** to make it the current multileader style in the drawing.
14. Click on **Close** to close **Multileader Style Manager**.

You now have an annotative multileader style in the drawing.

Tips and tricks #24

When working with annotation styles, especially dimension styles and multileader styles, it is a good idea to make the layer you want these annotation types to use current. Then, when you set the properties in the annotation styles to **ByLayer**, the preview in the relevant style manager displays on the appropriate layer. Look at *Figure 7.29*. The dimension style has adopted the layer properties in the preview panel, using the current dimension layer, which is red in color. This is a good habit to get into. Using the **ByLayer** setting for your multileaders ensures they all adopt the layer settings of the layer they are placed on. Then, if those layer settings need to change, all of your multileaders will update accordingly.

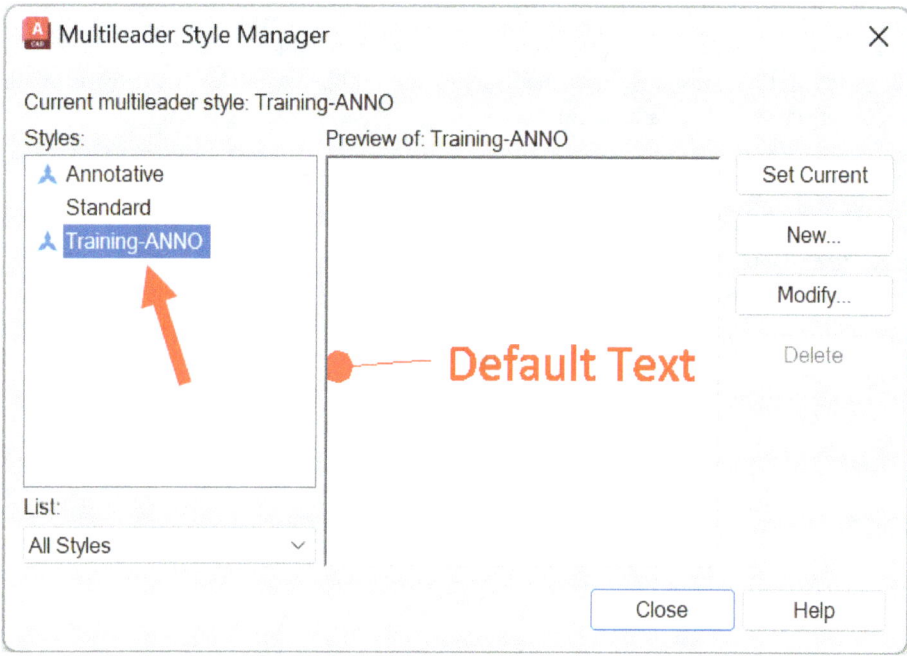

Figure 7.29: The current multileader style (Training-ANNO) shown previewed in Multileader Style Manager

The blue triangular symbol next to a text style indicates that it is an annotative text style.

AutoCAD for Mac

Based on *Tips and tricks #24*, AutoCAD for Mac also adopts the same methodology when using the **ByLayer** setting for annotation styles. The workflow for multileader styles is also very similar, using the Mac interface.

Leader styles are incredibly useful in your drawings. Leaders allow you to highlight specific areas of interest in a drawing that need further description and allow you to keep any descriptive text or symbology away from the objects that make up your design, providing clarity and making the drawing easy to read and understand.

In this section, you learned how to create and implement multileader styles. Both dimension and multileader styles allow you to annotate your designs, communicating design intent. In the next section, you will dive into another important feature of AutoCAD.

Working with accurate table styles

AutoCAD also allows you to tabulate data from your drawings in tables. These tables can be defined using table styles in the same way as dimension styles and multileader styles and provide tabulated annotation for effective design data communication.

You should still have the exercise file, `New Office Proposal.dwg`, open. Using this file, you will create a new, simple table style for room areas. The steps to do so are as follows:

1. To create new table styles, you need to access the **Table Style** dialog box. You can do this in two ways. The first is from the **Home** tab/**Annotation** panel, as shown in *Figure 7.30*.

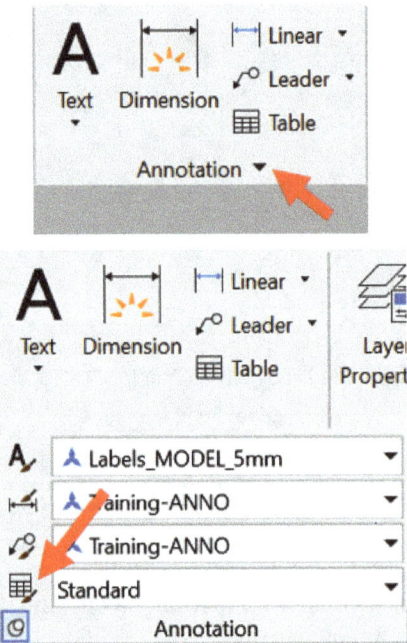

Figure 7.30: Expanding the Annotation panel on the Home tab and then clicking on the Table Style icon

You can also use the **Annotate** tab/**Tables** panel, as shown in *Figure 7.31*. Each method differs slightly, but you end up in the same dialog box.

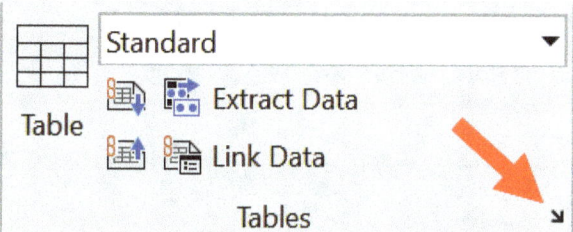

Figure 7.31: Clicking on the arrow icon on the Tables panel title bar in the Annotate tab on the ribbon

2. When creating the dimension and/or multileader styles, you can set various style properties to **ByLayer**. Create a new layer called `Tables` and set it to **Gray** as a color (*Color 8*). Set it as the current layer, and when you set any table style properties to **ByLayer**, they will display on the **Tables** layer in any previews.

3. Using either method to access table styles, you will end up with the **Table Style** dialog box being displayed, as shown in *Figure 7.32*.

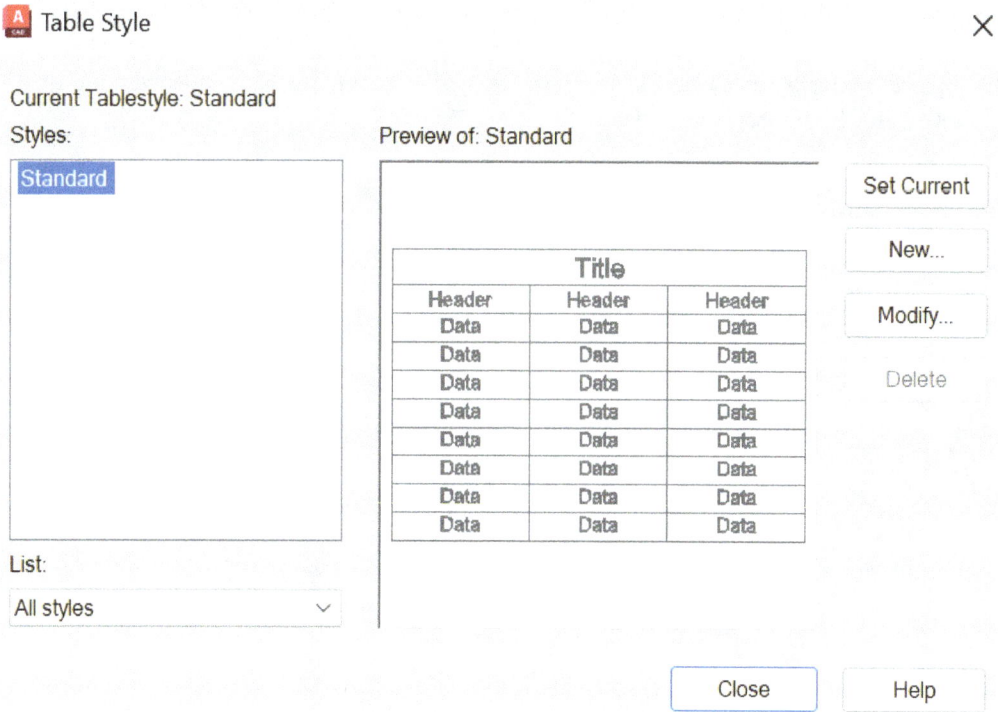

Figure 7.32: The Table Style dialog box

4. Click on **New…**.

5. In the **Create New Table Style** dialog box, add a new table style name, `Training`. Set **Start With** to **Standard** (the default table style), as shown in *Figure 7.33*.

Figure 7.33: The Create New table Style dialog box

6. Click on **Continue**.

   The **New Table Style** dialog box is displayed, as shown in *Figure 7.34*. Notice you can select an existing table style to start with (arrowed). This allows you to select an existing table in your drawing and use its table style as a template.

7. Make sure that **Table direction** is set to **Down**. This ensures that the **Title** and **Header** fields are at the top of the table. If it was set to **Up**, they would appear at the bottom of the table.

8. You will be creating a new table style from scratch, so make sure you have **Cell styles** (top-right) set to **Title** in the drop-down menu.

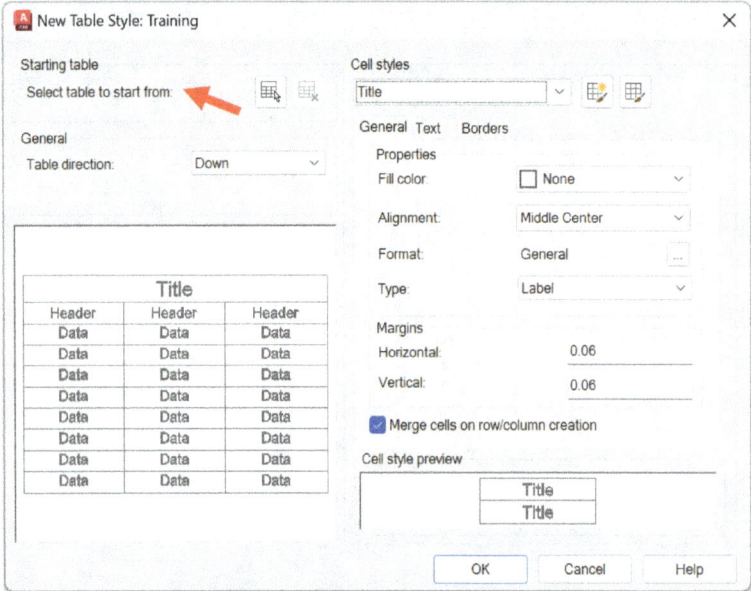

Figure 7.34: The New Table Style dialog box

9. You will be setting the table properties for the **Title** field (see the preview in the dialog box). Select the **General** tab first.

10. In **Properties**, set the following:

    - **Fill color**: **None**
    - **Alignment**: **Middle Center**
    - **Type**: **Label**
    - **Margins**: 25 (**Horizontal** and **Vertical**)

    Leave **Merge Cells on row/column creation** checked.

    You will see the **Cell style preview** update. It might look a bit odd initially (see the arrows in *Figure 7.35*) but this is because all the properties have not been updated in the table style yet.

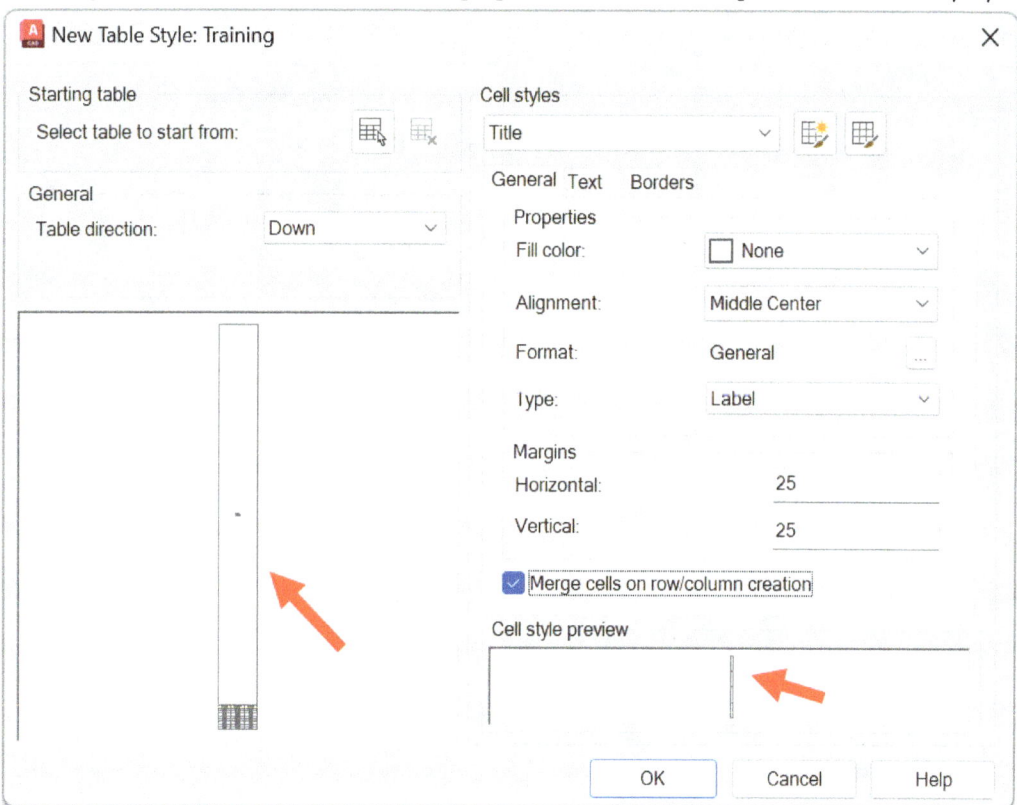

Figure 7.35: The Title cell style General tab

11. Now, select the **Text** tab and then set the following text properties for the **Title** cell style:

    - **Text style**: **Dims_MODEL**
    - **Text height**: `100`
    - **Text color**: **ByLayer**
    - **Text angle**: `0` (horizontal)

    Your table style and cell style previews should now look as they do in *Figure 7.36* (arrowed).

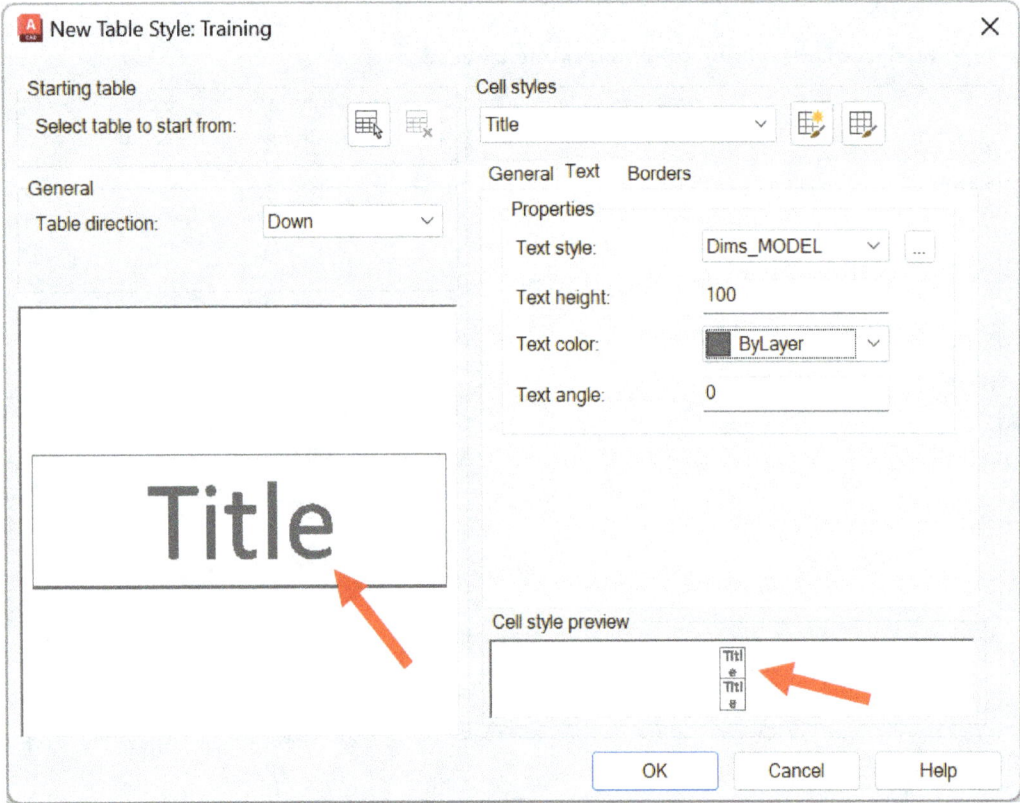

Figure 7.36: The Title cell style Text tab

12. Select the **Borders** tab.

13. Set the **Lineweight**, **Linetype**, and **Color** properties to **ByLayer**, as shown in *Figure 7.37* (arrowed).

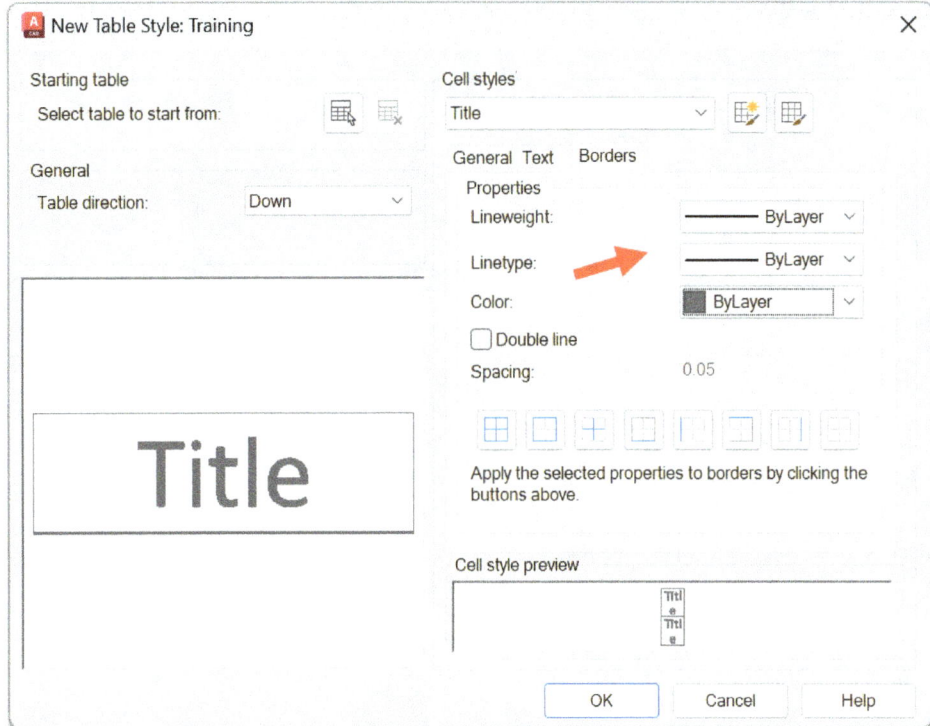

Figure 7.37: The Title cell style Borders tab

As you can see, the table style still looks odd in the table and cell style previews. Do not worry. The next steps will rectify this.

14. In the **Cell styles** drop-down menu, select **Header**, as shown in *Figure 7.38*.

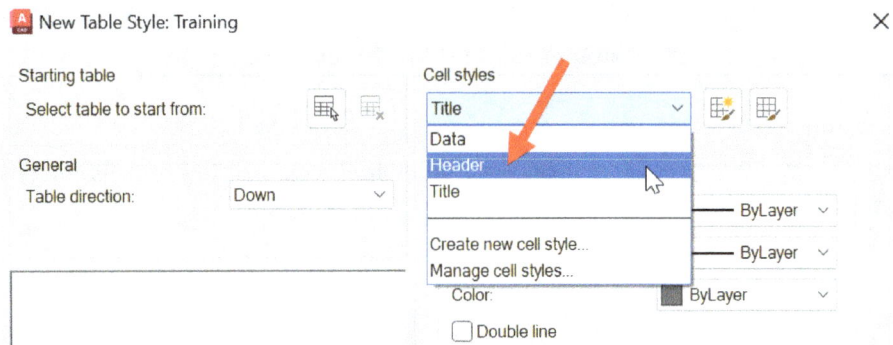

Figure 7.38: The Header cell style in the Cell styles drop-down menu

15. In the **General** tab, use the same settings as for the **Title** cell style.
16. In the **Text** tab, set **Properties** as shown in *Figure 7.39*.

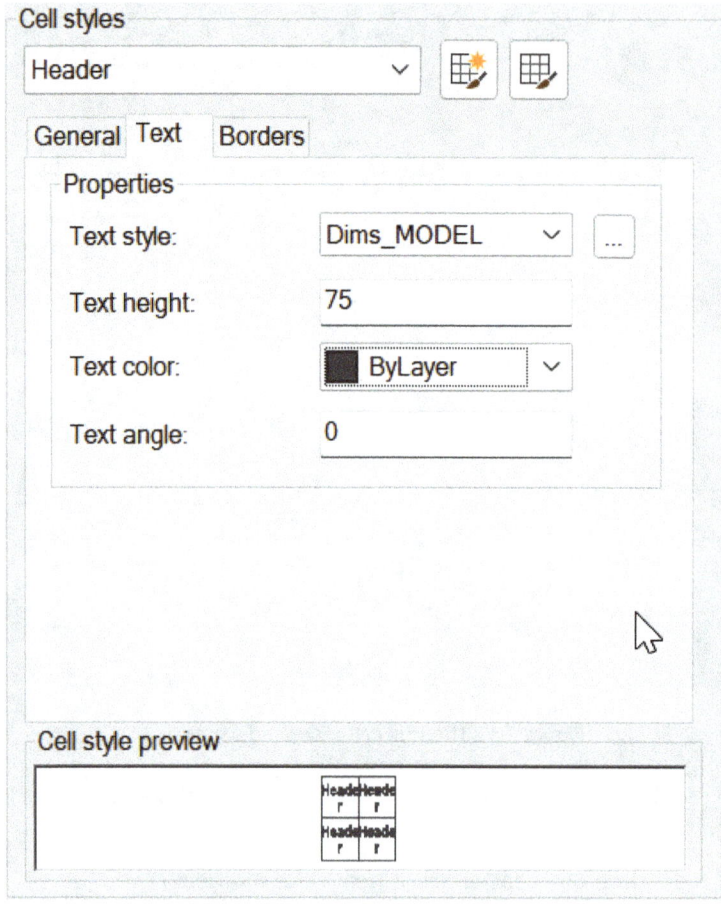

Figure 7.39: The Header cell style Text properties

17. In the **Borders** tab, set **Properties** to the same as those used for the **Title** cell style, with **ByLayer**.
18. Your table style is now looking more normal as the **Header** cell style looks sensible in the table and cell style previews, as it does in *Figure 7.40*.

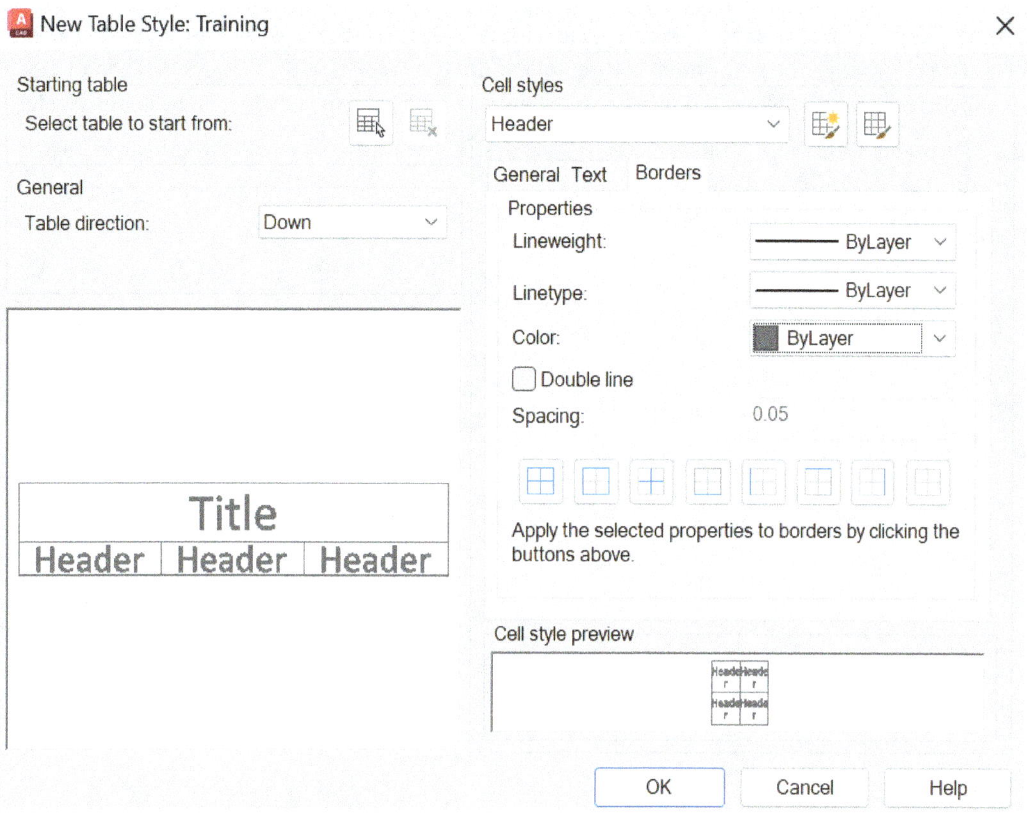

Working with accurate table styles   179

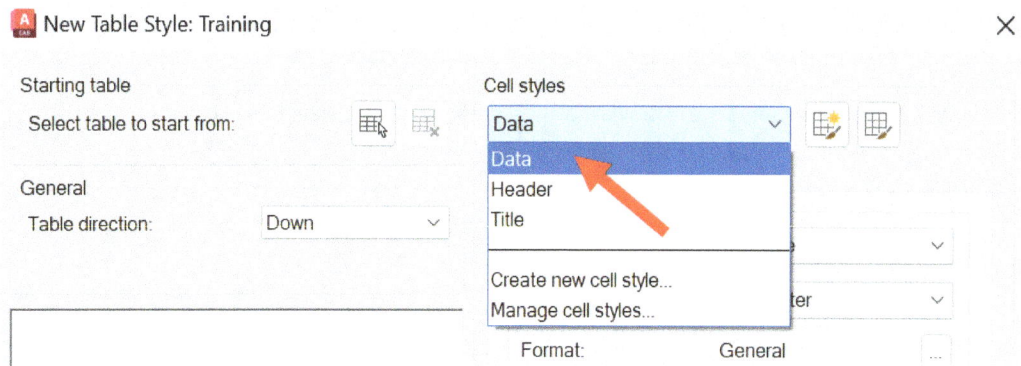

Figure 7.40: The Header cell style Borders tab

19. Now, select the **Data** cell style in the **Cell styles** drop-down menu, as shown in *Figure 7.41*.

Figure 7.41: The Data cell style in the Cell style drop-down menu

180 Developing Annotative Annotation Styles

20. Use all of the same **Properties** settings for the **Data** cell style as were used for the **Header** cell style but change the **Alignment** setting to **Middle Center**. AutoCAD always defaults to **Top Center** for **Data** cells, and **Middle Center** alignment tends to look that little bit neater in a table!

21. Your table style should now look like *Figure 7.42* in the preview (arrowed on the left side) in the **New Table Style** dialog box.

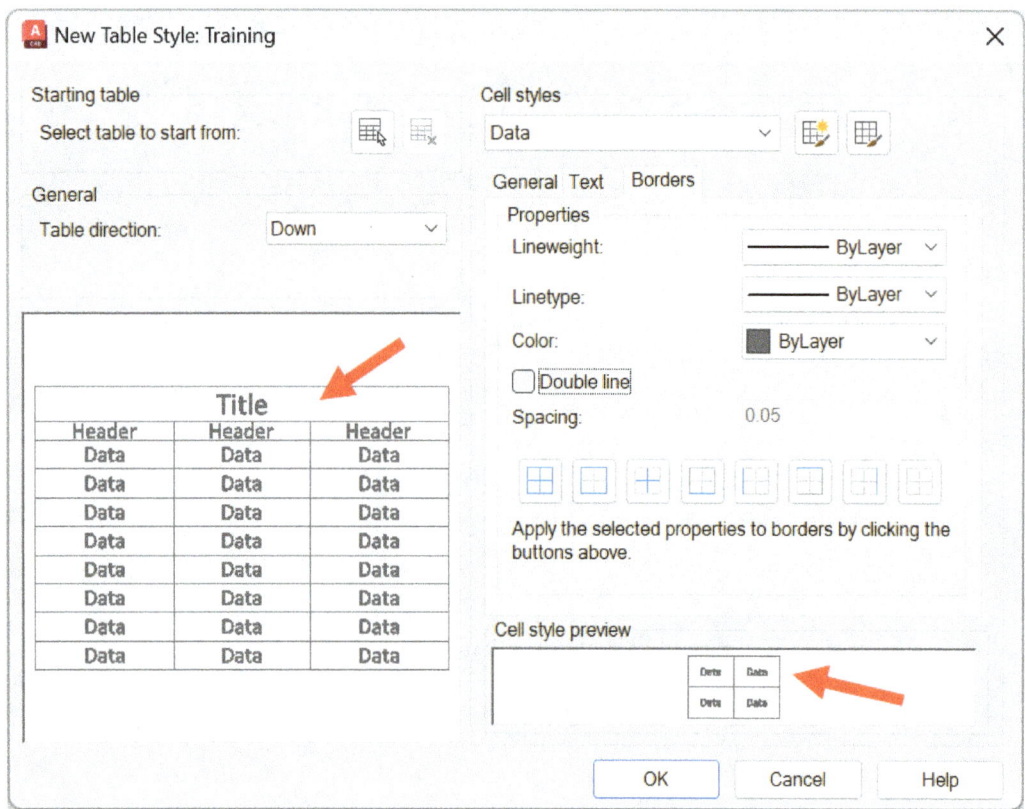

Figure 7.42: The new table style in preview with all properties in the New Table Style dialog box

22. Click on **OK**.

23. In the **Table Style** dialog box, you will see the new **Training** table style. Select it in the left-hand pane (see *Figure 7.43*) and click on **Set Current**. It is now the current table style in the drawing.

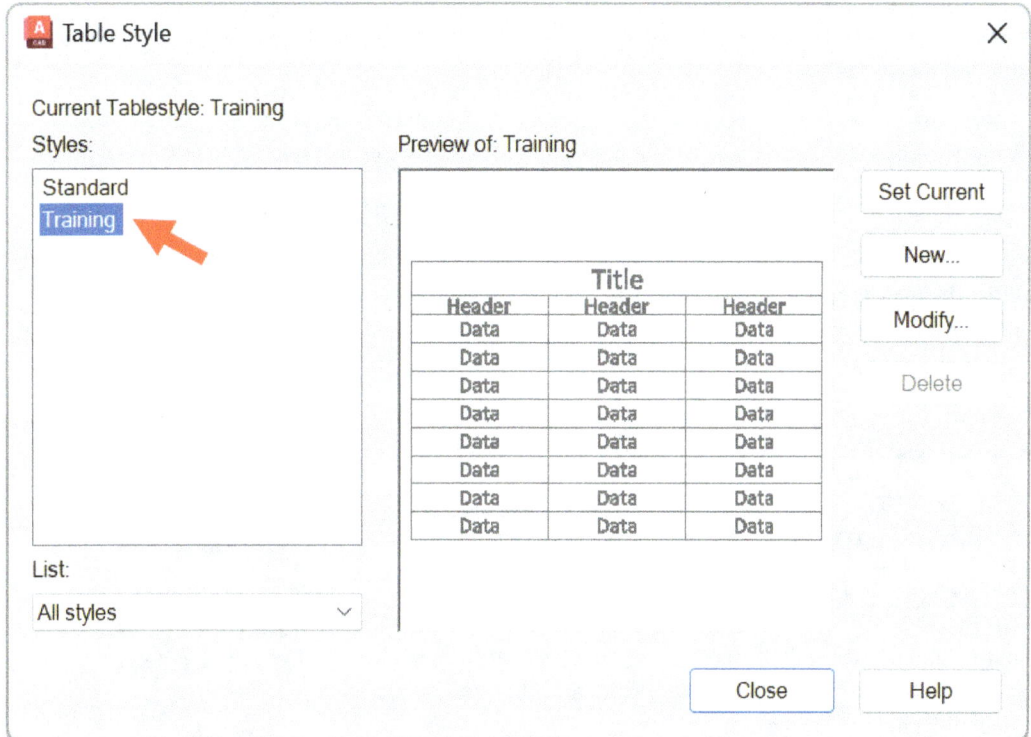

Figure 7.43: The new table style in the Table Style dialog box

24. Click on **Close** to close the **Table Style** dialog box.
25. Make sure to save your drawing to save the table style in the `New Office Proposal.dwg` exercise file.

In this section, you learned how to set up a table style in readiness to add table annotation to your drawings. This will enable you to tabulate pertinent data in your drawings in an easy-to-read format.

Summary

You now have a drawing with a text style, a dimension style, a leader style, and a table style. In this chapter, we have gained knowledge about how to create and implement new annotative and non-annotative text styles.

You have also learned how to set up an annotative dimension style to prepare for beginning work on a drawing, as well as working with a new annotative multileader style to enable labeling in a new drawing.

You have also learned how to configure a new table style in preparation for tabulating drawing information.

Through the exercises discussed in this chapter, you have learned that annotation styles must be created and implemented effectively and accurately to ensure that information and data are interpreted correctly. When building or manufacturing, for instance, the design intent and information must be precise to ensure that whatever is being built or made is made to the correct size, material, and specification.

In the next chapter, we will look at how you can utilize your annotative annotation styles to undertake annotation scaling in your AutoCAD drawings.

Get This Book's PDF Version and Exclusive Extras

Scan the QR code (or go to `packtpub.com/unlock`). Search for this book by name, confirm the edition, and then follow the steps on the page.

Note: Keep your invoice handy. Purchases made directly from Packt don't require one.

8
Working with Annotative Scaling

AutoCAD provides the flexibility and versatility to easily mix and match your annotative styles with your chosen annotation scales, making for an easy workflow when adding the necessary annotation to a drawing. Combining annotative styles with annotative scaling can help create a comprehensive drawing that is easy to read and understand.

Effective annotation ensures that your designs are understood and implemented precisely and accurately, whether a new building, a wiring connector in an electric vehicle, or a new landscape in a garden.

A significant amount of time in AutoCAD is spent annotating designs and annotation styles. When combined with annotation scales, users must, therefore, ensure all drawing information is presented accurately to the appropriate scale.

This chapter covers the following ways to utilize annotation styles with annotative scaling in your DWG files:

- Setting up viewports and varying viewport scales
- Working with annotation scales in the Model tab
- Adding and deleting object annotation scales

That annotation must be displayed appropriately to your project stakeholders and team members to communicate design intent effectively and accurately.

In the previous chapter, you learned how to create and manage annotative styles for text and dimension annotation. In this chapter, you will learn how to combine those annotative styles with annotative scaling when using scaled viewports in drawing layouts and title blocks.

Exercise files

You must ensure you have downloaded the exercise file, `Office Plan_GROUND FLOOR.dwg`, to follow the sections in this chapter.

Setting up viewports and varying viewport scales

Viewports are essential in an AutoCAD drawing. You need them in your layout tabs to display the essential elements of your design.

Viewports can be set to any scale that you require. For example, you may need a viewport at a small scale (say, `1:100`) for an overall, general arrangement of your design, and then add viewports at larger scales (say, `1:50`, `1:10`, etc.) for more detailed views of your design. Don't be confused by a `1:100` scale being called small. It means that one unit in the scaled viewport represents a hundred units in the **Model** tab. Hence, your view will be smaller, not larger, even though the numbers might not seem to reflect that. A `1:1000` scale would be even smaller, if that makes sense!

This section will teach you how to set up new viewports and scale them accordingly by means of an exercise. To get started, open the exercise file, `Office Plan_GROUND FLOOR.dwg`. It will be in the **Model** tab when it opens, displaying a simple office floor plan without annotation.

Your first step is to move to the layout tab in the drawing. Select the **ISO A3** layout tab, as shown in *Figure 8.1*:

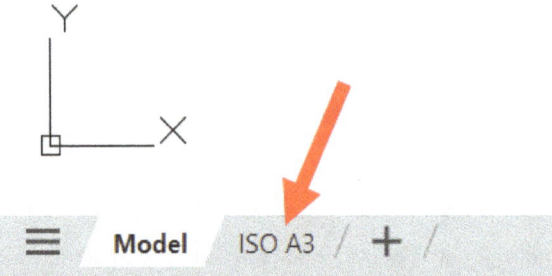

Figure 8.1: The ISO A3 layout tab (with the Model tab currently selected)

The **ISO A3** layout tab is set to an *ISO metric A3 sheet size*. You can set any sheet size in AutoCAD, whether metric or imperial. It all depends on your relevant standards and page setups. For the purpose of this chapter, it's recommended that you use the **ISO A3** sheet size.

You can define different page setups using sheet sizes and sheet orientations to plot and publish the various details from your drawings. You might have one page setup for plans, one for elevations, and one for details, for example.

The following URL takes you to an Autodesk web page explaining why page setups can assist you when working in AutoCAD:

https://www.autodesk.com/learn/ondemand/tutorial/understanding-page-setups-for-printing?msockid=063e61fa977165a339ee753f9664640d

You will see that there is one scaled viewport in the layout tab in the exercise file. If you hover over the edge of the viewport with the crosshair/cursor, AutoCAD will display the viewport properties, which are as follows:

- **Color**: ByLayer
- **Layer**: Viewports
- **Standard scale**: 1:40
- **Custom scale**: 0
- **Layer property overrides**: No

Figure 8.2 shows how this is displayed in AutoCAD:

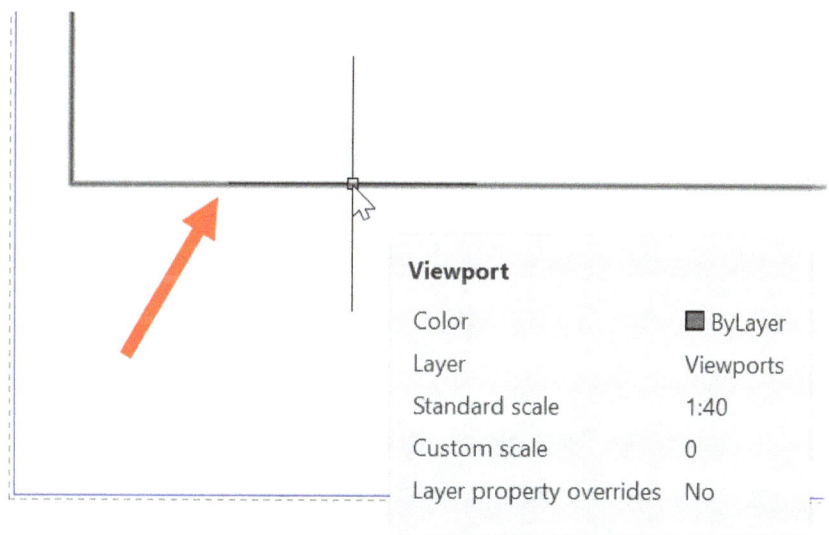

Figure 8.2: The viewport properties displayed

You will now learn how to create and manipulate new and existing viewports and viewport scales by following these steps:

1. Make sure you are in the **ISO A3** layout tab in the exercise file (`Office Plan_GROUND FLOOR.dwg`).
2. Click on the outline of the viewport to select it. The viewport object's grips will be displayed, as shown in *Figure 8.3*:

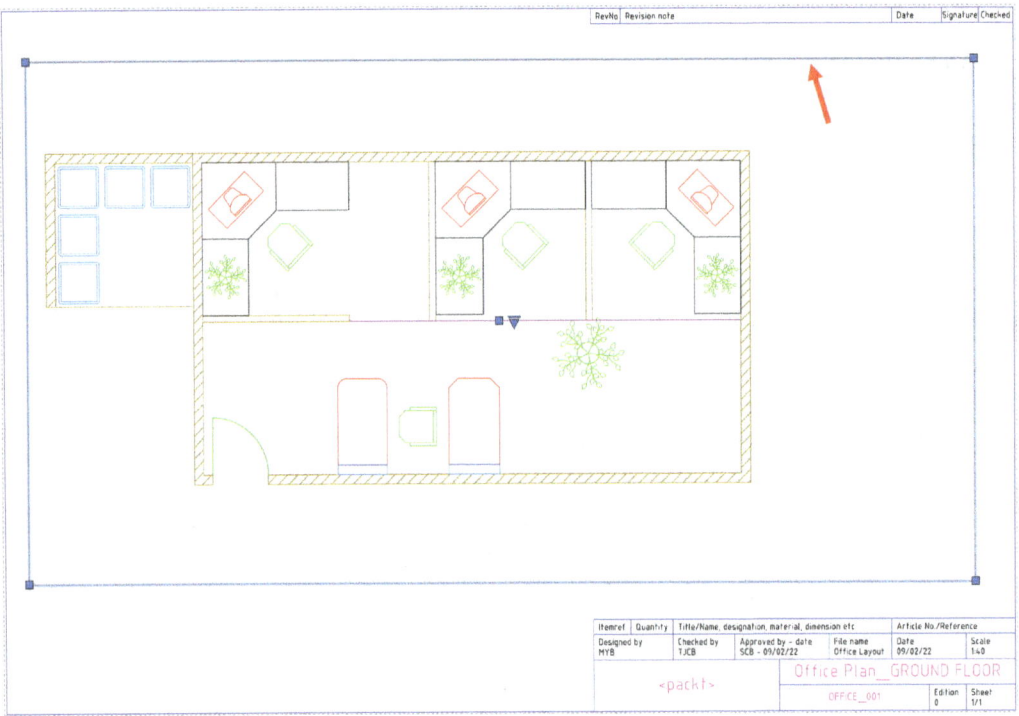

Figure 8.3: The original viewport in the ISO A3 layout tab

Sequentially click on each corner grip and move horizontally and vertically to resize the existing viewport until it looks like the viewport displayed in *Figure 8.4*:

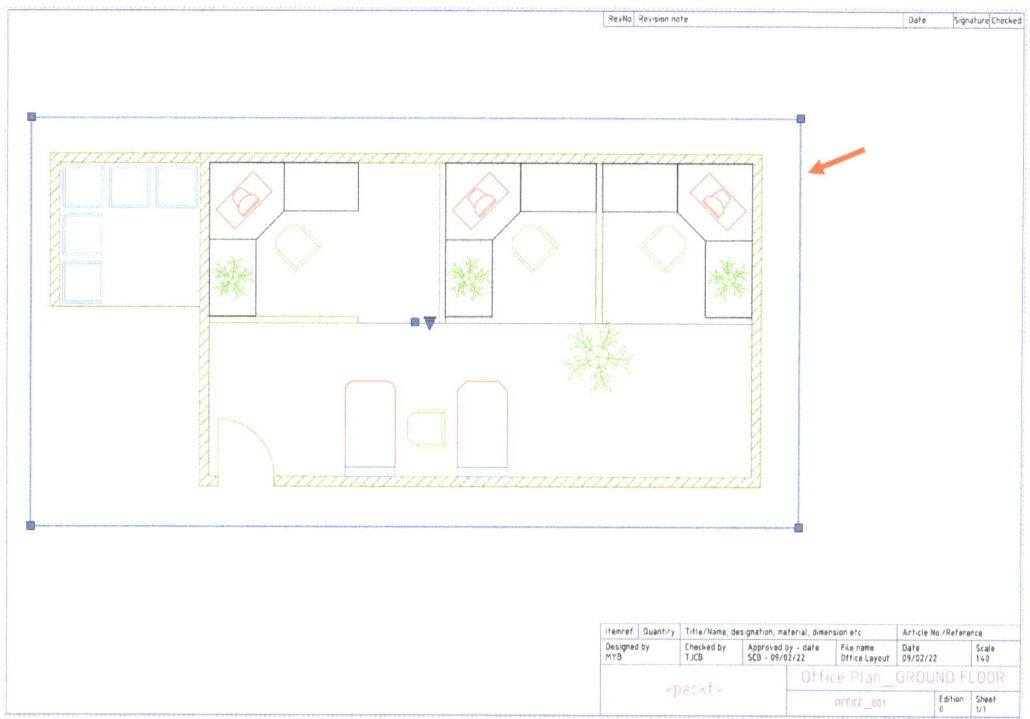

Figure 8.4: The resized viewport in the ISO A3 layout tab

You can toggle between multiple viewports in a layout tab, using the key combination of *Ctrl + R*.

> **Tips and tricks #25**
>
> When you select a viewport, it is not only the grips that are displayed. If you select the triangle dropdown in the center of the selected viewport, you will be able to see all available viewport scales. If you select a different scale from the existing viewport scale, the viewport will be resized and rescaled, as shown in *Figure 8.5*. This also works in AutoCAD for Mac.

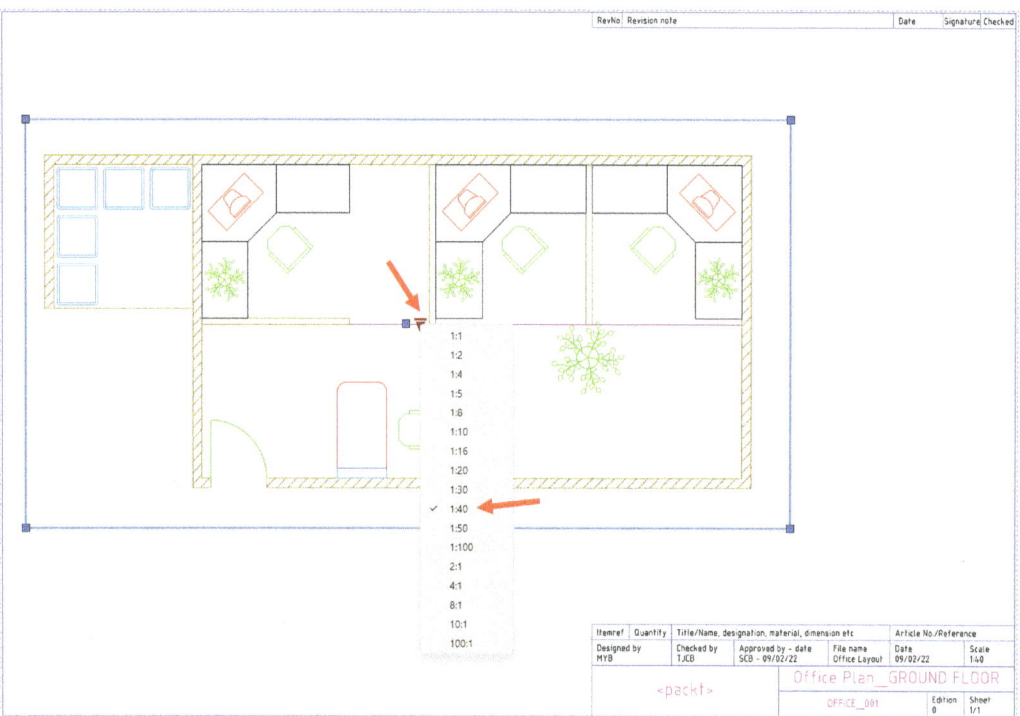

Figure 8.5: The viewport scale dropdown displayed

1. You will now learn another method of revising your viewport scale. With the viewport selected, look down at the status bar, and you will see the viewport scale displayed. At this point, it should still be **1:40**. If you changed it using *Tips and tricks #25*, you will need to use that same method to get the viewport scale back to **1:40**.

2. With the viewport scale displayed at **1:40** in the status bar, select the flyout arrow next to the viewport scale. The list of available scales is displayed in *Figure 8.6*:

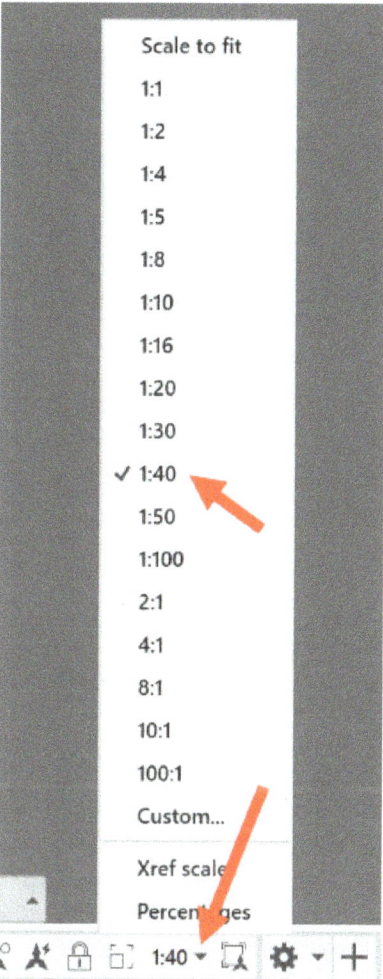

Figure 8.6: Available viewport scales in the displayed scale list

3. Select the **1:50** scale in the list, and the content displayed in the viewport will be resized to that scale, but with this scaling method, the viewport boundary remains the same, as shown in *Figure 8.7*.

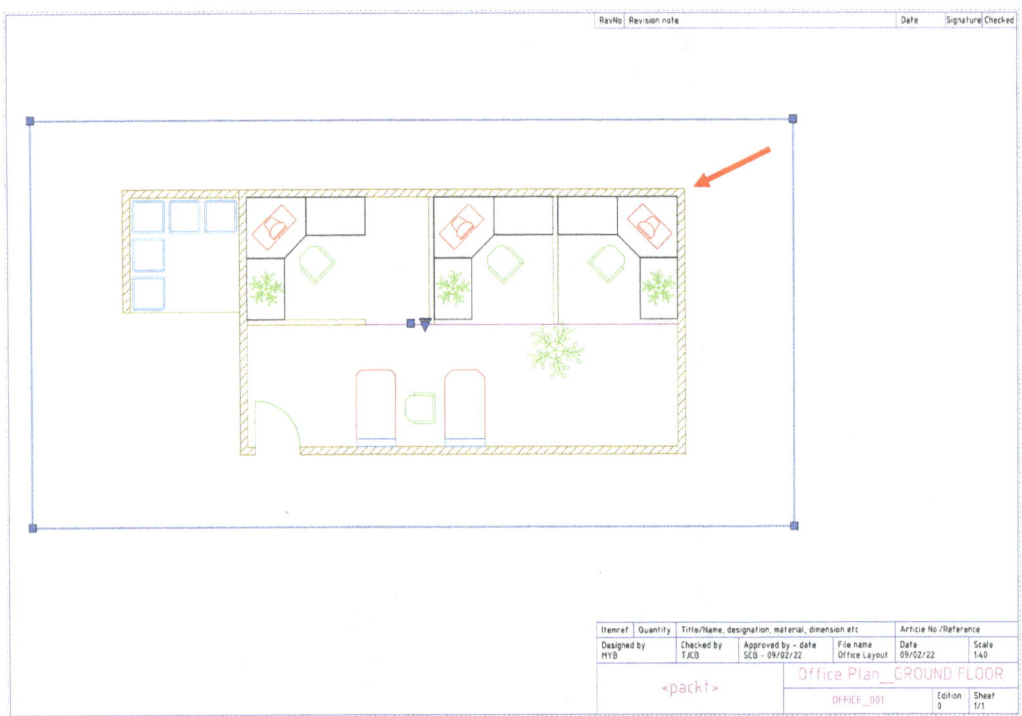

Figure 8.7: Scaling the viewport to 1:50 without resizing the viewport boundary

4. The next step is to rationalize space in your layout. The viewport can be moved like any other AutoCAD object. Ensure the viewport is selected (the blue grips at each corner will be visible, and the outline will go blue). This is also displayed in *Figure 8.7*:

5. Right-click to bring up the shortcut menu. Select **Move**, and then click on the top left corner of the selected viewport (it's an **Endpoint** object snap). Move the viewport upwards and to the left until it is close to the drawing title block, and then click again to place the viewport in the new position. It should look like it does in *Figure 8.8*:

6. It is important to lock the viewport scale. With the relevant viewport selected in the layout tab, make sure to click on the padlock icon in the status bar. It will be locked and turn blue. You can do this for each individual viewport.

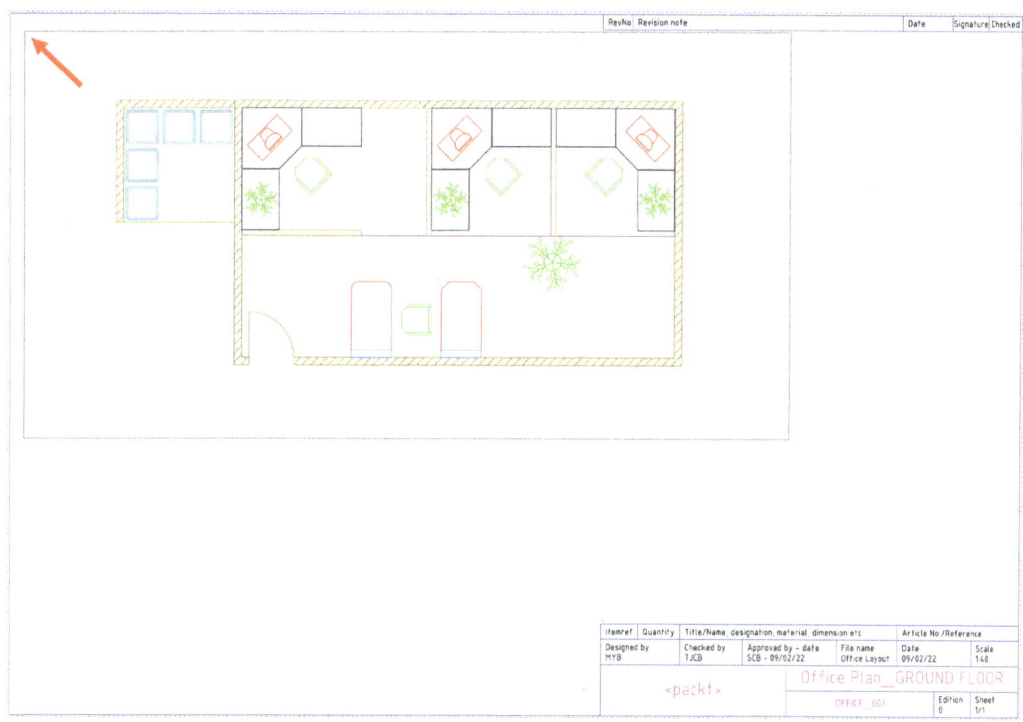

Figure 8.8: The viewport relocated to its new position

7. You now have more space to add other viewports to the drawing. Go to the **Layers** panel in the **Home** tab on the ribbon. Using the **Layer** drop-down menu, ensure **Viewports** is the current drafting layer, as shown in *Figure 8.9*:

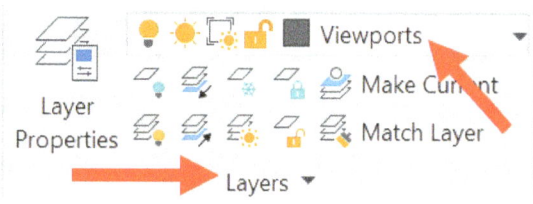

Figure 8.9: The Layers panel with the Viewports layer currently selected

8. You now have enough space in the title block to add another scaled viewport. Click on the contextual **Layout** ribbon tab (which appears in blue on the AutoCAD ribbon). This is displayed because you are in the **ISO A3** layout tab in the drawing.

9. On the **Layout Viewports** panel, select a **Rectangular** viewport type in the top-right dropdown. It is the default type, so it may already be displayed. You can also type `VIEWPORT` and press *Enter*. The **Viewports** dialog box will appear. Selecting the **New Viewports** tab in the dialog box will give you options for various viewport layouts, including single, two vertical, horizontal, and so on. *Figure 8.10* shows the **Layout Viewports** panel and how to select the **Rectangular** viewport type using the ribbon.

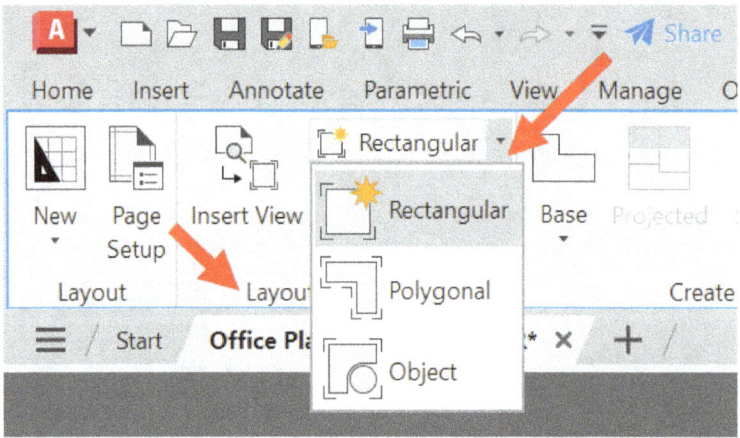

Figure 8.10: The contextual Layout Viewports panel with the viewport type drop-down menu displayed

10. You will now see the **Specify corner of viewport** prompt. Using object snaps, place a new viewport underneath the existing viewport. Use the bottom-left corner of the existing viewport (**Endpoint** snap) and the bottom-left corner of the title block description box (**Endpoint** snap), as shown in *Figure 8.11*. After clicking on the second point, the viewport will be placed automatically.

Setting up viewports and varying viewport scales   193

Figure 8.11: The new viewport with selected corners arrowed

11. The viewport will display a zoomed extents view of what is in the **Model** tab as soon as the viewport is placed. Double-click inside the boundary of the new viewport to activate it. You will see the viewport boundary highlight and you can now work within the viewport as if you were drafting in the **Model** tab. This is colloquially known as *floating modelspace*. *Figure 8.12* shows the viewport activated. When a viewport is active, navigation tools such as the **Navigation Bar**, **ViewCube**, and the **UCS icon** are displayed inside the active viewport.

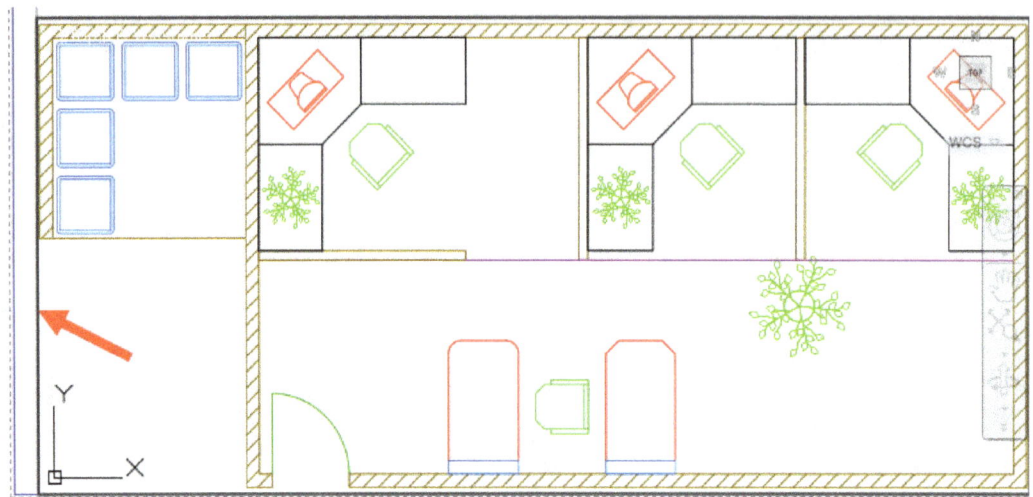

Figure 8.12: The new viewport activated with the Navigation Bar, ViewCube, and UCS icon displayed

12. You should be able to zoom and pan in AutoCAD and, using the mouse wheel to zoom and pan, you need to set a view of the **Executive Office** in the new viewport. This is the larger office area in the top row of cubicles. *Figure 8.13* shows how the viewport should now look with the **Executive Office** highlighted.

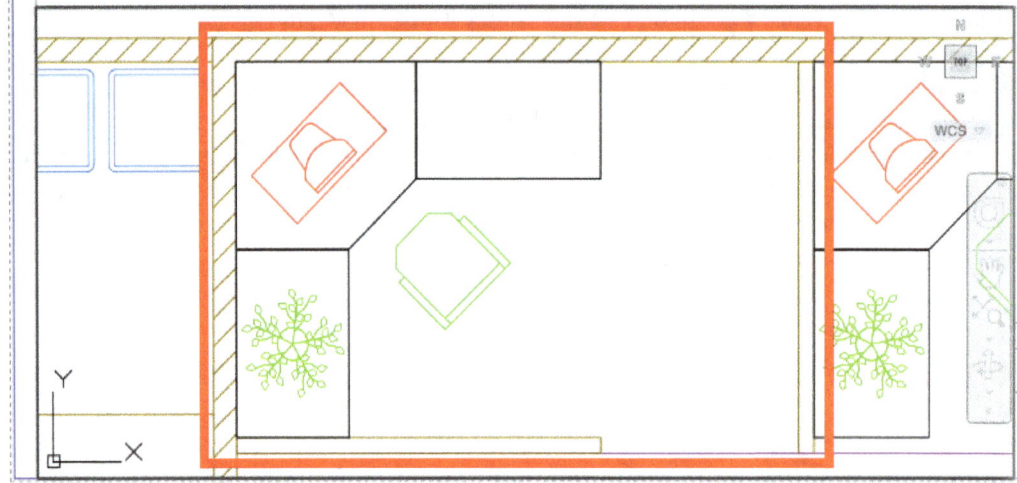

Figure 8.13: The zoomed view in the new viewport with the Executive Office highlighted

13. Select the viewport scale menu on the status bar by clicking the flyout arrow next to the scale value. The status bar scale will not display as a recognized scale value as you have just performed a manual zoom in the new viewport. Select **1:30** from the scale list displayed, as shown in *Figure 8.14*. The view in the new viewport will adjust to the selected scale, and **1:30** will now be displayed in the status bar.

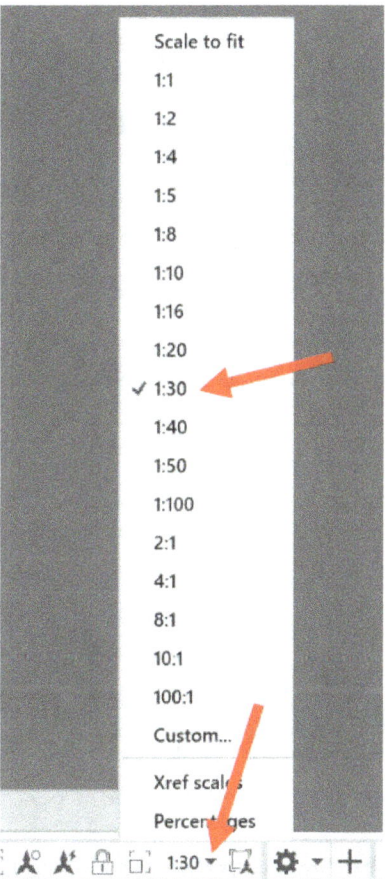

Figure 8.14: The viewport scale list with the flyout arrow and 1:30 scale display arrowed

14. You have now set up a new viewport with the required view from the **Model** tab to a standard scale (**1:30**). Move the cursor *outside* the sheet boundary (into the grey area) and double-click. This will deactivate the new viewport.

Working with Annotative Scaling

> **Tips and tricks #26**
>
> Once a viewport is placed and scaled, it can be locked to prevent any changes caused by errors. For example, a user might double-click inside a viewport boundary by mistake and zoom and pan, thus changing the viewport scale. The easiest way to do this is to use the padlock icon on the status bar when the viewport is selected in the layout tab. This is shown in *Figure 8.15*. When the padlock icon is blue, the viewport is locked.

Figure 8.15: The padlock on the status bar, set to blue, indicating that the selected viewport is currently locked.

Once a viewport is locked, its scale cannot be changed. This avoids accidental changes to viewport scales if a user activates a viewport in error and zooms in or out while the viewport is active.

> **AutoCAD for Mac**
>
> All the viewport functionality mentioned in this section works in the same way in AutoCAD for Mac. It is still located on the status bar, but the padlock/lock icon uses the MacOS iconography, and looks slightly different, as shown in *Figure 8.16*:

Figure 8.16: The viewport padlock displayed on the AutoCAD for Mac status bar

You now know how to work with existing viewports and how to create and scale new viewports. A good way to learn more about viewports is to experiment with them and discover their behavior when placing them and scaling them in your layout tabs in your drawings. A typical example might be to set a `1:100` viewport, and then rescale it to `1:50`. You will see that the `1:50` viewport shows more detail, as it is half of the `1:100` scale. Try using different scale values, and then resize the viewports when selected by using the blue grips.

In the next part of the chapter, you will learn how to utilize annotations in the Model tab, ensuring that it displays effectively in scaled viewports.

Working with annotation scales in the Model tab

You should already have the `Office Plan_GROUND FLOOR.dwg` exercise file open from the previous section. You will now add some annotative dimensions in the **Model** tab, using the appropriate annotation scale and making sure it matches the selected scaled viewport. These are the steps to do so:

1. Make sure you are in the **Model** tab of the drawing and are zoomed into the **Executive Office** area of the floor plan, as shown in *Figure 8.17*:

Figure 8.17: Zoomed into the Executive Office on the Model tab

2. You need to use an appropriate text style to place some labels in the **Executive Office** area of the drawing. Using the **Annotation** panel on the **Home** tab of the ribbon, use the flyout menu on the panel title bar. You can then use the text style flyout menu to ensure you use the appropriate text style for annotation. You need to be using **Labels_MODEL_5mm**, as shown in *Figure 8.18*. If it helps, you can pin the **Annotation** panel flyout open to stop it from disappearing back into the ribbon. It is also shown pinned open in *Figure 8.18*:

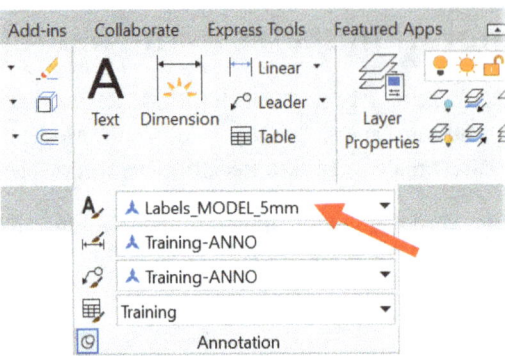

Figure 8.18: The Annotation panel pinned open with the text style arrowed

3. The **Labels_MODEL_5mm** text style is annotative (it has the blue annotative symbol next to it in the flyout menu), so it will adopt the current annotation scale set up on the status bar when in the **Model** tab. For the annotation text to be displayed as it should in the **1:30** viewport created in the previous section, the annotation scale must also be set to **1:30**. Select the annotation scale flyout in the status bar and select the **1:30** scale, as shown in *Figure 8.19*:

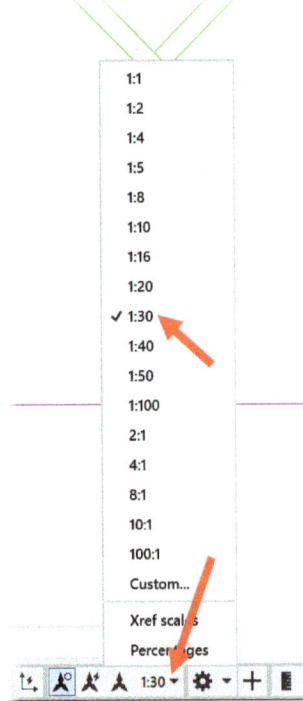

Figure 8.19: The annotation scale set to 1:30 in the status bar

4. Your annotation text can now be placed in the **Executive Office** area as a room label. Use the layer dropdown on the **Layers** panel to ensure you use the **Text** layer as the current layer.

5. Select the **Multiline Text** option from the text flyout in the **Annotation** panel on the ribbon, as shown in *Figure 8.20*:

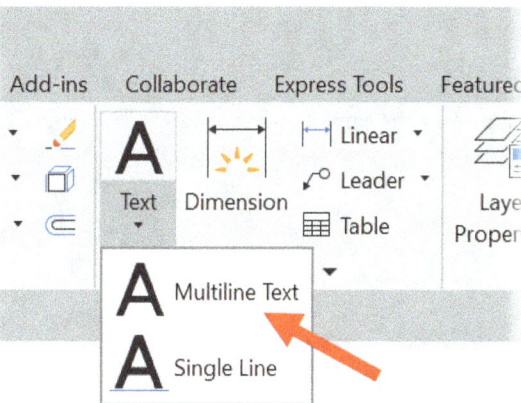

Figure 8.20: The Multiline Text (MTEXT) option on the text flyout in the Annotation panel

6. You will be prompted to place a rectangular area for the **Multiline Text** (*MTEXT*). Click the two points indicated in *Figure 8.21* in the top-right corner of the **Executive Office**. This will then create an area in which to place your text. Note the preview of your text style at this point (indicated by **abc** in the **Multiline Text** area being placed).

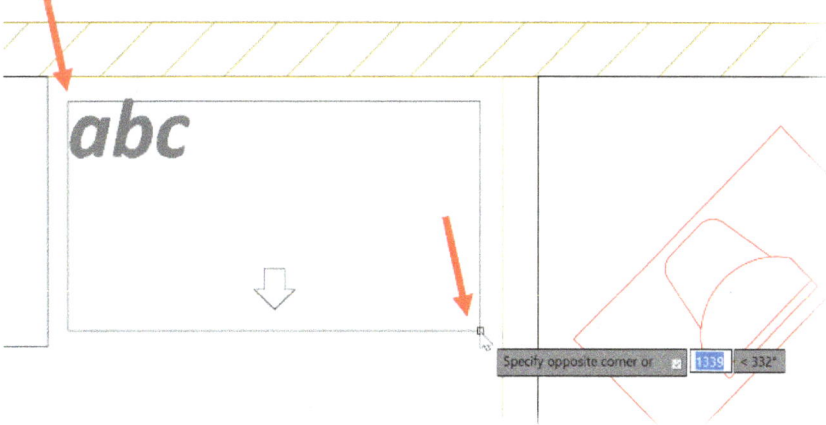

Figure 8.21: The Multiline Text area with the text preview displayed

7. Once you have placed the text area, you will see the cursor flashing and a contextual tab on the ribbon called **Text Editor** displayed. The ribbon tab is blue; you will see all the multiline text editing tools displayed. **Text Editor** is shown in *Figure 8.22*. It behaves just like a word processing application, such as Microsoft Word. To see how it works, type the following in **Text Editor**:

   - Executive (press *Enter*)
   - Office

   The text displayed will now be the same as what is shown in *Figure 8.22*:

Figure 8.22: The typed multiline text displayed in Text Editor

8. To close the **Multiline Text** (*MTEXT*) command, you can click outside **Text Editor**, or you can click on the **Close Text Editor** icon, displayed with a green tick on the **Text Editor** contextual ribbon tab. The text will now be displayed in the drawing as typed, and the **Text Editor** tab on the ribbon will close.

9. Double-click on the mouse wheel as a button, and you will zoom to the extents of the visible objects in the drawing in the **Model** tab. Roll back the mouse wheel to zoom out and get some space around the floor plan for easier dimension placement. You will now place some annotation dimensions around the floor plan.

10. As mentioned previously, you will need to set the annotation scale in the **Model** tab to suit the viewport scale in the viewport where the dimensions will be displayed.

11. Set the annotation scale to **1:50** in the annotation scale flyout on the status bar.

12. Using the layer dropdown on the **Layers** panel, make sure you set the **Dimensions** layer as the current layer.

13. You will also need to ensure you are using the correct annotative dimension style. Click on the flyout on the **Annotation** panel title bar and pin it open if you wish (like in *step 2*). Make sure you are using the **Training-ANNO** dimension style. It has the blue annotative symbol next to it, as shown in *Figure 8.23*.

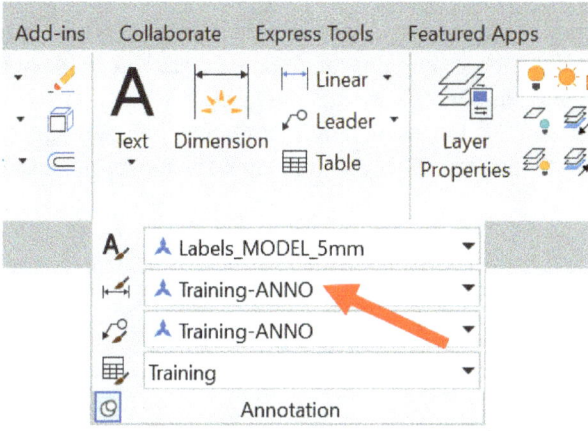

Figure 8.23: The Annotation panel flyout menu with the dimension style arrowed

14. You can now add dimension annotation to the drawing. You can access the dimension drop-down menu from the **Annotation** panel you have been using, or you will also find it on the **Annotate** tab in the **Dimensions** panel. *Figure 8.24* shows the dimension drop-down menu in the **Annotation** panel on the **Home** tab on the ribbon. Make sure **Object Snaps** are switched on in the status bar for accurate dimension placement, and then select the **Linear** dimension type, as also shown in *Figure 8.24*:

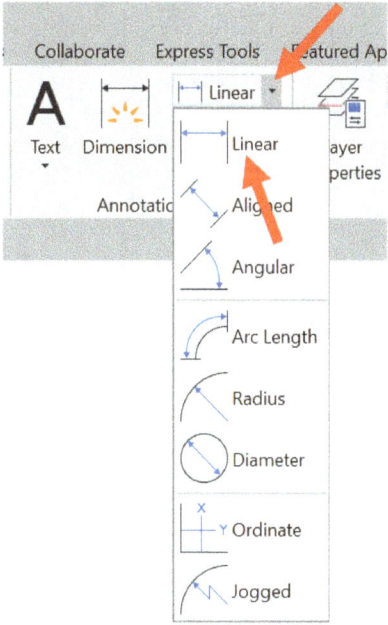

Figure 8.24: The dimension drop-down menu in the Annotation panel on the Home tab on the ribbon

15. You will now be prompted for two extension origin points. Use the **Endpoint** object snap and use the top-left and top-right points on the floor plan. You will then need to click a third time to place the dimension line. *Figure 8.25* shows the two points to select on the plan and an approximate position of the dimension line. Your placed dimension should look similar to the one in *Figure 8.25* when placed. After the third click, the **Linear** dimension command closes.

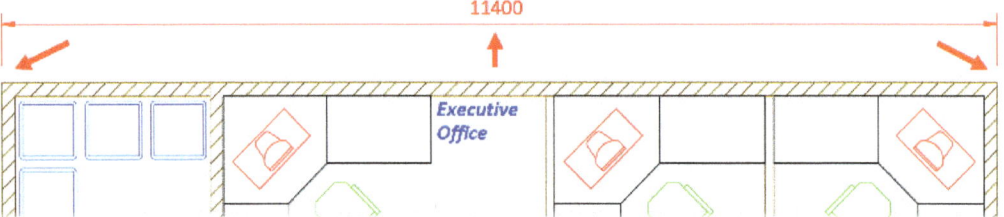

Figure 8.25: The placed Linear dimension type with placement points arrowed

16. Using the **Linear** dimension type, place a few more horizontal and vertical dimensions to get used to the dimension placement workflow. You should end up with a floor plan that looks something like *Figure 8.26*:

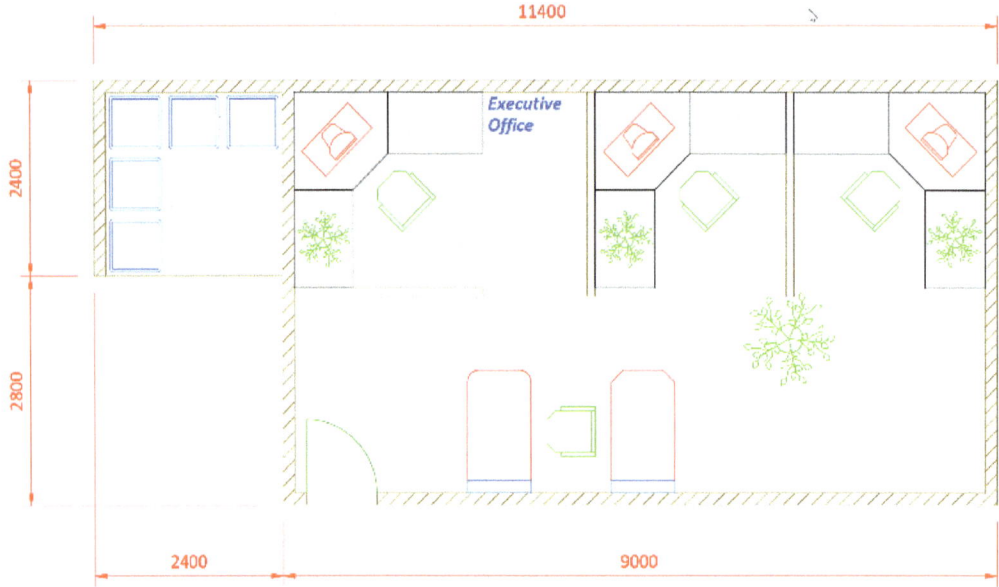

Figure 8.26: The floor plan with some more dimension annotation added

> **Tips and tricks #27**
>
> When placing **Linear** dimensions, you can line them up accurately using **Object Snaps** (*OSNAP*). Simply use the **Endpoint** object snap of the point of the arrowhead you want to line up with when placing the dimension line – the third click when placing a **Linear** dimension – and you will find that the arrowheads then line up regularly, keeping the dimension lines all in line. This works for both horizontal and vertical dimension placement.

Object Snaps are the most effective method to use to dimensions accurately and precisely. Make sure that the *OSNAP* setting is always **ON** when placing dimension annotation.

> **AutoCAD for Mac**
>
> Linear dimension placement works in the same way for AutoCAD for Mac. The only difference is that the dimension tools are in the vertical left-hand menu.

Notice that both the text annotation and the dimension annotation are displayed on the **Model** tab, using their appropriate annotation scales. Click on the **ISO A3** layout tab to see the drawing displayed in *Figure 8.27*:

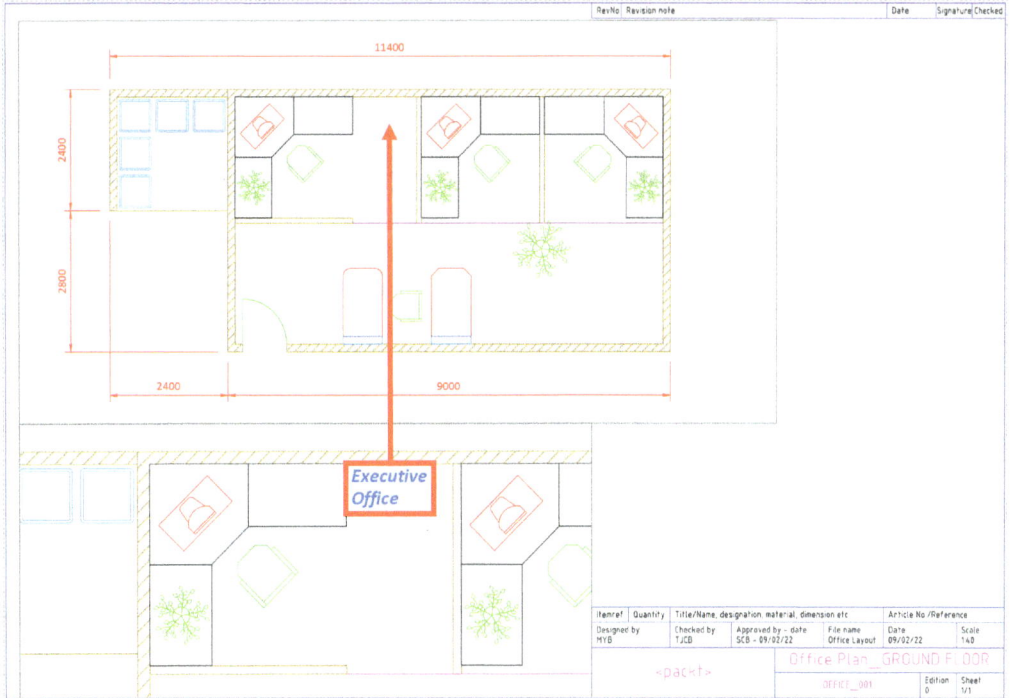

Figure 8.27: The ISO A3 tab with the drawing displayed

In *Figure 8.27*, the text annotation is highlighted, as it only appears in the **1:30** (lower) viewport and not the **1:50** (upper) viewport. This is because the text annotation only has a **1:30** annotation scale applied to it in the **Model** tab. In the same way, the dimension annotation is only set to display in the **1:50** (upper) viewport as it only has a **1:50** annotation scale applied to it in the **Model** tab. This is how annotative scaling works.

In this section, you learned how to use your annotative text and dimension styles with your scaled viewports. Both the text and dimensions placed used a single annotation scale in the **Model** tab to coincide with the scaled viewport where they were displayed in the drawing.

Annotation scales allow easy scaling of annotative objects, in this case, annotative dimensions. When using annotative dimensions, annotation scales can be applied to consistently scale dimension annotation in viewports of differing scales in your layout tabs.

In the next section of this chapter, you will learn how to add and delete annotation scales for annotative objects.

Adding and deleting object annotation scales

In this section, you will learn that annotative objects can have more than one annotation scale applied to them, thus being able to be displayed in more than one scaled viewport.

You will still have the `Office Plan_GROUND FLOOR.dwg` file open. With it open, follow these steps:

1. Return to the **Model** tab in AutoCAD and zoom to the **Executive Office** area.
2. Hover over the multiline text object that says **Executive Office**. You can see the annotative symbol visible in *Figure 8.28*:

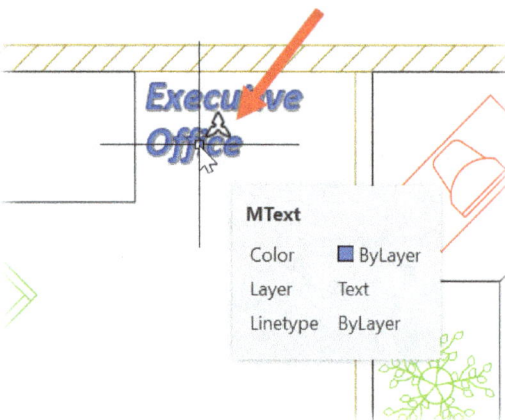

Figure 8.28: The annotative symbol is shown when hovering over the annotative text object

3. Select the annotative multiline text with a click. You will see the blue grips appear. Right-click to display the context-sensitive shortcut menu, as shown in *Figure 8.29*:

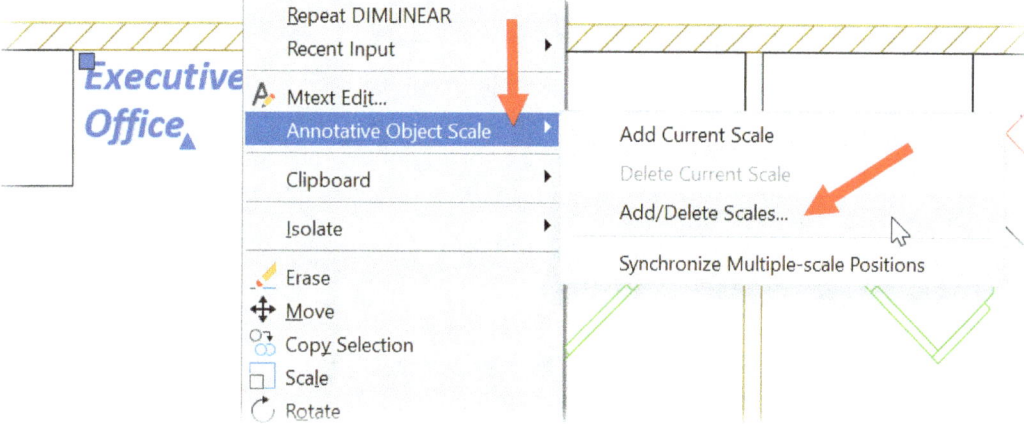

Figure 8.29: The shortcut menu with Annotative Object Scale - Add/Delete Scales… displayed

4. Select **Annotative Object Scale** from the shortcut menu, and then click on **Add/Delete Scales…** from the sub-menu.

5. The **Annotation Object Scale** dialog box is displayed, as shown in *Figure 8.30*. You will notice that the only annotation scale applied to the annotative text is the **1:30** scale. Click on the **Add…** button:

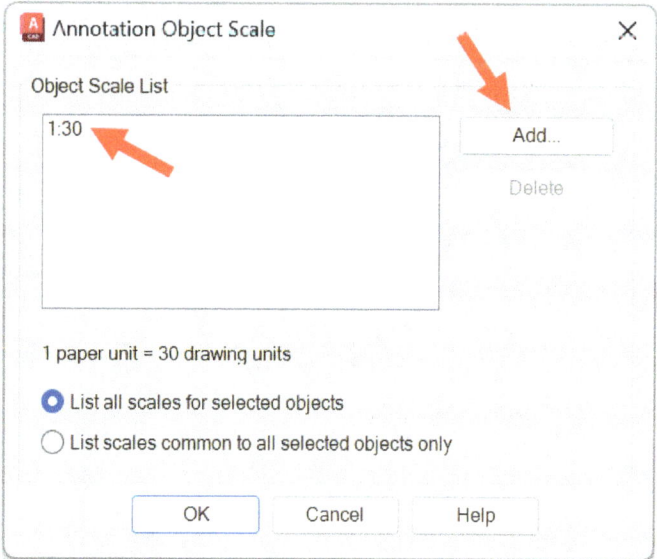

Figure 8.30: The Annotation Object Scale dialog box

6. The **Add Scales to Object** dialog box is displayed, as shown in *Figure 8.31*. Select the **1:50** scale and click on **OK**. The dialog box closes, and you are returned to the **Annotation Object Scale** dialog box:

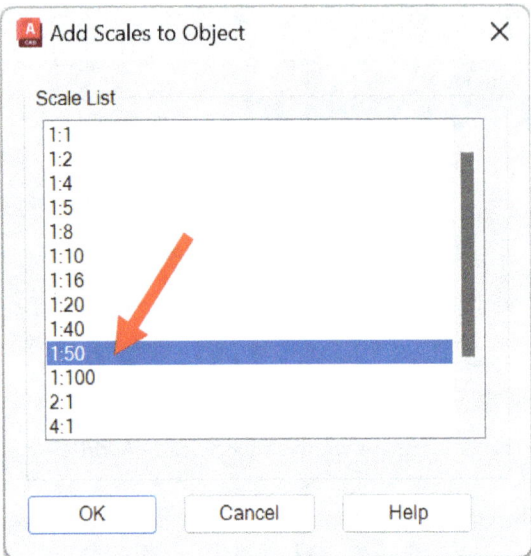

Figure 8.31: The Add Scales to Object dialog box

7. You can now see that two annotation scales are applied to your annotative text object, as shown in *Figure 8.32*:

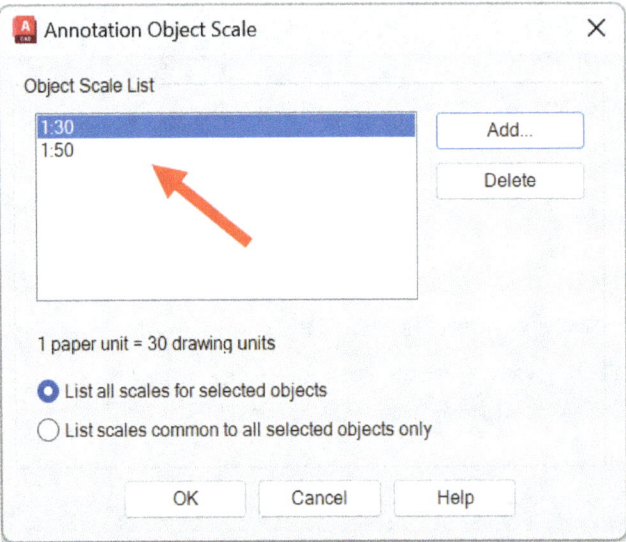

Figure 8.32: The Annotation Object Scale dialog box with two scales applied

8. Click on **OK** to close the dialog box. You will notice that the annotative text is now larger in the **Model** tab, as shown in *Figure 8.33*. This is because you now have two annotation scales applied, and the current annotation scale is **1:50**, which defines its size in the drawing. Also note that when hovering over the annotative text object, *two* annotative symbols are displayed, indicating more than one annotation scale has been applied.

Figure 8.33: The annotative text object with two annotative symbols displayed

9. If you return to the **ISO A3** layout tab, you will also see that the *Executive Office* text object is displayed in the **1:50** (upper) viewport. This is because it now has the **1:50** annotation scale applied to it in the **Model** tab. *Figure 8.34* shows this, and you can see that using that text style with the **1:50** annotation scale in that viewport causes it to cross geometry and look a bit untidy.

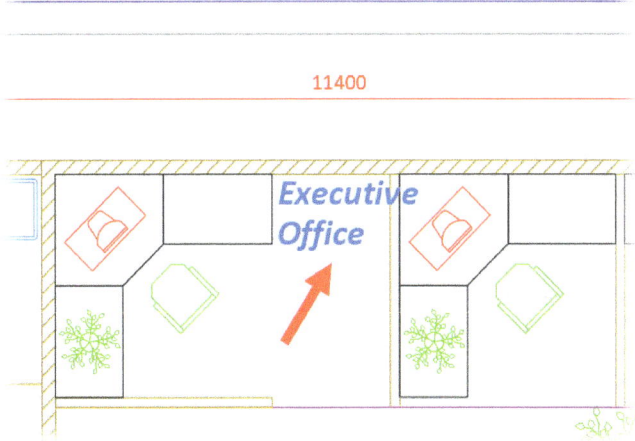

Figure 8.34: The annotative text object in the 1:50 viewport

10. Return to the **Model** tab. Select the **Executive Office** text object, and the blue grips will appear.
11. Right-click to display the shortcut menu. Select **Annotative Object Scale**. The **Annotative Object Scale** dialog box will be displayed as it was previously in the section.
12. Select **Add/Delete Scales…** in the sub-menu.
13. Select the **1:50** scale in the list.
14. Click the **Delete** button, and the **1:50** scale will be deleted as an applied annotation scale for the text object.
15. Click on **OK** to close the dialog box, like before.
16. The annotative text object now only has the one annotation scale applied, as before.
17. If you return to the **ISO A3** layout tab, you will see that the **Executive Office** text object is now only displayed in the **1:30** (lower) viewport, as shown in *Figure 8.35*.
18. Make sure to save your drawing as `Office Plan_GROUND FLOOR-COMPLETE.dwg`. That way, you save all of the revisions you have made, and you can refer to the file for future reference.

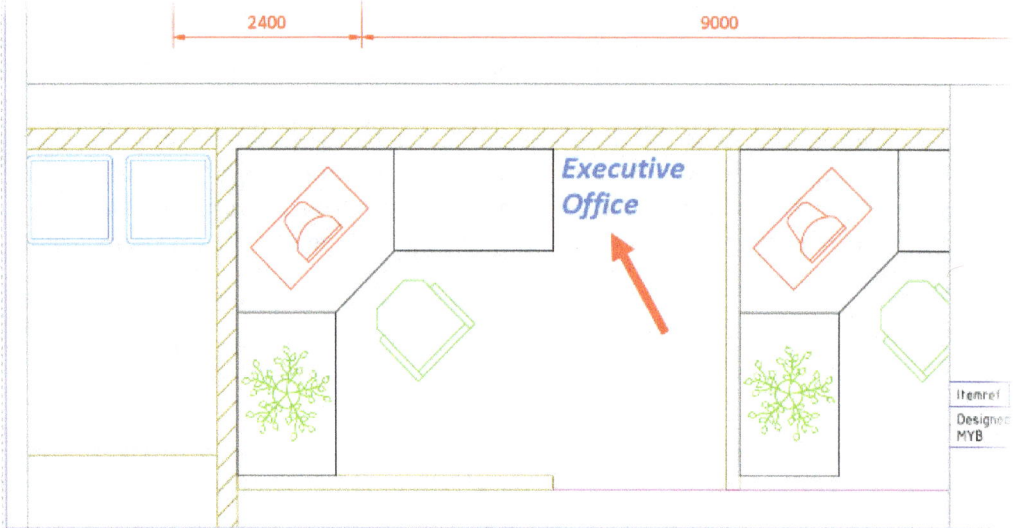

Figure 8.35: The ISO A3 layout tab with the annotative text object displayed

You can now add and delete annotation scales to your annotative objects, including text and dimensions. Provided you place the objects in the drawing using an annotative style, such as text and dimension styles, any annotative object can have more than one annotation scale applied to it, allowing it to be displayed in multiple viewports at differing scales in the layout tabs in a drawing.

You can apply annotative scaling to only the following AutoCAD objects:

- Text (single line and multiline) and text styles
- Blocks and attribute definitions
- Hatches
- Dimensions and dimension styles
- Geometric tolerances
- Multileaders and multileader styles

You can find out more about annotative objects in AutoCAD using this link:

`https://help.autodesk.com/view/ACD/2023/ENU/?guid=GUID-6D4A620B-30AB-4593-B168-F9FF084017C6`

Summary

You now know how to work with annotative scaling. In this chapter, you have learned how to set up viewports with varying viewport scales to ensure that viewports are maintained.

You have also learned how to work with annotation scales in the Model tab, making sure that the appropriate annotation scale is used, and how to add and delete object annotation scales when required.

Annotation scaling is essential when adding your designs to the layout tabs to communicate your design intent. Annotation scaling must be implemented effectively and accurately to ensure that information and data are scaled correctly.

The tools used in this chapter demonstrate how important annotation scaling is when working with annotating drawings in AutoCAD.

In the next chapter, we will look at how you can re-use design content with AutoCAD blocks to make effective use of regularly used content in your AutoCAD drawings.

Get This Book's PDF Version and Exclusive Extras

UNLOCK NOW

Scan the QR code (or go to `packtpub.com/unlock`). Search for this book by name, confirm the edition, and then follow the steps on the page.

Note: Keep your invoice handy. Purchases made directly from Packt don't require one.

Part 3: Content Re-Use Including Dynamic Blocks

Re-using design content in AutoCAD provides you with the flexibility to use similar content again and again. Working on a project that uses specific content that can be reused in another similar project saves valuable project time, reducing repetitive, onerous content creation. Re-using content from your DWG files also allows for the easy creation of content libraries using regular AutoCAD blocks and dynamic blocks that incorporate specific parameters and actions, allowing for easy manipulation of the dynamic blocks when working with them in your drawings.

This part has the following chapters:

- Chapter 9, Developing Block Libraries
- Chapter 10, Working with Block Attributes
- Chapter 11, Creating a Dynamic Block with Parameters and Actions
- Chapter 12, Creating a Dynamic Block with Visibility States

9
Developing Block Libraries

Content reuse is essential when working with CAD teams on multiple projects. Blocks are an essential part of any project, and this chapter explains how block libraries can be created and shared within a CAD team. Using blocks means that you only need to create the object once (the block) and then reuse it by inserting it as another instance of it in your drawings.

By the end of this chapter, you will be able to work with regular and dynamic blocks in drawings and create your own block libraries using various methods, including the *Clipboard*. You will also learn how to use the Blocks palette and utilize tool palettes with your blocks.

This chapter covers the following methodologies you will need to work with AutoCAD blocks in your DWG files:

- Bringing blocks and dynamic blocks into drawings
- Utilizing the Clipboard to create a new block library drawing
- Adding the blocks library to the Blocks palette
- Creating a new block library tool palette

Reusing drawing content and managing that content will save valuable drafting time, reducing the need for repetitive tasks, and allowing content sharing with your project stakeholders and team members.

In this chapter, you will learn how to work with regular blocks and dynamic blocks and discover numerous methods to manage blocks in your drawings for your CAD team.

Exercise file

You must ensure you have downloaded the exercise file, `New Office Design.dwg` to follow the sections in this chapter.

Bringing blocks and dynamic blocks into drawings

Blocks are objects made up of multiple AutoCAD objects, such as lines, arcs, and circles. A typical AutoCAD block might be a door or a chair that must be used many times in a drawing, such as a floor plan.

There are two types of blocks that can be used in AutoCAD: **regular blocks** and **dynamic blocks**. Regular blocks are one-off blocks that have a single use. Dynamic blocks can have specific parameters applied to them to recognize increments and iterations, such as a metric bolt of varying lengths or a door/window of varying shapes and sizes.

Blocks are the best way to reuse content in any AutoCAD drawing, and they will form many of the essential elements of your design.

When first created in a drawing, blocks remain saved in the drawing file they were created in, but they can also be set up in specific block library drawings that can then be put in a suitable location for not just you to use, but the rest of your CAD team. They can be stored locally on a hard drive, or a networked server. And with more use of the cloud, cloud-based block libraries can easily be set up and maintained.

Open the exercise file, New Office Design.dwg. The drawing is a simple plan of an office layout where you will utilize the blocks in the drawing. You will be bringing blocks and dynamic blocks into the drawing to reuse design content, so you won't need to re-draw and re-work AutoCAD objects. The drawing will be on the **Model** tab when it opens, displaying a simple office floor plan without annotation. Your first step is to bring a regular door block into the drawing. Zoom into the door opening and select the line and arc objects that make up the door, as shown in *Figure 9.1*.

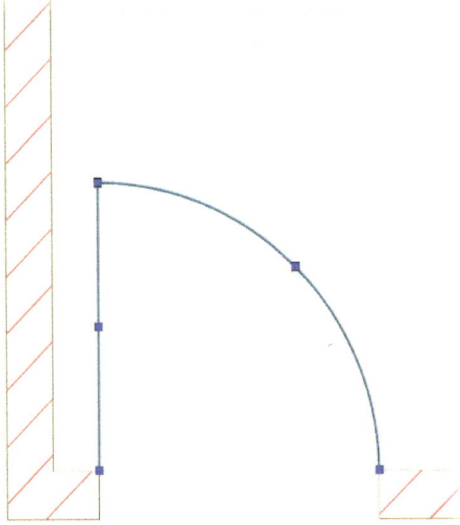

Figure 9.1: The door opening (with the line and arc selected)

You will see that the door is made up of a line and an arc. To duplicate this door, you must copy both objects and ensure they are in the correct layer, leaving this workflow open to error, even for such a simple combination of two AutoCAD objects. Copying requires you to make sure you have selected all necessary objects to be copied. An AutoCAD block can just be reused over and over again, in the knowledge that all required objects form part of the block.

The drawing already has a number of blocks saved in the DWG file. Some are regular blocks and some are dynamic blocks. In the next workflow, you will ensure that the correct layer is current and place a regular door block in place of the line and the arc objects.

Adding a regular door block

You will first need to go to the **Layer** drop-down menu and select the **Doors** layer, as shown in *Figure 9.2*. You will find the drop-down menu on the **Layers** panel on the **Home** tab on the ribbon. Select the **Doors** layer to make it current.

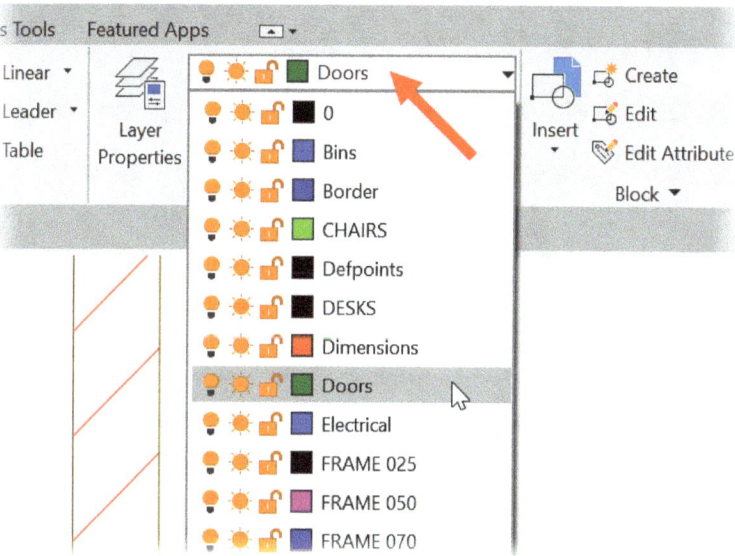

Figure 9.2: The Layer drop-down menu with the Doors layer current

Now that the **Doors** layer is current, the following workflow will allow you to insert a regular block representing a door:

1. Ensure you are on the **Model** tab in the exercise file (`New Office Design.dwg`) and zoomed into the door opening.

2. Ensure that the line and arc representing the existing door are selected. Then, using the **Erase** (*ERASE*) command, remove the line and the arc, to leave only the door opening in the wall. In this case, the right-click shortcut menu was used after the objects were selected, and **Erase** was selected on the shortcut menu, as shown in *Figure 9.3*.

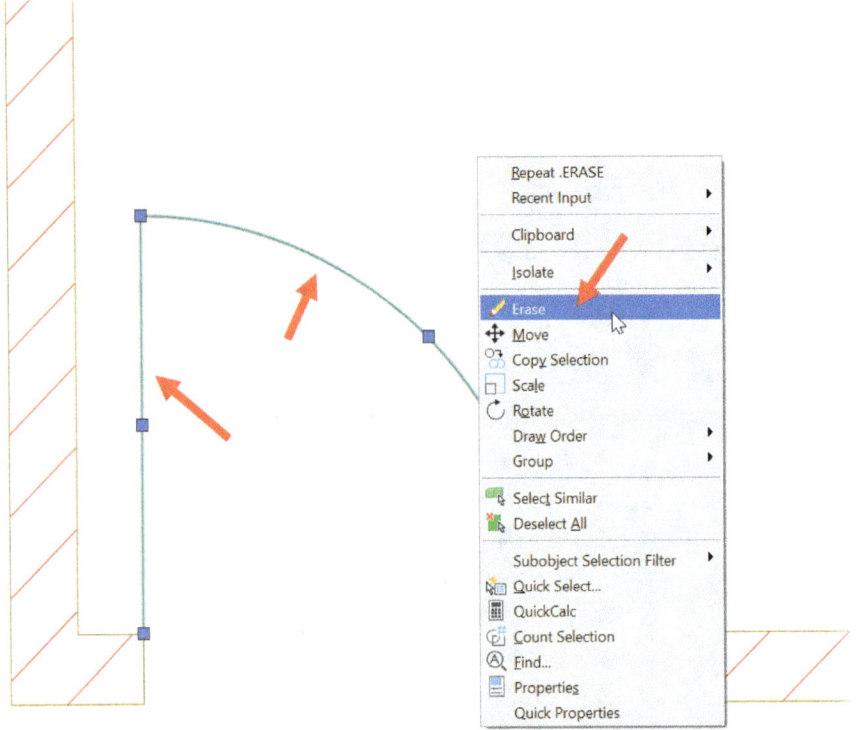

Figure 9.3: The original line and arc selected, ready to be removed using the Erase command in the shortcut menu

When erasing objects in a drawing, it is often easier to select multiple objects and then use the **Erase** (*ERASE*) command once, rather than erase objects one-by-one.

> **Tips and tricks #28**
>
> When you want to remove objects from your drawings, you use the **Erase** (*ERASE*) command. This can be expedited in several ways. You can use the **Erase** icon on the **Modify** panel on the **Home** tab on the ribbon, select the objects to be erased, and press *Enter* to confirm. You can also use the right-click shortcut menu once the objects to be erased are selected and select **Erase** (see *Figure 9.3*), or you can simply type ERASE and press *Enter*, select the objects to be erased, and press *Enter* again to confirm.

The *OOPS* command is a undo function for the **Erase** (*ERASE*) command only. If you erase something and realise it was a mistake, type OOPS and press *Enter*. The last use of the **Erase** (*ERASE*) command will be undone. Be careful, though, because you may have replaced the erased object with another object, and it will be superimposed on top of the original object that was erased.

> **AutoCAD for Mac**
>
> You can use methodologies such as *Tips and tricks #28* in AutoCAD for Mac to erase AutoCAD objects in drawings.

1. Make sure the drawing has been saved. Use the **Save** icon on the **Quick Access Toolbar**. Do this before selecting the **Insert** tab on the ribbon. This will ensure that the **Door** block is saved in the DWG file. Then, click on the **Insert** drop-down arrow, as shown in *Figure 9.4*. You will see available blocks in the drawing file, and there is a slider bar on the right to see further block content.

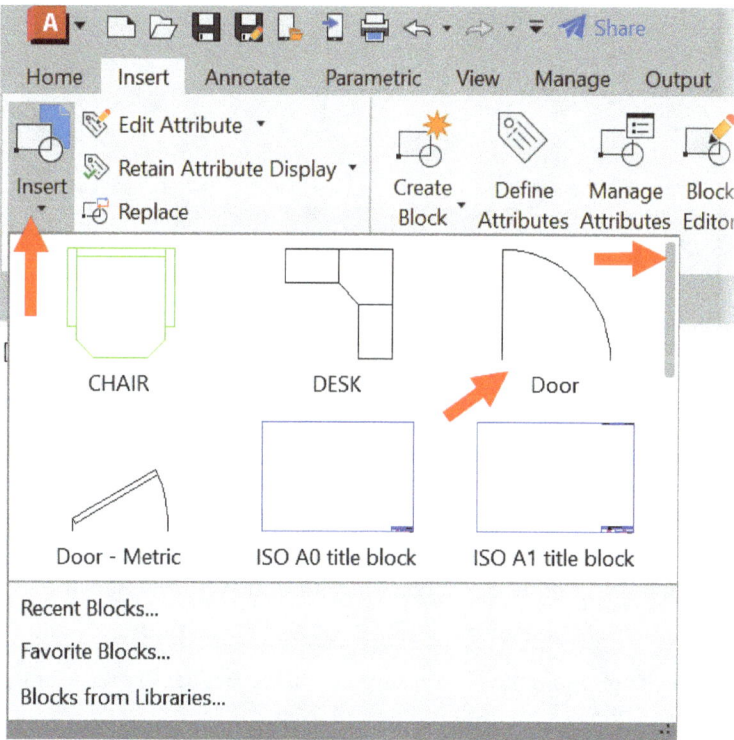

Figure 9.4: The Insert drop-down menu displaying available blocks

2. Click on the **Door** block on the **Insert** drop-down menu, as indicated in *Figure 9.4*. The **Door** block will appear on your cursor, and you will be prompted for an insertion point, as shown in *Figure 9.5*. Select the corner of the wall indicated by the arrow in *Figure 9.5* using the **Endpoint** object snap.

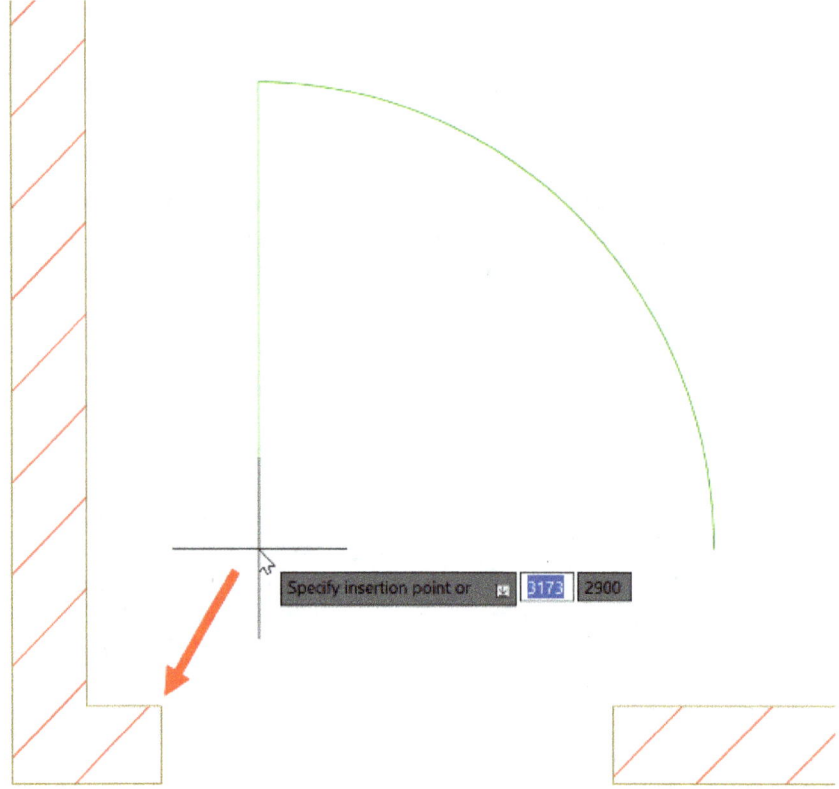

Figure 9.5: The Door block waiting on an insertion point

3. The **Door** block will now be placed in the door opening, and note that it is *one* object, not two. It is now an instance of block reference in your drawing. Make sure to save the drawing at this point.

You will see that the block now looks the same as the line and the arc that were previously there, and if you hover over the new door block, you will see the tooltip appear, letting you know that it is a **Block reference** on the **Doors** layer, as shown in *Figure 9.6*. Note that the block has adopted the current layer, **Doors**, as set previously.

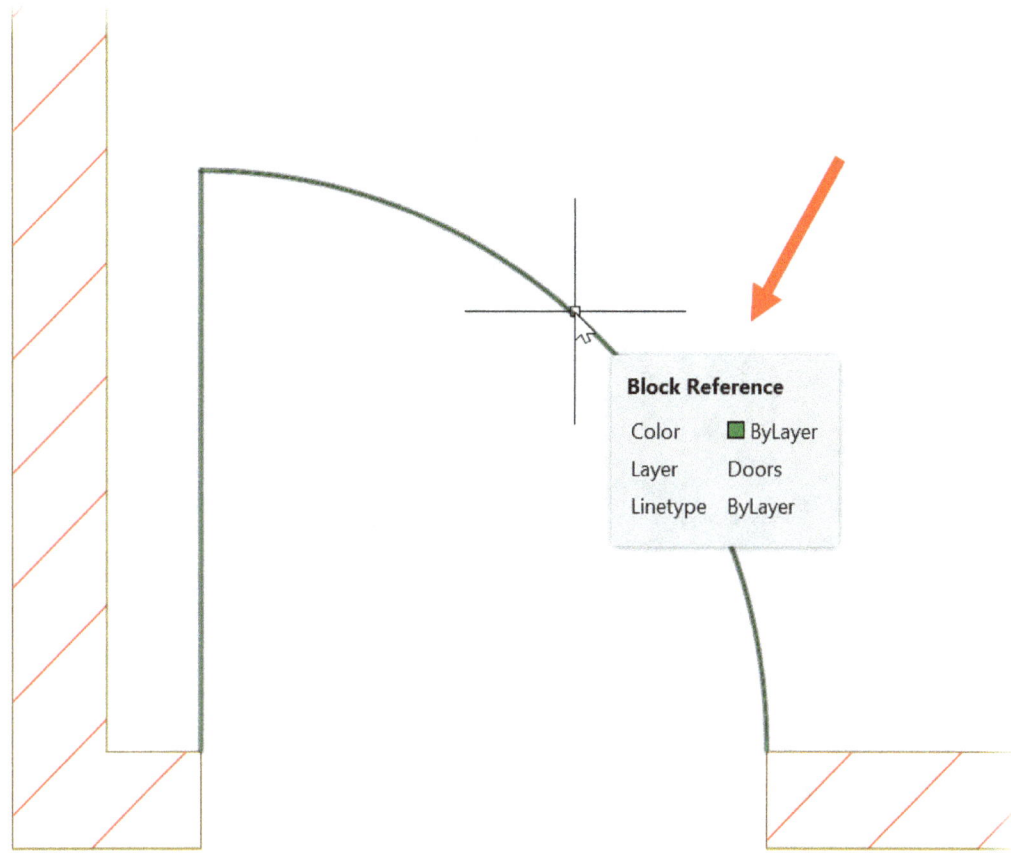

Figure 9.6: The new Door block with tooltip arrowed

You have now placed a regular **Door** block in your AutoCAD drawing.

Adding a dynamic Door block

Having placed a regular **Door** block in our AutoCAD drawing, it's time to move onto a dynamic **Door** block. Let's see how we can do that here:

1. In order to add a dynamic door block, you will now select the new **Door** block and remove it from the drawing. This may seem odd, as you have only just placed it, but you are now going to place a **DYNAMIC** block of a door to replace the regular block.

2. Use the previous *steps 1* and *2* to use the **Erase** command to remove the regular **Door** block, leaving the wall opening as before.

Developing Block Libraries

3. Select the **Insert** dropdown on the **Insert** tab on the ribbon and select the **Recent Blocks…** option, as shown in *Figure 9.7*.

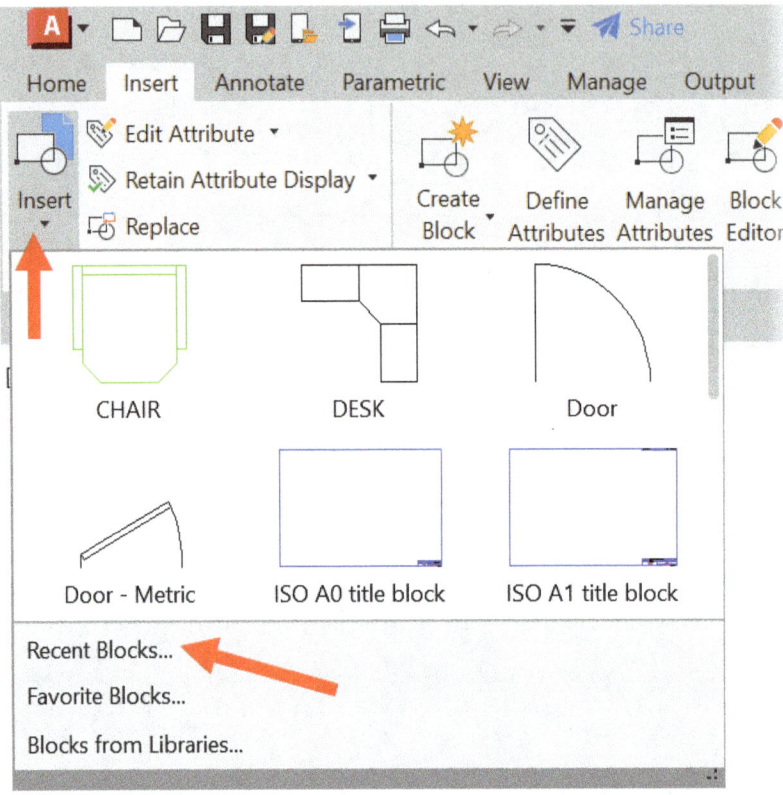

Figure 9.7: The Insert drop-down menu with Recent Blocks arrowed

The **Blocks** palette will now appear on the screen. The **Blocks** palette is a newer method of working with blocks in more recent versions of AutoCAD. It is also more versatile and allows you to develop block libraries. You can see the **Blocks** palette in *Figure 9.8*, displaying the blocks in the current drawing with the **Current Drawing** tab selected.

Bringing blocks and dynamic blocks into drawings   221

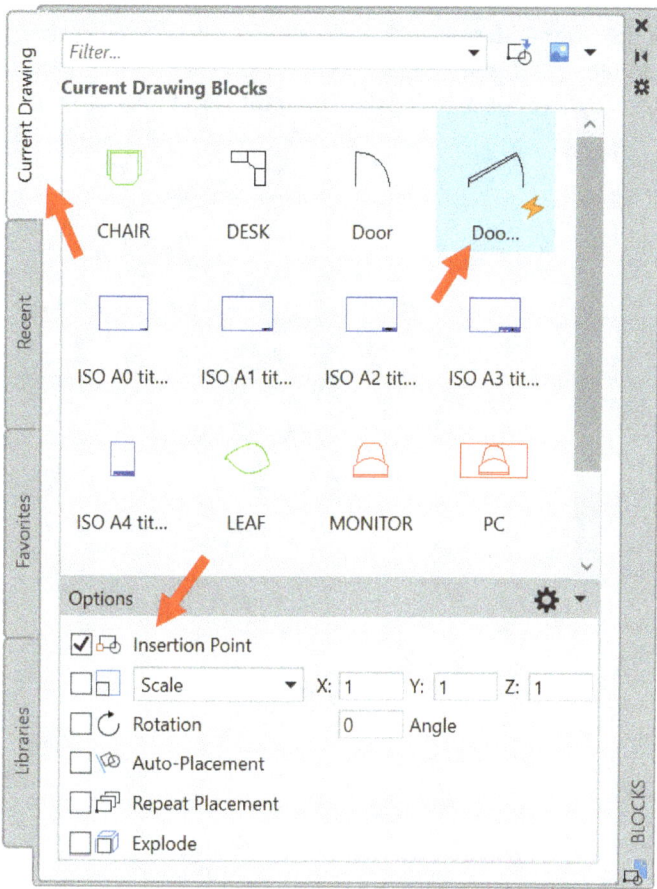

Figure 9.8: The Blocks palette with the Current Drawing tab current

1. Ensure that *only* the **Insertion Point** box is ticked in the lower area of the **Blocks** palette, as shown in *Figure 9.8*. This makes sure that you specify the insertion point as you insert the block.

2. You will notice that there is another door block on the palette (arrowed in *Figure 9.8*). This block has a yellow lightning symbol applied to it. This indicates that it is a *dynamic* block. The full block name is **Door – Metric**.

3. If you click on the **Door – Metric** block in the **Blocks** palette, you will see it appear on your cursor, like a regular block, and the placement method is the same. Place the block on the wall corner as you did previously, using the **Endpoint** object snap, as indicated in *Figure 9.9*.

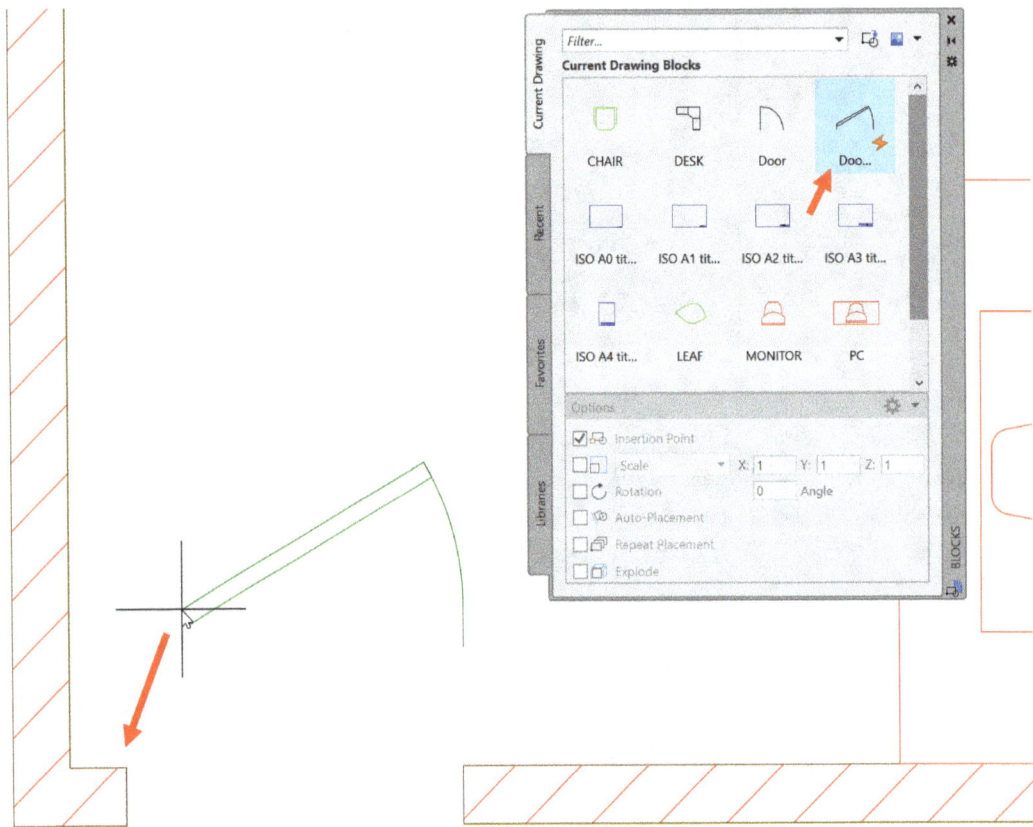

Figure 9.9: Placing the Door – Metric dynamic block

The **Door – Metric** dynamic block has a different appearance to the regular **Door** block, and you may find it difficult to orient the dynamic block on the corner of the wall, as shown in *Figure 9.10*. This is because an **Align** parameter built into the dynamic block is trying to align with the wall faces on the door opening.

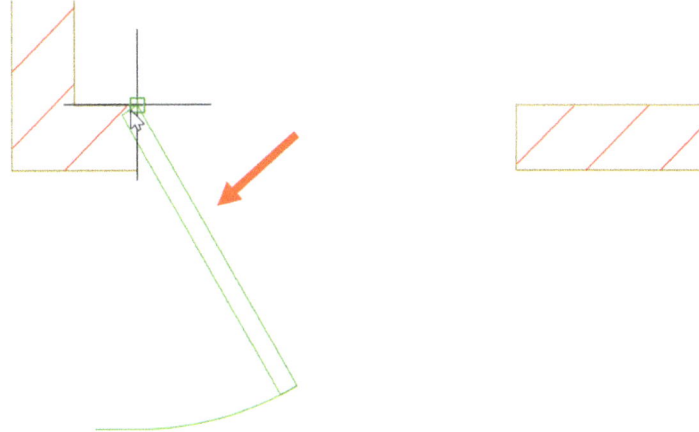

Figure 9.10: The Door – Metric dynamic block being difficult to place

4. A simple tactic here is to place the **Door – Metric** block away from the door opening and then use the **Move** (*MOVE*) command to move it after placement, utilizing object snaps to place the door block on the corner of the wall opening (using the **Endpoint** object snap). Use the **Endpoint** object snap shown in *Figure 9.11* as the basepoint to place the dynamic block on the wall corner.

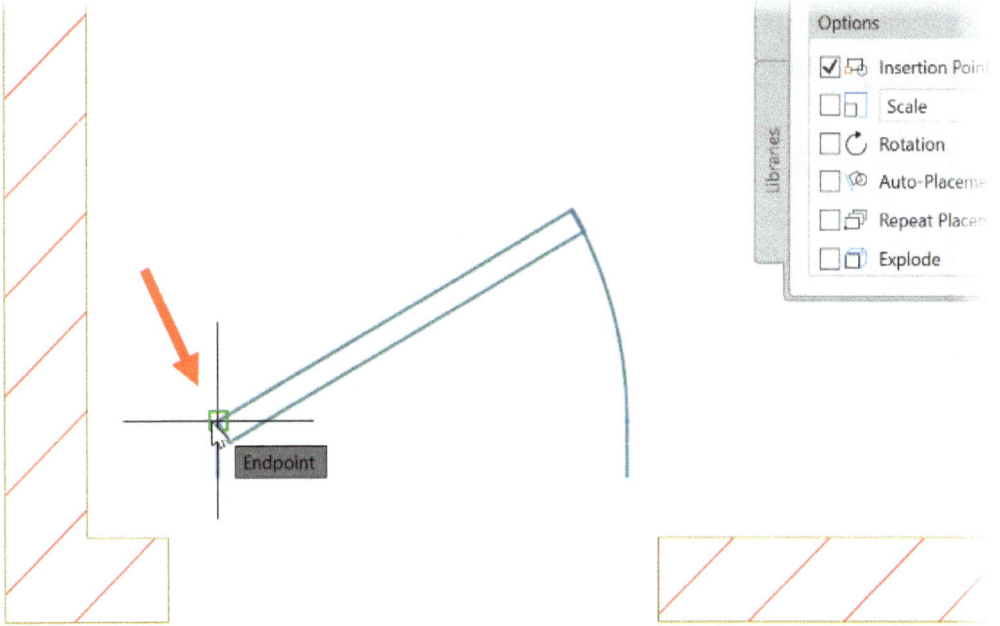

Figure 9.11: The Endpoint object snap used to move the dynamic door block

5. Once you have done this, you will find that the dynamic door block is now in place, as shown in *Figure 9.12*.

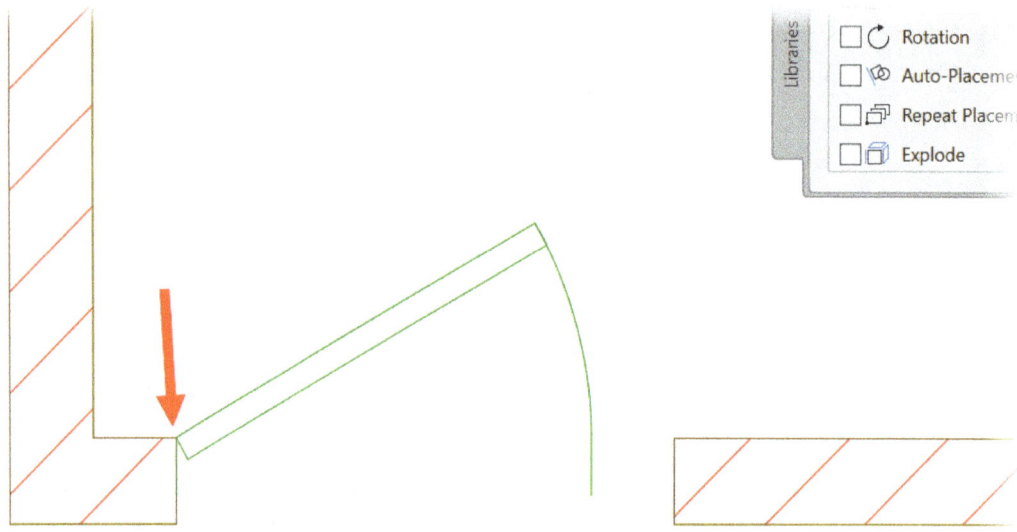

Figure 9.12: The Door – Metric dynamic block now in place

6. You will note that the dynamic door block does not fully close the door opening in the wall. This is where the *dynamic* in dynamic block kicks in. Select the block in the drawing, as shown in *Figure 9.13*. You will see numerous blue grips appear. These are all the dynamic block's built-in parameters, making it a highly versatile AutoCAD object.

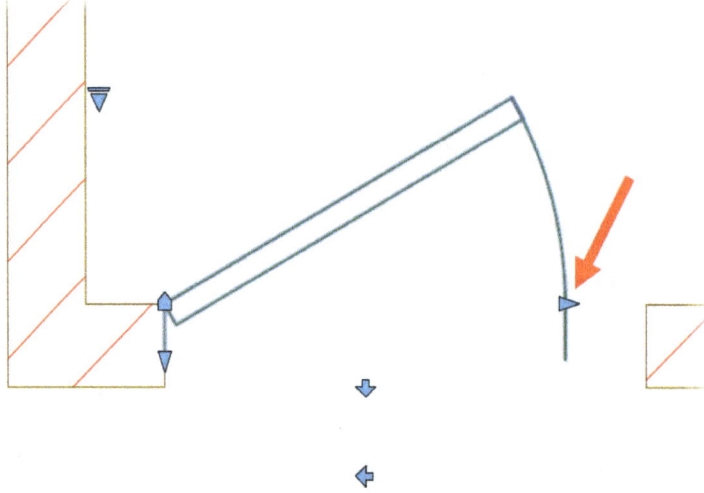

Figure 9.13: The dynamic block selected, with parameter grips displayed

7. Select the rightmost parameter grip (arrowed in *Figure 9.13*) and drag it towards the right-hand corner of the door opening. You will see the door block resize accordingly, and you can then click on the **Endpoint** object snap of the door opening to finish resizing the dynamic block, as shown in *Figure 9.14*.

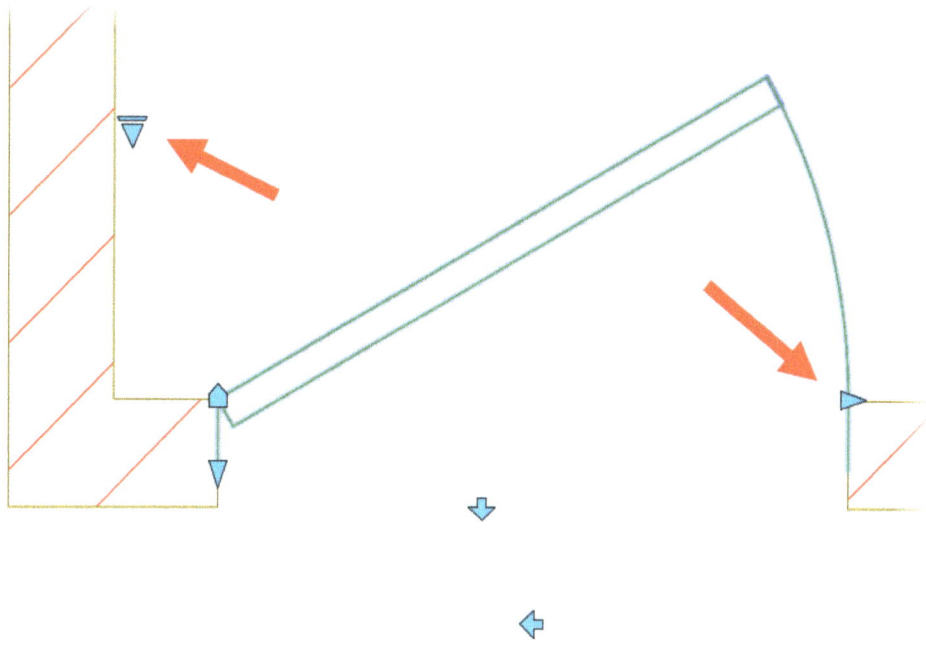

Figure 9.14: The dynamic block resized with the parameter grip

> **Note**
> Note that blocks like the dynamic door block can be added to a block library. This then allows for content reuse not only on the current project but on future projects as well.

8. With the block still selected, click on the larger, triangular parameter grip to the left, as also shown in *Figure 9.14*. You will see a menu displayed that provides options for the door swing angle, as shown in *Figure 9.15*.

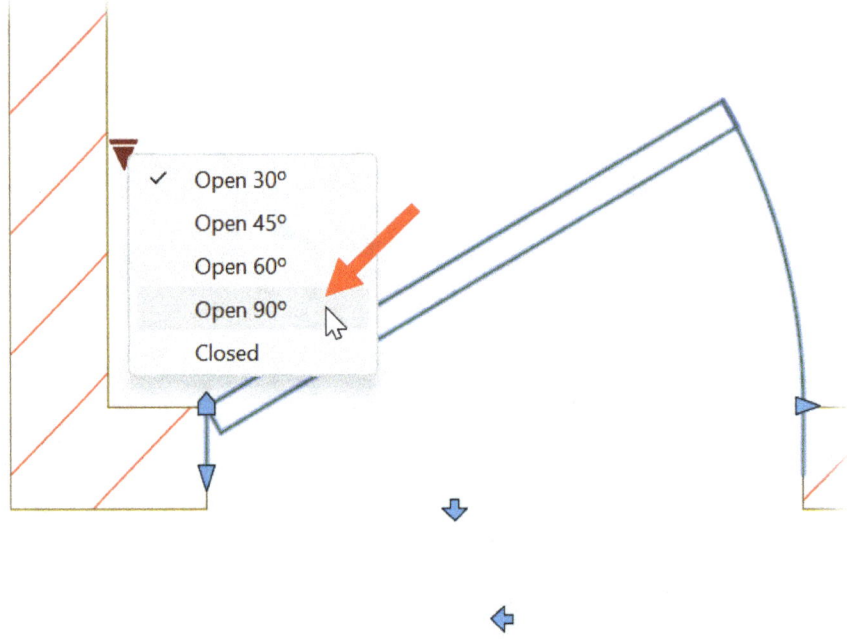

Figure 9.15: The door swing menu displayed for the dynamic block

9. Selecting the **Open 90°** option will update the dynamic door swing vertically, as shown in *Figure 9.16*. Press *Escape* a couple of times to ensure you have deselected the block.

You have now placed and used a dynamic block in your AutoCAD drawing.

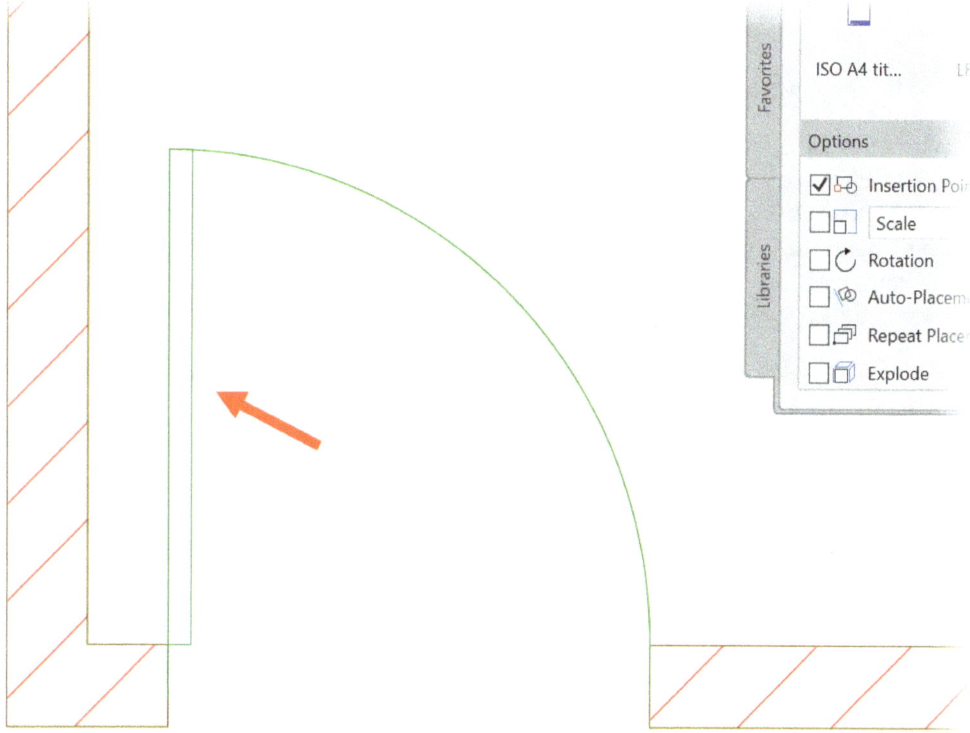

Figure 9.16: The dynamic door block with its 90° vertical swing

> **AutoCAD for Mac**
> You can use dynamic blocks in AutoCAD for Mac just as you can in AutoCAD for Windows as the workflow is virtually identical in both.

In this section, you learned how to work with regular blocks and dynamic blocks that were already saved in your DWG file. In the next section, you will create a new block library drawing consisting of blocks only so that it can be shared and become the location of a block library for content reuse.

Using the Clipboard to create a new block library drawing

The **Clipboard** function in AutoCAD works in the same way as it does in other Microsoft applications. In Microsoft Word, you might select a paragraph of text and copy and paste it to another part of the Word document. In AutoCAD, you can select an object (or objects), copy them to the Clipboard function, and paste them into the same drawing, or another drawing. There is also other AutoCAD-specific functionality in the Clipboard, such as selecting a specific base point to copy from, for example.

You should already have the exercise file, `New Office Design.dwg`, open from the previous section. You will now create a new blank library drawing, save it with a different filename, and add blocks to it.

You will do this by adhering to the following workflow:

1. With the `New Office Design.dwg` file still open, check the file tabs underneath the ribbon at the top of the AutoCAD screen, as shown in *Figure 9.17*. You will see the **Start** tab and the **New Office Design** tab. A tab with a + (plus) symbol is also displayed. Click on that tab to open a new blank drawing file (note that you may need to turn off the **Grid** setting on the status bar).

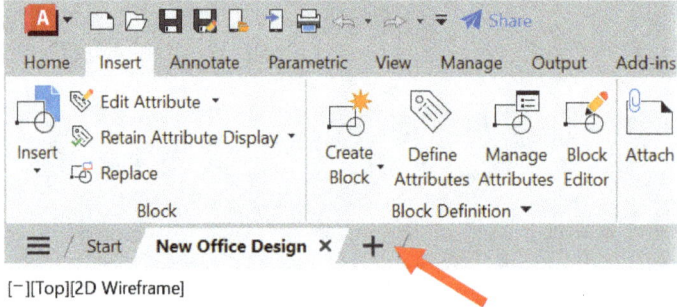

Figure 9.17: The file tabs in AutoCAD with the + tab arrowed

2. Select the dynamic door block you placed in the previous section of the chapter. Right-click to bring up the shortcut menu and select **Clipboard**. Select **Copy with Base Point** on the sub-menu, as shown in *Figure 9.18*.

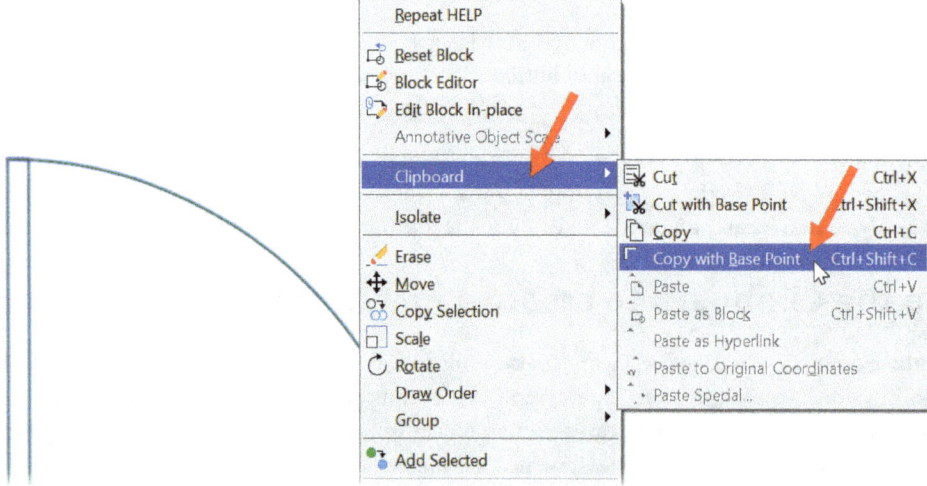

Figure 9.18: The shortcut menu with Copy with Base Point displayed

3. At the prompt, select the upper-left **Endpoint** object snap on the door block, as shown in *Figure 9.19*.

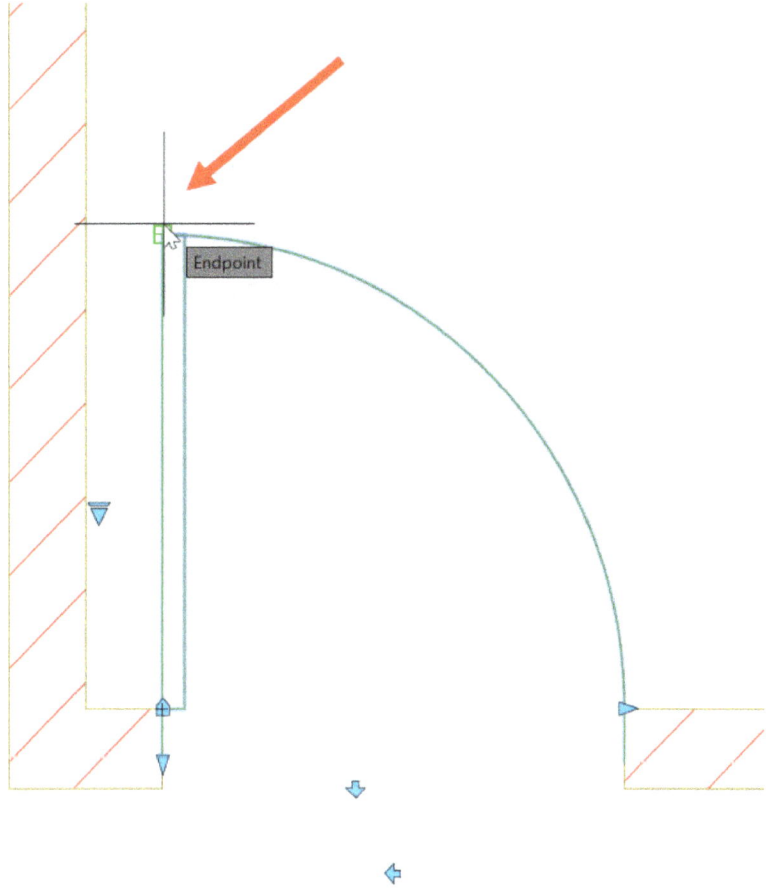

Figure 9.19: The door block selected with the Endpoint object snap

4. The door block will remain selected after clicking on the **Endpoint** object snap. Press the *Escape* key a couple of times to ensure it is deselected. The **Door – Metric** dynamic block is now on the AutoCAD Clipboard.

5. Click on the new drawing tab you created in the file tabs earlier. In the new blank drawing, right-click to display the shortcut menu and select **Clipboard** again. Select **Paste** from the sub-menu, and the door block appears on your cursor, as shown in *Figure 9.20*. As per the prompt, click anywhere in the drawing area as an insertion point. The block is now in the new drawing and has even brought along the layer it was on (**Doors** – you can check this in the **Layer** drop-down menu if you wish).

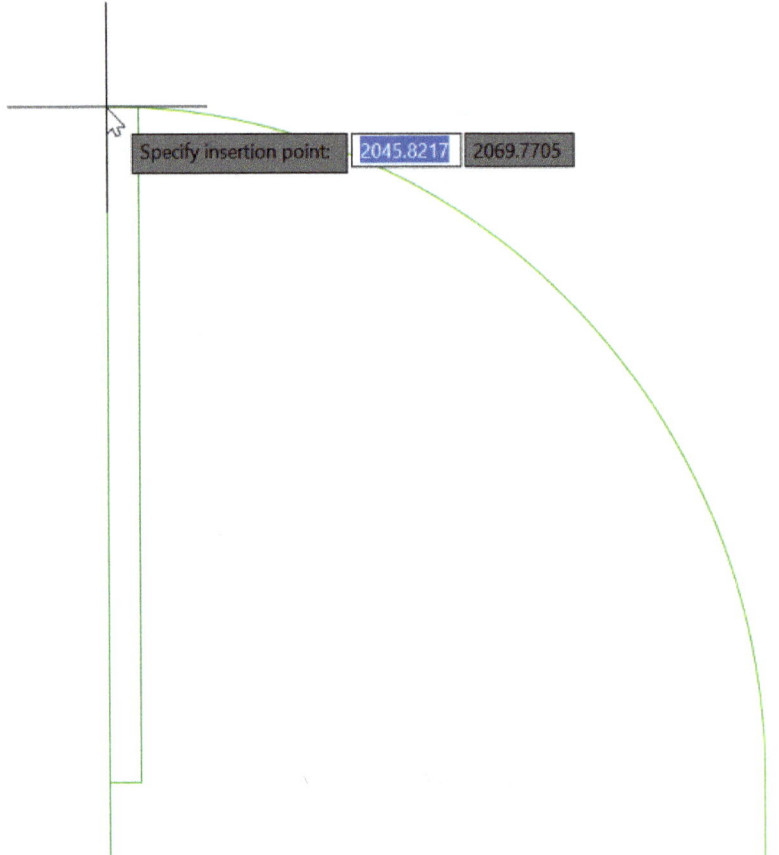

Figure 9.20: The door block with insertion point prompt displayed

6. With the new drawing current, you can now use **Save As…** and save the drawing with a suitable filename, such as `Architecture-LIBRARY.dwg`, for future use.
7. Return to the `New Office Design.dwg` file and experiment with other blocks in the drawing, copying them to your new block library drawing. Make sure to save your library drawing afterward to save the blocks in the new DWG file.

You have now created a block library drawing using the **Clipboard** function in AutoCAD. This drawing could now be placed in a shared location such as a network server or a cloud-based folder for others in your CAD team to use and copy and paste blocks from. This is a great time saver when you are all using the same blocks on the same project, saving hours of rework time.

> **Tips and tricks #29**
>
> When placing your blocks in the new block library drawing using **Paste** from the **Clipboard**, the copied block will also bring the layer it is currently on into the new drawing. It will also remain on that layer. It is often a good idea to put *all* your blocks in the new block library drawing onto their own neutral layer, avoiding any layer transfer into other working drawings.

The **Clipboard** in AutoCAD also uses the regular keyboard shortcuts, such as *Ctrl + C* for copy and *Ctrl + V* for paste. *Ctrl + X* will cut, and *Ctrl + Z* will undo the last operation.

> **AutoCAD for Mac**
>
> Copying and pasting blocks works in a virtually identical way for AutoCAD for Mac.

You have learned how to copy and paste existing blocks into a new block library drawing in this section. Next, let's look at how block libraries can be added to the Blocks palette.

Adding the block library to the Blocks palette

For the purposes of this section, I have saved the block library drawing as `Architecture-LIBRARY.dwg` in a known location.

In this section, you will learn how to add the block library to the **Blocks** palette so that it is always accessible via the **Blocks** palette at any time while working on any drawing in AutoCAD:

1. Currently, the `New Office Design.dwg` file and the `Architecture-LIBRARY.dwg` file are still open in AutoCAD. Make sure that the `New Office Design.dwg` file is the current drawing.

2. Click on the **Insert** tab on the ribbon and select the **Insert** dropdown, as you have done in previous sections in the chapter.

232 Developing Block Libraries

3. Select **Blocks from Libraries…** on the dropdown, and the **Blocks** palette will open with the **Libraries** tab current, as shown in *Figure 9.21*.

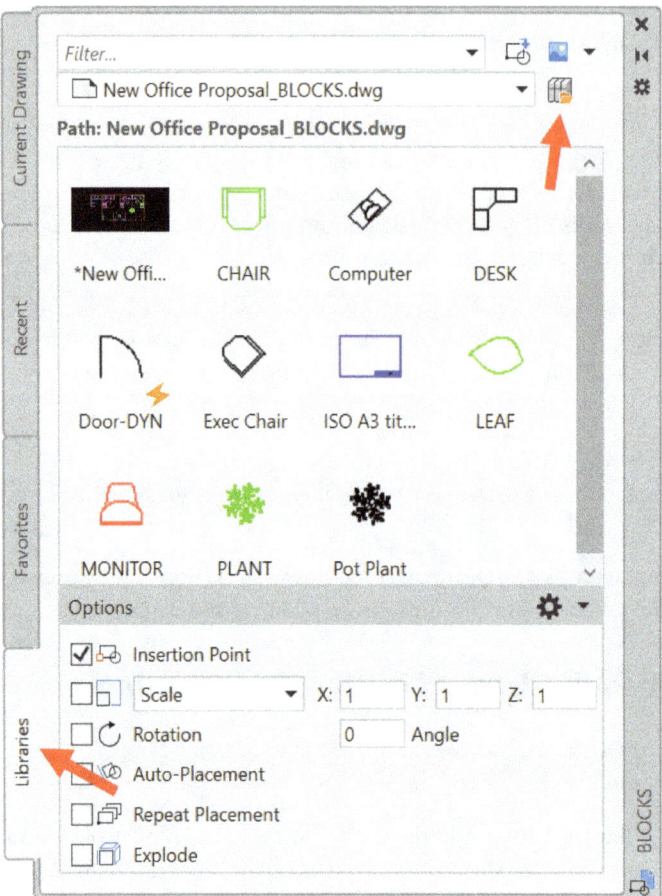

Figure 9.21: The Blocks palette with the Libraries tab current

4. To add `Architecture-LIBRARY.dwg` to the library list, you need to click on the small icon top-right in the **Blocks** palette. It looks like a little line of books and is arrowed in *Figure 9.21*.

5. You will now see a new dialog box appear, prompting you to select a folder or file for the new block library, as shown in *Figure 9.22*. Navigate to the location where you have saved your `Architecture-LIBRARY.dwg` file. You may have saved it with a slightly different filename, but you must still locate the file.

Adding the block library to the Blocks palette

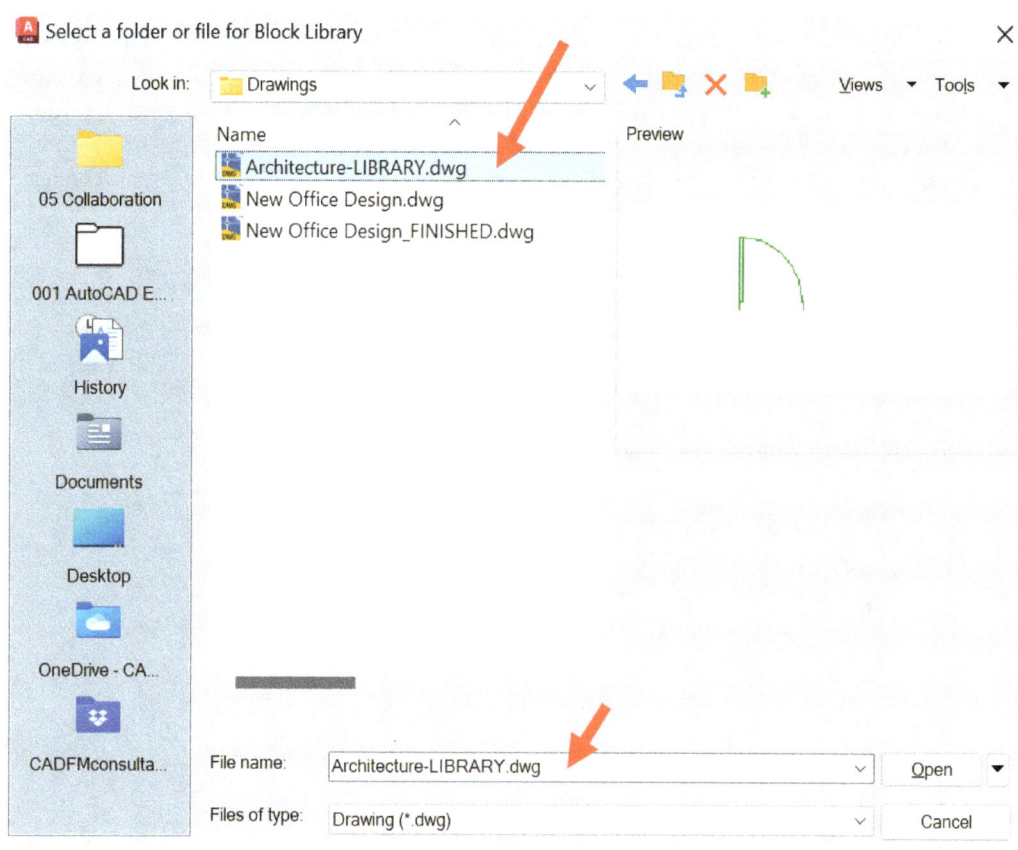

Figure 9.22: The dialog box used to locate the block library drawing

6. Select the block library drawing, as shown in *Figure 9.22*, and click on **Open**.

234　Developing Block Libraries

7. After a slight pause as AutoCAD locates your block library drawing, you will see that `Architecture-LIBRARY.dwg` has been added to the library list, displaying two icons: one icon is to use the whole drawing as a block (left), and the other icon represents the **Door – Metric** dynamic block with the lightning symbol, as shown in *Figure 9.23*. As you add more blocks to the `Architecture-LIBRARY.dwg` file, this view in the **Blocks** palette will update each time the **Blocks** palette is used.

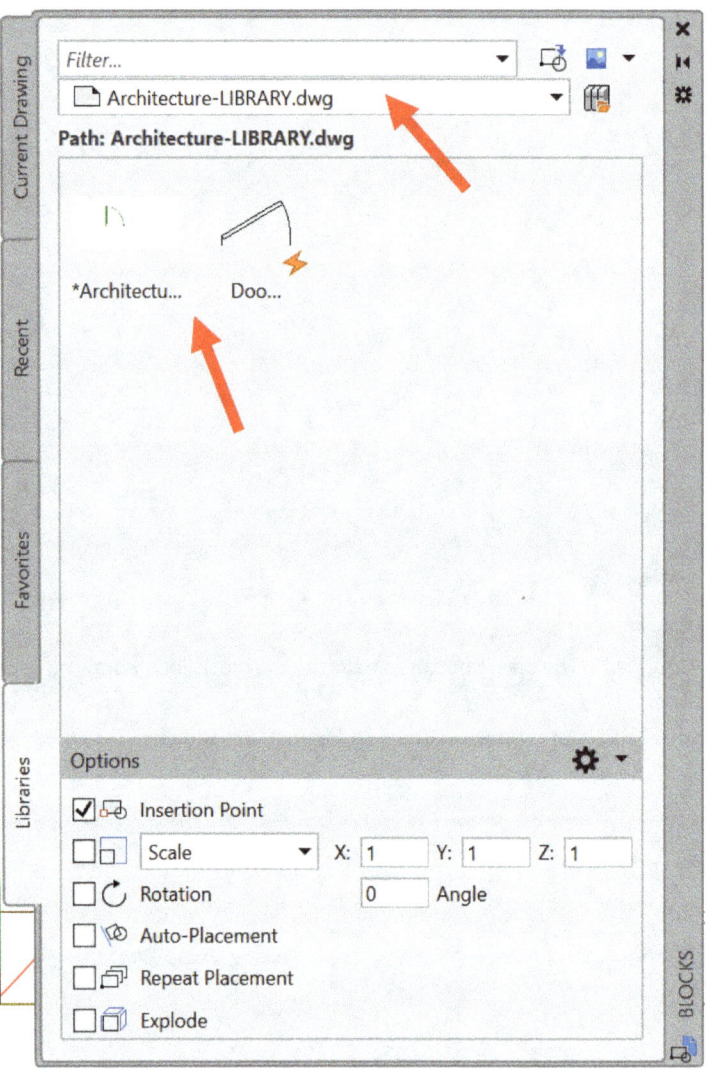

Figure 9.23: The block library drawing now added to the Blocks palette

8. As you build up your block libraries, you can locate them using the dropdown in the **Libraries** tab in the **Blocks** palette, as shown in *Figure 9.24*.

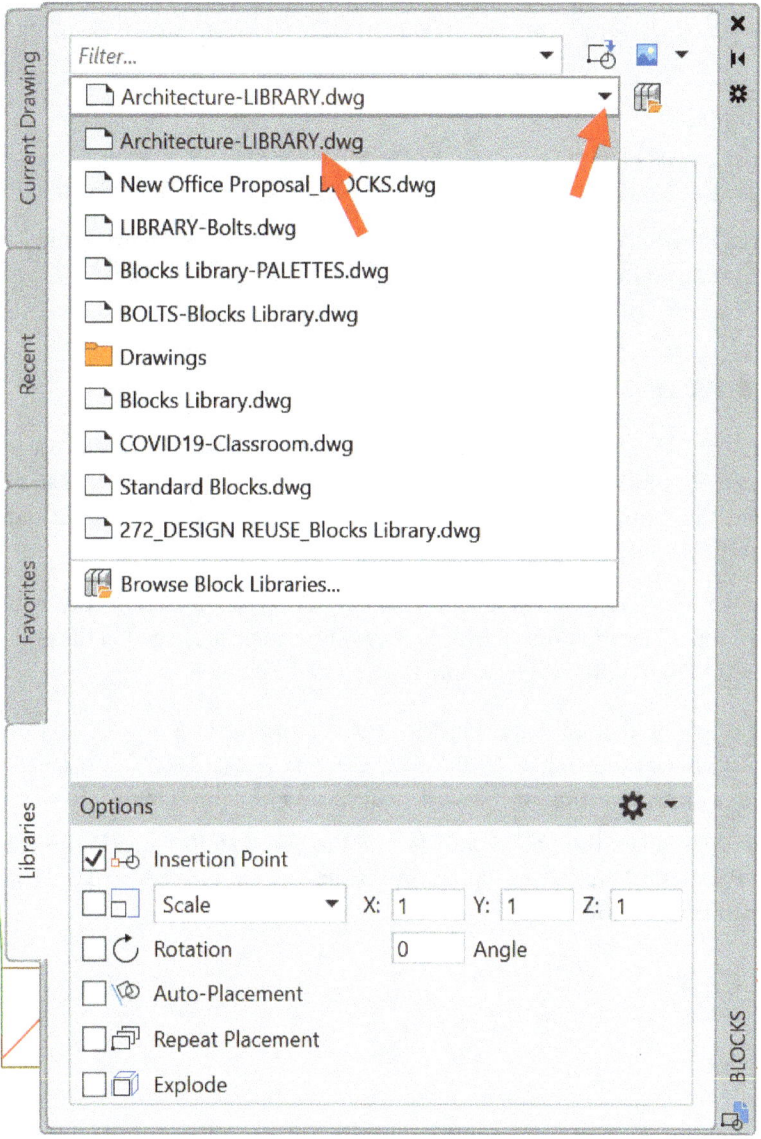

Figure 9.24: The Libraries tab showing the drop-down menu and the library drawing

9. You have now added your block library drawing to the **Blocks** palette. If you locate your library drawing in a central location, such as on a server network or in the cloud (using the likes of OneDrive, for example), anyone in your team can locate the library drawing and use the blocks in it. This saves rework time and time taken to locate the block library drawing file.

> **AutoCAD for Mac**
> The **Blocks** palette works in the same way in AutoCAD for Mac.

In this section, you learned how to add your blocks to a new block library drawing and include a path to that library drawing on the **Blocks** palette. In the next section, you will discover how to create a block library tool palette, using the **Tool Palettes** in AutoCAD.

Creating a new block library tool palette

Tool palettes in AutoCAD are another way in which to store your blocks for central use by your CAD team. If you store your block library drawings in a central location, you can drag and drop blocks onto a tool palette, and the tool palette will utilize that location. You can then import and export tool palettes to members of your CAD team.

In the following workflow, assume that the block library drawing `Architecture-LIBRARY.dwg` is stored in a central location. Use the block library drawing you created in the previous section to drag and drop the **Door – Metric** block onto the new tool palette:

1. Ensure that your block library drawing is the current drawing in AutoCAD. In this section, the current block library drawing is called `Architecture-LIBRARY.dwg`, and is assumed to be saved in a central location, such as a network server, or in the cloud.

2. Select the **View** tab on the ribbon and click on the **Tool Palettes** icon in the **Palettes** panel. The **Tool Palettes** palette will appear on the screen, as shown in *Figure 9.25*. You can also see the **Door-Metric** dynamic block.

Creating a new block library tool palette 237

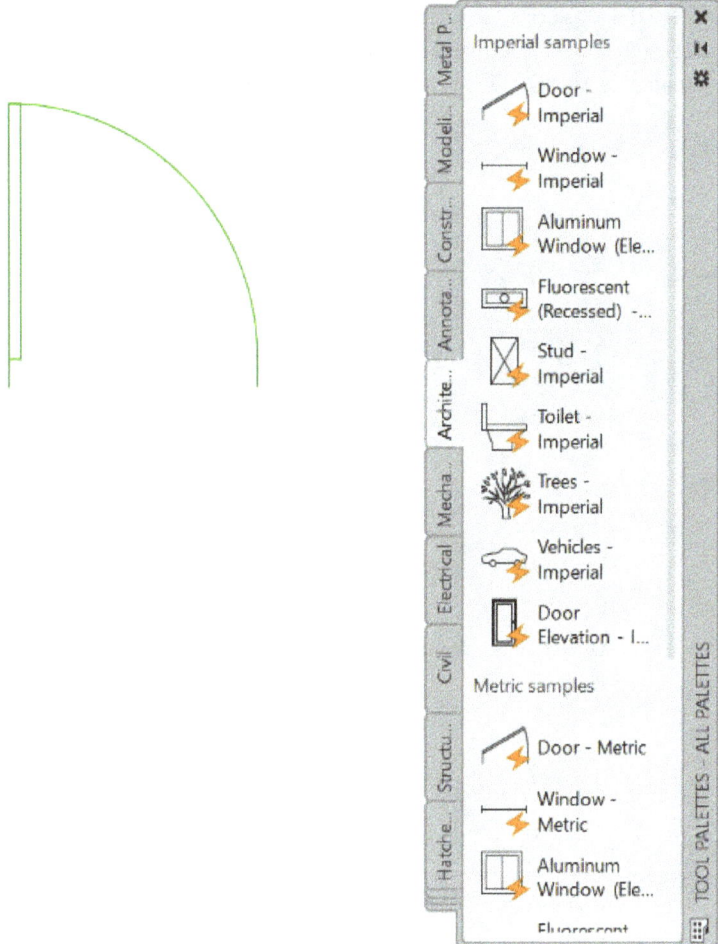

Figure 9.25: The Tool Palettes palette with the Door – Metric block

3. The **Tool Palettes** come with many pre-installed tabs and blocks; you can see the **Architecture** tab is current in *Figure 9.25*.

238 Developing Block Libraries

4. If you click where the tabs are all stacked up, you will get a list of all the available tool palettes, as shown in *Figure 9.26*. You can investigate all of these in your own time to get an idea of what comes pre-installed in AutoCAD.

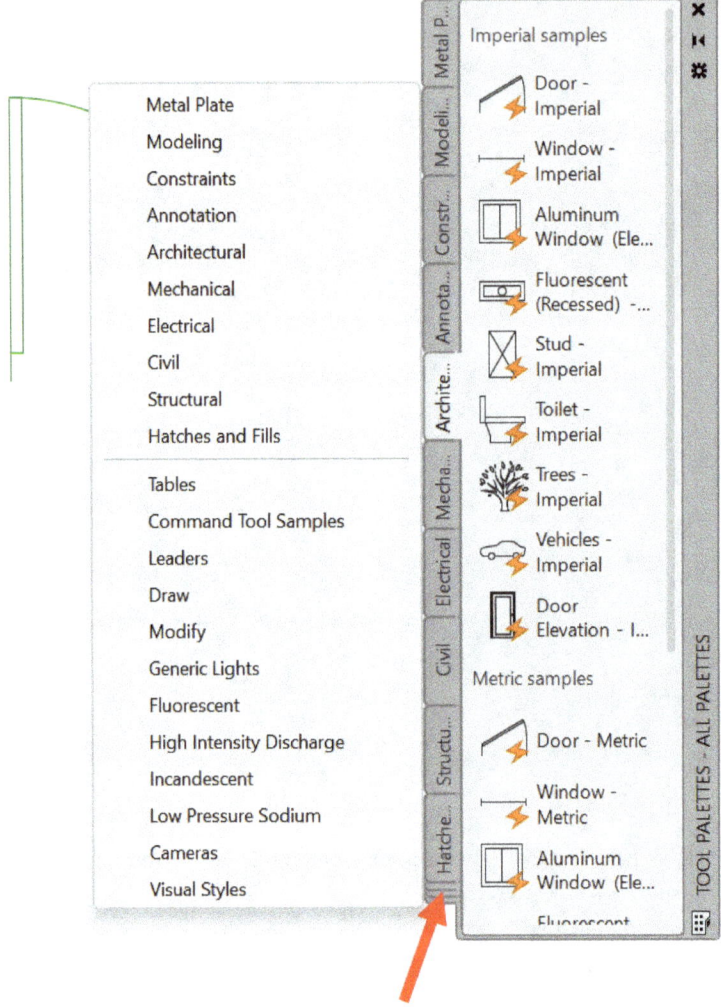

Figure 9.26: The Tool Palettes with tab list displayed

5. Click away from the **Tool Palettes** to close the tab menu.

6. Right-click on the **Tool Palettes** title bar, and another menu appears. Select **New Palette**, as shown in *Figure 9.27*.

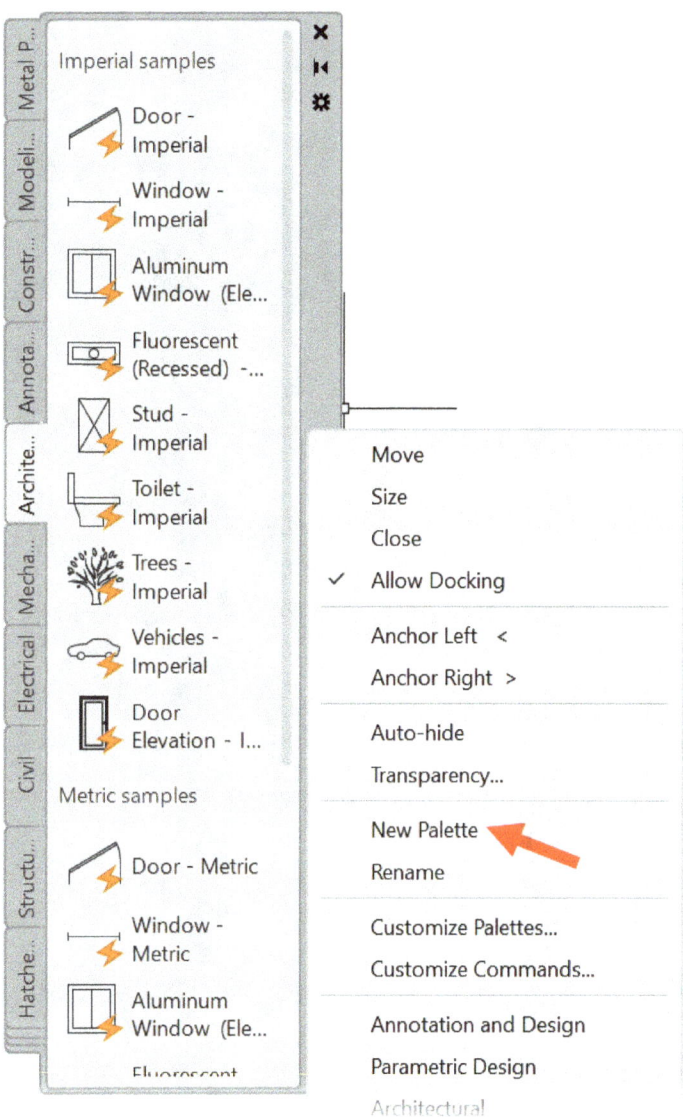

Figure 9.27: The Tool Palettes menu, with New Palette arrowed

7. A new palette tab is added to the **Tool Palettes**, and you are prompted to name it. Type in `Arch-LIBRARY`, as shown in *Figure 9.28*, and press *Enter* to confirm the tab name.

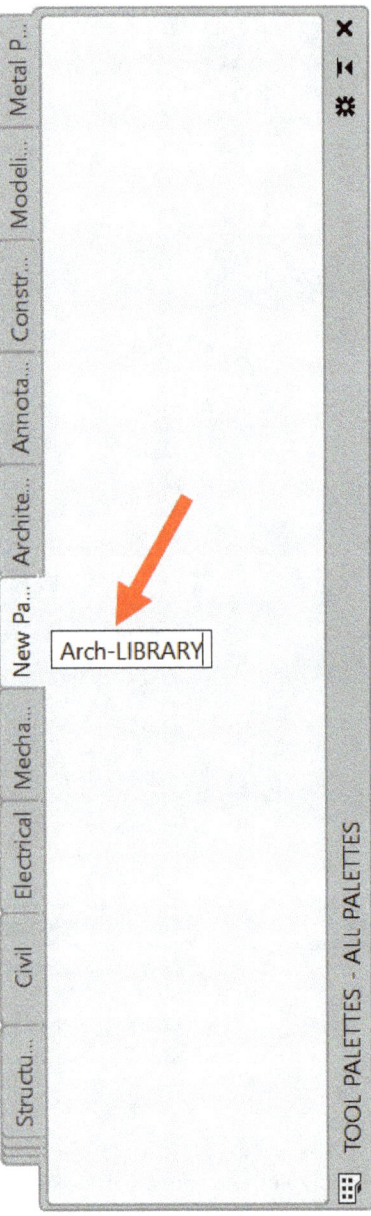

Figure 9.28: The new palette tab being named

8. Click on the **Door – Metric** dynamic block to select it. Click and drag the block over to the palette, making sure *NOT* to use any of the blue grips. If you select a grip, AutoCAD will assume you are editing using the selected grip, so click and drag using an edge line, for example.

9. As you drag over the new palette area, you will see a + (plus) symbol on the cursor and a line on the new palette, as shown in *Figure 9.29*.

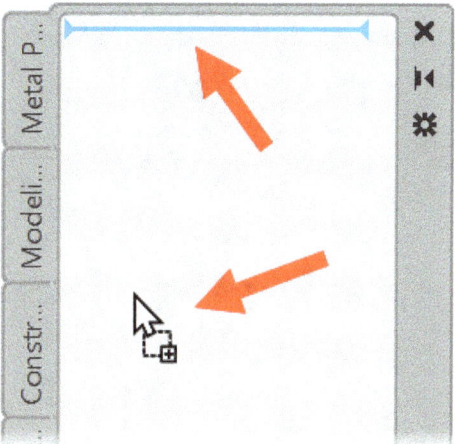

Figure 9.29: The + symbol and line on the new palette

10. Release the mouse button, and a **Door – Metric** block icon appears on the new palette, as shown in *Figure 9.30*. You can also see the lightning symbol, indicating it is a dynamic block.

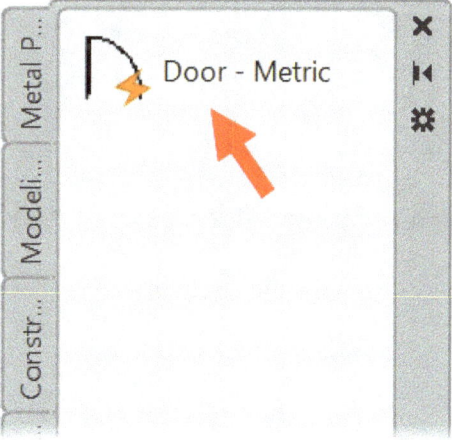

Figure 9.30: The Door – Metric dynamic block on the tool palette

Your block is now placed on the tool palette and can be dragged and dropped from the palette into any drawing from its central location. The palette remembers that location so make sure that if you do change the block library drawing location, you update the properties of the icon on the palette. You can do that by right-clicking over the palette icon and selecting **Properties** on the shortcut menu.

11. You can add text and separators to the new tool palette. Right-click in the tool palette area and select **Add Text** or **Add Separator** to do this, as shown in *Figure 9.31*.

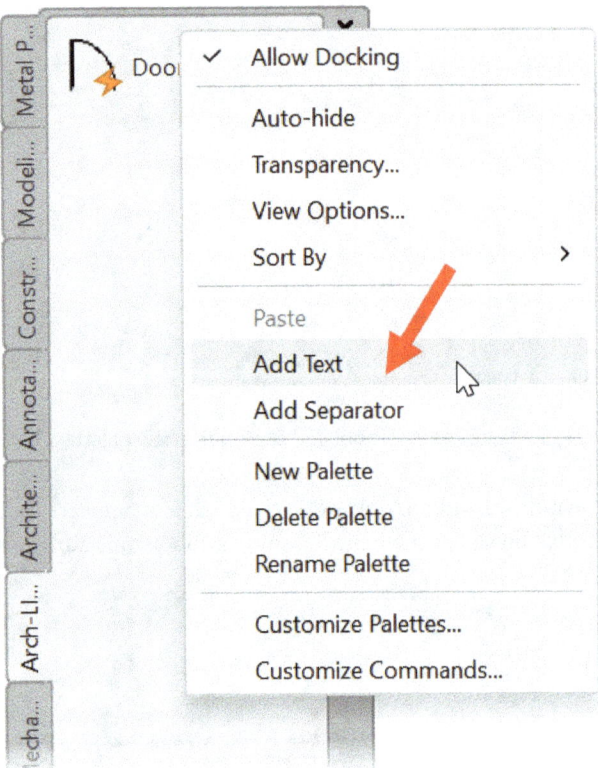

Figure 9.31: The tool palette menu displaying Add Text and Add Separator

12. Using the text and separator tools, you can specify areas on the tool palette for block types, as shown in *Figure 9.32*.

Creating a new block library tool palette   243

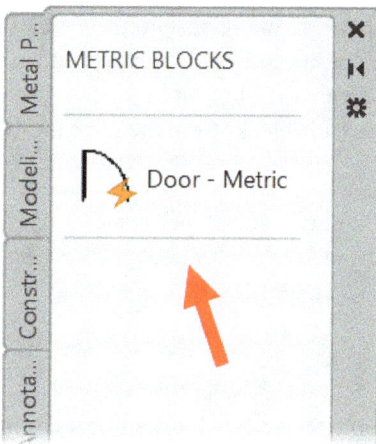

Figure 9.32: The new tool palette with text and separators added

13. To import and export tool palettes, you must click on the **Tool Palettes** title bar again. Select **Customize Palettes...** from the menu, and the **Customize** dialog box will appear, as shown in *Figure 9.33*.

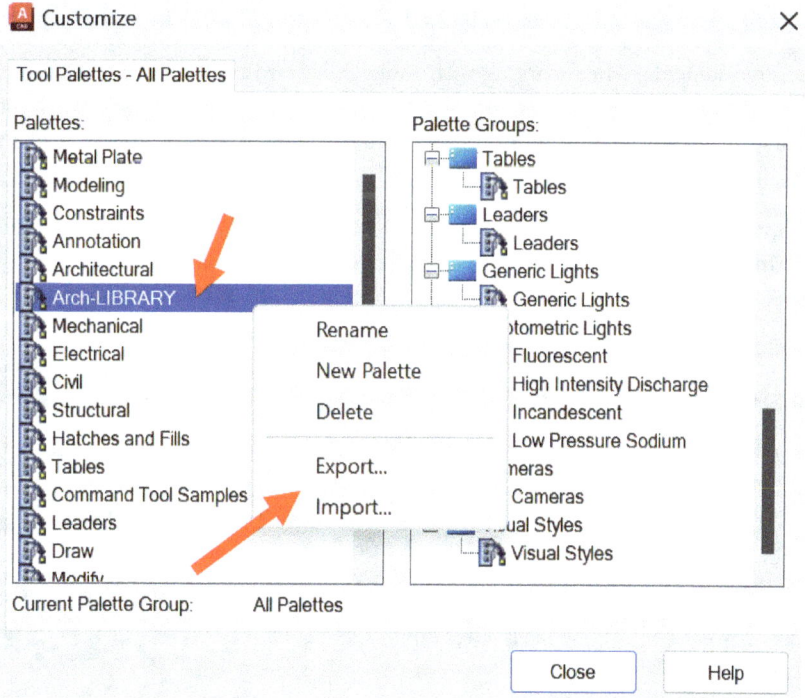

Figure 9.33: The Customize dialog box with the Arch-LIBRARY palette selected

14. Select the **Arch-LIBRARY** palette from the list on the left and right-click on it. The shortcut menu shown in *Figure 9.33* appears, and you can import and export your tool palettes as **XTP** files. Export an XTP file to a team member, and they can then import the XTP file into their own tool palettes and use the same blocks from the same location.

You can now create your own tool palettes, add your drawing blocks to those palettes, and import and export palettes within your team to reuse existing block content. To explore tool palettes further, use this link to access the Autodesk website: `https://help.autodesk.com/view/ACD/2021/ENU/?guid=GUID-167A8594-92CB-4FCC-B72C-0F546383E97C`.

Summary

You now know how to start developing your own block libraries, working with both regular blocks and dynamic blocks, adding them to libraries in the Blocks palette, and creating your own tool palettes with your own blocks. In this chapter, you have learned how to insert regular and dynamic blocks into drawings and use dynamic block parameters to change a dynamic block's appearance.

You have also learned how to use the Clipboard function in AutoCAD to copy and paste AutoCAD blocks between drawings to start developing block libraries. In addition, you have learned how to add a new block library drawing to the Blocks palette by accessing it from the **Libraries** tab.

You have also gained valuable knowledge on adding and managing blocks in new tool palettes.

Content reuse is fundamental when working with AutoCAD drawings in large projects as it can save valuable time and the onerous reworking of AutoCAD objects in project drawings. The skills learned in this chapter will give you a good grounding and understanding of how to start implementing content reuse and block libraries in the future.

In the next chapter, we will look at how you can add attributes to AutoCAD blocks when reusing design content in order to add and relay more detailed design information within your AutoCAD blocks in your AutoCAD drawings.

Get This Book's PDF Version and Exclusive Extras

Scan the QR code (or go to `packtpub.com/unlock`). Search for this book by name, confirm the edition, and then follow the steps on the page.

Note: Keep your invoice handy. Purchases made directly from Packt don't require one.

10
Working with Block Attributes

In the previous chapter, you learned how to work with AutoCAD blocks, manage them in your drawings, and create block libraries for content reuse. In this chapter, you will learn more about the blocks and how to add **attributes** to a block, providing detailed information within a drawing.

As you are aware, blocks are objects made up of multiple AutoCAD objects for content reuse, such as a chair or a desk, to avoid having to rework that particular chair or desk repetitively in a drawing. Attributes take that content reuse one step further by providing pertinent information about the block. Take a block that represents a chair, for example. Typical attributes of the chair block might be the manufacturer, the model type, and the serial number. You can even apply attributes for ownership, such as the department that owns the chair in the office and which employee uses that chair. The applications of attributes are endless, and you can easily extract and edit those attributes at any time.

Over time, drawings become occupied with more and more blocks. Attributes allow you to identify your blocks and provide valuable information to anyone using your drawings.

This chapter covers the following methodologies you will need to work with attributes in your AutoCAD blocks:

- Defining attributes within a block
- Editing attributes in a block using Enhanced Attribute Editor
- Using Block Attribute Manager (*BATTMAN*)

As in the previous chapter, reusing drawing content and managing that content will save valuable drafting time, reducing the need for repetitive tasks and allowing content sharing with your project stakeholders and team members.

In this chapter, you will learn how attributes in blocks give you the ability to give your blocks the relevant information needed for effective interpretation of your drawings.

Exercise file

You have already downloaded the previous chapter's exercise file, `New Office Design.dwg`. You will also use this exercise file for this chapter.

Defining attributes within a block

Blocks (regular and dynamic) can have attributes applied to them. This section will teach you how to apply attributes to a regular AutoCAD block. The same workflow will apply to a dynamic block.

There are already existing blocks in the exercise file, `New Office Design.dwg`. You will need to be in the **Model** tab when it opens, displaying the simple office floor plan.

Your first step will be to return the block to its original AutoCAD objects. You do this to enable the attributes to be added to the content of the block, and then save the block again.

To do this, you will need to zoom into the desk near the door opening and select the block that represents a computer, as shown in *Figure 10.1*.

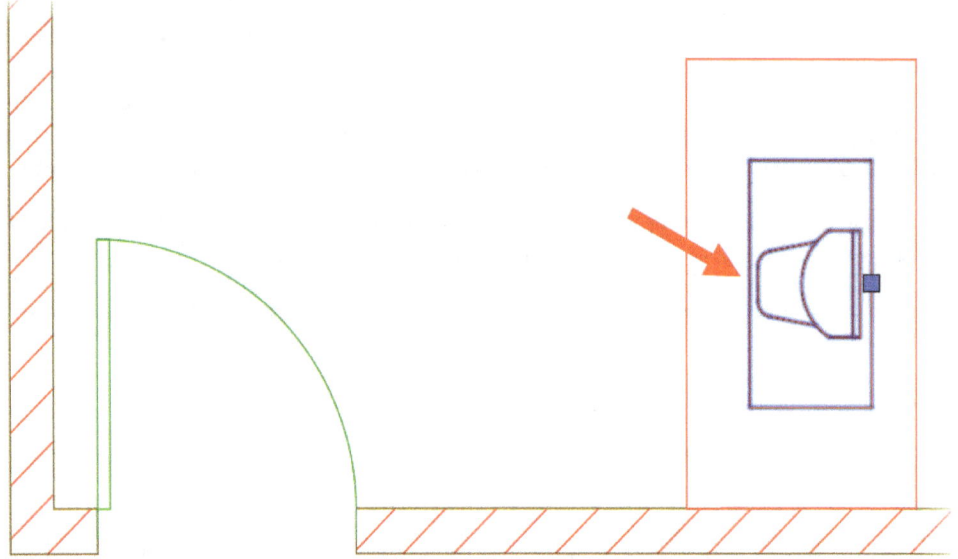

Figure 10.1: The PC block on the desk near the door opening (with the block selected)

You will see that the selected PC block is one object with one grip displayed. That grip is the block insertion point, and you can (if needed) use grip editing tools with the block by selecting the grip and right-clicking to bring up the shortcut menu. You don't need to do this right now, as you will be editing the block to add attributes to the block.

Defining attributes within a block   247

You will need to create a new block for the PC that includes attributes, and the quickest way to do this is to use the **Explode** (*EXPLODE*) command to explode the block back to its original AutoCAD objects. With the block still selected, click on the **Explode** icon on the **Modify** panel on the **Home** tab on the ribbon, as shown in *Figure 10.2*.

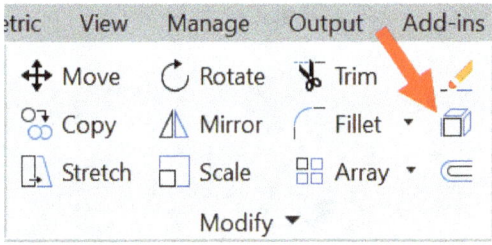

Figure 10.2: The Explode icon on the Modify panel

The exploded block had what is known as a *nested* block within it. You can make blocks of blocks, and these are known as **nested blocks**. The original PC block was made up of four lines and another block that represented the computer screen. The block will now be returned to its original AutoCAD objects, and you now need to start the workflow to create a new PC block that has attributes included:

1. Select the screen block and explode that as well. If you hover over any element of the screen now, it is an AutoCAD object, such as a line or an arc.
2. These objects are shown selected in *Figure 10.3*. Make sure you have all four lines, and the screen block selected as shown (the blue grips will be displayed).

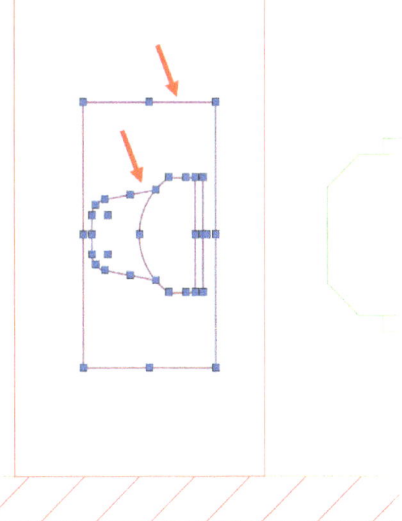

Figure 10.3: The AutoCAD objects selected after exploding the blocks

When creating a new block, a good practice to get into is to ensure that *all* objects that make up the new block start on layer **0** (*zero*). Then, once the block has been created, it will adopt the current layer each time an instance of the block is inserted in the drawing.

3. With all the now-exploded objects selected, go to the layer drop-down menu on the **Layers** panel and select layer **0** (*zero*). It is always at the top of the layer list as it is the AutoCAD default layer, as shown in *Figure 10.4*.

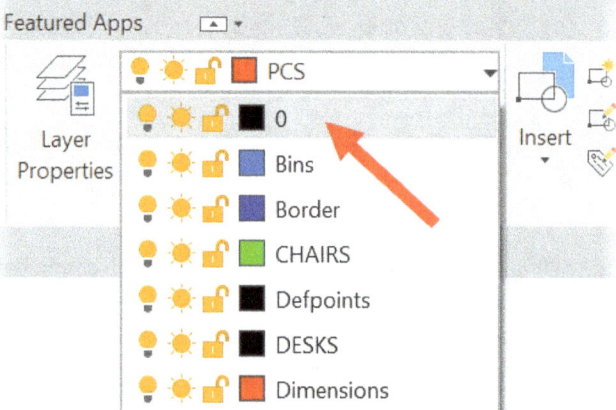

Figure 10.4: The layer drop-down menu with layer 0 (zero) indicated

4. When going to the layer drop-down menu with the exploded objects selected, you will note that they are all on the **PCS** layer. This is why the objects need to go to layer **0** (*zero*), as you may need to put them onto an alternative layer. Click on layer **0** on the dropdown, and you will see all the objects go onto that layer.

Press the *Esc* key several times to ensure the objects are deselected. Then, make sure that layer **0** is the current layer.

5. Click on the **Insert** tab on the ribbon. Click on the **Define Attributes** icon in the **Block Definition** panel, as shown in *Figure 10.5*.

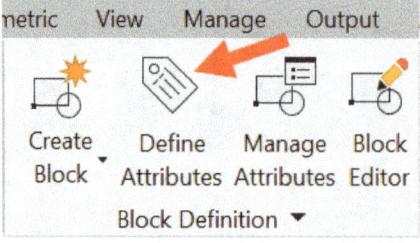

Figure 10.5: The Block Definition panel with Define Attributes indicated

6. This will start the **Define Attributes** (*ATTDEF*) command, and the **Attribute Definition** dialog box will appear, as shown in *Figure 10.6*.

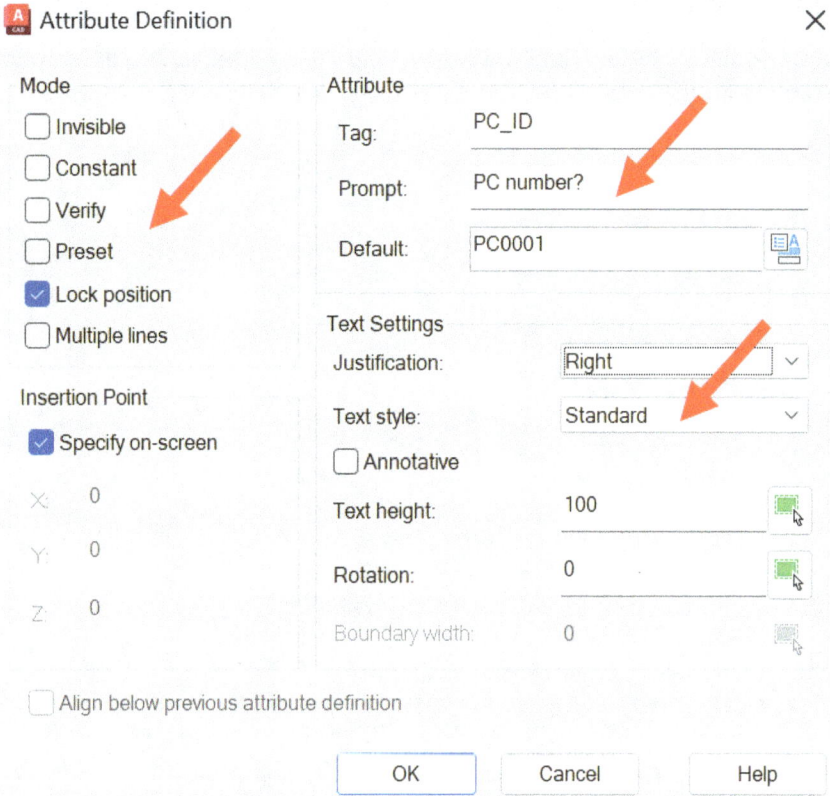

Figure 10.6: The Attribute Definition dialog box

7. There are three main areas in the dialog box where attribute settings can be set: **Mode**, **Attribute**, and **Text Settings**. There is also an area where **Insertion Point** can be defined. Make sure to check **Specify on-screen** in that area.

8. To set up the **PC_ID** block attribute, ensure that the following settings are defined for the block attribute:

   - **Mode**: Set this to **Lock position**. There are numerous settings here, but **Lock position** is the only one needed.

   - **Attribute**: Set **Tag** to **PC_ID**. Attribute tags cannot have spaces, so use the underscore character if a space is needed. **Prompt** is what appears in the dialog box when inserting the attributed block in the drawing, so it's useful to ask a question with a question mark. Add a **Default** setting, too, so that the field has data in the dialog box.

- **Text Settings**: Set **Justification** and **Text style** to what is shown in *Figure 10.6*. A **Text height** value of 100 is used as the drawing is in metric millimeters, which works as a suitable attribute size for this drawing.

9. Click on **OK**, and the dialog box closes, leaving you with the attribute attached to your cursor. Make sure to place the attribute to the left of the PC objects in the drawing, as shown in *Figure 10.7*.

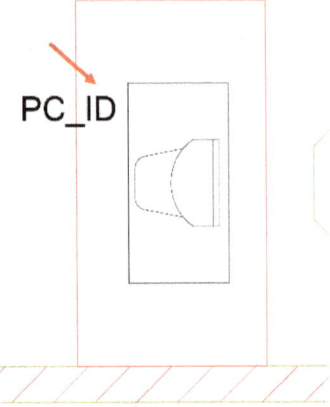

Figure 10.7: The placed block attribute

10. Using the previous steps, create two more attributes:

    - **PC_MANU**: Use the **PC Manufacturer?** prompt with a default of **Acme**
    - **EMP_ID**: Use the **Employee ID?** prompt with a default of **E999**

    Before placing the two new attributes, make sure to set **Justification** to **Right**, and then check the **Align below previous attribute definition** box. Placing the attributes, they automatically align below the **PC_ID** attribute, as shown in *Figure 10.8*.

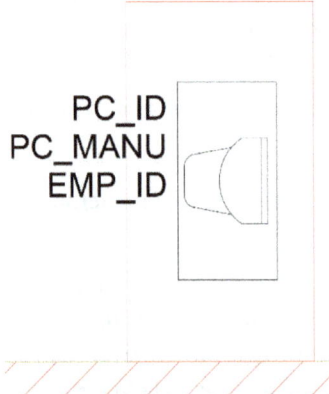

Figure 10.8: The three attributes placed to the left of the objects

11. Select all three attributes and all the objects that will make up the new PC block, as shown in *Figure 10.9*. You will see all the grips displayed.

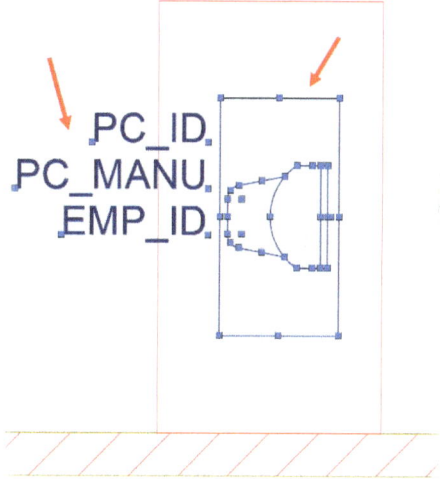

Figure 10.9: All attributes and objects selected

12. Click on the **Create Block** icon on the **Block Definition** panel, as shown in *Figure 10.10*.

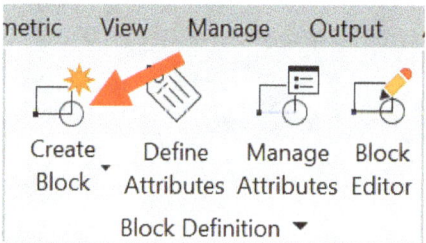

Figure 10.10: The Create Block icon on the Block Definition panel

13. The **Block Definition** dialog box will appear. Name the block PC_Attributes, in the **Name** field.
14. Select the **Pick point** icon in the dialog box, and in the drawing, select the top-right **Endpoint** snap of the objects, as shown in *Figure 10.11*.

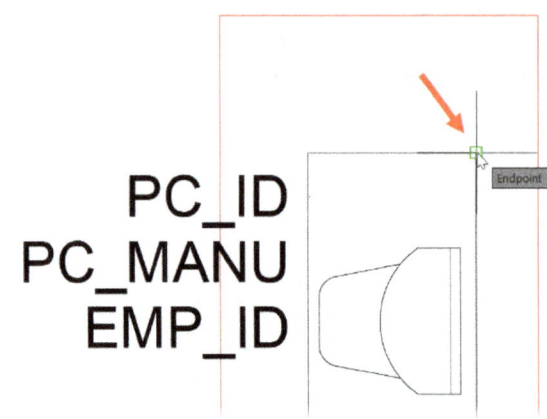

Figure 10.11 – The Endpoint object snap on the selected objects

15. Note that the X and Y coordinates are now set (ignore the numbers), and make sure that all other settings are set as they are in the dialog box in *Figure 10.12*. The objects were already selected before you started the **Create Block** (*BLOCK*) command, so there will be 17 objects selected.

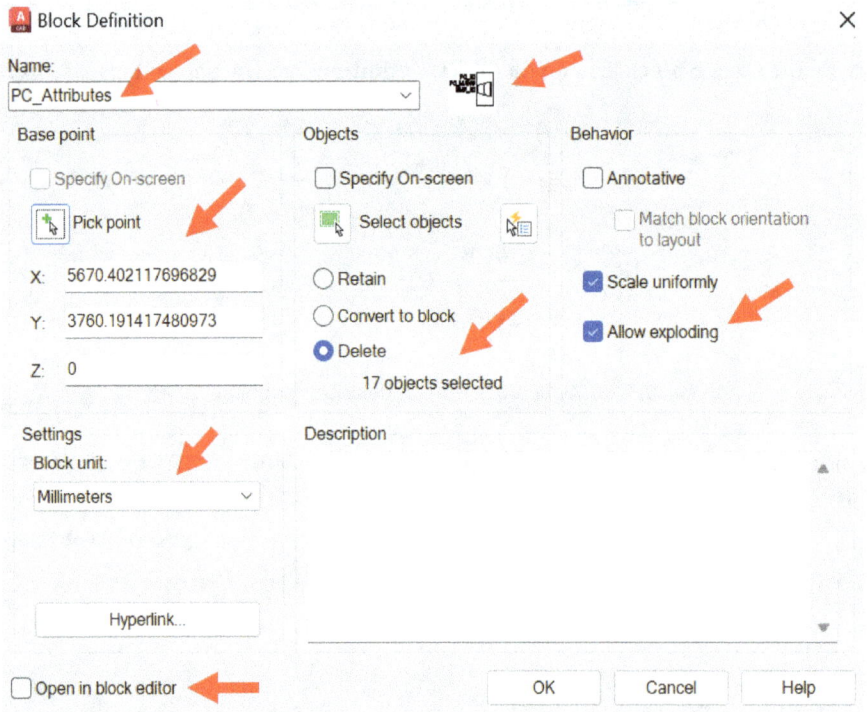

Figure 10.12: The Block Definition dialog box with settings

16. Click on **OK**, and the attributes and objects disappear. Do *not* panic at this point. The **Delete** option was set in the **Objects** pane in the **Block Definition** dialog box, so the objects forming the new block have been deleted, but the new block is still in the DWG file.

17. At this point, it is good practice to save your drawing. Then, the block, while not displayed, is saved in the DWG file.

18. You now need to insert the newly attributed block into the drawing. The block was created on layer **0** (*zero*) so it will adopt the current layer. Make sure you change the current layer to **PCS** on the **Layer** drop-down menu, on the **Layers** panel on the **Home** tab on the ribbon, first.

19. On the **Insert** tab on the ribbon, click on the **Insert** dropdown on the **Block** panel. Using the slider bar on the right of the drop-down menu, you can locate your new attributed block, PC_Attributes, as shown in *Figure 10.13*. Click on the block on the menu and you can then insert the block into the drawing.

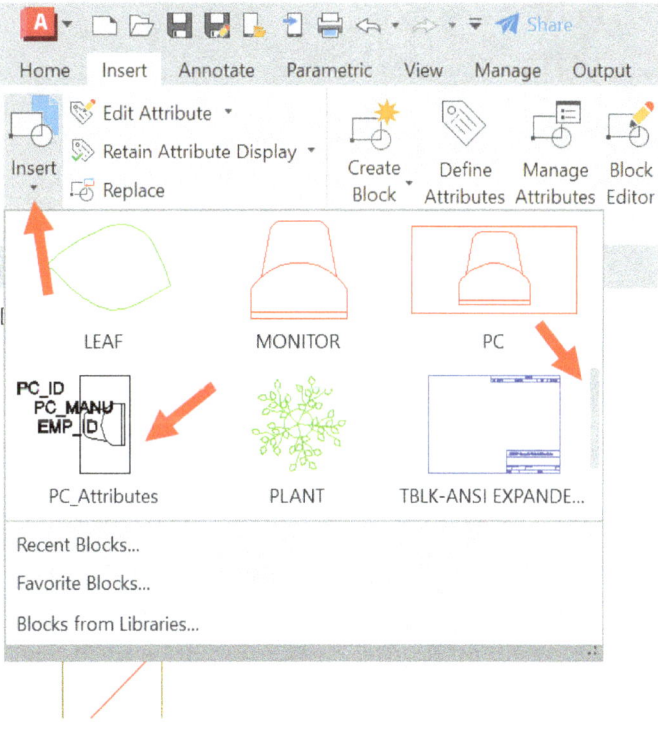

Figure 10.13: The Insert drop-down menu with the new attributed block pointed out using an arrow

20. The selected block appears on your cursor, and you can position it using the insertion point you selected when creating the block (top-right corner of the PC). Locate the new block centrally on the desk (don't worry too much about exact positioning, as you can rework that later with object snaps if you wish). *Figure 10.14* shows the block in position before you click to confirm. Note that it is displaying the attributes and is on the current layer (*PCS*).

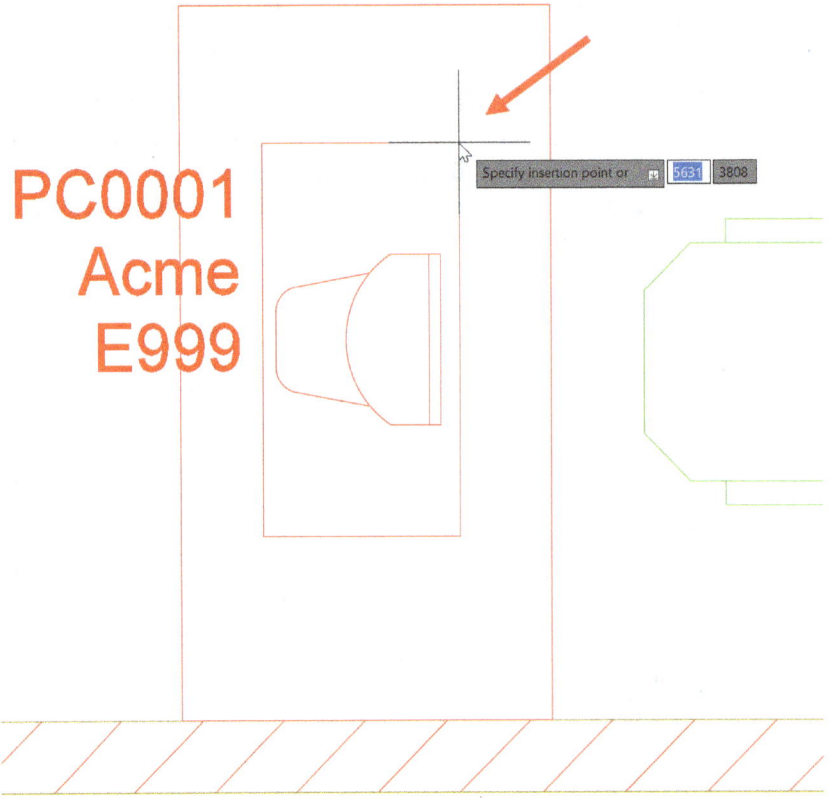

Figure 10.14: The PC_Attributes block just before the position is confirmed

21. Upon clicking, you will confirm its position and be prompted to edit the block attributes in the **Edit Attributes** dialog box, as shown in *Figure 10.15*. Note that the prompts are as you set them up in the original attribute definitions, along with the default attribute values.

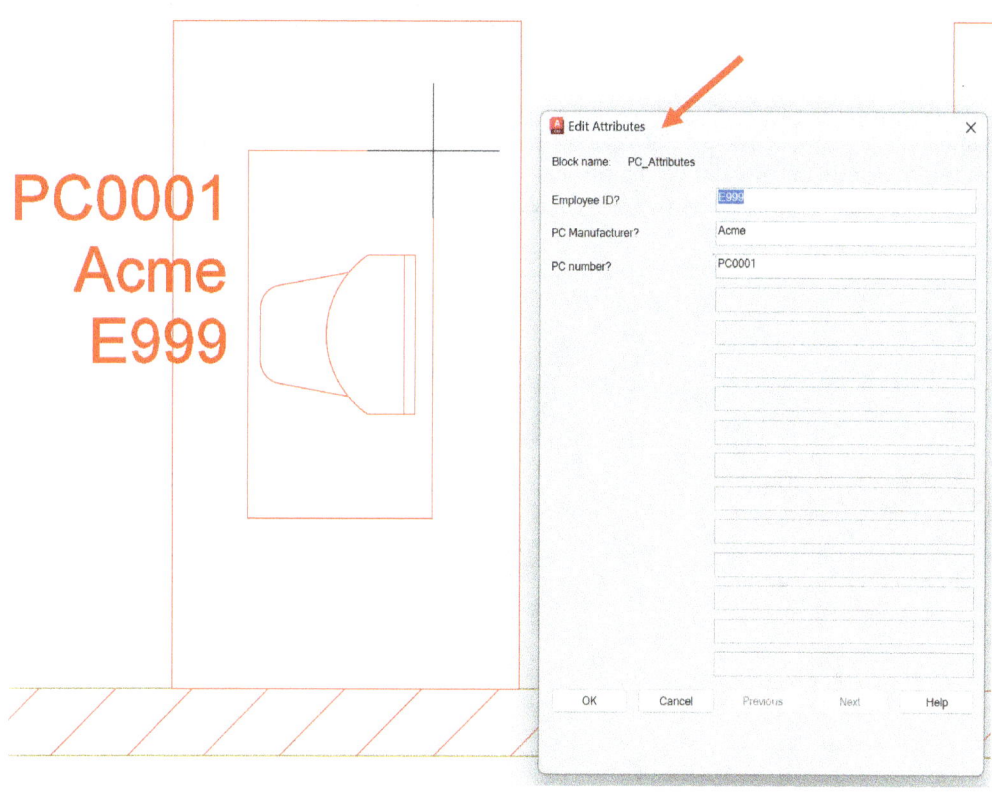

Figure 10.15: The Edit Attributes dialog box ready for any attribute editing

22. Edit the attribute values if you wish. For the purposes of the exercise, though, they will be left at their default values for the moment. Click on **OK** to close the **Edit Attributes** dialog box. You must click **OK**, as the dialog box will not close if you press *Enter* like other AutoCAD commands. You now have an attributed block placed in your AutoCAD drawing.

Tips and tricks #30

You might want to rotate blocks at various angles when you insert blocks into your drawing. Instead of inserting the block, confirming its position, and then using the **Rotate** (*ROTATE*) command afterward, consider right-clicking when prompted for the block insertion point. You can utilize **Rotate** (and **Scale**) on the shortcut menu as part of the block insertion workflow, saving you valuable time when you're on a deadline! *Figure 10.16* shows the block insertion shortcut menu in action.

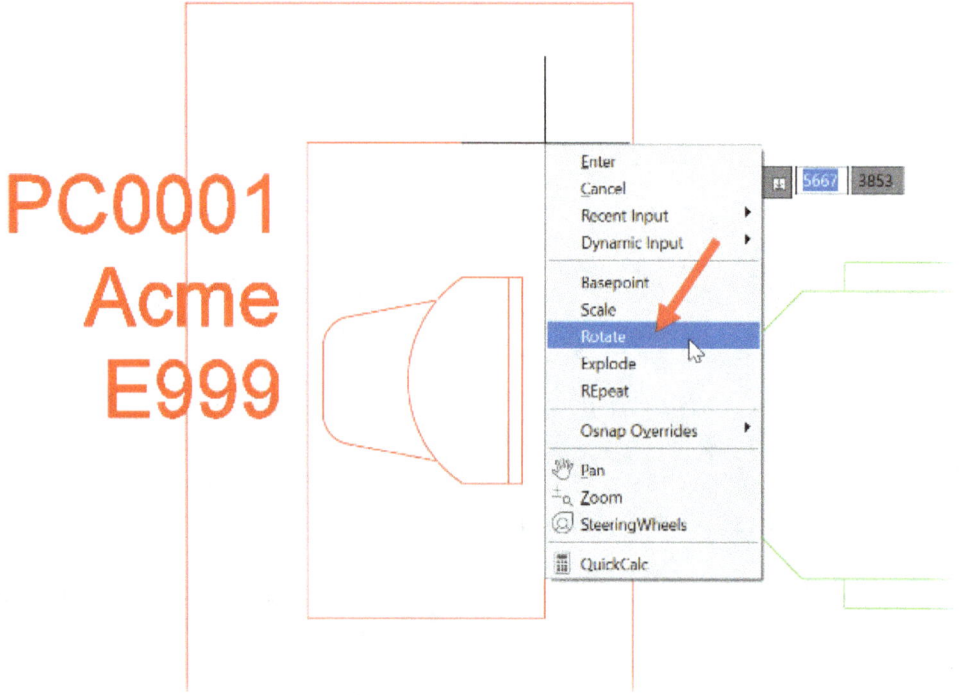

Figure 10.16: The block insertion shortcut menu with Rotate indicated

The right-click shortcut menu has many commands and tools that you can use when working with blocks. All of them allow you to be a little bit more productive, letting you have a more efficient workflow.

AutoCAD for Mac

AutoCAD for Mac uses the **Blocks** palette for inserting blocks into your drawings, and this tends to be the best method for the Mac interface.

In this section, you learned how to create and insert a new block with attributes. Attributes in blocks provide more information about the block, enabling recipients of the drawing to see and understand what the blocks represent and what data they carry. For example, a block representing a door could display attributes displaying the door size and manufacturer. In the next section, you will learn how to use **Enhanced Attribute Editor** to edit existing block attributes.

Editing attributes in a block using Enhanced Attribute Editor

You should already have the `New Office Design.dwg` exercise file open from the previous section. Make sure you are still zoomed into the part of the drawing where you inserted the `PC_Attributes` block onto the desk.

You will now work with **Enhanced Attribute Editor** in the drawing to make changes to the displayed block attributes. Editing attributes is sometimes useful for higher visibility in the drawing, or font sizes need to be reduced for clarity.

You will do this by using the following workflow:

1. Hover over the `PC_Attributes` block, and then double-click on it. Since it has attributes in the block, **Enhanced Attribute Editor** will appear, as shown in *Figure 10.17*. It defaults to the **Attribute** tab in the editor. You can now edit the attributes in the block without the need to explode the block and rework the attributes.

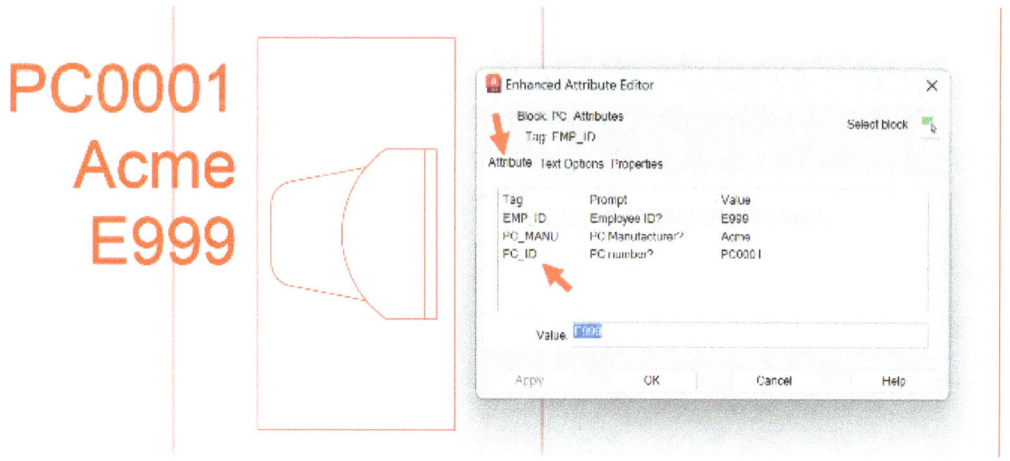

Figure 10.17: Enhanced Attribute Editor with the Attribute tab selected

2. Select the **PC_ID** attribute, and the attribute value will display in the **Value** field. Change the **PC_ID** attribute value to **PC100**. You will see this update in the editor and preview in the drawing.

3. Select the **Text Options** tab in the editor. Note that at the top of the editor, you can see which block and attribute you are working on (indicated using arrows). You can also select another attributed block to work on using the **Select block** icon (also indicated using arrows). This is all shown in *Figure 10.18*.

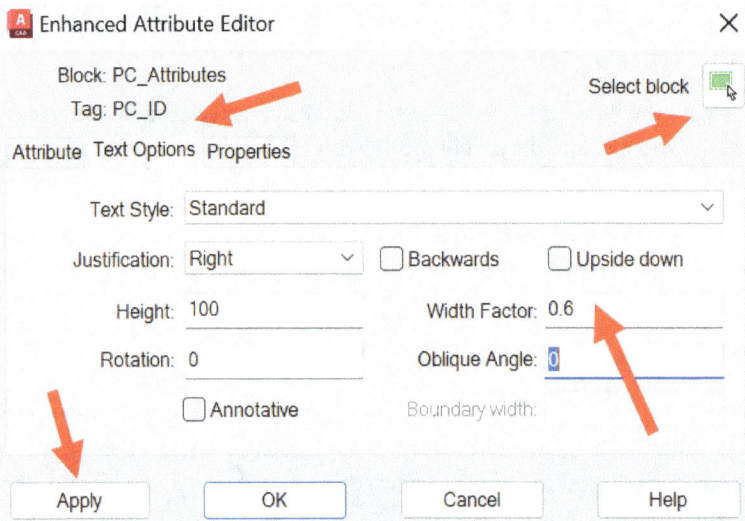

Figure 10.18: The Text Options tab settings

4. Change the **Width Factor** value from 1 to 0.6, as shown in *Figure 10.18*. Click on **Apply** to see the text width of the **PC_ID** attribute change. Do *not* click on **OK** at this point.

5. Select the **Properties** tab. Using the **Color** drop-down menu, change the color to **Green**, as shown in *Figure 10.19*. As before, click on **Apply** to see the change in the attribute.

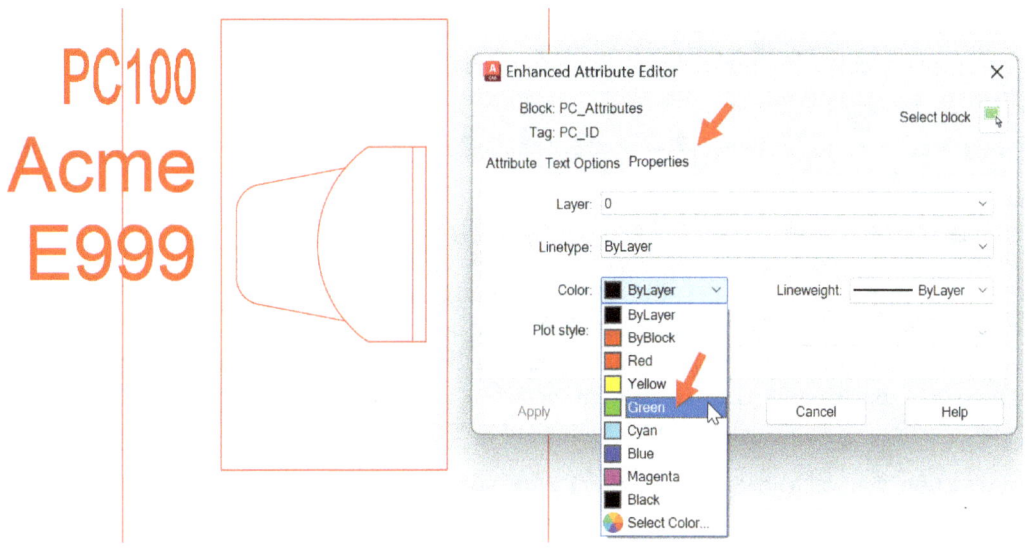

Figure 10.19: The Properties tab with the changes required shown

6. After seeing the **PC_ID** attribute display in green, click on **OK** to close **Enhanced Attribute Editor**. You now have a block with an edited attribute, as shown in *Figure 10.20*.

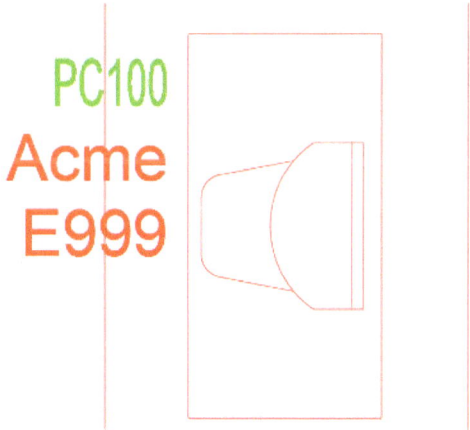

Figure 10.20: The PC_Attributes block, with the edited PC_ID attribute

In this section, you have learned how to use **Enhanced Attribute Editor** to edit individual attributes in your AutoCAD blocks. You can use the editor with any block with attributes simply by double-clicking on the block and editing the attribute values, text settings, and properties.

> **AutoCAD for Mac**
>
> **Enhanced Attribute Editor** works in the same way in AutoCAD for Mac.

The next section takes you to the next level of attribute editing using **Block Attribute Manager** (*BATTMAN*).

Using Block Attribute Manager (BATTMAN)

For this section, you can stay in the `New Office Design.dwg` file. However, before we begin in earnest, it's time for a little CAD humor. The Block Attribute Manager command is called `BATTMAN`. If you type `BATTMAN` and press *Enter*, you will activate **Block Attribute Manager**. You probably do not need to be told that this relates to a certain superhero, and there is always a bit of humor involved if you are struggling with block attributes; you call in `BATTMAN`, right?

In this section, you will learn how to use **Block Attribute Manager** to further edit attributes in your `PC_Attributes` block, learning more skills to work with the attributes in your blocks. Let's look at the steps involved:

1. Staying in the `New Office Design.dwg` file, make sure you are still zoomed in to where you placed the `PC_Attributes` block in the previous section.

2. With no commands running or objects selected, type `BATTMAN`. The dynamic input will automatically bring up the text on the suggestion menu. Press *Enter*, and the **Block Attribute Manager** dialog box will appear on the screen, as shown in *Figure 10.21*.

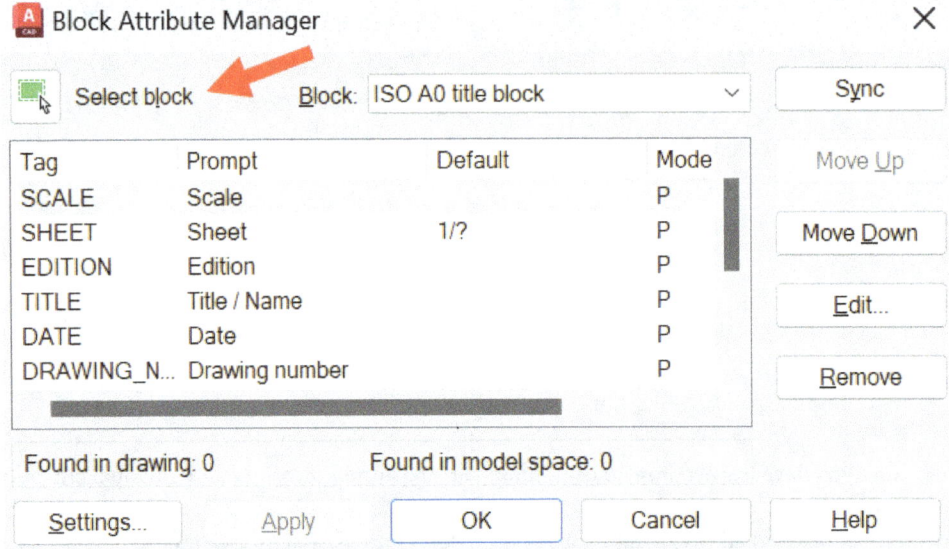

Figure 10.21: Block Attribute Manager (BATTMAN)

3. Using the **Select block** icon (shown in *Figure 10.21*), you can then select your `PC_Attributes` block.

4. You will be returned to the dialog box, and you can now see the attributes of the `PC_Attributes` block displayed, as shown in *Figure 10.22*.

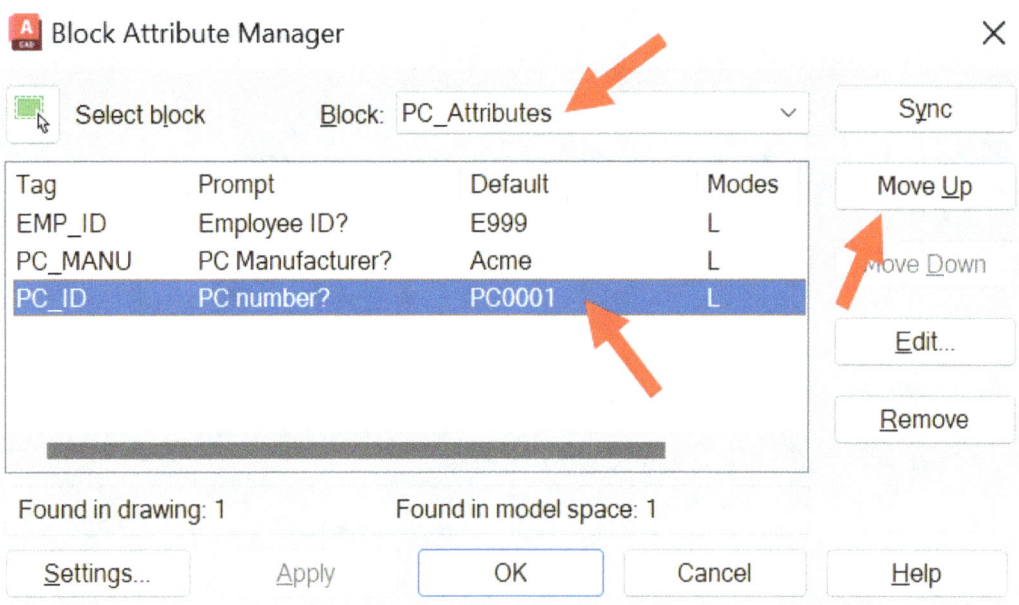

Figure 10.22: Block Attribute Manager with the block attributes displayed

5. You can perform many block attribute editing tasks in the **Block Attribute Manager** dialog box, and you are going to learn how to edit the order of the attributes in the **Edit Attributes** dialog box next time it appears when inserting a block with attributes into your drawing.

Note the order of the attributes in *Figure 10.22*. They are as follows: **EMP_ID**, **PC_MANU**, and **PC_ID**. This is how they display in the **Edit Attributes** dialog box. However, they display as **PC_ID**, **PC_MANU**, and **EMP_ID** in the drawing after the block is placed. You are going to re-arrange them using **Block Attribute Manager**.

6. Select **PC_ID** in the attribute list. Use the **Move Up** button in the dialog box and move it to the top of the attribute list. Using **Move Up** and **Move Down** as you select an attribute, change the list order to as it is displayed in *Figure 10.23*.

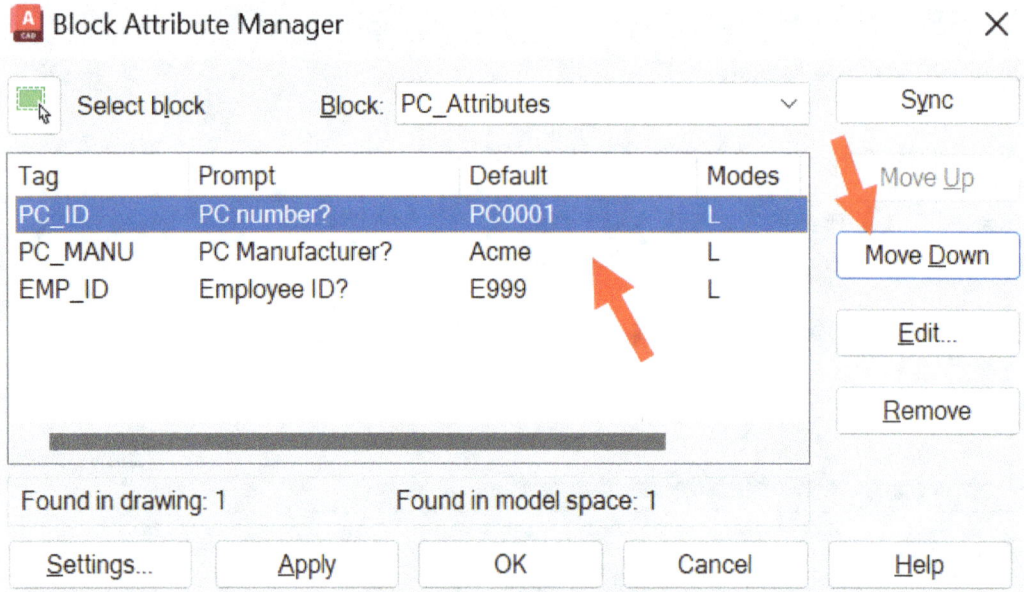

Figure 10.23: The reordered attribute list

7. Click on **Apply** and then on **OK**, making sure that the changes are applied. **Block Attribute Manager** will now close.

8. Using the skills learned in the previous section, insert another instance of the `PC_Attributes` block in the drawing. You can place it anywhere, as it is the attributes you need to look at. Repositioning can be sorted after the block is inserted using object snaps.

9. The **Edit Attributes** dialog box appears after clicking to position the block, as shown in *Figure 10.24*.

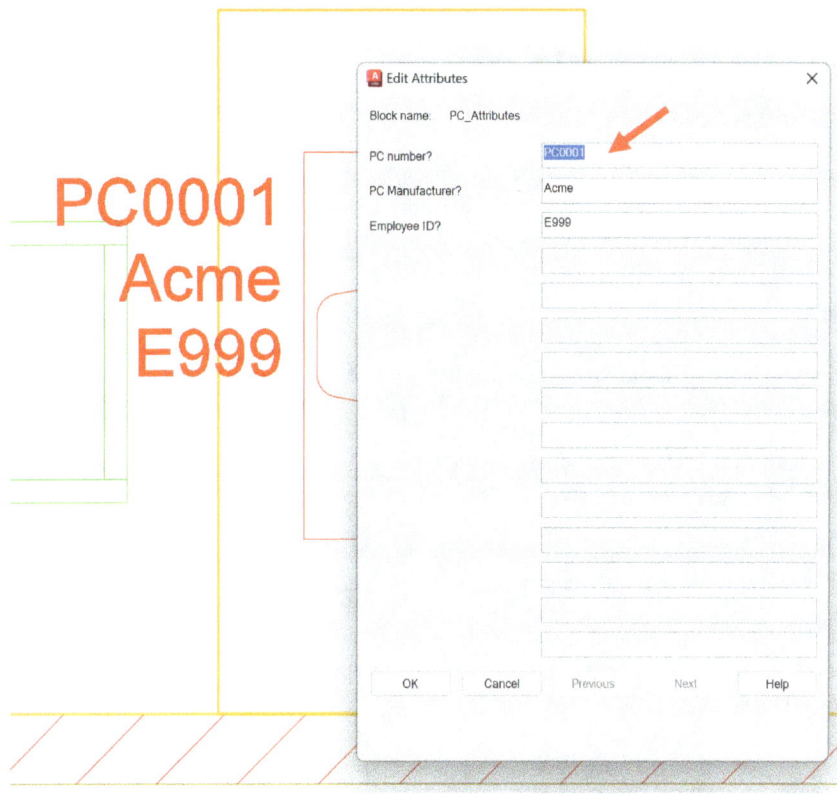

Figure 10.24: The Edit Attributes dialog box

10. The attribute order has changed in the **Edit Attributes** dialog box to match the display order of the attributes in the drawing, as per the changes made using **Block Attribute Manager** (BATTMAN). This a great visual timesaver as you can now check and edit your attributes in the same order as they are displayed in the drawing, thus cutting down on errors.

> **AutoCAD for Mac**
> The **Block Attribute Manager** (*BATTMAN*) palette works in the same way in AutoCAD for Mac.

You can now create and manage your own blocks with attributes, developing them from scratch, and saving them in your DWG files. You can also edit and manage your block attributes using **Enhanced Attribute Editor** and the **Block Attribute Manager** (*BATTMAN*).

As you build your AutoCAD knowledge, you can experiment with both tools to develop extensive block libraries, managing your libraries effectively using the skills learned in *Chapter 9* by creating block libraries for your blocks with attributes.

You can learn more about AutoCAD block attributes on the Autodesk website:

`https://help.autodesk.com/view/ACD/2023/ENU/?guid=GUID-67A2DDAD-2217-412F-8AEF-D4495192F45B`

You now know how to work with, edit, and manage your attributes in your AutoCAD blocks, and using the knowledge gained in *Chapter 9*, these attributed blocks can then be added to a block library drawing that is referenced in the **Blocks** palette, or you could develop your own tool palettes.

Summary

In this chapter, you learned about creating and editing attributes in an AutoCAD block and inserting the block into a DWG file.

You also learned how to edit individual attribute properties using **Enhanced Attribute Editor**. Also, using **Block Attribute Manager** (*BATTMAN*), you learned how to work with and manage block attributes.

Effective block attribute management is incredibly important when using blocks with attributes in your drawings. The information must be accurate and correct and displayed effectively in your drawings.

As you work with AutoCAD drawings on larger projects, the skills you learned in this chapter will give you a good grounding and understanding of how to start implementing blocks with attributes in your AutoCAD designs.

The tools used in this chapter demonstrate how important attributes can be to relay block information to the CAD team and project stakeholders using your drawings, saving valuable time. In the next chapter, we will look at dynamic blocks in more depth, so that you can learn how to create and manage dynamic blocks, adding parameters and actions.

Get This Book's PDF Version and Exclusive Extras

Scan the QR code (or go to `packtpub.com/unlock`). Search for this book by name, confirm the edition, and then follow the steps on the page.

Note: Keep your invoice handy. Purchases made directly from Packt don't require one.

UNLOCK NOW

11
Creating a Dynamic Block with Parameters and Actions

In the previous chapter, you learned how to create attributes in AutoCAD blocks. In this chapter, you will look at how those block attributes can be applied to the dynamic block you will create. However, you will concentrate on creating a dynamic block with parameters and actions.

As you know, blocks are objects made up of multiple AutoCAD objects for content reuse, such as a chair or a desk, to avoid having to rework that chair or desk repetitively in a drawing. Making a dynamic block of the chair or desk gives you even more versatility in the block itself, providing the ability to manipulate the block quickly and easily.

Dynamic blocks need both a parameter and an associated action, so if you were working with a block representing a door, you may need to add a parameter and action to control the swing direction of the door in the door opening in the drawing. Many parameters and actions are available in AutoCAD for dynamic blocks, and this chapter covers some of the methodologies you will need to start working with them in your drawings.

In this chapter, you will learn how adding dynamic parameters and actions to your blocks will make them more versatile and allow for much easier manipulation of the blocks in your AutoCAD drawings.

This chapter covers the following topics:

- Creating the regular door block
- Adding a vertical flip to the door
- Adding a horizontal flip to the door
- Testing the new dynamic block in the drawing

Exercise file

You will need to use the exercise file, `New Office_Dynamic Blocks.dwg`, for this chapter.

Creating the regular door block

In this section, we will be using AutoCAD objects to create a regular door block that can then be made dynamic. Open the exercise file in the **Model** tab and zoom into the door opening. Once zoomed into the door opening, you will see the objects that will be used to make the regular door block. There are two objects: a rectangular polyline and an arc. Both are on layer **0** (*zero*). When creating the regular door block, make sure to include both objects so that the block will be displayed in full visually when in use. You can see, in *Figure 11.1*, that both objects are selected, and the blue grips are displayed.

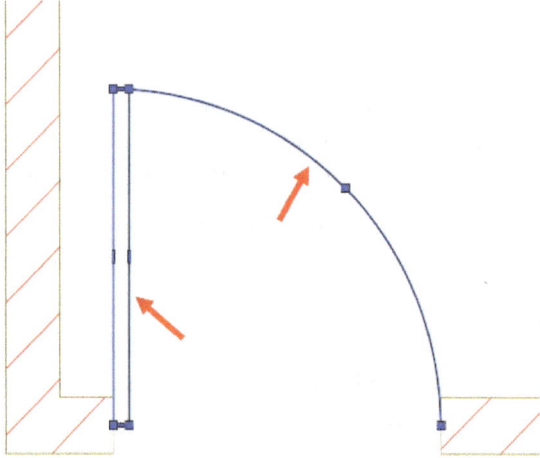

Figure 11.1: The objects to be used to make the regular door block

To create the door block, follow these steps:

1. Select the **Insert** tab on the ribbon with both objects selected. Then, click on **Create Block** (*BLOCK*) on the **Block Definition** panel, as shown in *Figure 11.2*.

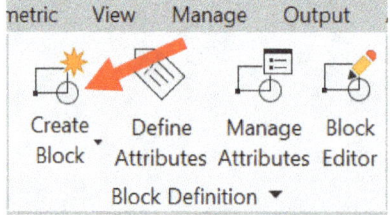

Figure 11.2: The Create Block (BLOCK) command on the Block Definition panel

2. The **Block Definition** dialog box will appear. In the **Name** field, type in the block name, Door-DYN (*DYN* is short for dynamic).
3. Click on the **Pick point** icon in *Figure 11.3*.

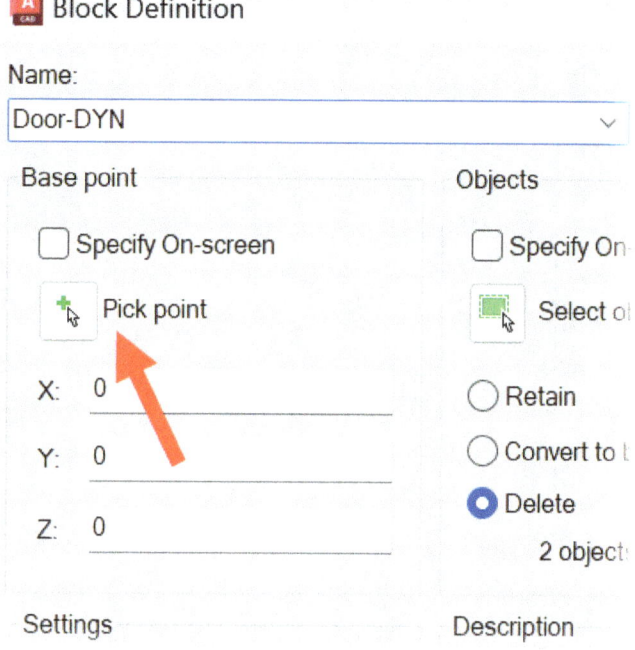

Figure 11.3: The Pick point icon in the Block Definition dialog box

4. You will be taken into the drawing to select an insertion point for your block. Select the **Endpoint** object snap, as shown in *Figure 11.4*.

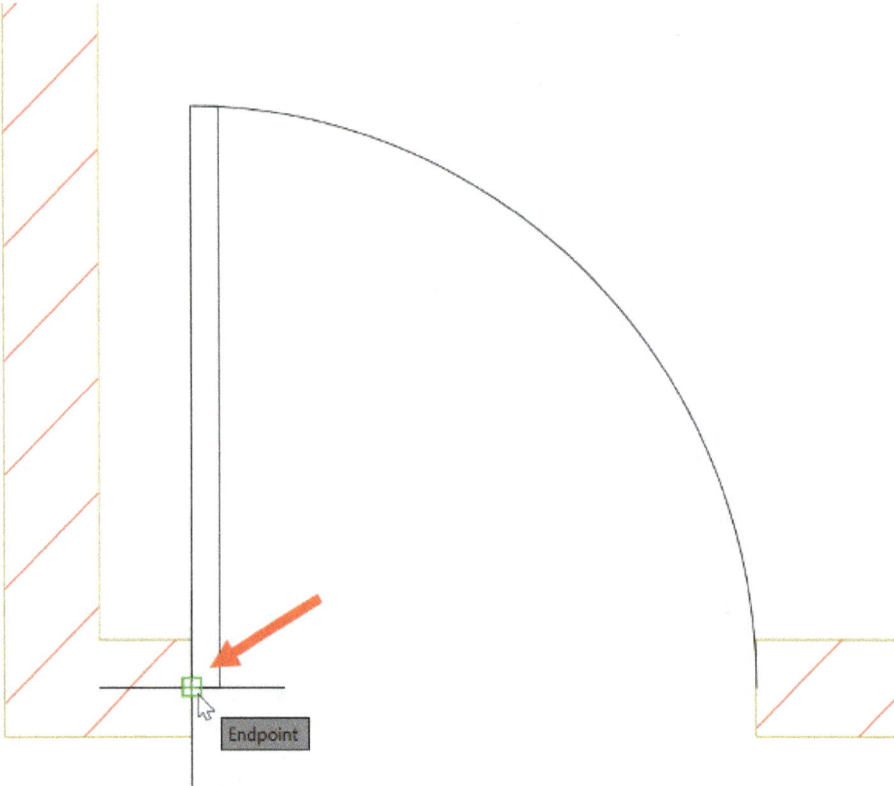

Figure 11.4: The Endpoint object snap to be used as the insertion point

5. Clicking on the **Endpoint** object snap will return you to the **Block Definition** dialog box. Note the exact precision of the **X** and **Y** coordinates in the dialog box due to using an object snap. You now need to set all the settings required to create your dynamic door block.

6. Refer to *Figure 11.5* and set all the necessary settings shown.

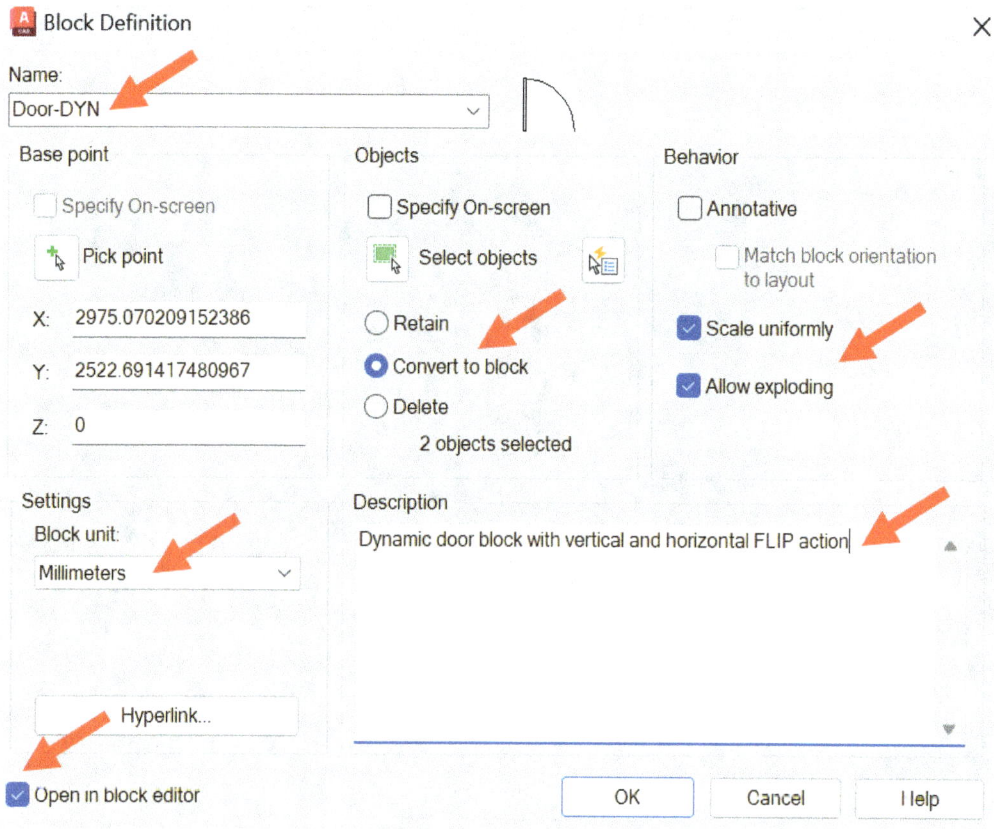

Block Definition

Name: Door-DYN

Base point
- ☐ Specify On-screen
- Pick point
- X: 2975.070209152386
- Y: 2522.691417480967
- Z: 0

Objects
- ☐ Specify On-screen
- Select objects
- ○ Retain
- ● Convert to block
- ○ Delete
- 2 objects selected

Behavior
- ☐ Annotative
- ☐ Match block orientation to layout
- ☑ Scale uniformly
- ☑ Allow exploding

Settings
Block unit: Millimeters

Description
Dynamic door block with vertical and horizontal FLIP action

Hyperlink...

☑ Open in block editor

[OK] [Cancel] [Help]

Figure 11.5: The Block Definition dialog box with all required settings

7. Once you have all the necessary settings in the dialog box, click **OK**.

8. With the **Open in block editor** box checked, AutoCAD will open **Block Editor**, as shown in *Figure 11.6*.

Creating a Dynamic Block with Parameters and Actions

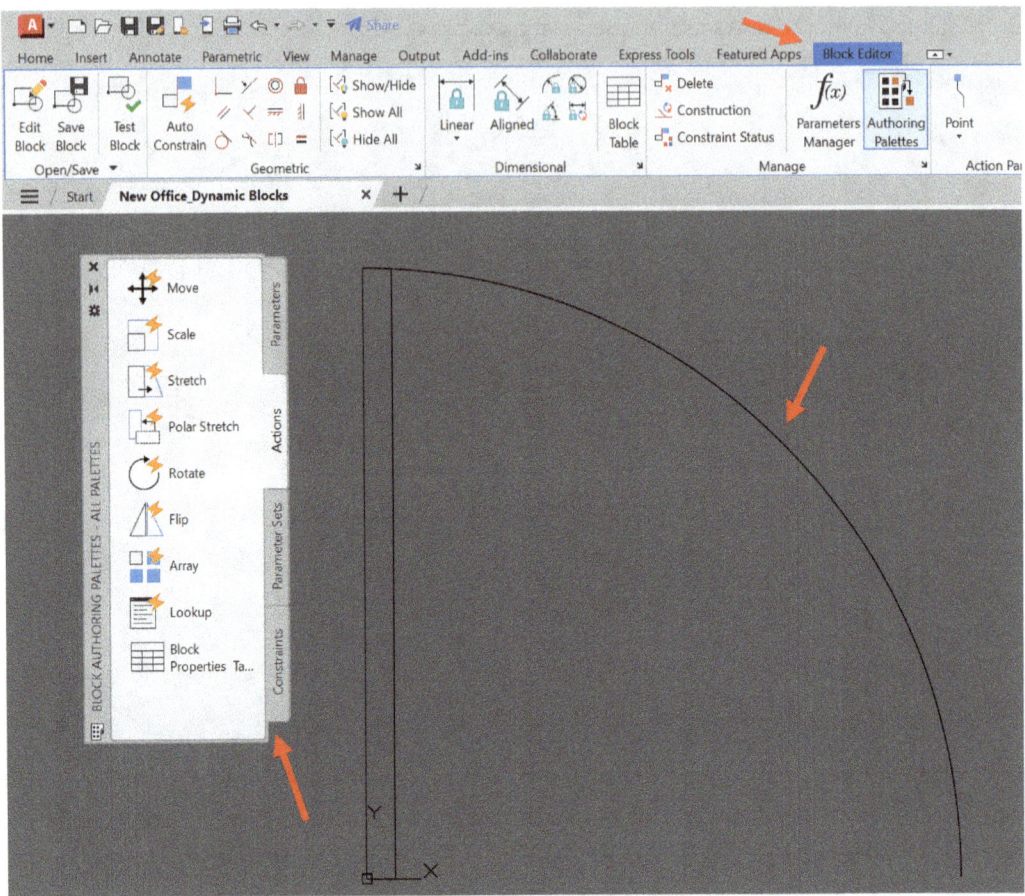

Figure 11.6: Block Editor open, ready to create the dynamic block

Your door block is now created and ready to start adding your dynamic parameters and actions. The next two sections will explain how to add parameters and actions to your dynamic door block while working in Block Editor in AutoCAD.

> **Tips and tricks #31**
>
> When selecting the objects to create an AutoCAD block, it is often more beneficial to select the objects that form the block *before* clicking on the **Create Block** (*BLOCK*) command. To make sure you can do this, you need **Noun/verb selection** checked in the **Selection** tab in the **Options** dialog box, as shown in *Figure 11.7*. You can open the **Options** dialog box from the **Application** menu, right-click the shortcut menu, or type OPTIONS and press *Enter*.

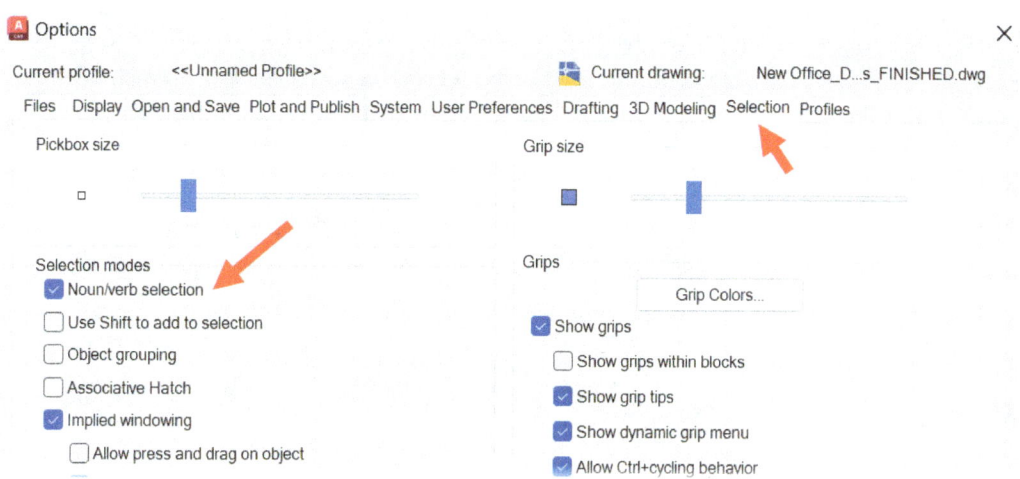

Figure 11.7: The Selection tab in the Options dialog box

Noun/verb selection should be on by default in your AutoCAD **Options** dialog box. It is always worth checking that this function is on before working with regular and dynamic blocks.

> **AutoCAD for Mac**
>
> AutoCAD for Mac uses a very similar method for creating blocks. The **Create Block** (*BLOCK*) command is in the left-hand menu.

Adding a vertical flip to the door

In *step 8* of the previous section of this chapter, you checked **Open in block editor** in the **Block Definition** dialog box, before clicking on **OK**. This opened **Block Editor** in AutoCAD, as shown in *Figure 11.6*.

In this section, you will learn how to add a vertical **Flip** parameter and apply the **Flip** action to it, enabling you to flip the dynamic block's vertical door swing in the drawing.

The main palette in the **Block Editor** is **Block Authoring Palettes** shown in *Figure 11.8* in **Block Editor**. It contains all the tools needed to create the vertical **Flip** parameter that we are going to add to our dynamic door block.

Note that a **Basepoint** parameter is required before placing any **Flip** parameters and actions. **Basepoint** does not have an associated action but, true to its name, it provides a *base point* with which to insert the dynamic block into the drawing. Staying in **Block Authoring Palettes**, follow these steps:

1. Select the **Parameters** tab and then select the **Basepoint** parameter, as arrowed in *Figure 11.8*.

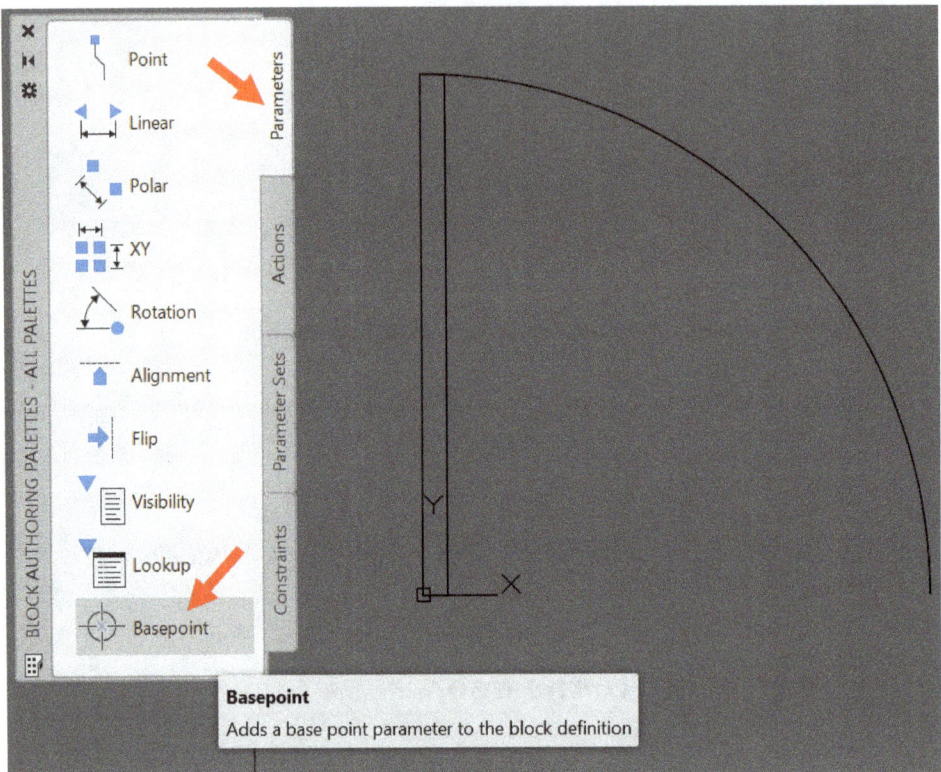

Figure 11.8: The Parameters tab with Basepoint arrowed

2. Select the lower-left **Endpoint** object snap on the door at the prompt. This will then display the **Basepoint** symbol on the door block, as shown in *Figure 11.9*.

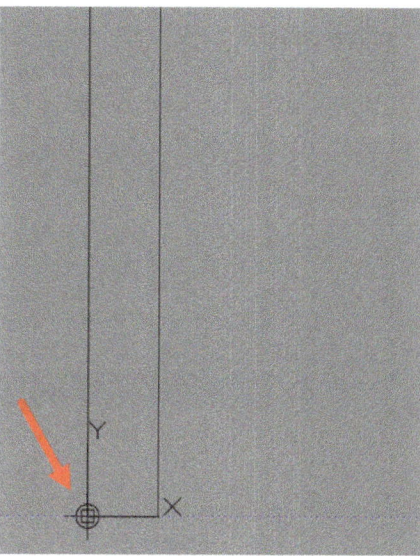

Figure 11.9: The Basepoint parameter displayed on the lower-left endpoint

3. Return to the **Parameters** tab and then select the **Flip** parameter, as arrowed in *Figure 11.10*.

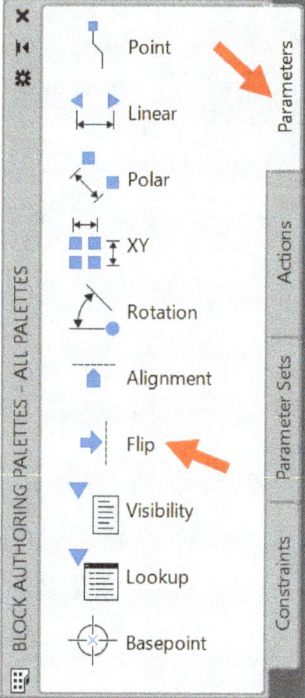

Figure 11.10: The Parameters tab on Block Authoring Palettes

274   Creating a Dynamic Block with Parameters and Actions

4. You will be prompted for the base point of the reflection line, and this is where you will need to use your object snaps. Right-click to bring up the shortcut menu. Select **Osnap Overrides**. It will display the **Osnap Overrides** menu, as shown in *Figure 11.11*.

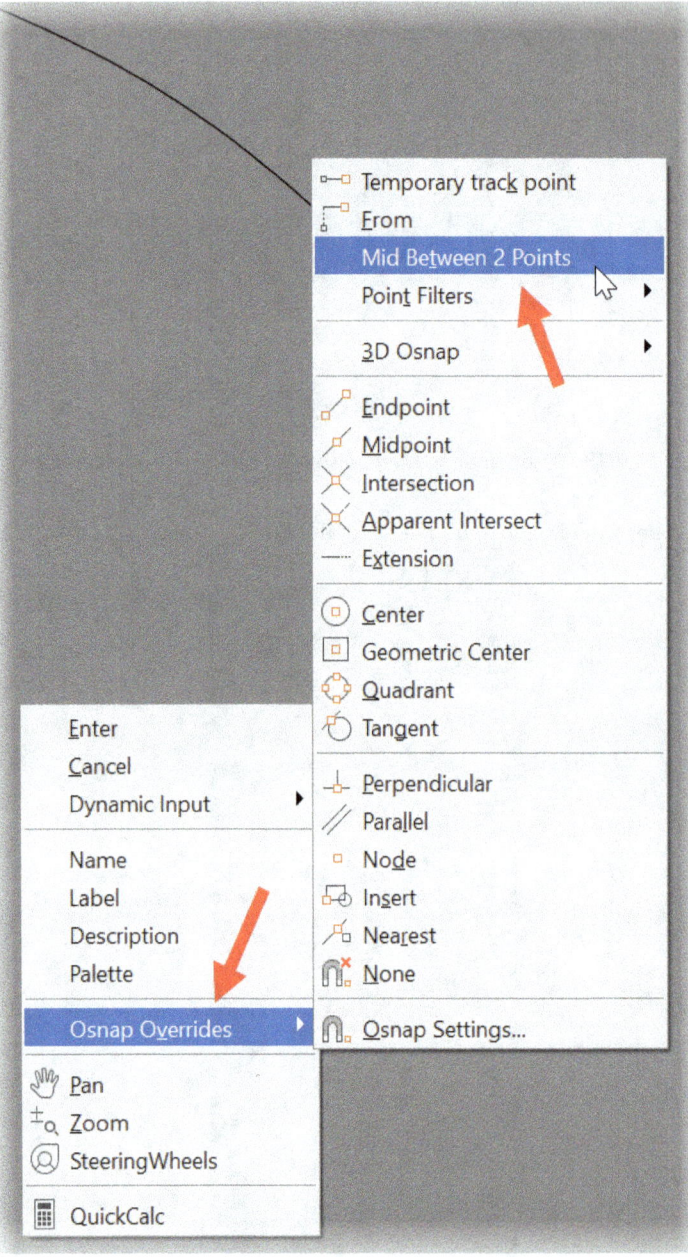

Figure 11.11: The Osnap Overrides shortcut menu

5. Select **Mid Between 2 Points** (*M2P*). You will be prompted for **First point of mid**. Select the lower-left **Endpoint** snap on the rectangle, as shown in *Figure 11.12*.

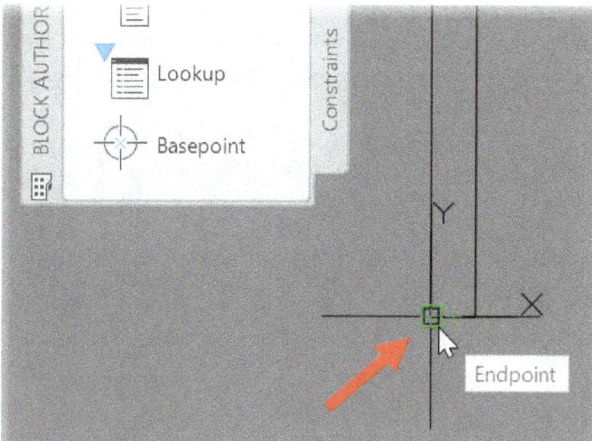

Figure 11.12: The Endpoint snap used as the first point of the mid between two points

6. You will then be prompted for the second point. Use the **Endpoint** snap at the end of the arc, as shown in *Figure 11.13*.

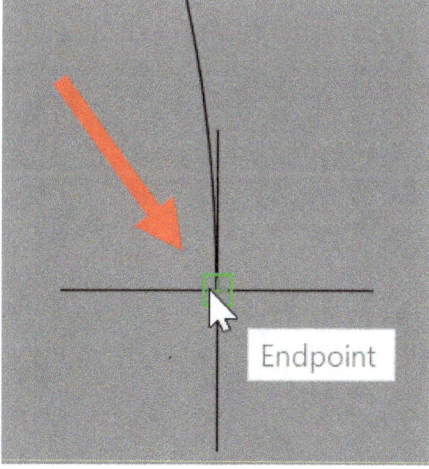

Figure 11.13: The Endpoint snap at the end of the arc

7. You will now see that you are working from a point selected that is exactly a midpoint between the previously selected points, hence the name **Mid Between 2 Points**. Move the cursor upward, ensuring that **Polar Tracking** (*POLAR*) is active on the status bar. Move the vertical reflection line up the polar tracking line through and over the arc, as shown in *Figure 11.14*.

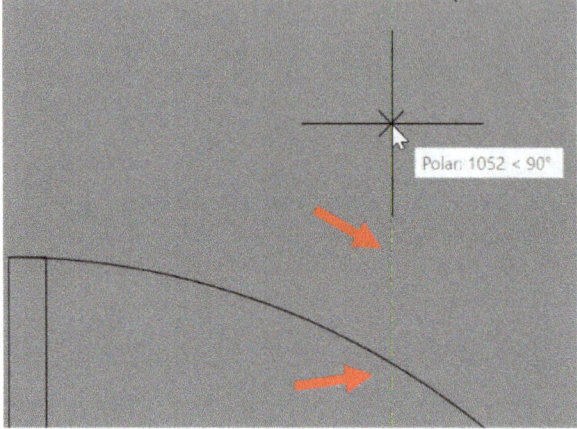

Figure 11.14: The vertical reflection line going through the arc, using Polar tracking

8. Click to position the vertical reflection line. You will be prompted to specify the parameter label location, as shown in *Figure 11.15*. Click to position the label near the reflection line.

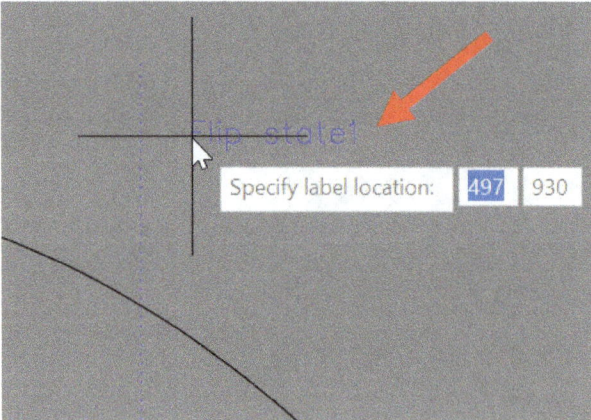

Figure 11.15: Positioning the vertical reflection line label

9. Your vertical **Flip** parameter is now placed. Select the parameter, right-click, and select **Properties** on the shortcut menu. In the **Properties** palette, rename the **Flip name** property label to Flip_VERT, as shown in *Figure 11.16*.

10. Press *Enter* to confirm the name change and close the **Properties** palette by clicking on the **X** symbol on the palette title bar. Press *Esc* a couple of times to deselect the parameter.

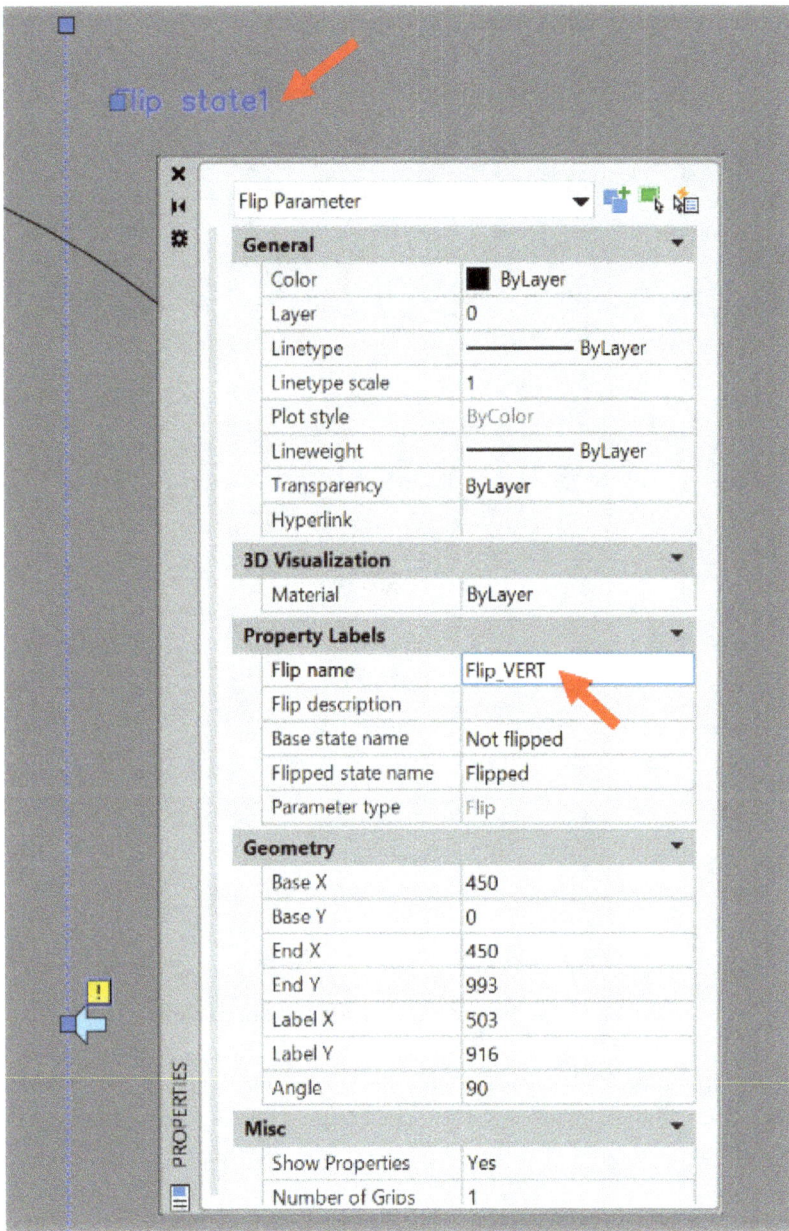

Figure 11.16: The property label name on the Properties palette

The **Flip** action now needs to be applied to the parameter, as indicated by the small yellow exclamation mark shown on the parameter.

11. Select the **Actions** tab on **Block Authoring Palette**, as shown in *Figure 11.17*. The **Flip** action is also shown.

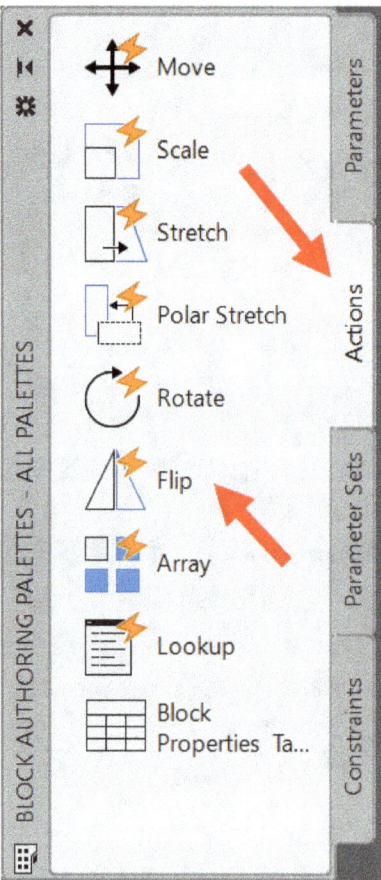

Figure 11.17: The Actions tab on Block Authoring Palette

12. Click on the **Flip** action, and you will be prompted to select a parameter. Select the **Flip_VERT** parameter. You will then be prompted to select objects. Make sure to select *all* objects that make up the door block and the **Flip_VERT** parameter. Press *Enter* to confirm the selection.

13. The small yellow exclamation mark disappears, and a **Flip** action symbol appears next to the blue arrow representing the **Flip** parameter (known as the **flip grip**), as shown in *Figure 11.18*.

Figure 11.18: The Flip action fully applied to the Flip parameter

You have now fully applied a vertical **Flip** parameter and a **Flip** action in **Block Editor**.

> **AutoCAD for Mac**
>
> AutoCAD users on the Mac will be able to apply the previous section workflow using the macOS interface. Adding parameters and actions in **Block Editor** follows a virtually identical workflow in AutoCAD for Mac.

In the next section, you will learn how to apply a horizontal **Flip** parameter and a **Flip** action to the dynamic door block, allowing for both vertical and horizontal flipping of the door swing. Remain in **Block Editor** for the upcoming section.

Adding a horizontal flip to the door

Staying in **Block Editor**, carry out the following workflow in order to place the horizontal **Flip** parameter and action:

1. Click on the **Parameters** tab in **Block Authoring Palette**.
2. Select the **Flip** parameter, as you did in the previous section. You will be prompted for the base point of the reflection line. Using object snaps, click on the lower-left **Endpoint** of the door rectangle, as shown in *Figure 11.19*. This is the same point you selected for the **Basepoint** parameter.

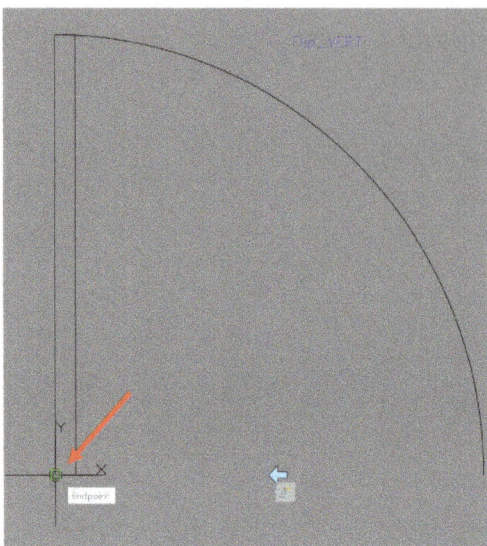

Figure 11.19: The Endpoint object snap on the door rectangle

3. At the prompt for the second point of the reflection line, click on the lower-right **Endpoint** object snap of the arc, as shown in *Figure 11.20*.

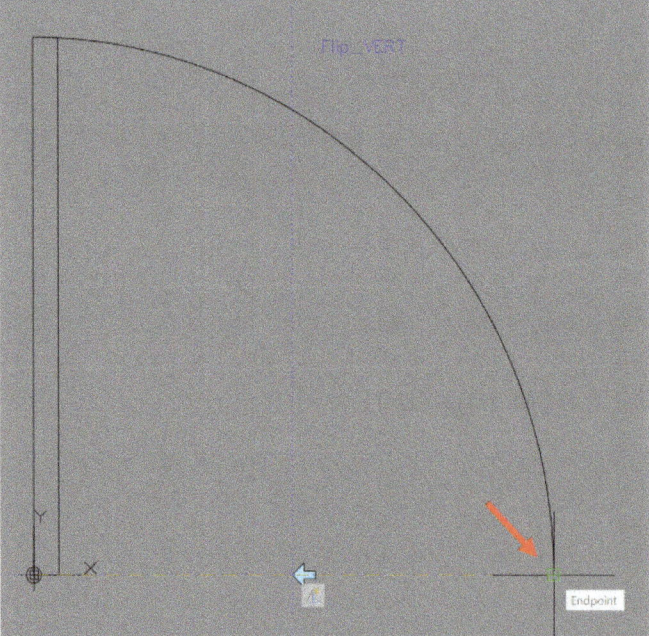

Figure 11.20: The second point of the horizontal reflection line

4. Click on a point to the right of the door arc. You will be prompted to place the default parameter label, as shown in *Figure 11.21*.

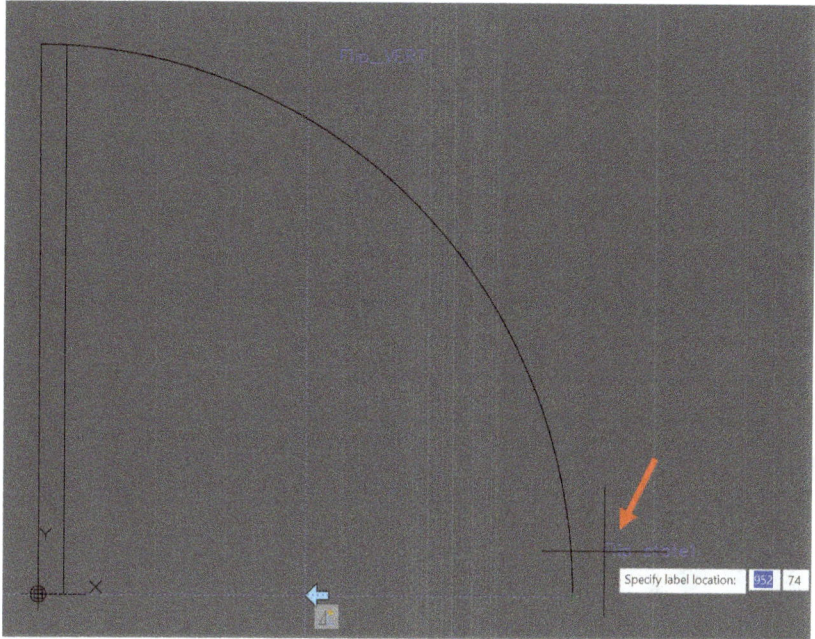

Figure 11.21: Positioning the parameter label

5. Click to position the parameter label. The *flip grip* appears to the left on the first point of the reflection line. It can be moved toward the middle of the door swing by clicking on it and positioning it using the blue grip that appears, just like any other AutoCAD grip. This is shown in *Figure 11.22*.

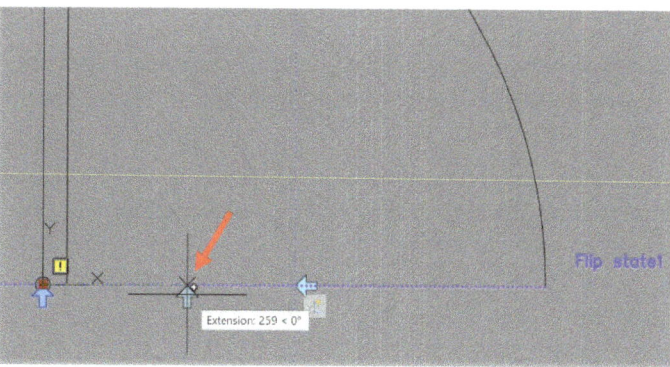

Figure 11.22: Repositioning the flip grip using grips

Creating a Dynamic Block with Parameters and Actions

6. Once the *flip grip* has been repositioned, press *Esc* a couple of times to deselect the grip.
7. Click on the parameter label and right-click. Select **Properties** on the shortcut menu to bring up the **Properties** palette. Rename the parameter label in the **Properties** palette to `Flip_HORIZ`, as shown in *Figure 11.23*.

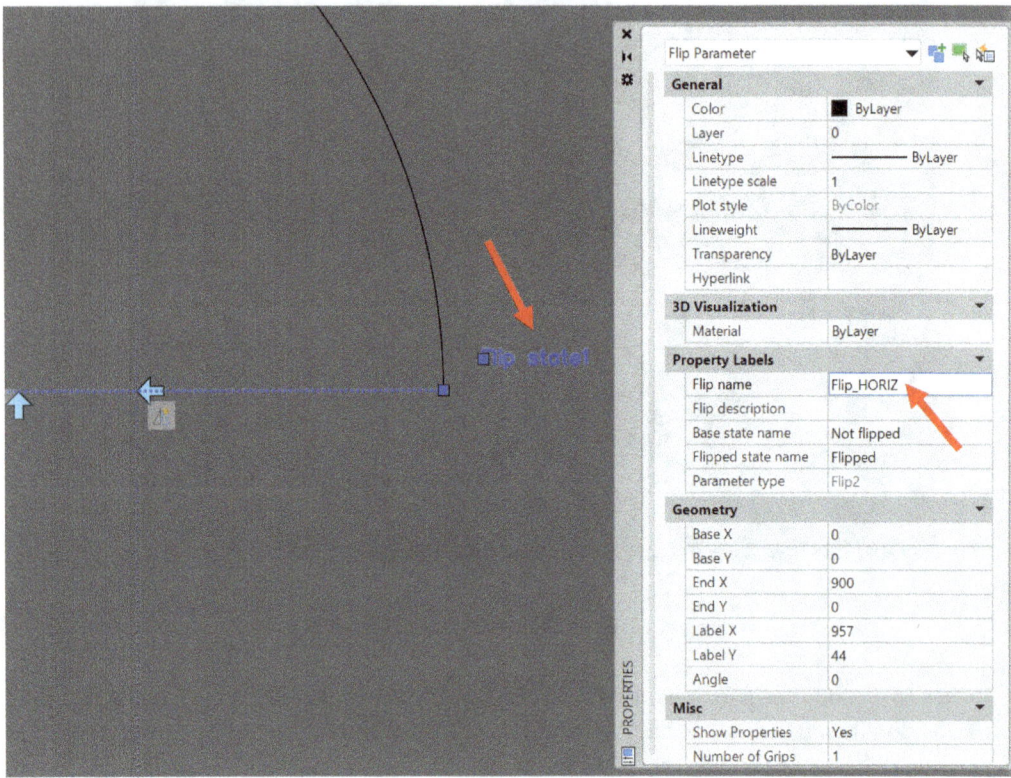

Figure 11.23: Renaming the parameter label in the Properties palette

8. Press *Enter* to confirm the new parameter name in the **Properties** palette, then close the palette. The new parameter name will be displayed in **Block Editor**. Press *Esc* a couple of times to deselect the parameter.
9. The yellow exclamation mark on the parameter indicates that an action needs to be applied. Select the **Actions** tab on **Block Authoring Palette**. Select the **Flip** action.

10. At the prompt, select the new **Flip_HORIZ** parameter. You will then see the **Select objects** prompt, as shown in *Figure 11.24*.

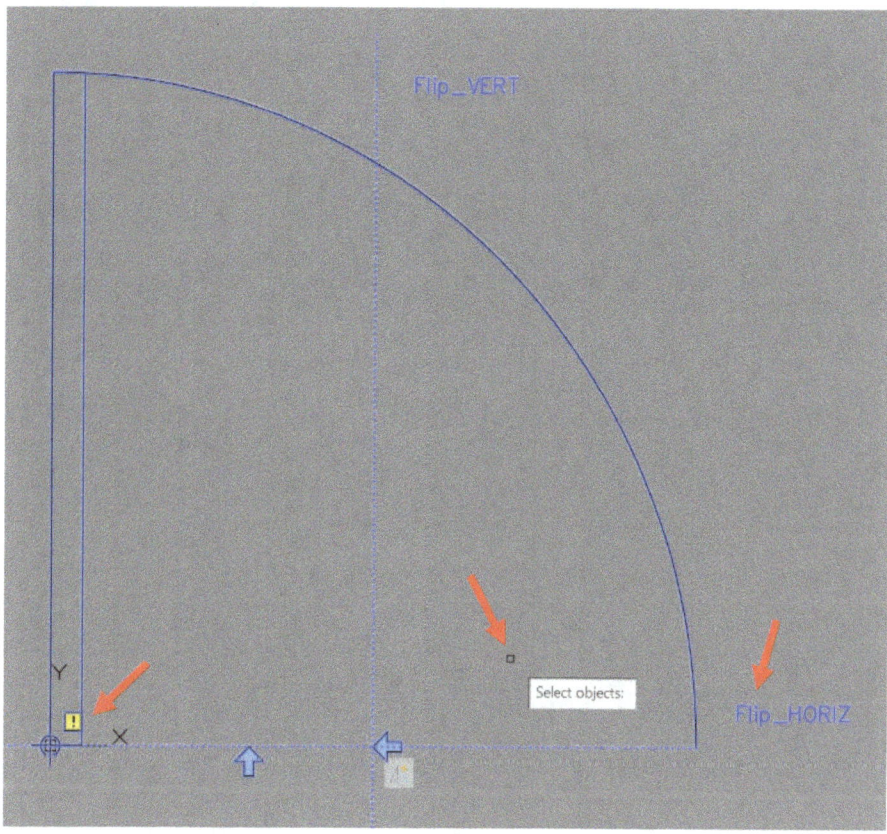

Figure 11.24: The Select objects prompt for the horizontal Flip action

11. Select *all* objects in **Block Editor**, including the **Basepoint** parameter (they are all shown selected in *Figure 11.24*) and the vertical **Flip** parameter and action. Press *Enter* to confirm selection, and your dynamic door block should now look as it does in *Figure 11.25*.

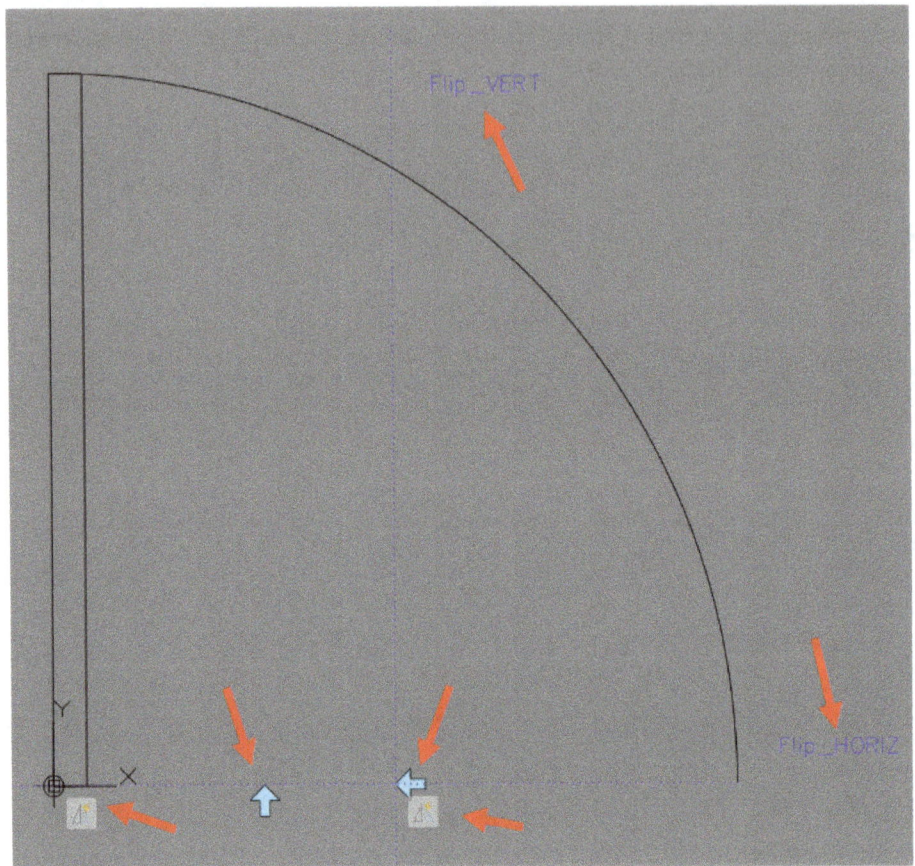

Figure 11.25: The door block with finished parameters and actions in Block Editor

To make sure that all parameters have an associated action, there will be no yellow exclamation marks. Also, note the renamed **Flip** parameters, **Flip_VERT** and **Flip_HORIZ**.

12. You can now test your new dynamic block using the **Test Block** function. Click on **Test Block** in the **Open/Save** panel in **Block Editor**, as shown in *Figure 11.26*.

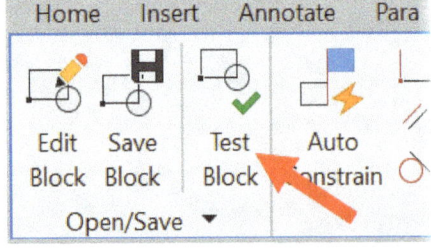

Figure 11.26: The Test Block function in the Open/Save panel

13. You are taken to the testing area after clicking **Test Block**. Click on the door block to select it. You will see the two *flip grips* and the lower-left grip. The lower-left grip was created using the **Basepoint** parameter. *Figure 11.27* shows the dynamic door block selected in the test area.

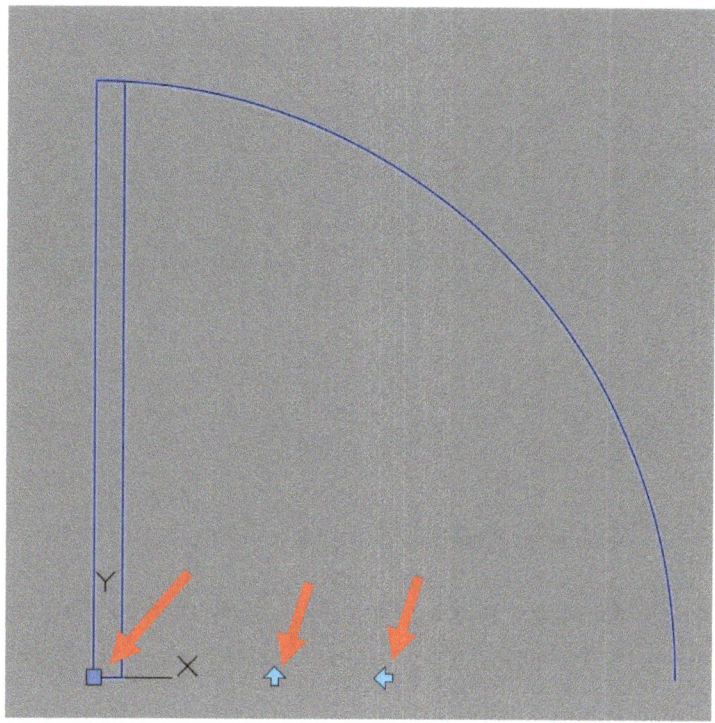

Figure 11.27: The dynamic door block shown selected in the test area

14. Click on the *flip grips*, testing that they both flip the door swing vertically and horizontally. Once testing is complete, click on **Close Test Block** on the ribbon (indicated by a green check mark).

15. You are returned to **Block Editor**. Click on **Close Block Editor** on the ribbon (also indicated by a green tick).

16. At the prompt, select to save the changes to the **Door-DYN** dynamic block. You are returned to the AutoCAD drawing.

17. The door block in the drawing is now your dynamic door block, **Door-DYN**. Select it and use the **Layer** dropdown on the **Home** tab on the ribbon to ensure it is on the **Doors** layer. Also, make **Doors** the current layer to ensure that any further blocks inserted will go on the appropriate layer. The **Door-DYN** block should look as it does in *Figure 11.28*.

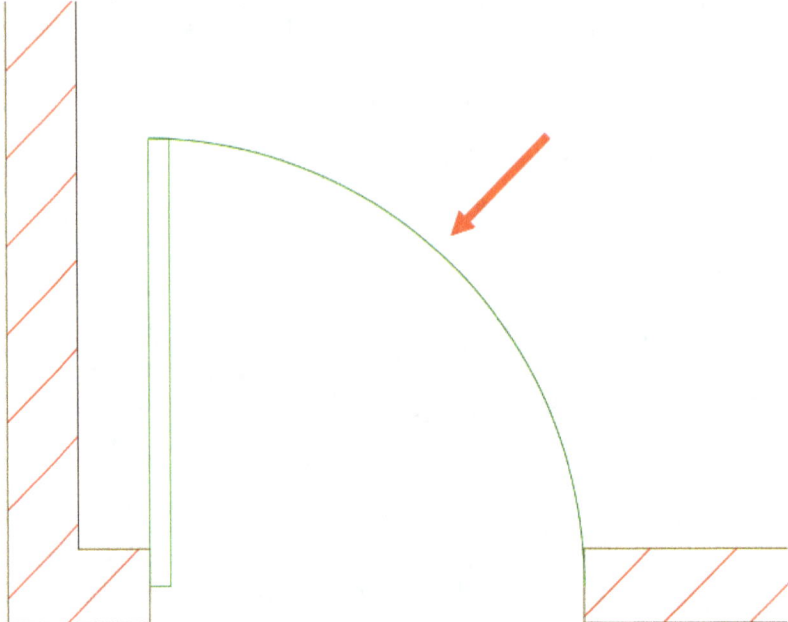

Figure 11.28: The Door-DYN block in the drawing

18. Press *Esc* a couple of times to ensure the **Door-DYN** dynamic block is deselected.
19. Make sure to save the drawing to ensure the block definition is saved in the DWG file.

You have now successfully created a dynamic door block with a vertical and horizontal **Flip** action to alter the direction of the door swing in both directions.

Testing the new dynamic block in the drawing

In the previous section, you learned how to convert a regular door block into a dynamic one using **Block Editor**. In this section, you will fully test the block by inserting it into the drawing on the current layer, using the **Flip** actions added to the dynamic block.

The following workflow will allow you to fully test the dynamic door block:

1. On the **Home** tab on the ribbon, check that the **Doors** layer is current on the **Layers** panel. Make sure you are zoomed to the area where the door block is in the drawing.
2. Select the door block and right-click. On the shortcut menu, click on **Erase** to remove the block instance. You should now only have the door opening remaining, as shown in *Figure 11.29*.

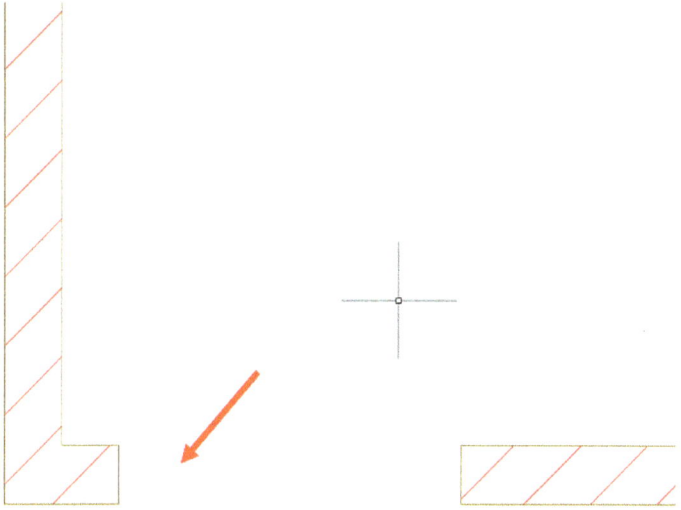

Figure 11.29: The door opening after the block is erased

3. Click on the **Insert** tab on the ribbon, then click on the **Insert** dropdown at the left-hand end. You can see the **Door-DYN** block shown in the dropdown in *Figure 11.30*.

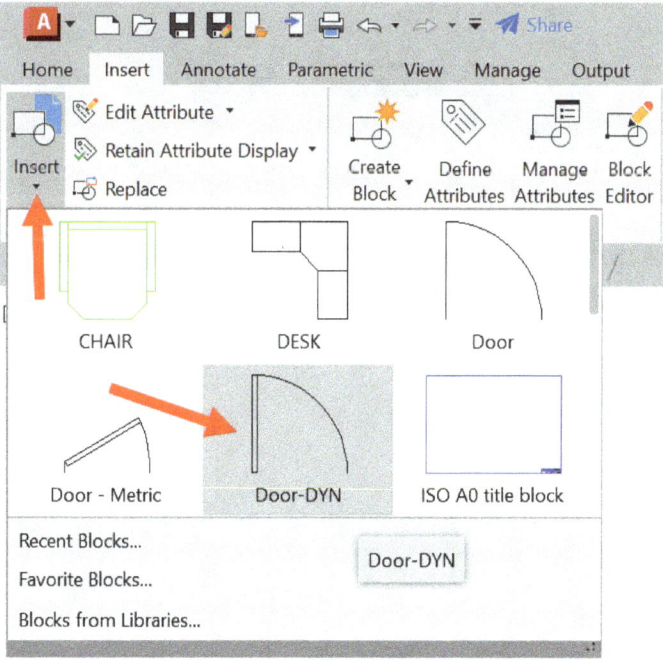

Figure 11.30: The Door-DYN dynamic block on the Insert dropdown

4. Select the **Door-DYN** block on the dropdown to insert it into the drawing. You will see the block on the cursor using the **Basepoint** parameter you set on the lower-left corner of the block. This is shown in *Figure 11.31*.

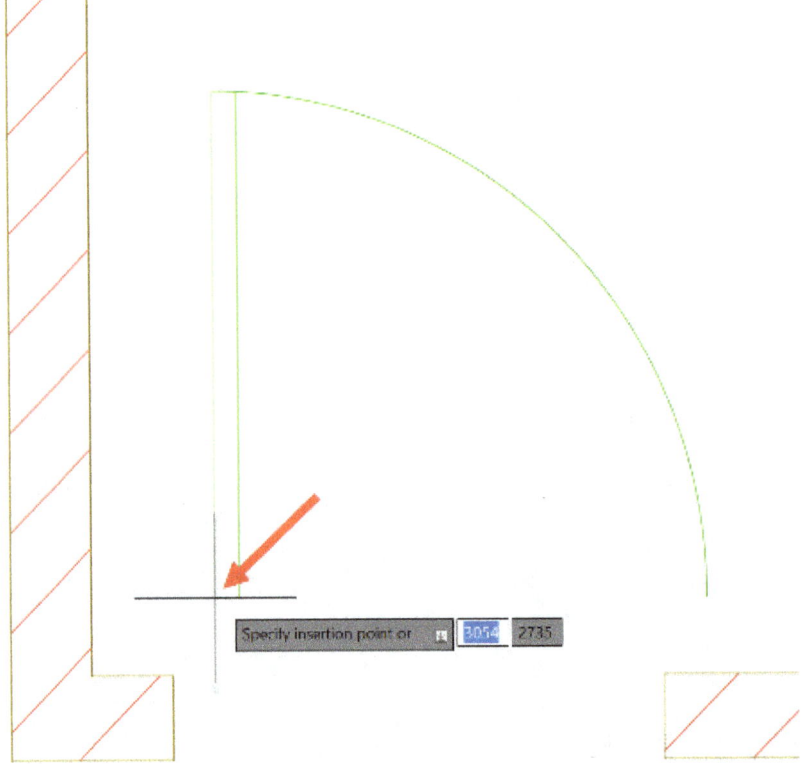

Figure 11.31: The Door-DYN block with the Basepoint parameter arrowed

5. Position the block on the **Midpoint** object snap on the left-hand side of the door opening, as shown in *Figure 11.32*. Click on **Midpoint** to confirm the block position.

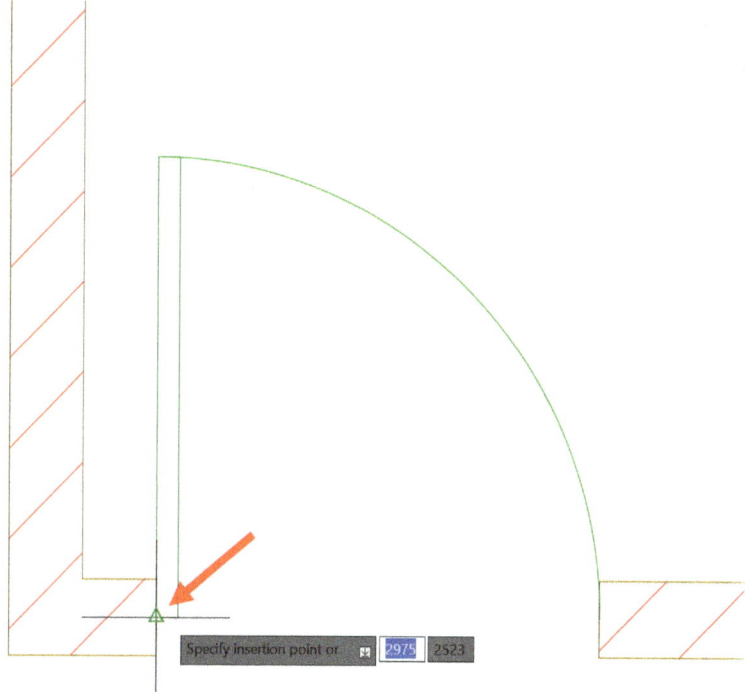

Figure 11.32: Using the Midpoint object snap to position the block

6. Now that the block is positioned, you can test the **Flip** actions in the dynamic door block. Click on the block to select it, and you will see the *flip grips* displayed, as shown in *Figure 11.33*.

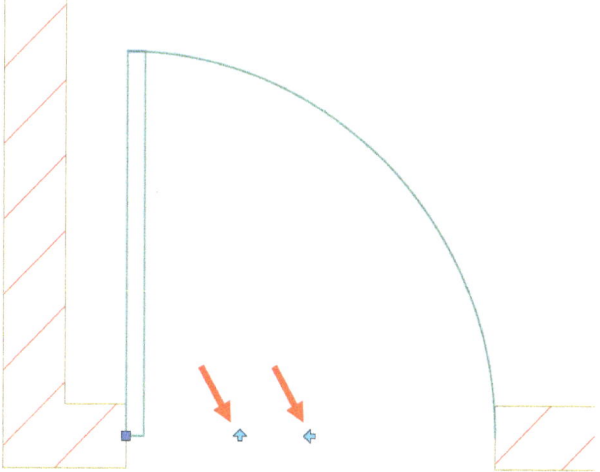

Figure 11.33: The positioned dynamic block with the flip grips displayed

7. Click on each *flip grip* once (once on the vertical, once on the horizontal), and the dynamic door block will adjust accordingly, as shown in *Figure 11.34*.

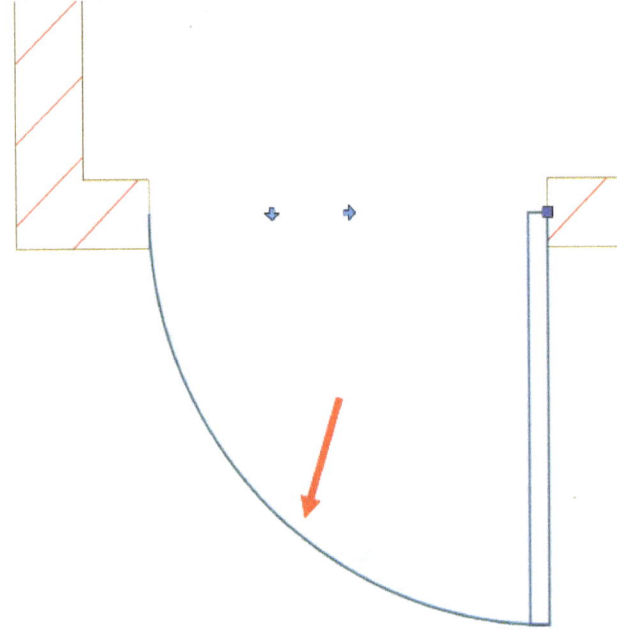

Figure 11.34: The Door-DYN dynamic block flipped using the flip grips

8. Repeat the process, clicking once on each *flip grip* and the **Door-DYN** block will return to its original position.

You have now ensured that the block is not only on the correct layer but also that the dynamic functionality within the block is all working as it should.

Congratulations! You have now created a dynamic block for use in your AutoCAD drawing.

> **AutoCAD for Mac**
>
> Dynamic blocks are created in the same way in AutoCAD for Mac. While the Mac interface is slightly different, the workflow is the same.

In this chapter, you have only scratched the surface of what you can do with dynamic blocks and the functionality they provide. Apart from **Flip**, there are multiple other actions available. You can bring in **Linear** parameters, **Rotation** parameters, **Visibility** (visibility states) and many more. In fact, you could write a whole book on them!

As you build your AutoCAD knowledge using this book, you might want to set aside some time to experiment with dynamic blocks and what they can do for you in your AutoCAD drawings. They can be used with block attributes to make blocks that save valuable drafting time.

You can learn more about dynamic blocks in AutoCAD here on the Autodesk website: `https://help.autodesk.com/view/ACD/2024/ENU/?guid=GUID-2A3D92B8-20E2-47B3-92CE-FB3EB03888C3`.

Summary

You now know how to work with, edit, and manage your dynamic blocks, and using the knowledge gained in previous chapters, you can now consider developing block libraries that contain not just regular AutoCAD blocks but also dynamic blocks with block attributes.

In this chapter, you have gained knowledge of using AutoCAD objects to create a regular door block and making that door block into a dynamic block.

Using parameters and actions, you learned how to add dynamic functions to a regular door block, by adding vertical and horizontal door swing directions.

You then tested the dynamic door block in the drawing to ensure the functionality of the dynamic parameters.

Dynamic blocks are a great way to reduce time spent on onerous editing tasks. You can develop dynamic blocks that can be rotated, lengthened, and flipped by using dynamic actions in the block rather than selecting the block and performing just one action from the **Modify** panel on the ribbon.

As you work with AutoCAD drawings on larger projects, the skills learned in this chapter will give you a good understanding of how much time can be saved by developing dynamic blocks for use in your day-to-day AutoCAD workflows and processes.

The simple tools used in this chapter demonstrated how important dynamic blocks can be for the CAD team when used in your drawings.

In the next chapter, we will examine dynamic blocks in more depth so that you can learn how to create and manage *visibility states* in dynamic blocks, adding the associated parameters and actions.

Get This Book's PDF Version and Exclusive Extras

Scan the QR code (or go to `packtpub.com/unlock`). Search for this book by name, confirm the edition, and then follow the steps on the page.

Note: Keep your invoice handy. Purchases made directly from Packt don't require one.

12
Creating a Dynamic Block with Visibility States

In the previous chapter, you learned how to create a dynamic block with two **Flip** actions applied and associated parameters. This chapter teaches you how to create another dynamic block with visibility states. **Visibility states** allow you to create a block with numerous views in the same block. For example, different variations of the same block might exist, such as a left- and right-handed desk. This chapter shows you how to create a washbasin block with three different views: top, front, and side.

As you know from previous chapters, blocks are objects made up of multiple AutoCAD objects for content reuse, and dynamic blocks give you even more versatility in the block itself, providing the ability to manipulate the block quickly and easily. In this chapter, you will be providing different views of the washbasin in one dynamic block, thus negating the need to bring in other regular blocks that have different views of the washbasin.

This chapter covers the following methods that you will need to work with a dynamic block of the washbasin in an AutoCAD drawing:

- Creating the washbasin block drawing
- Adding the necessary blocks for each view
- Adding visibility states in a dynamic block
- Using the new dynamic block with visibility states

As in the previous chapter, adding more functionality to AutoCAD blocks and making them dynamic allows for easy reuse of drawing content. In this case, you will learn how visibility states provide the ability to show different views of the object represented by the block.

Exercise file

For this chapter, you will need to use the exercise file titled `Washbasin-DYNAMIC.dwg`.

Creating the washbasin block drawing

In this section, we will be using AutoCAD objects to create the various washbasin blocks for use in the dynamic block. To begin, open the file in the **Model** tab and zoom in to see the three views of the washbasin. You will see the objects that will be used to make the regular washbasin blocks. From left to right, they are front, top, and side. Each view comprises AutoCAD objects on layer **0** (*zero*), as displayed in *Figure 12.1*.

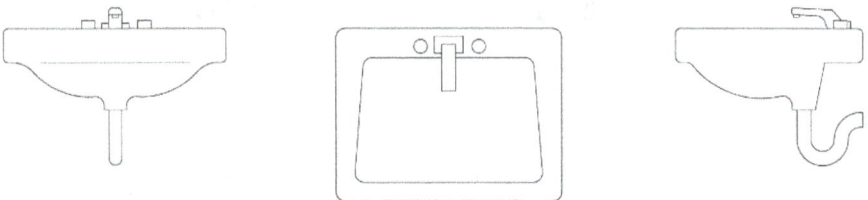

Figure 12.1: The objects to be used to make the washbasin blocks

Adding the front block

There are three visibility states in the dynamic block that need to be created. You will start with the front block first.

Follow these steps to create the front block:

1. Initially, you will create a regular block of the objects forming the front view on the left. With all the objects selected (as shown with all the grips displayed in *Figure 12.2*), select the **Insert** tab on the ribbon.

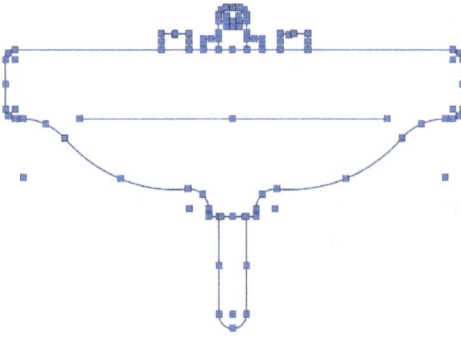

Figure 12.2: The objects for the front view selected, with grips displayed

2. Click on **Create Block** (*BLOCK*) on the **Block Definition** panel, as shown in *Figure 12.3*.

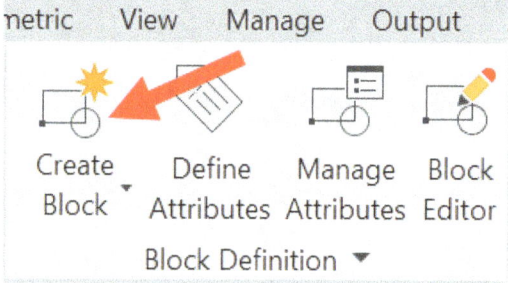

Figure 12.3: The Create Block (BLOCK) command on the Block Definition panel

3. The **Block Definition** dialog box will appear. In the **Name** field, type in the block name `Washbasin_FRONT`.
4. Click on the **Pick point** icon, as shown in *Figure 12.4*.

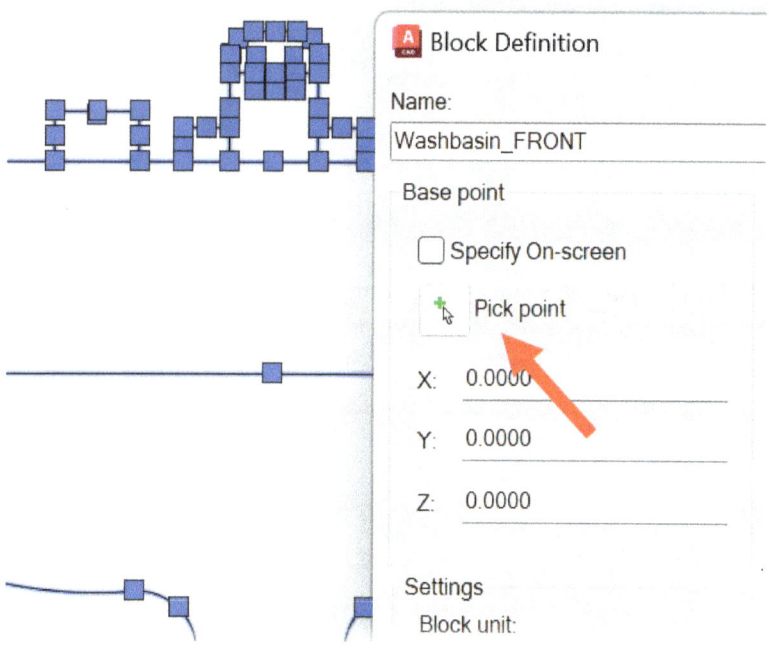

Figure 12.4: The Pick point icon in the Block Definition dialog box

5. You will be taken into the drawing to select an insertion point for your block. Select the **Midpoint** object snap shown in *Figure 12.5*.

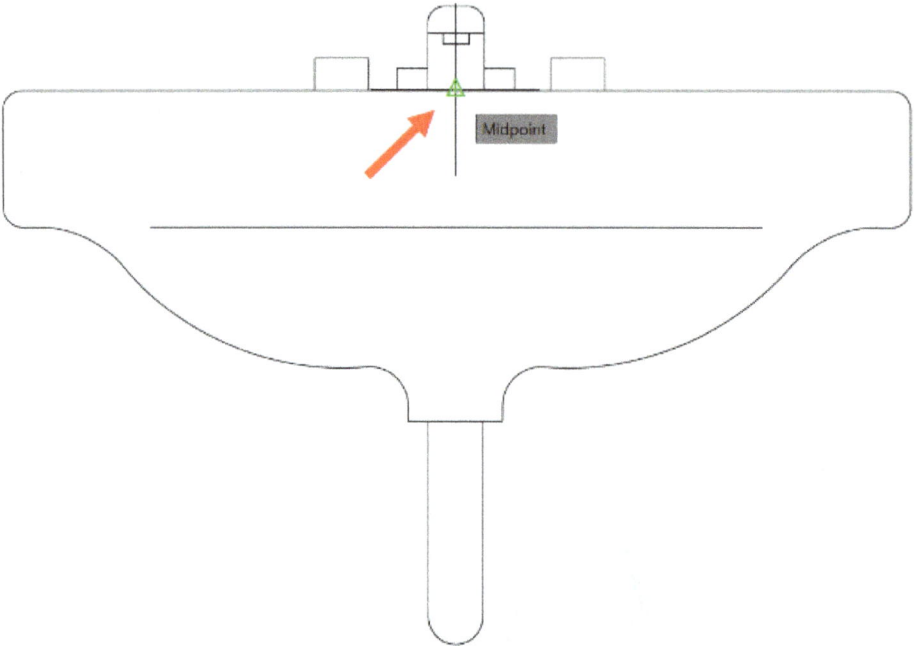

Figure 12.5: The Midpoint object snap to be used as the insertion point

6. Clicking on the **Midpoint** object snap will return you to the **Block Definition** dialog box. Note the exact precision of the **X** and **Y** coordinates in the dialog box due to using an object snap. You must now set all the settings required to create your dynamic door block.

7. Refer to *Figure 12.6* and set all the necessary settings in the **Block Definition** dialog box as shown.

Creating the washbasin block drawing   297

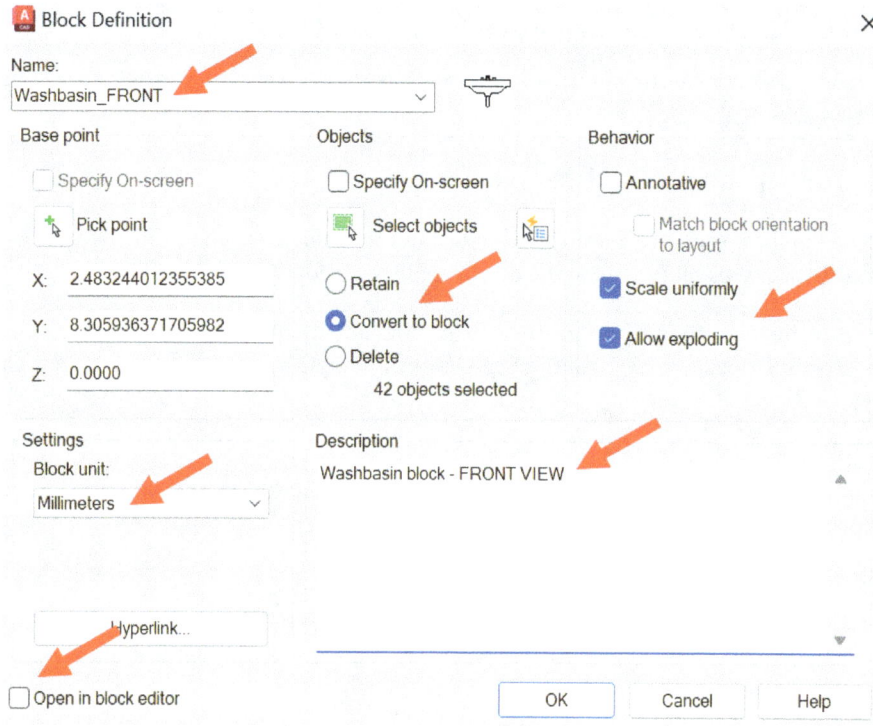

Figure 12.6: The Block Definition dialog box with all required settings

8. Once you have all the necessary settings in the dialog box, click **OK**.

9. The dialog box will close, and your objects will now be a block reference in the drawing. To check that the objects have been converted to a block, hover over the washbasin front view and AutoCAD will provide a tooltip, as shown in *Figure 12.7*. If that tooltip reads **Block Reference**, you know that the objects have been converted to a block.

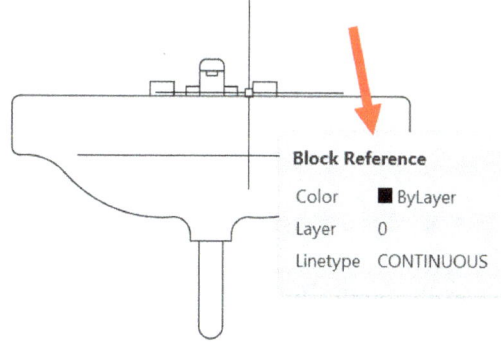

Figure 12.7: The Washbasin_FRONT block indicated by the tooltip

10. Press *Esc* several times to ensure you have deselected the block.

    You must now perform the same workflow (*Steps 1–10*) to create the `Washbasin_TOP` and `Washbasin_SIDE` blocks.

Adding the top and side blocks

You now need to repeat the workflow to add the top and side blocks. Each of these blocks, and the front block, will form a visibility state in the dynamic block. Follow these steps:

1. Repeating the preceding workflow from *Step 1* for the `Washbasin_TOP` block; make sure you select the objects that form the top view of the washbasin before clicking on **Create Block** (*BLOCK*).
2. Enter the name `Washbasin_TOP` in the **Name** field.
3. When using the **Pick point** tool in the **Block Definition** dialog box, you must select the **Midpoint** object snap shown in *Figure 12.8*.

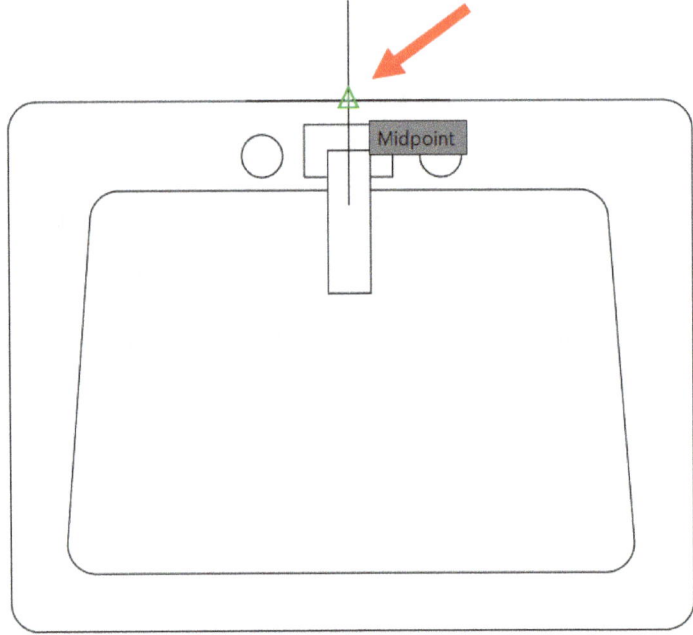

Figure 12.8: The Midpoint object snap for the Washbasin_TOP block

4. Check that all the other settings in the **Block Definition** dialog box match what is shown in *Figure 12.6* and click on **OK**.

Creating the washbasin block drawing 299

5. Hover over the new block to check that the tooltip displays **Block Reference**, as shown in *Figure 12.9*. If it does, you have created your `Washbasin_TOP` regular block.

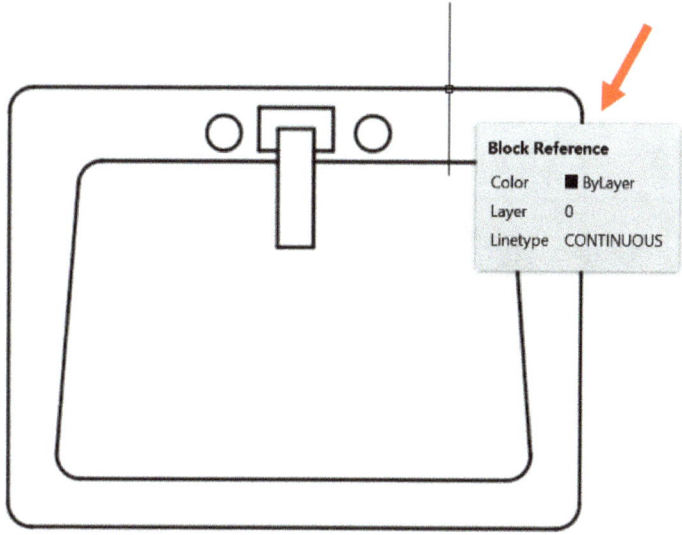

Figure 12.9: The finished Washbasin_TOP block

6. Again, repeating the block creation workflow from *Step 1*, you can now start to create the `Washbasin_SIDE` block.

7. Make sure you select the objects that form the side view of the washbasin before clicking on **Create Block** (*BLOCK*).

8. Enter the name `Washbasin_SIDE` in the **Name** field.

9. This block is a little more detailed, and you need to take into account the curved corner of the washbasin when using the **Pick point** tool in the **Block Definition** dialog box. You need to select an **Object Tracking** point, due to the curve on the corner of the washbasin.

10. You must ensure that **Polar Tracking** (*POLAR*), **Object Snap Tracking** (*AUTOSNAP*), and **Object Snap** (*OSNAP*) are active on the status bar, as shown in *Figure 12.10*. If they are active, they will be shown in pale blue. You can then use these drafting settings to select your **Object Tracking** point.

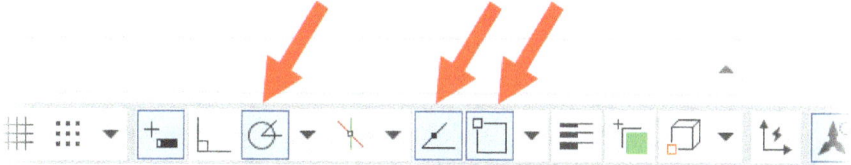

Figure 12.10: The settings required on the status bar

11. Zoom in to the upper-right corner of the washbasin side view objects, as shown in *Figure 12.11*.

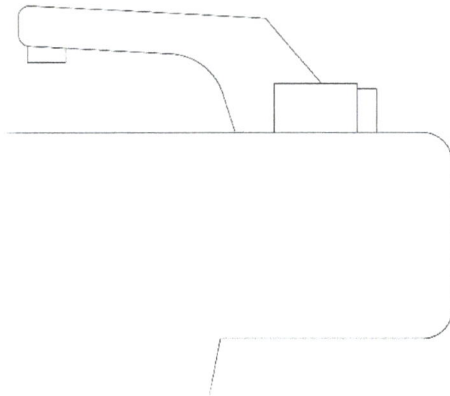

Figure 12.11: A zoomed-in view of the washbasin side view

12. Click on **Pick point** in the **Block Definition** dialog box.
13. Hover over the two **Endpoint** object snaps shown in *Figure 12.12*, and *do not* click on them. Hovering over the object snaps uses them as tracking points and not object snaps, allowing you to locate the **Object Tracking** point you need.

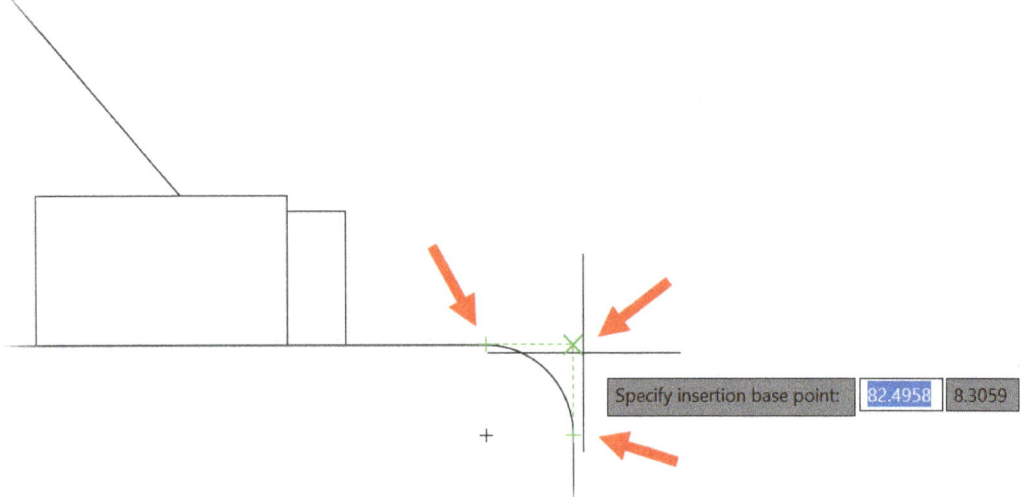

Figure 12.12: Using Object Snap Tracking to set the insertion point

14. As you move away slightly with the cursor, two polar tracking lines intersect, and an **Intersection** object snap displays, as shown in *Figure 12.12*.

15. Click when you see this intersection (shown as an **X** in *Figure 12.12*) to set it as the block's insertion point.

16. Check that all the other settings in the **Block Definition** dialog box match what is shown in *Figure 12.13* and click on **OK**.

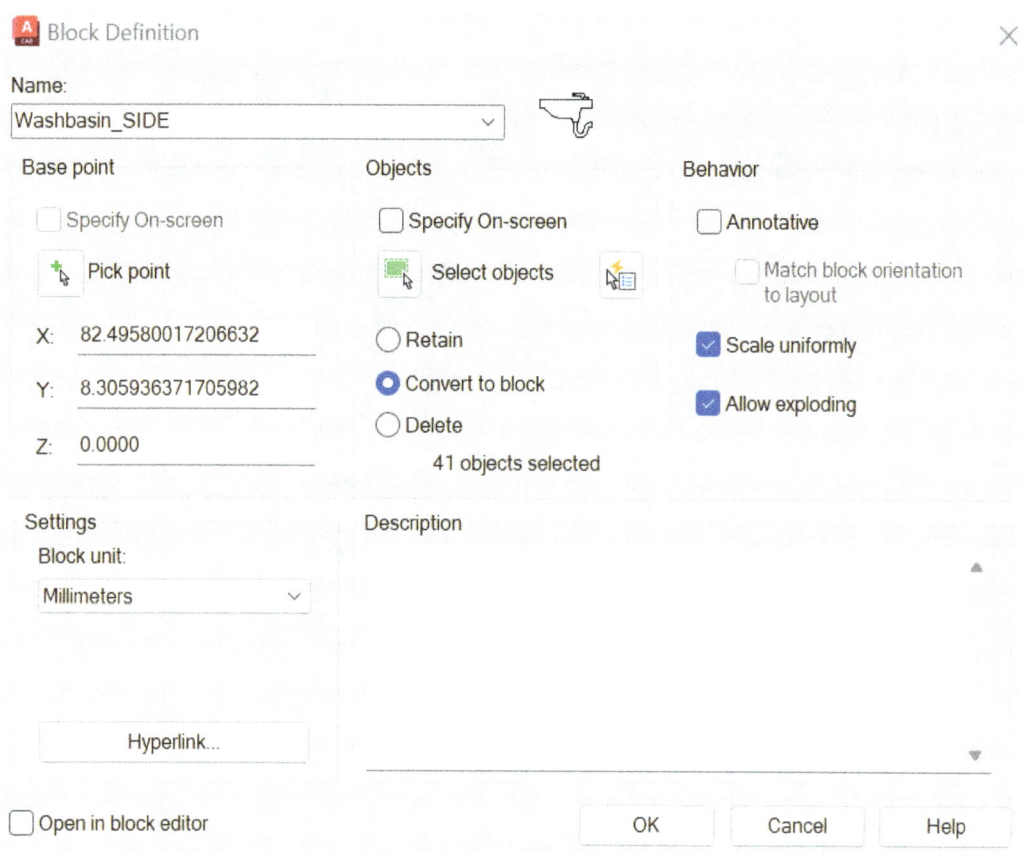

Figure 12.13: The settings in the Block Definition dialog box

17. Hover over the new block to check that the tooltip displays **Block Reference**, as shown in *Figure 12.14*. If it does, you have created your `Washbasin_SIDE` regular block.

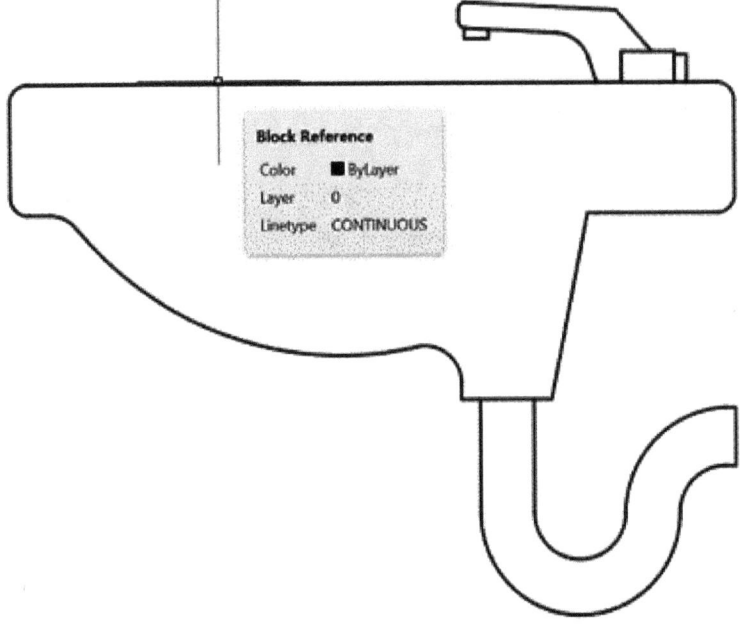

Figure 12.14: The finished Washbasin_SIDE block

You have now created all three regular blocks needed for the visibility states in the dynamic block. At this point, make sure to save the drawing to save the blocks in the DWG file.

The next section of this chapter will explain how to add these blocks to **Block Editor** as you develop the dynamic block.

> **Tips and tricks #32**
>
> Block naming philosophy is *important*. You want to ensure that all users of your blocks, both regular and dynamic, know what a particular block will be used for. A simple naming trick is as follows. When creating a dynamic block, use the suffix DYN. So, a dynamic block will have the name `Block_DYN`, rather than just `Block`. This way, your dynamic blocks are easily recognized when using the **Insert** block drop-down menu.

Effective management of your blocks is essential in your AutoCAD drawings. Make sure you document all of your block naming philosophy in a simple CAD standard for your team to use and follow. This makes sure you are all using the same blocks.

> **AutoCAD for Mac**
>
> AutoCAD for Mac uses a very similar method for creating dynamic blocks with visibility states. The **Create Block** (*BLOCK*) command is on the left-hand menu.

Adding the necessary blocks for each view

In the previous section of this chapter, you learned how to make the regular blocks that form each view of the washbasin. This section will bring these blocks into the new dynamic block for the washbasin, ready to form the relevant visibility states.

Staying in the `Washbasin-DYNAMIC.dwg` file, you now need to work through the following steps to start developing your washbasin dynamic block:

1. To create a new block in **Block Editor**, you can directly use the **Block Editor** icon in the **Block Definition** panel on the **Insert** ribbon tab, as shown in *Figure 12.15*.

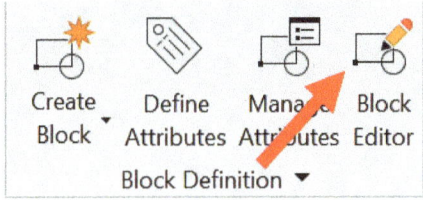

Figure 12.15: The Block Editor icon on the Block Definition panel

2. You will be prompted to edit a block definition with the **Edit Block Definition** dialog box, where all the regular blocks you created previously will be listed, as shown in *Figure 12.16*.

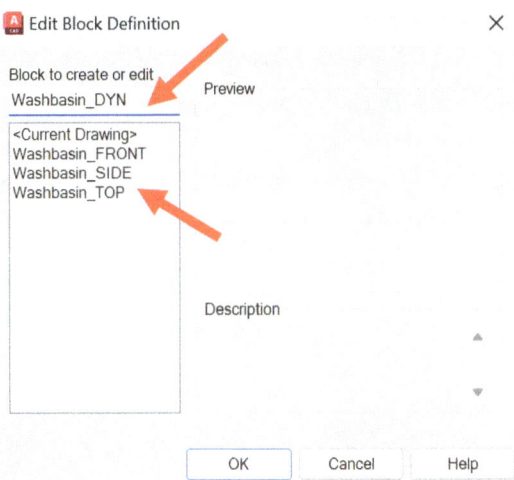

Figure 12.16: The Edit Block Definition dialog box

3. Also, add the new dynamic block name `Washbasin_DYN` in the **Block to create or edit** field, also shown in *Figure 12.16*, and click on **OK**.

4. You will now be in **Block Editor**, ready to start inserting the regular blocks you created in the previous section. Use the **Insert** tab on the ribbon to locate the **Insert** dropdown (far left on the ribbon). Click **Insert**, and the drop-down menu will appear, as shown in *Figure 12.17*.

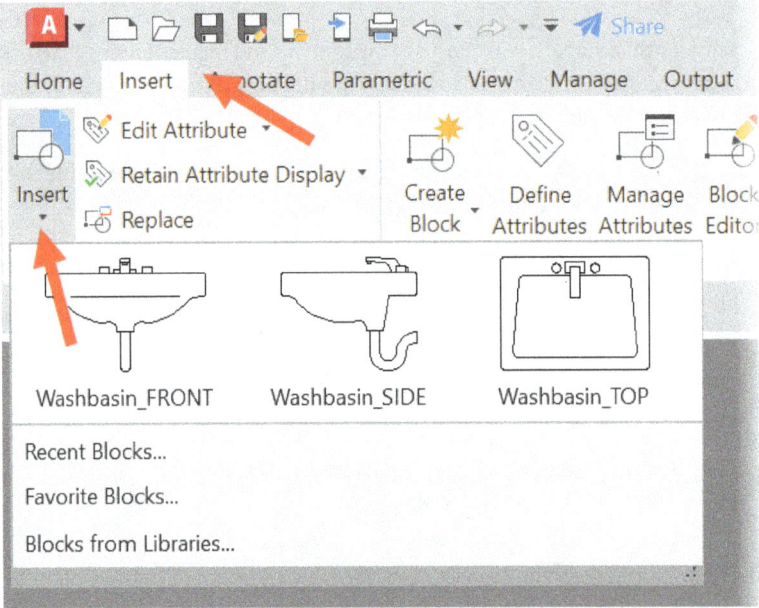

Figure 12.17: The Insert drop-down menu on the Insert tab

5. Select the **Washbasin_TOP** block. It will appear on your cursor. Click any point in **Block Editor** to locate it. The **Washbasin_TOP** block will be the base block for the other two regular blocks.

6. Repeating what you did in *Step 4* with the **Insert** drop-down menu, select the **Washbasin_SIDE** block. It will appear on your cursor as before.

7. At the **Specify insertion point** prompt, select the **Midpoint** object snap on the already inserted **Washbasin_TOP** block, as shown in *Figure 12.18*. This will insert the **Washbasin_SIDE** block.

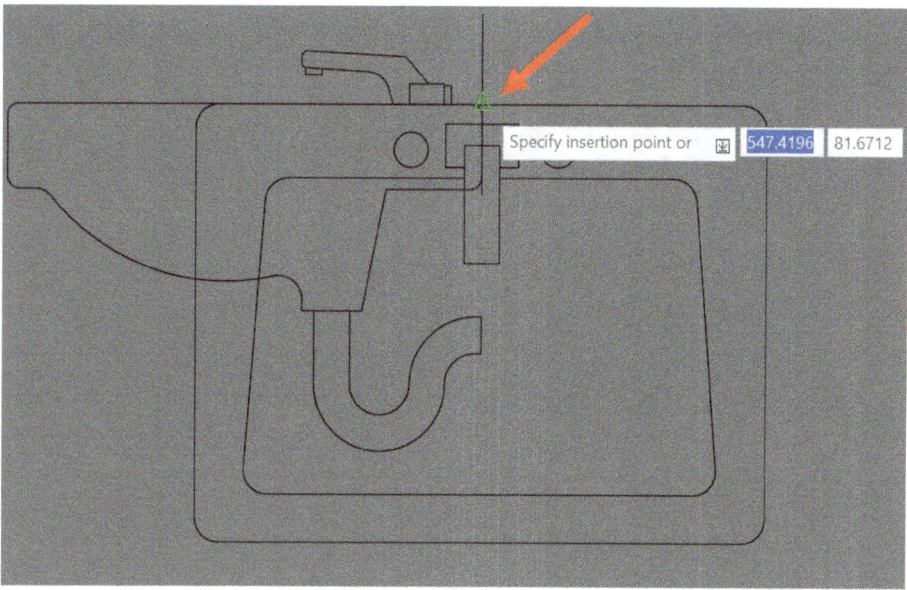

Figure 12.18: The Midpoint object snap on the Washbasin_TOP block

8. Repeat the process from the **Insert** drop-down menu, but this time, insert the **Washbasin_FRONT** block. Again, at the **Specify insertion point** prompt, use the **Midpoint** object snap on the **Washbasin_TOP** block to place the block as shown in *Figure 12.19*.

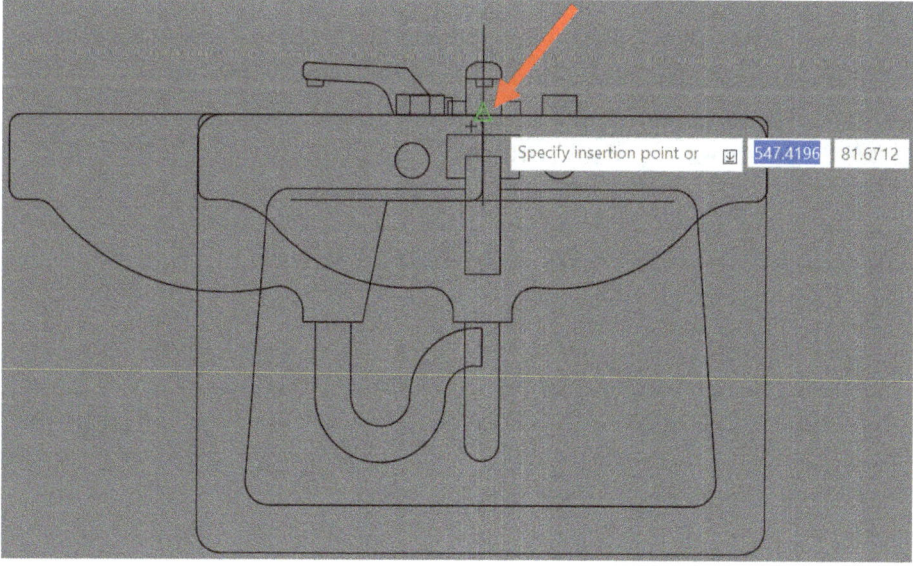

Figure 12.19: Reusing the Midpoint object snap on the Washbasin_TOP block

9. You now have a somewhat jumbled view in **Block Editor** of the three regular blocks, as shown in *Figure 12.20*.

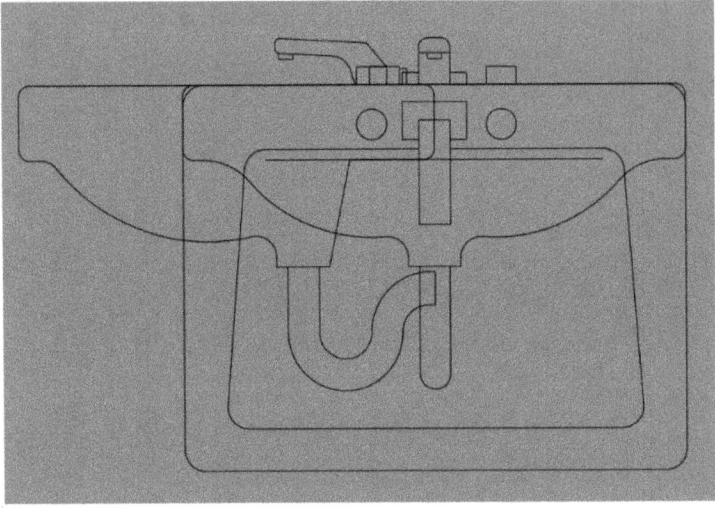

Figure 12.20: The three regular blocks placed in Block Editor

You have now placed the three blocks, and you need to start adding visibility states.

> **AutoCAD for Mac**
> Adding regular blocks to **Block Editor** follows the same workflow in AutoCAD for Mac.

At this point, stay in **Block Editor** and don't save anything because, in the next section, we begin the second part of the workflow, and you will start adding the visibility states for the **Washbasin_DYN** dynamic block.

Adding visibility states in a dynamic block

In the previous section, you learned how to insert the regular blocks into **Block Editor**, working toward creating the new **Washbasin_DYN** dynamic block. In this section, you will develop the relevant visibility state for each regular block, providing a view for each block in the **Washbasin_DYN** dynamic block. The visibility states are all stored in one dynamic block, and when that dynamic block is inserted into the drawing, you can select which visibility state is displayed. This saves time and avoids the need for three regular blocks, one for each washbasin view.

Setting up the first visibility state

The following workflow will take you through setting up the visibility states:

1. Staying in **Block Editor**, editing the **Washbasin_DYN** dynamic block, a **Basepoint** parameter needs to be set. The **Basepoint** parameter makes sure you have one specific insertion point for the dynamic block as a point of reference when bringing it into a drawing. Click on the **Parameters** tab in the **Block Authoring Palette**.

2. Select the **Basepoint** parameter. You will be prompted for the location of the base point. Using object snaps, click on the **Midpoint** object snap you used in the previous section to locate the regular blocks, as shown in *Figure 12.21*.

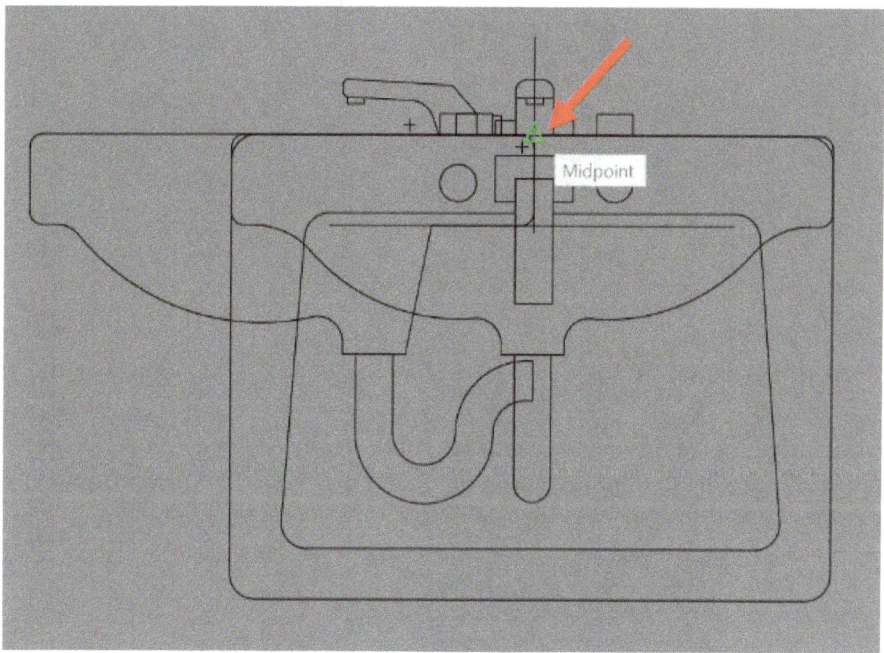

Figure 12.21: The Midpoint object snap used as a Basepoint parameter

3. The **Basepoint** parameter is now placed. You need to consider the visibility states, which are set up using only the **Parameters** tab in the **Block Authoring Palette**.

4. Click on **Visibility** in the **Block Authoring Palette**, as shown in *Figure 12.22*.

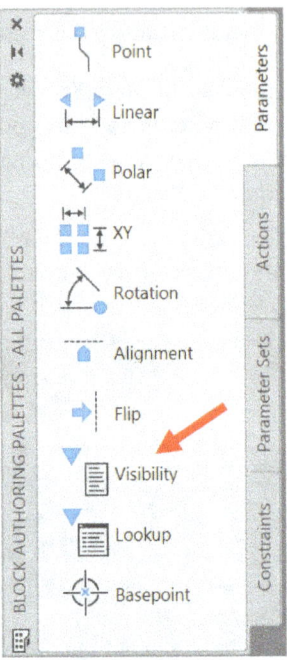

Figure 12.22: The Block Authoring Palette with the Visibility parameter indicated

5. You will be prompted for the parameter's location. You need to select a point close to the regular blocks but not directly on them, as shown in *Figure 12.23*. This is because the **Visibility** parameter will be displayed on the dynamic block when it is used in a drawing.

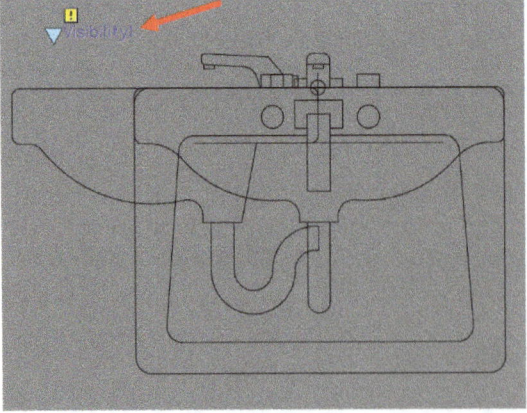

Figure 12.23: The Visibility parameter shown placed in Block Editor

6. You can see the *yellow exclamation* mark like in *Chapter 11*, which means that the **Visibility** parameter needs more information to function. In this case, it needs objects (the regular blocks) to represent each visibility state in the dynamic block. You don't need to name the parameter, but it can be done by selecting it, right-clicking and selecting **Properties** on the shortcut menu, and renaming it in the **Properties** palette.

7. Look at the ribbon. You are in the blue contextual **Block Editor** ribbon tab. Look for the **Visibility** ribbon panel, as shown in *Figure 12.24*.

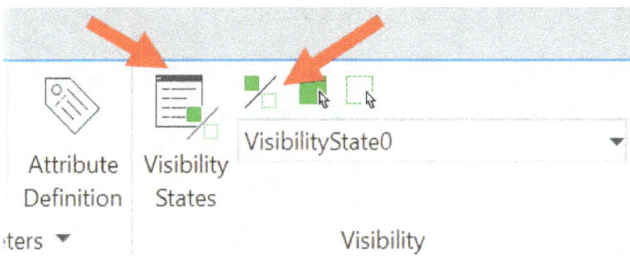

Figure 12.24: The Visibility panel on the ribbon

In *Figure 12.24*, there are two icons arrowed. The right-hand arrow points to the icon that sets the AutoCAD BVMODE system variable, called **Visibility Mode**. Clicking on this icon turns BVMODE either on (**1**) or off (**0**). You will need it on, as any visibility states set to invisible will then appear grayed out, rather than invisible, which is much easier to work with. If BVMODE is set to zero (**0**), you only see the current visibility state. This will become clearer as you go through this workflow. Click on the icon and look at the command line, and if you see BVMODE set to **1**, as shown in *Figure 12.25*, you are all set. If it says zero (**0**), click the icon again to set it to **1**.

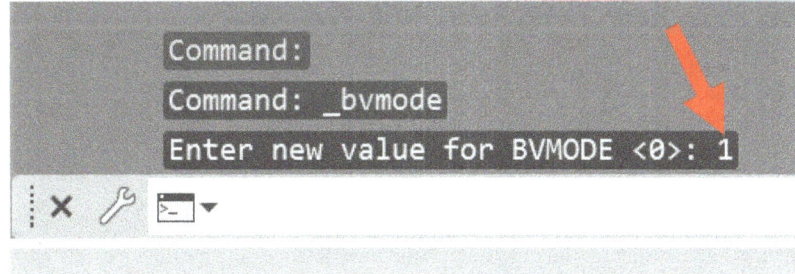

Figure 12.25: Setting the BVMODE system variable to 1

8. Click on the **Visibility States** icon shown in *Figure 12.24*.

9. The **Visibility States** dialog box will display a default visibility state called **VisibilityState0**. Click on **New**, and in the **New Visibility State** dialog box, set the new state name to **Washbasin-SIDE**. Set the visibility options to the third option, **Leave visibility of existing objects unchanged in new state**, as shown in *Figure 12.26*.

Creating a Dynamic Block with Visibility States

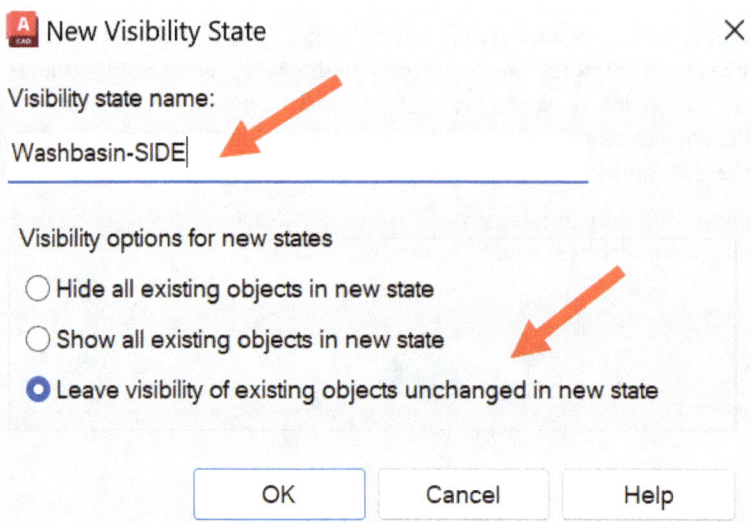

Figure 12.26: The New Visibility State dialog box with settings arrowed

10. Click on **OK**. The **Visibility States** dialog box will then be shown, as in *Figure 12.27*.

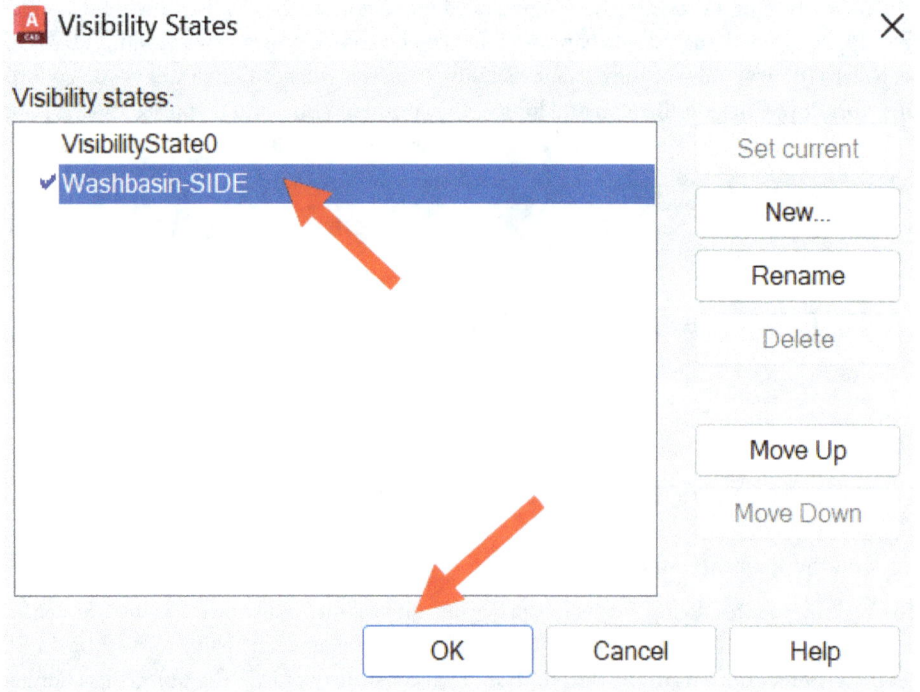

Figure 12.27: The Visibility States dialog box

11. The **Washbasin-SIDE** visibility state is current, as indicated by the check mark. You can now select the default state, **VisibilityState0**, and click **Delete** to remove it.
12. Click on **OK** to close the **Visibility States** dialog box. You are now in the **Washbasin-SIDE** visibility state and need to set which regular blocks are visible and invisible.
13. The ribbon's **Visibility** panel shows which visibility state you use. Select the regular block that displays the side view of the washbasin, as shown in *Figure 12.28*, and click on the green square icon, also shown in *Figure 12.28*. This sets that block as visible in the visibility state.

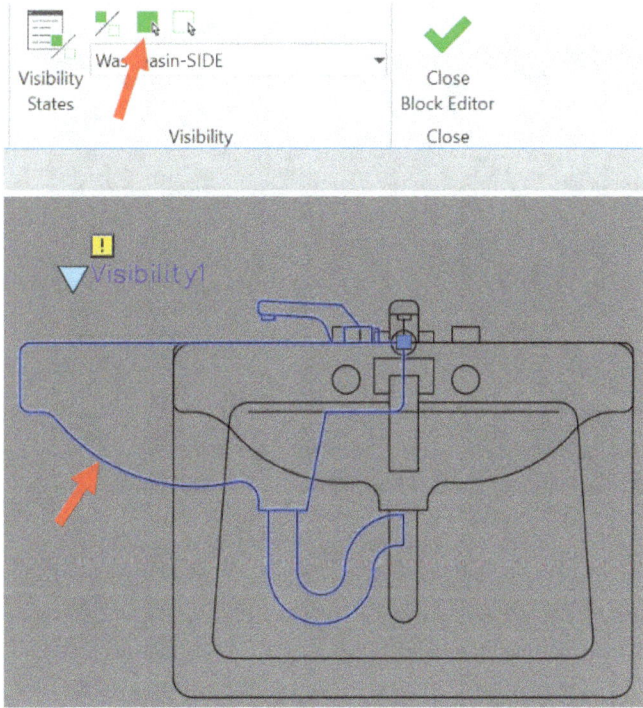

Figure 12.28: The selected side view block being made visible

The side view will be deselected and is now set as visible in the visibility state.

14. Select the two other blocks representing the top and front views, as shown in *Figure 12.29*. Then, click the green dashed icon, also shown in *Figure 12.29*. This will make them both to be invisible in the current visibility state.

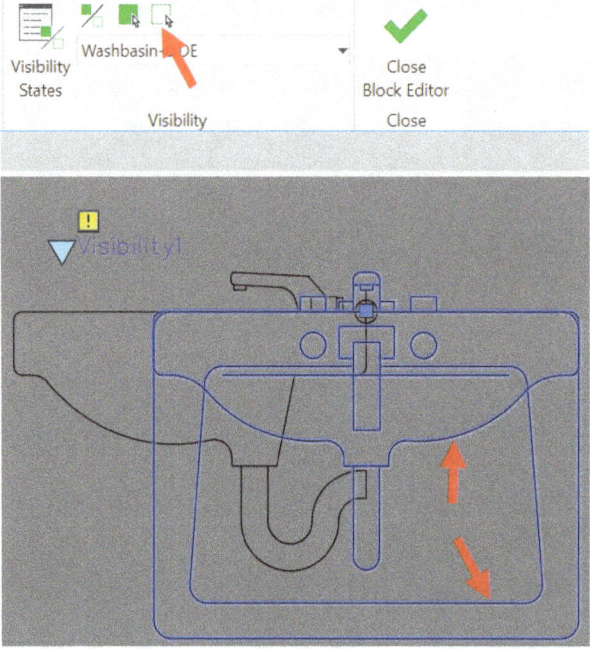

Figure 12.29: The other two blocks selected to be made invisible

15. Once you click the icon, the two blocks will be deselected and displayed grayed out due to the `BVMODE` system variable being set to **1** earlier. This is shown in *Figure 12.30*.

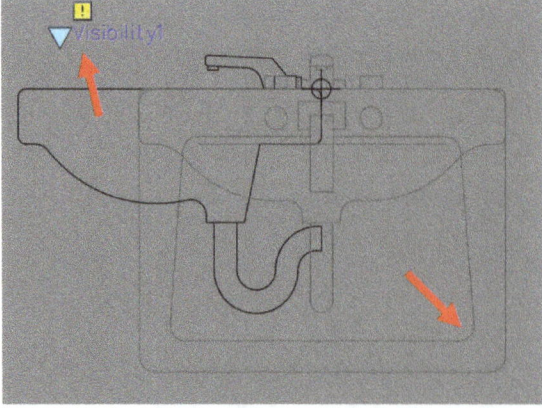

Figure 12.30: The visibility state with the side view visible

Adding visibility states in a dynamic block   313

You will note that you still have a *yellow exclamation* mark. This is because you only have one state set at present.

Adding two more visibility states

The two remaining visibility states must be set up in the dynamic block. This section will repeat the creation of the first visibility state, but you will create two more visibility states, using the other two regular blocks:

1. Click on the **Visibility States** icon again to display the **Visibility States** dialog box. Click on **New**.
2. In the **New Visibility State** dialog box, set another state name called **Washbasin-TOP**, using the same options as *Step 9* previously. Click on **OK**.
3. In the **Visibility States** dialog box, the new **Washbasin-TOP** state is now current (checked). Click on **OK**. You now need to repeat the visible/invisible process.
4. Check that the **Washbasin-TOP** state is current in the **Visibility** panel. Then, select the regular block showing the top view of the washbasin, as shown in *Figure 12.31*. Click on the green icon shown in *Figure 12.31* to make it visible in the current state.

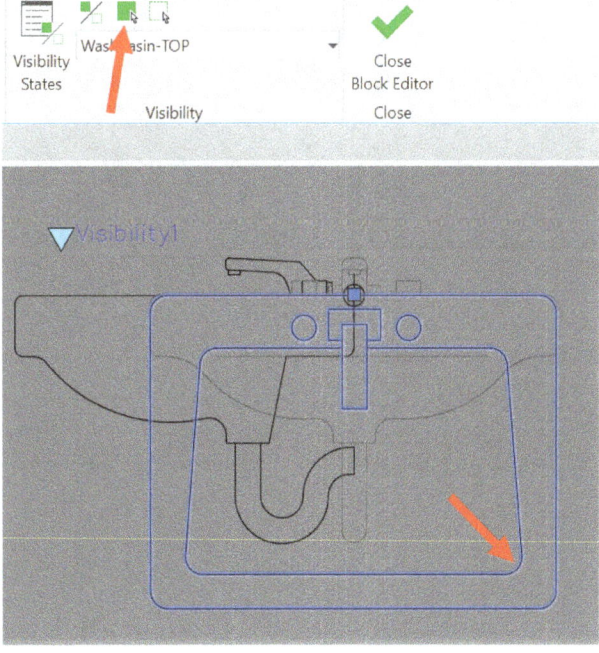

Figure 12.31: Setting the top view as visible

5. The top view block will be deselected automatically and is now set as visible in the **Washbasin-TOP** visibility state. Note that the yellow exclamation mark has gone because you now have more than one visibility state.

6. Like before, you must select the blocks representing the washbasin's side and front views and then click on the green dashed icon in the **Visibility** panel to mark them as invisible.

7. Again, they will automatically be deselected. They are now marked as invisible in the **Washbasin-TOP** visibility state and grayed out, as shown in *Figure 12.32*.

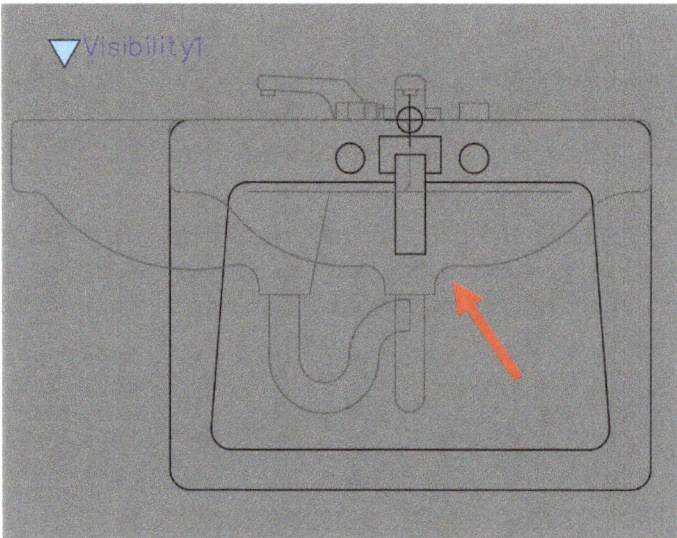

Figure 12.32: The visibility state with the top view visible

8. Repeat the preceding workflow (*Steps 1-7*) one more time, creating a third visibility state called **Washbasin-FRONT**, where the block displaying the front view of the washbasin is visible.

9. The **Washbasin-FRONT** visibility state should look like *Figure 12.33*, where the block displaying the front view is visible and the other two side and top blocks are invisible (grayed out).

Adding visibility states in a dynamic block   315

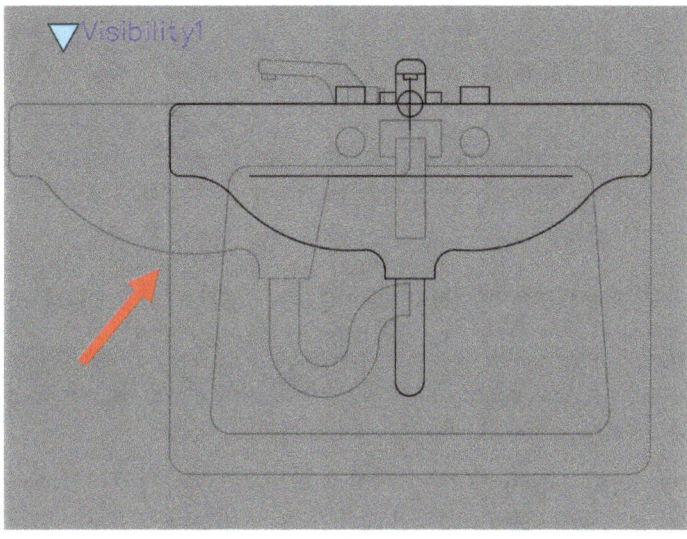

Figure 12.33: The visibility state with the front view visible

To toggle between visibility states, you can set the current state using the drop-down menu on the **Visibility** panel, as shown in *Figure 12.34*.

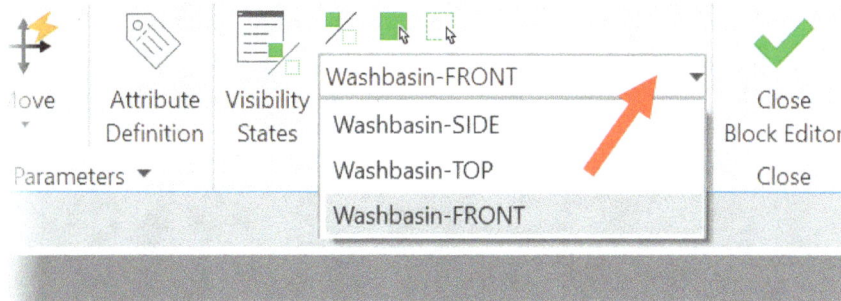

Figure 12.34: The visibility state drop-down menu

You have now set up all three required visibility states in the **Washbasin_DYN** dynamic block.

10. Click on **Close Block Editor** (the *green* check mark on the ribbon) to close **Block Editor** and return to the drawing.
11. Once you are back in the drawing after leaving **Block Editor**, a prompt will appear. Make sure to select **Save the changes to Washbasin_DYN**.

You are now back in the `Washbasin-DYNAMIC.dwg` file, and you can see the regular blocks you created previously that were used as visibility states in the new dynamic block.

Make sure to save the drawing so that your new dynamic block is saved in the DWG file.

> **AutoCAD for Mac**
>
> Adding visibility states in **Block Editor** follows the same workflow in AutoCAD for Mac.

You have now created your new **Washbasin_DYN** dynamic block with visibility states. In the next section of this chapter, you will bring the block into the drawing and use the visibility states to display different views of the washbasin.

Using the new dynamic block with visibility states

In the previous section, you learned how to use regular blocks to create visibility states of different views of the washbasin in a new dynamic block. In this section, you will learn how to insert the new dynamic block into the drawing and utilize the visibility states.

Throughout this chapter, you have worked on the default layer, layer zero (*0*). This means your new dynamic block will assume the current layer when inserted in the drawing. The following workflow will allow you to fully test the dynamic washbasin block:

1. On the **Home** tab on the ribbon, check that the **Sanitary** layer is current on the **Layers** panel.
2. Using zoom and pan functions, ensure you work in a space away from the existing blocks.
3. Click on the **Insert** tab on the ribbon, then click on the **Insert** dropdown at the left-hand end. *Figure 12.35* shows the **Washbasin_DYN** block shown in the dropdown.

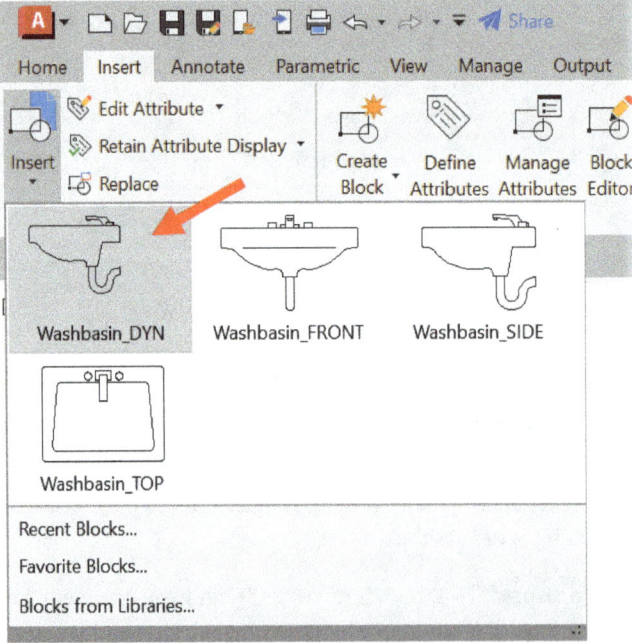

Figure 12.35: The Washbasin_DYN dynamic block on the Insert dropdown

4. Select the **Washbasin_DYN** block on the dropdown to insert it into the drawing. The block will appear on the cursor. You will see that the dynamic block has adopted the first current visibility state that was set, the **Washbasin-SIDE** view, as shown in *Figure 12.36*. This can be changed (if required) shortly.

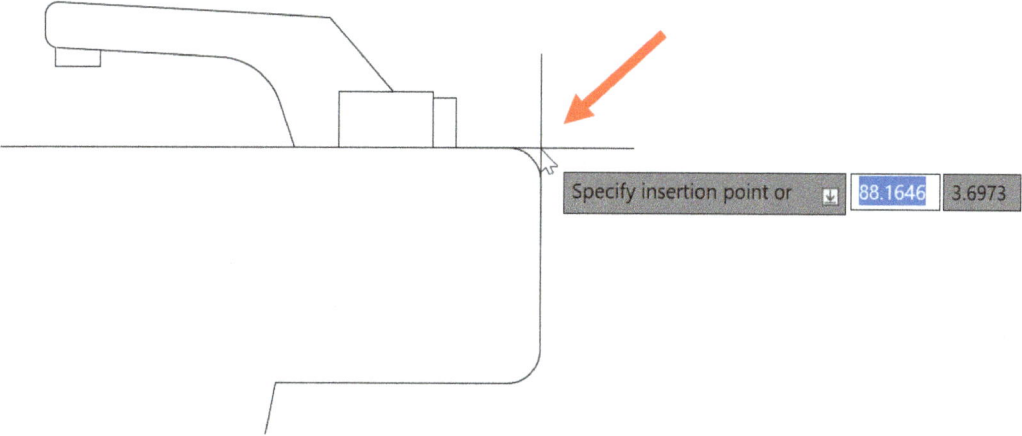

Figure 12.36: The Washbasin_DYN block inserted with the Washbasin-SIDE view current

5. Pick a point to insert the **Washbasin_DYN** block. Once placed, click on the block to select it, as shown in *Figure 12.37*.

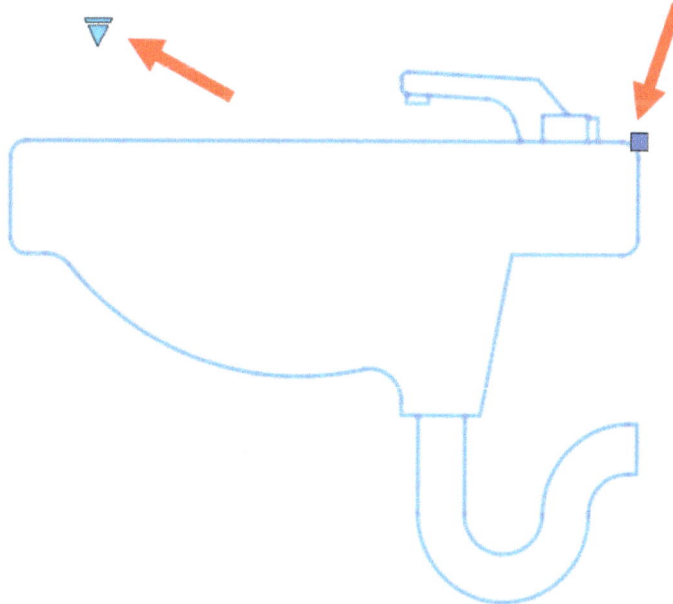

Figure 12.37: The selected Washbasin_DYN dynamic block

318 Creating a Dynamic Block with Visibility States

Note that the selected block has two blue grips. The right-hand *square* grip is the **Basepoint** parameter you added in **Block Editor**. The left-hand *arrow* grip is for the visibility states set inside the dynamic block.

6. Click on the arrow grip to display the available visibility states, as shown in *Figure 12.38*.

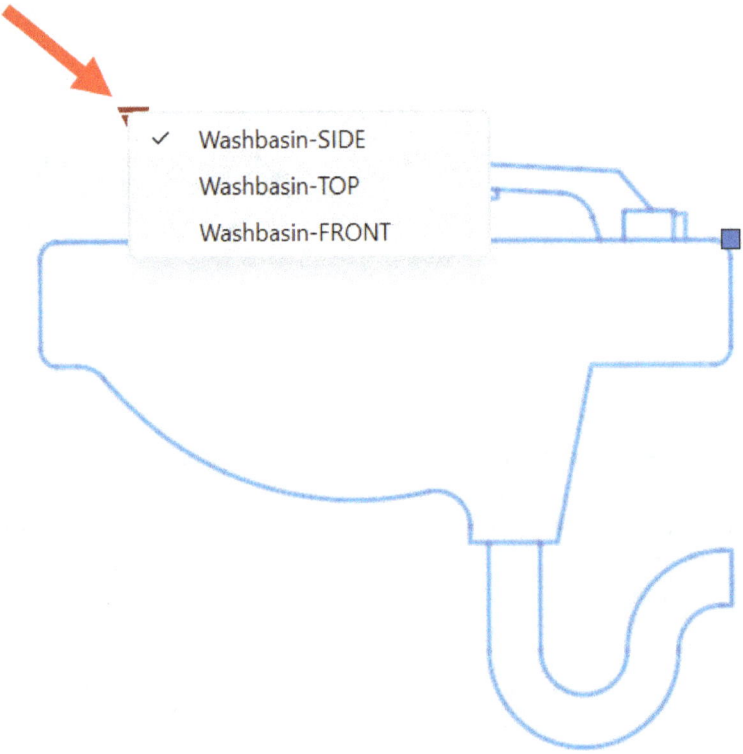

Figure 12.38: The positioned dynamic block with the visibility states displayed

7. On the menu displayed in *Figure 12.38*, select the **Washbasin-TOP** visibility state. The block's view will change to the washbasin's top view, as shown in *Figure 12.39*.

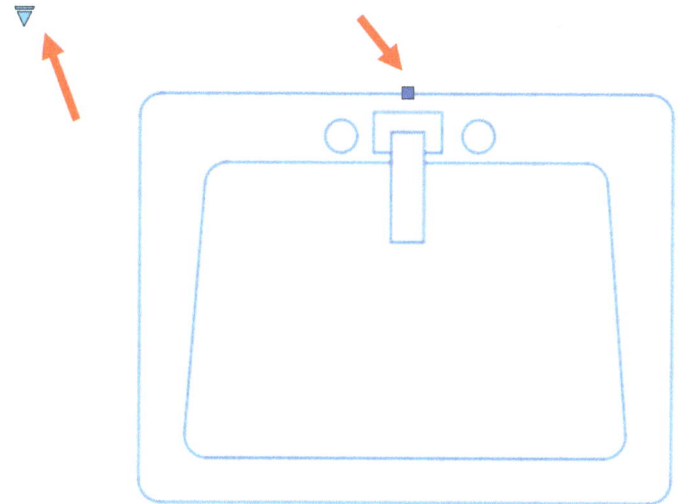

Figure 12.39: The Washbasin_DYN dynamic block using the Washbasin-TOP visibility state

You can now toggle visibility states using the menu on the arrow grip. This saves valuable time when drafting, as you now have three regular block views in one dynamic block, all representing the same drawing object, the washbasin.

Congratulations! You have now created a dynamic block with visibility states. As you build your AutoCAD knowledge, you might want to set aside some time to experiment with dynamic blocks that use visibility states. Consider using them with block attributes to make dynamic blocks that save valuable drafting time.

You can learn more about dynamic blocks with visibility states here on the Autodesk website: `https://help.autodesk.com/view/ACD/2024/ENU/?guid=GUID-B30B3B47-F93B-487E-998F-2E8C72D22CBD`.

Dynamic blocks with visibility states are a great way to reduce time spent on long-winded editing tasks. You can develop dynamic block families with visibility states, too. A good example would be a particular type of fixing bolt with differing lengths or threads with a visibility state for each length or thread. You could also consider length parameters in this case.

> **AutoCAD for Mac**
> Dynamic blocks with visibility states are created using the same workflow in AutoCAD for Mac.

Summary

In this chapter, you learned how versatile dynamic blocks can be. You also saw how visibility states provide incredible flexibility, allowing you to have numerous representative views of the same block in one dynamic block. Dynamic actions in a block, such as visibility states, provide a much quicker way of adding views of block objects in your drawings rather than inserting individual blocks for each view.

You now know how to work with, edit, and manage your dynamic blocks with visibility states, and using the knowledge gained in previous chapters, you can now consider developing more advanced dynamic blocks.

You have gained the knowledge of how to create a simple washbasin drawing that contains the necessary regular blocks you need to develop your dynamic block visibility states.

You learned how to utilize the regular blocks when adding the visibility states to a dynamic block and inserted the dynamic block into a drawing to test the assigned visibility states.

In the next chapter, we will look at ways to share your drawings with your project team and stakeholders using the **Share Drawing** tool and **Shared Views** palette.

Part 4: Communicating and Collaborating

AutoCAD has been around for over 40 years and has adopted new technology with each new version. AutoCAD 2026 is no different. Cloud-based technology and file storage now allow your AutoCAD DWG files to go mobile and travel with you. Using the AutoCAD mobile application and the browser-based AutoCAD Web, combined with cloud-based file storage, you can now take your drawings everywhere, allowing for easy, seamless, real-time communication and collaboration on your AutoCAD designs.

This part has the following chapters:

- *Chapter 13, Sharing Your AutoCAD Drawings*
- *Chapter 14, Comparing Drawings and External Reference Files*
- *Chapter 15, Working with AutoCAD Web*
- *Chapter 16, Collaborating Using Traces in AutoCAD*

13
Sharing Your AutoCAD Drawings

In the previous chapters, you learned how to work with blocks, attributes, and dynamic blocks to reuse design content in your drawings. This chapter teaches you how to share your AutoCAD drawing files with both AutoCAD users and non-AutoCAD users who may need to mark up and comment on the designs in your drawings.

Sharing drawings and drawing views will give you the capacity to share aspects of your design in real time, using the power of the internet and the cloud. This saves valuable drawing management and collaboration time by providing a much more dynamic drawing revision path.

AutoCAD has several methods for sharing drawings for easy collaboration, revisions, and changes to the design. In this chapter, you will see how **Share Drawing** and **Shared Views** can make your daily AutoCAD workflows and processes much quicker, allowing for faster and more efficient collaboration. You can use the **Share Drawing** (*SHARE*) command to share drawings via the browser-based version of AutoCAD: **AutoCAD Web**. You can also utilize the **Shared Views** palette, which provides views of drawings via Autodesk Viewer, allowing for comments and markups.

In a nutshell, we look at the following topics in the chapter:

- Using the Share Drawing tool
- Working with shared drawings in AutoCAD Web
- Using the Shared Views palette
- Working with shared views in Autodesk Viewer

Exercise file and requirements

For this chapter, you will need to use the `New Office Design_FINISHED.dwg` exercise file. Open the file in the **Model** tab, making sure you can see the full floor plan.

You will also need to ensure that you are logged in to AutoCAD using your Autodesk account. If you don't have an Autodesk account, you may need to set one up here: `https://accounts.autodesk.com/`. This chapter assumes you have an Autodesk account and that you are logged in to it.

Using the Share Drawing tool

The **Share Drawing** tool is used to share drawings to AutoCAD Web for viewing or editing, quickly and easily in real time. You will find the **Share Drawing** (*SHARE*) tool in two locations: on the **Collaborate** tab on the ribbon in the **Share** panel, and (conveniently) on the **Quick Access toolbar** (**QAT**), as displayed in *Figure 13.1*.

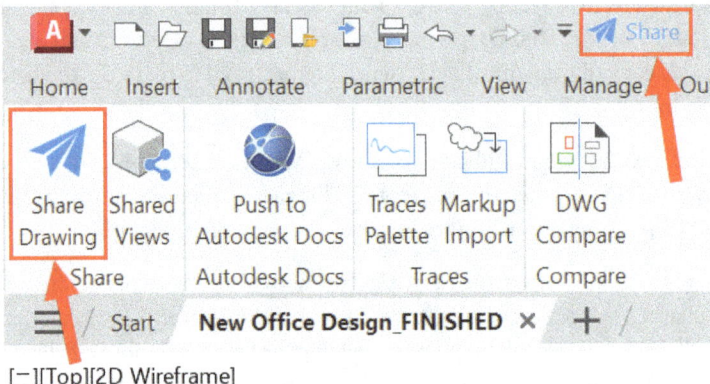

Figure 13.1: The Share Drawing tool on the Collaborate ribbon tab and QAT

In the following exercise, you will learn how to utilize the **Share Drawing** tool to share drawings via the cloud with the AutoCAD Web application:

1. You can click on either of the icons seen in *Figure 13.1* to activate the **Share Drawing** (*SHARE*) command. This will create a URL to share the DWG file in AutoCAD Web, and provide you with a dialog box, as shown in *Figure 13.2*.

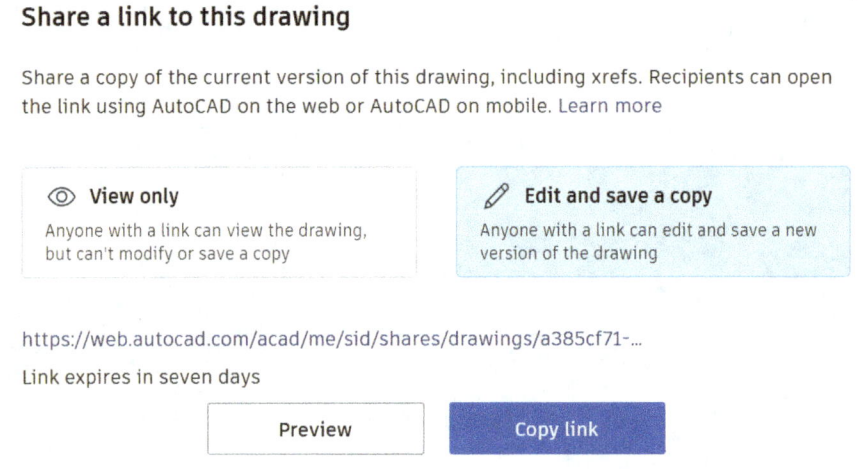

Figure 13.2: The Share a link to this drawing dialog box

Shared drawings can be set with two different levels of permission:

- **View only**: This means that anyone who receives this link can view the drawing but cannot modify or edit the drawing. They also cannot save a copy of the drawing.

- **Edit and save a copy**: This means that anyone who receives the link can modify and edit the drawing, and also save a copy of the drawing.

If you click on either of these in the dialog box, you will see the `https://` link in the dialog box change. Also, note that the links will expire in seven days from sending. The **Copy link** button does exactly that. It copies the `https://` link for you to insert into an email client, document, or even a text message.

2. Provided you are logged in to your Autodesk account, click on **Preview** in the dialog box, and you will automatically be taken to a new browser page with the drawing displayed in AutoCAD Web, as shown in *Figure 13.3*.

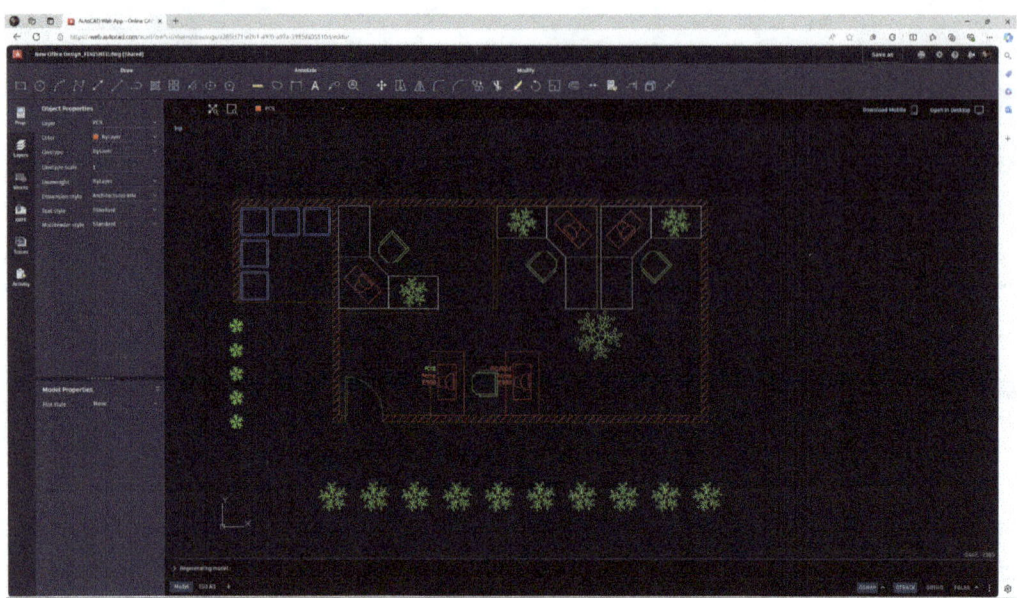

Figure 13.3: The drawing being previewed in AutoCAD Web

3. The browser used will be your default browser. In this case, the chosen browser is the latest version of **Microsoft Edge**, which works well with AutoCAD Web. **Google Chrome** is also a good browser to use. Be aware that AutoCAD Web functionality in other, more obscure browsers may not be as good.

4. Make sure that you have selected the **Edit and Save a Copy** option so that the recipient can edit and save a copy of the shared drawing, and then click on **Copy link**. You can now close the dialog box using the small cross in the top-right corner.

5. Copy the link into a blank Microsoft Word document and save it with a simple filename. For the purposes of this chapter, we will call it `AutoCAD Web-LINK.docx`. That gives you a record of the shared link provided and makes it easier to click on the link.

6. You can then hold down the *Ctrl* key and click on the link in the Word document to open up the drawing in AutoCAD Web.

You have now shared your drawing using the **Share Drawing** (*SHARE*) tool. You can now use AutoCAD Web to edit the drawing and save a copy of the drawing.

> **AutoCAD for Mac**
> The **Share Drawing** function is the same in AutoCAD for Mac and uses the same workflow.

In the next section, you will save a copy of the drawing in AutoCAD Web and make some simple edits to the drawing.

Working with shared drawings in AutoCAD Web

In this section, you will be using the web-based version of AutoCAD to edit and revise drawing files and make real-time edits to a web-based DWG file. Autodesk has added AutoCAD Web to the AutoCAD subscription, to allow for easy mobility and collaboration with AutoCAD DWG files.

> **Important Note**
> AutoCAD Web is a browser-based application and the interface changes regularly due to Autodesk development. It may look different to the figures in this chapter when you log in.

AutoCAD Web is browser-based, which allows your drawings to become mobile using a browser on the likes of a suitable tablet, such as an iPad Pro. You should be in the AutoCAD Web application in a browser window. The filename of the shared drawing will be displayed in the top-left corner. It should read New Office Design_FINISHED.dwg (Shared), as shown in *Figure 13.4*.

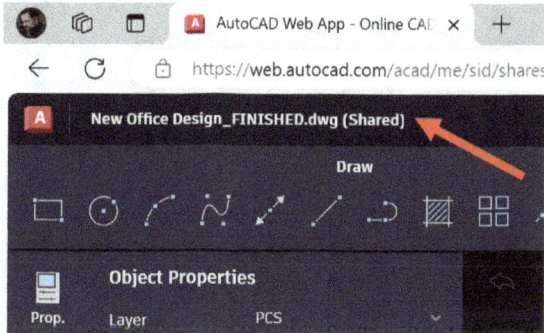

Figure 13.4: The DWG filename displayed in AutoCAD Web

Firstly, you must save the AutoCAD Web version of the shared drawing. Let's start the exercise by learning how to do this:

1. Click on the **Save as** button in the top-right corner of the AutoCAD Web screen, as shown in *Figure 13.5*.

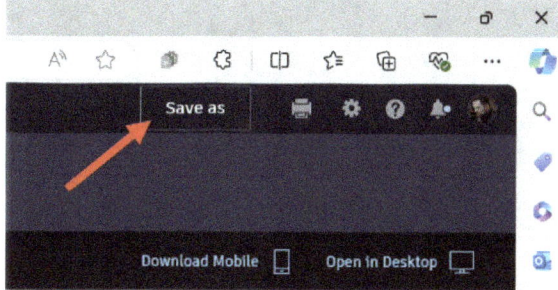

Figure 13.5: The Save as button in AutoCAD Web

2. The **Save As** dialog box will appear, as shown in *Figure 13.6*. Click on **New Folder** to create a new folder for your shared drawing.

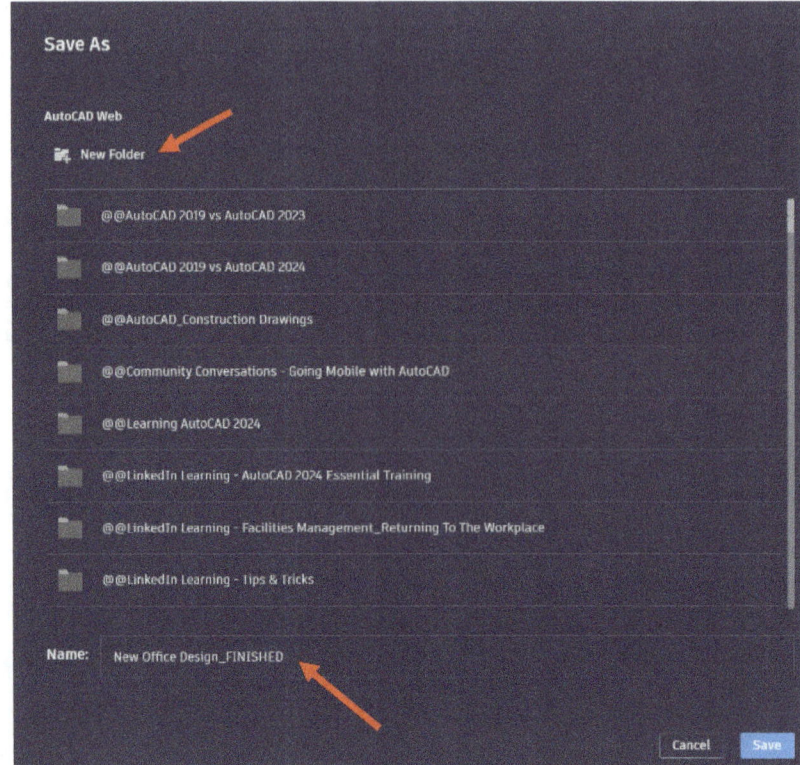

Figure 13.6: The Save As dialog box with New Folder arrowed

3. Name the new folder New Office Design, as shown in *Figure 13.7*.

Figure 13.7: Naming the new folder as New Office Design

4. Double-click on the new folder in the list, and it will open the folder, showing that it does not contain any files.

5. In the **Name** field, rename the shared drawing as `New Office Design_DESIGN1`. AutoCAD Web knows it is a DWG file, so no DWG suffix is displayed.

6. Click on the **Save** button, and the shared drawing is now saved in the new folder with the new filename. You can see this in the top-left corner of the AutoCAD Web screen, as shown in *Figure 13.8*.

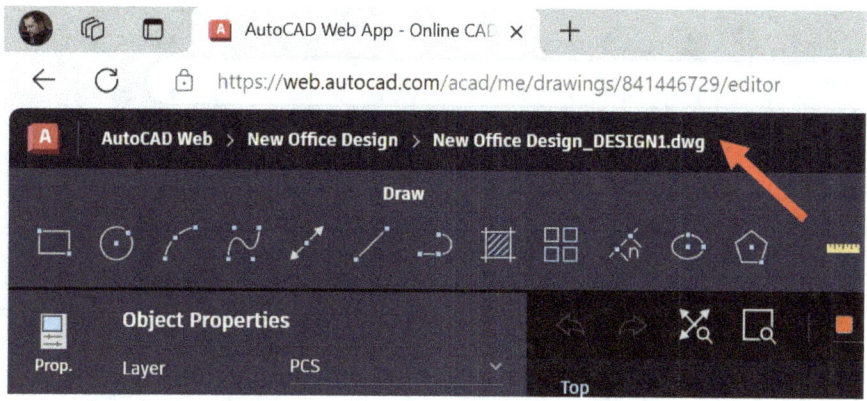

Figure 13.8: The name and location of the newly saved shared drawing in AutoCAD Web

The shared drawing is now a new drawing in a new folder, saved as per the permissions set when it was shared. You can now edit the drawing, make changes, and save those changes.

> **Tips and tricks #33**
>
> As you are logged in to AutoCAD Web via your Autodesk account, any drawings saved via AutoCAD Web will be saved to the cloud into the default **AutoCAD Web and Mobile** folders associated with your Autodesk account. You can use other cloud-based providers such as Autodesk Drive, Microsoft OneDrive, Google Drive, Dropbox, and Box. To access these, click on the *red* AutoCAD icon at the top left of the **AutoCAD Web** screen to re-locate where you want to save your drawing. Make sure to do this *after* you have saved your drawing. You can also access your saved drawing in the **AutoCAD Web and Mobile** folders through the AutoCAD desktop application, using the icons on the QAT.

1. AutoCAD Web uses a similar interface as the AutoCAD desktop application, so zoom into the top-left office cubicle using your mouse and select the chair by clicking on it. It will highlight and display the insertion grip, as shown in *Figure 13.9*.

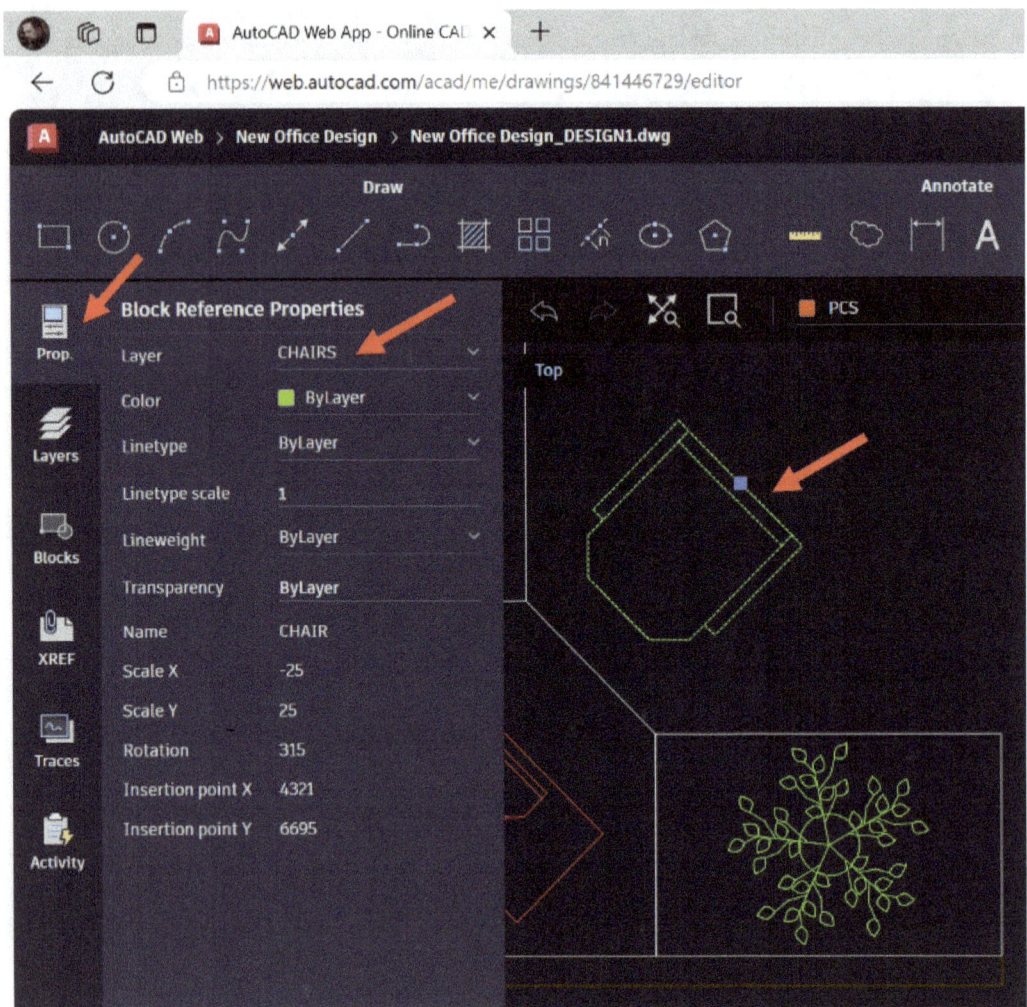

Figure 13.9: The selected chair in AutoCAD Web

The default tab on the left in AutoCAD Web is the **Properties** tab (**Prop.**). With that tab selected, and the chair block selected, you can see that the chair is on the **CHAIRS** layer, and the **Properties** tab is displaying **Block Reference Properties** due to a block being selected at the time

2. Click on the **Layer** dropdown and select the **Furniture** layer, as shown in *Figure 13.10*. Note that there is another **Layer** dropdown above the drawing area (also arrowed). That can be used to set the current layer, which is **PCS** in this case. Make sure you use the **Layer** dropdown in the **Properties** tab.

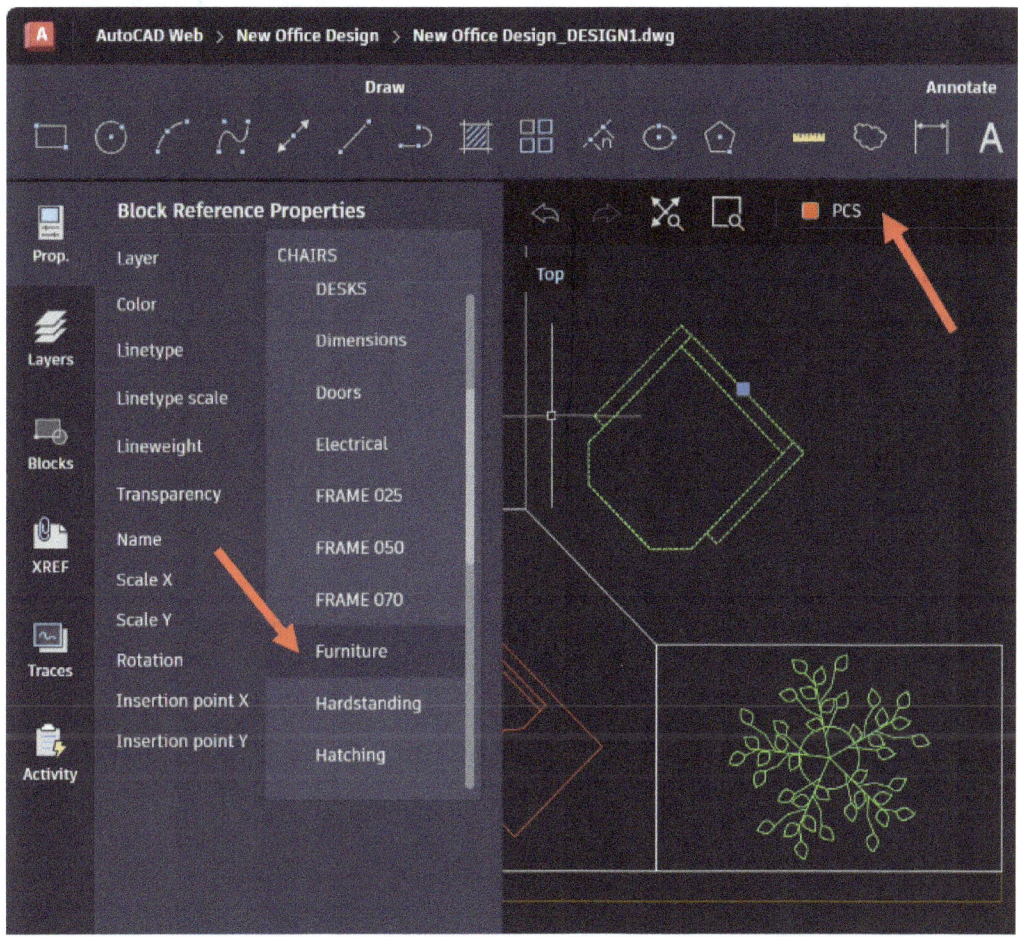

Figure 13.10: The Layer dropdown in the Properties tab

When you change the chair's layer to **Furniture**, you will see that the color of the chair block does *not* change. This is due to the block setting. You can check this by deselecting the block by pressing the *Esc* key a couple of times and then clicking on the chair again.

3. Save the drawing by clicking on **Save** (top right), as shown in *Figure 13.11*. You can also access **Save As** by clicking on the drop-down arrow next to the **Save** button. There will be a slight pause as the drawing is saved.

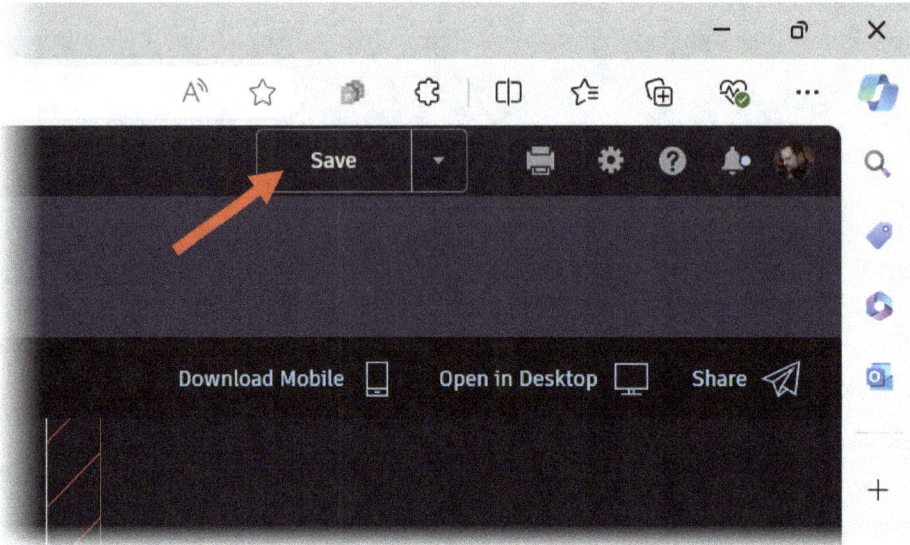

Figure 13.11: The Save button in AutoCAD Web

You have now saved, edited, and relocated your shared drawing in AutoCAD Web, as per the permissions granted when it was originally shared from the AutoCAD desktop application.

4. If you were to return to the AutoCAD desktop application and click on the **Open from Web & Mobile** (*OPENFROMWEBMOBILE*) icon (see *Figure 13.12*) on the QAT, you can open the saved shared drawing from its new location.

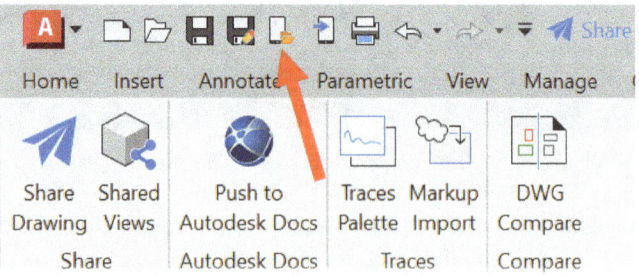

Figure 13.12: The Open from Web & Mobile icon on the QAT

5. In the **Open from AutoCAD Web & Mobile** dialog box, select the recently created `New Office Design` folder and click on **Open**, as shown in *Figure 13.13*.

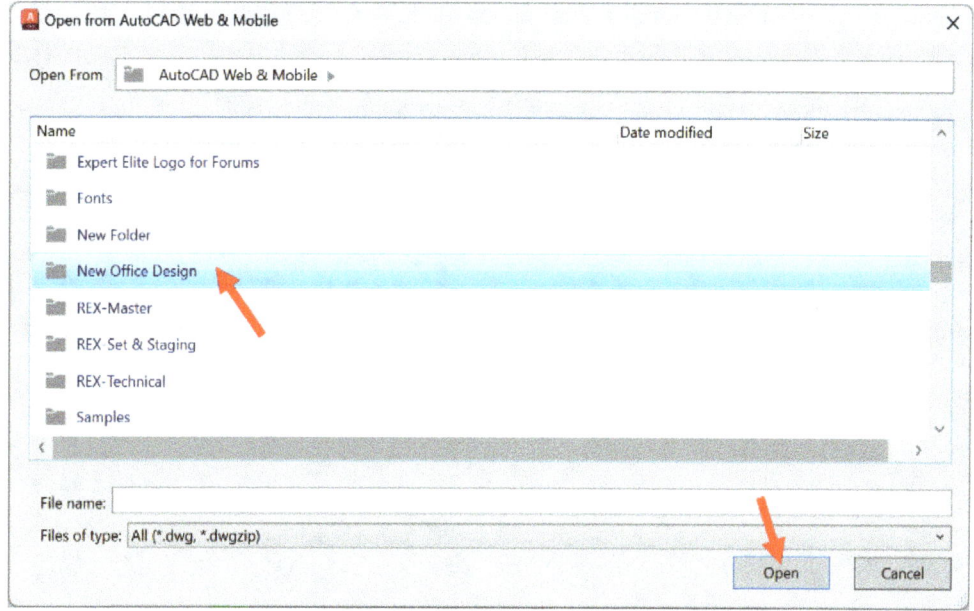

Figure 13.13: The Open from AutoCAD Web & Mobile dialog box

6. Once in the `New Office Design` folder, you will see your new drawing file, as shown in *Figure 13.14*.

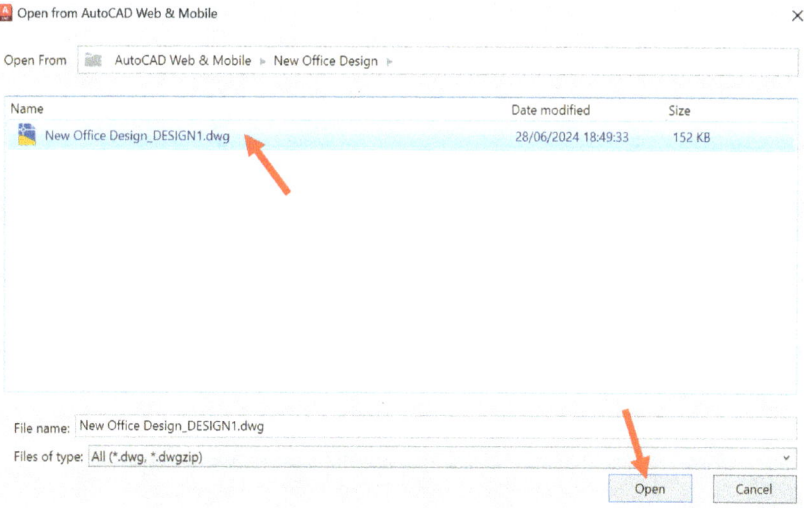

Figure 13.14: The new drawing in the New Office Design folder

7. Select the drawing file and click on **Open**. The drawing will open in the AutoCAD desktop application.
8. Zoom into the chair in the top-left office, as you did in AutoCAD Web.
9. Select the chair and check the **Layers** panel on the **Home** tab on the ribbon.
10. You will see that the chair is on the **Furniture** layer as saved when edited in AutoCAD Web, as shown in *Figure 13.15*.

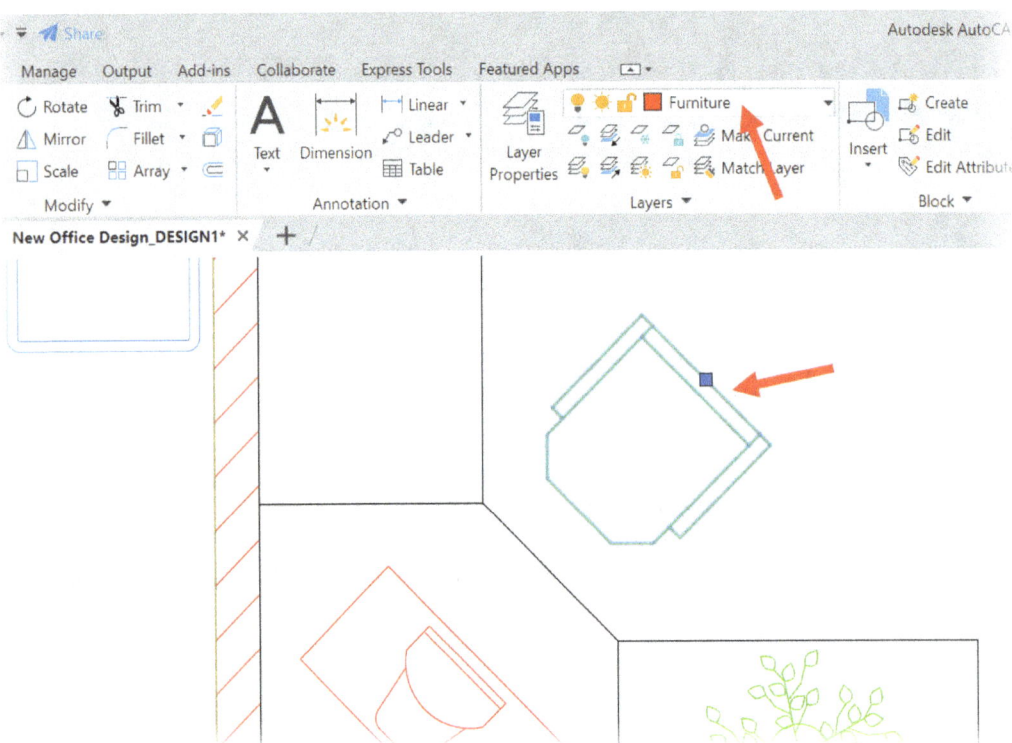

Figure 13.15: The selected chair in the Autodesk desktop application

AutoCAD for Mac

You can also share drawings using the same workflow in AutoCAD for Mac using the **Share Drawing (SHARE)** tool.

You can now share a drawing using AutoCAD's **Share Drawing** (**SHARE**) tool and then utilize AutoCAD Web to make edits and changes. In the next section, you will learn how to use the **Shared Views** palette to share views from your drawings.

Using the Shared Views palette

In the first section of this chapter, you learned how to share your drawings using the **Share Drawing** (*SHARE*) tool. There is also another way to share your views of your drawings using the **Shared Views** palette.

Sharing views is an alternative method of collaboration with your AutoCAD drawings using the browser-based Autodesk Viewer. You can find the viewer at any time at `https://viewer.autodesk.com`. The Autodesk Viewer is non-AutoCAD specific and can view many file formats, including the AutoCAD DWG file format. It is incredibly useful when working on projects that use multi-platform file formats, allowing non-application users to view and mark up files and comment on designs.

Let's go back to the `New Office Design_FINISHED.dwg` file. You will use this file for the next two sections of the chapter. Also, ensure you are signed in to your Autodesk account in AutoCAD and the Autodesk Viewer (you will sign in to the Autodesk Viewer later).

You now need to work through the following steps to start collaborating using the **Shared Views** palette:

1. With the drawing file open in the **Model** tab, go to the **Collaborate** tab on the ribbon. You will find the **Shared Views** icon on the **Share** ribbon panel, as shown in *Figure 13.16*.

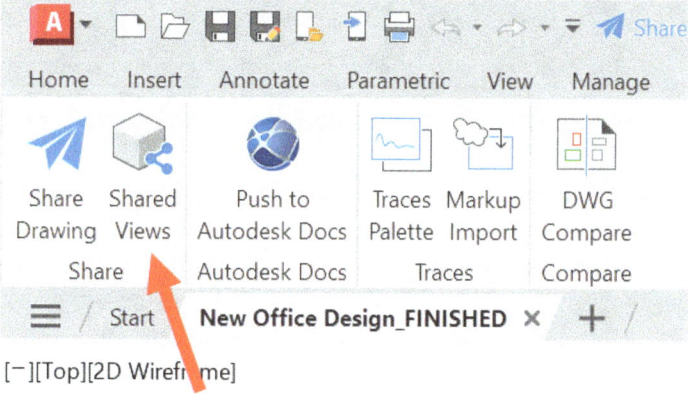

Figure 13.16: The Shared Views icon on the Share ribbon panel

2. Upon clicking on the **Shared Views** icon, the **Shared Views** palette will appear, as shown in *Figure 13.17*.

   Note that if you are not signed in to your Autodesk account at this point, you will be prompted to sign in. Usually, this won't be required, as most newer versions of AutoCAD are subscription-based, and you will be signed in already.

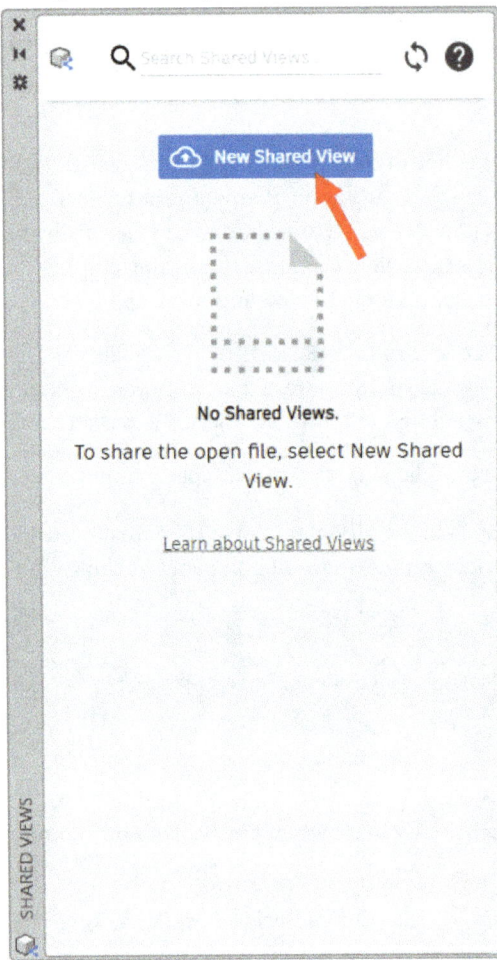

Figure 13.17: The Shared Views palette

3. Upon opening, no shared views will be displayed in the palette, so click the **New Shared View** button, as shown in *Figure 13.17*.

4. The **Share View** dialog box will appear, as shown in *Figure 13.18*.

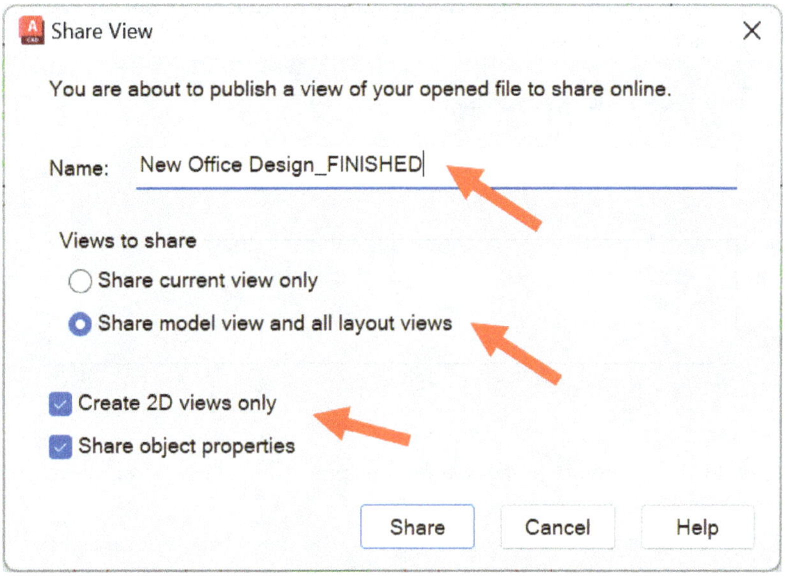

Figure 13.18: The Share View dialog box

5. The name of your drawing will be displayed in the **Name** field. You may want to change this filename to show that this is a shared drawing file, so change it to `New Office Design_SHARED`.

6. During the design development, you may only need to share the current view in the drawing (such as the **Model** tab), so in that case, you would select **Share current view only**. In this case, make sure you select **Share model view and all layout views** to see how it affects the views in the Autodesk Viewer.

7. The drawing being shared is 2D, so make sure **Create 2D views only** is selected. If working in a 3D model, this would *not* be selected.

8. Selecting **Sharing object properties** is useful, as it allows collaborators to see which layers are being used, which could be needed for standards checking. It can be turned off if not required.

9. Once your settings are ready, click on the **Share** button.

10. You will be prompted with a message that background processing of the shared view is about to start, as in *Figure 13.19*. Click on **Proceed**. Note that you can check the **Do not show me this message again** box to bypass this next time if required.

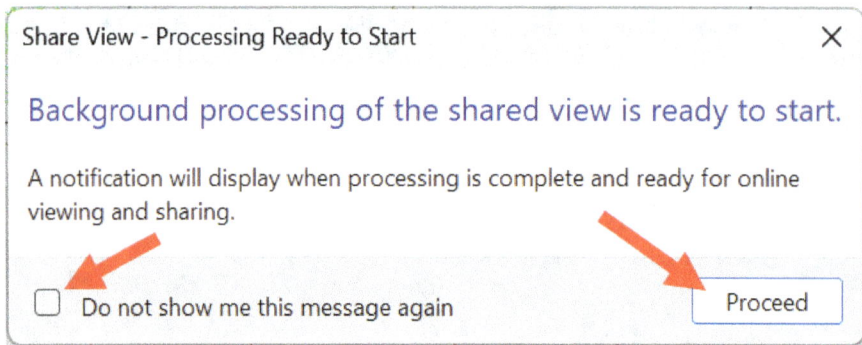

Figure 13.19: The prompt to start background processing of the shared view(s)

11. After clicking on **Proceed**, a new icon appears on the status bar (bottom right), showing the processing progress, as shown in *Figure 13.20*. This may take a few moments, depending on internet/cloud bandwidth and speeds.

Figure 13.20: The background processing icon on the status bar

12. A prompt appears once the shared view has been processed, as shown in *Figure 13.21*. Click on the **View in Browser** link to open the shared view in the Autodesk Viewer in your default browser.

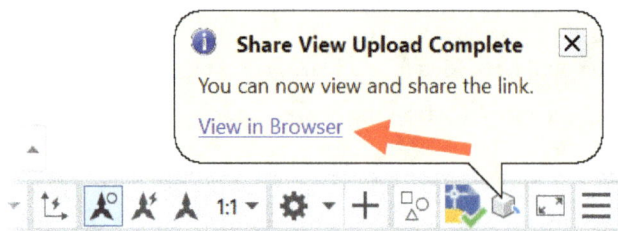

Figure 13.21: The prompt confirming background processing is complete

13. You have now opened your shared view drawing in the Autodesk Viewer. Note the file's name in the viewer, as shown in *Figure 13.22*. It is now `New Office Design_SHARED.collaboration`. Also, ensure you have signed in using your Autodesk account in the viewer to enable the full Autodesk Viewer functionality.

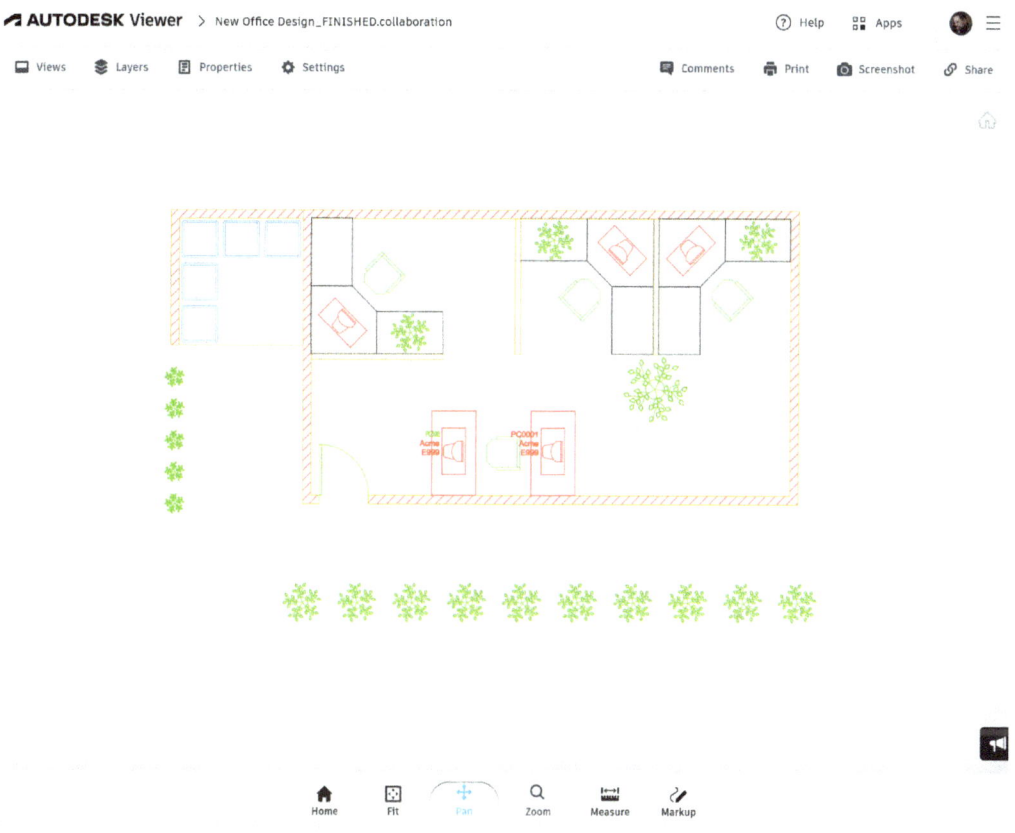

Figure 13.22: The shared view drawing displayed in the Autodesk Viewer

At this point, stay in the Autodesk Viewer, so that you can learn how to use the viewer functionality to collaborate with your newly shared drawing file. The next section will show you how to do that.

> **AutoCAD for Mac**
>
> You can share drawings using **Shared Views**, following the same workflow in AutoCAD for Mac.

Working with shared views in the Autodesk Viewer

In the previous section, you learned how to share your design using the **Shared Views** palette in AutoCAD. You are now in Autodesk Viewer, signed in with your Autodesk account, and ready to utilize some of the collaboration tools in the viewer.

As you are signed in through your Autodesk account, you will add some markup content in the viewer, which will then be reflected in the **Shared Views** palette in the AutoCAD desktop application. This will provide feedback on collaboration, similar to commenting on the shared design.

The following workflow will take you through adding the markup content:

1. While staying in Autodesk Viewer and ensuring you are signed in through your account, make sure you select the **Views** menu at the top left of the screen and check that you are in **Model | 2D View**, as shown in *Figure 13.23*.

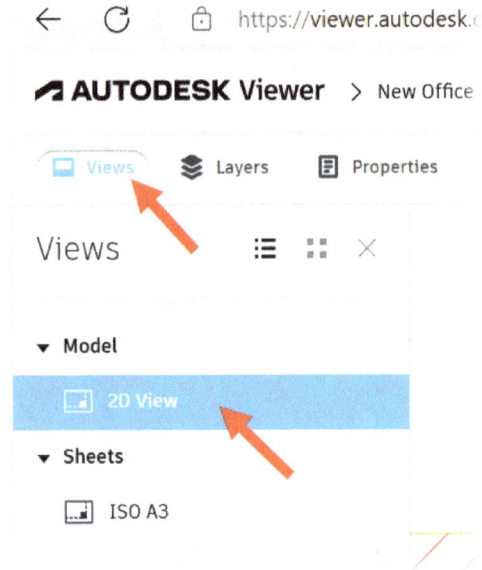

Figure 13.23: The Views menu and Model/2D View

2. Click on the **Markup** icon at the bottom of the screen, as shown in *Figure 13.24*.

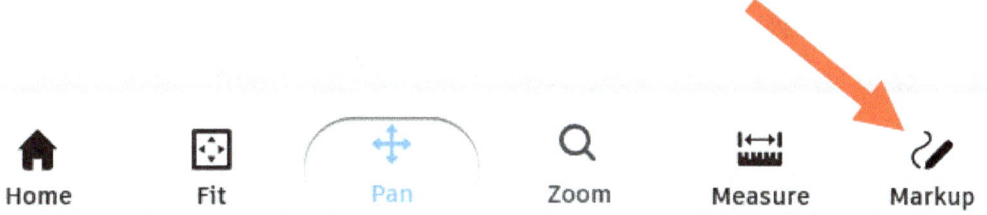

Figure 13.24: The Markup icon in the Autodesk Viewer

3. The **Markup** menu is now displayed, as shown in *Figure 13.25*.

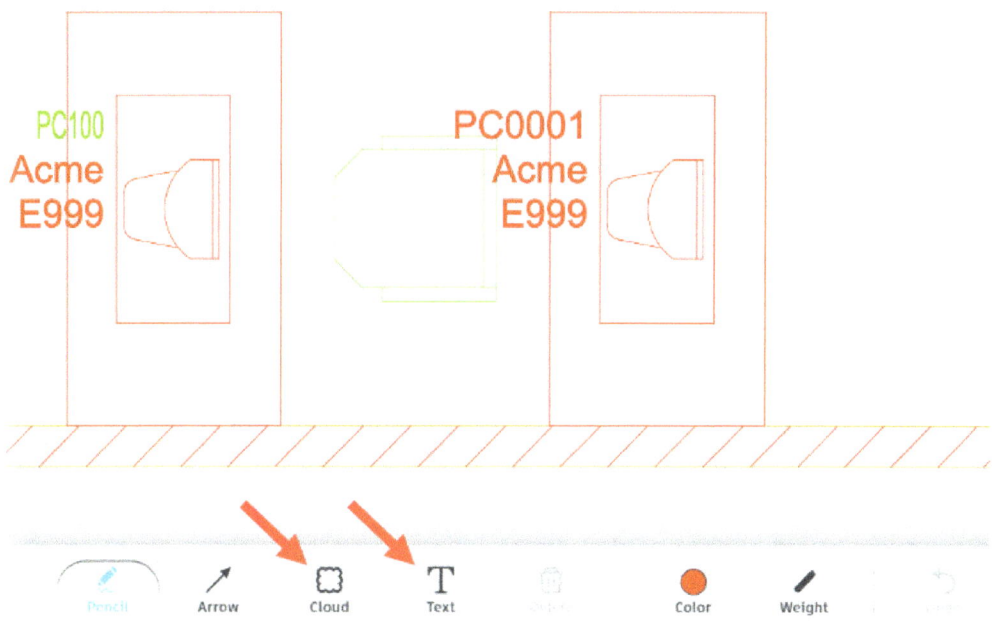

Figure 13.25: The Markup menu in the Autodesk Viewer

4. You can add markups to the shared view using the arrowed markup tools in the preceding figure, **Cloud** and **Text**. Add a cloud and text using these tools, as shown in *Figure 13.26*. Just drag and click to place the cloud and click and type to place the text using the default settings in the viewer. While working in the Autodesk Viewer, you will find the workflow to do this remarkably similar to working in AutoCAD.

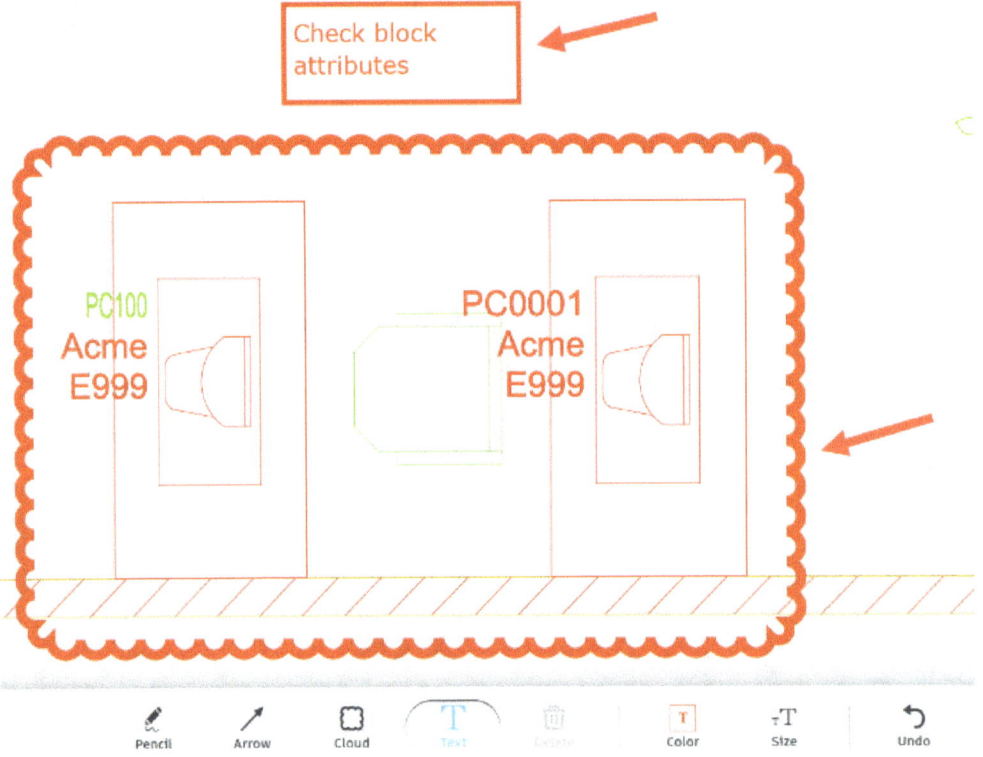

Figure 13.26: Markups added in the Autodesk Viewer

5. To save your markups, click on **Save** in the top-right corner of the viewer.
6. You will now see that the markups have been added to the **Comments** panel, which automatically appears on the right-hand side of the viewer screen, as shown in *Figure 13.27*. Note that there is a preview thumbnail of the markups and a URL to share the markups/comments. There is also a **Resolve** checkbox to check when the markups have been resolved. You can also use the filter called **Show Resolved** to view resolved comments at the top of the **Comments** panel.

Working with shared views in the Autodesk Viewer 343

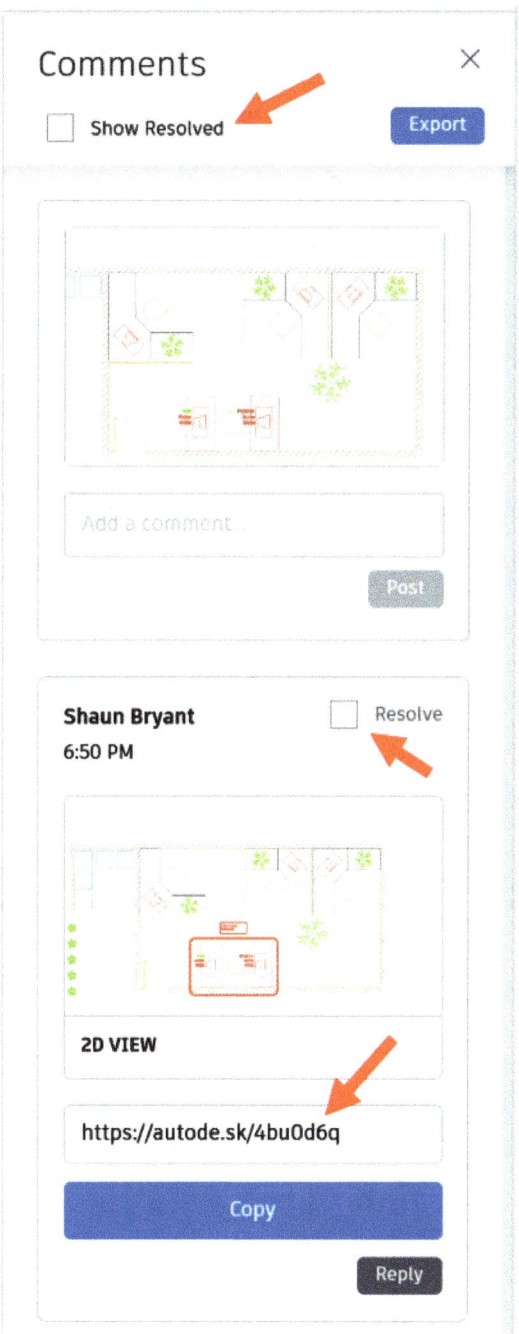

Figure 13.27: The Comments panel with markups shown

The markups and/or comments added are saved back to connect to the drawing file when you save the shared view(s) in the Autodesk Viewer.

If you now return to AutoCAD and the drawing and click on the **Refresh** icon in the **Shared Views** palette (top right, as shown in *Figure 13.28*), you will see the shared view, the date it was created, and its expiry period. All shared views last for 30 days. You will also see that it has one comment.

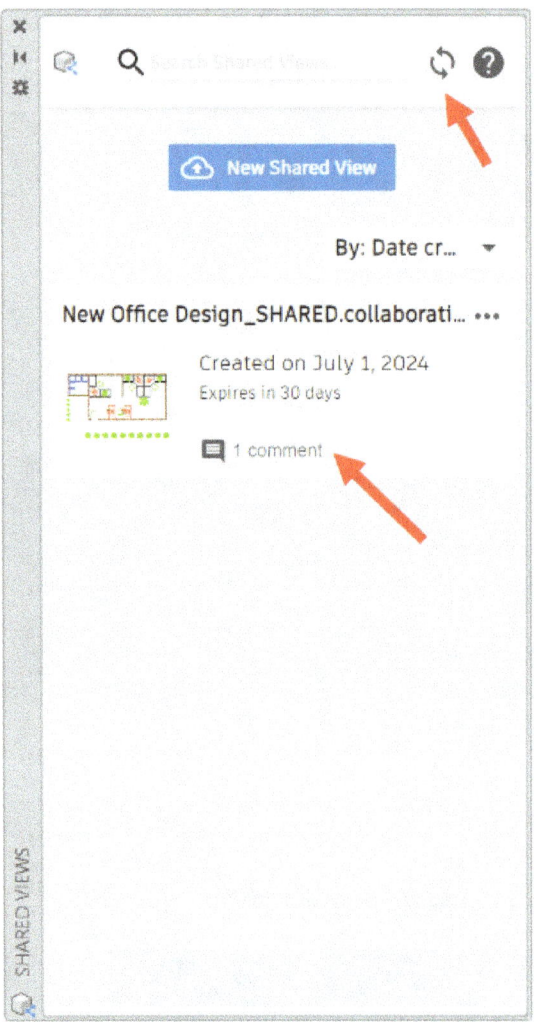

Figure 13.28: The Shared Views palette with the shared view displayed

Working with shared views in the Autodesk Viewer | 345

7. Click on the comment, and the palette will expand the comment to show the markup detail you created in Autodesk Viewer in a thumbnail image, as shown in *Figure 13.29*.

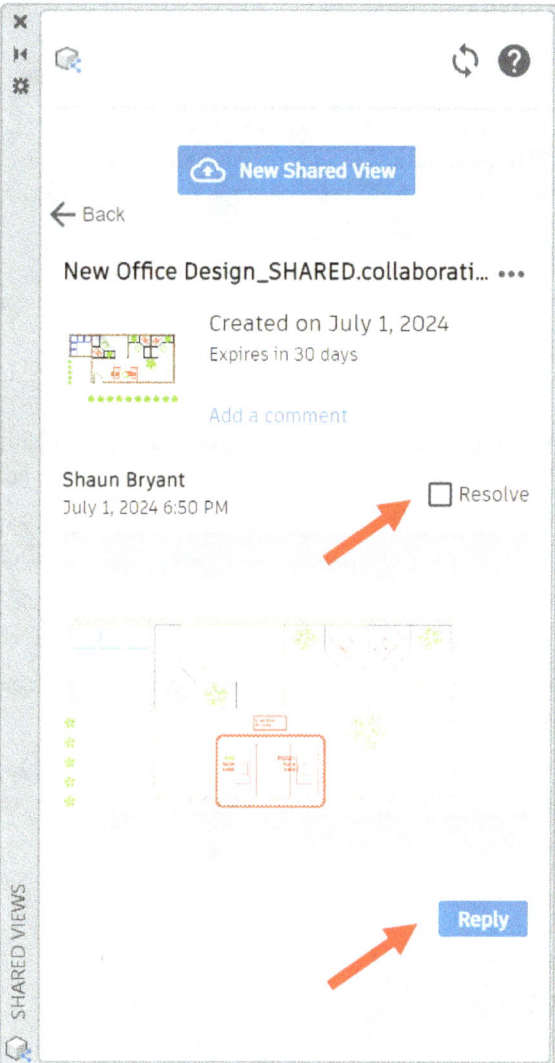

Figure 13.29: The Shared Views palette with comments displayed

8. You can now reply to the markups/comments in the **Shared Views** palette in AutoCAD, and these will then become available in the Autodesk Viewer collaboration file, thus allowing non-AutoCAD users to collaborate and provide input on the original design created in AutoCAD.

Sharing Your AutoCAD Drawings

> **AutoCAD for Mac**
>
> You can create shared views in AutoCAD for Mac using the same workflow and collaborate using the browser-based Autodesk Viewer.

You can now easily share drawings and views using the **Share Drawing** (*SHARE*) tool and the **Shared Views** palette. Using **Shared Views** and the Autodesk Viewer allows non-AutoCAD users to view and mark up shared drawings. The Autodesk Viewer provides a simple-to-use interface, with real-time marking up and commenting capabilities. These markups and comments can then be viewed and utilized in the AutoCAD desktop application.

Summary

In this chapter, you have learned how to quickly and efficiently collaborate on your AutoCAD designs with other Autodesk users with **Share Drawing** (*SHARE*) and AutoCAD Web. You have also learned how to collaborate and mark up your designs using the **Shared Views** palette and the Autodesk Viewer, which is browser-based, thus providing an easy way of sharing designs with non-AutoCAD users.

You can use either method to save valuable time when collaborating on your AutoCAD drawings and designs. You can learn more about **Shared Views** here on the Autodesk website: `https://help.autodesk.com/view/ACD/2023/ENU/?guid=GUID-459FD977-18F2-46C4-B238-B91E6DC27536`.

You can learn more about AutoCAD Web (part of your AutoCAD subscription package) at `https://web.autocad.com`.

In this chapter, you have learned how to use the **Share Drawing** tool quickly and efficiently when working with the **Share Drawing** (*SHARE*) command, sharing a DWG file to AutoCAD Web for easy collaboration in the browser-based version of AutoCAD.

You have also experienced different types of shared drawings, understanding how drawings can be viewed and revised in the AutoCAD Web application using the **Edit and save a copy** option. You also learned how to save and edit a new file in AutoCAD Web.

You utilized the **Shared Views** palette to create a collaboration file for use in the Autodesk Viewer and learned how to work with views/drawings by adding markups/comments in the Autodesk Viewer, and how to work with them in the AutoCAD desktop application.

Collaboration using cloud-based and browser-based tools such as AutoCAD Web and the Autodesk Viewer allows quick, simple, and effective communication between project stakeholders and your CAD team. They are tools that will enable you to work smarter, not harder. In the next chapter, we will look at ways to compare drawings and external reference files (*XREFs*) using **DWG Compare** (*DWGCOMPARE*) and **XREF Compare** (*XREFCOMPARE*).

14
Comparing Drawings and External Reference Files

In the previous chapters, you have learned how to work with blocks, attributes, and dynamic blocks and share your drawings. You now need to consider how you might compare the drawings and **external references** (**Xrefs**) that contain those blocks and attributes. You might also need to compare drawings and Xrefs when sharing drawings. This chapter teaches you how to compare your AutoCAD drawing files and Xrefs using the *COMPARE* and *XREFCOMPARE* commands.

Comparing drawings and Xrefs is much easier and less time-consuming than it used to be. It used to be a manual, visual comparison, but those days are long gone. You can now use AutoCAD to compare drawing files and Xref drawing files. This technology also allows you to make a drawing file of the comparison and incorporate the compared objects into the relevant drawing. In this chapter, you will see how **DWG Compare** and **Xref Compare** can improve your AutoCAD drawing approval workflows, making them much quicker and allowing more efficient document preparation.

This chapter covers the following ways of working with the *COMPARE* and *XREFCOMPARE* commands:

- Comparing drawings with DWG Compare
- Working with drawing comparisons generated with DWG Compare
- Comparing drawings with Xref Compare
- Working with reference file comparisons generated with Xref Compare

Exercise files

For this chapter, you must use the `New Office Layout_REV1.dwg` and `New Office Layout_REV2.dwg` exercise files. Open both files in the same AutoCAD session and ensure both display the office floor plan in the **Model** tab. You will notice subtle differences between the two drawings.

In the later sections of the chapter, when you work with and compare Xref files, you will be using the `New Office Layout_WITH XREF.dwg` file.

Comparing drawings with DWG Compare

The **DWG Compare** (*COMPARE*) tool is located in two locations: on the **Collaborate** tab on the ribbon in the **Compare** panel as displayed in *Figure 14.1*.

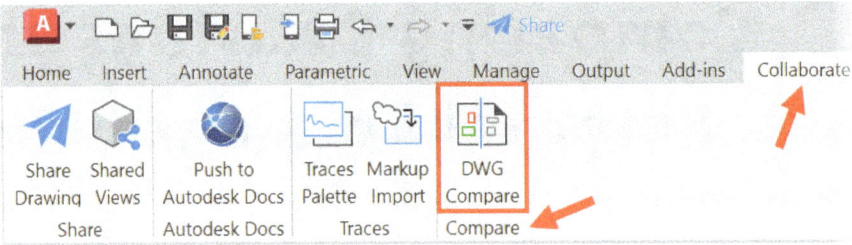

Figure 14.1: The DWG Compare tool on the Collaborate ribbon tab

It is also located in the **Drawing Utilities** menu in the application menu, as shown in *Figure 14.2*

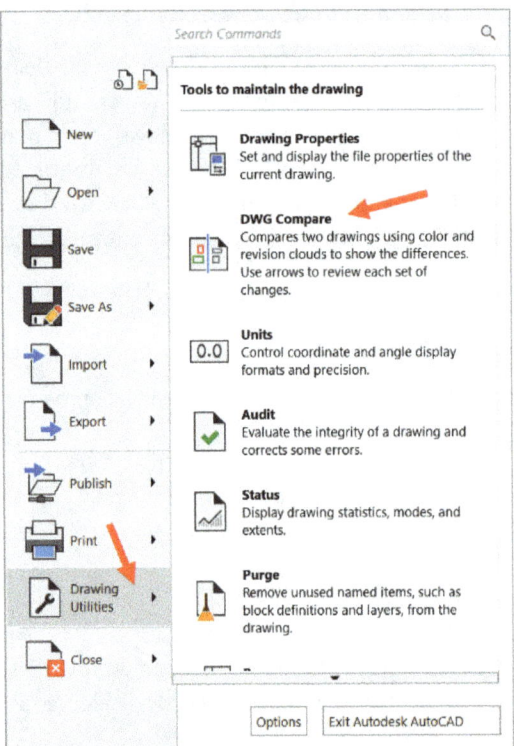

Figure 14.2: The DWG Compare tool in Drawing Utilities in the application menu

You can click on either of these icons to activate the *COMPARE* command, but as mentioned in the *Exercise files* section, you must have both exercise files open in the same AutoCAD session.

Let's start the exercise:

1. As shown in *Figure 14.3*, ensure the `New Office Layout_REV1.dwg` is current in the file tabs underneath the ribbon. It should be displayed in bold on the file tab. If it isn't bold, click on it to make it current.

Figure 14.3: The current drawing indicated in the file tab

2. As mentioned at the beginning of the section, start the **DWG Compare** (*COMPARE*) tool from either the ribbon or the application menu.
3. The **Select a drawing to compare** dialog box will appear, as shown in *Figure 14.4*. Select the `New Office Layout_REV2.dwg`. Once the file is selected, click on **Open** in the dialog box.

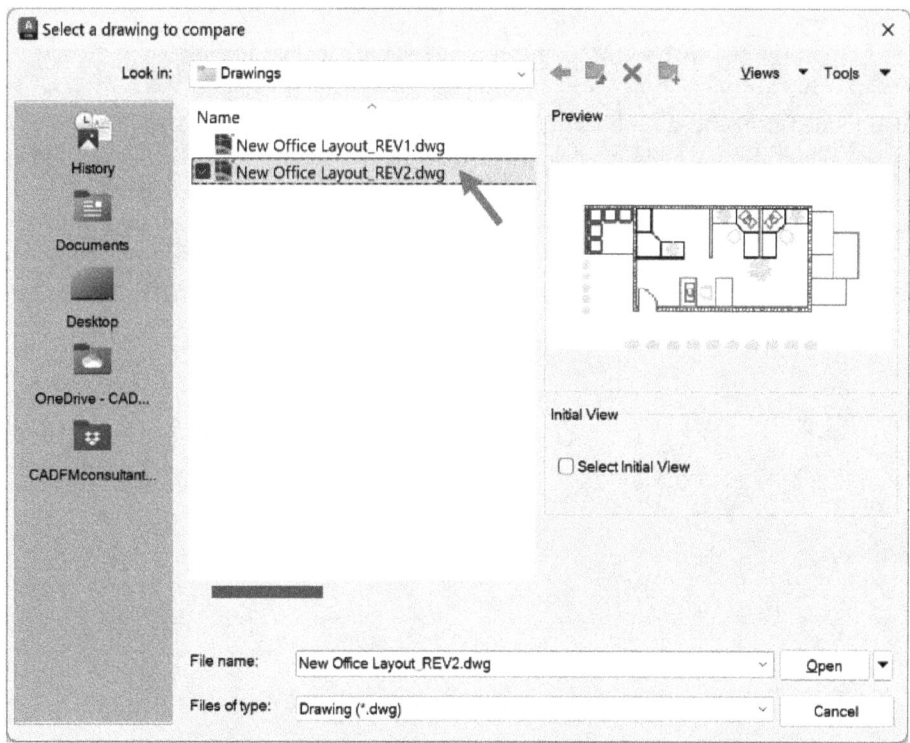

Figure 14.4: The Select a drawing to compare dialog box

4. The AutoCAD screen will change quite dramatically as you are taken into DWG Compare mode, with the **DWG Compare** toolbar at the top of the drawing area, as shown in *Figure 14.5*. The drawing looks greyed out, which is not the case. Anything grey (by default) is common to both compared drawings.

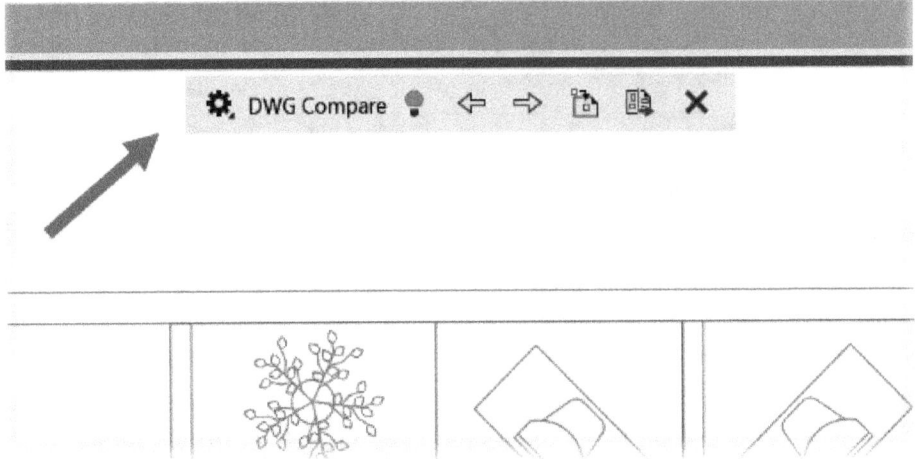

Figure 14.5: The DWG Compare mode with the toolbar arrowed

5. Click on the **Settings** icon (*gear wheel*) on the **DWG Compare** toolbar, as shown in *Figure 14.6*. You will notice that the highlight colors can be set there. Set the **Cloud Display** color to make the revision clouds stand out more. In this case, a dark blue cloud display color is selected as the background is white. The default cloud color is orange, which works well when using the default AutoCAD dark color theme in the AutoCAD Options. Colors are used in **DWG Compare** to make sure that the differences between drawings that are highlighted are organized and obvious.

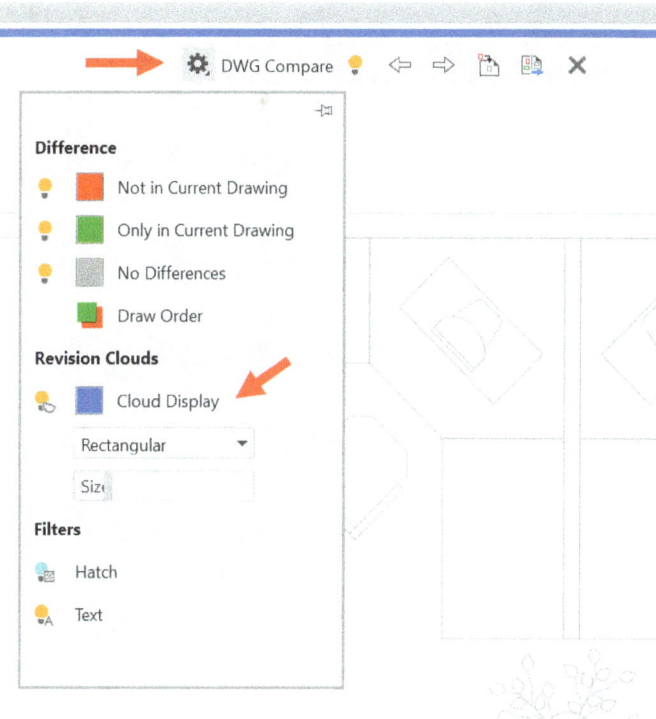

Figure 14.6: The DWG Compare Setting menu with Cloud Display arrowed

6. Now that the cloud color has been changed, you can make a clearer comparison between the two DWG files. Anything displaying a revision cloud shows a difference between the two drawing files. Objects shown in red are not in the current drawing, and anything shown in green is specific to the current drawing. *Figure 14.7* shows objects that are not in the current drawing.

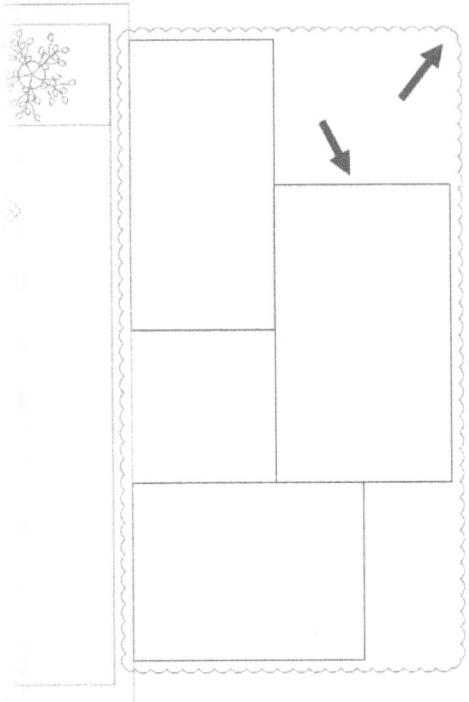

Figure 14.7: Clouded objects not in the current DWG file

While *Figure 14.8* shows objects specific to the current drawing.

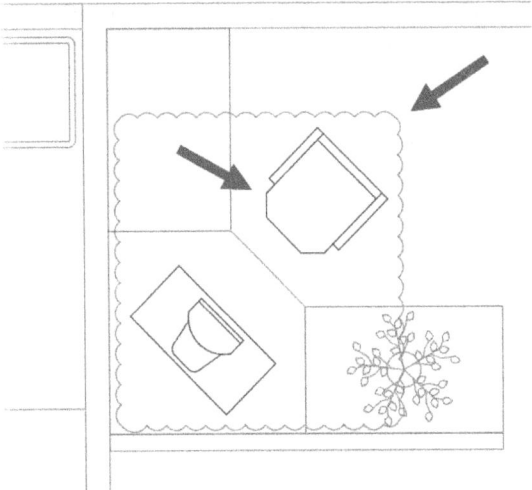

Figure 14.8: Clouded objects specific to the current DWG file

Using the arrows on the DWG Compare toolbar, you can toggle between the clouded differences between the two files. There are only two instances in this case, and each time you click on an arrow, **DWG Compare** will zoom into the extent of the clouded compared area. This is incredibly useful when navigating many clouded compared areas on a drawing.

You now know how to set up **DWG Compare** to compare two drawings and know how to interpret the results, including how to change colors in the DWG Compare settings.

Stay in the **DWG Compare** mode now, as you will need this functionality for the next section. Also, note that if you close down **DWG Compare** and have to restart it again, you will need to change the color settings.

In the next section, you will learn how to add compared results to the current drawing and how to save a comparison drawing as a separate DWG file.

Working with drawing comparisons generated with DWG Compare

In the previous section, you compared two DWG files using **DWG Compare** and noted the comparison results. In this section, you will add the drawing elements from the comparison, which are not in the current drawing, to the current drawing. You will also save a separate comparison DWG file. Follow these steps to begin the exercise:

1. While staying in DWG Compare mode, you can select the **Import Objects** icon on the **DWG Compare** toolbar, as shown in *Figure 14.9*.

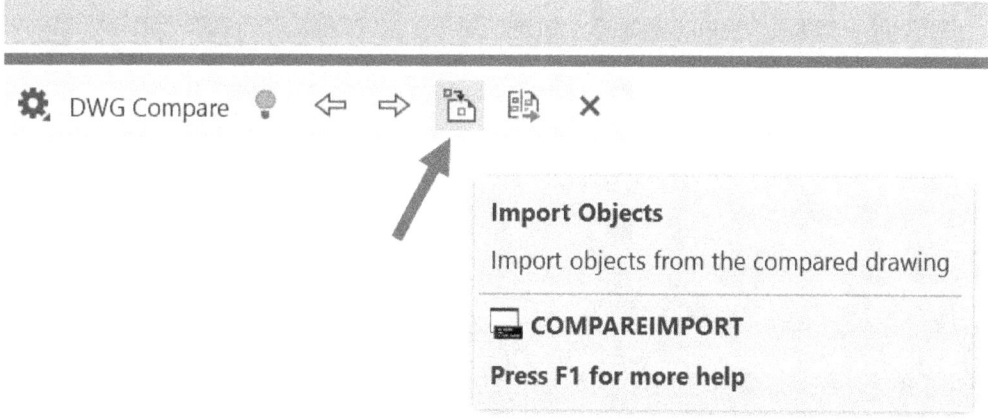

Figure 14.9: The Import Objects icon on the DWG Compare toolbar

2. After clicking on **Import Objects**, you will be prompted to select the compared objects you want to import into the current drawing, `New Office Layout_REV1.dwg`.

3. Select the objects, as shown in *Figure 14.10*.

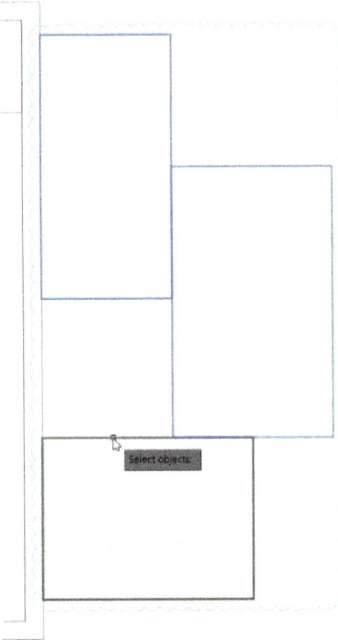

Figure 14.10: The selected compared objects

4. Press *Enter* to confirm the selection. The selected objects will go from *red* (not in the current drawing) to *grey*, indicating they are common to both compared drawings. This is shown in *Figure 14.11*.

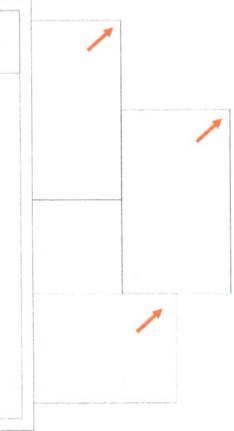

Figure 14.11: The selected compared objects now in the current drawing and common to both drawings (grey)

5. Save these changes in the New Office Layout_REV1.dwg file. You don't need to worry about the revision numbers (REV1 and REV2). They are simply there to distinguish between each separate compared drawing.

6. You now need to save a comparison DWG file. To do so, click on the **Export Snapshot** icon on the **DWG Compare** toolbar, as shown in *Figure 14.12*.

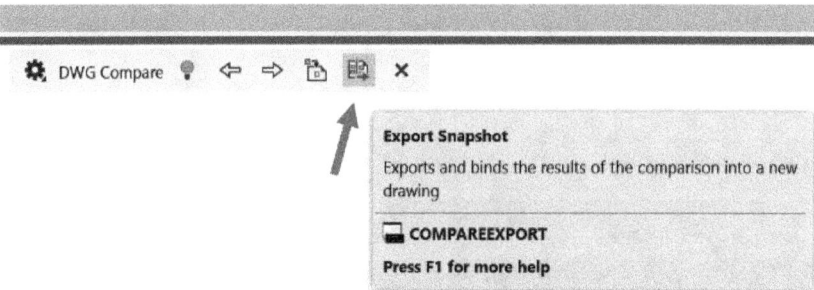

Figure 14.12: The Export Snapshot icon on the DWG Compare toolbar

7. You will be prompted to save your snapshot drawing in the **Save Drawing As** dialog box, as shown in *Figure 14.13*. The snapshot drawing will be named New Office Layout_COMPARISON.dwg. Save it in the same location as the two compared drawings.

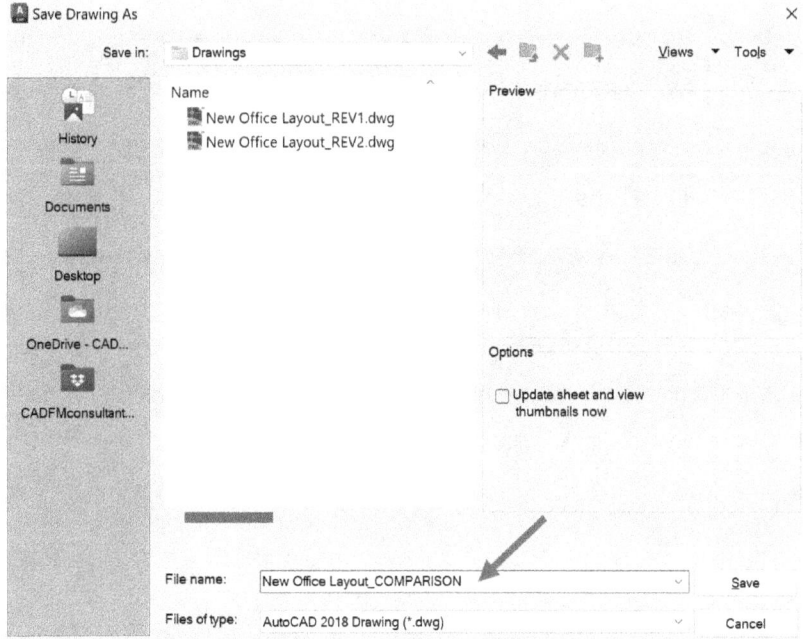

Figure 14.13: The Save Drawing As dialog box

8. You will see a prompt that lets you know that the comparison drawing is being processed in the background, as shown in *Figure 14.14*. Click on **Continue** to process the comparison snapshot drawing. Note that you can tick the box not to show this prompt again.

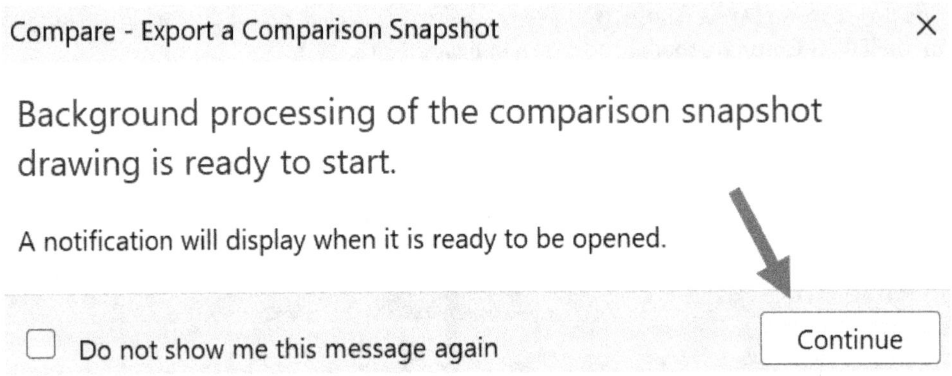

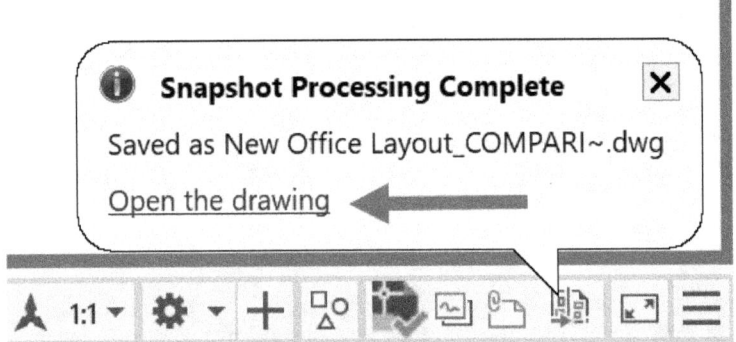

Figure 14.14: The prompt for background processing

9. After you click **Continue**, the drawing starts processing in the background, and a small icon displays on the status bar, indicating processing. Once the processing is complete, AutoCAD displays a notification in the bubble bottom-right of the status bar, as shown in *Figure 14.15*.

Figure 14.15: The notification bubble indicating that background processing is complete

10. Clicking on the **Open the drawing** link will open the comparison drawing in **DWG Compare Snapshot** mode, as shown in *Figure 14.16*.

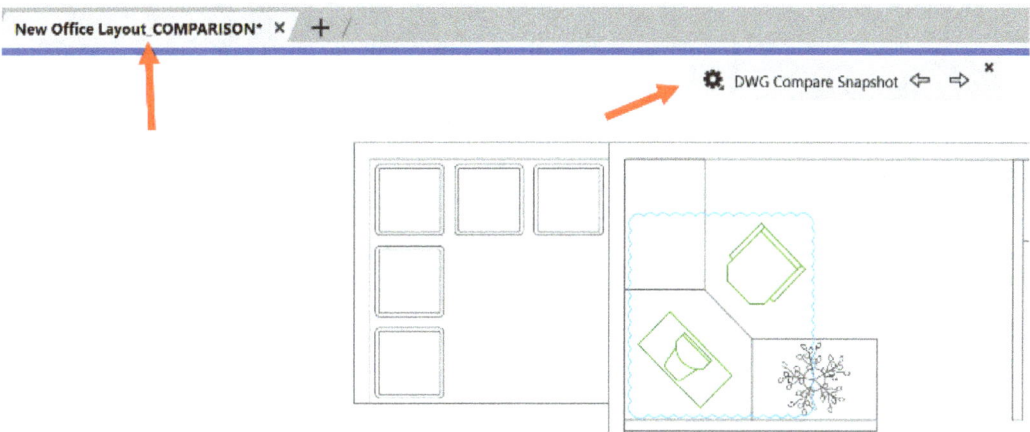

Figure 14.16: The saved comparison DWG file in DWG Compare Snapshot mode

DWG Compare Snapshot mode is similar to DWG Compare mode, but you are looking at the comparison drawing rather than the two previously compared drawings. You can still navigate between each comparison instance using the arrows on the DWG Compare Snapshot toolbar. Plus, the comparison snapshot drawing has been saved for future reference, which is great for creating an audit trail of changes, edits, and revisions to your drawings.

This brings this section to a close, and you have now learned how to utilize the DWG Compare tool in AutoCAD to compare DWG files and save a comparison DWG file for future reference.

In the next section, you will learn how to use the **Xref Compare** tool in AutoCAD to compare different iterations of XREFs attached to your AutoCAD drawings.

Comparing drawings with Xref Compare

This section will teach you how to use the Xref Compare tool. Like the DWG Compare tool, it provides a comparison interface, allowing you to view and work with differences between Xrefs attached to your host drawing. Xrefs are separate DWG files that are *paper-clipped* as a reference file to the current host drawing. Another AutoCAD user can work on an Xref DWG file, and the subsequent changes can be displayed on the Xref attached to the current host drawing.

You will use a different exercise file this time, so make sure you have the `New Office Layout_WITH XREF.dwg` file open in the **Model** tab. It should look like what's shown in *Figure 14.17*.

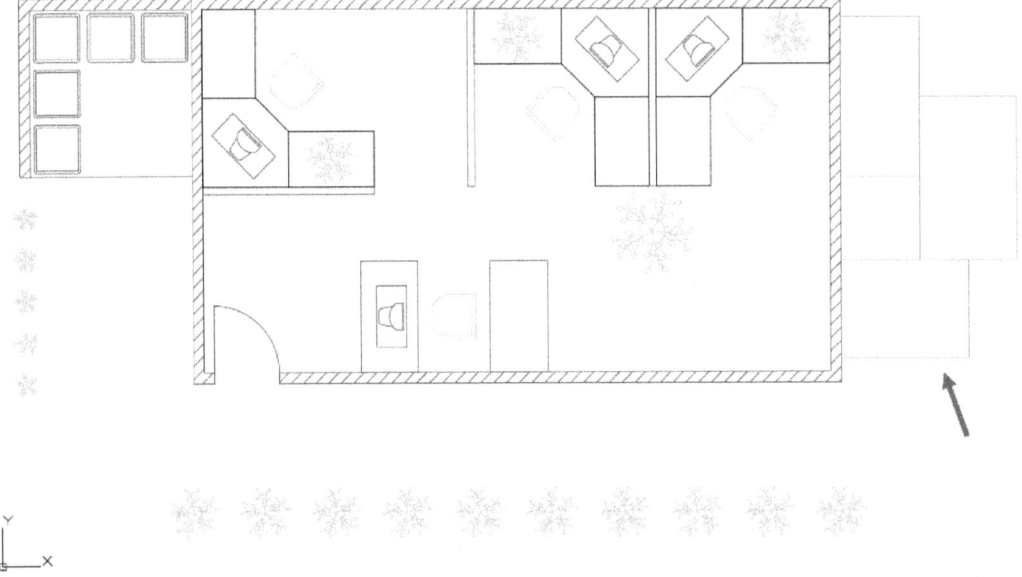

Figure 14.17: The New Office Layout_WITH XREF.dwg with the Landscaping_REV1.dwg file attached as an Xref (arrowed)

Note the arrowed landscaped area to the right of the building. That is an attached Xref, which is `Landscaping_REV1.dwg`. This Xref file must be in the same folder as the `New Office Layout_WITH XREF.dwg` file to be displayed as the attached Xref. Ensure you also have the alternative Xref file, `Landscaping_REV2.dwg`, in the same folder.

Now, let's begin the exercise by carrying out the following steps:

1. Go to the AutoCAD ribbon and click on the **Insert** tab. Click on the diagonal arrow button on the title bar of the **Reference** ribbon panel, as shown in *Figure 14.18*.

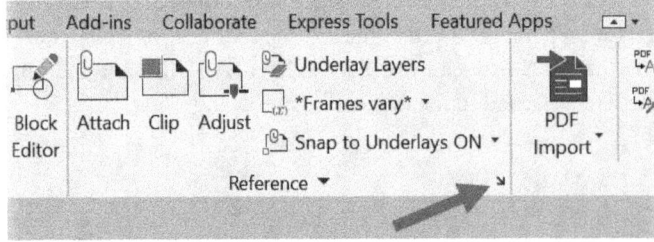

Figure 14.18: The diagonal arrow on the Reference panel on the Insert ribbon tab

2. The **EXTERNAL REFERENCES** palette will open, and you can see the attached Landscaping_REV1.dwg Xref on the palette, as arrowed in *Figure 14.19*. The Xref is also arrowed in the drawing for clarity.

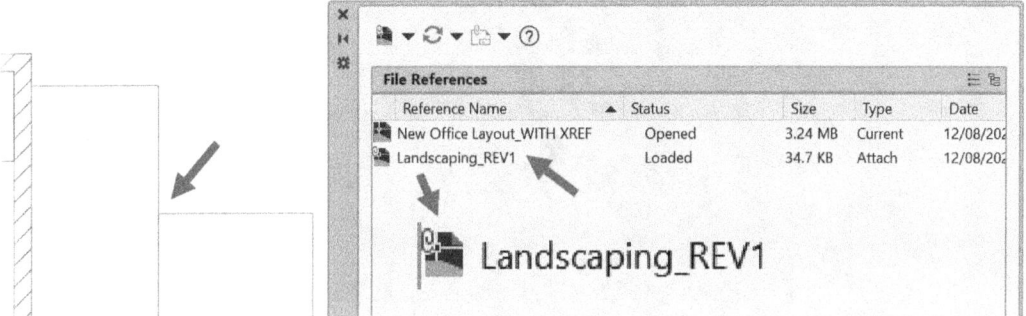

Figure 14.19: The EXTERNAL REFERENCES palette with the current Xref arrowed and the Xref filename enlarged

3. The host drawing, New Office Layout_WITH XREF.dwg, can also be seen in the palette. It will always be at the top of the list as the host drawing. This is the default setting in AutoCAD.

> **Tips and tricks #34**
>
> Looking closely at the attached Xref file in the **EXTERNAL REFERENCES** palette, as shown in *Figure 14.19*, you will see a *paper clip* symbol on the blue and yellow DWG icon to the left of the filename. This indicates an attached Xref file. The host DWG file (at the top of the list on the palette) does not have the paper clip symbol, indicating it is the host drawing file.

4. Select the `Landscaping_REV1.dwg` file in the **EXTERNAL REFERENCES** palette. It will be highlighted in blue on the palette and in the host drawing, as shown in *Figure 14.20*.

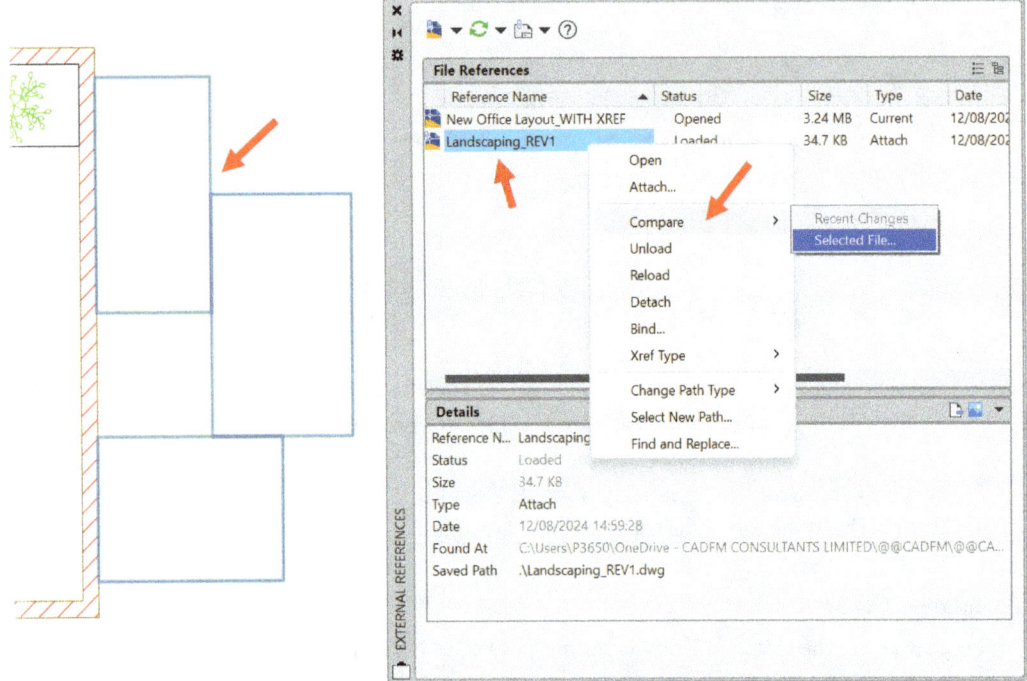

Figure 14.20: The selected Xref file in the drawing and on the palette

5. As also shown in *Figure 14.20*, right-click on the selected Xref file. The shortcut menu will appear. Select **Compare**, followed by **Selected File…**.

6. A dialog box will appear, allowing you to select another external reference file, Landscaping_REV2.dwg, from the folder. This exercise file should also be in the same folder as the host drawing and the current attached Xref, Landscaping_REV1.dwg. You will see all these files in the same folder in *Figure 14.21*.

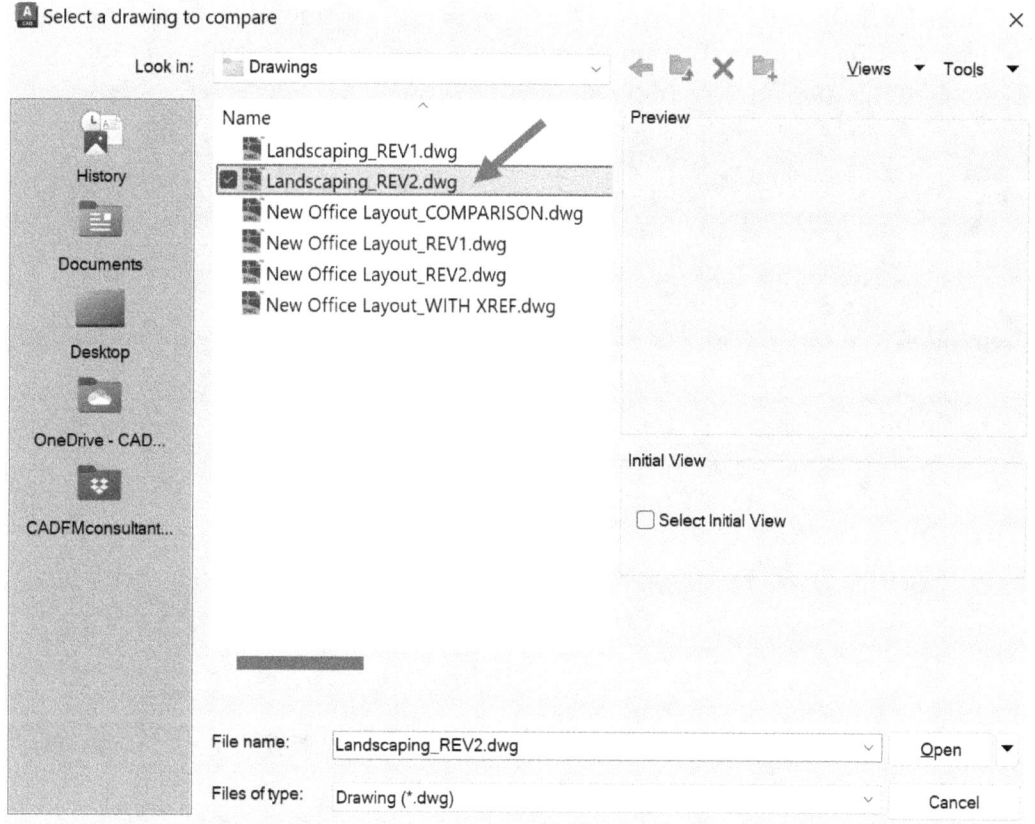

Figure 14.21: The dialog box, with the external reference (Xref) file to be compared (arrowed)

7. Double-click the Landscaping_REV2.dwg file to compare it to the attached Landscaping_REV1.dwg Xref file. You can also select it from the list and click on **Open**.

   You will now see that you are in a similar interface mode as **DWG Compare** in previous sections. This time, you are in **Xref Compare**, comparing an attached Xref file (Landscaping_REV1) to another file that might be used as an Xref (Landscaping_REV2). Note that the toolbar reads **Xref Compare**, not **DWG Compare**, this time around, as shown in *Figure 14.22*.

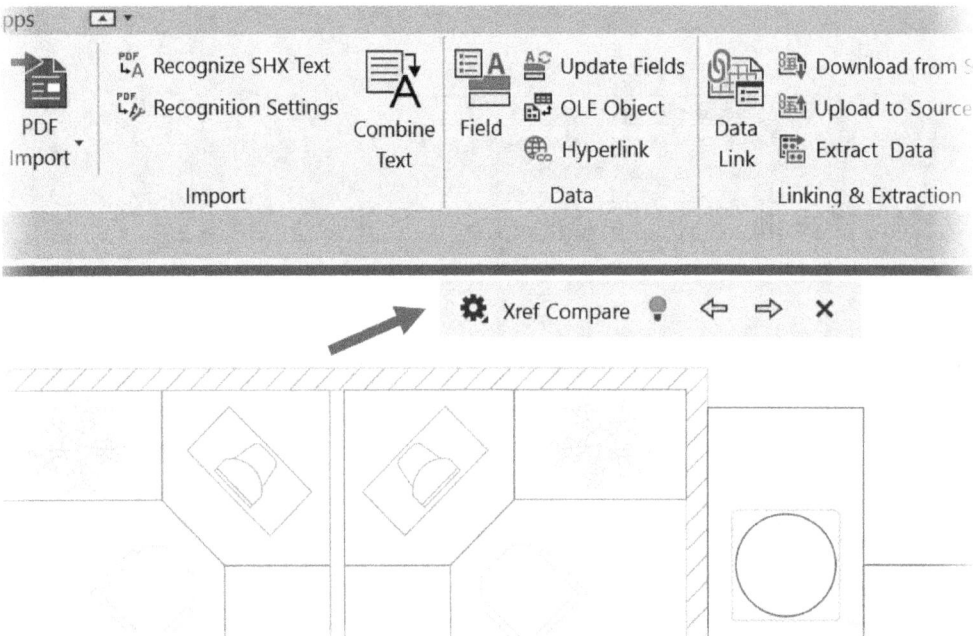

Figure 14.22: The Xref Compare toolbar in Xref Compare mode

8. Like DWG Compare, you can adjust the Xref Compare settings by clicking on the *gear wheel* icon on the toolbar, as shown in *Figure 14.22*.

9. Finally, click on the **Settings** icon and change the **Cloud Display** color in the **Revision Clouds** section of the **Settings** menu, as shown in *Figure 14.23*. This makes the clouds easier to see on a white background. If you are using a different background in AutoCAD, use a contrasting color for the clouds. I am using blue in this exercise.

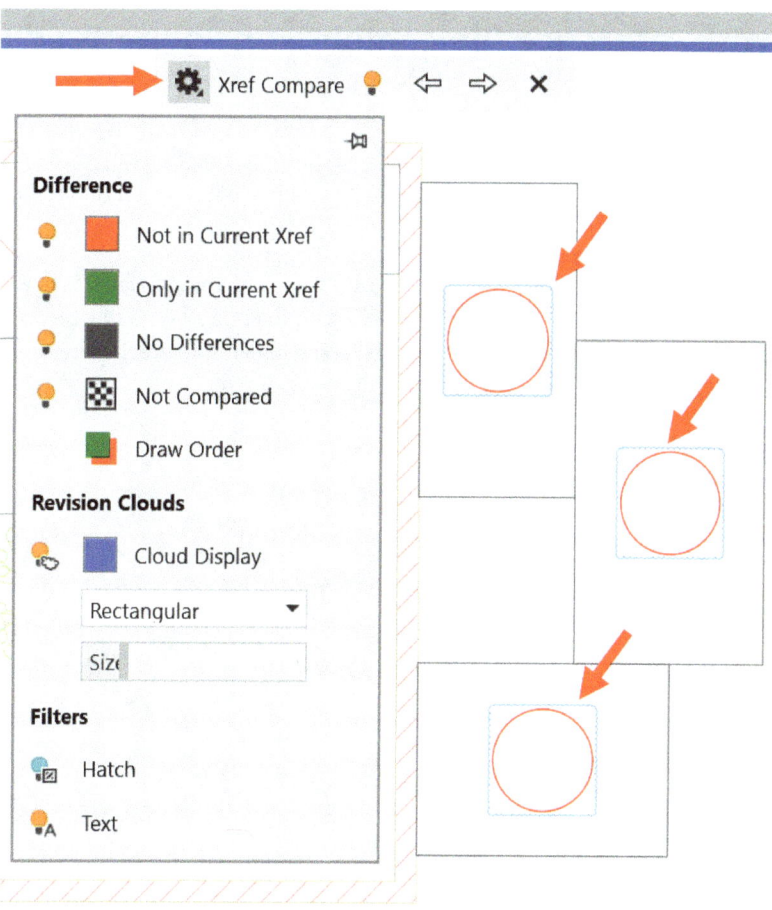

Figure 14.23: Changing the cloud color in the Settings menu

In this section, you have used the Xref Compare tool to compare Xref files, and you can see how similar it is to the DWG Compare tool. These tools are incredibly useful for this purpose and provide valuable time savings.

In the next section of this chapter, we will explore the functionality of the Xref Compare tool in more depth.

Please keep the `New Office Layout_WITH XREF.dwg` file open with the `Landscaping_REV1.dwg` file attached as an Xref and stay in Xref Compare mode.

Working with reference file comparisons generated with Xref Compare

In this section, you will explore the Xref Compare tool and utilize its functionality further. You cannot save a comparison DWG file with Xref Compare, but you do have other useful functions. Let's learn more about this feature:

- The Xref Compare interface is the same as the DWG Compare interface. When comparing the attached Xref file, `Landscaping_REV1.dwg`, to the other DWG file, `Landscaping_REV2.dwg`, the blue comparison clouds (as set in **Settings** in the previous section) highlight the differences between the two files, as shown in *Figure 14.24*.

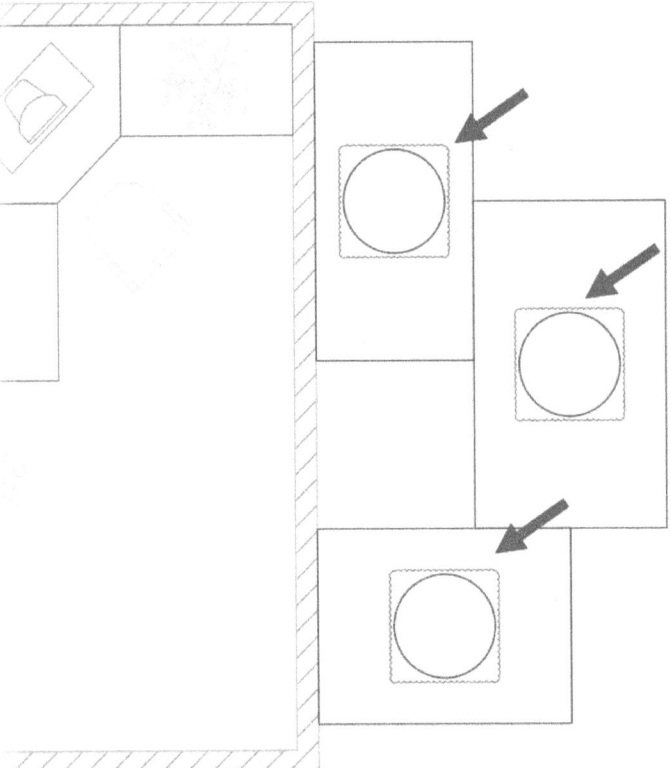

Figure 14.24: The compared differences highlighted by blue comparison clouds

- Like with DWG Compare, you can use the arrows on the Xref Compare toolbar to move between each comparison cloud, and AutoCAD will zoom to the extents of each cloud for easy viewing.

- As per the **Settings** on the toolbar, the red circles are marked so they are not in the current attached Xref file, Landscaping_REV1.dwg; they are in the compared file, Landscaping_REV2.dwg. This setting is shown in *Figure 14.25*. You can change any of these colors in the **Settings** menu.

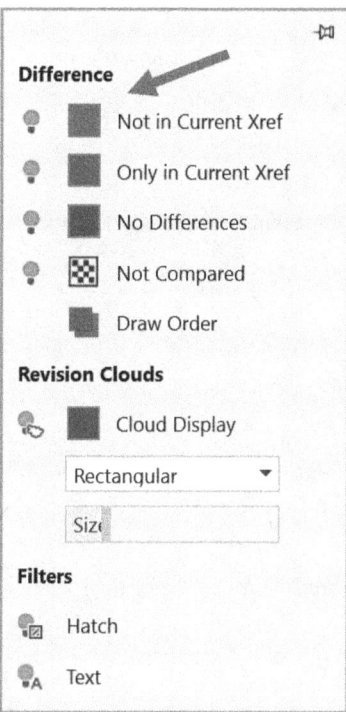

Figure 14.25: The Xref Compare Settings menu

- Another useful part of Xref Compare is that any **external reference file** (**Xref**) in comparison is noted as **In Compare** in the **EXTERNAL REFERENCES** palette, as shown in *Figure 14.26*. This is especially useful when you have more than one attached Xref file, and you must distinguish which ones are in the Xref comparison.

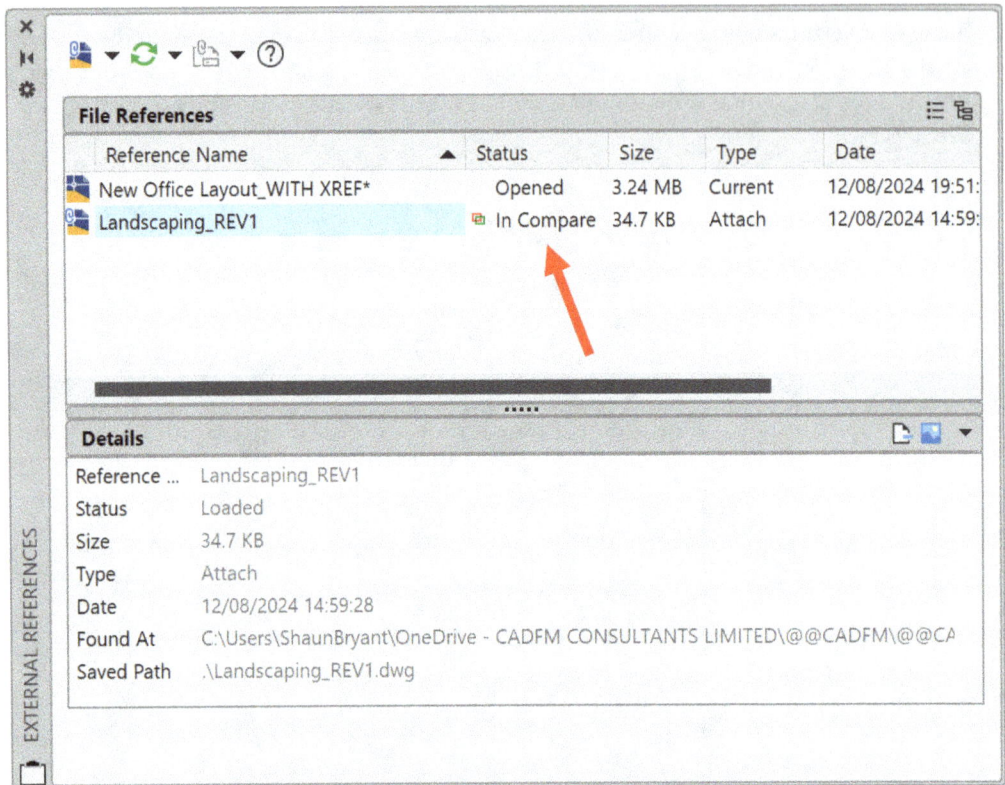

Figure 14.26: The External references palette showing the attached Xref file In Compare

- You can close the **Xref Compare** toolbar using the small **X** in the top-right corner of the toolbar. You can also do this in **DWG Compare**, coming out of the comparison mode, to be returned to the host DWG file.

The Xref Compare tool compares Xref files. While you cannot save a comparison DWG file, checking Xref files is still massively useful, especially when another CAD user might be working on an Xref file that might be attached to your host drawing.

You have now learned how to utilize the Xref Compare tool in AutoCAD, working quickly and effectively with the attached (and not attached) Xref files.

> **AutoCAD for Mac**
> DWG Compare and Xref Compare are also available on AutoCAD for Mac and are used in the same workflows using the MacOS interface.

Summary

You can now easily compare drawings and Xref files using the DWG Compare and Xref Compare tools. Consider using either method to save valuable time when comparing files and see edits, changes, and revisions in your AutoCAD drawings and designs.

You can learn more about DWG Compare (*COMPARE*) on the Autodesk website: `https://help.autodesk.com/view/ACD/2024/ENU/?guid=GUID-4B96F5FD-C9CF-4E2E-996E-E00914F8D99E`.

You can learn more about Xref Compare (*COMPARE*) on the Autodesk website: `https://help.autodesk.com/view/ACD/2023/ENU/?guid=GUID-84E4CED9-A52E-4F36-8D30-EB660DDC1086`.

In this chapter, you have gained knowledge about how to work with the DWG Compare (*DWGCOMPARE*) tool to compare different iterations/revisions of the same DWG file, and used DWG Compare (*DWGCOMPARE*) to save a DWG file that displays the comparison.

You have also learned about a similar workflow with the Xref Compare (*XREFCOMPARE*) tool to make comparisons between attached and non-attached Xref files, and how to spot the **In Compare** status in the **EXTERNAL REFERENCES** palette.

In the next chapter, we will examine in depth how to use **AutoCAD Web** effectively, developing drawings for easy collaboration via a browser and in the cloud.

Get This Book's PDF Version and Exclusive Extras

Scan the QR code (or go to `packtpub.com/unlock`). Search for this book by name, confirm the edition, and then follow the steps on the page.

Note: Keep your invoice handy. Purchases made directly from Packt don't require one.

15
Working with AutoCAD Web

In previous chapters, you learned how to work with attributes and dynamic blocks and share your drawings. You also learned to compare DWG files and **external reference files** (**Xrefs**). You are now at a point where you and your CAD team may need to collaborate on a drawing file to further your design. This is where you can utilize AutoCAD Web and the cloud.

AutoCAD is a subscription-based application. With that subscription comes the AutoCAD Web offering, which incorporates the AutoCAD web application and the AutoCAD mobile application. Both applications allow DWG file collaboration in the cloud, and the AutoCAD mobile application adds full mobility to your DWG files, utilizing the latest mobile devices, such as smartphones and tablets. This chapter will teach you how to use AutoCAD Web to provide a seamless, cloud-based collaboration experience, collaborate with DWG files that are based in the cloud, and check for current versions using the Drawing History tool. You will also learn how to save DWG files to the cloud and use them with AutoCAD Web and how to use the AutoCAD web and mobile applications.

Using the cloud for collaboration will not only save large amounts of time but also allow you to revise and change drawings on the fly in real time. In addition, it's a highly valuable DWG storage resource.

This chapter covers the following methodologies to work with AutoCAD Web and the cloud:

- Saving DWG files to the cloud
- Using the Drawing History tool
- Opening and working with drawings in the AutoCAD web application
- Opening and working with drawings in the AutoCAD mobile application
- Using drawings updated in AutoCAD Web or the AutoCAD mobile application

Exercise file

For this section, you must use the `New Office Layout.dwg` exercise file. Open the file and ensure that the office floor plan is displayed in the **Model** tab.

This chapter will display various images from a browser-based version of AutoCAD and the AutoCAD mobile application installed on a tablet (an Apple iPad Pro). Please ensure you have access to AutoCAD Web using your AutoCAD subscription details.

There is no essential requirement to have a mobile device with the AutoCAD mobile application installed for this chapter, but it will help to have one and install it. This will allow you to become familiar with the relevant mobile workflows. You can find the mobile application if you search for `AutoCAD` online in your relevant app store.

Saving DWG files to the cloud from the AutoCAD desktop

The AutoCAD desktop application allows you to save your DWG files to the cloud using the AutoCAD web and mobile folders. Provided you are signed in to your AutoCAD subscription, you can use the **Save To Web & Mobile** (*SAVETOWEBMOBILE*) command.

The *SAVETOWEBMOBILE* command is conveniently located at the top left of the **Quick Access Toolbar (QAT)**, as shown in *Figure 15.1*. You may be asked to install a driver file when you click on it for the first time. Make sure this is installed. It will install very quickly and won't take long.

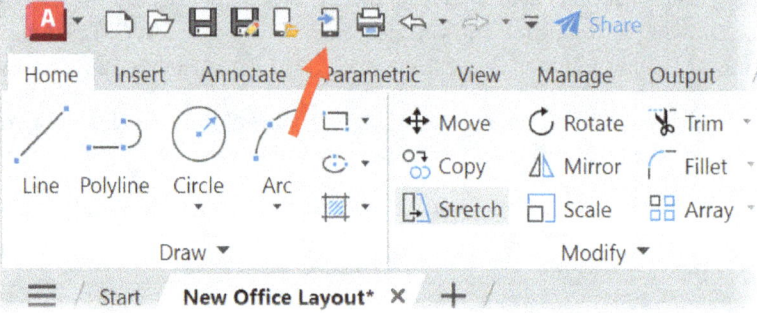

Figure 15.1: The SAVETOWEBMOBILE icon on the Quick Access Toolbar (QAT)

Once it's installed, follow these steps to save DWG files:

1. After clicking on the icon (and installing the driver), the **Save To AutoCAD Web & Mobile** dialog box will appear, as shown in *Figure 15.2*. The file location is displayed at the top of the dialog box (**AutoCAD Web & Mobile**: arrowed in the figure), and the preferred filename is displayed at the bottom (arrowed in the figure).

Saving DWG files to the cloud from the AutoCAD desktop   371

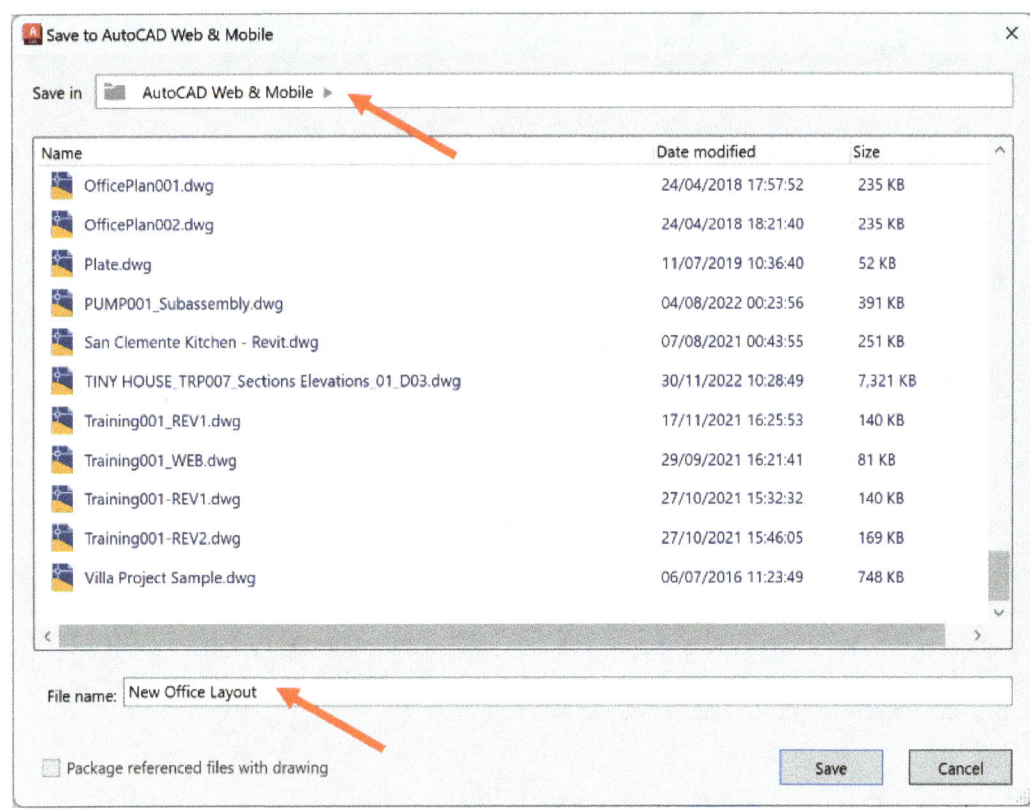

Figure 15.2: The Save To AutoCAD Web & Mobile dialog box

2. After typing in the preferred filename (just use `New Office Layout` at this point), you can click on **Save**. This will save the DWG file into the cloud space reserved for your AutoCAD subscription in the `AutoCAD Web & Mobile` folders.

After clicking **Save**, the drawing will look the same as the original file you opened, but your current drawing is now the cloud-based version with the same filename.

Look at the AutoCAD title bar. You will see a long-winded path for your newly saved DWG file, as shown in *Figure 15.3*. This path is the location of your **AutoCAD Web & Mobile** cloud space, defined by your AutoCAD subscription and the Autodesk account you use when signing into AutoCAD. Note that your file path will differ from the one shown in *Figure 15.3*, as it is specific to *your* account details.

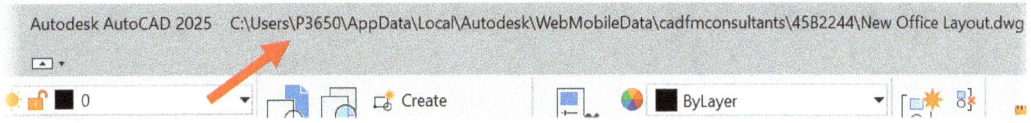

Figure 15.3: The new file path for the DWG file saved in the cloud

Your drawing is now in the cloud, ready for collaboration. Yes, it's that easy!

You now know how quick and easy it is to save your DWG file for collaboration in the cloud. Autodesk provides a very easy method using the `AutoCAD Web & Mobile` folders.

> **Tips and tricks #35**
>
> There are other proprietary cloud-based locations where your DWG files can be stored for collaboration. AutoCAD supports Autodesk Drive, Microsoft OneDrive, Google Drive, Dropbox, and Box. You can also connect your files using Autodesk Desktop Connector and Autodesk Docs. Using these other methods of cloud-based storage will require a subscription/account and will provide a separate location other than the default `AutoCAD Web & Mobile` folders.

If working for a large organization or company, it may be that they have an enterprise-wide proprietary cloud-based solution already. Microsoft OneDrive and Dropbox are common in larger companies, so check if these are available, as they will be readily accessible by the rest of your CAD team.

> **AutoCAD for Mac**
>
> The `AutoCAD Web & Mobile` folders are *not* supported in AutoCAD for Mac. You must save your DWG files from a Mac to one of the proprietary cloud-based solutions, such as Microsoft OneDrive, mentioned in *Tips & tricks #35*.

Using the Drawing History tool

When working with cloud-based DWG files, you need to know which version of the file is current. Sometimes, there might be a locally saved version of the file with the same filename. This is normally a case of checking a time and date stamp applied to the drawing. This is why you were asked to save the cloud-based version of your file with the same filename. You now have two versions of the `New Office Layout.dwg` file: one is stored locally, and one is stored in the cloud.

The following steps will take you through the Drawing History workflow, allowing you to use the **Drawing History** functionality in AutoCAD. This allows you to analyze the iterations of the same drawing and make sure you are using the appropriate version/revision of the drawing file.

1. Open the locally saved version of the drawing first. Then, using the **Open From Web & Mobile** (*OPENFROMWEBMOBILE*) command, open up the cloud-based version of the `New Office Layout.dwg` file. You will find the icon for the *OPENFROMWEBMOBILE* command on the **Quick Access Toolbar** (**QAT**), as shown in *Figure 15.4*.

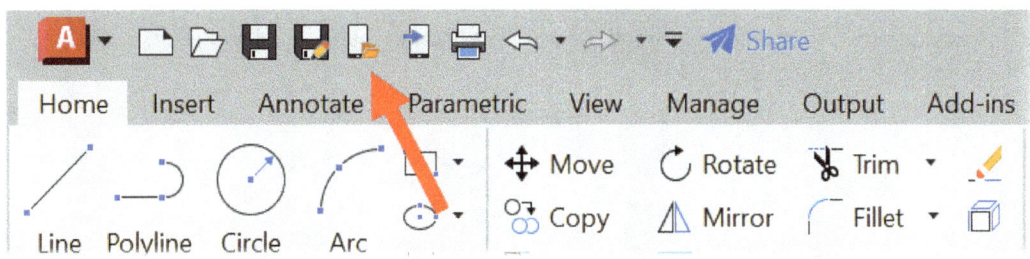

Figure 15.4: The Open From Web & Mobile (OPENFROMWEBMOBILE) icon on the Quick Access Toolbar (QAT)

2. You will now have *two* file tabs in AutoCAD that read the same. Take care to note which is which at this point. Click on the file tab for the locally saved DWG file first, as shown in *Figure 15.5*. In this case, the local file is the *left-hand* file tab, and you need to click on this file tab to make it the current DWG file.

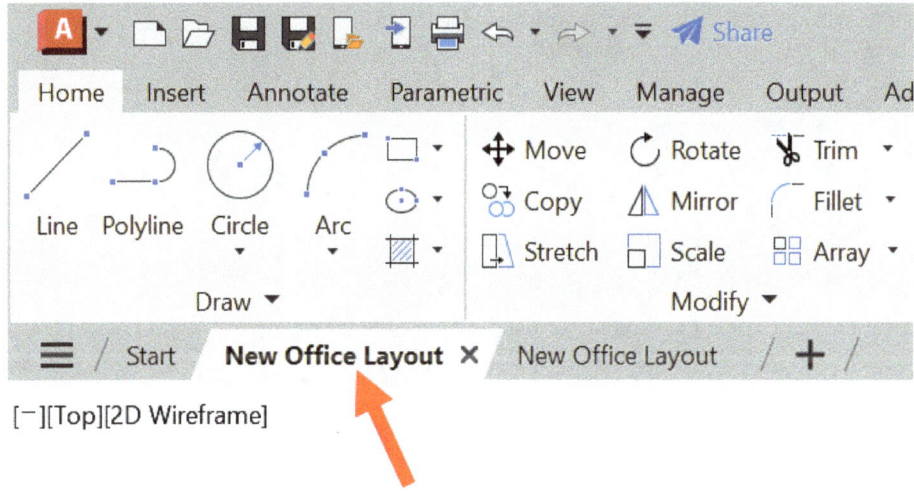

Figure 15.5: The file tab of the local DWG file is made current

3. Click on the **View** tab on the ribbon. Locate the **History** ribbon panel and click on **Activity Insights**, as shown in *Figure 15.6*.

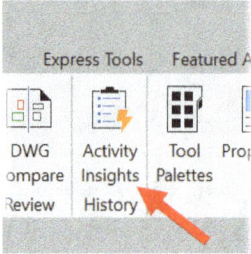

Figure 15.6: The Activity Insights icon on the History ribbon panel

In AutoCAD 2026, **Drawing History** (*DWGHISTORY*) is now part of the **Activity Insights** palette. In older AutoCAD versions, **Drawing History** is a separate palette activated by the *DWGHISTORY* command. If you type `DWGHISTORY` in AutoCAD 2026, the **Activity Insights** palette will automatically open, as shown in *Figure 15.7*.

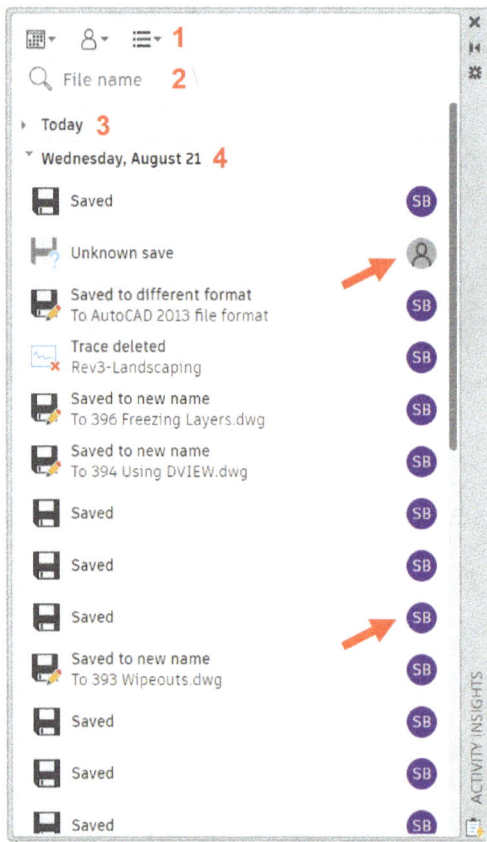

Figure 15.7: The Activity Insights palette for the locally saved DWG file

The new **Activity Insights** palette in AutoCAD 2026 has been enhanced to incorporate your drawing history, as shown in *Figure 15.7*. You can see various iterations of the DWG file there, which are numbered in *Figure 15.7*:

- **1**: Date, user, or activity
- **2**: File name
- **3**: Today's activities
- **4**: Activities on other relevant dates

Also, every time there is a key file save, the user is assigned to that save, as indicated by the circles on the right-hand side of the palette (arrowed).

4. Repeat *steps 2* and *3* with the other file tab (the cloud-based DWG file), and you will see that the **Activity Insights** palette displays slightly different information for the cloud-based DWG file, as shown in *Figure 15.8*. It also gives you the option to connect to **OneDrive** (arrowed).

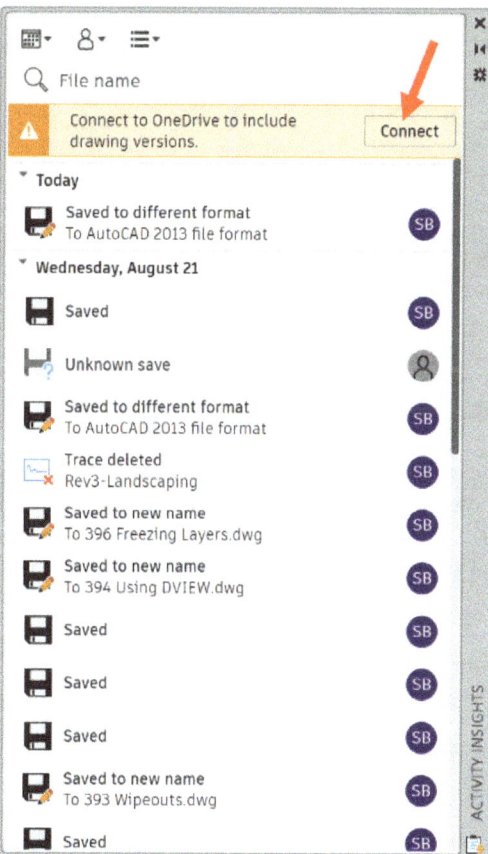

Figure 15.8: The Activity Insights palette for the cloud-based DWG file

AutoCAD 2026 allows you to check the history of your drawing files in the **Activity Insights** palette. Other versions of AutoCAD still have a **Drawing History** palette when the **DWGHISTORY** command is used.

Both methods provide a quick and easy way to check the DWG version history of a locally saved file, and the version history of a DWG file saved in the cloud.

> **AutoCAD for Mac**
>
> **Activity Insights** is also available in AutoCAD for Mac, providing the same levels of insight as AutoCAD for Windows.

In this section, you learned how to use **Drawing History** in the **Activity Insights** palette. This allows you to check for the most current iteration of a drawing file, and make sure you are using the most recent version.

Opening and working with drawings in the AutoCAD web application

AutoCAD Web is the collective name for both AutoCAD in a browser and AutoCAD on mobile, whether a smartphone or a tablet device. Both AutoCAD Web applications provide a similar user experience to the AutoCAD desktop application and allow for easy access and use of cloud-based DWG files.

This section will show you how to open and work on a DWG file using AutoCAD Web through a web browser. The example is viewed and worked on in the most recent version of the Microsoft Edge browser, but AutoCAD Web also supports other popular web browsers.

Let's begin the process by undertaking the following steps:

1. Open your web browser and navigate to `https://web.autocad.com`. The AutoCAD web landing page is shown in *Figure 15.9*. Note that you can utilize the QR code on the page to download the AutoCAD mobile application on Google and Apple app stores.

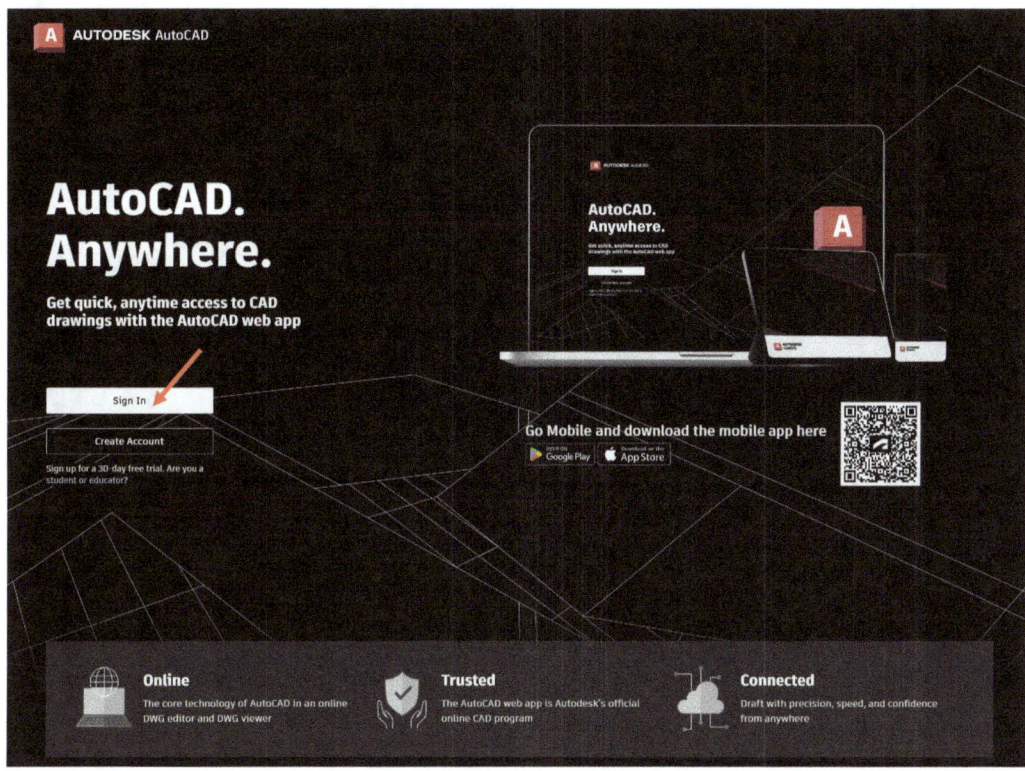

Figure 15.9: The AutoCAD web application landing page

2. Sign in to the AutoCAD web application with your Autodesk account. Click on **Sign In** as arrowed in *Figure 15.9*. You will be prompted to use your Autodesk account username and password.

3. Once signed in, you will be taken to the **AutoCAD Web** landing page, as shown in *Figure 15.10*. On the left, you will see that it has defaulted to the **AutoCAD Web** setting, which means that you are looking at files in the `AutoCAD Web & Mobile` cloud-based folders, and in the top-right corner, you will see your profile photo displayed. It is quite small, but it allows you to confirm you are using your Autodesk account. Scroll down the list of drawing files to locate the `New Office Layout.dwg` file.

Figure 15.10: The AutoCAD Web landing page with New Office Layout.dwg arrowed

4. Double-click on `New Office Layout.dwg` to open the file in AutoCAD Web. You can check the date the file was last modified and its file size.

5. The DWG file will now open in the AutoCAD Web application in the browser used. This will take a little bit of time (or not), depending on the speed and bandwidth of your internet connection. Once opened, you will see the main interface screen of AutoCAD Web with the DWG file displayed in the **Model** tab, as shown in *Figure 15.11*.

Opening and working with drawings in the AutoCAD web application 379

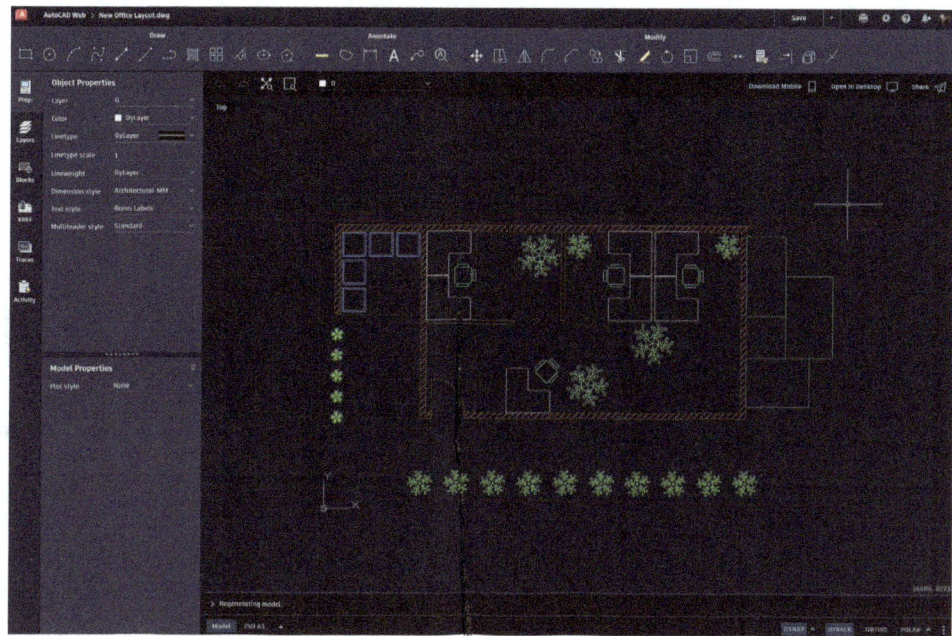

Figure 15.11: The DWG file open in the AutoCAD Web application

6. In the *top-right* corner of the AutoCAD Web interface, you will see a **Settings** icon represented by a small *gearwheel* symbol. Click on the gearwheel to open the **Settings** dialog box, as shown in *Figure 15.12*.

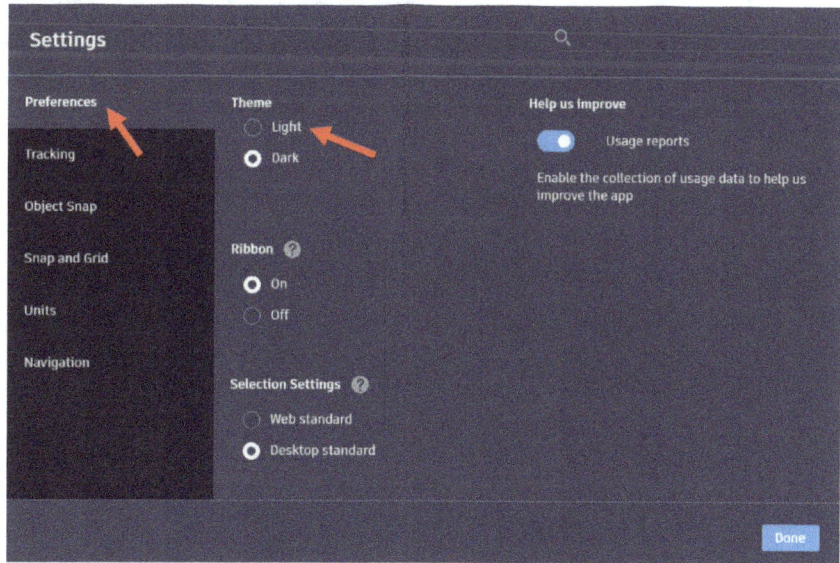

Figure 15.12: The Settings dialog box for AutoCAD Web

7. Upon clicking on the **Preferences** tab on the left of the dialog box, you will see that you can update **Theme**. The default theme is **Dark**. Select **Light** to make for a lighter interface in the browser, and then click on **Done**. As shown in *Figure 15.13*, you will notice that the menus are lighter, but the drawing area continues to use the darker theme. The **Light** theme makes for easier reading of the menus in AutoCAD Web.

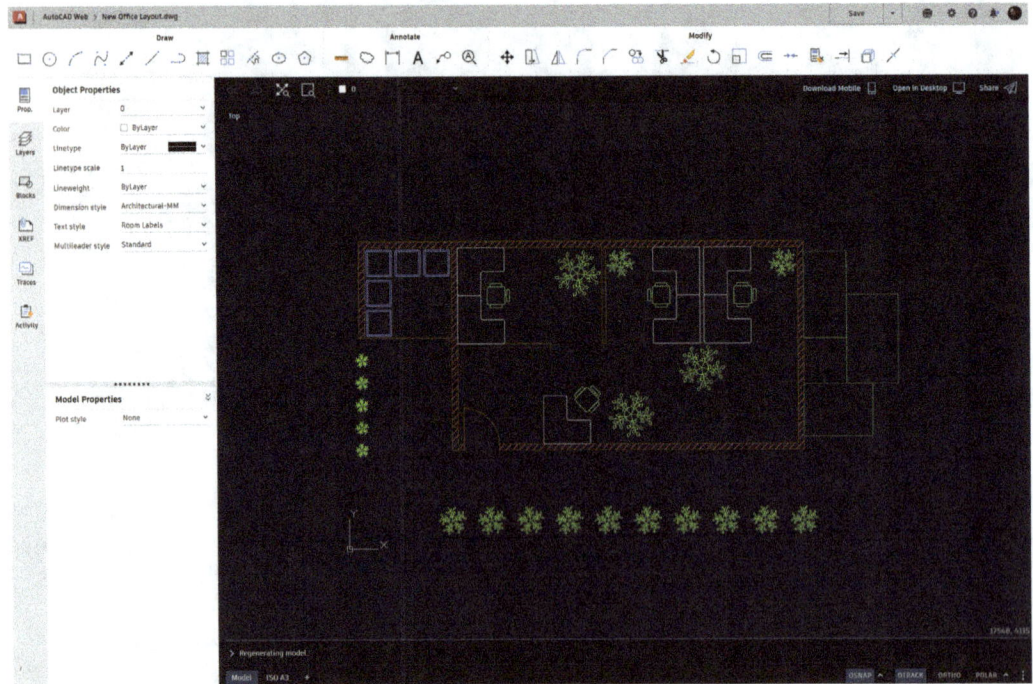

Figure 15.13: The Light theme when used in AutoCAD Web

Autodesk has tried to make sure that the AutoCAD interface used in AutoCAD Web is as close to the AutoCAD desktop interface as possible, to make the transition from desktop to web as easy as possible.

8. If you click on the icons on the icon menu to the left of AutoCAD Web interface, you will see that you can work with the **Properties**, **Layers**, **Blocks**, **XREF**, **Traces**, and **Activity** menus.

9. Click on the **Layers** icon to see the **Layers** panel appear, as shown in *Figure 15.14*.

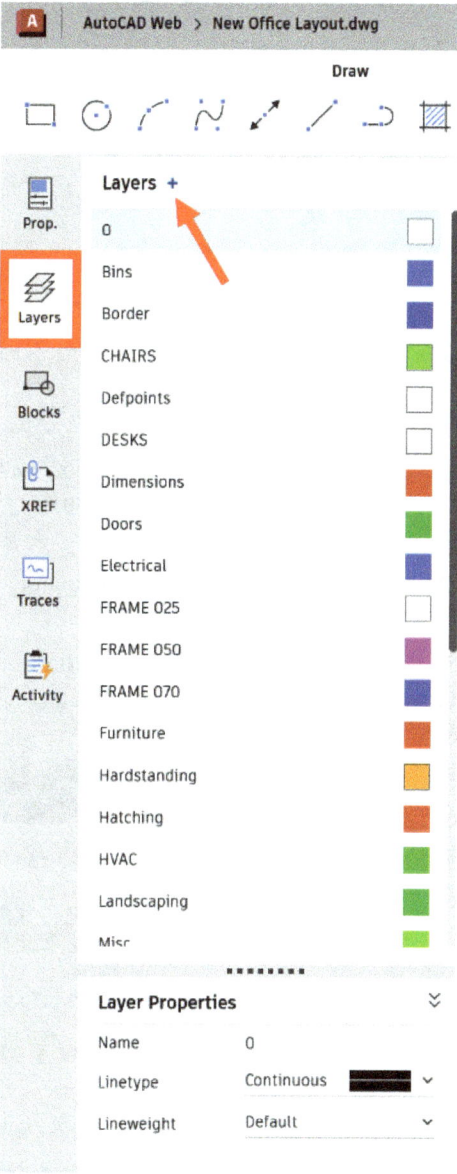

Figure 15.14: The Layers panel in AutoCAD Web

10. If you click on the + symbol next to the word **Layers** in the panel shown in *Figure 15.14*, you can create a new layer in the drawing, as shown in *Figure 15.15*.

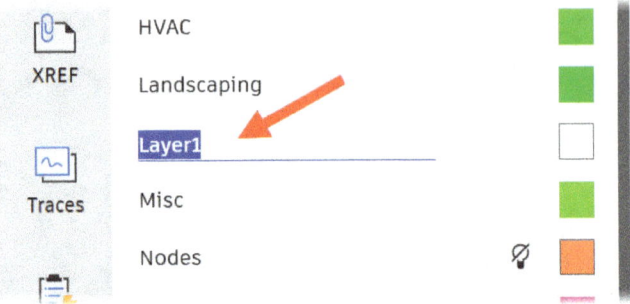

Figure 15.15: The new layer ready to be named in the Layers panel

11. By default, The new layer is named **Layer1** (or similar, depending on how many new layers have been created). It will be highlighted in blue (selected), so you can type in any name required to overwrite the default layer name.

12. Type in the layer name `Traces` and press *Enter*. The layer name will be added to the layer name list. Note that the layers shift alphabetically automatically.

13. The new `Traces` layer is by default white. Click on the color box to the right of the layer name to change the color, and the color palette will appear, displaying the colors in the drawing and the AutoCAD index colors, as shown in *Figure 15.16*.

Figure 15.16: The AutoCAD Web color palette

14. Should further colors be needed, click on **More colors…** in the palette. This will open the full AutoCAD index color palette, as shown in *Figure 15.17*.

Figure 15.17: The AutoCAD color index

15. Hover over a color in the index, and it will display the AutoCAD color number. Select color **10** (*red: on the index's left*) and click **Apply**. You will see the color change in the layer list for the **Traces** layer. When you hover over a layer, you will also see a lightbulb symbol. Clicking on the lightbulb will allow you to toggle the layer on and off in the drawing.

16. Click on **Save** in the top-right corner of the AutoCAD Web interface, as shown in *Figure 15.18*. The DWG file is now saved.

You have created a new layer in your cloud-based DWG file using AutoCAD Web, and the `New Office Layout.dwg` file is now saved in the `AutoCAD Web & Mobile` folders.

17. Click on your profile pic in the top-right corner and select **Sign Out** to sign out of the AutoCAD Web application.

In this section, you have learned how to open and work on a DWG file in the AutoCAD Web application. You have opened up a cloud-based DWG file, created a new layer, and saved the drawing in the cloud.

You can use numerous commands and workflows in AutoCAD Web, all of which follow similar workflows as the AutoCAD desktop application. Autodesk has done this to maintain the AutoCAD user experience. Also, note that AutoCAD Web is *not* a full working version of AutoCAD in a browser. There are a limited number of AutoCAD commands and features available, but there are enough in there for you to easily review, edit, and update any 2D DWG file.

> **Call to action**
> AutoCAD Web is an excellent tool for accessing your DWG files on the fly when they are stored in the cloud. Try saving a more complex DWG file to the cloud and working on it in AutoCAD Web. Experiment with AutoCAD Web's tools, features, and workflows to test how quickly and easily a DWG file in a browser can be edited.

AutoCAD Web democratizes AutoCAD, regardless of whether you are working on AutoCAD for Windows or AutoCAD for Mac. The DWG file is the same in AutoCAD Web, and all edits done in AutoCAD Web will reflect in the DWG when opened in the Autodesk desktop application when using either the Windows or the Mac version.

Opening and working with drawings in the AutoCAD mobile application

This section is based on using the AutoCAD mobile application on an *Apple iPad Pro*. The AutoCAD mobile application can be run on both iOS and Android mobile operating systems, but the interface can differ, so be aware of that.

Also, you are not expected to have access to a tablet such as an iPad. This chapter includes this section to give you an appreciation of how quick and easy it is to work on a cloud-based DWG file when mobile. You could (possibly) follow this section on a smartphone, but you might be limited by the size of the phone screen. If you have one of the larger smartphones on the market, it could be feasible.

It is assumed that the AutoCAD mobile application is already installed on the Apple iPad Pro. You can access AutoCAD (on a subscription basis) in the respective Apple and Google app stores. The following steps will take you through how to open and work with drawings using the AutoCAD mobile application.

1. Like AutoCAD Web, you must log in to the AutoCAD mobile application using your Autodesk account credentials, as shown in *Figure 15.19*. You can also use the **Create Account** button to create a new Autodesk account should it be needed.

Figure 15.19: The AutoCAD mobile application login screen

Upon logging in, you will see a page that displays a **Recent** panel showing recently accessed files and a **Sources** panel, where you can access other cloud-based file locations, as shown in *Figure 15.20*. You can see the New Office Layout.dwg file in the **Recent** panel, as it has been accessed on the iPad recently. You can also use **AutoCAD Web** in the **Sources** panel, which takes you to the AutoCAD Web & Mobile folders.

386   Working with AutoCAD Web

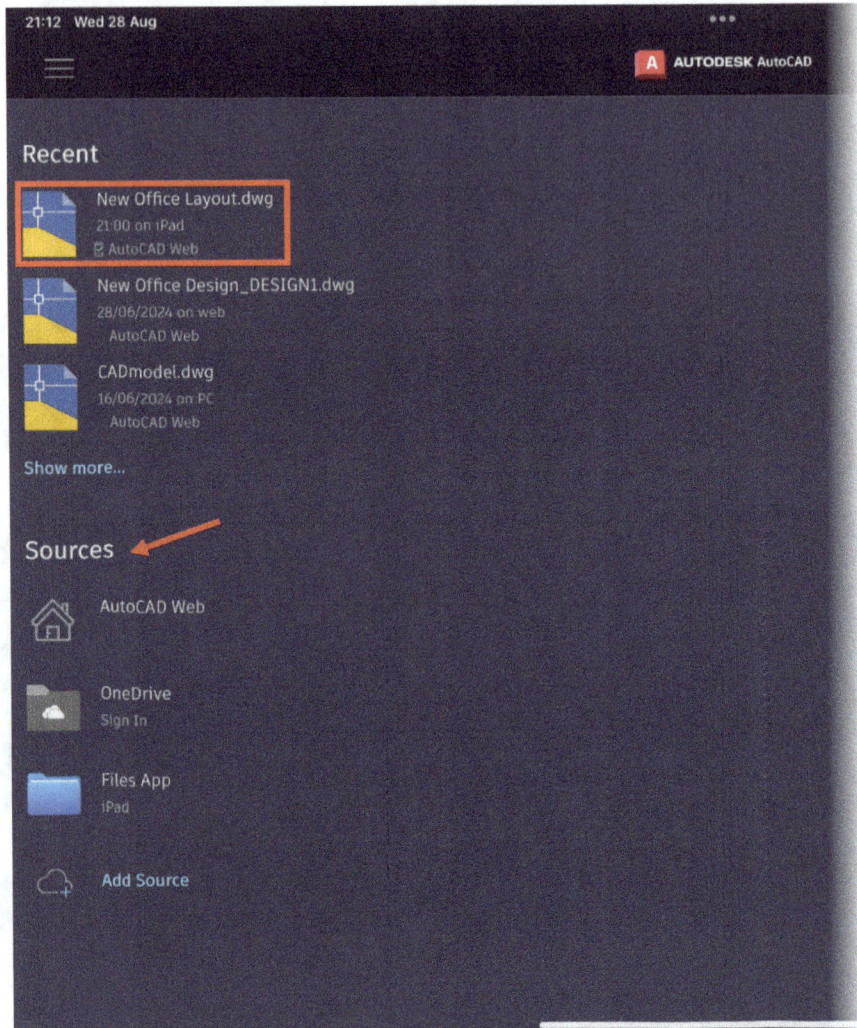

Figure 15.20: The AutoCAD mobile application front screen

2. Select the `New Office Layout.dwg` file. The AutoCAD mobile application will load the drawing. This may take a moment, depending on your mobile data coverage and the specification of your tablet. Once the DWG file has loaded, it will look as shown in *Figure 15.21*.

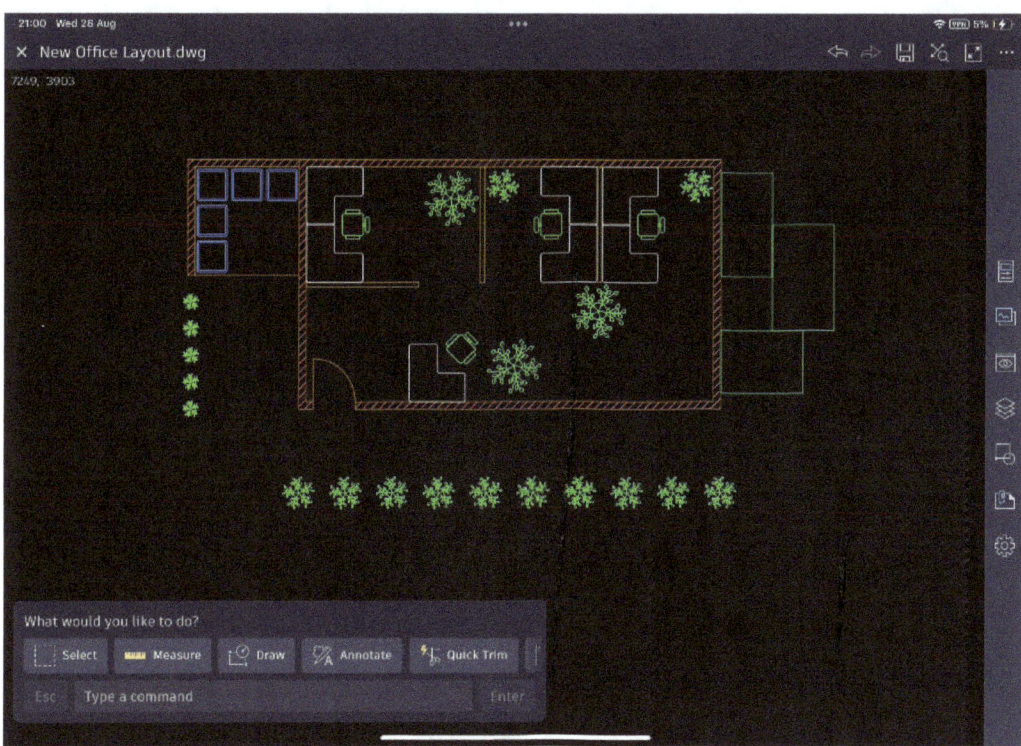

Figure 15.21: The cloud-based DWG file in the AutoCAD mobile application

The AutoCAD mobile application uses the standard iOS interface, including finger gestures for zooming and panning. It also supports the Apple Pencil with an iPad. If you have the Apple tech available (or similar), it is worth checking how it works.

The command panel is at the bottom left, and the icon menu is on the right-hand side of the screen. Note that the icon menu uses the same icons as the AutoCAD Web application. This is to maintain the consistency of the user interface across the AutoCAD Web offering and AutoCAD desktop.

3. Click on the **Layers** icon on the icon menu, as shown in *Figure 15.22*. Then, click on **New layer** (arrowed).

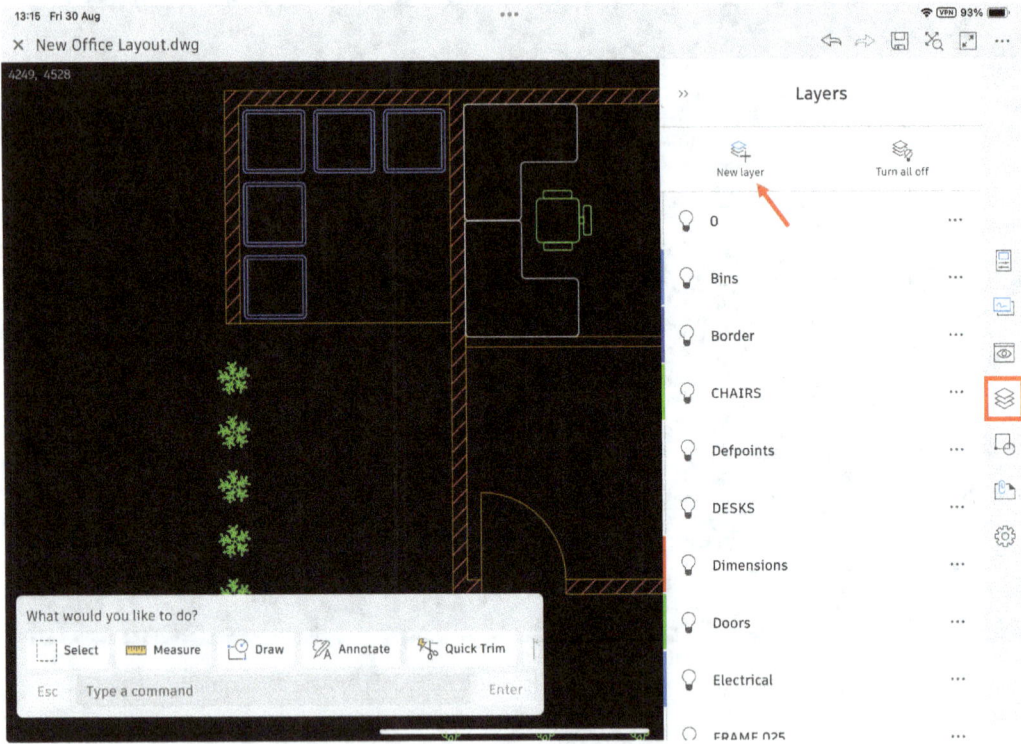

Figure 15.22: The Layers panel in the AutoCAD mobile application

4. Give the new layer the name `Threshold`, as shown in *Figure 15.23*.

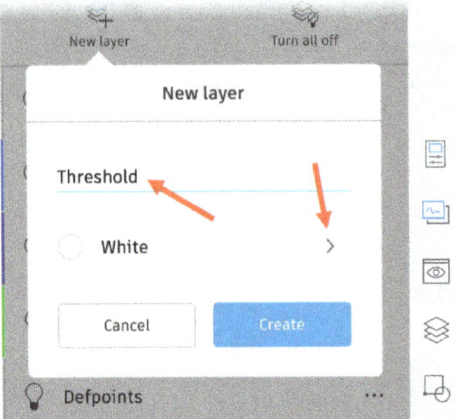

Figure 15.23: Naming the Threshold layer in the Layers panel

5. Click the arrow next to the new layer name (arrowed). You will be taken to the layer color panel, as shown in *Figure 15.24*. You can slide the layer color panel up and down to choose any AutoCAD index color (0-255). Red was chosen from the top of the list, a recently selected layout color.

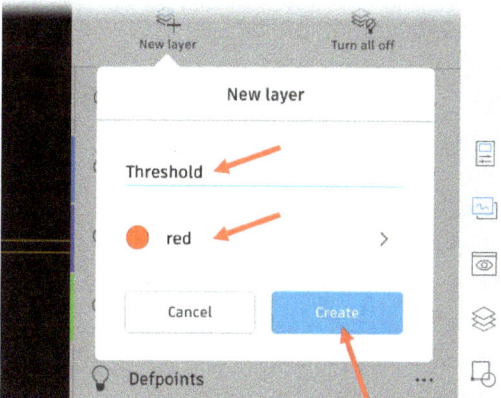

Figure 15.24: Selecting red as the layer color

After selecting the layer's color, you can see that the new **Threshold** layer now uses red, as shown in *Figure 15.25*.

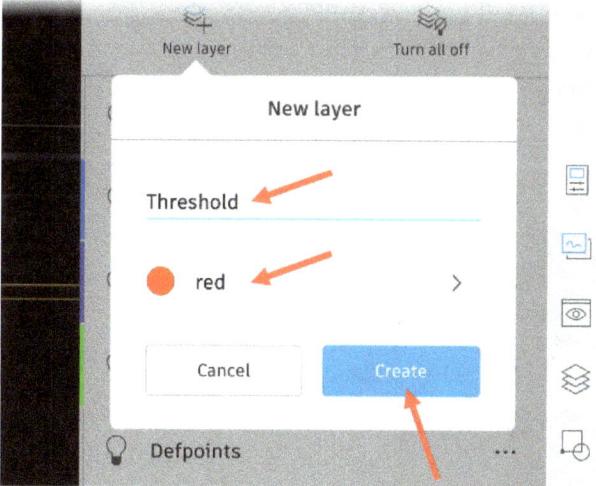

Figure 15.25: The Threshold layer with red layer color

6. Click on **Create** to add the new layer to the drawing's layer list. The new **Threshold** layer will now be added alphabetically to the layer list.

7. Scroll down the layer list to find the **Threshold** layer. The layer color is shown as a vertical highlight to the left of the layer name in the layer list, as shown in *Figure 15.26*.

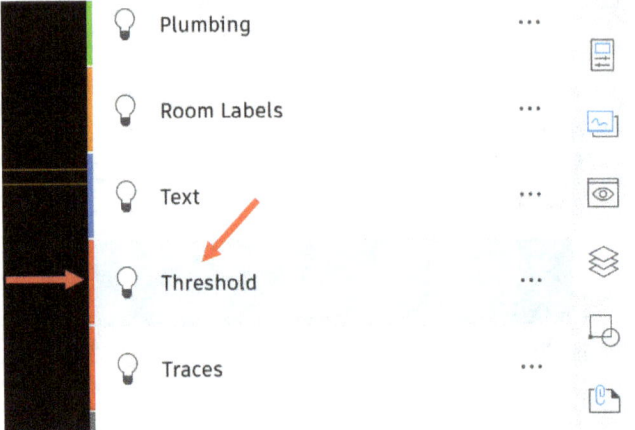

Figure 15.26: The Threshold layer in the layer list

Tips and trick #36

In both the AutoCAD Web and AutoCAD mobile applications, you can turn layers on and off in the drawing by clicking on the *lightbulb* symbol.

8. Click on the double arrow symbol in the layer list to minimize the **Layers** panel, as shown in *Figure 15.27*.

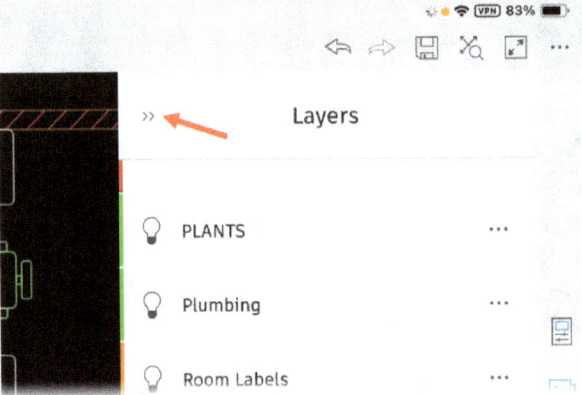

Figure 15.27: Using the double arrow to minimize the Layers panel

9. You can now save the DWG file to the cloud by clicking on the disk icon in the top-right corner of the AutoCAD mobile application window, as shown in *Figure 15.28*.

Figure 15.28: The AutoCAD mobile Save icon (disk symbol, top-right)

The `New Office Layout.dwg` file has now been saved back to the cloud in the `AutoCAD Web & Mobile` folders with the new `Threshold` layer.

Make sure you log out of the AutoCAD mobile application. This ensures that other users of the updated DWG file are using the latest version.

Autodesk has created the AutoCAD mobile application as part of the AutoCAD Web offering to allow DWG files to be used while mobile. This could be on a construction site or perhaps a factory floor setting. The AutoCAD user experience is maintained with an interface like AutoCAD Web, reminiscent of the AutoCAD desktop.

Also, note that the AutoCAD mobile application is *not* a full working version of AutoCAD on a smartphone or tablet. There are a limited number of AutoCAD commands and features available, but there are enough to easily review, edit, and update any 2D DWG file.

> **Call to action**
>
> The AutoCAD mobile application is an excellent tool for accessing your DWG files from the cloud when on the move. Experiment with the AutoCAD mobile application tools, features, and workflows to test how quickly and easily a DWG file in a browser can be edited when using your device, whether that be a smartphone or a tablet.

Regardless of whether you have edited drawings in **AutoCAD Web** or the AutoCAD mobile application, the edited DWG file can still be used in the AutoCAD desktop application as normal. The next section takes you through this particular workflow.

Using drawings updated in AutoCAD Web or the AutoCAD mobile application

Working with the AutoCAD Web or AutoCAD mobile application is great when you are in an unfamiliar office (AutoCAD Web: *using a browser*) or on the move (AutoCAD mobile application: *on a tablet*).

However, once you have made revisions and edits to a cloud-based DWG file, you will always need to return to the AutoCAD desktop environment to use the full version of AutoCAD.

In this section, we will open the cloud-based `New Office Layout.dwg` DWG file from the `AutoCAD Web & Mobile` folders to check that the changes made in AutoCAD Web and the AutoCAD mobile application are in place. Let's start by following these steps:

1. On the AutoCAD desktop, select the *OPENFROMWEBMOBILE* command using the **Quick Access Toolbar** (**QAT**) icon, as shown in *Figure 15.29*. Then, select the `New Office Layout.dwg` file and click on **Open**.

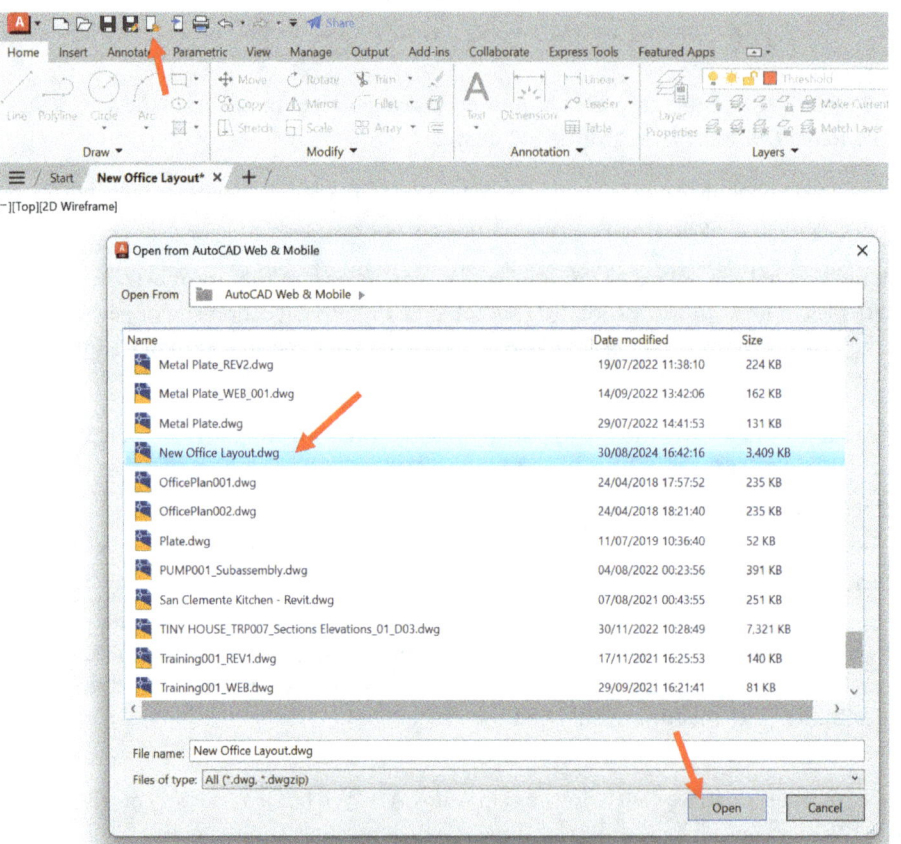

Figure 15.29: Opening the DWG from the AutoCAD WEB & Mobile folders

Using drawings updated in AutoCAD Web or the AutoCAD mobile application 393

The drawing will open. Ensure you are in the **Model** tab zoomed to a full view of the office floor plan.

2. Click on the **Home** tab on the ribbon and look at the **Layers** ribbon panel. Click on the **Layer Properties** icon, as shown in *Figure 15.30*.

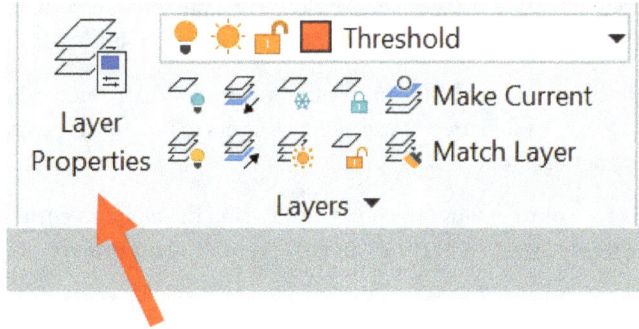

Figure 15.30: The Layer Properties icon

3. The **Layer Properties Manager** palette will appear on the screen, as shown in *Figure 15.31*. Notice that the layers **Traces** and **Threshold** are now available in the DWG file.

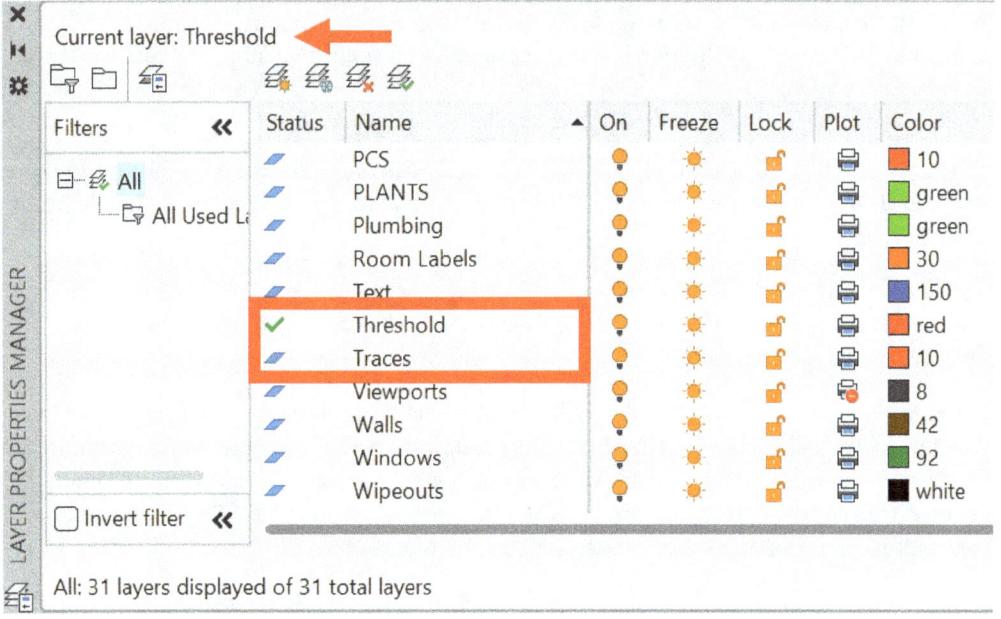

Figure 15.31: The new layers in the Layer Properties Manager palette

The **Traces** layer was added when the `New Office Layout.dwg` file was open in AutoCAD Web, and the **Threshold** layer was added in the AutoCAD mobile application. **Threshold** is the current drafting layer (arrowed in *Figure 15.31*), the last layer created in the AutoCAD mobile application.

You can now use the cloud-based DWG with those two new layers added from other alternative AutoCAD applications. This demonstrates that using a cloud-based DWG file, even for a simple workflow, such as adding a new layer, makes for easy, seamless collaboration on the cloud-based drawing.

This brief section demonstrates how easy it is to collaborate on a DWG file stored in the cloud. Using the `AutoCAD Web & Mobile` folders, you can add new layers to the drawing using both AutoCAD Web and the AutoCAD mobile application.

The applications of this type of workflow are endless, and using the cloud to ensure universal access to the DWG file being used saves lots of time when collaborating on projects that use DWG files in AutoCAD.

> **AutoCAD for Mac**
>
> The `AutoCAD Web & Mobile` folders and the *OPENFROMWEBMOBILE* and *SAVETOWEBMOBILE* commands are *not* available when using AutoCAD for Mac. However, you can still collaborate using other cloud-based, proprietary solutions such as **Microsoft OneDrive**. OneDrive is supported by AutoCAD Web and the AutoCAD mobile application, so when working on the AutoCAD desktop in AutoCAD for Mac, you would save your file to your chosen cloud-based location in OneDrive and then connect to it using AutoCAD Web or the AutoCAD mobile application by using the appropriate login credentials for your chosen cloud-based location.

You can save your DWG files to the cloud using the `AutoCAD Web & Mobile` folders. You can also save your DWG files to other cloud-based solutions, such as Microsoft OneDrive, Google Drive, Dropbox, Box, and Autodesk Drive.

You also know about AutoCAD Web, the web and mobile offering for AutoCAD that is included in your AutoCAD subscription. If you are using AutoCAD LT, it is also included in your AutoCAD LT subscription.

The AutoCAD Web and AutoCAD mobile applications provide superb browser-based and mobile tools for working on DWG files stored in the cloud. These applications allow for quick and easy, real-time collaboration on drawings. Consider using either application to save valuable time when collaborating on files that need edits, changes, and revisions by other members of your CAD team and working with project stakeholders, such as architects, engineers, and project managers.

- You can learn more about working with AutoCAD Web on the official AutoCAD blog: `https://www.autodesk.com/blogs/autocad/building-collaboration-with-autocad-web/`

- You can also learn more about AutoCAD Web here on the Autodesk website: `https://help.autodesk.com/view/ACD/2022/ENU/?guid=GUID-B4A46563-E5CA-4A34-918C-78ADEA2FEEB4`
- There is also more information about the AutoCAD mobile application here: `https://help.autodesk.com/view/ACD/2022/ENU/?guid=GUID-20A8F96D-0ACA-49F6-A6FF-D7DD71A8D03A`

Summary

In this chapter, you have gained knowledge about how to save DWG files using the *SAVETOWEBMOBILE* command, and subsequently open the saved files using the *OPENFROMWEBMOBILE* command. You have also learned how you can check the history of your DWG files using the **Activity Insights** palette.

You have also gained valuable knowledge of how to open and work on drawings in the AutoCAD Web application in a browser and in the AutoCAD mobile application on a mobile device such as a tablet or smartphone.

Subsequently, you have also learned how to open modified, cloud-based DWG files on the AutoCAD desktop, using changes made in the DWG file by AutoCAD Web and the AutoCAD mobile application.

Cloud-based DWG files make for seamless, real-time collaboration, whether that be through a browser or on a mobile device. The knowledge gained in this chapter will allow you to think about cloud-based strategies that utilize cloud-based DWG storage and use AutoCAD Web and the AutoCAD mobile application to collaborate effectively and productively.

In the next chapter, we will examine how to use the **Trace** functionality in AutoCAD and combine it with cloud-based DWG files to enhance collaboration on your drawings even further.

Get This Book's PDF Version and Exclusive Extras

Scan the QR code (or go to `packtpub.com/unlock`). Search for this book by name, confirm the edition, and then follow the steps on the page.

Note: Keep your invoice handy. Purchases made directly from Packt don't require one.

16
Collaborating using Traces in AutoCAD

In the previous chapter, you learned how to work with drawings stored in the cloud and collaborate utilizing AutoCAD Web and the AutoCAD mobile application. Now that the cloud can be used to store your AutoCAD DWG files, collaboration is key, and the trace functionality in AutoCAD has become an excellent way to communicate design changes, edits, and revisions.

The new trace function in AutoCAD used to be available only in AutoCAD Web and the AutoCAD mobile application. As of AutoCAD 2023, it is also available in the AutoCAD desktop application and is much enhanced in the AutoCAD 2026 version.

This availability provides full trace functionality across all three AutoCAD applications: desktop, web, and mobile. This chapter provides the user with an overview of the trace functionality in AutoCAD and how it can be used to their advantage.

This chapter covers the following methodologies that allow you to work effectively with the trace functionality across all three AutoCAD applications:

- Using traces with AutoCAD desktop
- Using traces in the AutoCAD mobile application
- Using traces in AutoCAD Web
- Reviewing traces in the AutoCAD desktop app

Using the cloud combined with the trace functionality for collaboration will save considerable reworking time and provide updates to DWG files in real time.

This chapter will show you how the cloud is now a fundamental part of the AutoCAD DWG workflow. It provides storage for DWG files and easy collaboration using tools such as the trace functionality in AutoCAD.

Exercise files

For this section, you must use the exercise `New Office Layout_TRACE.dwg` file. Open the file in the AutoCAD desktop application and ensure the office floor plan is displayed in the **Model** tab.

Ensure you save the `New Office Layout_TRACE.dwg` file to the `AutoCAD Web & Mobile` folder using the **SAVETOWEBMOBILE** command. Use the **Save to Web & Mobile** icon on the **Quick Access Toolbar** (**QAT**). You learned how to do this in previous chapters. You can then easily access the drawing file with AutoCAD Web and the AutoCAD mobile application later in this chapter.

In this chapter, we will display various images from a browser-based version of AutoCAD (AutoCAD Web) and the AutoCAD mobile application installed on a tablet (an Apple iPad Pro). Please ensure you have access to AutoCAD Web using your AutoCAD subscription details.

There is no essential requirement to have a mobile device with the AutoCAD mobile application installed for this chapter, but it will help to have one and install it. This will allow you to become familiar with the relevant mobile workflows. You can find the mobile application if you search for AutoCAD online in your relevant app store.

Using traces with AutoCAD desktop

AutoCAD gives you access to drawing files locally and those stored in the cloud. While having files stored locally can be preferred, making sure your DWG files are stored in the cloud (the `AutoCAD Web & Mobile` folder) allows for quick and easy collaboration using the trace tools in all three AutoCAD applications: desktop, Web, and mobile.

> **Tips and tricks #36**
>
> Adding a trace to a DWG file using the AutoCAD desktop application has only been available on the desktop since the AutoCAD 2023 version. Before that, you could only *view* traces on the AutoCAD desktop. Should you run an AutoCAD version before AutoCAD 2023, you must add traces using AutoCAD Web or the AutoCAD mobile application. The other solution here is to upgrade your AutoCAD version. Sometimes, this isn't the quickest way forward, as you might have to liaise with your organization's IT department to get this expedited. However, you should have access to AutoCAD Web and the AutoCAD mobile application through your existing AutoCAD subscription, so perhaps use those applications to add traces to your cloud-based DWG files in the meantime!

The following steps take you through how to use traces when working in the AutoCAD desktop application:

1. The *SAVETOWEBMOBILE* command is conveniently located at the top left of the QAT, as shown in *Figure 16.1*. You may be asked to install a driver file when you click on it for the first time. Make sure this is installed. It will install very quickly and won't take long.

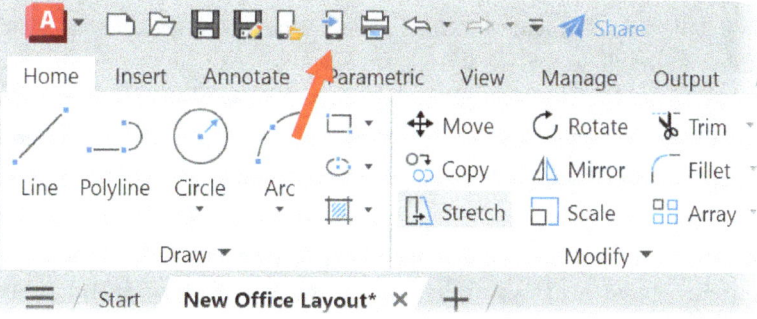

Figure 16.1: The SAVETOWEBMOBILE icon on the QAT

2. After clicking on the icon (and installing the driver), the **Save to AutoCAD Web & Mobile** dialog box will appear, as shown in *Figure 16.2*. The file location is displayed at the top of the dialog box (**AutoCAD Web & Mobile**), and the preferred filename is displayed at the bottom. You will notice that the figure shows the DWG file already saved in the **AutoCAD Web & Mobile** folder. You can overwrite existing DWG files in the cloud, and you will be asked whether you want to replace the file, just like a regular file on your hard drive or a server.

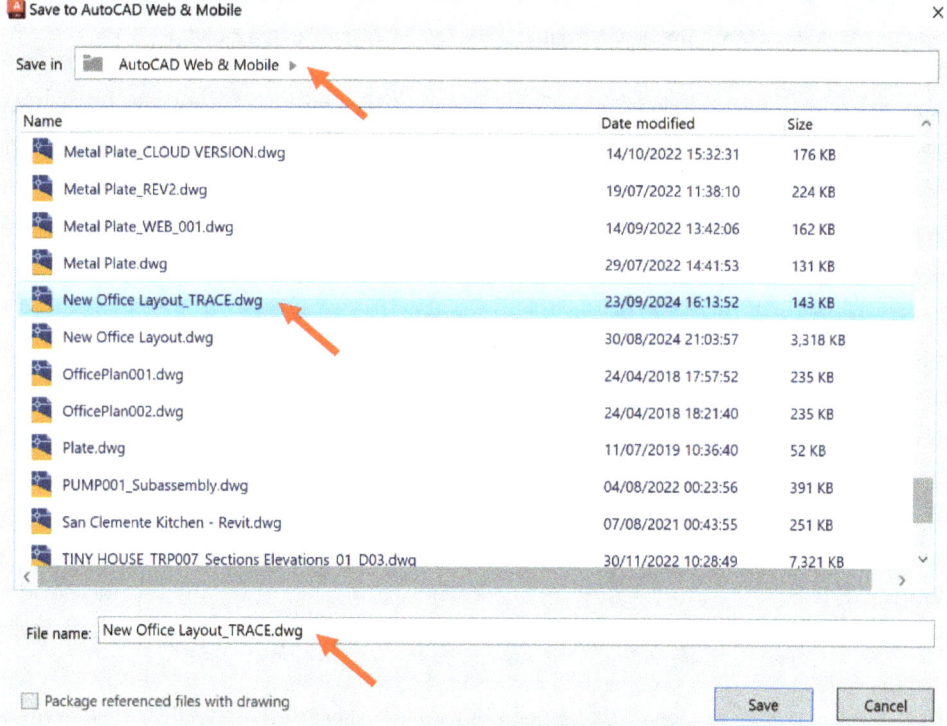

Figure 16.2: The Save to AutoCAD Web & Mobile dialog box

3. Use the `New Office Layout_TRACE.dwg` filename and click on **Save**. This will save the DWG file into the cloud space reserved for your AutoCAD subscription in the `AutoCAD Web & Mobile` folder. That way, any traces added to the DWG file are available to all the AutoCAD applications: desktop, web, and mobile.

4. After clicking **Save**, the drawing won't change. It is simply saved as a cloud-based version with that filename.

5. Look at the AutoCAD title bar. You may see a long-winded path for your newly saved DWG file, as shown in *Figure 16.3*. This path is the location of your **AutoCAD Web & Mobile** cloud space, defined by your AutoCAD subscription and the Autodesk account you use when signing into AutoCAD. Note that your file path will differ from the one shown in *Figure 16.3*, as it is specific to *your* account details.

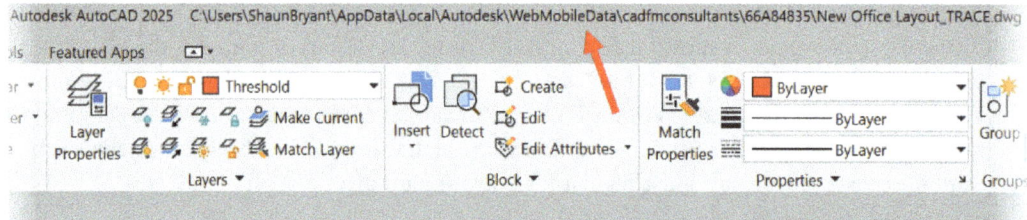

Figure 16.3: The new file path for the DWG file saved in the cloud

6. Your drawing is now in the cloud, ready for collaboration using the trace functionality in AutoCAD.

7. To add a simple trace to the drawing, click on the **Collaborate** tab on the ribbon and select the **Traces Palette** icon on the **Traces** ribbon panel, as shown in *Figure 16.4*.

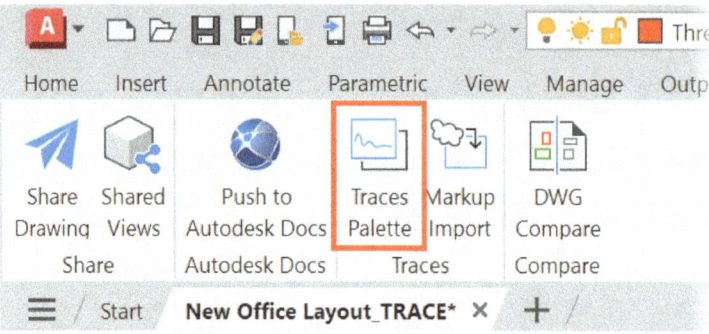

Figure 16.4: The Traces Palette icon on the Traces ribbon panel

When the palette opens, you will see that there are no traces in the DWG file. This is shown in *Figure 16.5*. Click on the **New Trace** button. This will start the workflow that allows you to add a trace to the DWG file when using the AutoCAD desktop application.

Using traces with AutoCAD desktop   401

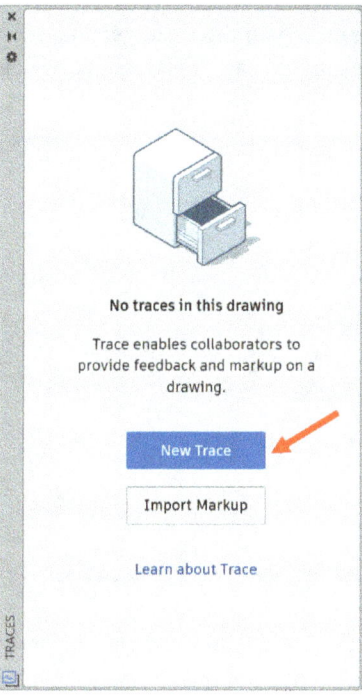

Figure 16.5: Traces Palette with the New Trace button

8. After clicking **New Trace**, you will go into trace mode, where the drawing displays any traces associated with it. You don't have any traces, so AutoCAD will add a default trace to the **Traces Palette**, as shown in *Figure 16.6*. In this case, it is called `Trace1`.

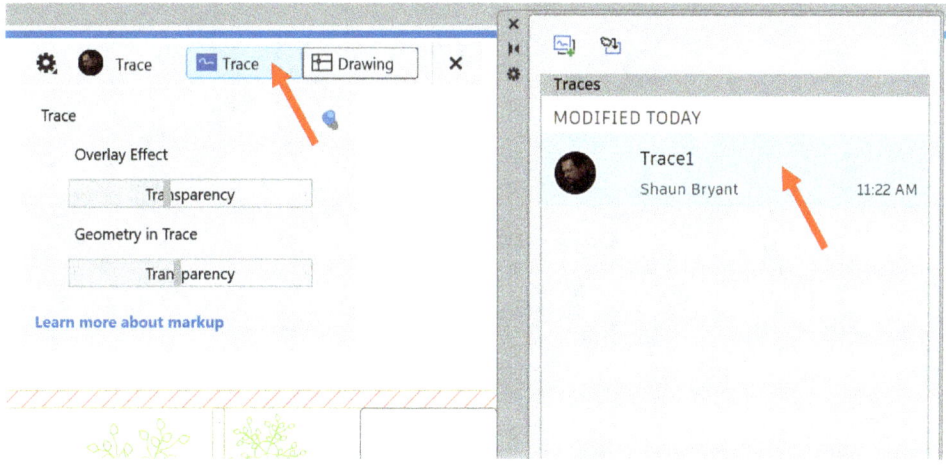

Figure 16.6: AutoCAD in trace mode with a default trace

9. The `Trace1` name is a default, so you can easily rename your trace by right-clicking on the trace name. The right-click menu lets you close, rename, or delete the trace. Select **Rename** as shown in *Figure 16.7*.

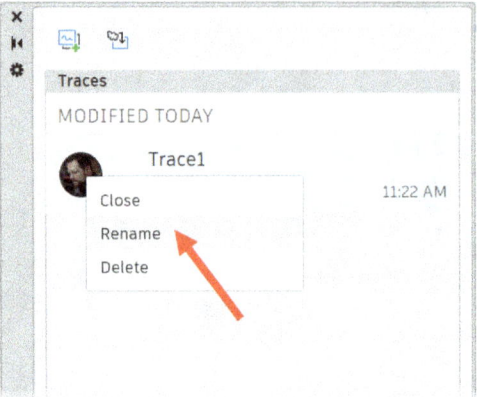

Figure 16.7: The right-click menu on Traces Palette

10. For the trace, use the `Revision1` name. After typing it in, press *Enter* to confirm the renaming.
11. If you now hover over the trace in the palette, you will see that AutoCAD gives you all the author information for the trace and other information, such as the trace creation date, as shown in *Figure 16.8*. It also displays the contributors to the trace, showing who else has collaborated on the trace. At the moment, only you should be shown as a contributor.

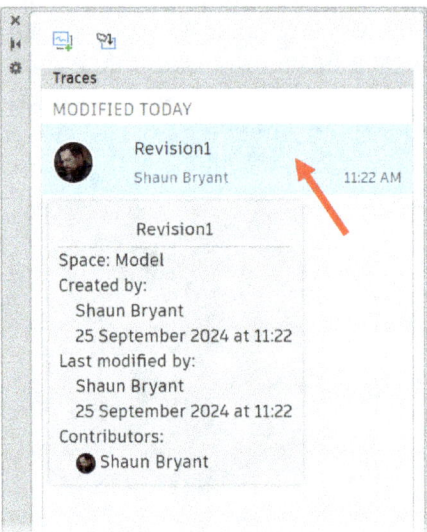

Figure 16.8: The trace information

12. Now that you have a named trace in the drawing, you need to add information to the drawing while in trace mode. In this case, you will be adding a simple revision cloud.
13. Using the **Home** tab on the ribbon, go to the **Draw** panel and click on the arrow on the **Draw** panel title bar to expand the panel icons. Select the **Rectangular** revision cloud on the **REVCLOUD** drop-down menu. You can see this in *Figure 16.9*.

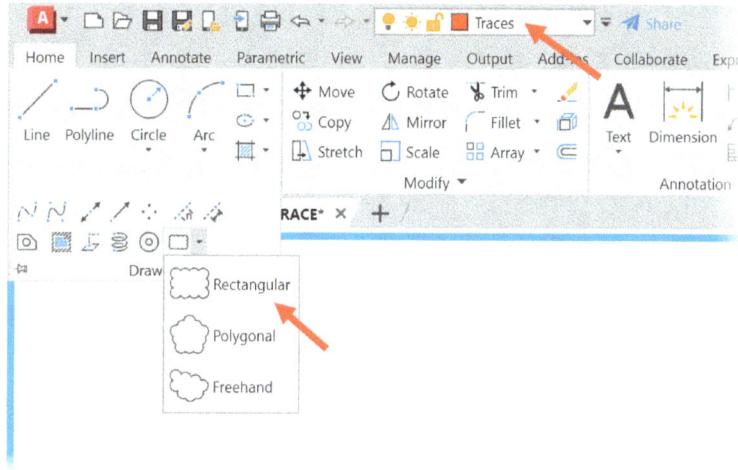

Figure 16.9: The Rectangular revision cloud option

14. You are now in the **REVCLOUD** command. AutoCAD will normally pre-calculate the arc length in the **REVCLOUD** command, but you can adjust it if you want to. Right-click to bring up the shortcut menu, as shown in *Figure 16.10*.

Figure 16.10: The REVCLOUD shortcut menu with Arc length selected

15. You will see a default arc length displayed at the prompt. For this exercise, set the arc length to 900, and press *Enter*. You will then be ready to place your revision cloud in the trace.
16. Zoom to the top-left executive office in the office floor plan and place your rectangular revision cloud around the double desk configuration in that office, as shown in *Figure 16.11*. Click the two opposing corners of the rectangular revision cloud, as if you were placing a rectangle using the **RECTANGLE** command.

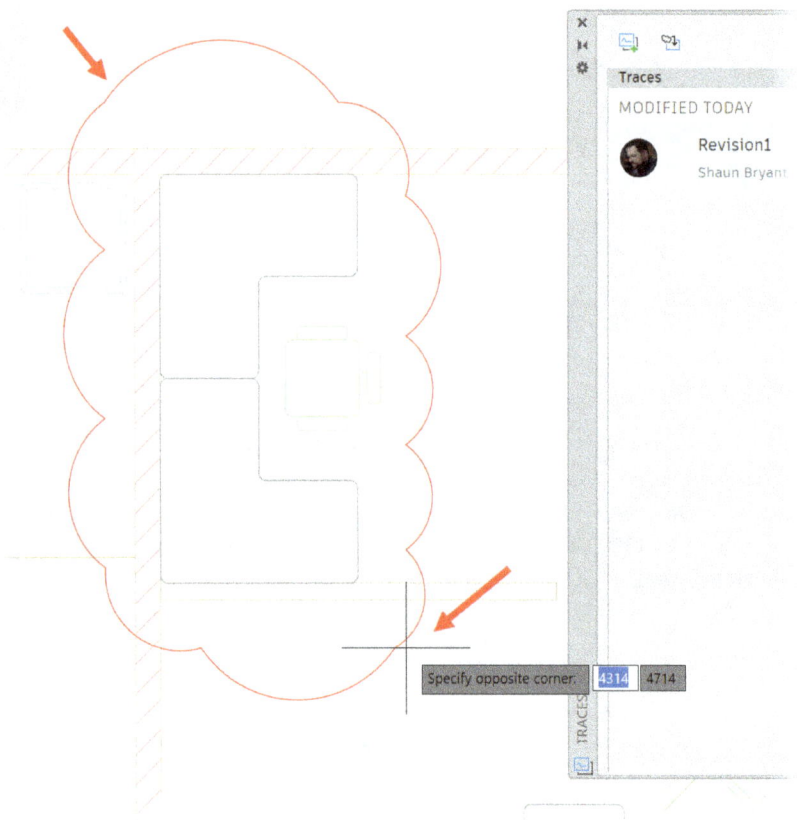

Figure 16.11: The placing of the rectangular revision cloud with both opposing corner points arrowed

17. After the second corner click, the revision cloud is placed on the **Traces** layer in the **Revision1** trace.
18. The trace will remain attached to the DWG file, so you can exit trace mode by clicking on the small **X** on the **Trace** toolbar, as shown in *Figure 16.12*.

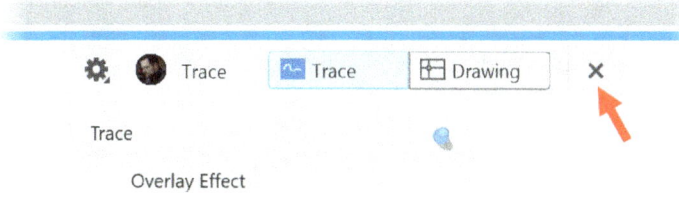

Figure 16.12: The X used to close the Trace toolbar

19. You can now click on **Save** on the QAT at the top-left of the AutoCAD screen, as shown in *Figure 16.13*. You can save normally like this, as you are working on a drawing that is based in the cloud, in the `AutoCAD Web & Mobile` folder. It is the same as saving a drawing file in a local location, such as on a hard drive or server.

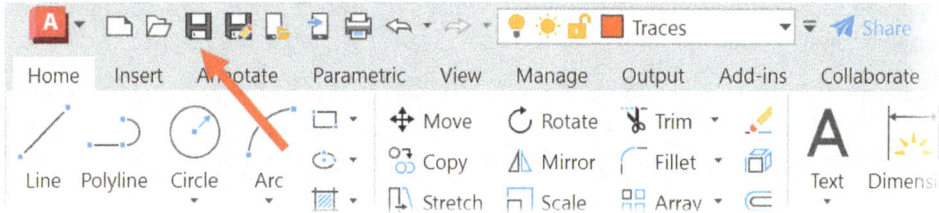

Figure 16.13: The Save icon on the QAT

20. After closing the **Trace** toolbar, you will return to the **Model** tab in the `New Office Layout_TRACE.dwg` file.
21. You have now applied a trace to the drawing file and saved it back to the cloud.

> **Tips and tricks #37**
>
> Adding a trace to a DWG file using the AutoCAD desktop application is a straightforward workflow, as demonstrated by the previous section in this chapter. However, there is one little thing you should *always* remember. You *cannot* save a DWG while a trace operation is active, so you *must* close the trace by closing the **Trace** toolbar, and *then* save the drawing file.

In this section, you initiated the collaboration workflow by adding a trace to a DWG file while working in the AutoCAD desktop application.

> **AutoCAD for Mac**
>
> The trace functionality is supported in AutoCAD for Mac. If you are using the 2024, 2025 or 2026 version, the workflows in the previous section are the same. Still, you must save your DWG files from a Mac to one of the proprietary cloud-based solutions, such as Microsoft OneDrive, as `AutoCAD Web & Mobile` folders are not supported in AutoCAD for Mac.

In the next section, you will add to that trace using the AutoCAD mobile application as if you were onsite, working on the new office layout in real-time in a real-world environment.

Using traces in the AutoCAD mobile application

This section is based on using the AutoCAD mobile application on an Apple iPad Pro. The AutoCAD mobile application can be run on both Apple and Android mobile operating systems, and the interface can differ, so be aware of that.

You are not expected to have access to a tablet such as an iPad Pro. This chapter includes this section to give you an appreciation of how quick and easy it is to work with traces in a cloud-based DWG file using AutoCAD mobile:

1. The AutoCAD mobile application is assumed to have already been installed on the Apple iPad Pro. You can access AutoCAD (on a subscription basis) in the Apple and Google app stores.
2. Like the AutoCAD desktop application and AutoCAD Web, you must log into the AutoCAD mobile application using your Autodesk account credentials.
3. Upon logging in, you will see a page that displays a **Recent** panel showing recently accessed files and a **Sources** panel, where you can access other cloud-based file locations, as shown in *Figure 16.14*. You can see the `New Office Layout_TRACE.dwg` file in the **Recent** panel, as it has been accessed on the iPad recently. You can also use AutoCAD Web in the **Sources** panel, which takes you to the **AutoCAD Web & Mobile** folder. Also, note that the listing for the `New Office Layout_TRACE.dwg` file shows you whether it has been accessed on PC (AutoCAD desktop) or via AutoCAD Web.

Using traces in the AutoCAD mobile application   407

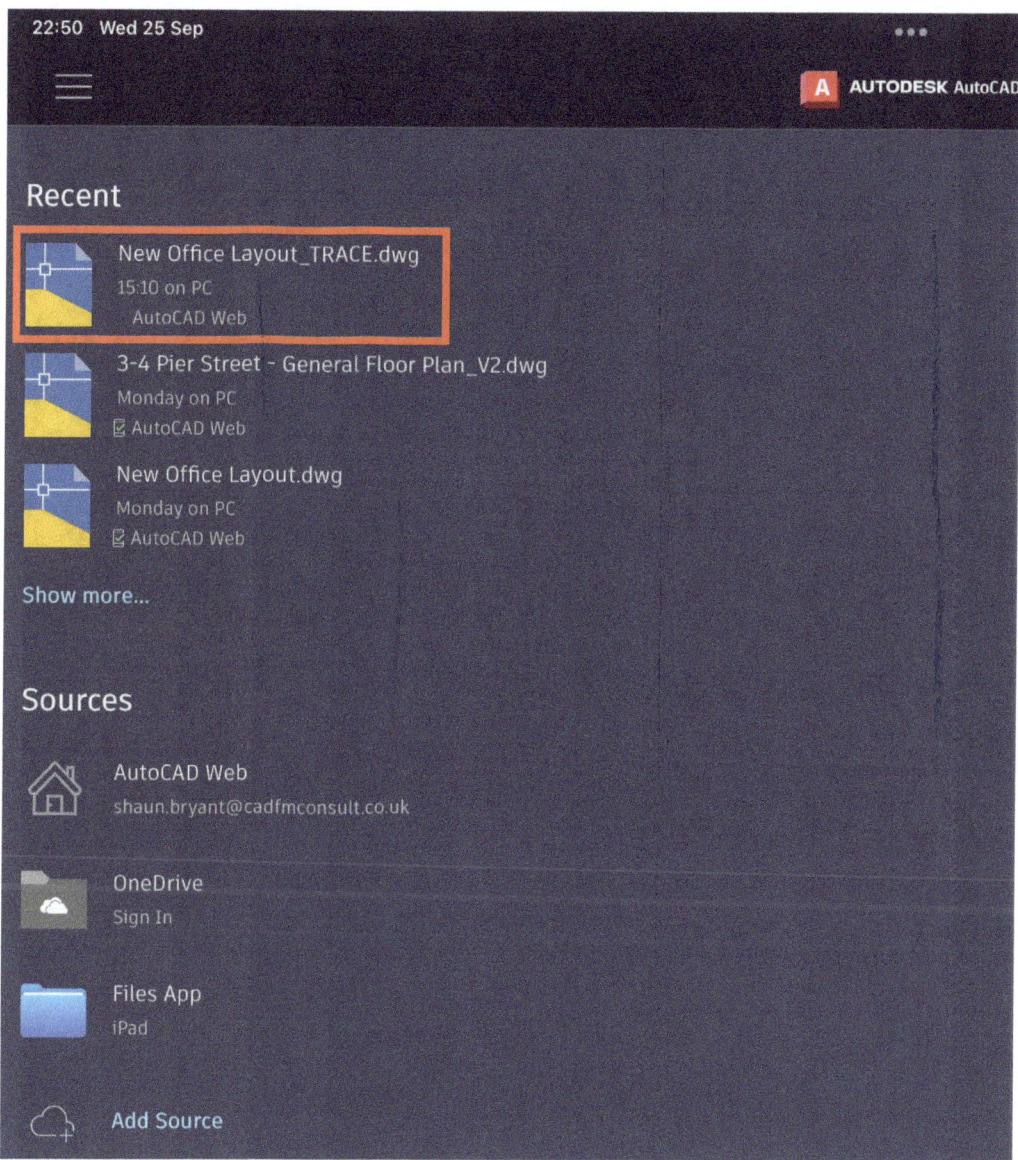

Figure 16.14: The AutoCAD mobile application's Recent and Sources screen

4. Click on the `New Office Layout_TRACE.dwg` file, which will open in the AutoCAD mobile application, as shown in *Figure 16.15*. The traces icon is shown arrowed on the right.

Figure 16.15: The drawing opens in the AutoCAD mobile application with the traces icon arrowed

5. Upon clicking on the traces icon, the **Traces** panel will expand into the iPad screen area, and any traces attached to the DWG file will be displayed in trace mode, as shown in *Figure 16.16*.

Using traces in the AutoCAD mobile application   409

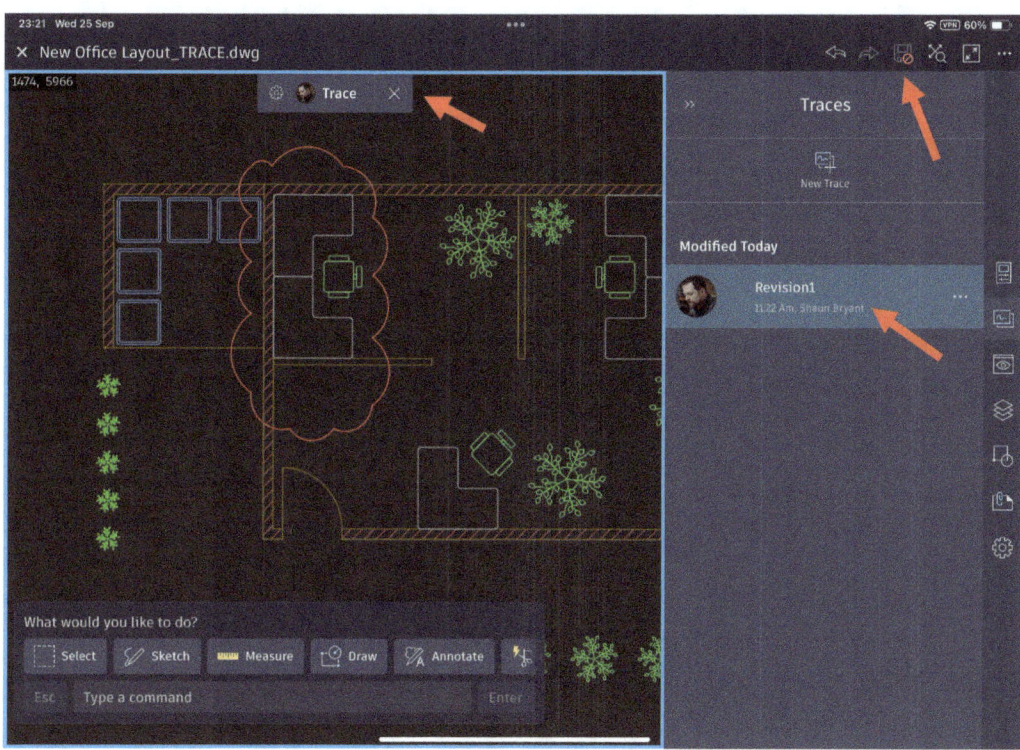

Figure 16.16: The Traces panel in the AutoCAD mobile application

6. The only trace in the DWG file is the **Revision1** trace that was added using the AutoCAD desktop application.

7. Using the drafting tools (bottom-left of the screen), select the **Annotate** option. One of the **Annotate** tools displayed will be **MText**. Click on **Mtext**.

8. Click next to the revision cloud to locate the **MText** position in the trace. You will then be prompted for the area the text annotation will occupy, as shown in *Figure 16.17*.

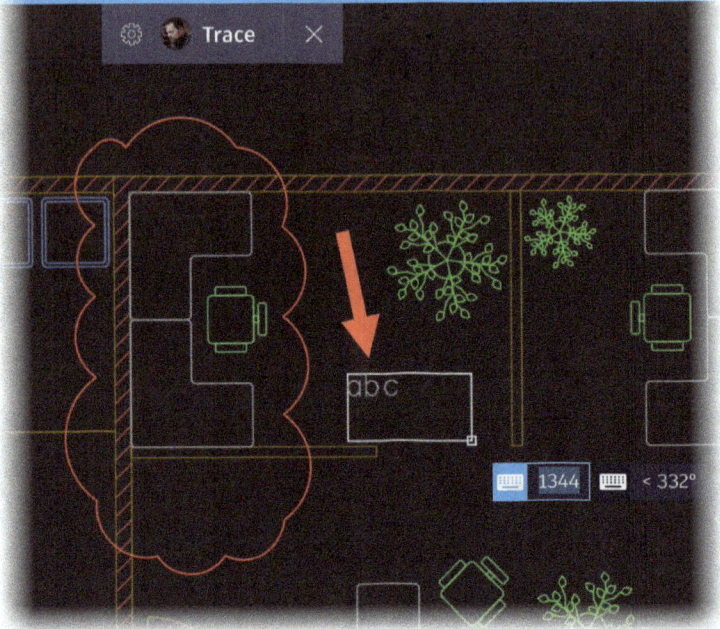

Figure 16.17: The MText area being specified on the screen

9. After clicking on the second corner of the MText area, you will see the text editor at the bottom of the iPad screen, as shown in *Figure 16.18*.

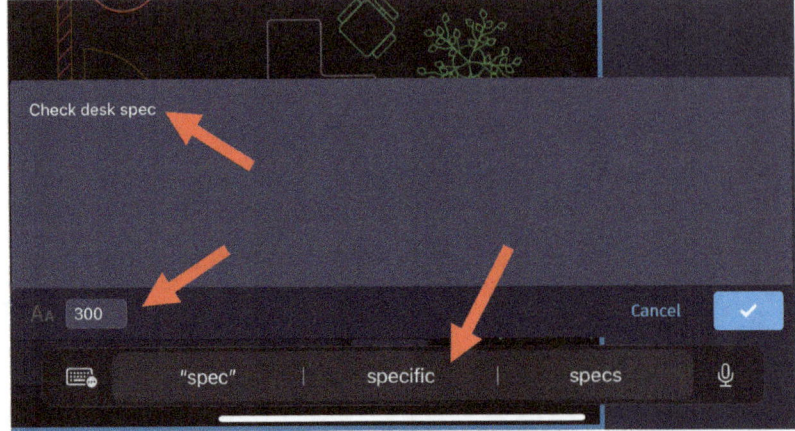

Figure 16.18: The text editor in the AutoCAD mobile application

10. You will be prompted to add the text using the text editor settings. In this case, you can see the text height is set to 300 with the **Check desk spec** text. Also, note that the iPad gives you predictive text, as shown below the text editor.
11. Click on the blue checkmark to confirm the text settings. The editor will close, and the text will be placed in the trace, as shown in *Figure 16.19*.

Figure 16.19: The MText placed in the trace in the DWG file

12. Using the **X** symbol on the **Trace** toolbar, you can now close the **Trace** toolbar and exit trace mode. You will then return to the drawing. If the **Traces** panel does not close, click the traces icon, as previously shown in *Figure 16.15*.
13. Make sure the drawing file is saved using the **Save** icon (top-right of the iPad screen), as shown in *Figure 16.20*. It will display a green checkmark to show that it has been successfully saved to the cloud.

Figure 16.20: The Save icon in the AutoCAD mobile application

14. You have now saved `New Office Layout_TRACE.dwg` in the AutoCAD mobile application after adding some **MText** annotation in the trace attached to the drawing file. The changes are now saved and ready for further collaboration.

In this section, you learned how the **trace** functionality in your AutoCAD subscription allows you to collaborate with new and existing traces in drawings via the AutoCAD mobile application. In the next section, we use traces in AutoCAD Web.

Using traces in AutoCAD Web

This section is based on using AutoCAD Web to collaborate on the trace you have been using in this chapter.

The `New Office Layout_TRACE.dwg` file was saved in the cloud in the previous section using the AutoCAD mobile application, so you know that it is current. You can check this after logging into **AutoCAD Web** using your AutoCAD subscription details. The drawing will display in the **Recent** list when you log in, as shown in *Figure 16.21*.

File Type	Name	Location	Last Opened	Size
	3-4 Pier Street - General Floor Plan_V3.dwg	AutoCAD Web	Monday on PC	79 KB
	3-4 Pier Street - General Floor Plan_V2.dwg	AutoCAD Web	Sep 27, 2024 on PC	78 KB
	New Office Layout_TRACE.dwg	AutoCAD Web	Sep 27, 2024 on PC	249 KB
	New Office Layout.dwg	AutoCAD Web	Sep 23, 2024 on PC	3.2 MB
	3-4 Pier Street - General Floor Plan_V1.dwg	AutoCAD Web	Sep 16, 2024 on PC	83 KB

Figure 16.21: The drawing listed in the Recent list in AutoCAD Web

The drawing file displays the date it was last opened, allowing you to check whether it is the most current version.

> **Tips and tricks #38**
>
> A very simple way of checking whether you are working on the most current drawing when collaborating using cloud-based DWG files is to have a sensible file-naming philosophy. The drawing currently being used in this chapter is called New Office Layout_TRACE.dwg. To track edits and changes in the DWG file, make sure the current revision of the file is in the filename. For example, you might name the file you are using New Office Layout_TRACE_REV1.dwg, where REV1 indicates the first revision of the drawing file.

You now need to open the drawing file in **AutoCAD Web**, to check the trace applied in the previous section, using the AutoCAD mobile application:

1. After logging in to AutoCAD Web, open the New Office Layout_TRACE.dwg file from the **Recent** list by double-clicking on it in the list.
2. The DWG file will open in AutoCAD Web, as shown in *Figure 16.22*.

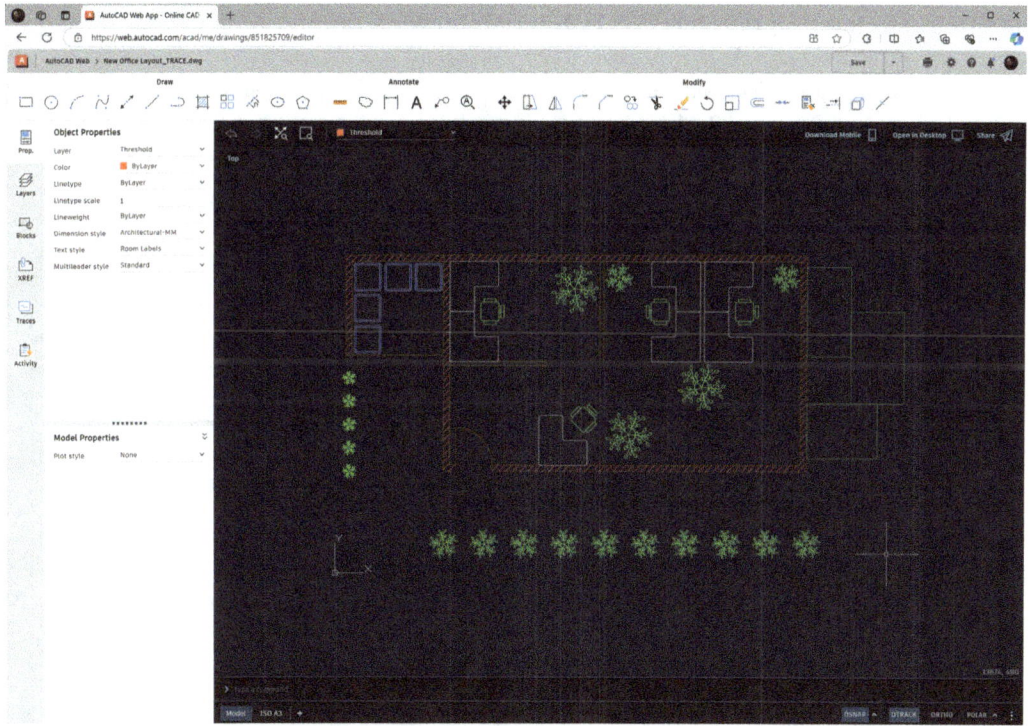

Figure 16.22: The DWG file open in AutoCAD Web

3. The **Properties** palette is always set up by default when opening AutoCAD Web.

4. To check the recently added trace, you must open the **Traces Palette**. Click on the traces icon in the menu bar on the left of the AutoCAD Web screen, as shown in *Figure 16.23*.

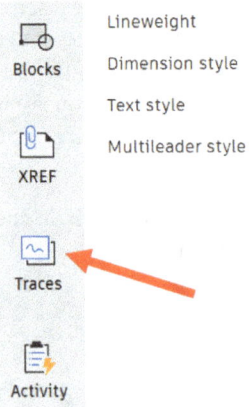

Figure 16.23: The Traces icon in AutoCAD Web

5. The **Traces** palette will display, and you will see the recent trace listed on the palette, as shown in *Figure 16.24*. Select the **Revision1** trace, and the drawing will enter trace mode, with the trace displayed. This will be the trace you saw when working with the AutoCAD mobile application in the previous section.

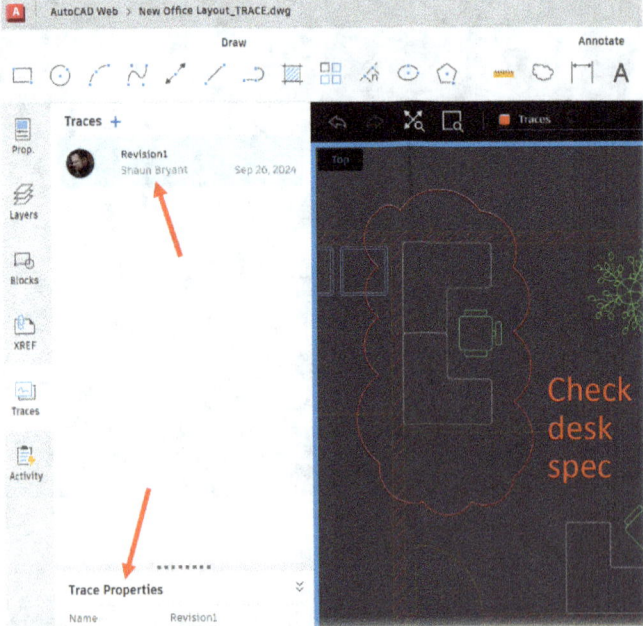

Figure 16.24: The Traces palette current with the trace selected

6. The trace properties are also displayed in the **Traces** palette. They are displayed under the **Traces** list, as arrowed in *Figure 16.24*.

7. As shown in *Figure 16.25*, you can check these trace properties to ensure they are current. You can also check who added the trace and who collaborated on it in the drawing.

Trace Properties	
Name	Revision1
Space	Model space
Created by	Shaun Bryant
Creation Date	Sep 25, 2024, 11:22
Last save	Sep 26, 2024, 00:29
Last saved by	Shaun Bryant

Figure 16.25: The trace properties for the Revision1 trace

8. Double-click on the text in the trace, and the AutoCAD Web text editor will display, as shown in *Figure 16.26*.

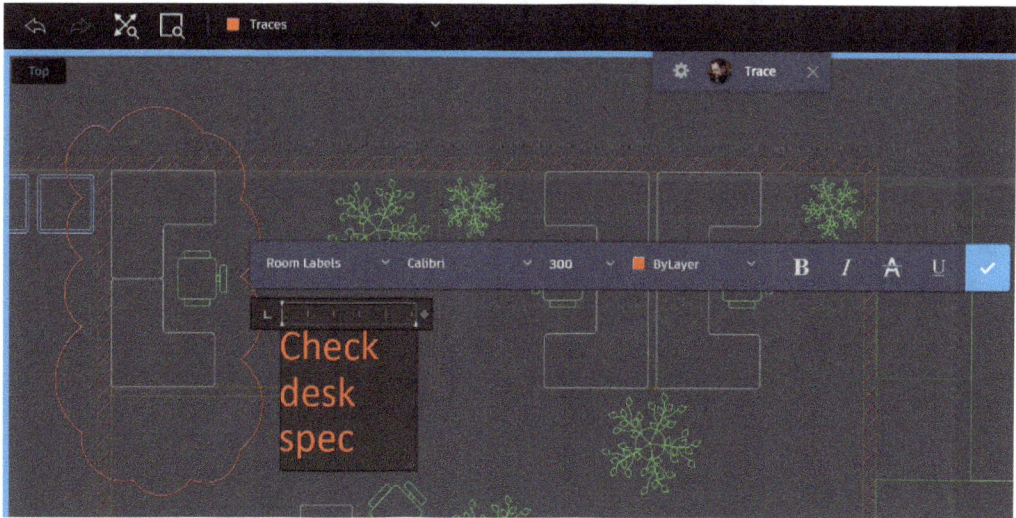

Figure 16.26: The text editor displayed in AutoCAD Web in trace mode

9. Edit the text to read Check desk spec and cost, and then click on the blue checkmark at the end of the text editor bar. This will close the text editor and update the text in the trace, as shown in *Figure 16.27*.

Figure 16.27: The updated text in the trace

10. You can now exit trace mode by clicking on the **X** at the end of the **Trace** toolbar, as shown in *Figure 16.28*.

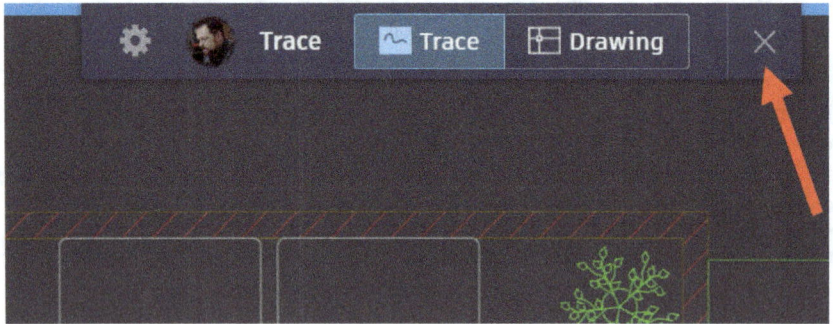

Figure 16.28: The trace toolbar with the X arrowed

11. The updated trace is now set in the DWG file, and you now need to save the drawing to the cloud to make sure that the updated trace is available to other collaborators. Use the **Save** icon in the top-right corner of the AutoCAD Web application window, as shown in *Figure 16.29*.

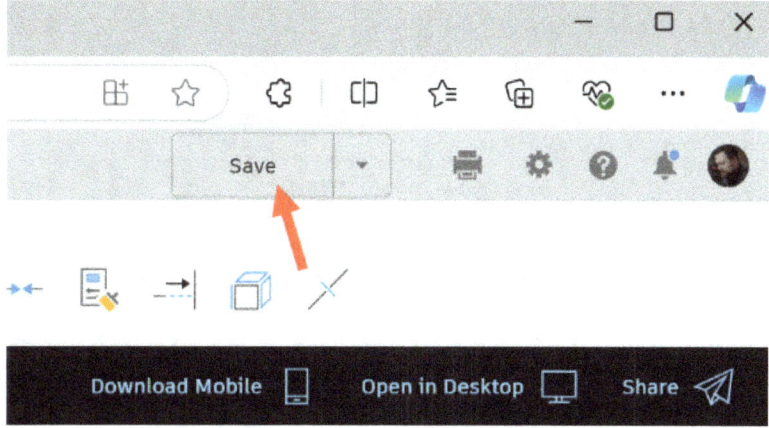

Figure 16.29: The Save icon in AutoCAD Web

12. Make sure to exit and log out from AutoCAD Web. You have now edited the trace in AutoCAD Web and saved the updated DWG file to the cloud.

In this section, you learned how to open a cloud-based DWG file that contained an existing trace in **AutoCAD Web**. You then edited the trace and saved the updated DWG file back into the cloud for further collaboration.

Reviewing traces in the AutoCAD desktop app

In the previous sections, you learned how to update traces in the AutoCAD mobile application and AutoCAD Web.

In this section, you will open the updated DWG file from the cloud in the AutoCAD desktop application and review the updated trace. You will still be using the same DWG file, New Office Layout_TRACE.dwg, and will be using the **Traces** palette:

1. Open the AutoCAD desktop application and click on the **Open From Web & Mobile** icon on the QAT, as shown in *Figure 16.30*.

418　Collaborating using Traces in AutoCAD

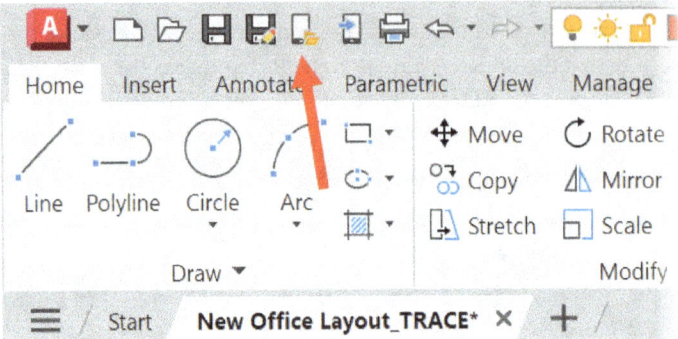

Figure 16.30: The Open From Web & Mobile icon on the QAT

2. The **Open from AutoCAD Web & Mobile** dialog box will display. Select the `New Office Layout_TRACE.dwg` file and open it, as shown in *Figure 16.31*. The drawing will open in AutoCAD.

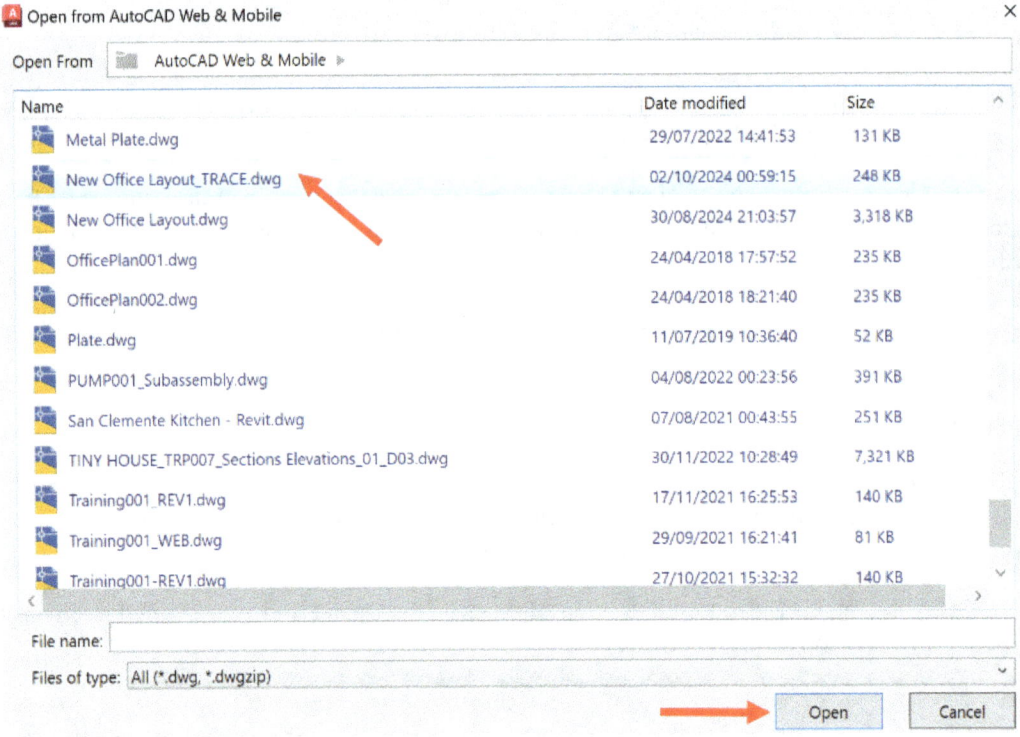

Figure 16.31: The Open from AutoCAD Web & Mobile dialog box

3. Click on the **Collaborate** tab on the AutoCAD ribbon and click on the **Traces Palette** icon on the **Traces** panel, as shown in *Figure 16.32*.

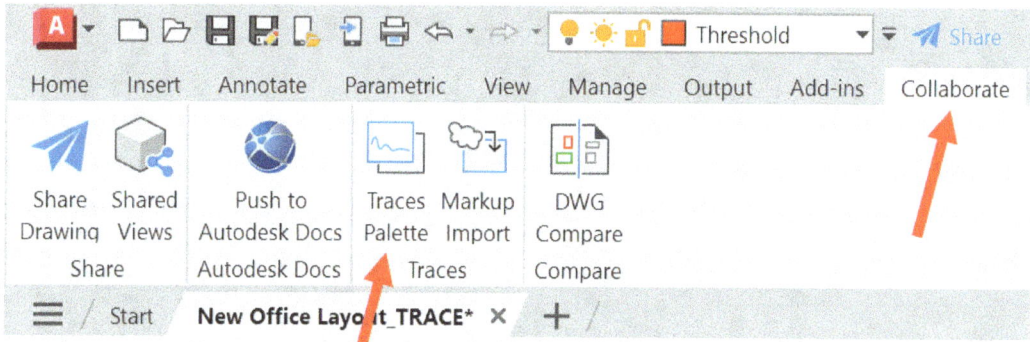

Figure 16.32: The Traces Palette icon on the Traces panel

4. **Traces Palette** will open in AutoCAD. Select the **Revision1** trace on the palette, as shown in *Figure 16.33*.

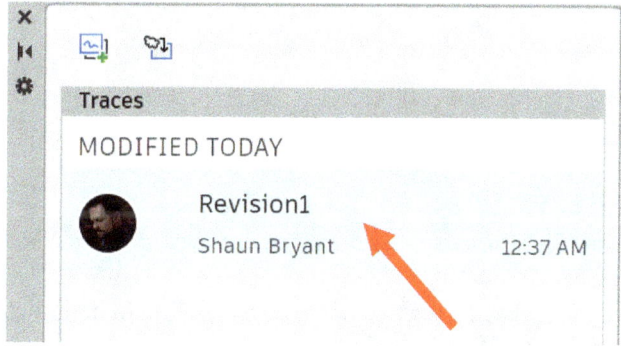

Figure 16.33: The Traces Palette with the Revision1 trace displayed

5. Once the trace is selected, you will enter trace mode in AutoCAD, and the trace will be displayed, as shown in *Figure 16.34*.

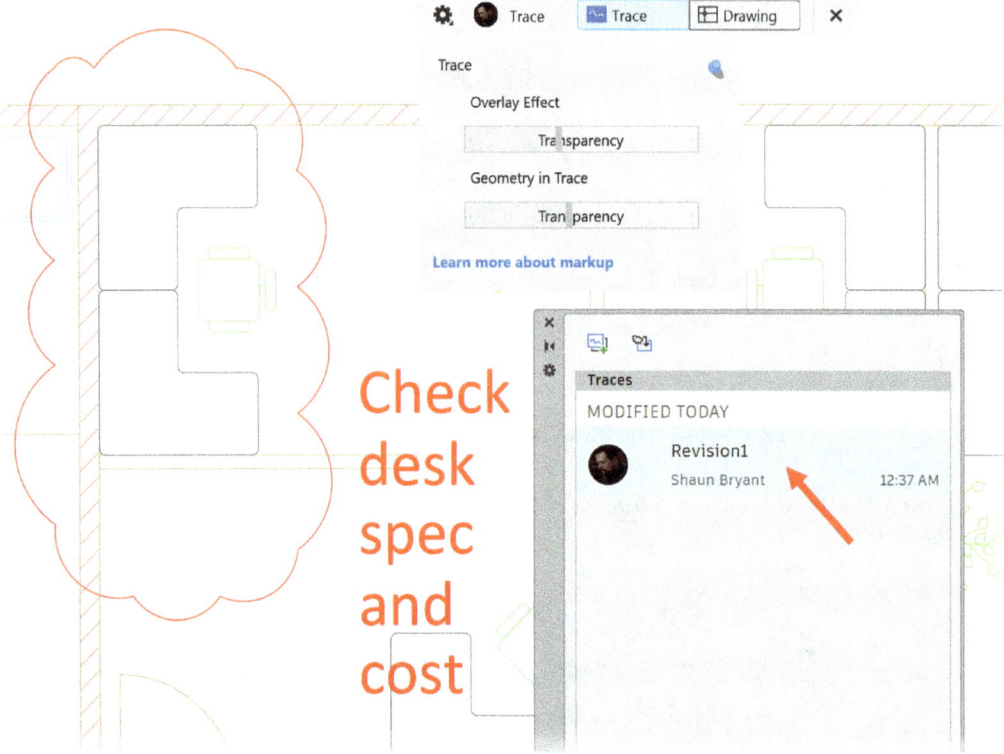

Figure 16.34: The trace in the drawing is displayed in trace mode

6. You can now see the updated trace that has been worked on in both the AutoCAD mobile application and AutoCAD Web. Note that the text has been updated, and those changes are now reflected in the trace displayed in the AutoCAD desktop app.

You can easily add to the existing trace as a collaborator by editing the text notes. Double-click on the trace text to activate the AutoCAD text editor, as shown in *Figure 16.35*. You will also see the contextual **Text Editor** tab appear on the ribbon.

Figure 16.35: The trace text selected for editing

7. Edit the text to read `Check desk cost`, and then click on the checkmark in the **Text Editor** tab on the ribbon. You have now edited the trace text.

8. You must also exit trace mode before saving and closing the drawing. To do so, click on the **X** at the end of the **Trace** toolbar, as shown in *Figure 16.36*.

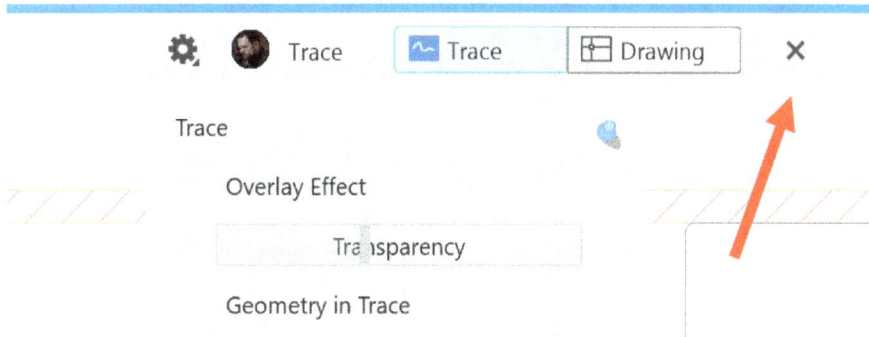

Figure 16.36: Closing the trace toolbar with the X

9. Make sure to save the drawing back to the cloud with the edited trace text. Use the **Save** icon on the QAT, as shown in *Figure 16.37*.

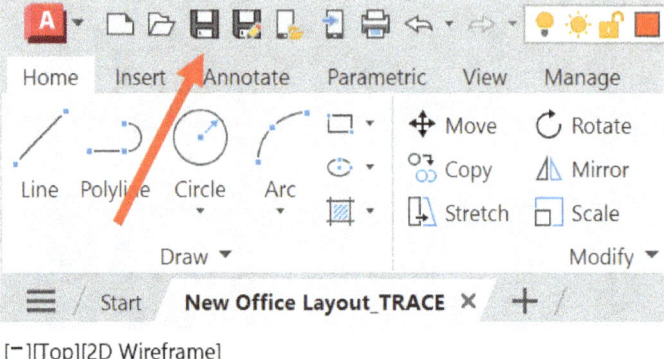

Figure 16.37: Using the Save icon to save the DWG back to the cloud

10. You have now edited the trace text and saved the drawing back to the cloud. Should the drawing be opened in either AutoCAD Web or the AutoCAD mobile application, those text changes will now apply.

> **AutoCAD for Mac**
>
> As mentioned in previous chapters, the `AutoCAD Web & Mobile` folder and the *OPENFROMWEBMOBILE* and *SAVETOWEBMOBILE* commands are not available when using AutoCAD for Mac. However, you can still collaborate using other cloud-based, proprietary solutions such as Microsoft OneDrive. OneDrive is supported by AutoCAD Web and the AutoCAD mobile application, so when working on the AutoCAD desktop in AutoCAD for Mac, you would save your file to your chosen cloud-based location in OneDrive and then connect to it using AutoCAD Web or the AutoCAD mobile application by using the appropriate login credentials for your chosen cloud-based location.

In this section, you learned how to review traces in cloud-based DWG files in the AutoCAD desktop app after trace changes had been saved through AutoCAD Web and the AutoCAD mobile application. You can now understand the benefits of not only saving drawings to the cloud but also using AutoCAD Web and the AutoCAD mobile application when it comes to collaborating on DWG files. Let's recap what we have learned in the chapter now!

Summary

You can learn more about working on a simple project with AutoCAD Web on the official AutoCAD blog:

`https://www.autodesk.com/blogs/autocad/tackling-a-new-workshop-build-with-autocad-web/`

You can also learn more about AutoCAD Web on the Autodesk website:

`https://help.autodesk.com/view/ACD/2022/ENU/?guid=GUID-B4A46563-E5CA-4A34-918C-78ADEA2FEEB4`

There is also more information about the AutoCAD mobile application at `https://help.autodesk.com/view/ACD/2022/ENU/?guid=GUID-20A8F96D-0ACA-49F6-A6FF-D7DD71A8D03A`. In this chapter, you learned how to add new traces in the AutoCAD desktop app. In doing so, you learned how to use the **Trace** tool to add a trace to an AutoCAD DWG file and make it ready for collaboration using the cloud for drawing storage.

You learned how to use the **Trace** tool in the AutoCAD mobile application, adding and editing traces using a smart mobile device like an iPad Pro, as well as learning how to use the **Trace** tool in AutoCAD Web, adding and editing traces using AutoCAD Web in a web browser.

You also learned how to review and edit existing trace information using the **Trace** tool in the AutoCAD desktop app, editing the trace text previously edited in the AutoCAD mobile application and AutoCAD Web.

Traces in AutoCAD provide a seamless, real-time collaboration experience when working with all iterations of AutoCAD, whether that be the desktop app, web app, or mobile application. This expands the user interface to not just the desktop but also a browser or a smart mobile device, making your DWG files completely mobile and easily accessible at any time. All changes can be updated and collaborated upon in real time using the trace functionality as well.

This chapter concludes the book, and you should now have gained an incredible amount of knowledge to enhance and improve your daily AutoCAD processes and workflows.

Happy AutoCAD-ing!

Get This Book's PDF Version and Exclusive Extras

Scan the QR code (or go to `packtpub.com/unlock`). Search for this book by name, confirm the edition, and then follow the steps on the page.

Note: Keep your invoice handy. Purchases made directly from Packt don't require one.

Index

Symbols

3Dconnexion icon 70, 71
3D modeling
  3D object snaps, utilizing 80-83

A

accurate table styles
  working with 172-181
Activity Insights 376
Angle tool
  used, for measuring precise angles 134-137
annotation scale
  used, to improve drawing legibility 87-92
  working with, in Model tab 197-204
annotative dimension style
  setting up 165-172
Area tool
  used, for area addition and subtraction 129-133
attributes 245
  defining, within AutoCAD block 246-256
  editing, with Enhanced Attribute Editor 257-259
AutoCAD
  default workspaces 4
  interface 4
  interface settings 4-6
  ribbon settings 6-12
AutoCAD block
  used, for creating regular door block 266-271
  used, for defining attributes 246-256
AutoCAD block attributes
  reference link 264
AutoCAD CUI
  redundant workspace, removing from 37-41
AutoCAD desktop
  DWG files, saving to cloud 370-372
  traces, reviewing in 417-422
  using, with traces 398-406
AutoCAD for Mac 152
  file tabs, using 47
  status bar, customizing 60
  ViewCube tools 66
  workflow, for Model and Layout 53
AutoCAD interface changes
  saving, to custom workspace 33-37
AutoCAD mobile application
  drawings, opening 384-391
  drawings, working with 384-391

traces, using in 406-411
updated drawings, using 392-395
AutoCAD navigation bar (navbar) 66, 67
   3Dconnexion 70, 71
   navigation wheels 67, 68
   Orbit (flyout) icon 70
   Real-time Pan tool 68
   ShowMotion tool 71-73
   Zoom icon 69
AutoCAD ViewCube 63-66
AutoCAD Web
   shared drawings, working 327-335
   traces, using in 412-417
AutoCAD Web application
   drawings, opening 376
   drawings, working with 376-384
   updated drawings, using 393-395
Autodesk Knowledge Network (AKN) 25
Autodesk Viewer
   reference link 335
   shared views, working 340-345

B

Block Attribute Manager (BATTMAN)
   using 260-263
block library drawing
   creating, with Clipboard function 227-231
blocks
   bringing, into drawings 214, 215
Blocks palette 256
   block library, adding to 231-236

C

CadMouse 70
Clipboard function
   using, to create block library drawing 227-231

Compact Discs (CDs) 16
Computer-Aided Design (CAD) 3
Computer Aided Manufacturing (CAM) 136
Customize User Interface (CUI)
   command 3, 21-26, 29, 35

D

dimension annotation
   managing, with dimension styles 152-164
Distance tool
   using, for length and angle calculation 125-129
drafting settings, status bar
   using 53-62
drawing comparisons, generated with DWG Compare
   working with 353-356
Drawing History tool
   using 372-376
drawings
   refining, with Modify panel 137-143
DWG Compare 347
   drawings, comparing 348-353
DWG Compare Snapshot mode 357
DWG files
   saving, to cloud from AutoCAD desktop 370-372
dynamic block
   bringing, into drawings 214, 215
   horizontal flip, adding to 279-286
   reference link 291
   testing 286-291
   using, with visibility states 316-319
   vertical flip, adding to 271-279
   visibility states, adding 306
dynamic Door block
   adding 219-227

E

Enhanced Attribute Editor
  used, for editing attributes 257-259
external reference file (Xref) 347, 365

F

file tabs
  working with 44-47
Flip actions 293
flip grip 279
floating modelspace 193

G

Geometric Center 108-112
Google Chrome 326

H

hamburger icon 44

I

ISODRAFT settings
  working with, to create
    isometric views 83-85
isometric drafting 83
isometric views
  creating, with ISODRAFT settings 83-85

L

Layout tab
  working with 47-53

M

**Measure (MEASUREGEOM)
    command** 129, 136
Microsoft Edge 326
Microsoft OneDrive 394
Mid Between 2 Points (M2P) 113
Model tab
  annotation scales, working with 197-204
  working with 47-53
Modify panel
  used, for refining drawings 137-143
multiple Osnaps
  working, with Object Snap Tracking
    (AUTOSNAP) 102-106

N

navigation wheels (steering wheels) 67, 68
nested block 247
noun/verb selection
  using, for object selection 122-125

O

object annotation scales
  adding 204-208
  deleting 204-208
object snaps (Osnaps) 95
Object Snap Tracking (AUTOSNAP)
  Geometric Center 108-112
  usage 106
  used, for multiple Osnaps 102-106
  working, with Snap Overrides 106-118
Orbit (flyout) icon 70
ORTHOMODE
  used, for orthogonal movements 100, 101

P

Polar Tracking
   need for 97
   used, for measuring angles 96-99
precise angles
   measuring, with Angle tool 134-137

Q

Quick Access Toolbar (QAT) 3, 83, 324
   customizing 16-18
   settings 18-21
   using, effectively 15
Quick Leader (QLEADER) command 165
Quick Measure
   using, for length and angle calculation 125-129

R

Real-time Pan tool 68
redundant workspace
   removing, from AutoCAD CUI 37-41
reference file comparisons, generated with Xref Compare
   working with 364-366
regular blocks 214
regular door block
   adding 215-219
   creating, with AutoCAD block 266-269, 271

S

selection cycling
   used, for object selection 76-79
shared drawings
   working, in AutoCAD Web 327-335
Share Drawing tool
   using 324-326
shared views
   working, in Autodesk Viewer 340-345
Shared Views palette
   using 335-339
ShowMotion tool 71, 73
Snap Overrides
   used, for Object Snap Tracking (AUTOSNAP) 106-118
SpaceMouse 70
status bar
   drafting settings, using 53-63
   units, changing via 85-87
sticky panels
   using 12-15

T

text styles
   creating, to manage text sizes and fonts 146-151
Tool Palettes
   used, for creating block library tool palette in AutoCAD 236-244
traces
   reviewing, in AutoCAD desktop app 417-422
   using, in AutoCAD mobile application 406-411
   using, with AutoCAD desktop 398-406
   using, with AutoCAD Web 412-417

V

viewports
   selecting 188
   setting up 184-196

viewport scales
   varying 184-196
visibility states 293
   adding, in dynamic block 306
   dynamic block, using with 316-319
   first state, setting up 307-313
   multiple states, adding 313-315

W

washbasin block drawing
   creating 294
   front block, adding 294-298
   top and side blocks, adding 298-302
washbasin dynamic block
   adding, for each view 303-306
workspace
   creating 32, 33
   selecting 30-32
   using 30

X

Xref Compare 347, 357
   drawings, comparing 357-363

Z

Zoom icon 69

www.packtpub.com

Subscribe to our online digital library for full access to over 7,000 books and videos, as well as industry leading tools to help you plan your personal development and advance your career. For more information, please visit our website.

Why subscribe?

- Spend less time learning and more time coding with practical eBooks and Videos from over 4,000 industry professionals
- Improve your learning with Skill Plans built especially for you
- Get a free eBook or video every month
- Fully searchable for easy access to vital information
- Copy and paste, print, and bookmark content

Did you know that Packt offers eBook versions of every book published, with PDF and ePub files available? You can upgrade to the eBook version at packtpub.com and as a print book customer, you are entitled to a discount on the eBook copy. Get in touch with us at customercare@packtpub.com for more details.

At www.packtpub.com, you can also read a collection of free technical articles, sign up for a range of free newsletters, and receive exclusive discounts and offers on Packt books and eBooks.

Other Books You May Enjoy

If you enjoyed this book, you may be interested in these other books by Packt:

Practical Autodesk AutoCAD 2023 and AutoCAD LT 2023 – Second Edition

Jaiprakash Pandey, Yasser Shoukry

ISBN: 978-1-80181-646-5

- Understand CAD fundamentals like functions, navigation, and components
- Create complex 3D objects using primitive shapes and editing tools
- Work with reusable objects like blocks and collaborate using xRef
- Explore advanced features like external references and dynamic blocks
- Discover surface and mesh modeling tools such as Fillet, Trim, and Extend
- Use the paper space layout to create plots for 2D and 3D models
- Convert your 2D drawings into 3D models

AutoCAD 2025 Best Practices, Tips, and Techniques

Jeanne Aarhus

ISBN: 978-1-83763-672-3

- Recognize hidden features in commonly used commands
- Explore innovative methods to make AutoCAD streamline your work for you
- Complete AutoCAD tasks in fewer steps using dynamic blocks and customizations
- Gain insider tips from AutoCAD veterans and gurus, saving you years of trial and error
- Use underutilized features of AutoCAD such as tables for data import and export
- Control how AutoCAD responds to your daily workflow and real-world environment

Packt is searching for authors like you

If you're interested in becoming an author for Packt, please visit `authors.packtpub.com` and apply today. We have worked with thousands of developers and tech professionals, just like you, to help them share their insight with the global tech community. You can make a general application, apply for a specific hot topic that we are recruiting an author for, or submit your own idea.

Share Your Thoughts

Now you've finished *Mastering AutoCAD*, we'd love to hear your thoughts! Scan the QR code below to go straight to the Amazon review page for this book and share your feedback or leave a review on the site that you purchased it from.

`https://packt.link/r/1-837-63969-8`

Your review is important to us and the tech community and will help us make sure we're delivering excellent quality content.

www.ingramcontent.com/pod-product-compliance
Lightning Source LLC
LaVergne TN
LVHW080304260326
834688LV00039B/1129